From

Italian Islands

1st Edition

by Sylvie Hogg

WILEY

Wiley Publishing, Inc

ABOUT THE AUTHOR

Sylvie Hogg has been collecting and sharing the best travel experiences in Italy for more than a decade. She is the author of *Frommer's Italy Day by Day* and *Frommer's Rome Day by Day* and has contributed to numerous other print and online publications about Rome and Italy, including *MTV Italy,* for which she received in 2007 the Society of American Travel Writer's Lowell Thomas Award. Working as a tour guide in Rome through much of her twenties, she developed an addiction to Italy's well-known history and culture and spent many a weekend exploring the country's best-kept secrets, its fabulous islands. Sylvie now lives in Kansas City, where she writes (*Food Lovers' Guide to Kansas City*), teaches Italian, and is a travel consultant. Her trusty "research assistants," her husband and young son, have also logged many nautical miles on ferries and hydrofoils around the islands of Italy.

Published by:

WILEY PUBLISHING, INC.

111 River St.
Hoboken, NJ 07030-5774

ISBN 978-0-470-50338-6 (paper); ISBN 978-1-118-03345-6 (ebk); ISBN 978-1-118-03346-3 (ebk); ISBN 978-1-118-03347-0 (ebk)

Editors: Alexia Travaglini with Elizabeth Heath
Production Editor: Heather Wilcox
Cartographer: Guy Ruggiero
Production by Wiley Indianapolis Composition Services
Front Cover Photo: Sunbathers enjoy one of Sardinia's many secluded beaches. © Franco Barbagallo/Hemis.fr/Aurora Photos.
Back Cover Photo: The Temple of Concordia at the Valley of the Temples, Agrigento, Sicily's most celebrated archaeological site. © Radius Images/Alamy Images.

For information on our other products and services or to obtain technical support, please contact our Customer Care Department within the U.S. at 877/762-2974, outside the U.S. at 317/572-3993 or fax 317/572-4002.

Wiley also publishes its books in a variety of electronic formats. Some content that appears in print may not be available in electronic formats.

Manufactured in the United States of America

5   4   3   2   1

CONTENTS

10 OTHER SICILIAN ISLANDS 224

11 AEOLIAN ISLANDS 249

12 EGADI ISLANDS 279

13 SARDINIA & SARDINIAN ISLANDS 294

14 FAST FACTS: ITALIAN ISLANDS 329

Index 333

LIST OF MAPS

HOW TO CONTACT US

In researching this book, we discovered many wonderful places—hotels, restaurants, shops, and more. We're sure you'll find others. Please tell us about them, so we can share the information with your fellow travelers in upcoming editions. If you were disappointed with a recommendation, we'd love to know that, too. Please write to:

Frommer's Italian Islands, 1st Edition
Wiley Publishing, Inc. • 111 River St. • Hoboken, NJ 07030-5774
frommersfeedback@wiley.com

AN ADDITIONAL NOTE

Please be advised that travel information is subject to change at any time—and this is especially true of prices. We therefore suggest that you write or call ahead for confirmation when making your travel plans. The authors, editors, and publisher cannot be held responsible for the experiences of readers while traveling. Your safety is important to us, however, so we encourage you to stay alert and be aware of your surroundings. Keep a close eye on cameras, purses, and wallets, all favorite targets of thieves and pickpockets.

FROMMER'S STAR RATINGS, ICONS & ABBREVIATIONS

Every hotel, restaurant, and attraction listing in this guide has been ranked for quality, value, service, amenities, and special features using a **star-rating system.** In country, state, and regional guides, we also rate towns and regions to help you narrow down your choices and budget your time accordingly. Hotels and restaurants are rated on a scale of zero (recommended) to three stars (exceptional). Attractions, shopping, nightlife, towns, and regions are rated according to the following scale: zero stars (recommended), one star (highly recommended), two stars (very highly recommended), and three stars (must-see).

In addition to the star-rating system, we also use **seven feature icons** that point you to the great deals, in-the-know advice, and unique experiences that separate travelers from tourists. Throughout the book, look for:

special finds—those places only insiders know about

fun facts—details that make travelers more informed and their trips more fun

kids—best bets for kids and advice for the whole family

special moments—those experiences that memories are made of

overrated—places or experiences not worth your time or money

insider tips—great ways to save time and money

great values—where to get the best deals

The following **abbreviations** are used for credit cards:

AE	American Express	DISC	Discover	V	Visa
DC	Diners Club	MC	MasterCard		

TRAVEL RESOURCES AT FROMMERS.COM

Frommer's travel resources don't end with this guide. Frommer's website, **www.frommers. com**, has travel information on more than 4,000 destinations. We update features regularly, giving you access to the most current trip-planning information and the best airfare, lodging, and car-rental bargains. You can also listen to podcasts, connect with other Frommers. com members through our active-reader forums, share your travel photos, read blogs from guidebook editors and fellow travelers, and much more.

BEST OF THE ITALIAN ISLANDS

Call it a cop-out, but the only category I can't bring myself to cover in this chapter is "Best Island." Wildly diverse in landscape, size, and atmosphere, each of the Italian islands has its own superlative features, which I've culled and compiled into the categories listed below. If your vision of an Italian island vacation is playing on a sandy beach, you'll find a carefully edited list of the best beaches right here. Perhaps nightlife is a priority, or art and history, or romance, or food and wine, or being one of the first to "discover" an island that's still untouched by international tourism, or doing nothing at all. I've presented my favorites for all these themes and more in this section, so that you can head straight for the all-stars in each category without wasting precious vacation time on the also-rans. Here's hoping you also find your own personal collection of "best" experiences while you're at it.

THE best BEACHES

- **Spiaggia dei Conigli** (Lampedusa): Simply cresting the hill of the hiking path that leads to this beach and beholding Spiaggia dei Conigli—a glorious crescent of sugary white sand—and its wide bay of swimming pool–like water may be the highlight of a trip to far-flung Lampedusa. The water here is shallow and always warm, and you can swim or wade the short distance to Isola dei Conigli islet, in the middle of the bay.
- **Biodola** (Elba): Sugary white sand that extends for 600m (1,969 ft.), a gentle offshore grade, and abundant services make this the best all-purpose sandy beach on Elba. The calm and shallow water is ideal for families with kids.
- **Citara** (Ischia): Buzzy social atmosphere meets dramatic headlands at this well-trod beach south of Forio. Combine your beach time with a thermal water experience at the Giardini Poseidon open-air spa, which occupies about a third of the coastline here. West-facing Citara has the best sunsets on Ischia.
- **Punta Molentis** (Sardinia): The beaches of Sardinia are in a league of their own. Sand is never in short supply, and the water has the color and clarity normally associated with Caribbean islands. Punta Molentis is a delicious slice of paradise near Villasimius, where a narrow isthmus,

bathed by beautiful water and fringed by sand on both sides, connects to a mountainous promontory. A lovely little thatched-umbrella snack bar completes the postcard image.

o **Cala Sinzias** (Sardinia): Near the popular flour-sand beach district of Costa Rei, but just far enough away to be blissfully uncrowded even in August, Cala Sinzias is a bit of the South Pacific right here in southeastern Sardinia. Fine beige sand seamlessly blends with the gentlest of crystal-clear breakers, and most of the beach is backed by a fragrant eucalyptus wood.

o **La Pelosa** (Sardinia): At the northwestern tip of Sardinia, La Pelosa is an extraplanetary seascape where the water achieves the most astonishing colors, from dappled grey to neon turquoise, that change with the position of the sun. The sandy bay is no deeper than knee height for hundreds of meters, as clear as rubbing alcohol and always calm, making it popular with families.

o **Tuerredda** (Sardinia): Of all the stretches of sand around beach-blessed Chia, none is more spectacular than Tuerredda. It's the stuff of island magazine cover photos, with leopard spots of indigo and electric aqua in a secluded bay with its own little islet, snow-white sand, and the brawny, green terrain of southwestern Sardinia all around.

o **Liscia Ruja** (Sardinia): Also known as "Long Beach," this is the unofficial headquarters of the Costa Smeralda beach scene and *the* place to be for movers and shakers (when they aren't out on a yacht). This beach is highly recommended for anyone in northeastern Sardinia who simply wants a wide expanse of golden sand, tourmaline water, and excellent people-watching.

THE best PLACES TO SWIM THAT AREN'T BEACHES

o **La Cattedrale** (Palmarola): On the northern tip of this practically virgin island, craggy cliffs plunge to the sea, and three side-by-side sea caves have earned the nickname "the Cathedral" for their striking resemblance to Gothic arches. The shimmering emerald waters just outside La Cattedrale are a favorite place for boat-trippers to dive in and glory in this little slice of Robinson Crusoe, just 20 minutes from Ponza and only 97km (60 miles) from Rome.

o **Cala Bianca** (Marettimo): The most remote island in the Egadi is short on beaches but big on gorgeous coves and grottoes that can be accessed only by sea. At Cala Bianca, a white rock wall continues underneath the water surface, imparting an opalescent tone to the cove. It's yet another example of the unending permutations of Mediterranean blue.

o **Cala Rossa** (Favignana): Its name may translate as "Red Cove" (from bloodshed here during the First Punic War btw. Rome and Carthage in the 3rd c. B.C.), but the colors here are grey and pale turquoise. Cala Rossa was once Favignana's most active quarry, and pillars and walls of the native grey stone stand as the otherworldly backdrop to this shallow bay. Brave the rocky entrance to swim in waters as clear and light as anything in the Caribbean.

o **Vasca Giulia** (Santo Stefano-Ventotene): On the classic day trip from Ventotene to historic prison island Santo Stefano, make sure your boat captain includes a visit to the Roman-era "Jacuzzi" that belonged to the imperial villa here. A hand-dug pool in the smooth rock of Santo Stefano's coastline, "Julia's Tub" is connected to the sea by narrow channels that allow the surging surf to come in at concentrated strength, creating the earliest known hydromassage jets. Not bad technology for the 1st century A.D., and yes, you can jump right in and feel the flow just like the ancients did.

- **Grotte di Pilato** (Ponza): It isn't every day you can swim—for free—in a Roman sea cave that was built for the express purpose of raising eels for the imperial dinner table. The so-called grottoes of Pilate are wonderfully atmospheric vaulted chambers with niches and underwater tunnels used to corral eels from one tank to another. The caves are just a short hop by boat from the island's main port, and thankfully, the morays are long gone from this spot.
- **Specchio di Venere** (Pantelleria): The bright and warm turquoise water of this volcanic crater lake really stands out on an island known for its rough black lava shores and dark blue seas. "Venus's Mirror" gets its eerily luminescent color from grey volcanic mud on the lake floor. The sulfuric mud is purported to have certain health benefits (though it stinks like rotten eggs), and it's common practice to slather yourself with mud on one side of the lake and rinse off on the opposite shore. Even Madonna has taken part in this classic Pantelleria ritual.
- **The Blue Grotto** (Capri): The most famous sea cave in the world, tinged Windex-blue by refraction of the sun's rays beneath the water, is normally visited as part of an overpriced (though very fun) boat trip, but it's a little known fact that you can also forgo the boats and just swim yourself in. Wait until all the tour boats have left—about 5pm in summer—and make sure the water is very calm. The cave entrance is a bit hairy, so it's a good idea to go in a group; but once you're in and surrounded by the extraordinarily lit water, it'll be the most memorable paddling and treading of your life.

THE best PARTY ATMOSPHERE

- **The Costa Smeralda** (Sardinia): Titans of industry and television starlets collide at the over-the-top discos of this luxury enclave in northeastern Sardinia. Paparazzi stalk canoodling celebrity neo-couples on the back of yachts and on beaches like Liscia Ruja. For the rest of us, there are also beachfront bars that welcome the plebes for gorgeous sunsets and impromptu dance parties.
- **Ponza:** The nightly ritual may be a bit repetitive—boat shuttle to Frontone beach for *aperitivo,* people-watching, and shopping promenade along Corso Pisacane, then a late dinner at one of the fish restaurants lining the marina—but Ponza's fun-loving energy is hard to resist.
- **Panarea:** After a day out on the water, vacationers on the most hedonistic of the Aeolian islands head straight for the buzzing drink scene at several waterfront bars and boutique-hopping in San Pietro village. When darkness falls, hit the shower and swap your bathing suit for a carefully assembled boho-chic ensemble and hit the open-air disco at the Hotel Raya. It's where everyone on Panarea congregates to dance and misbehave under the stars.
- **Capri:** This fabled jewel of the Mediterranean may not be the jet-set magnet it was several decades ago, but there is still a high celebrity quotient on Capri and an infectious sense of glamour at the bars on the famed Piazzetta. When the day-tripping hordes have set sail back to the mainland, Capri becomes an intimate playground for those lucky enough to spend the night.
- **Ischia:** Start with a sun-downer in charming Sant'Angelo, the tiny fishing port on the south side of the island, then make your way back around to Ischia Porto and find a spot at one of the happening waterfront bars along the Riva Destra, the right-hand side of the marina.

THE best HOTELS & RESORTS

o **Cave Bianche** (Favignana): Sexy South Beach meets the Flintstones at this contemporary hotel situated in a decommissioned tufa quarry. The quarry hotel concept is a bit of a trend on Favignana—what else to do with those striking cavities of the native stone?—and this is the best of the lot. Guest units occupy a tiered structure on one side of the quarry, while the grassy floor has palm trees, a swimming pool, and a stylish bar and restaurant set amid mood-lit tufa walls.

o **I Jardina Dammusi** (Pantelleria): On this chic and exotic island, most accommodations are either resorts or restored *dammusi,* the traditional stone dwelling of the Arabs who settled Pantelleria in the Middle Ages. I Jardina combines the best of both worlds—a boutique resort with lots of services and amenities, and the units are luxury interpretations of *dammusi,* each stylishly decorated and equipped with a private deck and swimming pool.

o **Il Pellicano** (Porto Ercole, Argentario): Ranking among the top luxury properties anywhere in Italy, this intimate cluster of orange stucco buildings cascades down through panoramic terraces (with swimming pool) to a private beach on the north side of the Argentario peninsula. Il Pellicano is the rare high-end resort that delivers impeccable service and style with genuine warmth, an immense credit to its management and staff. Even the most demanding of world travelers will be hard-pressed to find any nits to pick here. Although Il Pellicano is not technically on an island, it is very close to Porto Santo Stefano, and such a special property that it merits inclusion here.

o **Punta Tragara** (Capri): On an island endowed with an unfair number of stunning settings, this five-star property has the best location on Capri. The Punta Tragara is perched at the aerielike end of a footpath away from the hubbub of Capri town, and overlooking the famous Faraglioni rocks. The Punta Tragara's distinctive architecture—a ripple of pink stucco designed by Le Corbusier—blends with the native rock to gorgeous effect, and interiors are unique and classy, capturing the 1920s vintage of the place.

o **Regina Isabella** (Ischia): The grande dame of Lacco Ameno, the former fishing port developed in the 1950s into Ischia's fanciest resort enclave delivers old-school luxury with palatial public areas, a private cove, and—this being Ischia—a state-of-the-art thermal spa.

THE best BOUTIQUE INNS & GUESTHOUSES

o **Agave e Ginestra** (Ventotene): Named after the typical vegetation of the Pontine islands, agave plants and yellow broom, this boutique hotel is the epitome of chic and carefree island style. It's an oasis with cool, whitewashed rooms (though few frills) and an onsite restaurant that turns out sophisticated, light cuisine.

o **Villa Ducale** (Taormina): Set in the panoramic hills above Taormina town, this boutique country inn has just the right mix of pampering amenities and folksy Sicilian flair. Most rooms have ample private verandas overlooking the sea and the smoking top of Mt. Etna on the horizon, and staff is sunny and professional.

o **Villa Laetitia** (Ponza): This intimate and laid-back guesthouse above Ponza port is the creation of Anna Fendi Venturini, of the Fendi fashion house. From the cabinets to the floor tiles, each of the three rooms is eclectically appointed with antiques sourced on Ponza and in Naples.

THE best-kept SECRETS

o **Il Giglio:** Reached by ferry from Porto Santo Stefano on the Argentario peninsula, the diminutive Isola del Giglio has remained the vacation province of Romans and Tuscans. Like a miniature version of Elba, Giglio has a hilly interior, which means good hiking. The coastline offers few beaches beyond the smooth red sand of Campese, but a round-island boat tour will take you to Giglio's lovely swimming coves.

o **Salina:** Vulcano has its sulfuric spa devotees, Panarea its party animals, and Stromboli its volcano trekkers. Somehow, elegant Salina has stayed under the radar of Aeolian tourism. It may lack the kind of action that some summer travelers are looking for, and there are few beaches, but it has the Aeolians' best hotels (Signum and Capo Faro), splendid scenery and hikes, and it still feels authentic. For couples or anyone else seeking a low-key, romantic getaway, it's one of the best destinations in the Mediterranean.

o **Ventotene:** Like Ponza, its Pontine archipelago sibling to the north, Ventotene lies just far enough away from both Rome and Naples to be skipped over by foreign visitors to those cities. At just over 1 sq. km (⅔ sq. mile), Ventotene may be a mere speck in the sea, but it boasts some dramatic coastline, a picture-perfect pastel town, and a 2,000-year-old Roman port that's still in use.

THE best TOWNS & VILLAGES

o **Anacapri, Capri:** Yes, we love Capri town, too, but there's a more personal, cozy vibe to the whitewashed lanes of the town on the west end of the island. It may have agricultural roots, but Anacapri is no backwater—there are luxury hotels and boutiques here, yet there are also mom-and-pop groceries where you can get your wine, cheese, and bread at honest prices, and elegant coffee bars that still feel like the province of actual islanders.

o **Capoliveri, Elba:** On a hill high above the sea, Capoliveri isn't anywhere near the water, but it's still Elbans' and many a tourist's favored destination for sunset strolling, eating, and drinking. Capoliveri is exactly what you'd expect a mainland Tuscan village to look like, with its steep alleys, picturesque central piazza, and ochre-washed buildings.

o **Castello, Isola del Giglio:** A citadel of proud medieval architecture atop the central ridge of the second-largest Tuscan island, Castello is a lively island community and where most of Giglio's top restaurants are located.

o **Marettimo:** It's hard to find a more authentic fishing village than the port town of Marettimo. As the most remote town in the Egadi, it has kept its traditions intact, and visitors here can join in the rhythms of a real working maritime town.

o **Siracusa, Sicily:** Baroque Ortigia Island drips with Sicilian romance and has one of the best town squares in all of Italy. The stellar ancient sites in the city's own Parco Archeologico della Neapolis, good beaches nearby, and the opportunity for excursions to architectural gems like Noto make Siracusa a wonderful base for exploring southeastern Sicily.

o **Ventotene:** Follow the zigzagging Rampa della Marina up from the port to this tiny, adorable village (pop. 743), awash in Neapolitan Easter-egg pastels and firing on all Italian-hamlet stereotypes—laundry hanging from windows, kids playing soccer in the street, and gregarious old-timers gabbing over soccer- and politics-related headlines in lively cafes.

THE best ART & HISTORY

o **Valley of the Temples** (Southern Sicily): Even the ancient ruins of Greece itself have a hard time conveying the same sense of bygone grandeur as this celebrated complex of Doric temples, set on a ridge above Sicily's southern coast. Though most are fragmentary, the temples of Agrigento are a humbling and haunting testament to the power of Greece in Sicily 2,500 years ago.

o **Siracusa** (Eastern Sicily): An enormous Greek theater and a lush, primordial quarry make Siracusa's Parco Archeologico della Neapolis one of the most atmospheric ancient sites anywhere in Italy. Over in the *centro storico* of Ortigia Island, fanciful Baroque architecture lines the streets and piazzas and looks for all the world like an operatic stage set.

o **Palermo** (Northern Sicily): Sicily's cacophonous capital is like a scavenger hunt with masterpieces from nearly every significant time period of art and architecture. Arab-Norman monuments and the dazzling mosaics in the Cappella Palatina and Monreale cathedral (a short day trip from the city) command the most attention, but make time to seek out such gems as Serpotta's rococo oratories of Santa Cita and San Domenico, and the crumbling, nostalgia-inducing noble palazzi of the Kalsa district. The city's principal museums, the Museo Archeologico Nazionale and the Galleria Regionale at Palazzo Abatellis, are filled with important artifacts and Sicilian artworks.

o **Piazza Armerina** (Central Sicily): Tucked away in a rural part of the island, the Villa Romana del Casale might seem like an unlikely place to find the most intricate and amusing Roman mosaics ever discovered, yet here they are. The 3rd-century estate of a wealthy private citizen became a blank canvas for the most talented mosaic artists of the day, who decorated some 3,500 sq. m (37,674 sq. ft.) of floors with scenes of animal hunts, mythological battles, and bikini-clad women working out. The colors and sheer quantity of the mosaics here are enough to impress, but it's the attention to detail and the emotion rendered in the figures' faces that make this such an unforgettable detour.

o **Su Nuraxi** (Central Sardinia): Far and away the best preserved and most impressive of the Stone Age structures called nuraghi that dot the Sardinian countryside. Su Nuraxi is dominated by a central conical tower around which dozens of smaller, circular chambers spill over the hillside. A tour through the ruins is a mystical step back in time.

o **Villa Jovis** (Capri): Even in ancient times, Capri was a resort for the rich and famous. Eccentric emperor Tiberius built a whopping 12 personal villas on the island, and the "Villa of Jupiter" is the best preserved of them. On the vertiginous and pine-wooded northeastern tip of the island, wander among the skeletal remains of baths, dining halls, and terraces with sweeping views across to Sorrento—just don't get too close to the Salto di Tiberio, a notch in the cliffs 300m (984 ft.) above the sea where the emperor ordered "unpleasant guests" to take swan dives.

THE best EXCURSIONS

o **The Blue Grotto** (Capri): It's a Capri rite of passage, yet there are those who will find this outing repellent. And justifiably so: The Blue Grotto, after all, is an unabashed tourist trap and jostle of humanity where you pay upwards of 20€ to be in the cave for about 2 minutes. But the giddy, bumpy adventure—however brief—of being pulled by a rope underneath the grotto's tiny archway and into that dark cavern with its sloshing floor of mesmerizing blue, while boatmen sing Neapolitan sea chanteys that boom off the walls . . . it's a maelstrom of new sensations, and it's priceless.

o **Mt. Etna** (Sicily): It's hard to believe you're still on a Mediterranean island when you reach the desolate upper reaches of Etna. The wind whips hard at 3,300m (10,827 ft.), charcoal scree (and dead ladybugs) crunches underfoot, and even in August, you'll need to don a parka to tour the volcanic dunes and fumaroles near the summit. Approach the volcano from the north for more forested surroundings, or from the south for vast expanses of lava (from recent eruptions) and to ride the *funivia dell'Etna* cableway.

o **Sciara del Fuoco** (Stromboli): Get up close and personal with the fiery output of the last Aeolian volcano still in business. You don't even have to go to the summit; about 400m (1,312 ft.) up the mountain, the "Stream of Fire" is a thrilling encounter with nature, and one of few places in the world where you can get this safely close to lava flows, which perform reliably for visitors every 20 minutes. The molten rock slithering down the slopes of Stromboli, while the cone belches guttural moans above, is an indelible experience, especially at night.

o **Palmarola:** With a population of 1, Palmarola is all but uninhabited, and its craggy contours, covered with a shag carpet of lush vegetation, make it one of the most gorgeous islands in Italy. A boat trip here from nearby Ponza is a fabulous way to experience untouched coves and unspoiled nature, though you'll hardly have it to yourself in August. Swimming and bobbing around Palmarola feels like an elite privilege, and it's a rare glimpse of the Mediterranean as it used to be.

o **Santo Stefano:** The panettone-shaped former penitentiary island across the water from Ventotene is remarkable not only for its interesting "panoptic" (all-seeing) prison architecture but also for the opportunity to swim in an ancient Roman "Jacuzzi," the Vasca Giulia.

o **Round-Island Boat Tours** (any island under 100 sq. km/39 sq. miles): The *giro dell'isola* ("around-the-island") by sea is the classic way to explore the perimeters of the more modestly sized Italian islands (for example, all but Sicily, Sardinia, Elba, and Sant'Antioco), which often have long stretches of coastline not accessible by land. Do it yourself in a rented *gommone,* or join one of the organized trips from your island's main port.

THE best ISLANDS FOR ROMANCE

o **Capri:** Its neighbor to the east, the Amalfi Coast, may get the lion's share of honeymooners, but the quiet lanes, secluded restaurants, and vista points on Capri, which becomes very intimate after dark, beat anything in Positano in terms of setting the mood.

o **Pantelleria:** The "black pearl of the Mediterranean" may have a severe volcanic landscape that isn't everyone's idea of a romantic getaway, but there's no denying the exotic allure of staying in one of the island's luxurious *dammusi* resorts. Couples can toast their adventures on far-flung Pantelleria with the island's signature wine, the sweet passito, at one of the stylish, candle-lit restaurants here.

o **Salina:** The greenest and most elegant of the Aeolians was made for couples. A walk among the ferns of Monte Fossa delle Felci is a blissful way to enjoy some quiet time with a partner. On the shores of this island, you can actually tune into the sound of the waves, as opposed to the busy tourist activity on some other islands in this archipelago. Salina also boasts the Aeolians' two finest hotels, the boutique Signum and the chic miniresort Capo Faro, both gorgeous physical plants with services like massage and wine-tasting.

o **Sardinia:** On Sardinia, the romance is created by wild and windswept nature and endless sugary beaches. The quasi-Caribbean beach paradises around **Chia** and **Villasimius** were made for intimate relaxation *à deux,* while the luxury enclave of the **Costa Smeralda** (and the more rustic **La Maddalena** archipelago) presents a stunning landscape of pink granite and glittering emerald water in a tidy, amenity-filled package.

o **Sicily:** Chalk it up to several thousand years of hot-blooded cultures coming together here, but Sicily might just be the steamiest place in the Mediterranean. Hill towns like **Taormina** and **Erice** make you swoon, while the sea-fronting Baroque squares and alleys of **Siracusa** drip with romance. Even chaotic **Palermo** is sexy, with its sultry old cloisters, African-tinged gardens, and glamorous period-piece hotels like the Grand Hotel et des Palmes and the Villa Igiea.

o **Ventotene:** Itty-bitty Ventotene (it's just over 1 sq. km/²⁄₃ sq. mile) may be too small and slow for some tastes, but this cove-fringed speck of red tufa is utterly peaceful, and the pastel village and port have a way of making you feel like you belong here. Go for a walk after dark over Ventotene's rural spine, or explore the Roman ruins at sunset, and it becomes your own private island.

THE best SCENERY

o **Capri:** The entire island is a Mediterranean beauty queen that never fails to impress even repeat visitors. From the Faraglioni to the Blue Grotto to the forested limestone crags plunging into the deep blue sea far below, it takes your breath away every time. And though humans have been here for more than 2,000 years, the development on Capri only seems to exalt the place's natural splendor.

o **Elba:** What's not to love about an island that combines near-Alpine topography, the green hills of Tuscany, and hundreds of accessible beaches and coves? Portoferraio and its bay are just one of several sparkling blue ports around this geologically gifted island, and the corniche roads linking them have enough curves and precipitous edges to make anyone feel daring. The mineral and metallic riches that were Elba's lifeblood before tourism are still visible in dramatic decommissioned mines and quarries.

o **Marettimo:** Beyond the tiny fishing village and port, mountainous Marettimo is an unspoiled gem with big-time scenery that rivals even Capri. Hiking paths crisscross its rugged interior, which is overseen by the Italian Forestry Corps, and the coastline is grotto heaven, with dozens of sea caves to be explored on organized boat tours. The magnificent Barranche on the west coast—striking monoliths that stand perpendicular to the sea—are on par with the rock formations in the national parks of Utah and Arizona.

o **Ponza:** Its strange but beautiful lunar coastline—lots of milky white and yellowish escarpments, the grandest of which is Chiaia di Luna—is the result of a peculiar volcanic mineral profile, and it makes for some of the most fabulous swimming in the Tyrrhenian. Crescent-shaped and mountainous, with peninsular appendages stripped of their trees by deforestation centuries ago, Ponza looks like a lizard from afar, but its "scaly" silhouette is misleading: The slopes of Ponza are awash in colorful and fragrant *macchia mediterranea.*

- **Salina:** Introverted and gracious, and better suited to hikers than beach bums, Salina has two sensual volcanic peaks that are a verdant counterpoint to all the lavic surfaces in the Aeolians. Movie cameras loved this landscape in 1994's *Il Postino.*
- **Sardinia:** Whether it's the mesalike heights of the interior that call to mind the wild west, or the rugged mountain ranges, or the coasts fringed by long, sugary beaches, or the patchwork of verdant farmland in the interior, no other island in Italy has such geologic variety: It's no wonder the tourist board tagline for Sardinia is *quasi un continente* (almost a continent). And oh, the sea! In colors ranging from palest turquoise to deep emerald and with crystalline clarity, Sardinia has the most glorious swimming in the Med.
- **San Domino:** The greenest of the diminutive Tremiti has a jigsaw puzzle coastline of intimate coves where limestone meets San Domino's characteristic canopy of Aleppo pinewoods. It's a perfect recipe and scale for lazy days of exploring, and the pines that cover the interior offer welcome shade as you traipse between swimming spots. Views across the water to the east—framed always by the boughs of those pines— take in the formidable abbey-fortress and chalky cliffs of the island of San Nicola.
- **Sicily:** The massive headlands from Palermo to San Vito are thunderous sculptures of nature, while the delicious coastal hill towns of Erice and Taormina are prime examples of architecture's harmonious insertion into the well-endowed landscape. Inland, sun-baked hills dotted with medieval villages fully live up to your stereotypical visions of this island of Corleones and *cannoli.*

THE best FOOD & WINE EXPERIENCES

- **Da Adelina** (Panarea): It's hard to beat the setting alone, in a cozy dining room directly overlooking the intimate port of this chic island, but Adelina also delivers on the food front. The kitchen, helmed by an internationally seasoned Sicilian, conjures up reworked versions of typical Aeolian fare, making use of fresh vegetables from its own orchard and the delicious, delicate bounty of the surrounding sea.
- **Emanuele** (Elba): Snuggled into the beach at the Enfola headland west of Portoferraio, friendly, family-run Emanuele excels at marrying the catch of the day and pick of the crustaceans with fresh pastas and seasonal vegetables.
- **Fumarole-Cooked Chicken** (Ischia): Cooking your own picnic dinner of foilwrapped pollo delle fumarole al cartoccio in the naturally heated sand of Maronti beach is an unforgettable Ischian experience. The thermal jets, just a few inches under the sand, are warm enough to cook a whole chicken (add several sprigs of rosemary), plus a side of potatoes, in about an hour. It's inexpensive, easy to clean up, and you can go swimming right after you've digested.
- **La Nicchia** (Pantelleria): Set in a romantic courtyard with a gnarled old orange tree, "the niche" is a serious gourmet place that turns out tantalizing renditions of Pantescan cuisine with creative flair. Ingredients are rigorously local and the preparations exquisite, a true testament to the bounty of this island and the level of elegance it has reached.
- **Passito di Pantelleria:** No meal on Pantelleria goes without a finishing touch of sublime, sophisticated, sweet passito; it's practically a way of life. The refined flavor of Pantelleria's passito (the word is a generic term meaning raisin wine, since it's made from grapes dried in the sun, but Passito di Pantelleria has the prestigious

D.O.C. appellation) comes from this island's particular combination of highly lavic soil, sun, and salty air, and makes it sought after by international oenophiles.

o **Publius** (Elba): If Emanuele is the king of seaside dining on Elba, Publius reigns over the mountainous side of Elba's culinary scene. In the panoramic village of Poggio, it's an institution that draws VIPs for revisited Tuscan "surf and turf" dishes like pink gnocchi with seafood pesto and Etruscan-style boar, homemade desserts, and a wine list more than 350 labels long. Terrace dining offers sweeping vistas of the gulf of Marciana Marina down the hill.

o **Sella e Mosca Winery** (Alghero, Sardinia): The world of Sardinian wine is one that few foreigners know much about, and you'll get a great introduction to the island's grape varieties and winemaking methods at this well-run estate with multilingual tours and a modern tasting room and wine shop.

THE best HIKES

o **Capri:** When masses of day-trippers clog the streets of both Capri and Anacapri towns, don your walking shoes and hit one of the many trails, from easy to extreme, that flaunt the jaw-dropping natural beauty of the belle of the Bay of Naples. My favorite is the up-and-down Via Pizzolungo, which flanks the wooded heights just outside Capri town, from Punta Tragara to the Arco Naturale. There are rapturous sea views for much of the route, and you can rest in a Roman-era grotto along the way. You can also hoof it to the island's tallest peak, Monte Solaro (and give your feet a rest by taking the Monte Solaro chairlift on the way up or down). In fact, it's almost impossible to spend time on Capri without doing some moderate hiking—whether it's the hairpin path of Via Krupp to Marina Piccola, or the gentle grade that rises to the clifftop ruins of the Villa Jovis on the northeast tip of the island.

o **Monte Capanne** (Elba): No outdoorsy Italian worth his *scarpe da montagna* (hiking boots) will go through life without summiting Monte Capanne, at 1,019m (3,343 ft.), known as the rooftop of the Tuscan archipelago. The 3-hour ascent begins in lovely woods of chestnut and ilex where you might encounter *mouflon* (wild sheep), while the peak area has slick exposed granite slabs where bracing winds add to the sense of adventure. The views are 360-degree, taking in the mainland and other Tuscan islands, the toothy profile of Corsica, and even the snow-capped peaks of the Apuan Alps on a clear day. (Non-hikers can take a cableway to the top, where—this being Italy—there's a coffee bar.)

o **Monte Fossa delle Felci** (Salina): Higher even than the peak of volcanic Stromboli, and without all the messy smoke and lava, 962m-tall (3,156 ft.) "Mount Ferngully" is the roof of the Aeolian islands. Lush ferns carpet the gentle slopes of this dormant volcano, and a 2-hour hike (in the steps of the cast of *Il Postino*, which was filmed here) to the summit affords stunning views of the entire archipelago.

o **Stromboli:** Not content to watch the lava flows at the Sciara del Fuoco, extreme adrenaline junkies can make their way to the very top of Stromboli (926m/3,156 ft.), which belches and sputters around the clock, creating a continuous plume of smoke that can be seen from miles around. But the smoke is only half the story: Up close, Stromboli tosses volcanic bombs of molten rock up to several hundred meters into the air. As spectacular as these eruptions are, Stromboli can also be dangerous, which is why trips to elevations higher than 400m (1,312 ft.) can be made only with authorized guides and only when volcanic conditions permit. The hike itself is demanding and vertiginous, and takes the best part of 5 hours round-trip.

THE best PLACES FOR REST & RELAXATION

- **Giannutri:** The most exclusive of the Tuscan islands has few accommodations, but if you can score a place to stay, you can spend the days hiking on paths that cut through *macchia* as tall as you are (and intoxicatingly fragrant), and at night be lulled to sleep by the wind and waves.
- **Ischia:** Crowded and fun-loving Ischia may not seem very relaxing at first glance, but this is, after all, the island that the ancients turned to for the healing and restorative properties of its thermal waters. There are literally hundreds of spa establishments offering every possible permutation (both scientific and far-fetched) of hydrotherapy and good old-fashioned pampering wellness treatments like massages and body wraps.
- **Marettimo:** With a slow-paced fishing village that still lives by the rule of the sea, an uncontaminated interior with panoramic nature walks, and a stupendous coastline studded with sea caves and coves where you're often the only one present, the remotest of the Egadi is guaranteed to take your stress level down a few notches.

THE ITALIAN ISLANDS IN DEPTH

How to generalize more than 30 diverse islands that range from reclaimed marshland to exotic outposts of black lava that only by a fluke of history fly the Italian flag? Some are chic; some are everyman. Some are well known, while others are well-kept secrets. Some islands are easy hops from major cities, while others require lengthy boat journeys or uncommon flight routes.

The Italian islands are nothing if not a motley crew; even within the same archipelago, it's hard to make any blanket statements. Like any family, though, there are resemblances in addition to unique personality quirks. Today, the Italian islands share the common vocation, at least part of the year and in part of the territory, of being resorts in the Mediterranean.

Tourism is nowhere near as entrenched in the Italian islands as in the Greek or Spanish isles, where hordes of British, German, and northern European package tourists flock like bees to a hive, and where unsightly blocks of modern vacation developments have gone up, often blighting the coastline. Nature in the Italian islands is fiercely protected, and stringent laws limit how much and what kind of construction is allowed. Which isn't to say the Italian islands are virgin or primitive by any means; they heave with humanity in July and August. It's just that they've kept their native identities intact a bit better than, say, Majorca or Corfu. Even in the age of low-cost airlines and the European Union, the Italian islands are still very much of and for the Italians. This is less a function of deliberate exclusiveness than it is of the logistics required for foreigners to reach the islands. You have to really want to get there. You have to plan, and you have to go out of your way. You also have to forgo abundant beaches (except for Sardinia) in exchange for the privilege of getting into the character and the flavor of your chosen islands.

Unlike the Greek islands, which spread out from the Athenian port of Piraeus like a buffet and often have airports, the Italian islands aren't all that convenient to access nor particularly well suited for island-hopping (in high season, you have to stay at least 3 nights in any hotel), which makes them a bit of an unusual choice for international tourists. You can't fly to most of them, and no single mainland seaport serves them all. In many cases, the departure points for ferries and hydrofoils are well off the beaten track. Reaching the Tuscan islands, for example, is way more complicated than just being in Tuscany and deciding you want to catch a ferry to Elba. Within the Tuscan archipelago, the ferry lines are such that you have to set sail from three different offbeat cities to reach certain islands (Livorno for Capraia, Piombino for Elba, Porto Santo Stefano for Giglio and Giannutri). All of this has conspired to keep the Italian islands more authentic, more elite, more jealously guarded by those who love them. The fact that local culture reigns, undiluted by international tourism, is a huge part of the appeal of traveling to the Italian islands, and it's well worth braving some slightly cumbersome transportation issues.

I use, however sparingly, the words "insider" and "under-the-radar" when referring to certain less publicized, less developed islands in this book. However, the truth is that while plenty of Italian islands are *unspoiled,* none is completely *undiscovered* anymore. Each island has found its niche and its cadre of devout followers and life-long return visitors, whether it's the *bella gente* Romans who descend on Ponza every summer or the Germans who've set up vacation camp on the south coast of Elba. Just as many Italian islands devotees spend a lifetime trying to visit each and every one, as opposed to renting the same villa in Sardinia every year. The individual islands of Italy are national treasures, as cherished in the Italian consciousness as the Colosseum or the *David.*

As soon as you board a boat for an Italian island, you already have some sense of what's in store. Unlike the tricked-out mega-ferries sailing in some other parts of the Mediterranean, the ferries and hydrofoils that serve the Italian islands are old-school workhorses—the grizzled Marlboro men of watercraft—where fat coils of marine rope are haphazardly tossed underfoot, no doubt a fire hazard, but no one cares. The cloth seats are stained by salt and moisture, but the cabins are clean. The on-board bar—the one and only amenity on most Italian ferries—serves little but *caffè* and canned beer, which is all you really need. For the 1- to 2-hour crossing between mainland and island port, there is nothing to do but look out the window or roam the decks, feeling the sea spray and contemplating the strength and vastness of the water below. As the boat engines hum tirelessly over navigation routes than have been in use for thousands of years, you're being indoctrinated into island life. Laid-back, unvarnished, timeless, and with the essentials of civilization and a potent sense of nature all around—though each has its own personality, this is the fundamental atmosphere of the Italian islands.

HISTORY

Tourism may be the modern vocation of the Italian islands, but the modern era is only a drop in the bucket in the complex histories of these hardy Mediterranean souls. They've sheltered gods and heroes, martyrs and saints; they've withstood or succumbed to ferocious pirate incursions; they've harbored infamous criminals at maximum-security prisons—and at Elba, one very famous French exile.

The blacksmith of ancient Greek mythology, Hephaestus, crafted shields and arrows for the gods within the bowels of Sicily's Mt. Etna, while his Roman counterpart, Vulcan, set up his forge on the Aeolian island that now bears his name—Vulcano. In Homer's *Odyssey,* the sorceress Circe lured Odysseus to her island—Aeaea, or present-day Ponza—where she turned his men into pigs and carried on a yearlong affair with the hero, who was supposed to be sailing home to his wife. The dormant volcano that dominates Ischia, Monte Epomeo, is said to be where the hundred-headed, fire-breathing giant Typhoeus was imprisoned by Zeus, and the giant's grumbles and wails escape in the form of hot springs all around Ischia's coastline.

Just about every Italian island has a least a glancing association with ancient Mediterranean legend, but even those islands that aren't mentioned in myth nevertheless have very real, ancient human histories. It's well documented by ancient literary sources and by archaeological evidence that the Greeks, Phoenicians, Carthaginians, and Etruscans used the Italian islands as hubs of trade, transport, and defense in building their Mediterranean empires. Bloody battles were waged, such as that between Carthage and Rome off the Egadi islands in the 3rd century B.C., for control of these offshore territories. During Rome's domination of the Mediterranean, all of these islands came under imperial rule, and many of them were used as summer retreats—or exile—for the upper echelons of Roman society. You can see fantastic vestiges of the Roman era in the villas of Tiberius on Capri, the brilliant maritime engineering in the Pontine islands, the villas of the Ahenobarbi on Giannutri and Isola del Giglio. Other islands had more commercial than touristic value for the ancients: Elba had been exploited by the Etruscans for its iron and granite, and the Romans continued mining when they took over. Sant'Antioco, in the Sulcitan islands off southwestern Sardinia, was in fact called *Plumbaria*—"Leadville"—by the ancient Romans, who mined the valuable metal there.

In the transition from the Roman Empire to the Christian era, the Italian islands were often places of exile and martyrdom (such as that of St. Antiochus on Plumbaria) and hermitage (San Mamiliano on Montecristo), and in the medieval period, they became important religious sites; the majority of these islands have at one time harbored monastic communities. In the Tremiti islands, the Abbey-Fortress of San Nicola is the most impressive of these ex-island monasteries. The islands' hillsides and coves are also dotted with often lovely sanctuaries dedicated to the Virgin Mary. Whether for reasons of religious persecution or the old-fashioned pursuit of ducats and doubloons, nearly every island that belongs to Italy was subjected at one time or another to pirate raids or privateers' attacks. Many islands have at least one *Torre Saracena,* a squat masonry watchtower along the coast. Typical to central and southern Italy, these defenses were built in the 8th and 9th centuries to ward off incursions by Saracens, pirates from Muslim North Africa. The Saracens stopped hassling the Italian islands

---

DATELINE

15th c. B.C. The mysterious *nuraghi* are built by the Stone Age inhabitants of Sardinia.

1200 B.C. The Homeric hero Odysseus makes his epic voyage around the Mediterranean, stopping at Circe's island (now Ponza) for a year.

5th c. B.C. The Greek temples of the Valle dei Templi are built in ancient Akragas (Agrigento); this era is the apogee of Greek civilization on Sicily.

1st c. A.D. Roman emperor and hedonist Tiberius builds 12 imperial villas on Capri, where ancient biographers relate that he engages in all

sorts of sordid activities that have little to do with statecraft. (Consult Suetonius's biography of Tiberius in *The Twelve Caesars* for some insight into the salacious emperor.)

10th c. A.D. Arab settlers on Pantelleria invent the *dammuso* style of domestic architecture.

1200s The Abbey-Fortress of San Nicola in the Tremiti is fortified to withstand pirate attacks.

Mid-1500s Ottoman privateers Barbarossa and Dragut terrorize many Italian islands in their quest to in the 10th century, but the islands would be on their guard again in the 16th century, which is, not coincidentally, the date of construction of so many fortification walls and castles around the archipelagoes. The 1500s were the era of the legendary Turkish privateers Barbarossa and Dragut, who zigzagged their way around the Mediterranean, capturing galleons and sacking entire towns and islands in the name of the Ottoman Empire. Elba, Ponza, Capri, Procida, Montecristo, Sardinia, Capraia, Lampedusa, not to mention dozens of Greek and Spanish islands and several ports on the Italian mainland, all endured the terrorism of Barbarossa and Dragut.

In 1814, Elba became the most famous island in Italy (and crossword puzzle mainstay) when Napoleon Bonaparte was exiled here after his forced abdication from the French throne. Though he only spent 300 days on Elba, Napoleon stayed long enough to carry out social and economic reforms that still resonate for Elbani today and public works projects—such as the island's excellent roads—that tourists utilize every year. Elba was hardly a backwater before Napoleon arrived: Monuments from Roman and medieval times are strewn over the landscape, and the capital city of Portoferraio was fortified under Cosimo I de' Medici, Grand Duke of Tuscany, in the Renaissance.

Beginning with the unification of Italy in the 1870s and continuing through both World War I and World War II, the political wars of the 1970s, and the Mafia crackdowns of the 1980s and 1990s, several islands went the way of Alcatraz. Only one prison island, Gorgona in the Tuscan archipelago, is still open, with about 70 detainees. Asinara, off Sardinia, and Pianosa, near Elba, were both infamous *supercarceri,* or maximum security prisons for the most dangerous agents of the Mafia, political terrorists, and other big-time felons, who under article 41bis of the Italian Prison Administration Act had basically no rights while detained and were held in solitary confinement until they cooperated with authorities. Asinara and Pianosa both closed in 1998 (though there are still a few prisoners serving . . . spaghetti . . . on Pianosa; see p. 143), and the islands have just recently been reopened to the public. The military prison on Santo Stefano, in the Pontine islands, closed in 1965 and is now in private hands.

re-establish Ottoman domination of shipping routes.

1588 Dr. Giulio Iasolino publishes a treatise on the medical benefits of Ischia's thermal waters, launching the spa tourism that is still going strong on that island today.

1669 Mt. Etna's most catastrophic eruption in modern history destroys several villages in its path and buries part of Catania.

1738 San Pietro Island is colonized by Genoese refugees from Tabarka, an island of Tunisia. Tabarka was abandoned after repeated pirate incursions and exhaustion of the coral resources that had drawn the Genoese settlers there in the first place.

1814 Napoleon exiled to Elba.

1826 The Blue Grotto of Capri is "discovered."

Early 20th c. The organized crime syndicates of the Cosa Nostra rise around Palermo, Sicily.

1930s During the Fascist regime, Benito Mussolini deports homosexuals and other "enemies of state" to internment camps in the Tremiti islands.

continues

Of all the Italian islands, great and small, none has had a richer and more checkered run than Sicily, which is famously joked to have been conquered more times than any other place in Europe. Yet those who conquered it made it the theater of some of the greatest civilizations and unique cross-cultural influences in world history. From the formidable cities of Magna Graecia to the opulent and sophisticated Arab-Norman period to the Mafia-tinged present day, Sicily's story demands a book all its own. Accordingly, Sicily is hands-down the top Italian island destination for anyone with an interest in history, archaeology, architecture, and art. As a cultural treasure-trove, Sicily holds its own with even the monument-heavy mainland cities of Rome, Florence, and Venice.

You might expect Sardinia, which is as big as Sicily and just as strategically positioned in the Mediterranean, to be a history buff's haven—and it can be, if you use your imagination. But despite having been occupied and visited by a litany of empires and maritime republics, Sardinia doesn't feel ancient and doesn't have a whole lot to show for its lengthy history. Blame it on Sardinia's paradise-perfect beaches and waters, which have generated scores of ersatz "vacation villages" and created a sort of modern, Mediterranean-as-Caribbean holiday formula—gorgeous scenery minus must-do sights equals relaxation—that is totally unlike the dripping-with-antiquity, old-world atmosphere of Sicily.

With the exception of Capri, which has been a resort since the days of Julius Caesar, and Ischia, whose thermal waters have drawn travelers for centuries, tourism has only been a significant component of these islands' local economies for the past several decades. For places like distant Pantelleria, which has only ascended to the A-list of chic European hideaways in the past decade or so, locals regard the idea of their remote island as a hip summer destination with amused indifference.

ART & ARCHITECTURE

The lesser Italian islands (that is, all but Sicily and Sardinia) were never endowed with the great art that is found in so many mainland Italian cities, so unless you have

1941	The *Ventotene Manifesto* is written on the Pontine island of Ventotene by two political prisoners being held there. The document lays the groundwork for the idea of the European Union.	**1962**	Karim Aga Khan IV establishes the Consorzio Costa Smeralda and an enclave for the super-rich in northeastern Sardinia.
1949	Roberto Rossellini directs *Stromboli, Terra di Dio* on the Aeolian island of Stromboli. The filmmaker and his star, Ingrid Bergman, have an affair that results in a child out of wedlock; shockwaves of the scandal reach the floor of the U.S. Senate.	**1990s**	Thanks to VIP villa owner Giorgio Armani, Pantelleria climbs to chic getaway status despite its remote location, severe landscape, and down-at-heel port town.
		1998	The *supercarceri* of Pianosa and Asinara, where Italy's toughest criminals have been sent for decades, are closed.
1950s–1970s	Heyday of jet-set tourism on Capri. Jackie Kennedy Onassis is an island regular.	**1999**	Anthony Minghella's remake of *The Talented Mr. Ripley* is filmed on Procida and Ischia. Local

a hankering to see Bronze Age artifacts, you don't need to visit any museums while on the Italian islands. Architecturally, there are few standout monuments, and in all but a few instances, the architecture on the Italian islands is more or less analogous to the contemporary buildings you'd find in the nearest cities and towns on the mainland. The port towns of Ventotene and Procida have the feel of Neapolitan villages, all pastel houses jumbled together. Adorable Capoliveri and Marciana, also on Elba, could hold their own against any Tuscan hill town in a quaintness pageant. The only lesser islands with distinct architectural forms all their own are the Aeolians, off northeast Sicily, and Pantelleria, the lavic castaway off the north coast of Africa.

What you will see over and over in the **Aeolian Islands** (Lipari, Salina, Stromboli, Panarea, Vulcano, Filicudi, and Alicudi) is the so-called *stile eoliano* ("Aeolian style") house. Characterized by whitewashed cubic modules that are either coupled horizontally or stacked vertically, *stile eoliano* makes use of local materials—lava rock for the foundations, pumice for the exterior walls—and responds to the local climate. The typical Aeolian house has a *bagghiu* (terrace) shaded by a cane roof or vine-covered pergola that helps keep the outdoor living space cool and evening humidity out. A stone bench or *bisuola* runs the length of the *bagghiu*, which also originally had built-in ovens, wash basins, and cisterns. The roof or pergola of an Aeolian house's *bagghiu* is supported by fat columns of white pumice called *pulère*. Some multi-story houses in *stile eoliano* also have arcaded loggias. Traditionally, the roof terraces (*àstrico*) served to collect rainwater; now they're more commonly used as a place to watch the sunset.

On **Pantelleria,** the signature architectural form is the *dammuso*. The low-slung stone houses that are all over the island—and all over Pantelleria accommodations-booking websites—were invented in the 10th century by the Arabs who then inhabited the island. Responding to Pantelleria's particular weather and its available materials, they devised a totally original kind of dwelling that was never built anywhere else. Then as now, rain was scarce on Pantelleria, so *dammusi* were given gently domed roofs that connect to slightly concave flumes; originally, these collected rainwater and channeled it to a central cistern that was the source of the residents'

men line up to get a picture with Gwyneth Paltrow.

2001 Saadi Gaadafi (a son of Libyan leader Muammar) crashes his yacht into the marina at Porto Cervo, in the Costa Smeralda, Sardinia.

2003 *The Life Aquatic with Steve Zissou* is filmed in part on and around Ponza.

2007 *The Apprentice* first-season winner Bill Rancic and Naples-born *E! News* anchor Giuliana DePandi are married on Capri at the church of Santa Sofia.

2009 The G8 Summit scheduled to be held on La Maddalena Island, Sardinia, is moved to the Abruzzo city of L'Aquila to show solidarity for victims of the April 6 earthquake.

2010 Construction begins on the long-awaited Strait of Messina Bridge, a 4km-long (2½-miles) suspension bridge that will eventually link Sicily with Calabria, the toe of the Italian peninsula.

water for drinking and washing. The undulating rooflines of *dammusi* are washed with white plaster, which keeps interiors a bit cooler on this sun-beaten island. The dry-laid lava rock walls of a *dammuso* can be up to 1m (3¼ ft.) thick, also as a measure of insulation. *Dammusi* did not originally have discrete rooms with doors, consisting instead of a main living area off of which there were alcoves for sleeping. Most *dammusi* today have been modified to include modern comforts (for example, there were no bathrooms in the original structure), and most of the elaborate, villa-style *dammusi* on Pantelleria are not ancient at all, but built in the last decade to meet the demands of *dammuso*-seeking vacationers.

Integral to any Pantescan *dammuso* is a specific set of outdoor spaces, beginning with the terrace, outfitted on all sides with a stone bench called a *ducchena,* and shaded by a cane roof called a *cannizzato.* Today, the *ducchena* is softened with plush pillows, and there's almost always a hammock slung beneath the *cannizzato.* Not far from the actual *dammuso* is *u jardina,* a garden encircled by a high stone wall, to protect the fruit and citrus trees there from the omnipresent island winds. Nowadays, most *dammusi* or multi-*dammuso* resorts have swimming pools, a feature that was absent in the 10th-century blueprint.

The artistic heritage of **Sicily** is another story entirely, since it is one of the richest troves of tangible culture in Europe, with everything from Greek temples to Arab-Norman churches to Baroque palaces. **Sardinia,** on the other hand, may have its Stone Age *nuraghi,* and Pisan and Spanish fortifications, but on the whole, it has relatively little to offer the art hound. The Genoese enclave of **Carloforte,** on San Pietro island (in the Sulcitans off southwestern Sardinia), is built in the style of the Ligurian riviera towns, complete with gracious little white-balconied Art Nouveau *palazzi* done up in all the colors of the Easter basket.

THE LAY OF THE LAND

On the Tyrrhenian side, the Italian seacoast starts in Liguria, but there aren't any islands until you head south into Tuscany. This means that the Italian islands are the backyard destinations of central and southern Italy. Only the Venetian Lagoon islands and the Tremiti, in the Adriatic, lie off the eastern coast of Italy; the rest are scattered off the west coast in the Tyrrhenian, around Sicily, and off the coast of North Africa. Lampedusa, which is the southernmost point in Italy, belongs geologically to Africa and is only 113km (70 miles) from Tunisia (vs. 205km/127 miles to Sicily). Tunisia is also the nearest landmass to Pantelleria. Given the geographic "logic" of the Italian islands' distribution, Corsica and Malta also belong in this book, but due to the tangled web of Mediterranean history, the former belongs to France and the latter is its own country.

Over half of the Italian islands are totally volcanic in origin (the Aeolians, the Pontines, Ustica, Pantelleria, Linosa, Capraia, Ischia, Procida, San Pietro), while others are the result of limestone deposits (Capri, the Tremiti, the Egadi, Lampedusa, Pianosa, Giannutri), granitic intrusions (Gorgona, Montecristo, La Maddalena), an admixture of limestone and granite (Elba, Giglio, Sardinia), or of volcanic formation combined with other rocks (Sicily, Sant'Antioco).

Whether volcanic or sedimentary, almost all of the Italian islands are objectively beautiful, mountainous, and green, with significant stretches of rocky, impenetrable coastline. Stromboli has a perpetual column of smoke coming out of its volcanic cone; Pantelleria's coastline is a litany of jagged lava rock; Capri has sheer limestone cliffs hundreds of meters high that plunge straight down into the sea. Striking as they are, these geological profiles would be inhospitable if it weren't for the way the Italian islands are always relieved by some gorgeous access to the sea, and always some human component—a lively fishing village, a 1,000-year-old stairway leading down the steep terrain—that softens the landscape and telegraphs a reassuring sign of civilization as you approach from the sea.

Another major factor that makes the Italian islands so attractive is their manageable size. After Sicily and Sardinia, which at 25,000 sq. km (9,653 sq. miles) each are their own worlds with tremendously varied landscapes, the next largest island is Elba, 223 sq. km (86 sq. miles)—or 1% of Sicily or Sardinia. And beyond that, most of the Italian islands are much smaller. The average surface area (again excluding Sicily and Sardinia) is 24 sq. km (9 sq. miles; about the size of Isola del Giglio in the Tuscan archipelago), and the mean size is just 10.5 sq. km (41 sq. miles; equivalent to Capri or Filicudi). Given these diminutive measurements, it never takes very long to get from one side of the island to the other, and it makes that classic pastime, the round-island boat tour, an unhurried half-day excursion. These dimensions guarantee an intimate experience that makes you feel like an insider even with a few days' stay: You'll get to know the beaches, the shortcuts, the bus system, and the best coffee bars in no time at all. In a country known for its attention to tailoring and fit, the Italian islands are comfortably sized *a misura d'uomo* ("to the measure of man"). Distances from the mainland are usually just long enough to get that tonic sense of isolation, but short enough to count on regular transportation links and the prospect of continental comforts.

Beaches, in most cases, are a precious commodity in the Italian islands, and where they do occur, you don't always get sand (*sabbia*). The Italian word for beach, *spiaggia*, is a loose term that can refer to an inlet with fine pebbles (*ciottoli* or *ghiaia*) or a cove with smooth rock slabs (*lastroni*) just as easily as it can describe an actual sandy beach. Perhaps that's why when Italians talk about going for a day of sun and sea, the phrase is *al mare* (to the sea), not *in spiaggia* (to the beach). But take heart; all but a handful (Pantelleria, Ustica, the Venetian Lagoon islands) of the Italian islands have at least one sandy beach, and some (Elba, Ischia, Sicily, and the Mediterranean beach queen, Sardinia) have an embarrassment of golden sandy stretches. The spectacular beaches of Isola dei Conigli on Lampedusa and Chiaia di Luna on Ponza rank right up there with the Mediterranean's most fabulous swimming spots. Even the beach-poor islands usually redeem themselves with some preposterously beautiful cove (see Cala dei Briganti, Palmarola; and Cala Bianca, Marettimo) where you can go for a dip off a boat.

CULTURE & ECONOMY

Through the vicissitudes of the centuries, the lives and livelihoods of *isolani* (islanders) have remained inextricable from their finite allotments of dry land—what mineral resources they contained, or what crops could be grown. Above all, however, their lives have been tied to the sea: Every single day in the history of each of these islands, someone has pulled out of port before dawn with a boat full of nets, hooks, and pots. They've caught and hauled in fish that on both the local and international level have provided the income to feed their families. Even as fishing has been replaced by tourism as the backbone of the economy of some islands, true *isolani* have a connection to nature, resourcefulness and a work ethic, and a sunniness that are both admirable and increasingly rare in this day and age, and especially in modern Italy.

The remoteness of most Italian islands has kept their populations small: In total, the lesser islands count just over 165,000 residents, which amounts to .3% of the entire population of Italy. Fully half of these Italian island residents live in the Bay of Naples islands (Capri: approx. 14,000; Ischia: approx. 62,000; Procida: approx. 11,000), which have essentially become suburbs of Naples. The inhabited island with the smallest population, 1, is Palmarola in the Pontine islands. Sicily has a population of just over 5 million, representing nearly 10% of the overall Italian population, while Sardinia has 1.7 million.

In each archipelago, Roman Catholicism is the predominant religion, and islanders tend to be more of a practicing bunch than their mainland countrymen, perhaps because so much of their existence depends on factors—like the bounty of fish or tourist-friendly weather—that they cannot control. Every island has at least one annual feast day (if not several) dedicated to the local patron saint, which usually involves a solemn procession of the saint's effigy through town and then on a flower-bedecked barge through the marina, followed by fireworks over the harbor. Tourists who happen to be on an Italian island when one of these *feste* takes place may gawk at such a quaint cultural tradition, but the islanders, particularly the elderly, take this stuff very seriously and their eyes will cast daggers at anyone who talks too loudly during the procession or otherwise disrespects the saint on his or her special day.

Tourism represents the main source of income on many islands, but others still make most of their money through fishing. In the case of Sicily, Sardinia, Pantelleria, Salina, Elba, and Giglio, agriculture—namely wine and olive oil—is another major contributor to the island economy. Mining and quarrying, once so important in places like Elba (iron and granite), Favignana (*pietra di Favignana* limestone), Lipari (pumice), and Sardinia (lead, zinc, copper, iron, and especially silver), have ceased in the past few decades. The skeletons of decommissioned mining equipment and hollowed-out rock cavities now stand as poignant examples of industrial archaeology, often directly on the beaches of these islands. The most breathtaking of these is Cala Rossa, Favignana, a science-fictiony cove where the turquoise sea meets orthogonal columns and walls of the local yellow stone that bear the deep score marks of centuries of quarrying.

EATING & DRINKING

Cucina marinara reigns supreme around the Italian islands. This roughly translates as "seafood," but really refers to a specific set of dishes typical to all the Italian seasides, from seafood-based antipasti to pastas to main fish dishes.

The standard starters in *cucina marinara* might be a garlicky *zuppa* (sauté) of shellfish, or octopus salad, or a plate of steamed mixed fish. Some of the seafood antipasti may sound strange, but this is where I encourage you to branch out—you'll discover some wonderful flavors and preparations that are unique to these parts of the Mediterranean.

Just about everywhere, the pastas come with *vongole* (clams), *frutti di mare* (crustaceans, calamari, and fish), or lobster (*aragosta* or the more prized *astice*), and risotto with any number of local sea creatures. Most of these sauces have a base of *pomodorini* (cherry tomatoes), white wine, garlic, and olive oil. Some, like a classic spaghetti *alle vongole*, are *in bianco* ("white," no tomatoes), while the island favorite risotto *al nero di seppia* uses the black ink of cuttlefish to impart its special, delicate flavor.

Fish *secondi* (main courses) are almost always simply prepared—baked, grilled, fried—without many extra ingredients beyond the olive oil, lemon, and a few sprigs of local herbs. Other terms that often accompany fish on the menu are *acqua pazza* ("crazy water"—poached in herbed broth) and *guazzetto* (tomato, garlic, and herb sauce). The usual suspects of a fish *secondi* menu vary only slightly from region to region and typically include *branzino* (sea bass), *orata* (bream), *cernia* (grouper), *rombo* (turbot), *dentice* (dentex), and *grigliata mista* (mixed grilled fish, shrimp, scallops, octopus, squid, and so forth).

A full seafood meal, it must be noted, is always expensive, no matter what island you're on. The good stuff will cost you. Where it really adds up is in the fish *secondo,* or main dish. Often, the price of the entree is listed explicitly on the menu (for example, a fixed 30€ for a portion of grilled sea bass), but more often, the price listed is how much you'll pay per *etto* (hectogram, about a quarter of a pound) for that particular seafood item.

Say you want the *rombo al forno* (baked turbot), and the price listed is 10€ *all'etto.* Before sending your order to the kitchen, the waiter brings out the whole turbot for your inspection and approval (so you can see not just how handsome but how big it is). Italian customers tend to have this whole routine down pat and can tell by looking at the fish how much it's going to cost, how much meat it will yield once filleted, whether it makes sense to split it with another diner, and so on, and there are no surprises when the bill comes. If you aren't familiar with ordering fish this way, I strongly suggest you play the role of dense tourist and have the waiter tell you up front exactly how much the fish weighs and exactly how much it will cost. (This is what I do, every time.) Once it's cooked, it's on your bill. And while many restaurants are very fair and scrupulous about fish entree prices, others are unfortunately not as transparent, and you can end up with a shocking 100€ tab, when you most definitely did not eat an entire kilogram (2¼ lb.) of turbot.

A good way to keep costs within reason and still get a taste of the sea is to explore the antipasto menu: A variety of seafood items always appear as starters, and they're a good way to sample the specialties of *cucina isolana* without being a complete glutton and spending a fortune.

While seafood does dominate most island menus, there are other options for those who aren't big fish eaters and those who, after a few days of *cucina marinara,* cannot bear to see one more prawn on a plate. Relief from fish comes in the form of pizza, vegetable side dishes, salads, or meat dishes. You can always find an antipasto of cured meats and cheeses, and every restaurant serves plain tomato-based pastas.

Sicily has all the other islands beat with its desserts, like *cassata* (sponge cake with ricotta and chocolate or vanilla and covered with marzipan) and cannoli. Luckily, these are easy to find around the Aeolians, Egadi, Pelagie, and Ustica, too.

With all that dining guidance in mind, don't plan on eating every meal out. Island life is all about *leggerezza* (lightness), and you probably won't feel like a big lunch and a big dinner. Dinner is definitely the main event on Italian islands, as that's when you get to strut your tan and mix with everyone else out for the evening *passeggiata.* While restaurants do serve lunch, most island vacationers take their midday meal in the form of a *panino* (sandwich) on the beach or boat. At the ports and main squares of any island village, you'll find snack bars or kiosks where you can pick up to-go lunches before a day at the beach or a boat tour, or you can stop into the local grocer's and pick up fruit, prosciutto, bread, and water—whatever your heart desires. Pretty much every beach has at least one vendor selling simple sandwiches with mozzarella and

SPECIALTIES OF THE HOUSE, archipelago BY ARCHIPELAGO

Yes, you can get shrimp pasta anywhere, but there are a few culinary items that are unique to, or done especially well in, particular island groups.

Aeolian Islands: Spaghetti *ai ricci di mare* (with sea urchin eggs—trust me on this one; it's a delicate flavor!)

Bay of Naples Islands: *Insalata caprese* (with mozzarella, tomato, and basil); *coniglio all'ischitana* (stewed rabbit, a major feature on Ischia menus); *insalata di limoni* (made with Procida's huge and nonsour lemons); pizza (you're still in Naples, after all)

Egadi Islands: *Tonno* (tuna) in all its myriad forms, including *bottarga* (tuna roe); fish couscous; almond-based pesto; cassatelle (ravioli-like pastries filled with ricotta and chocolate and dusted with powdered sugar)

Pontines Islands: Legumes like *fave* (fava beans), *lenticchie* (lentils), and *cicerchie* (like chick peas)

Tuscan Islands: *Cacciucco* (fish soup); *schiaccia briaca* ("drunk torte" with pine nuts, raisins, and Aleatico wine)

tomato. For breakfast, an Italian island morning is no different from a mainland Italian morning: cappuccino, pastry, and *spremuta* (freshly squeezed juice). Hotels normally provide breakfast with the room rate, but—and this is a cardinal rule for Italian hotel coffee—the cappuccino and espresso are never as good as they are at the bar down the street.

WINES OF THE ITALIAN ISLANDS

Sicily (including the Aeolians and Pantelleria) and Sardinia are both significant producers of wine. Ischia, Ponza, and the Tuscan islands of Elba and Giglio also have well-established, if small-scale, winemaking traditions. Even good-quality bottles don't cost more than about 10€ in local wine shops, and are often priced well below that.

Except for the well-known Marsala (Sicily's fortified wine, analogous to port or sherry), Sicilian wines rarely made it off the island until relatively recently. Now you can find Sicilian wine on the shelves of liquor stores in Kansas City. They're even better and much less expensive at the source. Most common is the unpretentious **Nero d'Avola,** made from the indigenous red grape of the same name that grows in southeastern Sicily. Nero d'Avola is similar to Syrah/Shiraz and goes best with meat dishes. But don't neglect **Etna Rosso,** from the fertile slopes of Mt. Etna, or the tasty **Cerasuolo di Vittoria,** typical of Ragusa province. Noteworthy white wines include **Bianco d'Alcamo** and wines made from the **Inzolia, Grillo,** and **Grecanico** grapes. Among the dessert and aperitif wines, you can sample numerous versions of **Marsala** (they're not all as sweet as you think) or **Malvasia delle Lipari,** from white malvasia grapes grown in the Aeolian islands. The aristocrat of Sicilian sweet wines is actually from Pantelleria. Exotic, volcanic Pantelleria is home to the zibibbo grape, which is sun-dried to make the sophisticated raisin wine **Passito di Pantelleria.**

Sardinia's wines are often outstanding, but they're not widely exported, so be sure to sample as much as you can during your visit. The serious reds made on the island, Cannonau and Cabernet Sauvignon, may get more critical attention, but who wants to drink a big beefy red with grilled shrimp in the middle of the summer? That's where Sardinia's excellent white wines come in. Seek out Sella e Mosca's sublimely affordable **Terre Bianche,** a versatile, crisp, and dry wine made from the uncommon torbato grape, and **Vermentino,** which pairs wonderfully with seafood.

Elba has a burgeoning wine scene with some elegant, unique varietals—pair the white **Ansonica** with shellfish, and sip the sweet red **Aleatico** with dessert—that are hard to find off the island. **Giglio,** on the other hand, makes a robust white wine called **Ansonaco** (16%–17% alcohol) that is, shall I say, not for beginners. Your liver will be begging for mercy even before you've finished the first glass.

Ponza has a single vineyard—on lonely Punta del Fieno—where the island's local wine is made. Known as **Fieno,** it's a humble wine but worth a taste while you're here. The white is better than the red and goes well with seafood and vegetables.

WIND & WEATHER

Every Italian worth his sea salt is familiar with the winds of the Mediterranean and how they can make or break a day at the beach. There are eight distinct winds on the Italian wind compass, or *rosa dei venti,* so named for its multi-petaled shape. The major players are those that blow in from the north (the *tramontana*), the northwest (the *maestrale*), and the southeast (the *scirocco*). Less frequently cited winds, though they can definitely affect weather and sea conditions, are the *grecale* (from NE), the *levante* (E), the *ostro* (S), the *libeccio* (SW), and the *ponente* (W). On Capraia in the Tuscan archipelago, the only sand beach on the island disappears with the *grecale* and reappears only when the *libeccio* causes the water to recede.

The **scirocco** (from SE) originates in the Sahara desert and brings hot, dusty, dry air. While it is a significant meteorological factor mostly in Sicily and the Sicilian islands, its effects can be felt on any Italian island and throughout Europe. It is most prevalent in spring and fall and can blow for several hours or several days at a time. When the *scirocco* is at full throttle (typically in Mar and Nov, when gusts can reach speeds of over 100kmph/62 mph), the days are unseasonably warm and cars and windows from Palermo to Rome become coated with sand that flew all the way in from Africa. (The coarse particles also seem to make a beeline for the small working parts of cellphones and cameras, so make sure your electronics are well protected when the *scirocco* picks up.) But even in summer, the *scirocco* can be a pest, whipping arid heat into the already torrid days. Sicilians are so used to living with this wind that many houses have a room in the basement called the *camera dello scirocco* (*scirocco* room), where occupants can take shelter from the hot, sand-filled gusts. When visiting any of the Sicilian islands, it's always good to know where the *scirocco*-proof beaches are—look for anything that not only doesn't face south to the open sea but also has some sort of geographical barrier (for example, a promontory or a bay) between the beach and the southeast.

The **maestrale** (from NW) or mistral occurs when high-pressure air from the Atlantic between Spain and France meets low pressure in the gulf of Genoa. By the time the *maestrale* reaches the Mediterranean, it is a dry, clean wind that almost always heralds blue skies and exceptionally luminous sunshine. Photographers love the *maestrale* for its air-clearing properties, but beachgoers may not be as enamored of this stiff wind. In Sardinia especially, where thousands of wind-bent pines and junipers are testimony of the *maestrale*'s frequent visits, it can lift the sand on unprotected beaches. The corollary is that the *maestrale* also lifts sails—part of the reason why Sardinia is such a sailing and windsurfing mecca.

The cold **tramontana** (from the Latin *transmontanus,* "across the mountains") blows in off the mountains of France, similar in genesis to the *maestrale,* and can be a party-pooper for vacationers trying to tease a bit of Indian summer out of the islands of the Tyrrhenian. Though it's predominantly a winter phenomenon, when windchill effects can be serious for Mediterranean ship crews, the *tramontana* can also start as early as September or October. Early fall is a glorious time to visit the Italian islands—that is, until the *tramontana* decides to make its annual debut. When it does, forget going to the beach. You'll have clear weather, but it'll be too cold and blustery to swim: For many Italian island resorts, the *tramontana* is the death knell for the tourist season.

There is no way of knowing far in advance when, precisely, any of these winds will hit, so you won't be able to book your entire trip around them. The good news is that the prevailing winds during the traditional tourist season (May–Sept) are generally vacation friendly, clearing the air and providing gentle, refreshing breezes. Even if you do encounter that torrid *scirocco,* rarely does it upset your holiday plans for more than about a day. But in addition to having a good *scirocco* back-up beach plan, some healthy islander perspective and patience is a good thing. When an unexpected wind interrupts hydrofoil service to Capri in the height of August, don't freak out and get mad at the boat company staff, as if they conjured the *tramontana* just to mess you up. Instead, shrug like a savvy islander would, and do the next practical thing: Take the ferry. It's cheaper anyway.

FLORA & FAUNA

The destinations in this book may be spread far and wide, with diverse geological profiles, but in terms of biology, there are a few constants you can count on from Ponza to Pantelleria. Certain plants tend to flourish on Italian islands because maritime environments in the Mediterranean intrinsically share certain conditions that favor the growth of the same kinds of vegetation. With the exception of Sicily and Sardinia, which are so large they have their own diverse ecosystems, the Italian islands share the same basic environmental factors and small dimensions (even inland, you're never more than about 5km/3 miles from the water) and thus the same vegetation. If a plant or tree needs dry, hot summers and frost-free winters, and can tolerate salt-carrying moisture and strong winds, chances are you'll find it on the Italian islands. Likewise, the fauna of the Italian islands tends to include the same seabirds, small land mammals, and innocuous reptiles, and of course, sea creatures over and over. Fish, crustaceans, and mollusks represent a paycheck for many Italian islands, like Lampedusa, where the economy is still largely based on fishing. Good news for seafood lovers: The bounty of the Mediterranean is democratically distributed among the Italian islands, and the critters that wind up in your *frutti di mare* pasta are pretty much the same whether you're eating it on Ischia or Ustica.

Although many of these islands have been at least partially inhabited by humans for millennia—and thus, their ecosystems altered with the introduction of non-endemic animals or the planting of crops, and so on—there are nevertheless several zones in the archipelagoes of Italy where the native flora and fauna have survived mostly intact. Largely in the past few decades, these zones have been established as marine reserves and national parks where strict rules apply to their touristic use and development. These protected areas include the national parks of the Tuscan archipelago, of the Maddalena islands, of Circeo (including Zannone island in the Pontine archipelago), and of Asinara (Sardinia), and the marine reserves of the Tremiti islands, of Ustica, of the Egadi islands, and of the Pelagie islands.

Flora

In the world of Italian island flora, **macchia mediterranea** is far and away the dominant force. Similar to the way "chaparral" describes shrubland in parts of North America, *macchia* is a collective term that refers to the characteristic set of shrubs and small trees that blanket the wild stretches of Italy's coastline, both on the mainland and the islands. (On the mainland, however, development has reduced the prevalence of *macchia*, while the islands have more of it intact.) Literally, *macchia* translates as "stain," which has a negative ring in English but is an apt description because over and over, this tangle of shrubs and trees has indelibly marked the islands and coastal territories of the Mediterranean Sea.

The plants that most commonly show up in Italian island *macchia* are cistus (*cisto*, with its little white or pink flowers with a yellow center); heather (*erica*); euphorbia (*euforbia*); myrtle (*mirto*); rosemary (*rosmarino*); broom (*ginestra*—whose blooms explode into a sea of yellow, transforming the look of Italian islands in spring); and oleander. The shrubs of the *macchia bassa* can flourish practically alongside the surf because they're short in stature (no more than 2–3m/6½–10 ft. tall) with robust stems, and stiff, leathery leaves that can weather the wind, moisture and salt.

Macchia alta refers to the typical trees or taller shrubs (up to 4m/13 ft. tall) of these coastal settings, the most common of which are ilex (*leccio*—the most frequent tree species in the Mediterranean), cork oak (*sughera*), laurel (*alloro*), strawberry tree (*corbezzolo*; the fruit is a kind of spiny and sour berry, not a strawberry), lentisk (*lentisco*, or mastic), and juniper (*ginepro*). *Macchia* usually grows in dense clusters, where the stems of the myrtle are intertwined with that of the heather, but some species are more solitary, like capers, which cling to sheer rock faces.

A sensual attribute of most *macchia* species is that their leaves are coated with resins that together make up a heady bouquet that perfectly sums up the scent of the Italian islands. These resins are fragrant year-round but at their most potent in late spring. Italian island cuisine makes ample use of the flavors inherent in *macchia*; the aromatic herbs are gathered to infuse everything from baked fish to roast pork to pasta sauces. But cooks aren't the only ones taking advantage: The spas in fancy island resorts use essential oils derived from these leaves to infuse your massage oil. Whether the scent of rosemary can cure an aching back is another matter, but I'd like to think so.

Pinus pinea—the umbrella-shaped **stone pine**, or *pino domestico* in Italian—also makes frequent appearances on Italian islands, where they often occur in dense stands along the beach, from Elba to Ponza to Sardinia. It's the only Italian pine that yields edible pine nuts and is such an integral part of Italian life that just about every coastal town and island has a La Pineta (pinewood) hotel, a Via dei Pini, and a Bar del Pino. Similar to the domestic pine is the **Aleppo pine** (*pinus halepensis,* shorter with a less orderly branch system), which can be found in large numbers on San Domino island in the Tremiti. The so-called **maritime pine** (*pinus pinaster,* which has more of a column shape) also grows on some of the Tuscan islands but is not, despite its name, nearly as prevalent in the islands of Italy as the good old umbrella-shaped *pinus pinea*. Another common tree of the Italian islands is the **eucalyptus,** especially in the coastal regions of Sicily and Sardinia.

In the Pontine islands, the Aeolians, the Egadi, the Pelagie, and Sicily itself, **prickly pear cactus** (*fico d'India*) and **agave** lend an exotic, desertlike air to these coasts, where *macchia* also grows.

The underwater analog of *macchia*, at least in its prevalence, is ***posidonia,*** or Neptune grass. Nicknamed *l'oliva del mare* ("olive of the sea"), it is a widespread seagrass that occurs in great tufty meadows on the sea floor. *Posidonia* is the linchpin of marine ecosystems, producing oxygen and nourishing countless sea creatures, which feed off micro-organisms and bacteria that grow in the grass. Furthermore, *posidonia* acts as a sort of nursery for the sea: The tufts of grass provide ideal nesting sites for all kinds of fish, mollusks, crustaceans, and echinoderms.

Fauna

Admittedly, the Italian islands don't jump out as a prime destination for observing wildlife above the water line, but you can encounter some interesting creatures on Elba, where mouflon (sheep), hedgehogs, and wild boar populate the backcountry, and especially Sardinia, with its endemic pony, the *cavallino di Gesturi*, and the albino donkeys of Asinara. Seabirds are of course a common feature of Italian islands, and the species that recur in several of the archipelagoes are gulls, shearwaters, cormorants, egrets, herons, falcons, eagles, and buzzards. You can even find pink flamingos in the coastal ponds of Sardinia. Nearly every Italian island counts among its reptile life wall lizards and a few small harmless snakes; among the amphibians, tree frogs and common toads are typical. Land mammals you'll find on all but the smallest and most barren islands are rabbits, dormice and other rodents, and bats. The larger islands (Elba, Sardinia, and Sicily) host populations of deer, and many islands have wild goats and sheep.

As for seafood—um, I mean, marine fauna—there's a fairly predictable roster of fish, shellfish, and crustaceans you'll find over and over on the Italian islands, and on their restaurants' menus. Some of their English names are meaningless because these really are Mediterranean natives and not likely to be encountered in other oceans. Typical fish found close to shore are grouper (*cernia*); dentex (*dentice*); bream (*sarago, orata, musdea*); mullet (*cefalo, triglia*); amberjack (*ricciola*); sea bass (*branzino, spigola, corvina*); mackerel (*sgombro*); sole (*sogliola*); turbot (*rombo*); moray eels (*murena*); and conger (*grongo*). The king of Italian fish, tuna (*tonno*), and swordfish (*pesce spada*) prefer to swim farther out in the open sea. Among the crustaceans, the usual suspects are shrimp (*scampi*), prawns (*gamberi*), lobster (*astice*), spiny lobster or langouste (*aragosta*), and less commonly, spider crabs (*granseola*). Typical mollusks are striped Venus clams (*vongole*); blue mussels (*cozze*); scallops (*capesante*); octopus (*polipo* or *polpo*, and the smaller *moscardino*); squid (*calamari*); flying squid (*totano*); and cuttlefish (*seppia*, similar to squid). Sea urchins (*riccio di mare*—literally "sea hedgehog") also inhabit the reefs of many Italian islands and show up in recipes, especially on Sicily and its satellite island groups. For those who will be diving off the Italian islands, *buona immersione!* For the rest of us, *buon appetito!* Nearly all the sea creatures of the Mediterranean have the common characteristic of delicate flesh that, while retaining a certain marine flavor, never tastes too fishy.

There are, of course, a few marine animals that are not eaten. The *caretta caretta* (loggerhead sea turtle) nests on Lampedusa and Linosa. Around many islands of the

THE thug OF THE MEDITERRANEAN

Special mention must be made of the very ugly *scorfano* (scorpion-fish): If you met this 50cm-long (20-in.) fish in a dark alley—or dark reef crevice—you'd probably scream and run the other way, horrified at its spiky dorsal doodads, baleful underbite (punctuated by ghastly fleshy appendages), and general coloring, which is disconcertingly similar to that of raw meat. But try to look past his beastly exterior, because the *scorfano* is your friend: Its meat is among the most prized in all of Italian seafood for its wonderful flavor and consistency. Cooking *scorfano* is an art form that Italian island restaurants have mastered, so order it the next time you see it on the menu, usually as part of a soup or pasta sauce.

Mediterranean, the common dolphin (*delfino*) and porpoise (*tursiope*) swim both near the shore and farther out at sea. Occasionally, fin and minke whales (*balenottere*) and sperm whales (*capodogli*) can be in the open waters along ferry routes. Sharks, though common to the Mediterranean, are not likely to be encountered in the waters off the Italian islands. The most frequent species is the blue shark (*prionace glauca*), which can reach a formidable 4m (13 ft.) in length but is not known to attack humans and rarely ventures close to shore.

PLANNING YOUR TRIP TO THE ITALIAN ISLANDS

3

So you want to embark on a trip to the Italian islands—*benissimo!* But where to start? More than the well-known cities of the Italian mainland, where transportation connections are frequent and lodging is plentiful, travel in the Italian islands requires a bit of extra planning. Careful attention must be paid to boat schedules, as well as the unique rhythms of island tourism that sees certain islands all but shuttered for much of the year. In this chapter, I outline all kinds of general Italy-tourism information that's as valid in Rome as it is on Elba, but I also include lots of island-specific tips and logistical considerations—from when to go to what to wear to how much you'll spend—that will hopefully make your trip as smooth and free of unpleasant surprises as can be. Even armed with this primer, travelers to the Italian islands must still bear in mind that the best laid plans are always at the whim of mare (sea) and vento (wind). Along with your sunblock and flip-flops, bring some flexibility and pazienza.

VISITOR INFORMATION

The Italian Tourist Board, or **ENIT (Ente Nazionale per il Turismo),** has offices in major cities around the world, stocked with literature and maps, and staffed by native Italians who tend to be one of two extremes: enthusiastic resources for general information about travel in Italy, or totally disinterested government employees who would rather do a crossword puzzle or drink their coffee, anything besides helping prospective tourists plan a trip. However, in the hopes that you happen upon one of the helpful folks, contact information for some of ENIT's international offices is listed here.

United States

CHICAGO 500 N. Michigan Ave., Ste. 506, Chicago, IL 60611; ✆ **312/644-0996;** fax 312/644-3019; brochure hotline 312/644-0990; chicago@enit.it (Mon–Fri 9am–5pm).

LOS ANGELES   12400 Wilshire Blvd., Ste. 550, Los Angeles, CA 90025; ✆ **310/ 820-1898;** fax 310/820-4498; brochure hotline 310/820-0098; losangeles@enit.it (Mon–Fri 9am–5pm).

NEW YORK   630 Fifth Ave., Ste. 1565, New York, NY 10111; ✆ **212/245-5618;** fax 212/586-9249; brochure hotline 212/245-4822; newyork@enit.it (Mon–Fri 9am–5pm).

Canada

TORONTO   175 Bloor St. East, South Tower, Ste. 907, Toronto (Ontario) M4W 3R8; ✆ **416/925-4882;** fax 416/925-4799; brochure hotline 416/925-3870; toronto@ enit.it (Mon–Fri 9am–5pm).

United Kingdom

LONDON   1 Princes St., W1B 2AY London; ✆ **20 74081254;** fax 20 73993567; london@enit.it.

Australia

SYDNEY   46 Market St., Level 4, Sydney NSW 2000; ✆ **02 92621666;** fax 02 92621677; sydney@enit.it.

ENIT's website, www.italiantourism.com, contains a lot of information, if you know where to look and can put up with incomplete and sloppy translations, but does not have a ton of coverage for the lesser islands (meaning all of them besides Sicily and Sardinia). You're usually better off going directly to the official website for the local tourist board of that particular island or archipelago. Not every island group has an official tourism website, but those that do are listed here.

Aeolian Islands: www.aasteolie.191.it is one of those messy, blinking affairs but between the flashing buttons you'll find such handy information as ferry timetables and exhaustive listings of hotels, B&Bs, furnished rooms, campsites, and other accommodations for each island.

Bay of Naples Islands: www.infoischiaprocida.it and **www.capritourism. com** are both excellent resources that can help with all aspects of trip planning.

Egadi Islands: www.comune.trapani.it/turismo/tourism/surroundings.htm contains overviews in English of Favignana, Levanzo, and Marettimo, with links to tourism websites operated by private agencies.

Pontine Islands: www.latinaturismo.it has cursory information about Ponza and Ventotene, although most of it is in Italian.

Sardinia: www.sardegnaturismo.it gets the prize for most comprehensive regional website in Italy. Absolutely everything you could possibly need to know about the island is covered, although it may require some digging, so thorough and thick is the information here.

Sicily: www.regione.sicilia.it has plenty of tidbits to whet your appetite, but it's frustratingly incomplete as far as regional profiles and practical information, and the accommodations search function is difficult to use. However, there are a number of PDF brochures you can download, including a colorful 50-page treatise on Sicilian beaches.

Tuscan Islands: www.aptelba.it is the portal for the entire Tuscan archipelago and is fairly user friendly. It's packed with practical information, historical and cultural profiles, and databases for lodging and dining.

Additionally, many islands have a local brick-and-mortar government-sanctioned tourist information office, which is called the APT (Agenzia per la Promozione del Turismo), AAST (Azienda Autonoma di Soggiorno Cura e Turismo), or Pro Loco, where you can pick up maps and brochures, ask for itinerary ideas, and book accommodations. I've listed those individual addresses and phone numbers in each destination chapter.

ENTRY REQUIREMENTS & CUSTOMS

For non-European Union citizens, a passport is required to travel to Italy. Citizens of the U.S.A, Canada, Australia, and New Zealand, and many other countries, do not need a visa of any kind as long as you're staying for less than 3 months. If you don't already have a passport, you should apply for one at least 90 days in advance of your trip. (If you're short on time, you can opt for expedited processing, but you'll pay about double the standard fee.) In general, the post office is the easiest place to file your passport applications and renewal forms.

Passports must be valid for 3 months beyond the date of your final flight back home. (However, you will not be required to show a return travel document when you go through Italian immigration checkpoints.) Non-E.U. passports are stamped upon arrival at the airport, which effectively gives you a tourist visa good for 90 days. If you plan to travel in Italy for longer than that, you must leave and reenter Italy before the 90-day period expires, and your tourist visa will be renewed upon reentry for another 90 days. Technically, failure to comply with these time-limit regulations could result in deportation, although in practice this is uncommon.

All children traveling abroad must have their own passports. To prevent international child abduction, E.U. governments may require documentary evidence of relationship and permission for the child's travel from the parent or legal guardian not present. For up-to-date details on entry requirements for children, visit the U.S. State Department website: http://travel.state.gov/foreignentryreq.html.

For Residents of Australia: You can pick up an application from your local post office or any branch of Passports Australia, but you must schedule an interview at the passport office to present your application materials. Call the Australian Passport Information Service at ℂ **131-232,** or visit the government website at www.passports.gov.au.

For Residents of Canada: Passport applications are available at travel agencies throughout Canada or from the central Passport Office, Department of Foreign Affairs and International Trade, Gatineau, QC K1A 0G3 (ℂ **800/567-6868;** www.ppt.gc.ca).

For Residents of Ireland: You can apply for a 10-year passport at the Passport Office, Setanta Centre, Molesworth St., Dublin 2 (ℂ **01/671-1633;** www.irlgov.ie/iveagh). You can also apply at 1A South Mall, Cork (ℂ **021/484-4700**), or at most main post offices.

For Residents of New Zealand: You can pick up a passport application at any New Zealand Passports Office or download it from the website. Contact the Passports Office at ℂ **0800/225-050** in New Zealand or 04/474-8100, or log on to www.passports.govt.nz.

For Residents of the United Kingdom: To pick up an application for a standard 10-year passport (5-year passport for children under 16), visit your nearest passport office, major post office, or travel agency or contact the United Kingdom Passport Service at ℂ **0870/521-0410** or search its website at www.ukpa.gov.uk.

For Residents of the United States: Whether you're applying in person or by mail, you can download passport applications from the U.S. State Department website at http://travel.state.gov. To find your regional passport office, either check the U.S. State Department website or call the National Passport Information Center's toll-free number (© **877/487-2778**) for automated information.

For Children: To obtain a passport, the child must be present, in person, with both parents at the place of issuance; or a notarized statement from the parents is required. Any questions parents or guardians might have can be answered by calling the National Passport Information Center at © **877/487-2778** Monday to Friday 8am to 8pm Eastern Standard Time.

Visas

U.S., Canadian, U.K., Irish, Australian, and New Zealand citizens with a valid passport don't need a visa to enter Italy if they don't expect to stay more than 90 days and don't expect to work there. For more on visa applications, visit the Italian Ministry of Foreign Affairs website (www.esteri.it).

Customs

WHAT YOU CAN BRING INTO ITALY   Foreign visitors can bring along most items for personal use duty-free, including fishing tackle, a pair of skis, two tennis rackets, a baby carriage, two hand cameras with 10 rolls of film or a digital camera, computer, CD player with 10 CDs, tape recorder, binoculars, personal jewelry, portable radio set (subject to a small license fee), and 400 cigarettes and a quantity of cigars or pipe tobacco not exceeding 500 grams (1.1 lb.). There are strict limits on importing alcoholic beverages. However, for alcohol bought tax-paid, limits are much more liberal than in other countries of the European Union.

WHAT YOU CAN TAKE HOME FROM ITALY   Rules governing what you can bring back duty-free vary from country to country and are subject to change, but they're generally posted on the Web. So study up on your home country's regulations before you try to smuggle expensive wines and cheeses home in your suitcase. Also, be aware that anyone caught buying counterfeit products can be fined up to 10,000€, and anyone caught selling counterfeit products could face criminal charges.

U.S. Citizens: For specifics on what you can bring back, download the invaluable free pamphlet *Know Before You Go,* online at www.cbp.gov. (Click on "Travel," and then click on "Know Before You Go.") Or contact the U.S. Customs & Border Protection (CBP), 1300 Pennsylvania Ave. NW, Washington, DC 20229 (© **202/354-1000;** www.cbp.gov), and request the pamphlet.

Canadian Citizens: For a clear summary of Canadian rules, write for the booklet *I Declare,* issued by the Canada Border Services Agency (© **800/461-9999** in Canada, or 204/983-3500; www.cbsa-asfc.gc.ca).

U.K. Citizens: For information, contact HM Revenue & Customs at © **0845/010-9000** (from outside the U.K., 02920/501-261), or consult the website at www.hmrc.gov.uk.

Australian Citizens: A helpful brochure available from Australian consulates or Customs offices is *Know Before You Go.* For more information, call the Australian Customs Service at © **1300/363-263,** or log on to www.customs.gov.au.

New Zealand Citizens: Most questions are answered in a free pamphlet available at New Zealand consulates and Customs offices: *New Zealand Customs Guide for Travellers, Notice no. 4.* For more information, contact New Zealand Customs

Service, The Customhouse, 17–21 Whitmore St., Box 2218, Wellington (✆ **04/473-6099** or 0800/428-786; www.customs.govt.nz).

WHEN TO GO

The Italian islands have a shorter season than tourist areas on the mainland, and are at "full sail" only from June to September. Mid-July through August is peak season and when crowds and prices are at their highest. Some islands, like Pantelleria and parts of Sardinia, get going a little earlier (around Easter or May) and run a little longer (as late as mid-Nov), and some islands, like Sicily, Capri and Ischia, are year-round destinations (though, like the Italian mainland, are much quieter in winter). As a rule of thumb, however, don't expect to find comprehensive services up and running, or a wide range of hotels and restaurants open, from October to May.

If I were to plan my own Italian islands vacation and had the whole calendar available, I'd pick late June, early July, or early September—because I'd find just enough holiday atmosphere, reliable beach and boating weather, and my pick of accommodations at semi-reasonable prices. Unless you're a party-oriented type and craving the Italian summer horde scene—a cultural experience in and of itself—try to avoid August altogether. The heat, though not statistically much worse than in July, is oppressive due to the crowds, hotel prices will leave your wallet whimpering, and the atmosphere in most places resembles spring break. (If you're single, however, you'll love Aug in the Italian islands.) Things are much calmer in the other summer months, when the islands get more families and couples on holiday.

If you're willing to deal with much of the hospitality sector still boarded up from the winter, you can have a wonderful time on the Italian islands in the shoulder months of April, May, and October. The weather is often warm and sunny (though not always warm enough for swimming) with more depth of light (for vacation photos that "pop"), and you'll have a more intimate experience among real island locals. However, rough weather can also strike in the shoulder season, interrupting hydrofoil service and rendering activities like boat tours unpleasant or impossible.

Traveling to the Italian islands out of peak season also means serious savings. Ferry and hydrofoil ticket prices and tourist services like boat or scooter rentals are all more expensive in summer, but nowhere is the difference in cost more striking than in the accommodations sector. Most hotels' rates are broken down into calendar periods, A through D (and sometimes even F or G!). It varies from island to island, but A is the cheap off season (mid-Oct to Apr), B is the almost-as-economical shoulder season (May, early June, late Sept to mid-Oct), C is reasonably expensive high season (mid-June through July, early Sept), and D is the highest, most outrageously priced season of all (*altissima stagione,* which means Aug). Some places crank up the rates even higher (to F or G!) for August's most popular weeks of travel, which straddle the national holiday of Ferragosto, August 15. Prices in the highest bracket are typically double what you'll pay in period A or B.

Unfortunately, traveling to the Italian islands usually means flying to Italy in the peak airfare season of June to September, when ticket prices are 30% to 50% higher than the rest of the year.

WEATHER The Italian islands all have similar climates, and they're all nice and warm in summer. Daytime highs in the 90s (32°–37°C) are common in July and August, but the nights, mercifully, tend to be about 20°F cooler. The farther south you go, the more likely you are to have warm, beach-friendly weather in the shoulder months. Water temperatures can vary widely, even on the same island, but the Med is neither a bathtub nor an ice chest. Even in August, the water is cool and refreshing.

Average Monthly Temperatures

		MAY	JUNE	JULY	AUG	SEPT	OCT
PALERMO, SICILY	Temp (°F)	71	77	83	84	80	73
	Temp (°C)	61	67	73	74	71	64
CAGLIARI, SARDINIA	Temp (°F)	72	80	85	86	80	73
	Temp (°C)	54	61	65	66	63	57
CAPRI	Temp (°F)	73	79	85	85	79	71
	Temp (°C)	54	60	64	64	60	53
TREMITI ISLANDS	Temp (°F)	63	70	75	75	69	60
	Temp (°C)	51	57	62	62	57	50
PANTELLERIA	Temp (°F)	71	77	82	83	79	72
	Temp (°C)	58	64	70	71	68	63
ELBA	Temp (°F)	65	72	80	79	73	64
	Temp (°C)	53	60	65	66	61	55

Source: Weather Underground

Average Sea Temperature off the Italian Islands

	MAY	JUNE	JULY	AUG	SEPT	OCT
TEMP (°F)	66	72	75	77	72	66
TEMP (°C)	19	22	24	25	22	19

HOLIDAYS

Offices and shops in Italy are closed on the following national holidays: January 1 (New Year's Day), Easter Monday, April 25 (Liberation Day), May 1 (Labor Day), August 15 (Assumption of the Virgin), November 1 (All Saints' Day), December 8 (Feast of the Immaculate Conception), December 25 (Christmas Day), and December 26 (Santo Stefano).

GETTING THERE

In terms of easy international travel links, most of the Italian islands play hard to get, throwing down a gauntlet of out-of-the-way ports that are usually quite some distance from the nearest major airport and involve some combination of car, bus, or train just to get to the ferry. Indeed, the sometimes cumbersome connections and elapsed time in reaching the islands from major Italian cities is what has kept them from being mass tourism destinations. Because getting to many of these islands from overseas takes a long time, you can reduce some of the stress and fatigue of the journey with a night or two on the mainland before embarking on the odyssey of land transportation and boats it takes to reach the shores of the Italian islands. If you do elect to go straight through, expect to arrive at your destination late in the afternoon or evening, and very, very tired. But hey, at least you'll wake up the next morning already there!

By Plane

For international travelers heading to the Italian islands, Rome will likely be your first point of entry into Italy. There are, of course, a million permutations of possible flight structures—for example, you could also fly nonstop from Chicago to Frankfurt, Germany, and from there, direct to Alghero, Sardinia—but for North American travelers,

I am a big proponent of making an Italian airport your first landfall after crossing the Atlantic. The main reason for this is that European airport connections (London, Paris, Amsterdam, and so on) seem to be a Bermuda Triangle of lost luggage. If you fly through Rome en route to somewhere else in Italy and the luggage is delayed in Rome—say, on a layover between a flight from Toronto to Rome and Rome to Pantelleria—it's much easier to deal with because it's already in the right country.

High season on most airlines' routes to Rome is usually from June to the beginning of September. This is the most expensive and crowded time to travel. **Shoulder season** is from April to May, early September to October, and December 15 to December 24. **Low season** is from November 1 to December 14 and December 25 to March 31.

FROM NORTH AMERICA   Fares to Italy are constantly changing, but you can expect to pay somewhere in the range of $600 to $1,600 for a nonstop round-trip economy-class ticket from New York to Rome.

Flying time to Rome from New York, Newark, and Boston is 8 hours; from Chicago, 10 hours; and from Los Angeles, 12½ hours.

American Airlines (© 800/433-7300; www.aa.com) offers daily nonstop flights to Rome from Chicago's O'Hare, with flights from all parts of American's vast network making connections into Chicago. **Delta** (© 800/221-1212; www.delta.com) flies from New York's JFK to Milan and Rome; separate flights depart every evening for both destinations. **US Airways/AmericaWest** (© 800/622-1015; www.usairways.com) offers one flight daily to Rome out of Philadelphia (you can connect through Philly from most major U.S. cities). And **Continental** (© 800/231-0856; www.continental.com) flies several times a week to Rome and Milan from its hub in Newark.

Air Canada (© 888/247-2262; www.aircanada.com) flies daily from Toronto to Rome. Two of the flights are nonstop; the others may touch down en route in Montreal, depending on the schedule.

British Airways (© 800/AIRWAYS; www.britishairways.com), **Virgin Atlantic Airways** (© 800/821-5438; www.virgin-atlantic.com), **Air France** (© 800/237-2747; www.airfrance.com), **Northwest/KLM** (© 800/225-2525; www.nwa.com), and **Lufthansa** (© 800/645-3880; www.lufthansa-usa.com) offer some attractive deals for anyone interested in combining a trip to Italy with a stopover in, say, Britain, Paris, Amsterdam, or Germany.

Alitalia (© 800/223-5730; www.alitalia.com) is the Italian national airline, with nonstop flights to Rome from many North American cities, including New York (JFK), Newark, Boston, Chicago, Miami, Washington, and Toronto. Nonstop flights into Milan are from New York (JFK) and Newark. From Milan or Rome, Alitalia can easily book connecting domestic flights if your final destination is elsewhere in Italy. Alitalia participates in the frequent-flier programs of other airlines, including Continental and US Airways.

FROM THE UNITED KINGDOM   Operated by the European Travel Network, **www.discountairfares.com** is a great online source for regular and discounted airfares to destinations around the world. You can also use this site to compare rates and book accommodations, car rentals, and tours. Click on "Special Offers" for the latest package deals.

British newspapers are always full of classified ads touting slashed fares to Italy. One good source is *Time Out.* London's *Evening Standard* has a daily travel section, and the Sunday editions of almost any newspaper will run many ads. Although competition is fierce, one well-recommended company that consolidates bulk ticket purchases and then passes the savings on to its consumers is **Trailfinders**

(© 0845/050-5945; www.trailfinders.com). It offers access to tickets on such carriers as SAS, British Airways, and KLM.

Both **British Airways** (© 0870/850-9850 in the U.K.; www.britishairways.co.uk) and **Alitalia** (© 0871/424-1424; www.alitalia.it) have frequent flights from London's Heathrow to Rome, Milan, Venice, Pisa (the gateway to Florence), and Naples. Flying time from London to these cities is from 2 to 3 hours. British Airways also has one direct flight a day from Manchester to Rome.

The only island you can fly to directly from North America is Sicily, via **Eurofly's** nonstop service from New York-JFK to Palermo. These flights are only offered from July 1 to September 4, and only one to two times a week (either on Thurs evenings, or on Fri and Sat evenings). Eurofly is owned by **Meridiana** (© 866/387-6359 in the U.S. and Canada, 0789/52682 from other countries; www.meridiana.it). Sicily has three airports—Palermo, Catania, and Trapani—which are well served by domestic flights, major European airlines, and budget carriers like RyanAir and EasyJet (from within Italy, Europe, and the U.K.). Similarly, Sardinia has three main airports, Cagliari-Elmas, Alghero-Fertilia, and Olbia, that are served by domestic flights and a number of low-cost carriers from within Europe and the U.K. You can certainly take the ferry to Sicily and Sardinia from mainland Italy—and many Italians do, because they bring their cars—but for foreigners, air travel is generally the most economical and certainly the most time efficient way to reach Sicily and Sardinia.

Far-flung Pantelleria and Lampedusa both have airports, which represent the principal point of entry for visitors to those islands. There are sea connections from Sicily to Pantelleria and Lampedusa, but they're long and infrequent. Flights to those islands, however, are quite pricey, so anyone looking to visit Lampedusa or Pantelleria on a budget would do well to investigate ferry options, inconvenient though they may be.

Getting to the Seaport for Your Island

From Rome (or other major Italian airport with transatlantic service), you'll need to catch a train, bus, or plane to another city, and from there, to the appropriate seaport. Here, broken down for your convenience, are the sequence of connections necessary to reach the mainland seaports (in boldface type) that serve the various islands and island groups in this book. You'll find detailed versions of this in the "Getting There" section of each individual destination chapter.

Aeolian Islands: Flight to Catania or Palermo (1 hr.), bus to **Milazzo** (1–2 hr.), then hydrofoil or ferry to the islands (1–4 hr.).

Bay of Naples Islands: Flight (30 min.) or train (2 hr.) to Naples, bus or taxi to the seaport (15–30 min.), ferry or hydrofoil to the islands (30 min.–1 hr.).

Egadi Islands: Flight to Palermo or Trapani (1 hr.), bus or train to **Trapani** seaport (1–2 hr. from Palermo, 20 min. from Trapani airport), ferry or hydrofoil to the islands (30 min.–2 hr.).

Other Sicilian Islands: Lampedusa: Flight from Rome (1½ hr.); Linosa: Ferry from Lampedusa (3 hr.) or Porto Empedocle, Sicily, near Agrigento (6 hr.); Pantelleria: Flight from Rome (1½ hr.); Ustica: Flight to Palermo (1 hr.), bus or taxi to Palermo seaport (30 min.), ferry to the island (2½ hr.).

Pontine Islands: Ponza: Train to **Anzio** from central Rome (1 hr.), 5-minute bus or taxi to seaport, then ferry (2½ hr.); Ventotene: Train to **Formia** from central Rome (2 hr.), then ferry (2 hr.).

Sardinia: Flight to Cagliari, Alghero, or Olbia (1 hr.).

Sicily: Flight to Palermo, Catania, or Trapani (1 hr.).

Tremiti Islands: Drive (3 hr.) or take the train (5 hr.) to Termoli (1 hr.), then ferry or hydrofoil to the islands (2 hr.). You can also take a helicopter from Foggia (3-hr. drive or train ride from Rome) to the islands (15 min.).

Tuscan Islands: Consider flying into Pisa airport, which is served by Delta nonstop from New York–JFK, when planning travel to the Tuscan archipelago. Elba: Drive to Piombino port (3 hr. from Rome airport, or 1½ hr. from Pisa airport) or take train to Piombino (3 hr. from central Rome; then 10 min. bus or taxi from Piombino train station to the sea port), then ferry or hydrofoil (1 hr.); Isola del Giglio: Drive to Porto Santo Stefano (2 hr. from Rome airport) or take the train to Orbetello (2 hr. from central Rome; then 20 min. bus or taxi from Orbetello station to Porto Santo Stefano seaport); ferry or hydrofoil (1 hr.). Capraia: Train to Livorno (2½ hr. from Rome, or 20 min. from Pisa), then ferry (1½–2½ hr.).

Hydrofoils and Ferries

Detailed information about ticket prices, schedules, and travel times is given in each destination chapter's "Getting There" section, but here is some general information to keep in mind as you map out your trip:

o Hydrofoils are faster and more expensive than ferries, but ferries are the only boats that can operate in rough weather. You can walk around a ferry's exterior deck, but on hydrofoils you're confined to a clammy cabin. There are also fast boats called "jets" that have exterior decks where you can lounge.

o Whether by hydrofoil, ferry, or jet, crossing times to the islands from the mainland rarely exceed a few hours (although it takes 4 hr. to reach Stromboli from Milazzo), so the majority of boats don't have reserved seating or sleeping cabins.

o None of the boats serving the Italian islands is fancy (except some of the Sardinian mega-ferries), but there are always coffee bars and restrooms, and sometimes TV lounges and newsstands.

o Far more boat connections are offered in summer than in winter, spring, and fall.

o It's not necessary to make reservations for hydrofoil and ferry tickets in advance; foot passenger spots rarely sell out, even in August. If they do (or if you miss your boat), don't despair—the next boat is usually only an hour behind. In most ports that are served by multiple boat companies, the companies accept each other's tickets (for example, on Capri, if you miss the 3:10pm NLG boat, and the next boat is a Snav that leaves at 4:10pm, Snav will take the NLG ticket you already purchased).

GETTING AROUND

The islands where you definitely need a car are Sicily, Sardinia (including La Maddalena and the Sulcitans), and Elba (see the individual chapters for those islands for rental agency names and contact information); you'll find a car useful on Pantelleria and Lampedusa, too. The other islands are either too small to require a car, or so well-served by public transportation that a car is superfluous, or don't allow tourist vehicles ashore because of overcrowding. Ischia, for instance, permits visitors' cars only in the shoulder and off season. In the case of the Venetian Lagoon islands, they don't allow cars because they would sink in the canals! So, in the majority of cases on the "lesser" islands, expect to get around on your own two feet, or with fast, inexpensive, user-friendly public transportation.

Plan on walking a fair amount to reach various beaches and coves, although many islands have efficient bus systems that will drop you off right in front of a great swimming spot or other attraction. For islands where you'll have your own car, you'll find driving a pleasure: The roads are well maintained and signposted (for the most part—expect a few wrong turns here and there), though not well lit at night. Keep the driving to the daylight hours.

MONEY & COSTS

Since the advent of the euro (and many foreign currencies' waning strength against it), traveling in Italy can no longer be done on a shoestring, but I've created this table of typical costs to help you budget accordingly. Some islands, like Capri, are dramatically more expensive than the norm, while prices can also vary widely between lesser known and more famous parts of the same islands, like Sicily and Sardinia.

As with any overseas travel, you must notify your financial institution that you are planning to use your debit or credit card in a foreign country from, say, July 1 to July 15. A failure to make this call could result in your showing up on the shores of Pantelleria with no cash, credit, or buying power to your name. However, if you do find yourself in a cash bind, most islands have a Western Union or other money wiring office where you can receive funds from home. However, this is a hassle you want to avoid, so just be sure you make that quick call to your bank!

If you're going to any of the more remote islands, it's a good idea to bring a wad of cash with you. However, even on some of the more far-flung islands, credit cards are accepted at most restaurants, hotels, and bigger or nicer shops. Additionally, the agencies that sell ferry tickets almost always accept credit cards. You'll need cash for coffee, drinks, gelato, small grocery stores and delis, beach clubs, and the majority of boat trips and rentals.

WHAT THINGS COST	€
Double room in a mid-range hotel, high season	160€–220€ per night
Restaurant meal (pasta, shared appetizer, bottle of wine)	20€–25€ per person
Cappuccino, standing at the bar	1€–1.50€
Cappuccino, seated at a cafe table	2€–3.50€
Pint of beer in a pub	4€–5€
Glass of wine at a bar	3€–8€
Prosciutto and mozzarella sandwich, to-go from a deli	2.50€–3.50€
Small motorboat rental, high season	75€–100€ for a half-day
Margherita pizza in a sit-down restaurant	5€–7€
Round-island boat tour	15€–25€ per person
Beach club (lounge chair, umbrella, changing rooms, showers)	10€–18€ per day

GEAR & PACKING

A sun-and-sea vacation to the Italian islands requires some wardrobe items and toiletries you wouldn't necessarily pack for a summer trip to Rome or Florence. Yes, Italy is a shopper's heaven, and yes, you can buy almost everything you need for beach and boat time in the towns of any of these islands, but there are certain items you'll be glad you brought from home.

Number 1? Sunblock. Suncare products tend to be considerably more expensive in Italy (and especially in resort areas) and geared toward the majority of Italians who take their *abbronzature* (suntans) very seriously, which often means applying little or no sun protection before a day's baking under the Mediterranean rays. So, you'll find shelves stocked with SPF 2, 4, 6 oils, and *maybe* a bottle or two of SPF 15. If you want higher protection than that, you'll have to go to a pharmacy and invest in some sort of quasi-medical Swiss-made sunblock that costs 40€. After-sun soothing lotion (with purported tan-extending ingredients!) is widely available in Italy, although plain old green aloe vera gel is a bit harder to come by.

Beach Gear

Higher-end hotels provide guests with beach towels (*tela mare*, strictly separate from bath towels), but it's a good idea, if you're not going to be staying at resorts, to bring your own large terry towel. You can also buy brightly colored souvenir towels in town at any of the Italian islands for about 10€. An all-purpose beach tote will also serve you well. A word on bathing suits (*costumi da bagno*): They're a heck of a lot skimpier in Italy, so you'll probably want to bring one or two from home that provide a little more coverage. (This goes for men as well as women: Plenty of Italian guys now sport looser and longer board shorts, but just as many, of all ages, still rock the clingy 1940s-era trunks that are basically nylon boxer briefs.) Don't worry if your figure isn't that of a supermodel. Italian beachgoers don't let a little flab and cellulite keep them from exposing every possible inch of skin to those UV rays. Note also that many style-conscious vacationers wear one bathing suit for daytime sun and swim, and then shower and change into a fresh suit for the *aperitivo* hour at waterfront bars.

Key Wardrobe Pieces

Italian islands are generally laid-back, and that translates to the way people dress when on vacation there, but to a point—this is Italy, after all. There is an art to the way Italians do beach cover-ups, casual sandals, and island-night-out attire. The watchword is informal-chic, which for women often means ethnic prints (silk sarongs and pareos) and *Survivor*-inspired jewelry (leather cuffs with shells), while the men tend to opt for brand-name sportswear with a faded, broken-in look (cargo shorts that have that just-circumnavigated-the-Earth-in-a-hot-air-balloon patina before they even leave the store). Linen shirts and pants always cut a fine figure on the Italian islands, but also bring a few wrinkle-free shirts and dresses for evening.

As for footwear, rubber flip-flops are all you need during the day (also bring light-weight walking shoes if you plan on doing any hiking), but for hitting the town, upgrade to a slightly nicer pair of leather sandals (for women) or a clean pair of sneakers or hybrid sport shoes for men. (Guys, if you insist on wearing white socks, for the love of God make sure they are not visible. The archetypal Italian island lothario always goes sockless.) Women need not pack any heels, which in addition to being a liability on the cobblestone streets will also look out of place almost anywhere but the chichi shopping streets and nightclubs of Capri and the Costa Smeralda.

Finally, you need a killer pair of big sunglasses (this is something to consider buying in Italy) and a jaded gaze, and you'll begin to look the part.

Luggage Considerations

You can roll even the bulkiest of suitcases right onto the ferry or hydrofoil, but once you're on your particular island, the terrain may be a bit less wheel-friendly and make hauling your heavy bags around very cumbersome. All that means for anyone who, like me, is an incorrigible over-packer is that you'll need to pay for a taxi or one of those golf-cart-sized luggage vehicles when coming and going.

TRAVEL INSURANCE

In these days of never-ending Icelandic volcano eruptions, major airline strikes, and who knows what else, travel insurance isn't such a crazy idea. Check your existing homeowner's, medical, and automobile insurance policies as well as your credit card coverage before you buy, however. You may already be covered for lost luggage, canceled tickets, or medical expenses. If you're prepaying for your trip or taking a flight that has cancellation penalties, consider cancellation insurance.

The cost of travel insurance varies widely, depending on the destination, the cost and length of your trip, your age and health, and the type of trip you're taking, but expect to pay between 5% and 8% of the vacation itself. You can get estimates from various providers through **InsureMyTrip.com.** Enter your trip cost and dates, your age, and other information, for prices from more than a dozen companies.

U.K. citizens and their families who make more than one trip abroad per year may find an annual travel insurance policy works out cheaper. Check **www.money supermarket.com**, which compares prices across a wide range of providers for single- and multi-trip policies.

Most big travel agents offer their own insurance and will probably try to sell you their package when you book a holiday. Think before you sign. **Britain's Consumers' Association** recommends that you insist on seeing the policy and reading the fine print before buying travel insurance. **The Association of British Insurers** (✆ 020/7600-3333; www.abi.org.uk) gives advice by phone and publishes *Holiday Insurance,* a free guide to policy provisions and prices. You might also shop around for better deals: Try **Columbus Direct** (✆ 0870/033-9988; www.columbusdirect.net).

TRIP-CANCELLATION INSURANCE Trip-cancellation insurance will help retrieve your money if you have to back out of a trip or depart early, or if your travel supplier goes bankrupt. Trip cancellation traditionally covers such events as sickness, natural disasters, and State Department advisories. The latest news in trip-cancellation insurance is the availability of **expanded hurricane coverage** and the **"any-reason"** cancellation coverage—which costs more but covers cancellations made for any reason. You won't get back 100% of your prepaid trip cost, but you'll be refunded a substantial portion. **TravelSafe** (✆ **888/885-7233;** www.travelsafe.com) offers both types of coverage. Expedia also offers any-reason cancellation coverage for its air-hotel packages.

For details, contact one of the following recommended insurers: **Access America** (✆ 866/807-3982; www.accessamerica.com), **Travel Guard International** (✆ 800/826-4919; www.travelguard.com), **Travel Insured International** (✆ 800/243-3174; www.travelinsured.com), and **Travelex Insurance Services** (✆ 888/457-4602; www.travelex-insurance.com).

MEDICAL INSURANCE   For travel overseas, most U.S. health plans (including Medicare and Medicaid) do not provide coverage, and the ones that do often require you to pay for services up front and reimburse you only after you return home.

As a safety net, you may want to buy travel medical insurance, particularly if you're traveling to a remote or high-risk area where emergency evacuation might be necessary. If you require additional medical insurance, try **MEDEX Assistance** (✆ 410/453-6300; www.medexassist.com) or **Travel Assistance International** (✆ 800/821-2828; www.travelassistance.com; for general information on services, call the company's **Worldwide Assistance Services, Inc.,** at ✆ 800/777-8710).

Canadians should check with their provincial health plan offices or call **Health Canada** (✆ 866/225-0709; www.hc-sc.gc.ca) to find out the extent of their coverage and what documentation and receipts they must take home in case they are treated overseas.

LOST-LUGGAGE INSURANCE   On international flights (including U.S. portions of international trips), baggage coverage is limited to approximately $9.07 per pound, up to approximately $635 per checked bag. If you plan to check items more valuable than what's covered by the standard liability, see if your homeowner's policy covers your valuables, get baggage insurance as part of your comprehensive travel-insurance package, or buy Travel Guard's "BagTrak" product.

If your luggage is lost, immediately file a lost-luggage claim at the airport, detailing the luggage contents. Most airlines require that you report delayed, damaged, or lost baggage within 4 hours of arrival. The airlines are required to deliver luggage, once found, directly to your house or destination free of charge.

HEALTH

In general, Italy is viewed as a safe destination, although problems, of course, can and do occur anywhere. You don't need to get shots; most foodstuffs are safe, and the water in cities and towns is potable and often excellent. It is easy to get a foreign prescription filled at Italian pharmacies, and nearly all places throughout Italy contain English-speaking doctors at hospitals with well-trained medical staffs. The lesser Italian islands do not all have hospitals but are equipped with emergency responders and, if needed, can arrange for helicopter med-evac to another island, or the mainland, where there are better medical facilities.

For emergencies requiring immediate attention or specialized equipment, call ✆ **118** for an ambulance or go to the nearest *pronto soccorso* (emergency room). Note that non-critical cases seen at the *pronto soccorso* will be charged a fee of 25€ or more. For health issues that aren't emergencies but still need attention (for example, strep throat), get the name of a local doctor, who will usually be able to see you promptly and charge you a fee of 15€ for an office visit or 25€ for a house call. Outside of doctors' office hours, you can call the local *guardia medica* (phone numbers listed in each island's "Fast Facts" section). The *guardia medica* is a free service, open from 8pm to 8am. Some more heavily developed vacation areas have a *guardia medica turistica* that is open during daytime hours as well. Island medical offices aren't always staffed with English speakers, so it's a good idea to have an Italian speaker make the initial call, if possible.

For minor issues, the pharmacy is your best bet. Marked with a green or red cross, Italian pharmacies may look tiny, but they're stocked to the gills with everything from ankle braces and tampons to ibuprofen and blister-relief pads. You can also walk into a pharmacy, tell the pharmacist your complaint (or act it out if there's a language barrier), and he or she will produce some sort of remedy, pharmaceutical or natural, from behind the counter. (I have scored some great medicine cabinet standbys this way, including excellent heartburn tablets that look like pebbles of travertine.) While pharmacists are technically required to see a written prescription in order to sell prescription drugs, in practice it's a bit more relaxed than that: If your yeast infection flares up while you're on Elba, and you know the name of the drug you normally take for it back home, you can probably get the pharmacist to sell you that medicine with little hassle.

General Healthcare Information for Travelers

Contact the **International Association for Medical Assistance to Travelers** (**IAMAT;** ✆ **716/754-4883,** or 416/652-0137 in Canada; www.iamat.org) for tips on travel and health concerns in the countries you're visiting, and for lists of local, English-speaking doctors. The United States **Centers for Disease Control and Prevention** (✆ **800/311-3435;** www.cdc.gov) provides up-to-date information on health hazards by region or country and offers tips on food safety. **Travel Health Online** (www.tripprep.com), sponsored by a consortium of travel medicine practitioners, may also offer helpful advice on traveling abroad. You can find listings of reliable medical clinics overseas at the **International Society of Travel Medicine** (✆ **770/736-0313;** www.istm.org).

The following government websites offer up-to-date health-related travel advice:

Australia: www.dfat.gov.au
Canada: www.hc-sc.gc.ca
U.K.: www.dh.gov.uk
U.S.: www.cdc.gov

WHAT TO DO IF YOU GET SICK AWAY FROM HOME Any foreign consulate can provide a list of area doctors who speak English. If you get sick, consider asking your hotel concierge to recommend a local doctor—even his or her own.

Medical Insurance While Traveling

For travel abroad, you may have to pay all medical costs up front and be reimbursed later. Medicare and Medicaid do not provide coverage for medical costs outside the U.S. Before leaving home, find out what medical services your health insurance covers. To protect yourself, consider buying medical travel insurance.

Very few health insurance plans pay for medical evacuation back to the U.S. (which can cost $10,000 and up). A number of companies offer medical evacuation services anywhere in the world. If you're ever hospitalized more than 150 miles from home, **MedjetAssist** (✆ **800/527-7478;** www.medjetassistance.com) will pick you up and fly you to the hospital of your choice. Annual memberships are $225 individual, $350 family; you can also purchase short-term memberships.

U.K. nationals will need a **European Health Insurance Card (EHIC)** to receive free or reduced-costs health benefits during a visit to a European Economic Area (EEA) country (E.U. countries plus Iceland, Liechtenstein, and Norway) or Switzerland. The European Health Insurance Card replaces the E111 form, which is no longer valid. For advice, ask at your local post office or see www.dh.gov.uk/travellers.

If you suffer from a chronic illness, consult your doctor before your departure. Pack **prescription medications** in your carry-on luggage, and carry them in their original containers, with pharmacy labels—otherwise they won't make it through airport security. Carry the generic name of prescription medicines, in case a local pharmacist is unfamiliar with the brand name.

SAFETY

Just about the only places mentioned in this book where you'll need to keep your wits about you, crime-wise, are the cities of Palermo (Sicily), Cagliari (Sardinia), and occasionally Lampedusa. Palermo especially has a problem with petty street crime (pickpockets on buses and in crowded areas, and in bad areas after dark, muggers). Pickpockets can be an issue in Cagliari and Lampedusa, too, but to a much lesser extent. The best defense against pickpockets is not keeping anything valuable in a pocket or open handbag where deft hands can easily slide in. The pickpockets that work big Italian cities are amazingly adept at reaching for your stuff and making off with it before you even know it's happening. Some pickpockets are gypsy children who ask for money, which is just a distraction while they go pilfering through your belongings, while other pickpockets are "plainclothes" respectably attired Italians, who may "accidentally" bump into you on the sidewalk, bus, or train as a subterfuge, then liberate your wallet and iPhone as they effusively apologize for invading your personal space. Moral of the story? Keep your stuff within reach, in front of you and in your sight, at all times, and beware of any physical advances, "accidental" or otherwise. Dirty looks also tend to fend off these petty predators.

Anywhere in Italy, you should never leave valuables in a car, and never travel with your car unlocked. A U.S. State Department travel advisory warns that every car (whether parked, stopped at a traffic light, or even moving) can be a potential target for armed robbery. In these uncertain times, it is always prudent to check the U.S. State Department's travel advisories at http://travel.state.gov.

The coastlines of several Italian islands are prone to rock falls in certain stretches, so always pay attention to markers (*Pericolo: Caduta Massi*—"Danger: Falling Rocks") limiting access to particular beaches and coves. On some islands, like Capri, metal nets have been installed along fragile rock walls in busier pedestrian areas, thus eliminating much of the danger; but these measures aren't in place on less touristy islands, and unfortunately several people have been killed over the past decade by rocks that have broken off cliffs hundreds of feet above the beach. Such incidents are the reason Ponza's Chiaia di Luna beach is now closed indefinitely. When hiking along cliffs—and this should go without saying—never kick or throw rocks from the path. Also be careful of your footing (and especially that of any children you're with) when walking along heights, as there is seldom much in the way of walls or fences to keep you from falling a long way down.

The waters around the Italian islands don't present any extraordinary concerns for swimmers. Currents aren't generally very strong, but use extreme caution when swimming during periods of rough wind and weather, as the seas can get turbulent quickly and slosh swimmers into rocks and reefs. Jellyfish (*meduse*) can be a problem around some islands, like Pantelleria, making swimming a nuisance though not a life-threatening undertaking. Locals deal with jellyfish by wearing either a wetsuit or neoprene gloves and booties.

Sustainable Tourism/Ecotourism

Though they're not generally marketed as such, the Italian islands are excellent destinations for sustainable tourism and ecotourism. The simple fact that they are cut off to some degree from the mainland has made the Italian islands reliant on their own immediate resources and in most cases, these resources have been carefully managed and continue to sustain, as they have for hundreds of years, the local communities. Furthermore, a huge percentage of the land and sea areas in the Italian islands is protected by the government, whether as national parks or marine reserves, which ensures the preservation of these islands' natural treasures for generations to come.

For most who travel to the Italian islands, the flight to Italy represents the major environmental impact. After that, you're taking mass transit (ferry or hydrofoil) to the island, and in the majority of cases, you're using your own power (walking, swimming, or biking) to get around. If you do need to rent a car (as I recommend to see the best of Sicily and Sardinia), the good news is that European cars aren't gas guzzlers (the cost of fuel necessitates this); you can also inquire with the rental agency if any hybrids are available.

It's Easy Being Green

Many new hotels in Italy have been built with eco-friendly materials and low-impact physical plants, but here are a few simple ways you can help conserve fuel and energy when you travel, no matter where you go.

Each time you take a flight or drive a car, greenhouse gases release into the atmosphere. You can help neutralize this danger to the planet through "carbon offsetting"—paying someone to invest your money in programs that reduce your greenhouse gas emissions by the same amount you've added. Before buying carbon offset credits, just make sure that you're using a reputable company, one with a proven program that invests in renewable energy. Reliable carbon offset companies include **Carbonfund** (www.carbonfund.org), **TerraPass** (www.terrapass.org), and **Carbon Neutral** (www.carbonneutral.org).

Whenever possible, choose nonstop flights; they generally require less fuel than indirect flights that stop and take off again. Try to fly during the day—some scientists estimate that nighttime flights are twice as harmful to the environment. And pack light—each 15 pounds of luggage on a 5,000-mile flight adds up to 50 pounds of carbon dioxide emitted.

Where you stay during your travels can have a major environmental impact. To determine the green credentials of a property, ask about trash disposal and recycling, water conservation, and energy use; also question if sustainable materials were used in the construction of the property. The website **www.greenhotels.com** recommends green-rated member hotels around the world that fulfill the company's stringent environmental requirements. Also consult **www.environmentallyfriendlyhotels.com** for more green accommodations ratings.

At hotels, request that your sheets and towels not be changed daily. (Many hotels already have programs like this in place.) Turn off the lights and air conditioner (or heater) when you leave your room. Shutting off the A/C can also save you money, as some hotels charge up to 15€ per day for the use of it. Traveling in the shoulder season, when the weather is mild, eliminates the need for—and environmental impact of—heaters and air conditioners.

Use public transport where possible—trains, buses, and even taxis are more energy efficient forms of transport than driving. Even better is to walk or cycle; you'll produce zero emissions and stay fit and healthy on your travels. When touring by sea, take a group boat tour around the island instead of renting your own boat.

Eat at locally owned and operated restaurants that use produce grown in the area. This contributes to the local economy and cuts down on greenhouse gas emissions by supporting restaurants where the food is not flown or trucked in across long distances. This is normally not much of an issue on Italian islands: Anything with seafood and produce is almost always locally sourced. And of course, don't forget to be a green citizen by ordering a bottle of the local wine!

STAYING CONNECTED

Telephones

To call Italy from the United States, dial the **international prefix, 011;** then Italy's **country code, 39;** and then the city/region code (for example, **081** for Capri and Ischia), which is now built into every number. (Unlike some other international dialing sequences, you *do* need to dial with 0 that is part of the city code.) Then dial the actual **phone number.**

A short **local phone call** to a land line in Italy costs around .10€ to .20€. The orange **public phone** (*cabina telefonica*) is a dying breed, but if you find one whose cord and handset hasn't been ripped out by vandals, it can be used with precharged phone cards (*scheda* or *carta telefonica*), and sometimes coins. You can buy a *carta telefonica* at any *tabacchi* (tobacconists; look for shop signs with a white T on a brown, black, or blue background) in increments of 5€, 10€, and 20€. You must break off the perforated corner tab first for the card to work. To make a call, pick up the receiver and insert your card. Most phones have a digital display to tell you how much money you inserted (or how much is left). Dial the number, and don't forget to take the card with you when you're finished.

Otherwise, you'll need to use your hotel phone to make calls. Most hotel rooms have direct-dial phones (where you need to dial 0 to get an outside line, wait for the dial tone, and then compose the full phone number, 0 and prefix included); but before you go making a bunch of calls, get clear information from the hotel staff about their phone rates. Some hotels give you fair and square pricing and just charge you what the phone company charges them (so the hotel makes no profit), but the majority of hotels see guests' phone calls as a major cha-ching opportunity and charge ridiculously inflated rates.

Numbers in Italy range from four to eight digits, in addition to the two-, three-, or four-digit local prefix. Even when you're calling within the same city, you must dial that city's area code—including the zero. A Caprese calling another Capri number must dial 081 before the local number.

To **dial direct internationally from Italy,** dial **00** and then the country code, the area code, and the number. **Country codes** are as follows: the United States and Canada, 1; the United Kingdom, 44; Ireland, 353; Australia, 61; New Zealand, 64. Make international calls from a public phone, if possible, because hotels charge inflated rates for direct dial—but bring a fully loaded *scheda*. A reduced rate is applied from 11pm to 8am on Monday

Calling Cellphones Is Costly

While landline calls are cheap in Italy, calling from a landline to a mobile number (those with three-digit prefixes that start with 3—for example, 338, 347, 380, and so on) are quite a bit more expensive. A 5-minute phone call can easily drain your prepaid 5€ *scheda,* so be careful and try to call the landline number listed for a place whenever possible.

through Saturday and all day Sunday. Direct-dial calls from the United States to Italy are much cheaper, so arrange for whomever to call you at your hotel.

Italy has recently introduced a series of **international phone cards** (*scheda telefonica internazionale*) for calling overseas. They come in increments of 50, 100, 200, and 400 *unita* (units), and they're available at *tabacchi* and bars. Each *unita* is worth .15€ of phone time; it costs 5 *unita* (.75€) per minute to call within Europe or to the United States or Canada, and 12 *unita* (1.55€) per minute to call Australia or New Zealand. You don't insert this card into the phone; merely dial ✆ **1740** and then *2 (star 2) for instructions in English, when prompted.

To call the free **national telephone information** (in Italian) in Italy, dial ✆ **12.** **International information** is available at ✆ **176** but costs .60€ a shot.

To make **collect or calling-card calls,** drop in .10€ or insert your card and dial one of the numbers here; an American operator will come on to assist you. The following calling-card numbers work all over Italy: **AT&T** ✆ **172-1011, MCI** ✆ **172-1022,** and **Sprint** ✆ **172-1877.** To make collect calls to a country besides the United States, dial ✆ **170** (.50€), and practice your Italian counting in order to relay the number to the Italian operator. Tell him or her that you want it *a carico del destinatario* (charged to the destination, or collect).

Because you can't count on all Italian phones having touch-tone service, you might not be able to access your voice mail or answering machine from Italy.

Cellphones

The three letters that define much of the world's wireless capabilities are **GSM** (Global System for Mobile Communications), a big, seamless network that makes for easy cross-border cellphone use throughout Europe. If your cellphone is on a GSM system and you have a world-capable multiband phone, just call your wireless operator and ask for "international roaming" to be activated on your account. Per-minute charges are high—usually $1 to $1.50 in western Europe.

For many, **renting** a phone is a good idea. While you can rent a phone from any number of overseas sites, including kiosks at airports and at car-rental agencies, I suggest renting the phone before you leave home. North Americans can rent one before leaving home from **InTouch USA** (✆ **800/872-7626;** www.intouchglobal.com) or **RoadPost** (✆ **888/290-1616** or 905/272-5665; www.roadpost.com). InTouch will also, for free, advise you on whether your existing phone will work overseas.

Buying a phone can be economically attractive, as Italian cellphone companies have cheap prepaid phone systems. Once you arrive at your destination, stop by a local cellphone shop and get the cheapest package; you'll need to fill out some paperwork and allow an hour for the whole transaction. You'll probably pay less than 100€ for a basic phone and a starter calling card. Local calls and texts may be as low as .10€ per minute, and incoming calls and texts are free.

HEY, GOOGLE, DID YOU GET MY TEXT MESSAGE? It's bound to happen: The day you leave this guidebook back at the hotel for an unencumbered stroll through Siracusa, you'll forget the address of the lunch spot you had earmarked. If you're traveling with a mobile device, send a text message to ✆ **46645 (GOOGL)** for a lightning-fast response. For instance, type "don camillo siracusa" and within 10 seconds you'll receive a text message with the address and phone number. If your search results are off, be more specific ("giorgio armani shopping Milan"). For more tips and search options, see www.google.com/intl/en_us/mobile/sms. Regular text message charges apply.

Voice-Over Internet Protocol (VOIP)

If you have Web access while traveling, you might consider a broadband-based tele-phone service (in technical terms, **Voice-Over Internet protocol,** or **VOIP**) such as Skype (www.skype.com) or Vonage (www.vonage.com), which allows you to make free international calls if you use their services from your laptop or in a cybercafe. The people you're calling must also use the service for it to work; check the sites for details.

Internet/E-Mail

Just about every town in the Italian islands has at least one "Internet Point"—whether in a bar, hotel, or dedicated phone/Internet shop—where you can pay a fee to use a public terminal. Rates are typically in the ballpark of 5€ an hour, but it gets cheaper if you buy several hours up front. You'll normally be issued a hard plastic card that is encoded with your account information and balance. Due to international anti-terrorism measures, many Internet point businesses that aren't in your hotel require identification of users, so don't be surprised if they ask to see (and then photocopy) your passport before letting you log on.

Connection speeds at public terminals are never very fast, but they're fine for send-ing e-mails, uploading a few photos, and updating your Facebook status.

WITH YOUR OWN COMPUTER OR WIRELESS DEVICE More and more hotels, resorts, airports, cafes, and retailers are going **Wi-Fi** (wireless fidelity), becoming "hotspots" that offer free high-speed Wi-Fi access or charge a small fee for usage. To find public Wi-Fi hotspots at your destination, go to www.jiwire.com, or just turn on your machine periodically and see what pops up.

Lots of hotels have Ethernet hookups in guest rooms, though Ethernet cables aren't always on hand in the room, and it may be wise to pack your own. Do be aware that hotel charges for Internet use can, like direct-dial phone rates, be ghastly, so find out the charges up front, and read the fine print. On the other hand, there are many lovely hotels that don't charge anything at all for Wi-Fi or Ethernet use. On smaller and more remote Italian islands, Internet access in hotels may be spotty, so be sure to check if it's an essential part of your stay.

PACKAGES FOR THE INDEPENDENT TRAVELER

Booking flights, hotels, and, where applicable, rental cars as a bundle through online travel agencies like Orbitz, Expedia, Kayak, and Travelocity can save you up to 50% off the price of what these individual trip components would cost you a la carte. Granted, you don't always have quite as much flexibility to change plans, and your hotel choices are somewhat more limited, but the savings, not to mention the peace of mind of knowing everything's arranged at a fixed price up front, is rather appealing. The best deals are in the shoulder season months of May and October.

For many destinations, you can also add on extras like city tours or other organized excursions at discounted rates.

Escorted General-Interest Tours

Most of the Italian islands lie outside the scope of general-interest tours of Italy, but there are a few itineraries out there that call at the more well-known island destina-tions like Sicily, Capri, and the Venetian Lagoon islands.

The biggest operator of escorted tours for North Americans in Italy is **Perillo Tours** (© 800/431-1515; www.perillotours.com), family operated for three generations. Perillo's tours cost much less than if you arranged the same trip yourself. Accommodations are in first-class hotels, and guides tend to be well qualified and well informed. Nine-day Sicily tours start at $3,575 per person. **Trafalgar Tours** (© 866/544-4434; www.trafalgartours.com) is one of Europe's largest tour operators, offering affordable guided tours with lodgings in unpretentious hotels. One of Trafalgar's leading competitors is **Globus+Cosmos Tours** (© 866/755-8581; www.globusandcosmos.com). Globus has first-class escorted coach tours of various regions lasting from 8 to 16 days (for a more in-depth review of a Globus tour in Italy, check our website, Frommers.com). Cosmos, a budget branch of Globus, sells escorted tours of about the same length.

A few Italian tour operators, such as **Valtur** (www.valtur.it), offer escorted tours of Sicily, which may offer extensions to the Aeolian or Egadi islands. Your travel mates and tour guide may not speak a word of English, however.

SPECIAL-INTEREST TRIPS

Sailing & Yachting

You could argue that the most splendid way to experience the Italian islands is by boat—a floating base where you can roll out of bed and jump in the water, freely move from cove to cove (and eliminate the need to mix with the hoi polloi on the ferries and hydrofoils), stop in at the port when you feel like it, and best of all, be lulled to sleep by the gentle rise and fall of the Med.

Italy Yacht Charters (© 06/98181706 10am–2pm Italian time; www.italyyachtcharters.com) is a full-service outfitter offering **bareboat** (you pilot the boat yourself), **skippered** (you pay an extra 140€ per day for someone who knows what he's doing and knows these waters to helm the boat), or **crewed** (everything is taken care of, including food service and cleaning) formulas on sailboats, motor yacht, and catamarans ranging from standard to luxury class. They operate in all the islands and coastal areas of Italy (as well as Turkey, Croatia, Greece, and Corsica). Sample itineraries include 2- to 4-day tours of the Pontine Islands, 3- to 7-day tours of the Tuscan islands or the Bay of Naples islands, and 7- to 14-day tours of Sardinia and La Maddalena archipelago. Italy Yacht Charters works only with high-quality boats and reputable crews, and their responsive staff speaks excellent English.

Prices for skippered yacht vacations vary greatly depending on the time of year and class of boat; but as a general idea, you can expect to pay from 2,500€ per week for a three-cabin standard sailing or motorboat (6–8 persons), 3,400€ per week for a four-cabin standard sailing or motorboat (8–10 persons), 5,800€ for a four-cabin luxury yacht (8–10 persons), or 6,000€ per week for a 14m (46-ft.) catamaran (8–11 persons). I'll do the math for you: That works out to about 60€ to 110€ per person per day, which really isn't terrible even for the budget-minded. So, get a group together and book a boat (and if you can't find a taker for that fourth cabin, give me a call).

Cycling, Walking & Hiking

There are dozens of options for hiking and biking vacations in Sicily and Sardinia. The latter's diverse terrain and relative lack of compelling historical sights is particularly well suited for active types who'd rather feel the wind in their hair than tour a musty church. In Sardinia, **Dolcevita Bike Tours** (© 070/9209885;

www.dolcevitabiketours.com) is a cycling and hiking holiday specialist (leisure cycling, road cycling, and mountain biking) with a plethora of itineraries, both guided and self-guided. In Sicily, **Siciclando** (© **800/881-0484** toll-free in the U.S. and Canada, © **44/203/355-4186** in the U.K.; http://siciclando.com) has about a dozen different tours that combine cycling with hiking and art history, wine, geology, or spa-themed itineraries. Single travelers and all skill levels can be accommodated with either of these agencies.

Another specialist for hiking tours of Sicily, **Boundless Journeys** (© **800/941-8010;** www.boundlessjourneys.com) has weeklong tours suitable for most fitness levels along the country roads, panoramic seaside paths, and national park trails of that island.

Hiking enthusiasts interested in the Tuscan islands would do well to time their travel dates to coincide with the annual **Tuscan Coast and Islands Walking Festival** (early Apr to early May; © **0565/919411;** www.tuscanywalkingfestival.it), a month-long program of events in which hikes of all difficulties and lengths are organized on Elba, Giglio, Capraia, Giannutri, and Pianosa, often in concert with local restaurateurs, wineries, and specialty food producers.

TIPS ON ACCOMMODATIONS

The Italian islands are *gettonatissime* (in high demand) destinations in summer, and so it goes without saying that planning ahead when it comes to booking accommodations is essential, both in terms of securing the best deals, and finding a bed, period!

For each island in this book, I've listed my favorite hotels, B&Bs, and holiday rental agencies to suit a variety of tastes and budgets. In high season, renting a villa or apartment is the most economical way to stay in the Italian islands (short of a campground). Many require a minimum stay of 3 days, or even a week in August, but you'll usually be able save a bunch of euros off the cost of a traditional hotel. Sicily and Sardinia, due to their size alone, have the best range of villa and apartment rental options.

For more upscale villas and holiday rentals, there are a number of excellent agencies, including **Di Casa in Sicilia** (© **0941/361681;** www.dicasainsicilia.it), which has lovely properties all over Sicily, in the Aeolian and Egadi islands, and in Pantelleria. Another great resource for higher-end rentals is **Think Sicily** (© **800/490-1107** in the U.S. and Canada, © **44/020/7377-8518** in the U.K.; www.thinksicily.com), which also does bookings for Sicily's best boutique hotels, exclusive resorts, and accommodations at olive oil and wine estates. For villas in Sardinia, the aptly named **Sardinian Villas** (© **44/0870/2402367** [U.K. number only]; www.sardinianvillas.com) is a good place to start; the website has helpful breakdowns of its properties by key attributes, such as "walk to beach" or "child-friendly."

Other well-known islands like Capri and Ischia have a plethora of adorable villas and apartments for rent, which you can browse easily enough through a number of agencies on the Internet. On the lesser islands, there are fewer options, but it pays to be persistent. For example, if you want to rent a house in Ponza for a week in August, it won't be as simple as Googling "Ponza villas." You'll have to use some Italian terms, like *casa vacanza* (vacation house, which could be a villa or a studio apartment), and *affitto* (rent), and be prepared to employ the Google translate button to wade through the Web pages that you do find. Always look for the British or American flag icon or the "En" button, for those sites that have an English version; but if all else fails and everything is in Italian, just look for the word *"contatti,"* click on it, and send an e-mail in English to whatever address is shown. Chances are they'll be able to respond to your inquiry well enough, and then you can determine whether they're a good fit for you.

If you insist on going it vagabond style, booking nothing in advance and just waiting to see what's in store when your ferry pulls into port, you can probably still find a place to sleep, though it may be quite dreary, overpriced, or both. Again, this applies for the high-season months of July to September; out of that period, you'll have a much easier time arranging attractive, moderately priced sleeps ad hoc at the Italian islands. Nearly all islands have a tourist information booth or accommodations assistance desk at the port or in the airport that can help connect travelers with rooms in B&Bs and private homes.

WHAT THE STARS MEAN Accommodations in Italy are rated by regional council and awarded one to five stars, depending basically on the amenities offered. A two-star in Rome is not the same as a two-star in Sicily, but in general, the more amenities and stars a hotel has, the more expensive it will be. However, the number of stars isn't always a great indicator of how nice the place is overall: I've stayed in plenty of three-stars that had much better service and style than a staid old five-star that just happened to have a business center and conference facilities.

Tips on Dining

A huge part of the Italian experience, even on the islands, is food and drink. However, there are many more components to the world of eating and drinking than full-fledged restaurants. (And with the current economy and exchange rates, you probably won't want to be eating every meal in a full-fledged restaurant anyway.)

In many ways, the **bar** is the nexus of Italian life, and if you really want to get into the local culture, plan to log a lot of time at them. Although bars in Italy do serve alcohol, they function mainly as cafes and community gossip centers, where everyone stops in for coffee and socializing at some point, and sometimes several points, throughout the day. A bar visit never lasts more than about 10 minutes (they're not typically places where you can take a load off and read a book), but they always have a restroom that the public can use for free. You're not obligated to make a purchase but as a courtesy, consider buying a *caffè* or cold drink.

Espresso is king at Italian bars and the base of all coffee drinks. *Un caffè* gets you a standard espresso; *un cappuccino* has a few ounces of steamed and barely frothed whole milk (fat-free is a foreign concept in Italian bars). For just a dash of milk with your espresso, ask for a *caffè macchiato;* for a coffee drink with more milk than comes with a cappuccino, order a *caffellatte.* (Just saying *latte* will get you a tall glass of warm whole milk. Yummy, but maybe not what you had in mind.) A summertime standard at Italian bars is the *caffè freddo,* which is espresso that has been refrigerated for several

No Cappuccino After 11am

Order a milk-based coffee drink outside the morning hours in Italy and you might as well walk around with a sandwich board that says "I AM A TOURIST" strapped to your chest. Likewise, at restaurants, waiters will ask you if you want coffee after your meal; indeed, coffee is commonly ordered, but it's an espresso or maybe a *caffè americano* (espresso with more water), never a cappuccino.

hours (so, not chilled on the spot and diluted with ice cubes) and often pre-sweetened with lots of sugar. If you want something cold and even a bit fancier, ask for a *caffè shakerato* (shaken with ice and sometimes jazzed up with shots of chocolate, other flavorings, or booze). Note that there is only one size of any given drink at the Italian bar: Terms like *grande* and *venti* will get you nowhere.

Bars also have *panini* (ready-made sandwiches) on various kinds of rolls and *tramezzini* (giant triangles of white-bread sandwiches with the crusts cut off). These both run 1.50€ to 2.50€, depending on the filling, and are traditionally put in a tiny press to flatten and toast them so the crust is crispy and the filling is hot and gooey; microwave ovens have unfortunately invaded and are everywhere, turning *panini* into something resembling a soggy hot tissue. Needless to say, these are hardly gourmet sandwiches. For better *panini* made with top-quality Italian meats and cheese (but very simple—just served on a roll with no condiments or other toppings), go to the local grocery (*alimentari,* or the deli counter at supermarkets).

Some bars are also *gelaterie* (ice-cream parlors), though the quality of the gelato at bars is subpar and may just be mass-produced tubs of a dozen or so standard flavors. A much better choice when in the mood for a frozen treat is to seek out a dedicated gelateria that advertises *produzione propria* (made in-house). Bars are also the place to go for *spremuta di arancia* (freshly squeezed orange juice), and most have a blender where they'll whip up fresh *frullati* (smoothies) for you. You can always buy bottled water, bottled juice, and cans of beer at the bar. Most also serve wine and *prosecco,* Italian sparkling wine.

Prices at the bar have a split personality: *Al banco* is standing at the bar (what most people do, because it's fun and convivial, and cheaper), while *a tavola* (geared toward tourists and geezers) means sitting at a table where you'll be waited on and charged two to four times as much. In smaller, quieter bars, you can order your drink, sip it at the counter, and then pay on your way out; but in busier joints, it's better form to find the cashier, pay first, and then present your *scontrino* (receipt) on the counter when ordering your drink. Leave the barman a tip of .10€ to .20€—most Italians pre-tip, laying the coins on the receipt as they order for quicker service. As always in Italy, a simple greeting of *buon giorno* or *buona sera* as you walk in, and *grazie* all around when you leave, goes a long way.

Pizza a taglio or *pizza rustica* indicates a quick, counter-service place where you can order pizza by the slice, while *pizzerie* are casual sit-down restaurants that cook large, round pizzas in wood-burning ovens. Each person orders his or her own pizza, which is still a good 12 to 14 inches in diameter; sharing a pizza typically isn't done. This is a great way to save money and still go out to eat, as most pies cost from 5€ to 8€, and you can get inexpensive house wine or beer to wash it down with. A *tavola calda* (literally "hot table") serves ready-made hot foods (for example, single-portion *lasagne*) you can take away or eat at one of the few small tables often available. A *rosticceria* is the same type of place, and you'll see chickens roasting on a spit in the window.

A full-fledged restaurant will go by the name *osteria, trattoria,* or *ristorante.* Once upon a time, these terms meant something—*osterie* were basic places where you could get a plate of spaghetti and a glass of wine; *trattorie* were casual places serving full meals of filling peasant fare; and *ristoranti* were fancier places, with waiters in bow ties, printed menus, wine lists, and hefty prices. Nowadays, fancy restaurants often go by the name of *trattoria* to cash in on the associated charm factor; trendy spots use *osteria* to show they're hip; and simple, inexpensive places sometimes tack on *ristorante* to ennoble themselves.

The *pane e coperto* (bread and cover) is a 1€ or so cover charge that you must pay at most restaurants for the mere privilege of sitting at the table. Most Italians eat a leisurely full meal—appetizer and first and second courses—at lunch and dinner and expect you to do the same, or at least two out of three. To request the bill, ask *"Il conto, per favore."* A tip of 15% is usually included in the bill these days, but if you're unsure ask, *"È incluso il servizio?"*

You'll find at many restaurants, especially larger ones and in cities, a *menu turistico* (tourist's menu), sometimes called *menu del giorno* (menu of the day). This set-price menu usually covers all meal incidentals—including table wine, cover charge, and 15% service charge—along with a first course *(primo)* and second course *(secondo),* but it almost always offers an abbreviated selection of pretty bland dishes: spaghetti in tomato sauce and slices of pork. Sometimes a better choice is a *menu à prezzo fisso* (fixed-price menu). It usually doesn't include wine but sometimes covers the service and often offers a wider selection of better dishes, occasionally house specialties and local foods. Ordering a la carte, however, offers you the best chance for a memorable meal. Even better, forego the menu entirely and put yourself in the capable hands of your waiter.

The *enoteca* (wine bar) is a popular marriage of a wine bar and an *osteria,* where you can sit and order from a host of local and regional wines by the glass while snacking on finger foods (and usually a number of simple first-course possibilities) that reflect the region's fare. Relaxed and full of ambience and good wine, these are great spots for light and inexpensive lunches—perfect to educate your palate and recharge your batteries.

RECOMMENDED BOOKS & FILM

Books

The top-selling novel in Italian history is Giuseppe Tomasi di Lampedusa's **The Leopard** (*Il Gattopardo,* published posthumously in 1958), which tells the story of a Sicilian nobleman and his family caught up in the changes in society brought on by the 19th-century Risorgimento, or movement to unify Italy. It's an epic, sweeping book that assails both the decadence of the nobility and casts a disapproving glance at the rise of the working class, and as such, it was surrounded by controversy from all sides on its release. The novel was made into a film also called **Il Gattopardo,** by director Luchino Visconti in 1963. The big-budget cinematic adaptation of the novel stars Burt Lancaster (who is mouthing the words, spoken in Italian by another actor), Claudia Cardinale, and Alain Delon, and is a wonderfully nostalgic tribute to that bygone era of Sicilian life. It won an Academy Award for costume design, and the loving cinematography and saturated colors are enough to sell anyone a trip to Sicily. Be sure to see the Italian language version with English subtitles, not the English dubbed version.

Film

In addition to the epic **Il Gattopardo,** there are a number of smaller, more recent films that give you a taste of the landscape on the Italian islands. About a third of Roman director Nanni Moretti's **Caro Diario** (*Dear Diary,* 1993) takes place in the Aeolian islands. Chapter 2 of the film is entitled **Isole** (*Islands*) and sees Moretti visit Lipari, where there are too many tourists and he can't relax; they move to Salina, where a spoiled child and obsession with soap operas eventually drive Moretti to try out Stromboli. On Stromboli, there is a very funny scene in which Moretti's friend, while touring the island's fiery slopes, completely ignores the experience of being on a volcano and instead seeks out some American tourists so that he can ask them what's happening on *The Bold and the Beautiful,* since they're about a year behind on the soaps in Italy.

Anthony Minghella's lush 1999 remake of *The Talented Mr. Ripley* was shot all over Italy, from Rome to Venice to Naples to Palermo, and the islands of Ischia and Procida both played the part of fictional Mongibello, the quintessentially picturesque Bay of Naples seaside village.

Respiro (2002, directed by Emanuele Crialese and starring Valeria Golino), which chronicles a woman driven to madness on a small, isolated, and impoverished island, brought the severe landscape and societal constraints of Lampedusa to the big screen.

The Greek chorus scenes of Woody Allen's 1995 *Mighty Aphrodite* take place in the Greco-Roman Teatro Antico of Taormina, Sicily. Many of the sea-faring scenes of 2004's *The Life Aquatic with Steve Zissou* were shot around the coast of Ponza.

SUGGESTED ITINERARIES

Admittedly, the Italian islands as a collective group don't lend themselves to the kind of sampler-platter tourism that works so well in mainland Italy—say, 10 days split between Rome, Tuscany, and Venice or the Amalfi Coast. This is a factor chiefly of transportation logistics. Unlike the Greek islands, ferry and hydrofoil service to the Italian islands is very localized, and each lesser island group, though fairly close to the mainland, is served by lesser ports that are often quite some distance from the nearest major city. It can even be hard to island-hop within the same archipelago sometimes, as in the case of the Tuscan islands, because the ferries to them operate out of three different ports. Some islands, like Pantelleria and Lampedusa, are so remote and isolated that they're only really feasible to visit singly, whether it's for a long weekend, a week, or more. And Sicily and Sardinia, due to their size, demand at least 5 days each for even a superficial "greatest hits" tour.

Still, depending on how much time you can spend in the Italian islands and what sort of trip you're looking for, I've come up with several ways you might consider planning your travel. As any number of my extended family and friends of friends can attest, I love nothing more than helping people plan their trips to Italy: It's one thing to simply know about the best places in each destination, and quite another to craft a realistic itinerary that will expose you to the best of the Italian islands without overwhelming you with a too-busy schedule. If you're like most people, you probably want to see and do as much as possible—because who knows when you'll be here again—without going too crazy.

The itineraries below, organized by length or theme of trip, have been constructed with transportation issues very much in mind and include a cross-section of islands that will give you a great taste of the different personalities and assets of the Italian islands as a whole. Some are more practical than others, some more expensive and outlandish, but hopefully these suggested itineraries will be a helpful frame of reference or source of inspiration as you confront the dizzying possibilities that an Italian islands vacation presents.

If instead you'd rather narrow your focus to a single destination, I've sketched out the salient features of each island and island group in the following section, "The Regions in Brief."

THE REGIONS IN BRIEF

Italy has two major islands that are autonomous regions (that is, states or provinces of the Republic of Italy)—Sicily and Sardinia. At about 25,000 sq. km (9,653 sq. miles) each, Sicily and Sardinia are exponentially larger than the other islands, which are sometimes referred to as the "minor" or "lesser" islands. The minor islands are divided as follows: three groups in the Tyrrhenian, off the west coast of the mainland (the Tuscan islands, the Pontine islands, and the Bay of Naples islands); two off the east coast (the Venetian Lagoon islands; and the Tremiti islands, in the Adriatic off Puglia); two main archipelagoes off Sicily (the Aeolians to the northeast and the Egadi to the west); and a handful of other islands scattered singly well off the coast of Sicily (Pantelleria to the southwest, Ustica to the north, and the Pelagic islands of Lampedusa and Linosa to the south).

Sicily

The largest island in the Mediterranean, Sicily is a land of beauty, mystery, and world-class monuments. It's a bizarre mix of bloodlines and architecture from medieval Normandy, Aragonese Spain, Moorish North Africa, ancient Greece, Phoenicia, and Rome—you're as likely to encounter blonde-haired, blue-eyed natives as dark-skinned brunettes. On the eastern edge of the island is Mt. Etna, the tallest active volcano in Europe. Sicily's capital city, **Palermo,** is chaotic and sultry and loaded with art treasures, but for a more relaxed pace, try the east coast towns of **Taormina** and **Siracusa.** Sicily's mostly Greek ancient ruins, the most famous of which are the Valley of the Temples at Agrigento, are rivaled only by those of Greece itself.

Sicily does have some excellent beaches, which are well used by locals and visitors alike in summer, but what makes a trip here so compelling is the culture, both living and ancient; the food (you haven't lived until you've had a real Sicilian *cannolo*); and the spectacular scenery. Allow a week for a very superficial tour of selected highlights; a slower 10-day or 2-week itinerary will give you a much better sense of the soul of Sicily.

Sicily is also the gateway to the Aeolian islands (from the port of Milazzo on the northeast coast), the Egadi islands (from the west coast cities of Trapani or Marsala), Ustica (from Palermo), Pantelleria (flights from Palermo or Trapani, boats from Trapani), and the Pelagic islands of Lampedusa (flights from Palermo, ferry from Porto Empedocle in the south) and Linosa (boat from Porto Empedocle).

Sardinia

Only slightly smaller than Sicily but with a far different character, Sardinia is one of the more aloof souls in the Mediterranean. Its landscape is continent-like in its diversity, from rugged mountains to agricultural plains to striking mesas known as *giare,* but what draws most visitors here are its beaches. Sardinia has the best beaches in the Mediterranean—glorious expanses of soft white sand, evenly distributed around every coastal region of the island—and because the island is relatively bereft (as Italian regions go) of art and architecture for tourists to tick off, it's perfect for a relaxing sun-and-sea-themed vacation.

Cagliari is Sardinia's biggest and capital city, but Spanish-inflected Alghero is its prettiest. The luxury enclave of the Costa Smeralda is on the northeast coast, while both the southern regions of Chia and Villasimius, west and east of Cagliari, respectively, boast miles of sugary beaches and comfortable modern resorts. If beach time is your objective, even 4 days (in one spot, preferably) can be a satisfying trip to Sardinia, but to sample a few different parts of the island, plan to spend at least a week.

The Aeolians

For many, the seven volcanic stunners off the northeast coast of Sicily represent the quintessential Italian island vacation. From busy Lipari and elegant Salina to partying Panarea and smoking Stromboli, each has a different character, but all of the Aeolians offer exhilarating natural beauty and intimate dimensions with a real holiday spirit. Beaches are sorely lacking in this archipelago, but due to the Aeolians' small size, you can easily take a boat (whether your own rented craft or a group excursion) to putter around the coastlines and discover idyllic coves where the water is such a deep hue of turquoise and the rocky backdrops are so fabulous that you won't miss the sand. The Aeolians have great restaurants and accommodations both simple and sophisticated.

The main arc of the Aeolians, from Vulcano in the south to Stromboli in the northeast, is well served by ferry and hydrofoil from the Sicilian port of Milazzo, but the "satellite" islands of Filicudi and Alicudi, east of Salina, are more offbeat. Distances and travel times between islands (except between Vulcano, Lipari, and Salina) are longer than they might appear on the map, so think twice before planning an overly ambitious island-hopping itinerary in the Aeolians. Three or 4 days is sufficient for a quick getaway to one or two islands—say, Salina and Panarea—but you'll want a week or 10 days for a comprehensive tour that also takes in another island or two, like far-flung Stromboli.

The Bay of Naples Islands

The most famous islands in Italy, Capri and Ischia, are essentially geologic extensions of the backwards-C-shaped Bay of Naples; Ischia is off the northern tip of the bay, while Capri lies off the Sorrentine peninsula, immediately east of which is the celebrated Amalfi Coast. Tiny Procida lies between Ischia and the suburban Neapolitan port of Pozzuoli. Capri (pronounced CAH-pree) has been a resort since ancient times, and reached its heyday as a jet set getaway in the 1950s and '60s. It's not as exclusive as it used to be, though most hotel and restaurant prices beg to differ, but Capri very much deserves all the hype it's gotten over the years: It's still the most breathtakingly beautiful island in Italy, and there's an undeniable magic to the place once all the day-trippers (and there are many) stream out. The key to enjoying Capri is to spend the night. Several nights. Too many visitors give Capri short shrift and then walk away complaining about how crowded it was; I recommend staying at least 3 days, as there's surprisingly much more to do here than gawk at overpriced boutiques (which apart from the scenery is about all the Amalfi Coast offers).

Ischia is the most populous of the lesser Italian islands—with more than 60,000 residents, it's essentially a bedroom community of Naples. Tourism here, as in Capri, is also very entrenched; and Ischia draws boatloads of vacationers, whether Italian, northern European, or British, mostly for its beaches and thermal waters. Procida, the stepping stone between Ischia and the mainland, is a natural day trip from Ischia or detour on your journey back to Naples. All pink buildings and narrow cobblestone streets, Procida is the postcard image of a Neapolitan fishing village.

It's quite possible to island-hop within the Bay of Naples, as Capri and Ischia are only an hour apart. However, most people don't: Tourists on Capri tend to visit the island in conjunction with Pompeii, Sorrento, and the Amalfi Coast, while Ischia-bound vacationers tend to stay put there for a week at a time, maximizing their sand and spa time.

The Egadi

Not quite as "in" as the other main Sicilian archipelago, the Aeolians, the Egadi consist of three very different islands. Favignana is the nearest to the mainland (take a boat from Trapani or Marsala) and the best equipped for tourists, with a number of new and excellent hotels. Levanzo, immediately north of Favignana, is a bit of a hermit, with few tourist facilities but the islands' most important artistic attraction in the Grotta del Genovese, a cave with Neolithic wall paintings. Remote Marettimo is the most naturally stunning of the group, and its coastline is riddled with splendid grottoes and rock formations. It's a popular day trip from Favignana, but the fishing village on Marettimo also has a few guest beds. Because of the Egadis' relative proximity to the mainland and transit links (they're much closer to Trapani, a major transportation hub, than the Aeolians are to Milazzo, which is in the middle of nowhere), you could actually see and do a lot with just 4 or 5 days here.

The Pelagie, Pantelleria & Ustica

The four islands I've grouped into one chapter in this book, entitled "Other Sicilian Islands," are destinations with very different personalities. The Pelagie ("high-sea") islands of Lampedusa and Linosa lie south of Sicily, halfway to Africa and at the same latitude as Malta (which only by the vagaries of history isn't an Italian island). Severe and sere Lampedusa is an impoverished place that ekes out a living off the sea year-round and in summer, off about a month-long tide of wealthy Milanese tourists who've started building vacation villas here. Lampedusa has one of the most spectacular beaches in the Med, Isola dei Conigli. Diminutive and lush Linosa is about as far off the beaten track as any island in this book. Go there to really get away from it all, because your cellphone probably won't work. Pantelleria, off the southwest coast of Sicily, is about as exotic as Italy gets. Sometimes referred to as the "Black Pearl" of the Mediterranean, it's defined by its stark lavic landscapes (no beaches) and Arab-inflected architecture (the *dammuso* stone house) and place names like Rekhale and Khamma. VIPs like Giorgio Armani have been summering here for decades, and it's still quite an exclusive spot, where the glitterati of European fashion and media like to sunbathe poolside at their *dammusi* and slum it with the locals in down-at-the-heels Pantelleria town. Ustica, north of Palermo, is a bit of a loner; it's small and volcanic (read: no beaches), but it has a pleasant, village-y atmosphere, and for scuba enthusiasts, there is no better diving in the Italian islands.

The Pontines

Suspended in the Tyrrhenian, fairly far from shore but roughly equidistant from Rome and Naples, the Pontines are under-the-radar for non-Italians. Ponza is the main island in the group and a cherished summer haunt for upper-middle-class Romans and Neapolitans. Ponza's unique geological makeup gives it an endlessly surprising coastline of lunar-looking coves, the most jaw-dropping of which is the colossal Chiaia di Luna. During the day, everyone is out on the water, in rented boats or organized group tours—which includes a de rigueur jaunt over to the island of Palmarola, where pirate ships wouldn't look out of place. At night, Ponza town is a festive scene of shopping, waterfront dining, and people-watching. The rich kid scene may be a bit much in August, but outside of peak-peak season, Ponza is pure delight.

The much, much smaller Ventotene lies well south of Ponza (island-hopping between them is theoretically possible but uncommon). Its picturesque pastel village and still-operational Roman port are two of the most compelling things about Ventotene; it also has a pretty coastline of red tufa with several good swimming coves, though only a handful of small beaches. When on Ventotene, it's a must to add a short excursion to the nearby island of Santo Stefano, which has a now-defunct Bourbon prison and relics of Roman structures, including the Vasca Giulia, a rock-cut tub equipped with seawater "jets."

The Tremiti

The only Italian island group in the Adriatic is truly miniscule—the three islands in the Tremiti have just 3 sq. km (1 sq. mile) between them. Flung out to sea near the Gargano promontory of Puglia (the "spur" of Italy's bootlike shape), the Tremiti are, more than any other island group in this book, a relaxing getaway from civilization. San Nicola Island, all limestone bluffs, has the Tremiti's only requisite cultural stop in the fortress-abbey of Santa Maria a Mare, while pine-covered San Domino, just 500m (1,640 ft.) across the water, is where all the accommodations and tourist activities are. No one in the Tremiti is here to parade his or her designer beachwear, and most of your time will be spent bobbing in rented *gommoni,* picnicking under the pines in rocky coves, and swimming in bright turquoise waters.

The Tuscan Archipelago

The riches and charm of mainland Tuscany have cast a spell over international tourism, but there's more to this Italian region than duomos, rolling golden hills, and cypress-lined lanes. The Tuscan archipelago is an arc of seven widespread, diverse, and diversely employed islands, where you can get back to nature, rub your toes in the sand, and still experience that Tuscan trifecta of adorable hill towns, idyllic scenery, and great food and wine.

Elba is the largest and most visited, with a tourism infrastructure that makes travel here hassle free. Elba is an outdoor enthusiast's haven with lovely forests, mountains, and a squiggly coastline with more than 70 swimmable beaches and coves. Much smaller and more intimate is Isola del Giglio, a favorite weekend getaway of Romans, with a charming hill town in Castello and a beautiful coastline. The other inhabited islands, Capraia and Giannutri, are even smaller and more exclusive, usually visited as nature-outing day trips from Elba and Giglio, respectively, though they have a few overnight options. The former prison island of Pianosa is a day trip from Elba, with historical sights and a flat landscape for leisurely hikes. Finally, Gorgona is an active prison island with limited visitor access, while jagged Montecristo is a nature reserve that's even stingier with permits.

THE ITALIAN ISLANDS IN 1 WEEK

Assuming you're doing the common European vacation formula of flying there on a Friday night and flying back the following Sunday, that's 9½ days away from home but only 8 on the ground in Italy. With only a week to delve into the world of Italian islands, you can still see a broad range of landscapes and atmospheres: I recommend

Italy in 1 & 2 Weeks

focusing on the archipelagoes nearest Naples—the Pontine islands and the Bay of Naples islands. Feel free to tweak this itinerary depending on your travel personality. Add even more day trips and hotel changes if you're a who-knows-when-I'll-be-back-here-must-do-it-all type, or slow it down by adding more nights on fewer islands and eliminating some ferry hops and general stress. This itinerary can of course be reversed—that is, the Bay of Naples islands first, followed by the Pontines—but because sea connections are shorter and more reliable from Ischia and Capri back to the mainland (and your outbound flight), I've structured it from north to south.

Day 1: Naples to Ponza

On weekends in July and August, you can take Snav's 8am direct hydrofoil from Naples-Mergellina port to Ponza (2½ hr.; it stops at Ischia and Ventotene on the way); otherwise, you'll need to get to Formia, which is the main port for ferries to the Pontine archipelago. Whether by train or car, getting from central Naples to Formia takes about an hour. Sailing time from Formia to Ponza is another 1½ to 2½ hours, depending on which boat you take (hydrofoils at 8:45 and 10am, as well as 12:30pm on Sat; ferries at 9, 10am, and 2pm), but with any luck, you'll be in Ponza by mid-afternoon. Check into your hotel, then head back down to the port and hop on one of the shuttle boats to **Frontone,** the popular beach where everyone goes for afternoon swimming and happy hour. Cap the evening off with a people-watching promenade along **Corso Pisacane** and dinner a waterfront restaurant.

Day 2: Ponza & Palmarola

In the morning, head down to the port to rent a boat for the day (or just find an organized group excursion) and set out on a counterclockwise island-circumnavigation tour of Ponza's greatest hits. Start with the Roman-era **Grotte di Pilato** (caves that were used as eel farms), then make your way around Ponza's northern tip and stop at the **Piscine Naturali,** "natural swimming pools" in the rocks near Cala Feola. From there, set your motor on full throttle for the 10km (6-mile) crossing to **Palmarola,** the barely inhabited island where you can bob at anchor and swim in some of the Mediterranean's most gorgeous coves. After Palmarola, continue your tour around Ponza at Chiaia di Luna, where spectacular walls of yellow tufa tower above a crescent beach. (Due to rock falls, you can't access the beach, but you can swim in the bay and take in the sublime view.) Complete your island tour and return your boat to port. Back on land, toast your last night in Ponza with sunset drinks at the Hotel Chiaia di Luna's **Kibar,** perched romantically above Ponza's most celebrated beach.

Day 3: Ponza to Ventotene

Catch a boat to Ventotene in the morning (11:15am), and spend the rest of the day exploring this tiny island and its picture-perfect **pastel village.** At the 2,000-year-old **Roman port**—still very much in use—have a local fisherman ferry you over to **Santo Stefano,** the panettone-shaped island where you can visit the Bourbon-era former prison and, on the island's perimeter, swim in the **Vasca di Giulia,** a Roman-built seawater "Jacuzzi." In the evening, soak up the scene at one of the bars on the Roman port or up on the piazza in town.

If you'd rather spend most of the day in Ponza, there is a 6:15pm hydrofoil that stops in Ventotene and continues to Ischia Casamicciola, where you'd be arriving on Day 4.

Day 4: Ventotene to Ischia

Sea connections between Ventotene and Ischia are infrequent, so your time of departure from Ventotene will be dictated by the ferry companies' schedules. At present, there is a summertime hydrofoil to Ischia Casamicciola at 12:15pm. Upon arrival in Ischia, check into your hotel, then check out the scene at the big, sandy beaches of **Citara** or **Maronti.** Time permitting, indulge in the thermal park experience (such as Giardini Poseidon, on Citara beach), or just save it for tomorrow. In the evening, head over to **Ischia Porto** and grab a drink at one of the hip bars along the **Rive Droite** (right side) of the marina, then dinner at **La Baia del Clipper** (more casual) or **Alberto** (more romantic and expensive). Don't miss seeing the **Castello Aragonese** with its evening floodlights.

Day 5: Ischia

Ischia has been renowned since ancient times for the supposed therapeutic qualities of its thermal waters and hot springs: Today's the day to immerse yourself in Ischitan spa culture. The bigger **"thermal parks"** are veritable playgrounds of hydrotherapy, with prescribed courses through dozens of pools of different depths, shapes, and temperatures, and charge from 25€ to 30€ per day for the use of their facilities. Absorb the benefits of those waters for several hours or more; but if you want a change of scenery, cut your spa day short and use the rest of the afternoon to take in the star attractions of northwestern Ischia—the stunning gardens of **La Mortella,** the upscale hamlet of **Lacco Ameno** with its nostalgic 1950s-resort air, or the gorgeous beach of **San Montano.** This evening, go to the charming fishing village of **Sant'Angelo** for a sun-downer at one of its trendy bars, then head down to the **Fumarole** section of Maronti beach, where you'll **cook your own dinner of foil-wrapped chicken** in the volcanically heated sand.

Day 6: Ischia & Capri

Boats between Ischia and Capri are plentiful and frequent, but I recommend getting an early start: There's a lot to do on Capri. Once you've arrived at Capri's Marina Piccola and made your way to your hotel, grab a quick bite at a snack bar (don't bother with a restaurant for lunch, and don't waste time walking around Capri town, which is likely to be packed with day-trippers at this hour anyway). Head back down to the port for a **round-island boat tour,** which includes the uber-touristy but unmissable **Blue Grotto** and takes in all the best angles of this island's amazing natural beauty. By the time your tour is finished, the day-trippers are heading back to Sorrento and Naples, and Capri town is once again bearable. Explore its chic lanes and boutiques (be sure to check out Carthusia perfumery), and have a drink under the twinkling lights of the **Piazzetta.** Before the sun sets, take a short walk to the end of **Via Tragara,** with its achingly beautiful view over the Faraglioni rock stacks in the water far below.

Day 7: Capri

Spend the day over on the other side of the island, in **Anacapri** and around. Walk the whitewashed lanes of **Anacapri town,** take the chairlift to the top of **Monte Solaro,** then go for a swim at **Lido del Faro.** Back in Capri town, go for the short and undemanding hike to the **Arco Naturale,** and stop for dinner at **Le Grottelle,** immersed in the green heights of the island. (For more of a workout and even better views, start the hike to the Arco Naturale from Punta Tragara instead of from Capri town, but this path, called the **Pizzolungo,** has many ups and downs; plan to arrive at the dinner table a bit sweaty.)

Day 8: Capri to Naples

This morning, walk the gentle path from Capri town up to the ruins of the **Villa Jovis,** one of 12 villas built on Capri by the emperor Tiberius in the 1st century A.D. It's the second-highest point on the island and affords marvelous views over to the cliffs of Sorrento. Go for a quick dip at **Marina Piccola** (walk the hairpin Via Krupp down there from Capri town, but take the bus back up), then catch an afternoon boat to Naples. You'll have just a few hours in Naples, but they're evening hours; spend them strolling around the old quarter of **Spaccanapoli,** where you can stuff your face on Neapolitan pastries and soak up the decadent atmosphere of this crazy city. Have dinner at **Gino Sorbillo** (Via Tribunali 32), the best pizzeria in Naples, and spend the night at a centrally located hotel like **Costantinopoli 104** (Via Santa Maria di Costantinopoli 104; ℭ **081/5571035;** www.costantinopoli104.com) or **Palazzo Decumani** (Piazzetta Giustino Fortunato 8; ℭ **081/4201379;** www.palazzodecumani.com).

THE ITALIAN ISLANDS IN 2 WEEKS

With 2 weeks to devote to the Italian islands, follow the suggested 1-week itinerary above—from the Pontine archipelago to the Bay of Naples islands—then spend the next 6 days hopping around the Aeolians (with a dash of eastern Sicily on the tail end). You'll have 2 nights on Stromboli, 1 on Panarea, 2 on Salina, and 2 in Taormina, Sicily, and catch your first homeward flight segment out of Catania. So, it'll be a little whirlwind, but you'll be seeing unforgettable sights every day. Note that this itinerary only works from June to the first weekend of September, which is when the fast boat from Naples to the Aeolians is in operation.

Days 1–7

See the Italian Islands in 1 week, above.

Day 8: Capri to Stromboli, via Naples

Though it will involve careful timing and about 6 hours total at sea, you can leave Capri in the mid-morning and reach the Aeolian island of Stromboli before the sun sets. Make sure you're on a boat from Capri to Naples no later than noon, because the only boat from Naples to the Aeolians (operated by Snav from

May 29–Sept 5 only) leaves at 2:30pm. Note that the boats from Capri almost always arrive at Naples's main port, Beverello, but the Snav boat to the Aeolians leaves from Naples's smaller and prettier marina, Mergellina, 4km (2½ miles) away. (Though these two seaports are in theory only a 10-min. cab ride apart, allow 30–45 min. to get from Beverello to Mergellina. If you're early, you won't mind passing the extra time at Mergellina; there are cheerful cafes and restaurants where you and your luggage can hang out.) The 2:30pm boat from Naples-Mergellina arrives in **Stromboli** at 7pm, which leaves you time enough to wander about Stromboli town before having dinner (try **Punta Lena** or **Da Zurro**). Stay at the **Sirenetta Park Hotel.**

Day 9: Stromboli

While the main attraction on Stromboli is its active volcano (and the special privilege of being able to view it remarkably up close), volcanic tourism here is best done in the evening. So, you have the daytime free to explore the island and communities that exist below that smoking crater. Take the boat over to the rustic village of **Ginostra,** which has no electricity and is accessible only by sea, join a **round-island boat tour,** or rent a scooter to putter around Stromboli by land. At dusk, hike up to the **Sciara del Fuoco** to observe the fiery lava flows. The spectacular displays and collective sense of wonder among tourists there at the Sciara del Fuoco are plenty satisfying for most visitors, but more extreme adventurers can hike all the way to the top of the mountain, though only with an accredited guide.

Day 10: Panarea

Take a morning hydrofoil (7:15, 8:30, 10:05, or 11am) from Stromboli to Panarea (35 min.). Once you've dropped your luggage off at your hotel, waste no time getting out on the water for a round-island tour, in your own rented boat or with an organized group tour. Panarea is the prettiest of the Aeolians, so you'll want to maximize the time you have to swim and relax in its **myriad gorgeous coves.** In the early evening, browse the boho-chic **boutiques** in the village, then have **drinks and dinner on the waterfront.** Party animals will not want to miss the **open-air disco at the Hotel Raya,** which gets going after midnight.

Day 11: Salina

After a morning stroll along the whitewashed, prickly-pear and bougainvillea-lined lanes of Panarea, catch the 9:10 or 10:45am hydrofoil to Salina (25 min.). Check in at the **Hotel Signum** or **Capofaro Resort,** where you'll be tempted to while away many hours, days, weeks . . . . After lunch, walk through the ferns and forests to the top of **Monte Fossa delle Felci,** the highest point in the Aeolians with accordingly fabulous views. In the late afternoon, hire a fisherman in Malfa to take you to see the nearby village of **Pollara** and its stunning beach (no longer accessible by land because of its dangerously overhanging rock ledge, but you can swim in the bay). Have dinner at **Porto Bello** in Santa Marina Salina or **Alfredo's** in Lingua.

Day 12: Day Trip to Lipari (Overnight on Salina)

Take a mid-morning (9:40 or 11:10am) hydrofoil to **Lipari** (30 min.). The most populous of the Aeolians, Lipari has a bustling atmosphere that's quite a contrast from serene Salina. Traipse the streets of touristy Lipari town, check out the old citadel, then hop on a bus to some of the best sandy beaches in the Aeolians—the popular and pumice-y **Spiaggia Bianca** at Canneto and out-of-the-way **Valle Muria** on the island's wilder western coast. Back in Lipari town, before catching the boat back to Salina (hydrofoils at 3:50, 4:25, and 7:10pm), art and history buffs should stop in at the excellent **Archaeological Museum.** In Salina tonight, splurge on dinner at the **Capofaro Resort**—or keep it rustic with a meal at **Trattoria Cucinotta** in Santa Marina.

Day 13: Salina to Taormina

It's time to say *arrivederci* to the "lesser" islands and *buongiorno* to *la bella Sicilia,* even if it's only for a short stay. Plan to be on the 7:15 or 9:50am hydrofoil from Santa Marina Salina to Milazzo, Sicily (2 hr.). Rent a car in Milazzo and drive to **Taormina** (just over an hour if you take the *autostrada* all the way, via Messina). Assuming you've encountered no transportation snags, you'll be in Taormina by midday. Go for a quick orientation walk in town (admittedly not very Sicilian anymore but breathtaking anyway), take in the sweeping vistas over the Ionian sea and Mt. Etna from the ancient **Greco-Roman theater,** and then head for the **beach at Mazzarò or Isola Bella** (several hundred meters below town but conveniently accessible by cable car). This evening, join everyone else for the ritualistic *passeggiata* (stroll) down Corso Umberto I. My favorite hotel in Taormina is the **Villa Ducale,** which is actually a bit above town; a good moderate choice in town is the **Villa Schuler.**

Day 14: Mt. Etna & Flight Home from Catania

Check out of your hotel, load up the rental car with your luggage, and dedicate the morning to the volcanic giant that looms over eastern Sicily, **Mt. Etna.** Driving from Taormina, allow the best part of an hour to reach the visitor parking areas near the top, at least 2 hours to tour the summit area, and another hour or more to descend from the heights of Etna to Catania airport, where you'll return your rental car and catch the first leg of your air travel home.

SICILY & ITS ISLANDS IN 10 DAYS

You'll spend 2 nights in Siracusa, 1 in Taormina, 2 in Palermo, 2 on Pantelleria, and 2 on Favignana. If the Aeolians intrigue you more than the Egadi, it would be easy enough to adjust this itinerary to visit the Aeolians for a few days between Taormina and Palermo; with only 2 nights to spend, however, I suggest picking just one island, like Salina or Panarea.

Day 1: Siracusa

Fly into Catania this morning, rent a car, and drive down to **Siracusa** (1 hr.), my favorite town in Sicily. Check into a hotel on historic **Ortigia Island,** and spend the afternoon simply wandering the storybook lanes and squares of this Sicilian-Baroque town. There are enough cafes, restaurants, boutiques, and sigh-inducing vista points to keep you busy for days in Ortigia.

Sicily in 10 Days

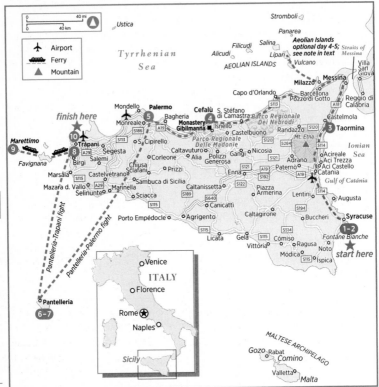

Day 2: Siracusa

Spend the morning touring the ancient riches in Siracusa's **Parco Archeo-logico della Neapolis,** then hit the beach at **Fontane Bianche** for a cooling-down. Not in a beach mood? Use that time instead to visit the hill town of **Noto,** arguably Sicily's finest Baroque gem. Have dinner back on Ortigia.

Day 3: Mt. Etna & Taormina

Get up early, and head north to **Mt. Etna** (about 1½ hr. by car from Siracusa). Visit the summit areas of the volcano, then head back down to **Taormina,** which you should reach by mid-afternoon. Go for a refreshing swim at one of the **beaches** below to rinse off that volcanic dust, but be sure to visit the **Greco-Roman theater** before sunset. In the evening, partake of the classic Taorminese nighttime ritual, the *passeggiata* down the main drag of Corso Umberto I, which is chockablock with tempting boutiques and lively cafes that stay open until the wee hours.

Day 4: Cefalú, Monreale & Palermo

After your very brief stop in Taormina, it's time to hit the *autostrada* once again—to Palermo (about 3 hr. on the A20). If you've gotten a very early start, you can even take a short detour en route to visit the charming seaside town of **Cefalù** (2 hr. from Taormina), with its impressive Arab-Norman cathedral set below the towering rock outcrop known as La Rocca. If you have lunch in Cefalù, **Ostaria del Duomo** is your best bet. Cefalù is nice, but you can skip it altogether for a more leisurely day. Palermo is 1 hour from Cefalù, but instead of stopping when you reach Palermo, overshoot it and head slightly inland to visit the hill town of Monreale, which holds perhaps the finest treasure of Sicilian artistic heritage in the **Byzantine mosaics of Monreale cathedral.** This is a must of Palermitan sightseeing, and since you have to take a bus or car to reach it from Palermo, you might as well do it now, while you have your car. After touring Monreale and dropping off your rental car in Palermo, it will probably be late afternoon or early evening by the time you check into your hotel. Don't do anything too ambitious tonight, because you'll need your strength tomorrow to take on the experience of being a tourist for 1 very busy day in Palermo. Go for dinner at the central, atmospheric, and delicious **Santandrea,** and get a good night's sleep. On that note, it's key to choose a hotel where a good night's sleep is likely—for sound-proof windows and comfortable mattresses, try the modern **Ucciardhome,** the classic **Grand Hotel et des Palmes,** or even the seaside **Villa Igiea,** removed from the hubbub of the city center.

Day 5: Palermo

As busy as today will be, I'm leaving out one very big sight—the Cappella Palatina in the Norman Palace—because it's essentially a repeat of Monreale cathedral, which you saw yesterday, and not making you go to any museums, because I think your time in this multi-faceted city is better spent soaking up the atmosphere in the streets and seeing the incidental, quick sights you can duck into without a huge commitment of time or money.

In the morning, fuel up on plump Sicilian pastries and a cappuccino or three, whether at the bar around the corner from your hotel or at the storied **Antico Caffè Spinnato,** where you are likely to rub elbows with Palermitan power-brokers on their way to work. Wander around the famous street market of **Vucciria,** where Palermo's pedigree as a Mediterranean trading post is on full display, and then stop into the **Oratorio of Santa Cita,** which is open only in the mornings, to see Serpotta's wonderful stuccoes. All of this must be accomplished by about 11am, because you have to be at the **Catacombs of the Capuchin Monks** (slightly out of the way; take a taxi) before they take their noon to 3pm *riposo;* with fully dressed cadavers hanging on the walls, these catacombs are an arresting mix of morbidity and camp and one of the most unique sights in all of Italy. (If the idea of paying 1.50€ to see dead people creeps you out, swap the Capuchin catacombs for a visit to one of Palermo's sultry Arab-Norman sights, like San Giovanni degli Eremiti or the side-by-side churches of San Cataldo and La Martorana.) Back in central Palermo, it may be time for a mini-siesta at your hotel or an air-conditioned cafe, but spend a few late-afternoon hours walking around the decaying **Kalsa** district (you don't want to be there after dark). In the Kalsa, don't miss the romantic shell of **Santa Maria dello Spasimo** or evocative old residences like **Palazzo Gangi.** (If you liked the stuccoes at Santa Cita this morning, get some more Serpotta at the **Oratorio di San Lorenzo,** which is open in the afternoons but with limited hours.) By now, your feet will be crying for mercy; rest them over dinner at one of the many good restaurants near San Lorenzo, including the elegant **Osteria dei Vespri,** wine-bar-with-creative-cuisine **Mi Manda Picone,** or the cafeteria-like institution of Palermitan peasant food, **Antica Focacceria San Francesco.**

Day 6: Pantelleria

Fly to Pantelleria this morning. (There is a 9:15am Meridiana flight from Palermo that arrives in Pantelleria at 10:05am.) Rent a car and drive to your *dammuso,* then hit the **northeast coast,** which has the best swimming spots and the famed **Arco dell'Elefante.** Or find a boat company in Pantelleria harbor that will take you by sea to the northeast coast. Repair from the afternoon heat in your *dammuso,* either within its thick stone walls or outside in the pool. In the evening, enjoy a sunset *aperitivo* at one of the portside bars in Pantelleria town. Have dinner in town or in the village of Scauri, on the west coast.

Day 7: Pantelleria

This morning, go for a swim and sulfuric mud bath (supposedly therapeutic) at the **Specchio di Venere** lake. After a scenic drive around the agricultural southern side and the mountainous interior of the island, and perhaps a stop on the slopes of **Montagna Grande** for a "dry bath" in the steam-vented rock grotto called the **Bagno Asciutto,** have lunch in Scauri at the water's-edge **La Vela.** In the afternoon, relax at your *dammuso,* or go for another swim at the Arco dell'Elefante. At dusk, it's back to the port for *aperitivo,* or just spend the evening in bar- and restaurant-rich Scauri. For a splurge, **La Nicchia** can't be beat. Be sure to toast your final night on Pantelleria with a good glass of *passito.*

Day 8: Pantelleria/Trapani/Egadi

Take the early morning flight to Trapani (departs 7am and arrives 7:50am), then head down to Trapani's seaport to catch a hydrofoil to Favignana (20 min.) in the Egadi Islands. (Try for the 9:20am sailing; otherwise, there's a boat at 10:45am.) If all goes smoothly, you should make it to Favignana by mid-morning, which gives you almost a whole day to **explore the coastline** by boat or from land (rent a bike for the latter). A swim in **Cala Rossa,** where stone pilasters of the old tufa quarries stand as a dramatic backdrop to crystalline turquoise waters, is a must. This evening, soak up the atmosphere of this ancient fishing community in Favignana town. See **Palazzo Florio,** the **Ex-Tonnara,** have a drink on **Piazza Madrice,** and eat dinner at **Aegusa.**

Day 9: Day Trip to Marettimo (Overnight on Favignana)

Today, treat yourself to the splendid scenery and isolation of the most remote Egadi, **Marettimo.** There are hydrofoils from Favignana to Marettimo (stopping at Levanzo on the way) at 8:40 and 9:55am, arriving at Marettimo

35 minutes later. At the port, find a boat to take you on a **round-island tour**—Marettimo is all about its dramatic coastline, grottoes, and gorgeous swimming coves. Depending on which tour you choose, you'll be back at port 3 to 5 hours later. With hydrofoils back to Favignana at 4:45 and 5:25pm, you'll also have time for a short wander around tiny **Marettimo town.**

If bad weather interrupts hydrofoil service, you won't be able to reach Marettimo, as the ferries that run in rough seas do not have schedules that permit day trips from Favignana. In that event, do a half-day trip to Levanzo and discover more of Favignana.

Day 10: Trapani, Erice & Flight Home

There are frequent boats from Favignana to Trapani (7:35, 8, 9:50, 10:10, 11:35am, and noon), so pick an earlier one if you want more time to explore Trapani and Erice, or a later one if you'd rather spend a few more hours on Favignana. Before heading up to the hill town of Erice (20 min. by taxi from Trapani port, 45 min. by bus from Trapani's Piazza Montalto), you might want to spend an hour or so exploring old Trapani, which is conveniently located within easy walking distance of the ferry landing. Up in **Erice,** which is breathtaking but doesn't take much time to explore end to end, **walk along the ancient walls,** visit the **Castello di Venere,** stop in at one of the town's celebrated **pastry shops,** and drink in those amazing **views.** After your tour of Erice, head back down to Trapani airport for the first segment of your flight home.

BAY OF NAPLES ISLANDS

Campania, with its stunning natural scenery and impressive lineup of world-class archaeological sites, and historic architecture and art, is in many ways the most all-around well-endowed region of Italy. This is the land of Mt. Vesuvius and Pompeii, pizza and Sophia Loren (both born in Naples), *mozzarella di bufala* and strong espresso, and the legendary Amalfi Coast. The Bay of Naples envelops in its crescent-shaped embrace some of the most alluring holiday islands in the entire Mediterranean: the legendarily chic Capri, the laid-back spa haven of Ischia, and the tiny villagelike Procida.

5 STRATEGIES FOR VISITING THE ISLANDS

Capri and Ischia offer plenty of diversions on their own, but travelers would be wise to combine their Bay of Naples island time with the stellar attractions of the nearby mainland. This is quite easy to do, as there are frequent boat connections between the islands themselves and from the islands to Naples, Sorrento, Positano, and Amalfi. Sailing times are also manageable (the trips between Capri and Naples, Capri and Ischia, and Ischia and Sorrento, for example, only take about an hour), but the process of getting to and from the ports, especially if you have luggage, can eat up a lot of the time. Moral of the story? Don't over-program your days, even if you're staying put on one island.

Many travelers make day trips out of Capri and Ischia, but it's just as valid, if you're in an island state of mind, to do a "reverse commute"—that is, to use the islands as your base and make a few forays to the mainland to explore Pompeii, Naples, or the Amalfi Coast. From Positano and Amalfi, you can catch a local bus to Ravello and other places along the Amalfi Coast, and up to Sorrento.

Although Capri is visited mostly from mid-morning to mid-afternoon by travelers on package tours or independent itineraries through Southern Italy, it's really best to stay here for at least a few nights: The island is totally different (read: *better*) when the day-tripping hordes empty out. Despite its diminutive size (10 sq. km/4 sq. miles), Capri has plenty to keep anybody busy for several days, and avid walkers will want to stay for the best part of a week. At 46 sq. km (18 sq. miles), Ischia is a much larger island than Capri and consequently more time-consuming to explore

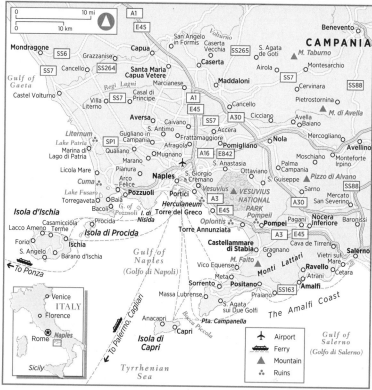

thoroughly; those who come here tend to stay for a few days to a week, though it's perfectly feasible to make Ischia a beach day trip, as Neapolitans often do in summer. Ischia is also the only Bay of Naples island onto which you can bring a car (by ferry only; hydrofoils don't carry automobiles). Having your own wheels is highly recommended here, but the municipal government sometimes limits tourist vehicles in high season—check with the ferry company before attempting to bring a car aboard.

A geological stepping stone between Naples and Ischia, Procida makes sense to visit en route to either of those places or from the northern Naples suburb of Pozzuoli. It's also possible to get here from Capri directly. Procida is tiny, so unless your objectives include getting to know every fisherman on the island, you don't need more than a day or two here. You might even find that a half-day of wandering around Procida, followed by lunch or dinner and the last boat back to your "base," is quite satisfying.

CAPRI ★★★

Two conjoined massifs of soaring limestone off the tip of the Sorrentine peninsula, Capri (*Cah*-pree) is Italy's most celebrated island, and for good reason. Its dashing good looks—rugged grey cliffs carpeted with dark green vegetation—and salubrious

Capri

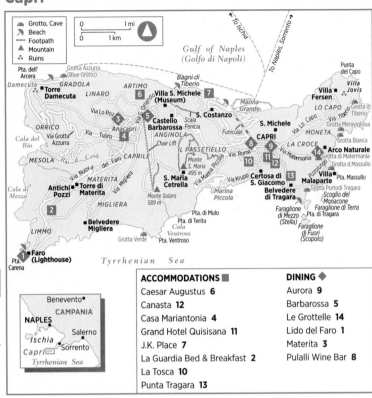

ACCOMMODATIONS ■

Caesar Augustus **6**
Canasta **12**
Casa Mariantonia **4**
Grand Hotel Quisisana **11**
J.K. Place **7**
La Guardia Bed & Breakfast **2**
La Tosca **10**
Punta Tragara **13**

DINING ◆

Aurora **9**
Barbarossa **5**
Le Grottelle **14**
Lido del Faro **1**
Materita **3**
Pulalli Wine Bar **8**

climate made Capri a favorite retreat of the rich and famous in antiquity (Emperor Tiberius built a dozen villas here). In the 1950s and '60s, jet-setters and movie stars revived the trend of vacationing on Capri, and the island has been a required stop on any tour through southern Italy ever since.

Why come to Capri? Sure, plenty of people are attracted by the island's fashionable reputation. There are some truly outstanding hotels on Capri, and high-fashion shopping abounds. But what ends up bowling you over isn't the five-star accommodations or the swanky boutiques; it's the stunning landscape, into which civilization has delicately inserted itself.

Capri is one of those rare travel destinations that is even more dramatic in person than in pictures. The entire island is a roller coaster of plunging rocks to which trees and shrubs and a great number of ingenious manmade structures cling. There are archaeological sites, manicured villas and gardens, boat tours, a chairlift ride, chic shopping and cafes, the famed Blue Grotto, and views, views, views. With dozens of panoramic paths that take you a world away from the madding daytime crowds, Capri is also a walker's dream-come-true.

This is still an elite island and much of it is priced as such, though you can do Capri on a budget if you're careful. Restaurants are frustratingly expensive for what you get, so consider getting picnic fare for some meals. Stay at a B&B on the outskirts of Anacapri, and use the money you save on lodging for Capri's necessary splurges, like drinks on the Piazzetta and a trip to the Blue Grotto.

If sun and sand figure high on your list of island priorities, bear in mind that Capri's craggy contours mean that most "beaches" here are either rocky coves or manmade bathing platforms. However, most upper-range hotels have spectacular pools, and the cerulean waters around Capri are clean and refreshing. I can think of no more fabulous place to take a dip in the Med than underneath the towering silhouettes of the Faraglioni (p. 109), on the south side of the island. If you've ever seen the magazine ads for Dolce & Gabbana's "Light Blue" fragrance, you'll get the idea.

Essentials

GETTING THERE

BY BOAT   Capri is served from mainland Campania and the other bay of Naples islands by abundant daily hydrofoils, jet boats, and ferries, operated by several different companies. All boats arrive at Capri's bustling port, Marina Grande. The "shipping timetable" page on www.capritourism.com has the most up-to-date schedules and fare information. Note that in bad weather, hydrofoils cannot sail; traditional ferries are the only means of reaching any of the islands when the seas are rough (which typically only happens in the off season).

With dozens of daily sailings, Naples's Molo Beverello and Sorrento are the two main ports of embarkation for Capri, though you can also get here directly from Ischia and Procida, and boats arrive in Capri from the Amalfi Coast ports of Positano, Amalfi, and Salerno.

Between Capri and Naples (20+ boats per day each way): From Naples–Molo Beverello, the boats are nearly all hydrofoils or fast jet boats, run by **Snav** (in Naples ℂ 081/4285555; in Capri ℂ 081/8377577; www.snav.it), **NLG** (in Naples ℂ 081/5527209; in Capri ℂ 081/8370819; www.navlib.it), and **Neapolis** (in Naples ℂ 081/4285111 or 081/7611004; in Capri ℂ 081/8377577 or 081/8376995). **Caremar** (in Naples ℂ 081/5513882; in Capri ℂ 081/8370700; www.caremar.it) runs the slower traditional ferries. Hydrofoils and jets cost 17€ one-way; ferries are 8.70€ to 9.60€; for all departures from Naples, there is an added .40€ harbor tax. Trip time is 45 minutes by hydrofoil or jet, or 1½ hours by ferry.

Between Capri and Sorrento (15+ boats per day each way): Consorzio LMP (in Capri ℂ 081/8376995; in Sorrento ℂ 081/8781430; www.consorziolmp.it) is the main hydrofoil operator from Sorrento. **Caremar** (in Capri ℂ 081/8370700; in Sorrento ℂ 081/8073077; www.caremar.it) runs the ferries. Fares from Sorrento are 15€ for hydrofoil, 9.80€ for ferry. Trip time is 15 minutes by hydrofoil, or 45 minutes by traditional ferry.

Between Capri and Ischia (1–3 boats per day each way): Alilauro (ℂ 081/4972238; www.alilauro.it) runs hydrofoils (16€ one-way) from April to October, while the ferries **Capitan Morgan** (ℂ 081/985080) and **Rumore Marittima** (ℂ 081/983636) also sail between the two islands (15€) year-round. Trip time between Capri and Ischia is about 30 minutes by hydrofoil, or an hour by ferry.

Between Capri and Procida (1 boat per day each way): M/N Brianza Trasporti Marittimi (ℂ 081/4972278) handles the route between Capri and Procida, stopping at Ischia's Forio harbor along the way. The fare is 25€ one-way and the trip takes about 1½ hours.

Between Capri and the Amalfi Coast (1–4 boats per day each way): Consorzio LMP (in Capri ☏ 081/8376995; in Positano ☏ 089/811986; in Amalfi ☏ 089/873301; in Salerno ☏ 089/227979; www.consorziolmp.it) runs ferries and jets that stop at Positano (15€/17€), Amalfi (15€/17€), and Salerno (16€/18€). Trip time is 35 to 45 minutes to Positano, 45 minutes to an hour to Amalfi, and about 1½ hour to Salerno.

It's not necessary to book your boat tickets to or from Capri far in advance, but you can buy them from the dock ticket offices or travel agencies (usually with a few euros' fee) at any time. Otherwise, just arrive at the dock ticket office 30 minutes or so ahead of sailing time to purchase your tickets; both cash and credit cards are accepted.

Don't freak out if travel snags cause you to miss the boat you'd been planning to take: There's almost always another one heading to Capri within a short while.

GETTING AROUND

BY BUS & FUNICULAR   Capri's frequently running public buses, along with the funicular railway that connects the port of Marina Grande with Capri Town, make getting around the island—and seeing a lot in a short amount of time—a breeze. Typically, it takes less than 30 minutes to get anywhere on the island by bus, though the buses can be quite crowded in high season (June–Aug). Technically, two different agencies (Sippic and Staiano) operate the buses and funicular, but they're all covered under the same basic ticketing system: A one-way bus ticket (including transfer) or a single funicular ride (no bus transfer) costs 1.40€. A 60-minute pass (good for the funicular and a bus ride, or for a short round-trip bus ride, as an example) costs 2.20€. The daily tourist pass is 6.90€ and covers two funicular rides and unlimited buses. If you're staying on the island a full 24 hours and doing any shuttling between Anacapri and Capri, this is definitely the best value. Single-ride tickets can be bought on board buses or in the funicular station, while day passes can be purchased at the funicular station or the main ticketing offices at Marina Grande and in Via Roma, just down from Capri Town's Piazzetta. **Sippic** (☏ **081/8370420**) operates the funicular and Capri Town–based bus lines, while **Staiano** (☏ **081/8372422** or 081/8371544; www.staiano-capri.com) operates the buses from Anacapri to Faro and the Grotta Azzurra (Blue Grotto).

ON FOOT   Walking is the only way to explore the narrow streets of both Capri Town and Anacapri. (For either one, the ground is flat and the distances aren't great.) The island is full of spectacular hiking and walking paths, and some of Capri's main attractions, like the Villa Jovis and the Arco Naturale, can be accessed only on foot. Some routes are easy, some quite demanding; see "Walking" (p. 91) for more details.

BY BOAT   Apart from the ferry or hydrofoil you'll take to Capri's Marina Grande, there are a number of local boat services available for island sightseeing. The most popular by far is the 11€ round-trip shuttle service operated by **Gruppo Motoscafisti** (☏ **081/8377714**; www.motoscafisticapri.com) from Marina Grande to the cove outside the Blue Grotto (once there, you'll pay another 11€ to actually enter the grotto; see p. 73 for admission details). A much better value and more intimate experience, if you have the time, is Gruppo Motoscafisti's Full-Island Tour (15€, and it includes the same stop outside the Blue Grotto), which goes counterclockwise around Capri and takes about 1½ hours. See p. 74.

Adventurous types can rent a *gozzo* (small motorboat) and putter around the island on their own or with a skipper. In warm weather, sea conditions are usually calm enough to make this an easy and stress-free experience even for nautical neophytes. Practically everyone on Capri has, or has a buddy who has, a motorboat of some kind that can be made available for island tours, and at Marina Grande you'll find several charter outfits that can tailor private excursions in nicer vessels with cabins and comfortable sun decks. Kayaks, pedal boats, and rowboats can also be rented by the hour at most of the bathing establishments, though these self-powered craft are not a practical means of getting all the way around the island.

BY MOPED As long as you don't have a fear of heights (or of buses that make hairpin turns at insane speeds), the tried and true Italian *motorino* is a fun and efficient way to see Capri. **Capri Scooter** (www.capriscooter.com) has three locations: near the ferry and hydrofoil docks at Via Don Giobbe Ruocco 55 (✆ **081/8378018**); west of the Marina Grande at Via Provinciale Marina Grande 280 (✆ **081/8377941**); and in Anacapri at Piazza Barile (✆ **081/8373888**). Their two-seater models rent for 30€ for 2 hours, 50€ for 4 hours, or 55€ for a full day, and they provide a handy map marked with vista points and parking areas. Frommer's readers get a 5€ discount.

BY TAXI Capri's expensive cabs are "boats" of a different kind—oversize sedans with convertible *(cabriolet)* tops where you'd be wise to do like Jackie O and don a headscarf and sunglasses to protect yourself from the sun and wind. Taxi stands are at Marina Grande and adjacent to Capri Town's Piazzetta; you can also call a cab at ✆ **081/8370543** in Capri and ✆ **081/8371175** in Anacapri. Do note that many points of interest on the island cannot be reached by taxi. The fare is determined by the meter for point-to-point trips, but for excursions like island tours, you should agree upon a fee before setting out. **Capri Drive,** Via P. S. Cimino, 1/5 (✆ **335/5651218;** www.capridrive.com), specializes in sightseeing tours in open-top sedans.

VISITOR INFORMATION

The local tourist board, with the long-winded name of **Azienda Autonoma di Cura Soggiorno e Turismo dell'Isola di Capri,** has information points in Capri Town (Piazza Umberto I; ✆ 081/8370686), Marina Grande (Banchina del Porto; ✆ 081/8370634), and Anacapri (Via G. Orlandi 59; ✆ 081/8371524). These kiosks can give you current information like reports on when the Blue Grotto is closed due to weather and when it reopens. The main Capri **tourism office** is a few hundred feet west of Piazza Umberto I ("the Piazzetta") at Piazzetta Ignazio Cerio 11 (✆ 081/8375308; Mon–Fri 8:15am–4pm). The tourist board's website, www.capri tourism.com, is an excellent general resource, with tips on itineraries and comprehensive listings of all the accommodations on the island.

The Top Attractions

Capri's breathtakingly beautiful scenery and chic atmosphere is what makes the island so unique and is in itself a principal attraction. Simply allowing yourself time to wander around and take in the lofty vistas, breathing in the salty marine air mixed with the aroma of pines, lemons, and geraniums, is plenty rewarding. Having said that, there are a number of stand-alone sights and experiences well worth seeking out.

Blue Grotto (Grotta Azzurra) ★★★ A natural sea cave where the effects of refracted sunlight turn the water a remarkable shade of neon blue, Capri's touristic pièce de résistance is on the one hand a touristy cliché, but on the other hand, one of the giddiest things you can do in Italy. The countless postcards you'll see of the *Grotta Azzurra* do not do justice to the experience of seeing the electric-blue water in person. Even the process of getting to and inside the grotto is an adventure and a great part of the fun of this attraction. Most people visit the grotto as part of a boat excursion from Capri's main port (see below) of Marina Grande, but you can also arrive by land by taking the Grotta Azzurra bus (1.40€) from Anacapri. The light effects are best and the crowds lightest after 3pm. Unless you swim in (see "Outdoor Pursuits"), every stage of the Blue Grotto requires cash, so make sure you come prepared.

At the cove where the Blue Grotto is located, near the western end of the northern coast, little suggests that a great natural wonder is just beyond the rock wall. However, the flotilla of tourist boats and money changing hands should tip you off that you've arrived at a major attraction. Whether you've arrived by sea or land, you and three other passengers will be loaded on a manned rowboat that will take you into the cave. (Pay the boatman 6.50€ per person at this time, and then pay another 4€ at the floating ticket office before going in the grotto.)

The only way to get into the Blue Grotto is through a tiny sea-level arch in the rock wall—at only 1m (3 ft.) high, it's barely big enough for your rowboat to pass through, and only when the sea is calm. Grotto-bound rowboats queue up in the cove, and for every boat that exits the cave, one boat is allowed in. When the critical time comes for your boat to slip into the cave—and I do mean critical, as the sloshing of the sea means that precision is key—your trusty boatman will ask you to lie all the way down (noncompliance results in being manhandled into position) so that you don't crack your head open on the low ceiling. (Claustrophobics take heart, once you're in the cave, there's a lot more breathing room.) Then he'll set down his oars and pull the boat inside with the aid of a chain strung below the vault of the entrance. A few dark and thrillingly bumpy seconds later, you're in, and the full splendor of the Blue Grotto appears as your eyes adjust.

The constant demanding of money at the Blue Grotto is certainly annoying, and the experience as a whole may seem completely overpriced and too touristy, but it remains a not-to-be-missed Capri experience. If you look at it as paying 12€ (more, with transportation) for the mere privilege of being inside a neat-looking cave for a few minutes, well, yes, you'll feel like you got hoodwinked. But you can take solace in the fact that *everyone* (except swimmers) pays this much, and you can amortize some of the expense of seeing the Blue Grotto by making it part of the full-island tour from Marina Grande (below), which covers every nook and cranny of Capri's dramatic perimeter. The cost of the island tour is only 15€, compared with 11€ for the water shuttle service that only goes from Marina Grande to the Blue Grotto and back.

Località Grotta Azzurra. No phone. 4€ admission fee plus 6.50€ rowboat fee; transportation (boat or bus) to the grotto is additional. Cash only. Daily 9am–5pm, only when the sea is calm.

Full-Island Tour by Boat ★★★   Here's where you can brag about being a smart traveler, escaping the masses and seeing more of Capri than the average day-tripper. For just a few euros extra (15€ vs. 11€), the same company that runs the shuttle boats from Marina Grande to the Blue Grotto and back will take you all the way around the island (including a stop at the Blue Grotto). Capri's coastline is more diverse than it would immediately appear, and the salty skippers who do this fun, full-island tour are a lot less surly than those stuck on the Blue Grotto run. You'll be regaled with colorful commentary (and tall tales of ancient Roman antics) throughout—providing you can understand your skipper's Neapolitan accent—and will be taken to lesser-known sea caves (like the emerald-toned Grotta dello Smeraldo and the stalactite- and stalagmite-rich Grotta Meravigliosa) and up close and personal with Capri's iconic Faraglioni rock stacks. (Your skipper may even "thread the needle" underneath the arch of the middle Faraglione di Mezzo.) Gruppo Motoscafisti di Capri runs the tours in their fleet of mostly small, 25-passenger wooden launches. They're zippy and intimate but offer no shade, so bring sun protection, and prepare to get a little sea-sprayed.

Tours, which last about 1½ hours, usually depart every half-hour from the central dock at Marina Grande (look for the wooden kiosk marked "Blue Grotto" and "Full-Island Tours"), but you can book through your hotel for a guaranteed departure time. If booking through a hotel or other agency, be sure it's the 15€ Motoscafisti tour, not something more expensive with lunch included—unless that's what you want and you don't mind paying extra.

Marina Grande. © **081/8377714.** www.motoscaficapri.com. 15€ does not include admission (4€) or rowboat fee (6.50€) at the Blue Grotto.

Monte Solaro ★★★   At 589m (2,062 ft.), Capri's highest peak affords top-of-the-world views over the island's craggy topography and the surrounding Mediterranean. From Anacapri, you can ride the rickety old chairlift to the summit or make the trek on foot (along a shady, gradual path). A small snack and coffee bar is at the top.

Chairlift: Via Caposcuro 10, Anacapri. © **081/8371428.** 8€ round-trip. Daily 9am–5:30pm; service suspended in high wind or heavy rain.

Villa Jovis ★★   Even in Roman times, Capri was a favorite summer retreat for the rich and famous: The emperor Tiberius (A.D. 14–37) built a dozen villas on the island, and this one, at an elevation of 334m on the craggy eastern tip of Capri, is the largest and best preserved. Granted, the walls of the once-splendid palace stand at a fraction of their former height and are overgrown with vegetation, but as you explore the intricate outlines of the buildings, which were built over multiple levels of a dramatic cliffside setting, it's not difficult to imagine its former luxury. There were elaborate cisterns for collecting rainwater for the sumptuous baths, vaulted atriums embellished with bronze and marble statuary, and colonnaded walkways that took in views of the Bay of Naples and the Amalfi Coast, as gorgeous then as they are today (though perhaps not as ominous—Vesuvius hadn't yet erupted in Tiberius's time).

Parts of the site are not recommended for sufferers of vertigo, as the land drops off abruptly to the sea at the upper perimeter of the complex. In fact, there's one jutting rock here called the *Salto di Tiberio* (Tiberius's Leap), perched some 300m (1,000 ft.) above the water, off which the emperor supposedly had traitors and enemies pushed for a final, bracing dip in the Mediterranean. Less scary, a balustraded vista point overlooks the tawny cliffs of Sorrento.

Getting to the Villa Jovis is part of the fun: From Capri Town, it's a gently climbing 45-minute walk past agricultural smallholdings, lemon and olive groves, and pine forests. Just follow the signs for "Villa Jovis" from the Piazzetta.

Via Tiberio, Capri. © **081/8374549.** 2€. Daily 9am–1 hr. before sunset. No credit cards.

Villa San Michele ★   Swedish doctor and writer Axel Munthe's (1857–1949) Anacapri manor boasts a wealth of antiquities and objets d'art as well as sultry gardens and sublime cliff-edge views. This is another favorite among package-tour day-trippers, so it's best to visit the villa in the first or last hour of its opening times.

Viale Axel Munthe, Anacapri. © **081/8371401.** 5€. Daily 9:30am–4:30pm. No credit cards.

Outdoor Pursuits
WALKS
Walk just about anywhere on Capri, and you'll get great views and a great workout without overexerting yourself. Do bring sunblock, water, and maybe even picnic fixings. The **Scala Fenicia** staircase and the **Passetiello** and **Anginola** hikes are vertiginous and strenuous routes best left to diehards. For your safety on these very

vertical, exposed paths, tackle them in the uphill direction and avoid them completely in wet or windy weather.

FROM CAPRI TOWN & AROUND   The classic "nature walk" from Capri Town is the easy jaunt to the **Arco Naturale ★** (a limestone arch in the forest). Along the way to this picturesque geologic formation, there are precipitous views down to the sea. The walk is almost completely in the shade but involves moderate ups and downs in each direction. Allow about 20 minutes each way.

A longer, more spectacular walk—if you have the time and energy—is the **Pizzolungo ★★★**, which begins or ends at the Arco Naturale or Punta Tragara. Wending its way along the high terrain of the southeastern end of the island, this is a well-groomed, paved path with a series of *saliscendi* (ups and downs, ranging from gentle to strenuous) and lots and lots of stairs. The rewards for your physical effort are breathtaking views over Capri's most dramatic edge, where dense groves of pines perilously cling to the limestone cliffs that plunge to the sparkling cerulean sea below. Nature is so unspoiled and rugged here, it's hard to believe there are Gucci and Prada boutiques less than a mile away. Along the Pizzolungo walk, you'll pass a natural cave called the **Grotta di Matermania ★**, which the Romans used as a *nymphaeum* (a fountain-grotto for religious and leisure use); some reticulate masonry from that era survives inside the grotto. Starting the walk from the Arco Naturale end (in Capri Town, follow signs to "Arco Naturale") is a bit less taxing than departing from Punta Tragara. Allow an hour each way, wear sunblock, and bring plenty of water.

The hairpin turns of **Via Krupp ★★**, tucked against the rock wall on the south side of Capri Town, are another classic island postcard, connecting the end of Via Matteotti with the water at Marina Piccola. It takes about 15 minutes to walk down the wide and sheltered stone path. If you don't care to climb back up, you can catch a bus at Marina Piccola back to Capri Town.

The most difficult hikes on the island, **Passetiello ★★★** and **Anginola ★★**, both begin from behind the hospital (Ospedale Capilupi) on the western outskirts of Capri Town. A few hundred meters beyond the hospital, take a sharp left turn (marked in red on the ground) to the Passetiello, or continue straight for the Anginola, also marked in red. Both paths merge again later, at the Cetrella hermitage, but not before some very challenging and exposed terrain. You'll be ascending sheer rock faces (proper footwear is essential, as is good balance!) where, in some stretches, there are cables and chains to assist you. Heartstopping views abound throughout, and lovers of "extreme" experiences will want to check at least one of these hikes off their list. From the top, it's a gentle walk into Anacapri. Allow 3 hours for either route.

FROM MARINA GRANDE   Until 1874, the **Scala Fenicia ★★★** ("Phoenician Staircase," in reality built by the Greeks) was the only route between the port and Anacapri. The path begins above Palazzo a Mare, to the west of Marina Grande, and ends near Villa San Michele in Anacapri. Most who arrive at Villa San Michele get there by bus and are shocked by those who cover this vertical distance on foot. In all, there are 800 steps of varying steepness and an altitude rise of 290m (951 ft.). On its way up, the Scala Fenicia crosses the main Capri–Anacapri road at the chapel of Sant'Antonio, where you can pray to Anthony, patron saint of lost things, to find some more strength to carry on (it's only another 40m/131-ft. climb from here). Or, if your stamina is flagging, you can just flag down a bus.

FROM ANACAPRI & AROUND   Most make the ascent of 589m (1,932 ft.) **Monte Solaro ★★★** by chairlift (see "Attractions," above), but you can also do it on foot from

Anacapri. The gradually ascending trail is mostly wooded and not terribly taxing, though it is time-consuming and does climb nearly 300m (984 ft.). Allow at least an hour for the ascent, then come back down on the chairlift to save your knees for more hikes.

Walking along Via Caposcuro (past the lower station of the Monte Solaro chairlift), you'll join **La Migliera ★★**; this panoramic road passes vineyards and cultivated land, and—after an easy 45 minutes—puts you at the **Belvedere della Migliera ★★★**. Perched atop steep white rocks on the south side of the island, this stunning lookout affords views of the Faraglioni, Punta Carena, and even Ischia.

Running along the western coast of the island, between the Grotta Azzurra area and Punta Carena lighthouse, the **Sentiero dei Fortini ★★** or "Forts Path," linking three historic blockhouses, has recently been reopened to the public. This is the "lonely" side of Capri, with gentler terrain that is less dramatic than the rest of the island, but you're likely to have it all to yourself except for the odd goat.

It's also possible to walk from Anacapri down to the Blue Grotto, though it takes the better part of an hour (downhill), is not the most scenic of routes, and you could just take the bus. It is interesting, however, to see the simplicity of agricultural life in this part of the island; it's the complete opposite of all the glitz over in Capri Town. Along the way, you can pay a visit to the remains of the 1st century A.D. **Villa Damecuta** (free entrance; always open), yet another of Tiberius's Capri pleasure palaces.

BEACHES

Get those erroneous images of sand and palms, promulgated by Capri Sun juice pouches, out of your head: The word "beach" on Capri usually means a bathing platform on a protected cove or bay fringed with rocks and gravel. Swimming in the waters off Capri is generally possible from May to October, but for abundant expanses of sand, you're much better off taking your towel and swimsuit to Ischia.

The most popular place for a land-based swim in the sea is **Marina Piccola ★**, the calm but often crowded bay on the south side of the island, below Capri Town. The cove, which is punctuated by the rocky Scoglio delle Sirene jutting out of the water, is gravelly, but the water is a clear, deep turquoise. Swim out beyond the point (50m/164 ft.) for views of the Faraglioni (p. 109). Several restaurant/beach clubs are at Marina Piccola, where you can pay for the use of lounge chairs, changing facilities, and showers, but there's also public access to the water. A number of vendors also rent kayaks and pedal boats for exploration beyond the cove.

At the base of the striking rock formations known as the Faraglioni (p. 109), two beach club/restaurants offer bathing platforms and accoutrements, both charging a hefty 16€ for the use of their facilities. **Da Luigi ai Faraglioni (✆ 081/8370591)** faces east and has the more dramatic setting directly beneath the Faraglioni. **La Fontelina (✆ 081/8370845)** faces west and has more sun and wide-open vistas. Either one will send a boat to collect you (that is, paying customers) at Marina Piccola, sparing you the steep walk down from Punta Tragara.

On the undervisited western end of the island, **Lido del Faro ★★**, Località Punta Carena (✆ 081/8371798; www.lidofaro.com), is a friendly restaurant and beach club with bathing platforms on a protected bay and a swimming pool cut into the rock terraces. This is a particularly special place to be at sunset.

In a pinch, the little **spiaggia di Marina Grande** (the sandy cove below J.K. Place hotel) is a fine place for a dip, with clear and shallow aqua water. (The beach is a bit dirty near the road but much cleaner where it meets the water.) You'll often find swarthy boat crew guys sunning and swimming here over their afternoon break, fully satisfying the romantic myth of Italy.

Last but not least, for the most memorable of Capri dips, you can swim into the **Blue Grotto ★★★** (p. 73), but there are a couple of important caveats. First of all, the Blue Grotto is, in the eyes of the Capri municipal government, a "museum" that closes at 5pm. During the day, the dense boat traffic here precludes the possibility of swimming in, but it's technically illegal to do so after 5pm. No one will arrest you, however, and there is a brief window, until about 6pm, when you will have the day's most gorgeous light effects inside. Secondly, the miniscule opening in the rock wall that is the grotto entrance is very sensitive to sea changes; it's very dangerous to swim anywhere near the grotto in rough seas or you risk being slapped against the jagged rocks. Go only when the water is glass-still. Finally, never swim into the Blue Grotto alone, as there is no lifeguard on duty; however, there are almost always a few locals going for a swim at this hour, and everybody watches each other's back.

Exploring the Island

Everyone arrives at chaotic **Marina Grande,** on the north side of the island. Marina Grande is also the port from which island boat tours depart, but there's no reason to hang around here unless you're waiting to catch a boat. If you do have some time to kill, resist the temptation to plop down at one of the tacky cafes. Instead, do some gawking at the mega-million-euro yachts moored in the eastern end of the harbor. *Mamma mia!* There's also a fairly clean (considering the boat traffic nearby) sandy **beach** to the west where you can go for a swim before your boat leaves. A bit farther west are the grey rubble walls known as **Palazzo a Mare,** remnants of an ancient Roman villa.

Otherwise, leave Marina Grande behind and head straight up the hill to Capri Town, by funicular or bus. If you've brought luggage to Capri, ask your hotel if they can meet you at the port; smaller hotels may tell you to haul your stuff as far as the Capri Town bus or funicular stations, at which point they'll load your bags onto a golf cart-size vehicle that can navigate the narrow alleys of the town.

CAPRI TOWN & AROUND

Perched 138m (453 ft.) above Marina Grande, **Capri Town** is a saddle of relatively flat ground on the eastern end of the island. In this labyrinth of pastel and white-washed buildings are most of Capri's hotels and restaurants. Heavily trodden thoroughfares like Via Vittorio Emanuele can feel overwhelmingly touristy, especially during the peak hours from 11am to 4pm. Venture off the main drag and into the backstreets, and you'll discover affordable pizzerias and the simple groceries and delis where real *Caprese* shop.

As you exit the upper funicular station, walk out to the right and look over the balustrades for spectacular views of the towering western end of the island, and on most days, the silhouette of Mt. Vesuvius across the bay. Heading back into town, on the left past the clock tower, is ground zero of the Capri Town social scene: the **Piazzetta ★★**. Officially called Piazza Umberto I, the "little square" of Capri is a rectangle no bigger than a basketball court, where white lights are strung overhead and four mostly identical alfresco bars vie for your business. Cafe-sitting and people-watching in the Piazzetta is an essential part of the Capri experience, especially after 5pm. The cafe I always end up at, **Al Piccolo Bar** (**℃ 081/8370325**), seems to have the most charming staff and prime viewing angle from the left rear corner of the Piazzetta. Although you can get light food at the Piazzetta cafes, the scene is more for *aperitivo* (pre-dinner) or *dopocena* (after-dinner) drinks.

Bearing south from the Piazzetta, the main "street" running through Capri Town is **Via Vittorio Emanuele III,** a busy pedestrian thoroughfare filled with hotels and boutiques. When you reach the five-star Grand Hotel Quisisana (a Capri institution, it was built as a sanatorium in the 19th century; *qui si sana* means "here you get healthy"), turn left onto **Via Camerelle** for even more tony shopping.

After a few minutes' walk Via Camerelle converges on **Via Tragara ★★,** a quiet street with exclusive boutique hotels and the easiest panoramic walk on Capri. Leaving the crowds of central Capri Town behind, follow Via Tragara to the end. Here, **Punta Tragara ★★★** offers phenomenal views over the southern side of the island, including a close-up of the **Faraglioni ★★★,** limestone stacks jutting out of the water from far below; sweeping vistas to the west take in the beach and small boat harbor of Marina Piccola and the 589m (1,932 ft.) Monte Solaro. The three Faraglioni feature in just about every Capri postcard or promotional material; the iconic, 100m-tall (330 ft.) formations can even be seen from the Amalfi Coast, so to see them from this zoomed-in perspective is especially impressive. If you're feeling energetic, take the path from Punta Tragara down to water level to admire the Faraglioni (follow signs to *spiaggia* or *mare*—beach or sea, respectively). The two beach-club-cum-restaurants—Luigi ai Faraglioni and La Fontelina—will let you, for the princely sum of 16€ per person, use their bathing platforms for a swim in these gorgeous waters. Just below the Punta Tragara is the southern terminus of the Pizzolungo trail, one of the most spectacular hikes on the island (p. 76).

Back in Capri Town, if you turn right at the Hotel Quisisana, onto Via Ignazio Cerio, instead of left on Via Camerelle, it leads down to the **Certosa di San Giacomo ★** (© 081/8376218; free admission; Tues–Sat 9am–2pm, Sun 9am–1pm), a 14th-century Carthusian monastery that includes a church, a cloister, and a garden with splendid **vistas ★.** Nearby, down Via Matteotti, are the **Giardini di Augusto ★,** terraced public gardens with blissful **views ★★** of the Faraglioni. The red-brick paths are lined with geraniums, pines, and manicured lawns. Continue downhill, to the end of Via Matteotti to access spectacular **Via Krupp ★★.** An engineering marvel with hairpin turns set snug against a sheer rock wall, this pedestrian path descends 100m (330 ft.) from the south end of Capri Town to the sea at Marina Piccola (see "Beaches," above).

ANACAPRI & AROUND

The higher, quieter town (elevation 290m/951 ft.) on the western end of the island has long been touted as "the real Capri." That's not to say there aren't fancy hotels and overpriced shops here; it's just that Anacapri gets far fewer tourists than Capri Town, and the overall feel is less glossy, more down-to-earth.

Buses from Capri Town make a few intermediate stops on the outskirts of Anacapri, but stay on the bus until the end of the line, which is Piazza Vittoria. At this two-tiered square is the lower station of the **Monte Solaro chairlift** *(seggiovia),* which takes you up to the highest point on Capri.

The center of Anacapri is all narrow, whitewashed lanes with a cozy, festive feel. In addition to tourist-oriented retailers of luxury goods, you'll find bakeries, green grocers, delis, and coffee bars, all of which still cater mostly to island residents.

Sights within Anacapri include the **Villa San Michele** (see "Attractions," above) and the **Casa Rossa ★,** Via G. Orlandi 78 (© 081/8372193; 2.50€; May–Sept 10:30am–1:30pm and 5:30–9pm; hours vary off season), an eclectic work of architecture—with out-of-place mullioned windows and crenellations—painted Pompeian red. The house belonged to an American Confederate army veteran, John Mac-Kowen, who filled it with antiquities. It now also houses a permanent exhibition of 18th- and 19th-century paintings of Capri.

Where to Stay

As to be expected on an island with a reputation for such luxury, Capri specializes in high-end lodging, with an astonishing number of rooms that go for well over 500€ per night. However, there are some excellent values to be had, especially if you book well in advance and can be flexible with your travel dates. Some hotels close for much of the winter, only opening over Christmas, New Year's, and Easter.

CAPRI TOWN

Canasta ★★ 🍃 Definitely one of the island's best values, the Canasta offers elegant island style and comfortable surroundings at a moderate price. The white-washed hotel, a converted villa, is set amid lush gardens in the quiet higher part of Capri Town. The recently restored rooms are bright and cheerful, employing the tile work, white linens, and wrought iron typical of Campania. A patio and breakfast area is enveloped by Mediterranean shrubs and flowers, guaranteeing privacy and a heady dose of the island's perfumes. Unusual for such a small, affordable hotel, the Canasta also has a swimming pool, which overlooks the Certosa.

Via Campo di Teste 6. ✆ **081/8370561.** www.hotel-canasta.com. 16 units. Doubles 100€–170€ low season (late Oct to mid Dec, late Mar); 150€–210€ medium season (Apr, May, Oct, 2nd week of Jan); 170€–230€ high season (June–Sept, last week of Dec, 1st week of Jan, Easter). Closed Dec 25-26, and from mid-Jan to mid-Mar. Rates include full breakfast. AE, DC, MC, V. **Amenities:** Bar; indoor lounge; outdoor patio; pool. *In room:* A/C, TV, hair dryer, minibar, free Wi-Fi, radio.

Grand Hotel Quisisana ★★ Movers and shakers who like to be in the middle of things and have a budget for luxury need look no further than the historic "Quisi," an institution of old-style Caprese hospitality that was overhauled in 2007. Each guest room is unique but all are light and airy, with majolica floors, private terraces, and great views. (Super-VIPs like Madonna book the 1,900€-per-night penthouse suite, with its gold-plated room key.) Given its setting in the heart of Capri Town, the property is remarkably expansive, with a particularly large pool and sun deck surrounded by meticulously kept gardens. The poolside bar (open to non-guests) is usually packed in high season, giving the Piazzetta cafes a run for their money.

Via Camerelle 2, Capri. ✆ **081/8370788.** www.quisisana.com. 150 units. Doubles from 400€. AE, DC, MC, V. **Amenities:** 3 restaurants; 3 bars; concierge; fitness center; pool; room service; spa; transfers. *In room:* A/C, TV, hair dryer, Internet (fee), minibar.

La Tosca ★★ Beloved by island habitués on a budget, this simple inn run by the *gentilissimo* Ettore Castelli is the antithesis of the showy consumerism so prevalent in Capri Town. Rooms are basic but immaculate and homey, and you will always feel well taken care of by the staff, who are happy to help you arrange island excursions or plan an itinerary. A small patio has views of the Faraglioni through the trees and rooftops. Always book well in advance, as this tiny place fills up fast.

Via Birago 5, Capri. ✆ **081/8370989.** h.tosca@capri.it. 11 units. Doubles 70€–140€. Rates include buffet breakfast. AE, DC, MC, V. **Amenities:** Lounge; library; patio. *In room:* A/C, hair dryer, free Wi-Fi.

Punta Tragara ★★★ Practically cantilevered over the Faraglioni at the end of Via Tragara, this five-star has the most stunning location in Capri Town. The Le Corbusier–designed edifice (c. 1920), a salmon-colored wave of arcaded stucco, is practically an island monument in its own right. Inside, the hotel rejects the cookie-cutter approach of so many luxury properties. Instead, the guest rooms all have a different layout and decor; all feel impeccably stylish and special, and nearly all have a terrace with sea view. Works of art, from archaeological artifacts to Neapolitan baroque paintings to modern sculptures, add unique flair to each unit. The two seawater pools are amid tall trees and rough-hewn rock and antique masonry on three sides, creating a romantic feel, while the fourth edge is open to the incomparable vistas over the southern coast of the island. This is truly one of the most outstanding hotels in the Bay of Naples.

Via Tragara 57, Capri. 📞 **081/8370844.** www.hoteltragara.com. 44 units. Doubles from 300€ low season, from 420€ high season. Rates include full breakfast. AE, DC, MC, V. **Amenities:** Restaurant; bar; concierge; fitness center; 2 pools; room service; spa; transfers. *In room:* A/C, TV, hair dryer, minibar, free Wi-Fi.

ANACAPRI & AROUND

Caesar Augustus ★★★   Bright yellow on the outside and tastefully muted inside, this converted villa is fronted by gardens and backed by terraces that hang over sheer 300m (1,000 ft.) cliffs, and it's the plummeting views (vertigo-sufferers, book elsewhere!) that make this place such a showstopper. You'll want to spend a lot of time at the two-tier infinity pool if you stay here. Luxury hotels with more obvious glitz exist on Capri, but for a discreet retreat without forgoing cushy amenities, the Caesar Augustus is your best bet. Ivory-toned rooms, with wrought iron and cool tile throughout, have an appropriate islandlike feel, and all have private balconies or terraces (some frighteningly perched right over the cliffs). Staff are professional and personable.

Via G. Orlandi 4, Anacapri. 📞 **081-8373395.** www.caesar-augustus.com. 56 units. Doubles 430€– 550€. AE, DC, MC, V. **Amenities:** Restaurant; bar; concierge; exercise room; room service; spa. *In room:* A/C, TV, hair dryer, minibar, free Wi-Fi.

Casa Mariantonia ★★   This super stylish guesthouse makes an ideal base for those wanting to experience the more authentic side of the island. The immaculately restored, peach-toned villa is surrounded by fragrant lemon trees, and the fresh and airy rooms open onto a communal terrace. Proprietress Vivica Canale and her staff will personally help you make the most of your stay.

Via G. Orlandi 180, Anacapri. 📞 **081-8372923.** www.casamariantonia.com. 9 units. Doubles 140€– 220€. Rates include breakfast. AE, DC, MC, V. **Amenities:** Garden; pool; free Wi-Fi. *In room:* A/C, TV, hair dryer, minibar.

La Guardia Bed & Breakfast ★★ 🎁   This little Mediterranean aerie is what southern Italian warmth is all about. Both bedrooms have a sea view at this tiny, wonderfully welcoming inn near Punta Carena lighthouse (about 10 min. by bus southwest of Anacapri), and the property has a panoramic pool and terrace where you'll be tempted to while away many hours; but it's the hosts who earn this place such rave reviews. Umberto and Ciro are the very hands-on owner/managers, greeting all new arrivals with wine and snacks, treating guests like family, and helping you plan out your island itineraries.

Via La Guardia 47, Anacapri. 📞 **081/8372667.** bblaguardia@virgilio.it. 2 units. Doubles 120€ Apr–June, Oct–Nov; 140€ July–Sept. Rates include breakfast. **Amenities:** Patio; small outdoor pool; sun deck. *In room:* A/C, hair dryer, minibar.

MARINA GRANDE

J. K. Place ★★★   The swanky J.K. hospitality minibrand began with a flagship boutique hotel in Florence, but the Capri incarnation far outshines the original. Beautifully situated at water's edge just west of the port, this white mansion is an all-around stunner, with ultra-fashionable decorative accents in the common areas, and cosmopolitan flair and clever design in the guest rooms. J.K. Capri has been featured in *Architectural Digest* and offers a more sophisticated version of luxury than Capri's other high-end accommodations—there's not a majolica tile in sight. Expansive teak terraces, outfitted with comfy lounge chairs, wrap around the building, providing guests countless cozy spots from which to gaze over the sea to Vesuvius. The property as a whole is quite large, fringed by well-kept lawns and gardens, and there's a large rectangular pool to the rear, with attached spa and fitness center. From the front desk to the pool bar, the staff is wonderfully attentive and engaging. The only drawback, and it's a minor one, is that you can't really walk to the action of Capri Town; but for many guests, the superb style and comfort of J.K. is all the "action" they need.

Via Provinciale Marina Grande 225, Marina Grande. ℰ **081/8384001.** www.jkcapri.com. 22 units. Doubles 500€–700€. Rates include full breakfast. AE, DC, MC, V. **Amenities:** Bar; concierge; exercise room; large outdoor pool; room service; spa. *In room:* A/C; TV/DVD; free Wi-Fi movie library; CD player; hair dryer; minibar.

Where to Dine

The bill at Capri restaurants can be a shocking sight—once the *coperto* (cover) and *pane* (bread) charges are tacked on to already-high entree prices, eating out on this island is almost always an expensive affair. A cost-cutting measure that I personally employ is getting picnic fixings for at least one meal per day. Great little *alimentari* (delis) in the backstreets of both Capri Town and Anacapri will make up simple sandwiches for you for about 3€, or you can buy ingredients—freshly sliced prosciutto, all manner of domestic cheeses, bread, and wine—a la carte at those delis or grocery stores. Capri has no shortage of benches and panoramic spots at which to enjoy your DIY meal.

CAPRI TOWN & AROUND

Aurora ★★ CAPRESE   Capri Town is full of restaurants that look pretty similar, serve basically identical menus, and cost way too much for what you get. Aurora isn't one of them. The family-run restaurant, on a pretty street east of the Piazzetta, is a venerable culinary institution and consistently turns out top-notch cuisine with warm, impeccable service to boot. Unless you order the pizza, this place isn't cheap, but you'll get a great meal for your splurge. Menu offerings adhere mostly to Caprese tradition, though ingredients are a bit more creative here than anywhere else, and the presentations are gorgeous.

Via Fuorlovado 18/22. ℰ **081/8370181.** Reservations recommended in high season. Entrees 10€–20€. AE, DC, MC, V. Daily Apr–Dec noon–3:30pm and 7:30–11pm.

Le Grottelle ★ CAPRESE   This restaurant is a good 10-minute walk from the "civilization" of Capri Town, immersed in the pines, and with sublime views from its terrace, over the trees and down to the sea. The plates are small and pricey, but the homemade *ravioli alla caprese* are perfection: exquisite pillows of pasta filled with the freshest tomatoes and ricotta. Le Grottelle, which means "the little caves," is along the Pizzolungo walking route between the Grotta di Matermania and the Arco Naturale (p. 76), and is an ideal place to rest your feet and refuel mid-hike. In summer, reservations are recommended for alfresco terrace seating; otherwise, the interior dining room is set against a half-exposed cave wall, which is also quite atmospheric. The views are best before the sun goes down, but it's also fun to come here for dinner and walk back to town through the dark woods (the path is lit).

Via Arco Naturale (a 10-min. walk from the Piazzetta). © **081/8375719.** Reservations recommended in high season. Entrees 11€–20€. AE, DC, MC, V. Apr–Oct noon–3:30pm and 7:30–10pm.

Pulalli Wine Bar ★★ WINE/SMALL PLATES   A fantastic low-key alternative to the overpriced traditional *ristoranti* of Capri Town, this enoteca below the clock tower, adjacent to the Piazzetta, offers wines by the bottle or glass, antipasti, and an abridged menu of hot food, mostly Neapolitan standards. The location is wonderful, with a terrace overlooking the bustle of the Piazzetta and the floodlit town cathedral. The food is always top-quality at a fair price, and the wine list is a well-edited catalog of the best and most interesting Italian labels. I always spend at least part of an evening here whenever I'm on Capri.

Piazza Umberto I, 4. © **081/8374108.** Entrees 8€–15€. AE, MC, V. Wed–Mon noon–3pm, 7–11pm, later on weekends in summer.

ANACAPRI & AROUND

Barbarossa ★ ☺ PIZZA/ITALIAN   You almost forget you're on glamorous Capri when you come to this *ristorante-pizzeria* opposite the Anacapri bus terminus, and that's a good thing. With TVs that broadcast all the big soccer games, this is a down-to-earth joint that could be anywhere in Italy. Order one of their reliable Naples-style pizzas and a carafe of house wine, and you'll fill up for less than 15€ a head—no easy feat for a sit-down meal on this island.

Via Porta 1 (Piazza Vittoria). © **081/8371483.** Entrees 5€–10€. AE, DC, MC, V. Daily noon–3:30pm, 7–11pm.

Lido del Faro ★★ CAPRESE/ITALIAN   Those who make the trek out here, to the remote southwestern corner of the island, are rewarded with a magnificent and totally secluded waterside setting amid the jagged rocks below Capri's lighthouse. Lido del Faro is a multi-tasking joint—part *stabilimento balneare* (beach club), part restaurant and special events venue—but is always exceptionally friendly, turning out solid renditions of regional cuisine with an emphasis on local seafood. Call ahead before taking a bus or taxi out here for dinner, as the restaurant is often booked. This is an ideal place for lunch, as you can precede or follow your meal with a dip in Lido del Faro's seawater pool or protected Mediterranean cove.

Località Punta Carena. © **081/8371798.** Entrees 8.50€–16€. AE, MC, V. May–Sept daily 12:30–3pm; open for dinner (call for times) on weekends in June and July and every night in Aug.

Materita ★ CAPRESE/ITALIAN   Materita lures many with its alfresco seating on the church piazza of Santa Sofia. The food—a pan-Mediterranean menu of pastas and fish secondi, plus brick-oven pizzas—can be wonderful (try the *bruschetta al pomodoro* for a starter), but the setting, in the cozy crossroads of quaint Anacapri town, is what's really memorable.

Via Giuseppe Orlandi 140. © **081/8373375.** Reservations recommended for dinner in high season. Entrees 8€–16€. AE, MC, V. Wed–Mon 12:30–3pm and 7:30–10:30pm.

Shopping

Via Camerelle and Via Vittorio Emanuele, both in Capri Town, are the main thoroughfares for luxury goods. All the biggest names in European fashion are represented here. Naturally, the boutiques tend to stock more resort-oriented merchandise (500€ plastic Louis Vuitton beach tote, anyone?) than the same stores in the big cities. Sale periods, as in the rest of Italy, are July (for spring and summer collections) and February (for fall and winter collections), when the ending season's items are marked down by 30% to 75%.

In high season, most shops are open every day from 10am to 8pm, and often until midnight on summer weekends—the better to take advantage of inebriated vacationers on their way back from the Piazzetta!

Classy **Carthusia Profumi di Capri ★★★**, Viale Matteotti 2 (✆ **081-8370368;** www.carthusia.com; open 9:30am–6pm), makes the island's signature perfumes and you can visit their shop and laboratory near the Giardini di Augusto. Carthusia sells a variety of island-inspired scents for women, men, and the home, but to me, nothing captures Capri better than their classic women's fragrance *Aria di Capri,* a blend of marine air, lemon, peach, bay laurel, and Mediterranean flowers like mimosa, iris, and jasmine. The beautifully packaged products make wonderful souvenirs.

Speaking of lemons, who can leave the Bay of Naples without a souvenir bottle of limoncello? The classic local liqueur, made from lemon zest, alcohol, sugar, and water, was supposedly invented by a Caprese family, the Canalis. Now made in high-tech distilleries and marketed worldwide, the Canalis' Limoncello di Capri (www.limoncello.com) is the best-selling limoncello at Italian bars and restaurants. You can buy some at **Limoncello di Capri ★**, Via Roma 79, Capri (✆ **081/8375561**), or Via Capodimonte 27, Anacapri (✆ **081/8372927**). Convenient for travelers, the bottles come in small sizes and make easy-to-carry, affordable gifts.

"Capri sandals" have also become a trademark fashion item here, worn by such past and present island regulars as Maria Callas, Jackie Onassis, Sophia Loren, and Naomi Campbell. The sandals are almost exclusively *infradito* ("between toes;" that is, thongs), though some have a leather big-toe loop. They start out as simple leather soles and straps, to which all kinds of embellishment can be added. Pre-made pairs are sold, or you can order your own custom design, at **Amedeo Canfora ★** in Capri (Via Camerelle 3; ✆ **081/8370487;** www.canfora.com) or **L'Arte del Sandalo Caprese di Antonio Viva ★** in Anacapri (Via Giuseppe Orlandi 75; ✆ **081/ 8373583**). The sandals are handmade and prices start at 180€ per pair.

For more practical footwear that will still seem like a good purchase when your vacation is over, **G4 ★★**, Via Roma 47 (✆ **081/8389527**), is my favorite shoe store on the island, selling fabulous boots and pumps by cool, mid-range Italian labels that are hard to find back home.

Jewelry is another mainstay of the island's luxury retail offerings, and you can admire—and purchase—fine examples at **La Perla Gioielli,** Piazza Umberto I, 21 (✆ **081/8370641**).

ISCHIA ★★★

Ischia's velvety slopes, green with pine woods and vineyards, have earned it the nickname *Isola Verde* (Emerald Isle), while its fame as a healthy retreat has earned it another nickname, Island of Eternal Youth. Hot mineral water springs, steam vents, and mud-holes dot the island's slopes and shores, fueled by volcanic activity underneath Ischia, although its volcano, Mount Epomeo, has been dormant for 700 years. Cashing in on the island's geologic gifts, spa activities abound here, from the thermal theme parks to an embarrassment of traditional wellness centers offering all kinds of health and beauty treatments. The spa focus tends to steal thunder from another of the island's important attributes: Ischia's is the only coastline in this part of Italy with a decent number of sandy beaches.

The largest of the Bay of Naples islands, Ischia (pronounced *Ees*-kee-ya) may have a less recognizable name than Capri, but don't think you're going to have the island to yourself. There are hundreds of hotels island-wide, many of which fill to capacity

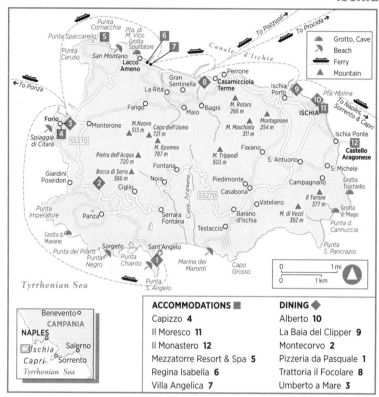

ACCOMMODATIONS ■
Capizzo **4**
Il Moresco **11**
Il Monastero **12**
Mezzatorre Resort & Spa **5**
Regina Isabella **6**
Villa Angelica **7**

DINING ◆
Alberto **10**
La Baia del Clipper **9**
Montecorvo **2**
Pizzeria da Pasquale **1**
Trattoria il Focolare **8**
Umberto a Mare **3**

5

BAY OF NAPLES ISLANDS

Ischia

in summer. Tourism exploded in the 1960s when the glamour set decided they liked the spa scene, but Ischia never really caught on among Americans. Most vacationers here are Italians and northern Europeans, especially Germans. *Ischitani* love tourists of all stripes, greeting everyone with the same exuberance, week after week, year after year (try finding the same general welcome on Capri).

Because of their proximity and symmetrical positioning opposite the mainland, Ischia (at the northern end of the bay) and Capri (at the southern tip) are often compared, but they're apples and oranges. Ischia may lack the intense drama and chic timelessness of Capri, but with its laid-back atmosphere and gentler, greener topography, not to mention all those spas and beaches, Ischia is its own brand of Mediterranean island vacation paradise.

Essentials

GETTING THERE
BY BOAT   Ischia's three main harbors—Ischia Porto (the largest), Forio, and Casamicciola—are very well connected to the mainland through frequent ferries (slower, but with an open deck) and hydrofoils (faster, but you're confined to a clammy cabin). Some of the hydrofoil lines are suspended during the winter because of rough seas.

If you want to bring your car (non-resident vehicles are only permitted from Oct to the week before Easter), ferries are the only means available; hydrofoils are passenger-only. Also, always check with the transport company as, even in the off season, local authorities sometimes restrict the number of cars allowed on the island. Reserve well in advance for car transport because space is at a premium; however, regular passenger tickets need not be booked more than an hour or two before your desired departure. All the boat companies have easy-to-find ticket offices, which accept major credit cards, at each of the ports listed here. If you're just planning to visit Ischia as a day trip, keep in mind that the last Naples-bound boat of the day normally leaves around 7pm.

Between Ischia and Naples (30 boats per day each way): Note that most departures are from Naples's main port, **Molo Beverello,** while a much smaller number of boats (hydrofoils only) leave from the smaller **Mergellina** harbor. **Caremar** (© **081/991953** or 081/984818; www.caremar.it) runs ferries (90 min.; 5.60€) and hydrofoils (1 hr.; 11€) from Naples's main port of Beverello to Ischia Porto, often stopping at Procida along the way. **Snav** (© **081/4285111;** www.snav.it) operates hydrofoils (50 min.; 16€) from Beverello to Ischia Porto and Casamicciola, usually stopping at Procida en route. **Alilauro** (© **081/991888** or 081/761004; www.alilauro.it) runs hydrofoils (45 min.; 16€) from Naples's main port, Beverello, to Ischia Porto and Forio. Alilauro also operates hydrofoils (35 min.; 16€) to Ischia Porto from Mergellina harbor (a pretty district of Naples, and much less chaotic than Beverello). **Medmar** (© **081/5513352;** www.medmargroup.it) runs traditional ferries from Beverello to Ischia Porto (90 min.; 6.30€).

Between Ischia and Pozzuoli (12–14 boats per day each way): **Medmar** (© **081/5513352;** www.medmargroup.it) and **Caremar** (© **081/991953;** www.caremar.it) both offer traditional ferries from Pozzuoli (a major port north of Naples, also with its own cultural attractions) to both Ischia Porto and Casamicciola. The trip takes 50 minutes and costs 3.60€.

Between Ischia and Capri (1–3 boats per day each way): **Alilauro** (© **081 /4972238;** www.alilauro.it) runs hydrofoils (16€ one-way) from April to October, while the ferries **Capitan Morgan** (© **081/985080**) and **Rumore Marittima** (© **081/983636**) also sail between the two islands (15€) year-round. Trip time between Capri and Ischia is about 30 minutes by hydrofoil, or an hour by ferry.

Between Ischia and Procida (16–18 boats per day each way): Procida is an intermediate stop on many hydrofoils and ferries between Ischia and Naples. You can get there by hydrofoil with **Snav** (© **081/4285111;** www.snav.it) and **Caremar** (© **081/991953** or 081/984818; www.caremar.it) or by ferry with **Caremar** and **Medmar** (© **081/5513352;** www.medmargroup.it). Most of the Procida-bound boats leave from Ischia Porto, though a few per day also leave from Forio and Casamicciola.

Between Ischia and Sorrento: From May to September, Alilauro operates one hydrofoil per day to Ischia Porto. It leaves Sorrento at 9:30am; the return boat leaves Ischia at 5:20pm. Trip time is 1 hour each way, and tickets are 17€.

Between Ischia and the Amalfi Coast: These connections are only offered in summer and usually aren't the most direct way to Ischia. **Navigazione Libera del Golfo** (© **081/5520763;** www.navlib.it) operates from Salerno to Ischia. **Alicost** (© **089/234892** in Salerno; 089/871483 in Amalfi; and 089/811986 in Positano; www.amalficoastlines.com) offers connections to Ischia Porto from Salerno, Capri, Amalfi, and Positano.

GETTING AROUND

Although larger than the other islands, Ischia can easily be toured via public transportation. SEPSA's public **bus system** (℃ **081/991808** or 081/991828) is very well run and organized: One of its lines tours the island toward the right (*circolare destra,* marked CD), and one circles toward the left (*circolare sinistra,* marked CS); other lines crisscross the island between its major destinations. Tickets are 1.20€ and are valid for 90 minutes; a daily pass costs 4€. You can get a printout of the bus schedule from the tourist office.

You can find **taxis** at the stands strategically located around the island, including all harbors and main destinations, or call ℃ **081/984998,** 081/992550, or 081/993720. Some of the taxis are picturesque three-wheelers—*microtaxi* or *motorette*—but they are rapidly disappearing. A 10€ minimum charge applies inside the town of Ischia (it's pretty much a flat rate), but drivers use the meter for trips outside town.

Bringing your own car to the island is prohibited from Easter through the end of September, but you can rent a car once on Ischia. Driving your own car or scooter around Ischia is the easiest way to see a lot in a short amount of time, and of course to get off the beaten track where the buses don't go, but in many busy areas, parking a car can be a challenge. For **small car** and **scooter rental,** try **Fratelli del Franco,** Via A. de Luca, Ischia Porto (℃ **081/991334;** www.noleggiodelfranco.it), which also rents bicycles, and **euroscootercar,** Via Iasolino, Ischia Porto (℃ **081/982722**).

Finally, getting around the island **by sea** is also an option worth considering. Agencies at any of the island's ports will rent you small motorboats (no experience or license required; from about 50€ for a half-day). At the helm of your 4- to 6-person, easy-to-pilot craft, you can putter around the island, stopping at the hard-to-access swimming coves. If you want to leave the skippering to someone else, there are also organized boat tours of the island as well as day excursions to nearby destinations like Procida, Capri, and even the Amalfi Coast. **Capitan Morgan** (℃ **081/985080** or 081/4972222; www.capitanmorgan.it) is one such operator: Their 3-hour afternoon island tours (12€) depart Forio at 2:30pm, picking up passengers at Lacco Ameno, Casamicciola, and Ischia Porto, before continuing around the island. The tour includes a 1-hour stop for swimming or refreshments at Sant'Angelo. Capitan Morgan's minicruise to the Amalfi Coast (29€, includes 2-hr. stop at Positano and Amalfi) departs at 8:45am and returns by 5:30pm.

VISITOR INFORMATION

The AACST (official) **tourist office** is in Ischia town at Corso Vittoria Colonna 116 (℃ **081/5074231;** fax 081/5074230; www.infoischiaprocida.it). They also maintain **information booths** on Via Sogliuzzo 72 in the center of Ischia Porto and by the harbor (℃ **081/5074211;** Mon–Sat 9am–noon and 2–5pm). Definitely stop at one of these information centers before hitting the rest of the island, as they provide free maps, printouts of bus and boat schedules, and brochures about everything from spas to nature walks to watersports.

The Top Attractions

For many vacationers, Ischia's big draws and defining characteristics are its **thermal waters** and the whole culture of *benessere* ("well-being") that goes along with them; yet for others, Ischia is a garden island of beautiful **sandy beaches** (a commodity that's hard to come by in the Bay of Naples and the Amalfi Coast) that also happens to have thermo-mineral spas and pools everywhere. A handful of historic monuments, museums, and villas, listed in "Exploring the Island," round out the island's offerings.

SPAS & THERMO-MINERAL SPRINGS

Suffering from arthritis, gout, fibromyalgia, tonsillitis, asthma, or eczema? Is cellulite hindering your bikini confidence? Stop wasting your time with doctors, medicines, and creams, Ischitan spa operators say, and come to this island! There is scarcely a respiratory, rheumatic, or dermatologic malady under the sun that Ischia's *acque termali* (thermal waters)—a veritable mosaic of water types with different mineral profiles—don't purport to palliate. Spa culture is all-consuming on this island and probably its most unique feature. With more that 56 mineral springs (not to mention the hot mud, hot sands, and numerous steam holes), harnessed by over 150 spa operators and hotels, Ischia is a spa lover's Shangri-La.

While I don't recommend you spend every waking minute on Ischia doing hydrotherapy and spa treatments (that would get expensive), you'd be seriously missing out on the Ischitan experience if you didn't spend at least a day at one of the wonderful *parchi termali* (thermal parks) like **Giardini di Poseidon** or **Negombo.** Even if you don't have any ailments, or you don't buy into the claims about the waters' curative properties, who cares? It's impossible not to enjoy the gorgeous settings and the just-plain-fun novelty of going from pool to pool and subjecting yourself to the various water jets and temperature changes.

The best spa facilities, in my opinion, are the *parchi termali*: These open-air "thermal parks" are veritable playgrounds of hydrotherapy, with prescribed courses through dozens of pools of different depths, shapes, and temperatures—some with strong hydromassage jets, some with steamy natural rock grottos, but all with specific supposed health benefits that come from the chemical make-up of that zone's hot springs. The largest parks occupy acres and acres of prime beachfront real estate, making them great destinations for sun and swim, too. A daily fee (average 25€) covers the use of the pools and basic facilities, and they also offer a huge range of beauty, relaxation, and therapeutic treatments from both western and eastern traditions (massages, mud wraps, and so forth), which are priced separately.

Spa season runs from April to October, giving Ischia a much longer tourist season than other Italian islands—even if the air is chilly in spring or fall, the thermal water, found in every hotel pool on the island, is nice and warm. As you explore the spa scene, you'll see some disconcerting black and yellow signs warning you about "radio-active water"—not to worry, the radon present in Ischia's springs has a short half-life

The Monster in the Mountain

Sure, geologists will tell you that volcanic activity under the Bay of Naples is responsible for Ischia's thermal waters, but the mythological explanation is more fun. According to Greek legend, Zeus himself imprisoned the monster Typhoeus in the ground underneath Ischia's Monte Epomeo. Whenever Typhoeus got particularly angry, the volcanic mountain would erupt; and whenever he wept, his tears would emerge at the island's surface as hot springs and fumaroles. Fortunately for islanders and tourists, Typhoeus hasn't lost his temper in several hundred years, but he still sobs around the clock.

(no danger of radiation or negative health effects) and is apparently a great antidote to stress. (Who knew?)

THE BEST PARCHI TERMALI

The most famous thermal park on Ischia is **Giardini Poseidon,** Via Giovanni Mazzella Citara, Forio (© **081/907122** or 081/907420; www.giardiniposeidonterme.com; daily 9am–7pm; 28€ per day), an open-air facility south of Forío, on the pretty bay of Citara. "Poseidon's Gardens" have 22 pools (both relaxing and curative), a large private beach, and several restaurants. The other preeminent thermal facility on the island is on the promontory of Monte Vico near Lacco Ameno: **Negombo** (© **081/986152;** www.negombo.it; daily 9am–7pm; 28€) is nestled on the island's most picturesque cove, Lido di San Montano, and has magnificent gardens, a secluded beach, and elegant thermal pools. Between Ischia Porto and Casamicciola, **Parco Termale Castiglione,** Via Castiglione 62 (© **081/982551;** www.terme castiglione.it; daily 9am–7pm; 25€ per day) is a state-of-the-art facility offering thermo-mineral waters and mud treatments in a mix of indoor and open-air facilities. The scenic outdoor pools range in temperature from 82° to 104°F (28°–40°C). Finally, to the east of Sant'Angelo, is the **Giardini Aphrodite-Apollon** (© **081/ 999219;** www.hotelmiramare.it; daily 8am–6pm; 25€ per day), an indoor-outdoor facility with lovely grounds and pools that is part of the Park Hotel Miramare.

For a more traditional spa experience, I recommend the state-of-the-art **Ischia Thermal Center ★**, Via delle Terme 15, Ischia (© **081/984376;** www.ischia thermalcenter.it; prices a la carte), an indoor facility (open year-round) offering a wide range of health and beauty treatments. I also like the four historical spas of Casamicciola Terme—**Terme Manzi, Belliazzi, Elisabetta,** and **Lucibello**—opening onto the famous Piazza Bagni in the hamlet of Bagni. For an even more exclusive experience, head to the **Terme della Regina Isabella ★**, a hotel and thermal resort (see "Where to Stay," below) in Lacco Ameno; this is one of the most elegant spas on the island.

WINE COUNTRY

Ischia's countryside is dotted with vineyards producing excellent D.O.C. wines (the white Ischia Bianco and red Ischia Rosso). Biancolella and Forastera are the island's principal white grapes, while Guarnaccia and Per'e' Palummo (Piedirosso) are the reds. The best winemakers on the island are **D'Ambra,** in Panza (© **081/907246;** www.dambravini.com); **Perrazzo,** in Ischia (© **081/982981**); Cenatiempo, in Ischia (© **081/981203**); and **Pietratorcia,** in Forio (© **081/907232**). Visits and tastings at these wineries are generally only possible the first week of June, in late September, and in early October.

Outdoor Pursuits

BEACHES

Ischia's coastline alternates between rugged cliffs and sandy stretches of shore, to the delight of sunbathers and swimmers. Nearly all **beaches and swimming coves** are accessible by land; they're either a short distance from a bus stop or can be reached by foot paths of varying lengths and difficulty. However, going by sea (with your own rented boat or with a water taxi or island tour; see "Getting Around," above) is the most efficient way to try out different spots and follow the sun.

At least part of every beach on Ischia is a free public area where you can spread a towel gratis; the rest is occupied by the standard Italian lineup of *stabilimenti* (beach clubs, with restaurants, changing rooms and showers, lounge chairs and umbrellas; and sometimes watersports equipment), which charge between 10€ and 15€ per day for the use of their facilities. The following section is a clockwise tour of the island's beaches, starting from Ischia Town. All of these beaches are directly along, or a short walk from, stops on the CD or CS bus lines. Alternatively, take a water taxi from any of the marinas (Ischia Porto, Ischia Ponte, Sant'Angelo, Forio, Lacco Ameno, or Casamicciola Terme).

BEACHES IN ISCHIA TOWN & EASTERN COAST New arrivals at Ischia Porto may be tempted to go for a dip right away, and three decent beaches offer the opportunity to do so. Just remember that it's only a short bus ride away from the busy harbor to much better beaches (see below).

Spiaggia degli Inglesi (English Beach) is several hundred meters east of Ischia Porto's circular marina (take the footpath that hugs the coastline, or take a water taxi) and got its name from the British travelers who used to frequent it in the 1950s, before mass tourism hit Ischia. Some locals still refer to it by its original name, Spiaggia di Sant'Alessandro, for the eponymous verdant hill nearby. It's a rather short swath of sand and tends to be cooler than elsewhere because of its northern exposure— hence its other nickname, *Spiaggia Fredda* (Cold Beach)—but it's almost entirely a free-access public beach and uncrowded.

Ischia's main town beach, **Lido d'Ischia,** lies on the eastern side of the harbor and is longer (though not very wide) and better equipped with beach clubs and services. As a "city beach," it also tends to be quite crowded, but the shallow waters are great for families, and you can watch all the comings and goings of the port.

My favorite beach in Ischia town is **Spiaggia dei Pescatori** ★ (Fishermen's Beach), which is farther west of Lido d'Ischia, but still on the town side of the Castello Aragonese promontory. Not only is there a great view of the castle from here, but you can also see Procida from this east-facing beach; and the sandy shore is punctuated by colorful wooden fishing boats. All in all, it's a charming scene, and the seafood restaurants lining the beach are some of the most authentic in town.

About a kilometer's walk south of Ischia Ponte (though it's much easier to access this beach by boat) is the small **Spiaggia di Cartaromana,** which consists of a narrow stretch of fine sand as well as steep drop-offs once you're in the water, making it popular with divers, who come here to look at the underwater archaeological remains of Roman buildings.

BEACHES ON THE SOUTHERN COAST OF ISCHIA Most locals will tell you that Ischia's beach par excellence is **Spiaggia dei Maronti** ★★, a 3 km-long (2 miles; Ischia's longest) stretch of soft golden sand in the middle of the southern coast, just west of the village and promontory of Sant'Angelo. Maronti has dozens of beach clubs as well as public stretches with lifeguards, and watersports galore. Toward the western end of the beach is the *Fumarole* section, so named because hot vents of steam come up through the water and sand—be careful not to burn your feet! It's actually possible to cook food in the hot sand here; see "Cooking Dinner in the Sand," p. 96. Though some prefer Citara (see below), Spiaggia dei Maronti is probably Ischia's best "all-around" beach.

With its chic bars and restaurants, **Spiaggia di Sant'Angelo** ★ is a surprisingly trendy strip of sand on the western side of the narrow isthmus connecting the promontory of Sant'Angelo to the rest of the island. A public stretch of beach is at the northern tip, but the rest (about 100m/400 ft.) is given over to beach clubs frequented by the yacht crowd, who moor at the little marina opposite. A bit farther west past Sant'Angelo is **Cava Grado,** a tiny and relaxing free beach that gets very little traffic (perfect for a tranquil day out).

For a free spa-on-the-beach experience, take the bus to Panza and head down the stone staircase to **Sorgeto ★**. The tightly enclosed bay of Sorgeto is lined with thermal springs and mineral-rich mud, making for great fun and relaxation among the vapors. The seawater is heated by the springs, making wintertime swimming totally feasible. With its hot, sometimes muddy sand, Sorgeto is not particularly recommended for catching rays.

BEACHES ON THE WESTERN COAST Citara **★★★**, on the southern outskirts of Forio, is my favorite Ischitan beach both for its natural beauty and its unmistakable holiday spirit. The fine, white sand stretches for nearly a kilometer (½ mile), and the water is almost Caribbean blue-green. It also faces due west, which is good news for tan-seekers and sunset-watchers. With lots of beach clubs, bars, and restaurants, Citara is Ischia's most happening beach, especially come sundown. Citara is also a thermo-mineral hot spot, home to the famous Giardini Poseidon thermal park; some public-access hot springs are at the southern end of the beach.

A bit farther north, just before Forio, is a short wedge of sandy beach called **Cava dell'Isola,** *the* place to be for the younger crowd. On the northern edge of Forio marina is **Spiaggia della Chiaia,** a pleasantly busy town beach with calm and clear water for swimming. **Spiaggia di San Francesco** is essentially a northerly extension of Chiaia, filled with beach clubs and services, and terminates with the dramatic lava-rock contours of Punta Caruso at the northwestern tip of the island.

BEACHES ON THE NORTHERN COAST OF ISCHIA Shaped like a slice of sandwich bread, **San Montano ★★** bay has the prettiest beach on Ischia, framed by profuse green vegetation and wildflowers and the promontories of Zaro and Monte Vico (near Lacco Ameno). The shore isn't huge, but it's almost as wide as it is long. The sand is deep, sugary soft, and the tropical-turquoise water is calm and shallow, even well away from the shore. San Montano is very popular and, due to its diminutive size, can be quite crowded in high season.

WALKING

Though the nature hikes on Ischia aren't nearly as dramatic as those on Capri (p. 76), there are still some worthwhile itineraries that alternate between lush flora and lovely sea views. Furthermore, a refreshing walk on the slopes of Monte Epomeo is a nice complement to all the spas and baths you may be partaking in down by the sea. Before setting out, I suggest you procure the diminutive brochure *Lizard Trails* from the tourist office in Ischia (p. 87); it has descriptions and maps of the island's best trails. Tourist office staff can also tell you what bus to take to a given trail head, which are mostly uphill or downhill, and other useful information.

Exploring the Island

Ischia is more or less round, covering about 46 sq. km (18 sq. miles), with a perimeter of 34km (21 miles). So, even though it eclipses Capri and Procida in size, it's not a behemoth; and with the island's handy bus connections, you can easily sample Ischia's many facets even during a short stay.

The largest town on the island is Ischia, developed around the main harbor on the island's northeastern corner. The town is divided into **Ischia Porto** (the busy touristic and commercial district built around the circular port where most island-bound hydrofoils and ferries arrive) and **Ischia Ponte:** Just east of the port, this is the district

A Fiery Festival

If you happen to be in Ischia in late July, you may be in for a real treat: The island's biggest festival, **La Festa di Sant'Anna**, takes place on July 26. The night begins with a nighttime parade of elaborately decorated rafts (designed by the six different municipalities of Ischia) in the waters beneath the castle. When the boats have all passed by (the order of appearance is determined by a swimming race between the municipalities the day before) and been judged (one will win a hotly contested *palio*, or award for best decorations), the festival's marquee event commences. Around 10pm, the Castello Aragonese is engulfed in flames (carefully controlled fires burn in containers around the fortress, but the effect is totally convincing of a raging *incendio*). A spectacular fireworks display caps off the evening.

adjacent to the bridge (*ponte*) that connects "mainland" Ischia to the fortress promontory known as Castello Aragonese. In between runs the pleasant promenade of Via Roma and Corso Vittoria Colonna, stretching about 2km (1¼ miles).

The promontory with its small natural harbor was the site of the original settlement, fortified by a castle as far back as the 5th century B.C. The castle on the promontory today, the **Castello Aragonese ★★**, Piazzale Aragonese, Ischia Ponte (✆ 081/992834; www.castellodischia.it; 10€; winter 10am–4:30pm, summer 9am–7pm) was built by the Aragonese over the ruins of the earlier fortifications. I encourage you to climb up for a visit (though you can take an elevator), since it is quite scenic and picturesque. The last eruption of Mount Epomeo in 1301 destroyed most of the village that had grown around the small natural harbor. The population resettled, but closer to the castle and bridge.

Ischia Porto was founded by the Bourbons on a whim. When they took over the island in the 18th century, there was just a scenic volcanic lake (originally a volcano crater) and a few villas. The new kings fell in love with a villa-cum-spa built by a doctor, Francesco Buonocore, and decided to establish their residence there. They refashioned the villa overlooking the lake into a small palace—what happened to the doctor is unknown; maybe he graciously donated his home to their majesties—the Casina Reale Borbonica, which today houses a military spa (not open to the public). They also cut a channel into the outer shore of the lake, transforming it into a large harbor. Inaugurated in 1854, it has been the island's main port ever since, and a lively town has developed around it, with many nice bars and a few restaurants.

A short distance west of Ischia (6.5km/4 miles) on the north shore is the small village of **Casamicciola Terme,** with its marina served by boats from Capri and Naples. The Villa Ibsen, where the famous Norwegian writer wrote *Peer Gynt,* is also here. Founded in the 16th century to take advantage of the area's thermo-mineral springs, Casamicciola Terme is where the first modern spa was opened on the island in 1604. The village, though, suffered a reversal of fortunes when it was destroyed by the earthquake of 1883. It was immediately rebuilt, but closer to the shore, in its current position by the marina. The remains of the original town are in the inland hamlet of Bagni, with the island's oldest spas opening onto its main square, and the village of Majo, farther up the slope.

Adjacent to Casamicciola, 8km (5 miles) west of Ischia Porto, is the picturesque **Lacco Ameno,** famous for its mushroom-shaped rock a few yards from the sandy shore. The ancient Greeks established their first settlement on this coast; although, daunted by the then-frequent earthquakes and eruptions, they never developed a colony. An unassuming fishing harbor until the 1950s, it was then shaken out of its sleep by Italian publisher Angelo Rizzoli. He built his villa on the promontory of Monte Vico, overlooking the village to the west, and decided to invest in the area and transform it into an exclusive resort. His plan was successful and the promontory has become the most haute spa destination in Italy, offering many luxurious hotels and villas. Villa Arbusto, Angelo Rizzoli's own summer home, is today a museum—**Museo Civico Archeologico di Pithecusae ★** (℅ **081/900356;** 3€; Tues–Sun 9:30am–1pm and 4–8pm)—displaying the findings of local archaeological excavation. It is worth a visit, if only to admire the famous **Coppa di Nestore ★★★**: Dating from 725 B.C., it bears one of the oldest known Greek inscriptions, which, appropriately, celebrates the wine of Ischia. Nearby is an important Catholic pilgrimage site, the **Sanctuary of Santa Restituta** (℅ **081/980706** or 081/980538; daily 10am–1pm and 4–7pm), with its archaeological excavations and museum. The original church was created in the 4th or 5th century A.D. by adapting an ancient Roman water cistern, and later restructured.

On the west side of the Monte Vico promontory are the lovely gardens of **Villa La Mortella ★★★**, Via Francesco Calise 39 (℅ **081/986220;** www.lamortella.it). Covering 2 hectares (5 acres), the gardens were designed by Russell Page, though they were the brainchild of Susana Gil, the Argentinean wife of British composer William Walton. Gil, who still lives here, has made it her vocation to create and sustain these gardens. Admission is 10€ adults, 8€ children ages 8 to 12, 6€ children ages 5 to 7, and children under 5 are admitted free (Apr 1–Nov 15 Tues–Thurs and Sat–Sun 9am–7pm; ticket booth closes 30 min. earlier).

Near La Mortella is **Villa La Colombaia,** Via Francesco Calise 73 (℅ **081/ 3332147;** daily 9:30am–12:30pm and 4–7:30pm), the former home of Italian film director Luchino Visconti. Set in a beautiful park with dramatic cliffside sea views, the Moorish-style villa now hosts various art shows and cultural events. A museum dedicated to Visconti's life and cinematic oeuvre is in the works.

On the western coast of the island, 13km (8 miles) west of Ischia Porto, is the lively town of **Forio,** with its wealth of bars and beautiful beaches; the best beach on the island, Citara, and the famous Poseidon thermal park, are just south of town. A favorite retreat of writers and musicians for centuries, it is also appreciated by those who come to enjoy the locally produced wine and the views of its watchtower. The tower—built in the 16th century to defend the town from Saracen attacks—was once a prison, and now houses a small museum (℅ **081/3332934**) of the work of local poet and sculptor Giovanni Maltese.

The southern half of Ischia is more agricultural, with only one town on the southern shore: the tiny harbor of **Sant'Angelo,** 11km (7 miles) south of Ischia Porto. Shaded by a promontory jutting into the sea and connected to the shore by a sandy isthmus (100m-long/300 ft.) that is closed to vehicles, it is one of Ischia's most picturesque sights, and a world away from the hype of the high-priced spa resorts. The other villages on this part of the island are nested on the steep slopes of the mountain, overlooking the sea. **Serrara Fontana** (9.5km/6 miles southwest of Ischia Porto) is a tiny hamlet centered around a lookout terrace affording spectacular views. Inland, the hamlet of **Buonopane** (part of Barano) is worth a detour, especially in the morning, when the ovens of the village, whose name means "good bread," emit an aroma of freshly baked *pane* that's positively intoxicating.

Ischia's unusual volcanic characteristics have produced more than spa-perfect conditions. The fertile soil and unique subtropical climate have been so favorable to flowering plants and shrubs that the island is host to 50% of the entire European patrimony of flower species, a number of them indigenous to Ischia.

Where to Stay

Ischia has an absurd number of hotels in all price ranges, and just about anywhere you sleep will have a swimming pool fed by the island's thermo-mineral waters. The highest season is July through August, and it's also quite busy in June and September. Though much less crowded, May and October are beautiful months, too, and better hotel deals are available. *Note:* In high season, most accommodations have a minimum stay of 3 nights.

Capizzo ★ FORIO   In a panoramic position above the gorgeous beach of Citara Bay, an easy walk to the Poseidon thermal park, this hotel is great for moderate budgets. Capizzo's interiors won't win any design awards (you've seen this honey-toned, vaguely contemporary wood paneling at dozens of other mid-range hotels in Italy), but each double has a sea view, and the hotel has many (mostly Italian) return guests, a good sign. The outdoor thermal pool and sun deck, surrounded by palm trees, have beautiful views of the bay below. It's about a 10-minute walk to the sea.

Via Provinciale Panza-Citara. ✆ **081/907168.** www.hotelcapizzo.it. 34 units. Doubles 105€–135€. Prices include buffet breakfast. AE, DC, MC, V. Closed Nov–Mar. **Amenities:** Garden; outdoor thermal pool; terrace. *In room:* A/C; TV; hair dryer; minibar.

Il Moresco ★★ ISCHIA PORTO   The most elegant digs in Ischia Porto, this hotel with Moorish style architecture is sandwiched between the beach and the main pedestrian drag Corso Vittoria Colonna. Rooms are cheery with hand-painted majolica floor tiles; the only sour note is the unfortunately dowdy curtains and bed linens. All units have at least a balcony; many have semi-private garden terraces. Only superior doubles and suites have full sea views. The extensive grounds contain thermal pools, one carved out of natural rock grottoes that used to be a wine cellar. Il Moresco's small private "beach" (a sandy patch set against a rocky shore, with a bathing platform) is convenient and has great views of the castle and Procida.

Via Gianturco 16. ✆ **081/981355.** www.ilmoresco.it. 72 units. Double 230€–460€. AE, DC, MC, V. **Amenities:** Restaurant; 3 bars; concierge; fitness room; 1 outdoor and 2 indoor thermal pools; room service; spa; garden; terraces. *In room:* A/C, satellite TV, hair dryer, minibar, balcony or terrace.

Albergo Il Monastero ★ ISCHIA PONTE   In the Castello Aragonese, this is the island's most picturesque hotel. The atmosphere—it was a former monastery—is unique, the reception warm and welcoming, and the views are quiet are superb. Guest rooms are spacious, especially considering they were monk cells, and are decorated with stylish sobriety, from the whitewashed walls and tiled floors to the solid dark wood or wicker furniture. The bathrooms are small but fully tiled with tasteful design (some are downright tiny with space for only showerheads and a drain in the tile directly below). A few rooms boast small but delightful private terraces, while others open onto a common terrace.

Castello Aragonese, Ischia Ponte. © **081/992435.** www.albergoilmonastero.it. 13 units. Doubles 120€–150€. Rates include continental breakfast. AE, DC, MC, V. Closed Nov–Jan. **Amenities:** Concierge; terrace. *In room:* A/C, hair dryer.

Mezzatorre Resort & Spa ★★ LACCO AMENO

On the promontory of Monte Vico near Lacco Ameno, this is among the best hotels on the island. The rocky point looks straight down to the sea and is surrounded by a 3-hectare (7-acre) wooded complex; the hotel shares these grounds with a 15th-century watchtower. The elegant outdoor spaces include tennis courts and an infinity pool on a cliffside terrace. Spacious guest rooms are individually decorated in a tasteful mix of Mediterranean and contemporary style, with tiled floors, quality furnishings, and warm-colored fabrics. All have state-of-the-art bathrooms, many with Jacuzzi tubs. Many rooms enjoy private terraces or gardens, and a number have sea views.

Via Mezzatorre. © **081/986111.** www.mezzatorre.it. 60 units. Doubles 420€–560€. Rates include buffet breakfast. AE, DC, MC, V. Closed Nov–Apr. **Amenities:** 2 restaurants; bar; babysitting; concierge; health club; outdoor pool; room service; spa; tennis. *In room:* A/C, TV, hair dryer, minibar.

L'Albergo della Regina Isabella ★★★ LACCO AMENO

Beautifully located, with views over the village and harbor, this prestigious historical hotel offers fine accommodations, a state-of-the-art thermal spa, and a private cove. The whole place has a vintage, Gina Lollobrigida-goes-to-the-sea feel. The public spaces are palatial, with many original furnishings, and the extra amenities will make your stay idyllic. The large guest rooms are decorated with a mix of contemporary and antique, with hand-painted ceramic floors and luxurious bathrooms. Many rooms have private balconies that open onto views of the sea or the gardens. The hotel's private cove is equipped with floating chairs, suitable for lounging.

Piazza Santa Restituta 1. © **081/994322.** www.reginaisabella.it. 132 units. Doubles 540€–740€. Rates include buffet breakfast. AE, DC, MC, V. Free parking. Closed Nov–Mar. **Amenities:** 2 restaurants; 2 bars; babysitting; children's programs; concierge; 2 outdoor pools; indoor thermal pool; room service; spa; tennis; beach. *In room:* A/C, satellite TV, hair dryer, minibar, free Wi-Fi.

Villa Angelica ★ LACCO AMENO

This small, family-run hotel is an excellent, moderately priced choice. In a whitewashed Mediterranean building with arched doorways and passages, it has a welcoming atmosphere that extends from the public spaces to the guest rooms. The latter are quiet and cozy, with tiled floors and wrought-iron beds. Most have private terraces. The hotel offers a beautiful thermal swimming pool with a Jacuzzi in the garden.

Via IV Novembre 28. © **081/994524.** www.villaangelica.it. 20 units. Doubles 130€–170€. Rates include buffet breakfast. AE, DC, MC, V. Closed mid-Nov to mid-Mar. **Amenities:** Restaurant; bar; babysitting; concierge; outdoor pool; room service; spa. *In room:* A/C, TV, hair dryer, minibar.

Where to Dine

For an island in the fish-rich Bay of Naples, traditional Ischitan *cucina tipica* has a surprisingly strong "turf" component. Rabbit (*coniglio*) is the specialty par excellence (cooked in a terracotta pan with tomatoes, garlic, wine, and local herbs); you'll also find the local snails (*'e maruzze*) on many menus. Of course, seafood is also ubiquitous here, and Ischia (as the rest of the Bay of Naples) is famous for its *frittura di paranza* (mixed small fish fry), which consists of a medley of minnow-sized whole fish, breaded, fried, and served—head, tail, bones, and all.

Alberto ★ ISCHIA ISCHITAN/SEAFOOD

This traditional restaurant, with a veranda right on the beach promenade between the harbor and the Castello Aragonese, is an excellent spot for sampling this coast's freshest seafood. The menu is small and focuses on local specialties as interpreted by the chef. I highly recommend the *marinata mista,* a medley of fish marinated in a tangy and delicate citrus sauce, to be followed by the superb linguine *alle vongole* (with clams) and the delicious *pesce all'Alberto,* oven-baked fish with potatoes, olives, and capers. The wine list offers an ample choice of local wines.

Via Cristoforo Colombo 8, Ischia Porto. © **081/981259.** Reservations recommended. Entrees 12€–24€. AE, MC, V. Daily noon–3pm and 7–11pm. Closed Nov–Feb.

La Baia del Clipper ★ ISCHIA PORTO ISCHITAN/PIZZA Directly on the happening "Rive Droite" of the busy harbor, this is a good spot for a light dinner after an *aperitivo* at one of the elegant bars in the vicinity. The menu features Neapolitan-style pizzas and tasty seafood appetizers.

Via Porto 44, Ischia Porto. © **081/3334209.** Entrees 7€–16€. AE, MC, V. Tues–Sun noon–3pm and 7–11pm.

Montecorvo ★★ NEAR FORIO ISCHITAN It is perhaps futile to try to avoid seafood when on any Italian island, but if you ever do reach fish overload, head up to Montecorvo, in the countryside above Forio. Choose from dining alfresco in a romantic garden terrace, or inside an evocative "cave" of moss-covered green tufa. Popular among locals in the off season, it's a good choice for traditional Ischitan food any time of year. The seafood is uniformly delicious, but you can also choose meat dishes, from a very good *coniglio all'Ischitana* (rabbit cooked with tomatoes and herbs in a terracotta casserole) to excellent roasted chicken with herbs.

Via Montecorvo 65, Panza (take a bus to Panza, then a 10-min walk north). © **081/998029.** Reservations recommended. Entrees 12€–20€. AE, MC, V. Nov–Mar: Tues–Sun 7–10:30pm, Sun also 12:30–2:30pm; Apr–June and Sept–Oct daily 12:30–2:30pm, 7–11pm; July–Aug daily 7–11:30pm.

Pizzeria da Pasquale ★ SANT'ANGELO PIZZA The picturesque fishing port of Sant'Angelo has fancier and more romantic places for a bite, but they'll also charge you an arm and a leg. Instead, family-run Da Pasquale serves excellent pizza at honest prices in an informal, cozy atmosphere. The house specialty pies (all cooked in a wood-fired oven) are *pizza con pomodorini* (cherry tomatoes) *e mozzarella di bufala,* pizza *ai fiori di zucchine* (zucchini blossoms), and stuffed pizza *ripiena* with prosciutto, ricotta, and vegetables. They also do delicious eggplant parmigiana and homemade desserts.

Via Sant'Angelo 79. ⓒ **081/904208.** Entrees 5€–[10€. AE, MC, V. Daily 12:30-3pm and 7pm-midnight. Closed Dec-Mar.

Trattoria il Focolare ★★ CASAMICCIOLA ISCHITAN This homey restaurant's hearty seasonal menu offers masterfully prepared dishes from the local tradition, including amazing antipasti that utilize fresh veggies from the island's orchards. Don't miss Il Focolare's prosciutto (made in-house). The best main dishes are the *tagliata* (sliced steak), the *tagliatelle al ragu di cinghiale* (fresh ribbon-shaped pasta with wild boar ragu), and the *coniglio all'Ischitana* (a local rabbit dish, which is a specialty of the chef). The desserts are also good, including Neapolitan favorites such as *pastiera* (pie filled with ricotta and orange peels).

Via Cretajo al Crocefisso 3. ⓒ **081/902944.** www.trattoriailfocolare.it. Reservations recommended. Entrees 8€–16€. AE, MC, V. Thurs-Tues 7:30-11:30pm; Fri-Sun also 12:30-3pm.

Umberto a Mare ★★ FORIO CAMPANIAN/SEAFOOD This historic restaurant that has been drawing diners for decades is still going strong. The beautiful terrace—which affords a matchless panorama and is so romantic at sunset—combines with the gourmet cuisine for a perfect dinner. Book well in advance, since there are only 10 very-in-demand tables. The menu is large and changes daily with the market offerings, with a strong focus on seafood. From the copious choices of antipasti, I loved the *insalatina di mare* (seafood salad) and the *tartare di palamito al profumo d'arancia* (marinated local fish with citrus). Follow it with the delicious *pennette all'aragosta e agli asparagi* (short penne with lobster and asparagus) or with the catch of the day, which varies in preparation from classic grilled or *all'acqua pazza* (in a light herb broth), to the more imaginative.

Via Soccorso 2, Forio. ⓒ **081/997171.** Reservations recommended. Entrees 14€–32€; prix-fixe menus 55€ and 65€. AE, DC, MC, V. Daily 7:30-11pm; Fri-Sun also noon-3:30pm. Closed Nov-Mar.

Nightlife

The sweet Ischitan nights are best spent outdoors, enjoying a bit of people-watching from the terraces of the many strategically located cafes on picturesque seaside promenades and panoramic outlooks. The east or "right" bank of the harbor, known by the French nickname **"Rive Droite,"** is *aperitivo* central, and many of the happening bars here also attract a late-night crowd of fun-seekers (read: young Ischitan men on the prowl for young German tourists of the female persuasion). I like the unassuming **Da Lilly** (no phone), a shack on the rocks with a simple terrace overlooking the Spiaggia dei Pescatori in Ischia Ponte. **La Floreana** (ⓒ **081/999570**), at the belvedere of Serrara Fontana, is perfect for a sunset *aperitivo* (they also have a simple restaurant). Other pleasant cafes line the seaside promenade of Forio and Lacco Ameno; I enjoy **Bar Franco,** Via Roma 94, Lacco Ameno (ⓒ **081/980880**), where you can sit at the pleasant outdoor terrace facing the beach or simply sample their excellent ice cream. **De Maio,** Piazza Antica Reggia 9; Ischia Porto (ⓒ **081/991870**), is the best ice-cream parlor on the island, claiming 80 years of experience. A few doors away is **Da Ciccio,** Via Porto 1, Ischia Porto (no phone), which conjures creative flavors by adding in nuts, chocolate bits, and so on.

I recommend the **outdoor concerts**—including classical and jazz—organized by the William Walton Foundation in the lovely gardens of Villa La Mortella, Via F. Calise 35, Forio (ⓒ **081/986220;** www.lamortella.it). The season runs from April to November; concert tickets include admission to the garden and are 15€ adults and 12€ children ages 8 to 12. If you are lucky enough to be on the island for the **Ischia**

Jazz Festival (www.ischiajazzfestival.com) in September, make reservations for the scheduled concerts, which usually include some famous international names.

PROCIDA ★★

Many film buffs are already in love with Procida and don't even know it. Remember that irresistibly picturesque, Italian seaside village from *The Talented Mr. Ripley*? Those pastel buildings and cobblestone streets are on Procida. Ditto for the "town" scenes of *Il Postino* (the rest of that 1994 film was shot on Salina, in the Aeolians). Pretty much unknown among foreign tourists, Procida is a low-key yet exclusive resort, popular among the rich and famous who have villas here, but also with local tourists, who often come just for the day or for dinner.

Procida's landscape is dotted with pretty houses in tones of pink and yellow, contrasting with the green of citrus groves and gardens. There are a few hotels and restaurants catering to various budgets, and you won't be competing with the kinds of crowds that can envelop Capri, or even Ischia, in high season.

Essentials

GETTING THERE & AROUND

Most ferries and hydrofoils running between Ischia and Naples stop at Procida. Many boats also connect Procida with the port of Pozzuoli, north of Naples and well connected to it by trains and buses. In summer, the late boat to Naples leaves Procida at 10:40pm, making dinner on the island a nice possibility, even if you're not staying overnight.

Caremar (© 081/0171998 from abroad, or © 892123 from anywhere in Italy; www.caremar.it) and **Medmar** (© 081/5513352; www.medmargroup.it) run ferries and hydrofoils to Procida from Naples (4.50€ ferry, 7.60€ hydrofoil), Ischia (2.30€ ferry, 3.10€ hydrofoil), and Pozzuoli (2.60€ ferry, 3.10€ hydrofoil). **SNAV** (© 081/4285555 or 081/4285500; www.snav.it) runs hydrofoils (13€) to Procida from Naples (Mergellina and Molo Beverello), Ischia Porto, and Ischia Casamicciola. Trip time to Procida from Naples is 45 minutes to an hour; from Pozzuoli, about 30 minutes; between Ischia and Procida is only about 15 minutes. **M/N Brianza Trasporti Marittimi** (© 081/4972278) handles the route between Capri and Procida, stopping at Ischia's Forio harbor along the way. The fare is 25€ one-way and the trip takes about 1½ hours.

Given Procida's diminutive size (4 sq. km/1½ sq. miles), the best way to see the island is definitely on foot. You can also take one of the four public bus lines run by **SEPSA** (© 081/5429965). All of the buses start from Marina Grande; tickets are 1€ per ride. Or you can use an open **minitaxi**—you'll find stands at each of the three marinas and at the ferry terminal. Unfortunately, the island's short distances have not discouraged the use of cars by locals, so traffic jams are regular, especially in the summer months.

VISITOR INFORMATION

The AAST maintains a small **tourist office** in Marina Grande near the ferry dock (© 081/8101968; www.infoischiaprocida.it or www.procida.net), open May to September, Monday to Saturday from 9:30am to 1pm and 3:30 to 6pm; the rest of the year it's only open mornings. The nearby travel agency **Graziella,** Via Roma 117 (© 081/8969191; www.isoladiprocida.it), is another good resource for help with hotel reservations and boat rentals.

Exploring the Island

Marina Grande, or Marina di Sancio Cattolico, is the major harbor of the island, and the location of the ferry terminal. A few steps away, along the main street, **Via Principe Umberto,** is **Piazza dei Martiri,** the village's main square. From it you can climb to **Torre Murata,** the highest point of the island, fortified by 16th-century walls. This is where Procida's rulers had their residences, and where you can enjoy some of the most magnificent views of the island and its surroundings. As you climb, you will find a **belvedere ★** affording good views of the Marina di Corricella; farther up beyond the Piazza d'Armi, you enter the **medieval citadel of Terra Casata ★★** and its belvedere with a magnificent view over the Gulf of Naples. On the square is the island's main church, **San Michele Arcangelo,** originally from the 11th century but redone in later times.

From Piazza dei Martiri, it is a short walk to **Marina della Corricella ★★**, a picturesque and charming fishing harbor originally established in the 17th century. Its colorful houses and narrow streets surround the small port.

If you continue toward the southwestern tip of the island, you should not miss the detour to the left for **Punta Pizzaco ★★★**, where you can enjoy one of the best views on the whole island.

Farther on, you'll finally reach **Marina di Chiaiolella ★★** at the southwestern tip of the island. This crescent-shaped harbor was once the crater of a volcano and now is a pleasant marina, lined with little restaurants and bars. The harbor is dominated by the tiny island of **Vivara ★★**, a 36-hectare (89-acre) half-moon of rugged, forested terrain that is the lip of an ancient crater. Attached to Procida by a metal and masonry foot bridge, Vivara is a wildlife refuge run by the World Wildlife Fund. Italian fashion house Pucci also named their signature perfume after the island. Check with the tourist office for guided tours of Vivara, or just explore the paths by yourself.

Sign up for a **boat excursion ★★** around the island at any of the three harbors: Marina Grande, Marina della Corricella, or Marina di Chiaiolella. You'll spend about 25€ per person for a 2-hour trip with a boat and driver; or about 50€ to rent your own small boat for a half-day.

Where to Stay & Dine

Procida isn't overflowing with accommodations options, so if you have a mind to sleep here, book early.

Where Can I Swim?

Though not particularly famous for its beaches, Procida nevertheless offers a few good spots for taking a dip. **Spiaggia della Chiaiolella** is the most popular, for its all-day sun and afternoon breezes, and its numerous snack bars, pizzerias, and beach clubs. **Spiaggia della Chiaia** is another good bet; backed by cliffs and protected by Chiaia Bay on the east side of the island, these are some of Procida's calmest waters for swimming. (To get here, you'll have to take a path with 182 steps from Via Pizzaco.) Near Marina Grande is the family-friendly **Spiaggia della Silurenza;** easy to reach on foot from the port, it also has basic facilities.

Caracalè ★ ISCHITAN   This picturesque restaurant on Marina Corricella offers traditional cuisine and a lively atmosphere. The delicious food includes many local specialties, most focusing on seafood, but vegetarian and meat choices are also available. I love the risotto *ai frutti di mare* (seafood risotto) and the catch of the day *all'acqua pazza* (poached in herb broth).

Via Marina Corricella 62. ℂ **081/8969191.** Reservations required. Entrees 7€–12€. AE, DC, MC, V. Daily noon–3pm, 7–11pm.

Conchiglia ★ ISCHITAN   Somewhat more formal in atmosphere and elegant in decor than Caracalè, above, this is a good restaurant in the classic mold, serving dishes prepared according to tradition and seasonal seafood choices. My favorites are the linguine *all'aragosta* (with local lobster) and the *spiedini di mazzancolle* (prawn skewers), but I also recommend the grilled catches of the day.

Via Pizzaco. ℂ **081/8967602.** Reservations recommended. Entrees 12€–23€. AE, DC, MC, V. Daily 12:30–3pm, 7:30–11pm. Closed Nov–Mar.

Hotel Celeste   This pleasant, family-run hotel near Marina di Chiaiolella is a traditional structure where guest rooms open onto the outdoors. Some have private terraces, but others face the veranda, the inner courtyard, or the terrace/garden. All are simply furnished with tiled floors and small outdoor spaces with a table and chairs. The service is warm and welcoming; Signora Concetta and her family give you individual attention. The view from the terraces and the solarium is nice.

Via Rivoli 6. ℂ **081/8967488.** www.hotelceleste.it. 35 units. Doubles 110€–150€. Rates include buffet breakfast. AE, DC, MC, V. Closed Oct–Mar. **Amenities:** Restaurant; bar; babysitting; room service. *In room:* A/C, TV, hair dryer.

Hotel Ristorante Crescenzo ★★ ISCHITANO   Popular and romantic, this is probably the best restaurant on the island. Overlooking the picturesque bay of Chiaiolella, right on the marina, it is moderate in price yet offers a well-rounded menu of traditional dishes, including both meat and seafood. The large array of antipasti includes such delicacies as *tortino di pesce spada* (swordfish cake) and *schiacciatine pesce spada e melanzane* (swordfish and eggplant fritters). You'll have a difficult time choosing among the many pasta dishes, but I recommend spaghetti *cozze e broccoletti* (with broccoli-rabe and mussels) and spaghetti *granchio e zucchine* (with crab and zucchini). Above the restaurant are 10 simply furnished rooms, with plain but scrupulously clean bathrooms. Some units have balconies, and others enjoy sea views. The nightly rate is 120€ for a double, including breakfast.

Via Marina di Chiaiolella 33. ℂ **081/8967255.** www.hotelcrescenzo.it. Reservations required. Entrees 6€–16€. AE, MC, V. Daily 12:30–2:30pm and 7:30–10:30pm.

La Casa sul Mare   In a typical 18th-century building at the foot of Terra Murata (the historic borgo or village of Procida), this little-known, small hotel offers high-quality accommodations with beautiful views over the Marina di Corricella. The elegant guest rooms are furnished with taste, with beautiful tiled floors, wrought-iron bed frames, and good-size bathrooms. Each opens onto its own private terrace enjoying a beautiful view over the sea.

Salita Castello 13. ℂ **081/8968799.** www.lacasasulmare.it. 10 units. Doubles 170€. AE, DC, MC, V. **Amenities:** Bar; babysitting; bicycle rental; concierge; garden; Internet (5€/day). *In room:* A/C, satellite TV, hair dryer, minibar.

PONTINE ISLANDS

Imagine waking up to a chaotic morning in one of Italy's busiest cities, and a few hours later, before it's even lunchtime, lounging in a fabulous cove and swimming in the crystalline sea of one of the Mediterranean's most authentic and naturally spectacular vacation spots. For the Romans and Neapolitans who have become lifelong devotees of the Pontine Islands, that dreamy scenario is a fabulous reality.

Mention "Pontine Islands" anywhere outside Italy, and you're likely to draw blank stares. The treasures of this archipelago—inhabited Ponza and Ventotene plus the islands of Palmarola, Zannone, and Santo Stefano—lie just far enough from a major port to have stayed under the radar of mass tourism. It takes 3 hours to reach Ponza from Rome, and 2 hours to reach Ventotene from Naples. Whenever an island is a bit of a pain to reach, it stays true to its roots. Outside of July and August, you'll find Ponza and Ventotene empty except for those who actually live there, and you'll be able to participate in their traditions and rhythms—slow, relaxing, and insular being the keywords. In peak summer, there are slightly different traditions, involving a surge in population and the very ingrained social rites of the beautiful city folk who descend here en masse.

The Pontine Islands are somewhat arbitrarily grouped together; in fact, they consist of two distinct island groups, north and south. Ponza, Palmarola, and Zannone in the north are closer to Rome and geologically part of the mainland, while Ventotene and Santo Stefano in the south are closer to Naples, both in their red-tufa mineral makeup and their pastel architecture. It's an hour-long boat ride to cover the distance between Ponza and Ventotene.

Ponza is the largest and most populous of the group (though by no means big—only 8 sq. km/3 sq. miles and with just over 3,000 permanent residents) and has the most tourist facilities. In July and August, it is the playground of moneyed Romans (especially) and Neapolitans (to a lesser extent). A geological marvel with all kinds of lunar volcanic rock, Ponza has spectacular and strange coves and beaches, and days are spent bobbing around the striking coastline in private yachts or rented *gommoni.* In the evenings, Ponza town is a pageant that involves everyone on the island; the portside walkway becomes a *passerella* (runway) on which vacationers flaunt their tans and carefully assembled-to-look-carefree island outfits. There is no shortage of *aperitivo* bars and waterfront restaurants at which to pursue or observe this behavior.

The de rigueur day trip from Ponza is boating over to the island of Palmarola (not served by the ferry companies); 10km (6 miles) to the west and all but uninhabited, it's the most naturally gorgeous of the Pontines, with coves straight out of a pirate movie and water a shade of emerald unique in the Mediterranean. Also an easy hop from Ponza is the nature reserve island of Zannone, which has shade (an important commodity in these islands) and panoramic hiking trails and rounds out the three islands of the "northern" Pontines.

Ventotene may be the main island of the southern Pontines, but it's a sleepy, wonderfully old-fashioned place that makes Ponza look like Manhattan by comparison. Ventotene is a tiny sliver of red volcanic stone capped by fertile land and fringed by intimate, mostly rocky coves. One of the most simple and delightful seaside villages in all of Italy is Ventotene town, built by the Bourbons of Naples in the 18th century. In antiquity, the Romans used Ventotene as a place to exile embarrassing imperial family members, and evocative ruins of their villas remain among overgrown prickly pear and agave plants. The Roman port of Ventotene is going strong after 2,000 years, harboring the fishing and tourism fleet of the island.

One nautical mile from Ventotene is the panettone-shaped islet of Santo Stefano, famous for its now-defunct prison, built in the late 18th century. Though the island is privately owned and the prison is not technically open to the public, Santo Stefano is easily visited with boatmen from Ventotene and home to a singular swimming opportunity in a Roman-era seawater "Jacuzzi" tub called the Vasca di Giulia.

PONZA ★★★

The principal island in the Pontine archipelago is one of the most naturally gorgeous and downright fun islands of Italy, and just far enough from the mainland to be an impractical destination for mass tourism. So much the better for those who do go to the trouble of making a trip here, because what you'll find is a rare Mediterranean gem that has kept its Italian identity intact and undiluted. It's not that Ponza is "undiscovered." On the contrary, it's a summertime escape that enjoys feverish devotion among the *bella gente* (the "nice"—that is, financially sound and good-looking—people) of Rome and Naples, who descend by the hordes here in July and August. This state of affairs is nothing new: Ancient Roman emperors favored Ponza as a summer retreat from their stifling urbs, and there are wonderful remains of that era in the so-called Grotte di Pilato, sea caves that were used as an eel farm, very near the port.

Long and skinny with scalloped bays that reduce its average width to about 1km (¾ mile), Ponza is shaped like a sickle that's been chipped away by time and the elements. Though it was deforested centuries ago to reveal mostly arid, lizardlike contours, nature is quite striking on Ponza. The island's intricate 22km (14-mile) coastline is big on coves and promontories with weird and often spectacular rock formations that provide an endless supply of dramatic swimming breaks. The grandest of them all is the stunning bay of **Chiaia di Luna ★★★**, backed by an enormous sheer wall of lunar-yellow volcanic tufa.

Going to Ponza is all about living and breathing *il mare* (the sea). You either own or rent a boat (small, easy-to-pilot motorboats abound), and you spend your days puttering up and down the coast, swimming in coves and grottoes that aren't accessible by land, picnicking under the unrelenting Mediterranean sun, and developing a killer tan that you can be proud of when night falls and it's time to strut your stuff for fellow

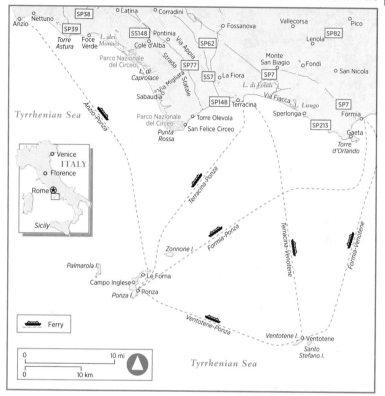

vacationers. By sunset, everyone goes for the evening *passeggiata* on the same street and for *aperitivo* drinks at the same bars.

Ponza has one main town, Porto, which is picturesque in a lived-in way; among the faded pastel houses stacked up behind the ferry landing are stylish independent boutiques, cheek by jowl with gritty marine hardware stores. This is a refreshing difference from more overtly charming Italian seaside towns, like Capri or Positano, that exist for tourism only. Ponza has a brief holiday season (July and Aug), but the rest of the year, it is a working island. There are no resorts on Ponza, no world-class hotels; the majority of accommodations are vacation rentals where function wins over form.

The repeat, moneyed visitors on Ponza, combined with the fact that there are very few foreign tourists to interfere with the entrenched rhythms and habits of the place, can make for a bit of a clubby atmosphere, especially in peak season. However, this microcosm of Italian privilege can also be great fun to watch. Of course, if you want to avoid that scene altogether, just come in the gorgeous shoulder months of May, June, and September. Locals will tell you this is when their island really shines. Days are warm but mornings and evenings are crisp, and the colors of the flora and sea are all the more vivid outside of high summer.

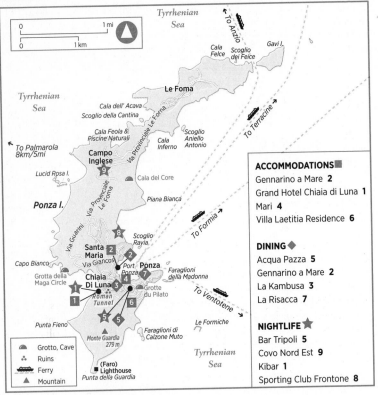

Two other islands in the Pontine archipelago not served by regular ferry, Palmarola and Zannone are classic day trips from Ponza, each just 30 minutes away by boat. To the west, Palmarola is an unexpected slice of *Robinson Crusoe* in the Mediterranean; its turquoise seas and splendid coves, evocative of pirates and castaways, seem like they've been transplanted from the South Pacific or the Caribbean. To the northeast, Zannone is a nature reserve with quiet hikes, dense forests, and wild sheep running free.

ESSENTIALS

GETTING THERE Several ports along the coast south of Rome—Anzio, Terracina, San Felice Circeo, Formia, and Naples—have boat service to Ponza. Only Anzio, Formia, and Naples are connected with nearby train stations, making transit from Rome relatively uncomplicated.

Anzio is the nearest point of departure from Rome (62km/39 miles, 1 hr. by train or car). From Anzio, **Caremar** (www.caremar.it) runs ferries to Ponza from mid-June to mid-September (1 hr., 45 min. each way; 19.20€). **Vetor** (in Anzio at Via del Porto

Innocenziano 40; © **06/9845083;** www.vetor.it) operates hydrofoils year-round (weather permitting); the journey takes 1 hour, 10 minutes and costs 27€.

From **Terracina** (a bit south of Anzio), **Navigazione Libera del Golfo** (in Terracina © 0773/725536; in Ponza © 0771/700710; www.navlib.it) runs fast jets to Ponza from April to September (75 min.; 19€). **SNAP & SNIP** (in Terracina © 0773/790055; in Ponza © 0771/820092; www.snapnavigazione.it) runs jets (70 min.; 15€) and ferries (2 hr., 30 min., 10€) between Terracina and Ponza, also from April to September only.

The closest port to Ponza is **San Felice Circeo,** a popular seaside resort within the Parco Nazionale del Circeo, though well away from the train lines and highways that connect Rome and Naples. From San Felice Circeo, **Linea Talamata** (© **0773/661423;** www.talamataviaggi.it) runs ferries (1 hr.; 18€; daily mid-June to mid-Sept; weekends only mid-May to mid-June and mid-Sept to Oct).

Farther south on the Italian coast, the port of **Formia** (167km/104 miles from Rome, 101km/63 miles from Naples) is connected to Ponza year-round by **Caremar** (in Formia at © **0771/22710;** www.caremar.it), with regular ferries (2 hr., 30 min.; 10.80€) and hydrofoils (80 min.; 18€), and by **Vetor** (in Formia at Banchina Azzurra; © **06/9845083** [central info and reservations line]; www.vetor.it) hydrofoils (70 min.; 24€).

From **Naples, Snav** (© **081/4285555;** www.snav.it) runs hydrofoils (July and Aug only) to Ponza, stopping at Ischia-Casamicciola and Ventotene along the way. Naples-Ponza takes 2½ hours and costs 40€. (Note that this service is from Naples's smaller, more elegant Mergellina harbor.)

For travel **between Ponza and Ventotene,** a few of the companies listed have boat connections in July and August only, although service is rather limited (about three boats per week for each company). **Navigazione Libera del Golfo** jets take 1 hour and cost 13€. **SNAP & SNIP** jets take 1 hour and cost 10€. **Snav's** hydrofoils (July and Aug only) link Ponza and Ventotene (20€).

GETTING AROUND   You'll need your feet, a bus ticket, and a boat to discover the best of Ponza. Around town, walking is the only way to go, and when the island's best beach, Chiaia di Luna, isn't closed for safety reasons (see "An Endangered & Potentially Dangerous Beach," below), you can reach it on foot from town. The rest of the island is long and thin with only one main road, which is served by **Autolinee Ponza** buses from Ponza port (Via Dante; © **0771/804470;** 1€ one-way; 6:30am–3:30am in summer). But because much of Ponza's 22km (14-mile) coastline and its most alluring coves are only accessible by sea, you really need to rent a small motor-boat (*gozzo, gommone*) to do the island justice. More than 20 different companies, at most of the major coves and beaches, rent boats to tourists, but **Diva Luna** (Spiaggia Sant'Antonio, just north of the ferry landing; © **338/2347608** or 0771/809906; www.divaluna.com) is by far the best, with friendly service and fast, new boats (*gommoni* from 50€–110€ for a full day; 30% discount for a half-day). In a day of calm seas, you can go all the way around Ponza as well as zip over to nearby Palmarola, stopping for a few swims and pausing for a picnic along the way. Be sure your boat has a sun shade (*tendalino*), and if you're going over to Palmarola, a slightly larger motor will come in handy. Organized island-circumnavigation tours are also offered by a number of outfitters at the port—see "Around the Island by Sea," below. Scooters and cars are also widely available for rent on Ponza, but they're more of a liability than convenience here.

VISITOR INFORMATION   The **Pro Loco** is at Molo Musco 2 (✆ **0771/80031;** www.prolocodiponza.it). They can furnish you with island maps and provide informa-tion about nontraditional accommodations options like room rentals.

FAST FACTS   The banks San Paolo IMI (Corso Pisacane; ✆ **0771/820554**) and Monte dei Paschi di Siena (Corso Pisacane; ✆ **0771/80654**) both have **ATMs.** The **carabinieri** are at Molo Musco (✆ **0771/80130**). The main **pharmacy,** Farmacia Mazzella, is at Piazza Pisacane 9 (✆ **0771/80708**); a **medical clinic** and the **Guar-dia Medica** are in Località Tre Venti (✆ **0771/80687**). The **post office** is in Piazza Pisacane (✆ **0771/80672**).

EXPLORING THE ISLAND

Ponza is long, thin, and crescent-shaped, with wide scalloped bays on the east coast and a more jagged profile on the west coast. Near the southern end of the island, facing east, is Ponza town, often referred to simply as **Porto.** This is the only part of the island with comprehensive services, and in summer, Porto heaves with activity. The main square is **Piazza Pisacane,** from which the main drag of Ponza, **Corso Pisacane,** runs west, with one side open to the marina. The street and piazza are lined with shops, cafes, and services like banks, pharmacies, and the post office.

In the evening, Corso Pisacane is the prime venue for the Ponzese *passeggiata* rit-ual. On Ponza, however, it's not so much about strolling up and down the street as doing a "static" version of the *passeggiata*—by leaning or sitting on top of the long ochre wall that follows the outer curve of Corso Pisacane and the old fishing marina. Throughout the day, locals and vacationers alike take a break along the wall, gelato or *granita* in hand, either facing the water to watch the boat activity or inland to watch the parade of people go by on Corso Pisacane. (This being Italy, most people choose to face inland.) Back down at the water, busy **Via Dante** skirts the port, where there are dozens of boat rental agencies and waterside restaurants.

The semi-circular marina of Porto is mirrored on the west coast by Ponza's most famous beach, Chiaia di Luna. Only 500m (1,640 ft.) of land separates them, so it's only a 10-minute walk from hectic port to spectacular beach, by way of a 2,000-year-old Roman tunnel. (Chiaia di Luna is closed as of press time but may be reopening in the near future: See "An Endangered & Potentially Dangerous Beach," below.) When it is open, this is one of a few good swimming areas on Ponza where you don't need a boat, and, in fact, it's better to come by land.

Not much else is within practical walking distance from Porto, so you'll need to take a bus or hop on a boat to see the rest of the island. Buses run from Via Dante to points north; if you want to take the bus simply as a way of sightseeing by land, allow about 45 minutes round-trip (without getting off). A few of the stops along the way put you within a short walk of swimming coves, including Cala Feola and the Piscine Naturali (see "Beaches & Coves Accessible by Land," below), although for others it's a significant hike, in which case you're much better just taking a boat around the island. When trying to reach a beach by bus, always ask the driver where to get off. The end of the bus route is the tiny village of Le Forna, where there are a few sleepy shops to serve the vacation rental community here.

Beaches & Coves Accessible by Land

Boating is a way of life on Ponza, but if you don't feel like bobbing your way around the island, not to worry: Some of Ponza's coolest swimming spots are best accessed by land. First and foremost is spectacular **Chiaia di Luna ★★★**, truly one of the most amazing beach settings in Italy. (Although it was closed for security reasons when this guide was researched, I—and the Ponzese—hold out hope that it will reopen again someday soon, so I'm writing about it as if it were open.) Walk up Via Panoramica Tre Venti (it's the road leading straight inland and uphill) for about 300m (984 ft.), then look for the pedestrian underpass on the left that takes you back under the road and to the right. This path leads to the ancient, 100m (328-ft.) tunnel (aka *galleria*) that the Romans bored under the mountain to allow easy access between the two sides of the island. At the end of the tunnel—an attraction in its own right—you step into the gorgeous tableau of Chiaia di Luna beach. A dark turquoise bay laps at a long crescent of golden sand and fine pebbles, immediately behind which is the beach's most impressive and distinctive feature, a 500m-long (1,640-ft.) and 100m-tall (328-ft.) wall of luminescent tufa. The strip of beach is narrow, but nevertheless equipped with snack bars and umbrella rentals.

The other major swimming destination on Ponza that is preferably reached by land is **Cala Feola,** home to the **Piscine Naturali ★★** ("natural swimming pools"). To get there, take the bus toward Le Forna; stay on past Cala Feola until the church of Le Forna, then take the pretty up-and-down footpath toward the water. Formed by volcanic sinkholes and connected to the bay and each other by arches in the rock, the seawater *Piscine* were traditionally used as havens for fishing boats, and still carry out this function to some extent; they're also now a favorite swimming spot, with incredibly clear water and smooth stone platforms for sunning and lounging.

The very social beach at **Frontone ★**, just north of Ponza port, isn't accessible by land, but because it's so convenient to town and served by handy water taxis throughout the day and evening, I'm putting it in this category. Frontone is a cushiony strip of fine pebbles and extremely popular with the young crowd, who stay for an *aperitivo* of champagne and oysters (or just a beer) here when the sun sets. The Sporting Club is the only beach establishment here, and it has a restaurant and bar. For 15€ per day, you can use their changing rooms, sun beds, and umbrellas; otherwise, just pick a

AN ENDANGERED & POTENTIALLY DANGEROUS beach

The dramatic lunar-looking cliffs of Chiaia di Luna beach are its greatest asset—and its greatest menace. The cliffs are prone to constant erosion, which means periodic rock falls. Due to several tourist injuries and one death from these rock falls over the past decade, Chiaia di Luna is currently closed, even though a metal reinforcement net has been installed over the cliffs at the southern end of the beach, which is the only part of Chiaia di Luna where tourists are normally allowed anyway.

But the cliffs aren't the only problem facing Chiaia di Luna. Because the Roman tunnel to the beach is essentially an archaeological site and subject to periodic restoration, the tunnel can on occasion be closed to the public for safety reasons. When it and the beach are closed—as is the situation at press time—the only way to reach Chiaia di Luna is by boat, and even then, you must keep well away from the shore. Alternatively, just enjoy the breathtaking view of the bay over sunset drinks at Kibar at the Grand Hotel Chiaia di Luna (see "Ponza After Dark," later in this chapter).

spot of public beach. Kayak and pedal boat rentals are also available at Frontone, which sits at the end of a large, calm bay, frequently filled with yachts. To get there, take a shuttle boat (operated by Cooperativa Barcaioli Ponzesi; ✆ **0771/809929**) from Molo Santa Lucia, adjacent to the ferry landing. The boats leave every 10 minutes all day long; round-trip tickets cost 4€.

Around the Island by Sea

Group *giro dell'isola* excursions are plentiful from Porto, usually leaving at 11am and returning by 5 or 6pm and including several stops for swimming. **Cooperativa Barcaioli Ponza** (Tunnel S. Antonio; ✆ **0771/809929;** www.barcaioliponza.it) offers round-island tours of Ponza and excursions to Palmarola (22€ each Apr–July and Sept–Oct; 25€ each in Aug) or a **combination tour of Ponza and Palmarola ★★** (25€ or 30€ in Aug). Sometimes lunch on board is included; otherwise, pick up a sack lunch (there is a **panino kiosk** on Via Dante that is legendary). But for more adventurous types, the 22km (14-mile) perimeter of Ponza is very easy to circumnavigate with your own small motorboat (available for rent from 70€ per day—I recommend Diva Luna; see "Getting Around," earlier in this chapter), which will permit you a more intimate and customized tour of the island's many distinctive coves. Provided the sea is calm, it's also a piece of cake to zip over to Palmarola with your rental boat and explore that island's magnificent coastal features. You can also hire a small private yacht and skipper to do the driving for you, and you'll find an embarrassment of yacht charter outfits at Porto eager to put such packages together for you, but of course this is much more expensive—from 200€ for a half-day's outing.

The organized group tours usually head south from the port and go clockwise around the island. However, to follow the sun, and encounter a little less sea traffic, I suggest DIY-island-circumnavigators motor around Ponza in a counterclockwise direction, with one caveat: Visit the Grotte di Pilato, the Roman sea caves immediately clockwise from Porto, first, as the light is best in the morning, then head back to the north.

In addition to simply covering the perimeter of Ponza, I highly recommend a detour to Palmarola off the northwest coast. If you opt for this extended itinerary, with a few swimming stops along the way, it takes the best part of 6 hours (picnic provisions, bottled water, and a sun shade are musts). Otherwise, a quick tour around Ponza's coastline can be done in about 3½ hours.

To reach the first stop on the round-island tour of Ponza, simply follow the southern edge of the harbor and around the point to the south. Clearly visible in the sea-level rock wall of Punta della Madonna promontory are the arched entryways of the ancient Roman sea caves commonly referred to as the **Grotte di Pilato ★★★** ("Pilate's Caves," though they have nothing to do with the Roman general of Judea who condemned Jesus to death). Drop anchor outside the caves and swim in; bring a mask if you have one. These atmospheric caverns (four in all, connected by underwater tunnels) were hand-excavated by the Romans and used as a *murenario* (eel farm) as early as the 1st century A.D., when the emperor Augustus first built a villa on the hill above. Archaeologists hypothesize that the sea caves were also used by the *haruspices* (readers of animal entrails in ancient Roman religion) to divine the prophecies of eel innards; cult statues of Roman gods would have been placed in the niches around the grottoes' inner walls. Remember that it's important to visit the Grotte di Pilato in the morning, because once the sun goes over the island to the west in the afternoon, you can't see much in here.

Now, back to that counterclockwise itinerary: The first sight you'll encounter heading north from the port is the beach of **Frontone** ★. The beach itself, made of fine pebbles, is pretty enough, but above the beach is a huge rock wall in the shape of a triangle, resembling the front of a Roman temple, which gives the beach its name and makes this such a dramatic spot. The northern tip of Frontone bay is delineated by the defunct Forte di Frontone, beyond which there is a striking formation known as **Piana Bianca** ★. It looks like a giant foot made of pale grey pumice, and its smooth top, accessible only from the water, is where serious sun seekers come to ramp up their tans.

Farther north, **Cala del Core** (Heart Cove), named for a heart-shaped formation in the rock wall, has a small, rocky beach and a sea-level grotto. Just ahead is **Cala Inferno** ★ (Hell Cove), with visible ruins of a Roman staircase hewn into the white tufa cliffs.

Past the promontory of Punta Nera, keep close to the coast so that you pass the rock outcrop of **Scoglio Aniello Antonio** on your right; look for fragments of a cargo ship that washed up here decades ago. In the middle of the next bay is a natural arch known as **Spaccapurpo** or **Spaccapolpi** ★ (Octopus-Killer, but also referred to by some by the more banal name *Arco Naturale*). After the arch, pick up speed and set a course toward the uninhabited islet of **Gavi**, just off the northern tip of Ponza. Turn left so that you pass between the islands (Ponza on the left, Gavi on the right), and begin your tour of the western coast of Ponza.

The semi-enclosed bay of **Cala Felce**—"Fern Cove," from the *osmunda regalis* (royal fern) that grows here—faces north, with a few picturesque golden rocks jutting out of its shallow, light green waters. The loose stones on the beach contain sulfur, which locals rub on themselves to form a sort of mud mask, purported to have beneficial dermatologic properties.

Continuing down the west coast, you'll pass the wide inlet of **Cala dell'Acqua,** where bentonite was extracted up until a few decades ago, significantly altering the landscape. The curious name of this bay, "Water Cove," derives from a natural spring of fresh water that was first exploited by the Romans, who built an aqueduct in this zone. Past the next promontory is the halfway point of the island circumnavigation tour, **Cala Feola** ★, favorite refuge of boaters and a sort of secondary port for the island. This area is fairly developed but a worthwhile stop nevertheless for the **Piscine Naturali** ★★. (See "Beaches & Coves Accessible by Land," above.)

Any point between here and Punta Fieno is a good jumping-off point for the 10km (6-mile) crossing to Palmarola.

Leaving Cala Feola, and rounding Punta Capo Bosco to the south, next up is the bay of **Lucia Rosa,** with its small pebble beach and enchanting offshore **Faraglioni** ★★. This spot is named for a certain 18th-century Ponzese girl named Lucia Rosa who, spurned by her beloved, jumped off the top of these rocks to her death. Beyond this bay, come upon the otherworldly tongue of milky rock known as **Capo Bianco** ★★, sculpted into a smooth slide formation by the wind and waves. In this zone there are many little grottoes, some of which can be navigated with your boat (motor off, using oars) and some only by dropping anchor in the cove outside and swimming in. The most famous of these is a slanted cleft in the rock known as the **Grotta della Maga Circe** ★ (Circe's Cave, where, according to legend, the Homeric enchantress cast her spell on Odysseus).

Beyond this point, you enter the magnificent bay of **Chiaia di Luna** ★★★ with its iconic curtain wall of blond tufa towering above the beach (see "Beaches & Coves

Accessible by Land," above). The bay is often crowded with boats at anchor, making it less enjoyable for a swim from the boat than from the beach itself.

Chiaia di Luna is delineated on the south by **Punta Fieno**—Ponza's mini-wine region; you'll see vineyards clinging to the terraces here—at which point begins the steepest terrain of the island. The next promontory is the southernmost tip of Ponza, **Punta della Guardia,** with its lonely, lofty lighthouse.

Heading back north along Ponza's eastern coast, you'll sail between the **Faraglioni del Calzone Muto ★**, triangular monoliths jutting out of the waters just offshore. Past the rock stacks of **Faraglioni della Madonna,** you're soon back at the **Grotte di Pilato** and the outer harbor of Ponza port.

Hiking

For most people on vacation here, Ponza is all about the sea, but there are nonetheless several opportunities for low-key, panoramic hikes. The classic Ponzese trek is the **walk from Porto (Ponza town) to Punta della Guardia ★★** and the lighthouse, Faro della Guardia, at the southern extremity of the island. This hike is about 7.5km (5 miles) round-trip, with a vertical change of about 200m; allow about 2 hours to do the whole thing, more if you want to stop for a swim at **Bagno Vecchio** along the way. You can also cut the hike short (trimming the distance by two-thirds) by only going as far as the panoramic Parata area, before the Faraglioni di Calzone Muto. In summer, I recommend going in the early morning—or for an outing dripping with romance, after sunset.

Some of the most pleasant nature hiking in the Pontine archipelago is among the woods on the nearby island of **Zannone,** part of the Parco Nazionale del Circeo (Circeo National Park), and within easy day-trip distance of Ponza. See "Sidetrips," below.

WHERE TO STAY

The Romans and Neapolitans who vacation on Ponza do not bother with hotels; they either own summer houses here or, more likely, book one of the many *case vacanza* (short-term apartments or houses) on the island, available for a minimum 1-week rental. If you can commit to that length of stay and don't come in peak-peak season (when prices across the board increase by 50%), this is a very economical option, particularly if you're traveling with a family or group. A four-bedroom villa (sleeps 10) costs from 800€ to 1,200€ per week outside of August and the last week of July, while a two-person flat costs from 200€ to 350€ outside those peak periods. A good agency is **Turistcasa** (Via Roma 2; Ponza 04027 Italy; ✆ **0771/809886;** www.turistcasa.it).

Note that the highest hotel rates listed below are only valid in August. For midweek stays in other months, you'll often find that hotels are willing to sell you rooms for even less than the lowest rack rate.

Gennarino a Mare ★ Above the renowned restaurant of the same name, this palazzo on stilts above the water is a boutique hotel with 12 rooms, all with balconies and sea views. Decor is tasteful and fresh, with a maritime feel. Guests are treated to the sounds and scents of the sea, which washes against three sides of the structure, as well as those of the kitchen and restaurant below. I can't imagine getting any sleep here in August (the restaurant is busy until midnight or later, and the streets nearby get a lot of pedestrian traffic), but it's delightful any other month and one of few Ponzese accommodations open year-round.

Via Dante 6. ℰ **0771/80071.** www.gennarinoamare.com. 12 units. Doubles 120€–270€. AE, DC, MC, V. **Amenities:** Restaurant; bar; babysitting; car, scooter, and boat rentals; Wi-Fi. *In room:* A/C, TV, minibar.

Grand Hotel Chiaia di Luna ★   Panoramically positioned at the top of the hill west of the port, overlooking Chiaia di Luna beach, this is a pastel- and white-washed complex with seawater pool, sun terraces, and a fabulous outdoor bar (Kibar; see "Ponza After Dark," later in this chapter) perched at cliff's edge. Those common areas far outshine the guest rooms, which are attractive enough with simple and sober Mediterranean furnishings, but tend to be quite cramped. Only a small fraction of rooms—the *vista mare* units—have a view of the sea and Chiaia di Luna beach; others face the port and town. Although it's way overpriced in July and August, rates go down by almost 50% in May, June, and September.

Via Panoramica. ℰ **0771/80113.** www.hotelchiaiadiluna.com. 78 units. Doubles 130€–300€. AE, DC, MC, V. Free parking. Closed Oct–Apr. **Amenities:** Restaurant; bar; saltwater pool; shuttle to port; terraces; *In room:* A/C, TV, hair dryer, minibar, Wi-Fi (fee).

Mari ★   With a prime position on the main drag of Porto, Mari is a *pensione*-style inn popular with younger travelers who love the extra energy in this busy pedestrian zone. The hotel opened in 1959 and still has that kitschy, retro European-seaside-holiday feel in common areas, while guest units have been updated with anonymous modern decor. However, most rooms are very spacious, with views over the port, and staff bend over backward to make you feel at home.

Corso Pisacane 19. ℰ **0771/80101.** www.hotelmari.com. 17 units. Doubles 92€–182€. AE, DC, MC, V. Closed Nov–Feb. **Amenities:** Bar; free Wi-Fi. *In room:* A/C, TV, hair dryer, minibar.

Villa Laetitia Residence ★★   Hands down the most stylish choice on Ponza is this guesthouse in the Scotti district (just above the port) owned and overseen by Anna Fendi Venturini (of the Fendi fashion house). A Roman and longtime summer fixture on Ponza, Fendi Venturini renovated this Bourbon *palazzetto* and decorated it with recovered tiles from Naples and pieces from the original 18th-century interiors. The overarching result is a homey island chic (homey for a fashion luminary, that is), though the three rooms, each named after a spice, are totally different in look and feel. All have sea views.

Salita Scotti. ℰ **06/3226776.** www.villalaetitia.com. 3 units. Doubles 150€–230€, including breakfast. AE, DC, MC, V. Free parking. **Amenities:** Garden terrace; shuttle service to port. *In room:* Ceiling fan, TV, minibar.

WHERE TO DINE

Almost no one goes out to eat for lunch on Ponza, opting instead for a mozzarella and tomato panino or other simple to-go fare on the beach or boat. Dinner, however, is a big social affair, so it's essential to book a table far in advance.

Acqua Pazza ★★   A prime location on the main square of Porto and elegant cuisine makes this one of the most well-known on the island for a splurge. Acqua Pazza specializes in whole fish, though crustaceans and shellfish are also served, and local vegetables, with only ingredients at the apex of freshness. Try the exquisite fish *carpacci* or one of the pastas with delicate sauces made from halibut or grouper. The dining room has a contemporary nautical feel, eschewing the old-fashioned maritime look typical of Ponza's restaurants.

Piazza Pisacane 10. ℰ **0771/80643.** www.acquapazza.com. Reservations required. Entrees from 15€. AE, DC, MC, V. Daily 8–11:30pm. Closed Nov–Easter.

Gennarino a Mare ★   With the most in-demand tables on the water in Porto, this is where you're most likely to spot any visiting celebrities. The dining room is an outdoor platform on stilts above the water, and fare is a solid Mediterranean lineup of seafood-based pastas, simple fish *secondi,* and a serious wine list. *Tip:* The hip crowd on Ponza likes to eat dinner late, so you have a better chance of scoring a last-minute table earlier in the evening. In August, service can be harried and food not up to the same standards as in less chaotic periods.

Via Dante 6. ℂ **0771/80071.** Reservations required. Entrees 15€–22€. AE, DC, MC, V. Daily 8:30pm–midnight. Closed Nov–Easter.

La Kambusa   On a side street near the ferry landing, this festive *bar-ristorante* with a thick ivy pergola is a good spot for light fare and drinks if you find yourself in the port area and needing to rest your feet and fuel up. In the evening, a rich buffet includes seafood-based antipasti, pastas, and grilled fish mains.

Via Banchina Nuova 15. ℂ **0771/80280.** Entrees from 10€. AE, DC, MC, V. Daily noon–3pm and 7:30–11pm; bar 8:30am–11:30pm. Closed Oct–Apr.

La Risacca ★   At the far eastern edge of Ponza harbor, this is a classic choice for typical Ponzese cuisine; try the *linguine al sugo di scorfano* (with scorpion fish and tomato sauce) or the *frittura di paranza* (mixed fish fry). It's a family-run place and always welcoming.

Molo Musco 24. ℂ **0771/80109.** Reservations recommended. Entrees 12€–18€. AE, DC, MC, V. Daily 8–11:30pm. Closed mid-Oct to Apr.

PONZA AFTER DARK

If you're under 35 or want to act like those who are, it is practically against the law not to go for an *aperitivo* at **Frontone ★★**. Though it's less than 1km (¾ mile) north of the port, the beach at Frontone is not accessible by land, so you have to take a shuttle boat from Ponza port (4€ round-trip from Molo Santa Lucia). Hopping on one of these small motorboats at sunset is part of the fun. Once you arrive, make your way to the decks of the Sporting Club Frontone (ℂ **0771/80755**), which is the rustic outdoor bar set up among the trees just behind the sand. The scene here is sun-kissed Roman girls with bikini-perfect bodies, swaying to the music, cocktail in hand, and hipster Roman guys looking like they've shown up to audition for "The Real World." The dress code at Frontone is strict: You must be in your bathing suit. Not the bathing suit you wore all day, mind you, but a clean one, unsullied by sweat and saltwater, that shows off your figure and your tan to maximum effect. Women may choose to don a sarong for more modesty, and men may wear a loose-fitting T-shirt, but that's it as far as cover-ups. Frontone is not overtly flashy at all, but the atmosphere here feels like a very exclusive party.

Besides mixing with the trendy and tanned at Frontone, there are plenty other places on Ponza for drinks before and after dinner. The classic coffee bar in Ponza port, **Bar Tripoli** (Corso Pisacane; ℂ **0771/809862**) serves cocktails and munchies at the *aperitivo* hour and well into the night. By far the most romantic spot is **Kibar ★★** at the Chiaia di Luna hotel (ℂ **0771/80113**). Alfresco, theater-like terraces are outfitted with boho chic benches and pillows and surrounded by lush bougainvillea (none of which interferes with that stunning vista of the bay and towering rock wall below). Yes, you'll pay 15€ for a mojito, but oh, that view!

After dinner, it's time to go dancing at **Covo Nord Est** (Via Campo Inglese, 4km/2½ miles north of Ponza port; ✆ **0771/808827;** open mid-June to mid-Sept). In the tradition of the Italian seaside *discoteca*, it's a little cheesy but full of eye candy for both sexes.

SIDE TRIPS

Palmarola ★★★

Most everyone who sets foot on Ponza also finds time for a visit to the nearby, all but uninhabited island of Palmarola—and for many, this is the highlight of the entire archipelago. Just 10km (6 miles) north and west (30 min. by boat) from Ponza, craggy Palmarola is the second largest (1⅓ sq. km/½ sq. mile) of the Pontine islands. With mountainous slopes carpeted in green *macchia* and limestone cliffs plunging to the Caribbean-turquoise sea, Palmarola is astonishingly beautiful; it could be Capri's more tropical sibling. Even when Ponza is swamped in summer, Palmarola feels intimate. The transparency and pale blue-green color of the coastal water here is remarkable, as are the island's natural features, which look like they've been sculpted and styled to suit an "island paradise" movie set or magazine cover.

There is no regular ferry service to Palmarola, but if you've rented a boat to putter around Ponza, it's easy enough (as long as the sea is calm) to motor over to Palmarola yourself. Allow about 20 minutes at full throttle for the crossing from the Chiaia di Luna area over to Palmarola. Otherwise, there are regularly scheduled shuttle boats (22€, 25€ in Aug; or 25€/30€ for the *gita doppia* that includes the boat tour around of Ponza) to Palmarola from Molo Musco in Ponza port, which make it easier to explore Palmarola's *terra ferma* if that's of interest to you. The tours are offered by Cooperativa Barcaioli Ponzesi (✆ **0771/809929**).

Setting a straight course off the west coast of Ponza, the first glimpse you'll have of Palmarola is a V-shaped cove called **Cala Brigantina ★★**. This protected bay with imposing cliffs and the most gorgeous emerald water was once a refuge for Mediterranean pirates, hence the name "Brigand's Cove." Cala Brigantina is riddled with tiny grottoes, some of which you have to swim underneath the water and through narrow rock tunnels to reach. (I've always been too scared to try this, but Italians do it all the time.) Even more like the set of a pirate movie, however, is a rock formation on the opposite (northern) end of Palmarola, Punta Tramontana. Here, three tall arches known as **La Cattedrale ★★★** have the uncanny look of some kind of a Gothic cathedral standing before the glittering turquoise water.

To explore Palmarola by land, pull into the "port" (really, just a beach) on the island's west coast. The extent of the settlement here is a few restaurants on the beach, including **O' Francese** (✆ **0771/80080** or 380/2542553; which also rents a few rooms in summer) and private houses, behind which the rugged rocks of Palmarola soar skyward, pierced by ancient cave houses—now mostly abandoned. A network of narrow paths and stairs lead ever upward into the dense vegetation, providing a glorious view over the island's dramatic contours and the sea below. Another worthwhile walk is to the top of the rock jutting out into the water below Palmarola beach; here are the ruins of a chapel dedicated to the patron saint of the Pontine islands, San Silverio.

Zannone ★

The green isle of Zannone (1 sq. km/¾ sq. mile) is part of the Parco Nazionale del Circeo. Although it's only 9km (5½ miles) from Ponza (so, slightly closer than

Palmarola), Zannone has a totally different nature from its neighboring islands. Along the coast of the lima-bean-shaped Zannone, there are few coves and inlets; brawny cliffs rise to a plateau covered in ilex woods and *macchia mediterranea:* Zannone isn't about idling on a boat but about going ashore and immersing yourself in its flora. Zannone was never deforested like the other Pontine islands, and the only human inhabitants on Zannone were a brief community of monks, whose 1213 **Monastero di Santo Spirito e Santa Maria** is in evocative ruins on the west side of the island. Boats land at **Il Varo,** on the southwest coast, from which a 20-minute footpath leads to the old monastery and park headquarters (at 121m/397 ft.), where there's a small museum. From here, there are two paths: One, leading east and north (45 min. round-trip), takes you to the *faro* (lighthouse) of Capo Negro; the other is a 90-minute loop that takes you due east, to the summit of Zannone, **Monte Pellegrino** (192m/630 ft.), before descending to the southeast coast of the island and back up toward the park headquarters. Along the way, you're likely to encounter mouflon, wild sheep brought here from Sardinia in 1924. Zannone's vegetation is evergreen, but the island is at its best in the spring, when wildflowers explode with color and the *macchia* explodes with the resiny aromas of rosemary, lavender, bay laurel, and myrtle.

To visit Zannone, a permit is technically required, but boat tours organized from Ponza port are already equipped with these permits. Cooperativa Barcaioli Ponzesi (© **0771/809929**) runs tours to Zannone (22€) from May to July and September to October. Tours are suspended in August. For more information, contact the park service of **Parco Nazionale del Circeo** (Via Carlo Alberto 107, 04016 Sabaudia, Italy; © **0773/511385;** www.parcocirceo.it).

Ventotene ★★

Forget international tourism—Ventotene is barely even on the radar of Italians. For those who have made it to this utterly relaxing and authentic island, Ventotene draws the same words of praise—*deliziosa, carinissima,* and more permutations of "delightful"—conveying the surprise of having found this *gioiellino* ("little jewel") of an island right here in Italian waters, mere hours from the chaotic cities of Rome and Naples. In an archipelago where the largest island, Ponza, is only 7.5 sq. km (3 sq. miles) with a population of 3,100, Ventotene brings new meaning to "diminutive," with only 1.5 sq. km (½ sq. mile) of surface area and year-round residents numbering 600.

Ventotene's isolation appealed to the ancient Romans, who established an exile colony here where they sent several embarrassing female members of the imperial family on extended "time-outs." The ruins of the sumptuous villa built for Julia, the wild-child daughter of Augustus, can be visited on the northern tip of Ventotene. But the Romans' most salient legacy on Ventotene is the port they built by hand, excavating a basin of tufa on the northeast coast. The *porto romano* was a triumph of engineering then as now; it's still in use for the small boats of Ventotene, and still the heart of the tight-knit seafaring community here.

The narrow squiggle of porous brown tufa that is Ventotene (highest elevation: 18m/59 ft. above sea level) takes less than an hour to walk from end to end. Along the coast, the tufa drops off to create suggestive coves ideal for exploring by sea—and excellent diving—but only one sandy beach of any size, Cala Nave, which is crowded in July and August. Ventotene town, adorable and authentic though it is, is a one-piazza affair that offers plenty of charm but not a whole lot of excitement. Visible from the eastern coast of Ventotene is the former prison island of Santo Stefano, where after a 7-minute crossing (informally arranged with local boatmen) you can explore the defunct 18th-century Bourbon prison, as well as some Roman ruins, and marvel at the rampant vegetation on this *panettone*-shaped tufa spur.

Ventotene may be the best island in Italy for adopting the unhurried rhythms of real *isolani*. Stressed-out city folk and hopeless romantics love it, as will anyone looking to unplug and inhale the sublime isolation of this little Mediterranean paradise. If that sounds good, book a weeklong stay. But if you're an action-and-amenities sort of traveler, 1 day and evening on Ventotene, before continuing on to Ponza or Ischia, will be just right.

ESSENTIALS

GETTING THERE Formia (150km/93 miles south of Rome; 90km/56 miles north of Naples) is the main port for boats to Ventotene and the only port offering year-round passenger service to the island. In summer, you can also reach Ventotene from Naples, Ischia Casamicciola, Ponza, and Terracina.

From Formia, **Caremar** (in Formia at Banchina Azzurra ✆ **0771/22710;** in Ventotene ✆ **0771/85182;** www.caremar.it) operates ferries (2 hr.; 12.20€) year-round, while both Caremar and **Vetor** (in Formia ✆ **0771/700710;** in Ventotene at Porto Nuovo ✆ **0771/85253;** www.vetor.it) run hydrofoils (1 hr.; 18€) from June to August. In July and August only, **Alilauro** (in Formia ✆ **0771/267098;** in Ventotene at Porto Nuovo ✆ **0771/85253;** www.alilauro.it) runs additional hydrofoils between Formia and Ventotene; tickets cost 17€ one-way or 30€ round-trip.

From Naples, **Snav** (in Naples at Via Giordano Bruno 84 ✆ **081/7612348** or 081/4285555; www.snav.it) runs hydrofoils to Ventotene, stopping first at Ischia's Casamicciola port (✆ **348/7013471**), then Ventotene (✆ **0771/85253**), then Ponza (✆ **0771/80549** or 0771/80743). Trip time from Naples to Ventotene is 1 hour, 50 minutes; Ischia to Ventotene is 50 minutes; and Ventotene to Ponza is 50 minutes. The set fare for any leg along that route is 15€.

From Terracina, SNAP & SNIP (in Terracina ✆ **0773/790055;** in Ventotene 0771/85253; www.snapnavigazione.it) runs ferries from mid-July to early September only, a few times per week. The trip takes 3 hours and costs 25€ one-way or 40€ round-trip. The boats stop at Ponza en route.

GETTING AROUND Ventotene is small and flat enough to be explored easily and completely on foot. Most hotels offer a shuttle service to and from the port to help with luggage. To get around by sea (recommended), either hire one of the boatmen down at the Porto Romano to take you for a tour, or rent your own *gozzo* or *gommone* (try **Raffaele Taliercio** at Porto Romano; ✆ **340/5558857**).

VISITOR INFORMATION The Pro Loco is at Via Roma 2 (✆ **0771/85257;** www.prolocoventotene.com).

FAST FACTS For police emergencies, the *carabinieri* are on Via Olivi (✆ 0771/85018). For medical emergencies, the *pronto soccorso* is on Via Luigi Iacono (✆ 0771/779381); the **pharmacy** is at Piazza Castello 29 (✆ 0771/85261). The **post office** is on Via Roma 31 (✆ 0771/85282). The **bank,** Monte Paschi di Siena, is on Piazza Castello (✆ 0771/85120), and has an **ATM.**

Exploring the Island

Ferries and hydrofoils pull into the **Porto Nuovo** (new port), an artificial extension of Cala Rossano on the northern tip of the island. Although this is not the most picturesque introduction to Ventotene, you will immediately see the striking red-brown tufa walls that characterize the entire perimeter of the island. Much more interesting than Porto Nuovo is the **Porto Romano** ★★★ (Roman port) to the south. The circular boat basin, lined with brightly painted fishing boats, was created in the Augustan era, 2,000 years ago, by excavating some 60,000 cubic meters (2,118,880 cubic ft.) of tufa from this section of the island. The Porto Romano is where most tourist excursion boats are moored, and is where you should come to arrange boat rentals and day trips around the island or over to Santo Stefano. On the inland side of the harbor is the Porto Romano's most distinctive feature, **arches** in the volcanic stone that served as offices and storage sheds during Roman times; today, they shelter fishing and boating gear for the *marinai* (seamen) of Ventotene. The waterfront **Bar Mariposa** (Porto Romano 22; ☏ 0771/85144) is the collective hangout for one and all down here. By day, it's a coffee and gelato joint; by night, it's a piano bar that sees a fair amount of action.

The town of Ventotene lies directly above the Roman port. To get from sea level to the main square of town, everyone uses the zig-zagging **Rampa Marina** ★, a lemon-yellow switchback climbing three stories up to Piazza Alcide de Gasperi, also known as Piazza Chiesa for the presence of the Bourbon church of **Santa Candida** (1769). Along the Rampa Marina are a few "rest stops" in the form of boutiques selling sun and swim gear and faux-hippie island duds.

At the top of the ramp, walk south to **Piazza Castello** ★★, the epicenter of Ventotene town and a textbook example of authentic Italian seaside village charm. The coffee bar here, with tables out on the square, is **Da Verde** (Piazza Castello 19; ☏ 0771/85235), which sees some nighttime traffic in high season. The Bourbon

ROMAN ventotene

Outside of the simple pleasure of strolling Ventotene town and watching village life play out in Piazza Castello, there are some interesting ancient ruins that round out the cultural side of things on the island. Immediately south of the Porto Romano, below the lighthouse, is the **Peschiera Romana** ★★ (Roman fish pool). Here, the Romans devised an ingenious system of manmade "tanks" (like the Porto Romano, dug out of the existing tufa) in which they corralled and cultivated seafood to be consumed at the elaborate banquets held by the exiled imperial family on the island. This fascinating ruin, along with the "Grotte di Pilato" eel farm on Ponza (p. 108), is one of the few surviving examples of Roman "fish engineering." The Peschiera Romana is best visited from the water and, if possible, with a snorkel or diving gear.

The most extensive Roman remains, those of the 1st century A.D. **Villa Giulia** ★★, occupy 30,000 sq. m (322,917 sq. ft.) at Punta Eolo, the northernmost tip of Ventotene. (The archaeological park is always open, free admission, no phone; to get there, take the ramp that leads from Cala Rossano toward Ventotene cemetery.) This was the principal residence for the exiled progeny of Augustus; in accordance with the *Lex Julia*—laws passed to improve morals in Roman society—adulterers were punished by banishment or worse. Julia, daughter of the emperor Augustus himself, was among the dissolute of Rome and promptly sent to Pandataria (the ancient name for Ventotene) for her infidelity. When she got here, she lived in style. Though the structure is now reduced to skeletal brickwork, the villa was equipped with sumptuous nymphaea and baths overlooking the sea, and their foundations can be clearly discerned around the site.

castello that gives the square its name houses the *comune* (city hall) and the **Museo Archeologico** (© **0771/85193**), in which finds from the Villa Giulia (see below) and other Roman structures on the island are exhibited.

From Ventotene town, **Via Olivi** runs southwest along the central axis of the island. End to end, the street is 2.5km long (1½ miles), and it takes 30 minutes to walk the full length in either direction. Out on the island, you'll find a few guest-houses and hotels strewn among the fields of lentils, as well as some raggedy Roman ruins, including cisterns and a necropolis. The silence and sense of isolation out here, combined with rampant growth of agave, broom, and particularly fat ferns, is sublime.

Beaches & Coves

Ventotene is not an island of wide sandy beaches, but it has plenty of lovely places for a swim. All along the coast, the reddish tufa meets the crystalline emerald sea to dramatic effect. The best way to explore the perimeter of Ventotene is by boat (see "Getting Around," above), but there are a few beaches you can reach on foot. The main *spiaggia* here is the dark sand **Cala Nave ★★**, immediately south of the Porto Romano. In high season, it's horribly crowded here, but otherwise, this is a gorgeous spot—a striking cove of striated tufa cliffs capped by lush Mediterranean vegetation. Cala Nave is equipped with a beach club, restaurant and bar, and kayak and pedal boat rentals. Nearby (between here and the port) is the swimming area known as **La Peschiera,** which consists of tufa platforms adjacent to the Roman fish tanks.

Beaches less convenient to reach by land are **Cala Battaglia** (on the southeast coast, a rocky beach accessible by a steep trail) and **Punta Eolo** (near the cemetery and Villa Giulia at the northern tip of Ventotene, it has smooth rocks for sunning and occasional nudists). You can also reach Parata Grande (on the west coast; see below) via a tiring series of staircases built into the tufa amphitheater.

If you're able to go by sea around Ventotene, whether with your own boat or with a guided excursion, many more options exist for swimming (but expect rough surfaces underfoot). The best coves are along the southern half of the island, both along the west and east coasts.

South of Cala Battaglia is **Parata Postina,** an intimate black pebble beach with semi-submerged tufa arches. Farther along are **Acqua Dolce** and **Le Saliere,** largely deserted coves with coarse black rock formations but beautiful water. At the southernmost tip of Ventotene, the **Piscine di Punta dell'Arco ★** are natural swimming pools, carved by the elements in the black basalt rock. There's no comfort-able place to lounge here, and you can easily burn your tootsies on the hot stone while getting into the pools, but the Piscine are a unique geological feature and very popu-lar stop for boaters nonetheless.

About a third of the way up the eastern coast is **Paratella ★**, a tiny beach famous for the sheer black rock wall directly above it and the chromatic effect of the deep blue water below. The next major cove, about two-thirds of the way up the eastern coast, is **Parata Grande ★**. Especially enchanting at **sunset ★★**, this is a narrow strip of sand and rocks backed by a high undulating wall of red tufa that sets geolo-gists' hearts aflutter. Rounding Punta Mamma Bianca, you enter **Cala Bosco ★**, a delightful and deserted little cove with rocks and sand. It's best in the morning, as the sun leaves this north-facing spot rather early in the day.

Side Trips

The former prison island of **Santo Stefano** ★★★ is the classic excursion from Ventotene. Tiny, 27-hectare (67-acre) Santo Stefano lies just 1 nautical mile east of Ventotene. There are many former prison islands in this book, but what makes Santo Stefano a standout among them is the unique architecture of the penitentiary, built in 1795 under the Bourbon Ferdinand IV, king of Naples. From above, the entire structure looks uncannily like a handcuff. The prison architect, Francesco Carpi, designed the cellblock buildings (which are rather attractive, with three stories of arcaded loggias painted sunny yellow) in a horseshoe shape; the cells face an inner courtyard where the guards' chapel-like watchtower had a 360-degree view of the inmates. Carpi was following prison design theory laid out by English philosopher and legal reformist Jeremy Bentham, who postulated that the *panopticon* ("all-seeing," round and inward-facing) prison not only made for easy supervision but also that the very nature of the architecture exacted a psychological toll on the prisoners—"a new mode of obtaining power of mind over mind," as he described it. A very deliberate feature of Carpi's architecture is that none of the cells has even a sliver of a sea view. The prison was closed in 1965, but during World War II it was used as a holding facility for such outspoken anti-Fascist "hindrances" as socialist Sandro Pertini, who went on to become president of the Italian Republic (1978–85). The prison is technically private property, not a museum or monument (no admission fee, no contact information), but visitors can get as far as the inner courtyard of the cellblocks.

The other must-do on Santo Stefano requires a bathing suit, so be sure you've brought one: At water's edge on the southeast part of the island, below the ruins of a Roman villa, is the **Vasca Giulia (Julia's Tub)** ★★★, one of the most memorable places in the Pontine archipelago for a swim. This circular pool was hewn into the smooth basalt in the 1st century B.C. and connected to the sea by means of curved canals in the rock. When the surf comes into the cove, the force of the waves is channeled into those narrow passageways, creating jets of water and a sort of Jacuzzi effect inside the tub. Roman hydro-engineering never ceases to amaze!

There are no regular ferries to Santo Stefano, but it's simple to arrange sea transport there and back with any of the boatmen down at the Porto Romano on Ventotene. They'll typically charge 10€ to the island and back, or a few euros more if you want them to make a stop at the Vasca Giulia.

Where to Stay

Agave e Ginestra ★★   The chicest sleeps on Ventotene are at this peaceful oasis a 15-minute walk south of town. The property is all whitewashed, vaulted spaces with cool tiles and colors in keeping with the surrounding sea. As understated and stylish as it is, this isn't a luxury, though it enjoys great word of mouth among well-to-do Italians who come here to unplug from their creature comforts. Half of the rooms have private patios with hammocks and views over to Santo Stefano. Management is Italian, while the staff is mostly Brazilian, including a chef whose delicious light fare at the onsite restaurant draws raves.

Via di Calabattaglia 10/12. ℗ **0771/85290.** www.agaveginestra.it. 14 units. Doubles 160€–270€. MC, V. Closed Nov–Mar. **Amenities:** Restaurant; bar; excursions; terrace. *In room:* Ceiling fan, free Wi-Fi, hammock, patio.

Lo Smeraldo ★   Close to Piazza Castello and the heart of Ventotene town yet surrounded by vegetation, the pink-stucco "Emerald" is a fine choice. Rooms are Mediterranean-modern, airy, and comfortable (either with terrace or garden) but do not have TVs or hair dryers. Common areas include a panoramic roof terrace and, at ground level, an ample communal garden for guests' use.

Via Olivi 64. ℂ **0771/85130.** www.maresmeraldo.it. 38 units. Doubles 130€–220€ per night for half-board treatment; 15%–20% discount for weeklong stays. AE, DC, MC, V. **Amenities:** Restaurant; bar; garden; excursions; terrace. *In room:* A/C or ceiling fan, minibar, terrace or garden.

Where to Dine

In addition to the restaurants below, the bar-cum-restaurant **Da Verde** ★ (Piazza Castello 19; ℂ **0771/85235**) in the main square of Ventotene town serves lunch and dinner and is a place everyone on the island finds himself or herself returning to again and again, for coffee, gelato, *aperitivo,* or a nightcap.

Da Benito ★   Benito serves up reliable regional cuisine at fair prices, but it's the atmosphere—the restaurant is literally in the base of the tufa cliffs near the Porto Romano—that is the real selling point here. Try the island specialty *zuppa di lentic-chie* (lentil soup) or one of the plates, like eggplant with shrimp, that marry the best of the local surf and turf.

Via Pozzillo. ℂ **0771/85267.** Entrees from 11€. MC, V. Open for lunch and dinner.

Le Grotte di Mast'Aniello ★   With a panoramic terrace on Cala Nave beach, this spot does good seafood and delicious Neapolitan-style pizza. Feel free to show up with sand between your toes.

Via Luigi Iacono 12. ℂ **0771/85227.** Pizzas from 5.50€. Entrees from 9.50€. MC, V. Open for lunch and dinner.

TUSCAN ARCHIPELAGO ISLANDS

7

I f nature and outdoor pursuits rank high on your list of island criteria, the Tuscan Islands are a no-brainer. Elba, along with its tourist-friendly sisters, Giglio, Capraia, and Giannutri, are not only the best Italian islands for an active vacation but also among the top spots in Italy, period, for hikers, bikers, and watersports enthusiasts. This being Italy, there's nothing terribly extreme about the outdoors activities, and a hearty meal and a good glass of wine are always close at hand—good news for those of us who only don our "outdoorsy" caps when on vacation.

In Italy's northernmost holiday archipelago, evergreens predominate, the light is crisper, temperatures take longer to warm up in spring and are quicker to cool in fall, and the air is just . . . different—even on a hot day in the middle of August. Yet the Tuscan sun shines brightly on the archipelago (and it's milder here in winter than on the mainland), and you can get just as wet and tan here as in more southerly locales.

Many things that have made traveling in mainland Tuscany so enormously popular—the gentleness of the land and its people, the ease of doing things, to name a couple—also carry over on Elba and the gang. Excellent wine is produced on Elba, and if you're smart about where you eat, you can have gourmet experiences every day in the archipelago. Elba's Capoliveri, Marciana, and Poggio, and Giglio's Castello are inland hill towns as charming as any in the Tuscan countryside. The archipelago doesn't offer too much in the way of cultural sights beyond a few historic fortresses and Napoleonic residences—but who wants to spend his or her island time indoors anyway?

Much of the archipelago, both land and surrounding sea, is designated parkland of the **Parco Nazionale dell'Arcipelago Toscano.** That translates to wild landscapes of Mediterranean forests and flowers, rich bird and mammal life on land, teeming populations of fish undersea, and protected geological treasures—from the granite massif of Elba's Monte Capanne to the red volcanic rock of Capraia. Locals are passionate about their protected status; even your hotel desk clerk is likely well informed about the nearby seagull colony or the unusual outcrop of feldspar down by the beach. Opportunities abound to get out and experience the park one-on-one throughout the archipelago.

Elba (*l'Elba* for Italians) is the largest of the Tuscan islands and the closest one to the mainland; it's also the most developed and frequented by travelers, accounting for about 90% of the archipelago's tourists every year. Geographically speaking, think of it as the eastern vertex from which the other islands are arranged in a fanlike pattern. From north to south, drawing a sort of half-moon around Elba, the other Tuscan islands are **Gorgona, Capraia, Pianosa, Montecristo, Giglio,** and **Giannutri.** Due west of *il Giglio* (and the gateway to Giglio and Giannutri) is the mountain promontory of **Argentario,** connected to mainland Tuscany by the wispiest of isthmuses. So, the Argentario isn't technically an island, but as a resort essentially surrounded by water, it's functionally an island.

Remarkably lovely **Elba** is Italy's third largest island—though only a pea in comparison to Sicily and Sardinia, which outrank it handily. Its name may be internationally synonymous with Napoleon's place of exile, but one look at Elba and you realize that this would be a wonderful place to be forced to live if your country ever kicked you out. However, Elba is not Italy's chicest resort destination. There are no "it" hotels, no hot spots where you're likely to rub elbows with supermodels, no gleaming yachts in the harbor (though a few VIPs call at Portoferraio from time to time)—and that's what island devotees love about it. With its abundance of campgrounds and affordable accommodations, Elba is like the summer camp of Italian islands; it has an especially laid-back vacation atmosphere and endless opportunities to get out and enjoy nature.

Giglio *(il Giglio)*, the next most visited island in the group, is at the southern end of the archipelago, served by ferry from the Argentario peninsula's Porto Santo Stefano. Geologically, it's almost a miniature Elba—a granitic formation with a mountainous inland that slopes gently down to an intricate coastline (28km/17 miles) of countless bays and coves. Plenty of accommodations, restaurants, and services make for easy travel, but even with those conveniences Giglio feels like more of a hidden treasure than its well-trodden sibling.

Exclusive **Giannutri** is directly west of Giglio and is typically visited as a day trip from that island. There are two restaurants but no hotels on Giannutri, just a very small number of vacation rentals; the rest of the island is privately owned by rich Romans.

Pancake-flat **Pianosa** was, until 1997, a prison island, and some of the most notorious *mafiosi* in Italian history did time here. Tourism here is limited to day trips (most often from Elba, 12km/7 miles to the east), which take in the picturesque old port, early Christian catacombs, nature hikes, and, of course the defunct penitentiary structures.

Rough and wild **Capraia** prides itself on being the least tamed of the visitable Tuscan isles. Hikers will find utter solitude, and boaters can explore the rugged coastline in blessed peace, even in high season.

Gorgona is the northernmost of the group and still an active penal colony—the last remaining prison island in Italy. The number of public visitors is carefully controlled, and those who do make it ashore are strictly limited to guided tours, which are escorted by prison wardens.

STRATEGIES FOR SEEING THE ISLANDS

Given the infrequent ferry connections between the Tuscan islands and the lack of facilities on all but a few, it makes the most sense, unless you have a week or more to devote to the archipelago, to pick just one island and stay put, perhaps making a day trip to one of the lesser islands. Elba has a ton of accommodations options in all categories, and Giglio is also fairly well equipped with hotels, B&Bs, and vacation rentals; Capraia and Giannutri have much more limited lodging. For travel in high season, always book well in advance. Visits to Pianosa, Gorgona, and Montecristo are restricted to day trips with guided tours and permits only; they have no overnight facilities. Elba and Giglio are the only Tuscan islands where you can bring a car.

Elba is a delight to visit off season, when you can trade the beaches for cozy *trattorie* and cool mountain hikes, and the scenery is no less stunning. A popular holiday weekend getaway for Romans and southern Tuscans, the Argentario also gets its share of winter visitors. The rest of the islands are all but deserted from November to March; even in April, May, and October, they're pretty empty, and you'll be hard pressed to find accommodations that aren't closed for the "winter."

As for the reliably warm summer months, June and September are the golden periods for a vacation, as with so many Italian islands. You'll have plenty of sun, the water is warm enough for swimming (though much more so in Sept), and hotels aren't charging their highest rates. *Altissima stagione* (highest season) is July and August (especially the last 2 weeks of Aug), when the islands are at their busiest and most expensive. For the smaller islands (Giglio, Capraia, and Giannutri) with fewer accommodations options, it's a must to book your travel well in advance.

ELBA ★★

Though it would probably win the tiara in a natural-beauty-plus-activities pageant of Italian islands, Elba doesn't have the most glamorous reputation in the Med. Chances are, you know it as the island where a certain vertically challenged French ruler was exiled—and not much else about it. Plenty of image-conscious Italians even turn their noses up at Elba, because it's basically a "proletarian" resort that doesn't have the prestige of Sardinia's Costa Smeralda, or the chicness and drop-dead stupendous terrain of Capri, or the cache of smaller Tuscan islands like Giglio and Capraia. Let them be snobs, because Elba has big surprises in store for anyone who thinks a Napoleonic stint is its only claim to fame.

Looks-wise, imagine the green hills and valleys of Chianti country mixed with craggy mountain peaks and dramatic coastlines. Lovely natural scenery and a well-established tourist infrastructure make Elba a delicious treat for both outdoor lovers and relaxation-seekers alike. Fully half of Elba's rugged landscape is designated parkland of the Parco Nazionale dell'Arcipelago Toscano (established in 1996): There are mountains to climb, secluded coves to swim and paddle in, sandy beaches to laze upon, and historic towns to wander. Whether you want to break a sweat taking in the sights, or just watch the scenery play out from a car window along one of the island's panoramic roads, mellow Elba is always a feast for the eyes.

Thanks to the existence of the Tuscan Archipelago National Park, much of Elba remains protected from the blights of mass tourism. Nevertheless, this is still an island that's been "discovered" in a big way, especially by middle-class Italians and northern Europeans. Don't come seeking solitude in July and August, but if you can get past the crowded beaches and traffic-clogged roads in those months, Elba is great fun in high season, when the vacation atmosphere is at fever pitch.

As for Napoleon, history buffs might be disappointed to know that there's not a whole lot left—besides a few rather dilapidated villas—from his tenure on Elba (although you can thank him for the island's good road system): He only spent 10 months here, after all, a mere drop in the bucket of Elba's geologic and human history.

Essentials

GETTING THERE

BY BOAT   Ferries, from the Tuscan mainland port of Piombino (9km/5½ miles away), are the most common way to reach Elba. (Piombino is an hour's drive south from Livorno; 1½ hr. south of Pisa; 2 hr. southwest of Florence; and 3 hr. northwest of Rome. If traveling by rail, take a train to Campiglia Marittima, then a bus to Piombino seaport.) Nearly all boats from Piombino sail nonstop to the principal Elban port of Portoferraio, though a few offer service to the smaller marinas of Cavo and Rio Marina. Two companies, **Moby** and **Toremar,** handle the Piombino–Elba passage, offering 15 boats per day in the off season and boats every 30 minutes from May through September. Both Moby and Toremar have easy-to-find ticket offices in Piombino and Portoferraio: **Moby** (www.moby.it), in Piombino: ✆ 0565/221212; in Portoferraio, Calata Italia: ✆ 0565/914133). **Toremar** (www.toremar.it): in Piombino (✆ 0565/31100 or

0565/226590); in Portoferraio, Calata Italia 44 (℃ 0565/960131); in Rio Marina, Calata Voltoni 20 (℃ 0565/962073); in Cavo, Via Michelangelo 54 (℃ 0565/949871). Crossing time between Piombino and Portoferraio is about an hour, slightly less from Piombino to Rio Marina. In calm weather, Toremar also operates a hydrofoil (for foot passengers only; no cars) from Piombino to Cavo (15 min.) and Portoferraio (30 min.).

Mid-season fares along the main Elban ferry routes are as follows: Piombino-Portoferraio costs 11€ (Toremar) or 14€ (Moby) each way for single passengers; 40€ (Toremar) or 44€ (Moby) each way for automobile and driver. Piombino to Rio Marina with Toremar is 8.50€ each way for passengers; 38€ each way for cars. Prices are slightly higher in "high season" (Fri–Sun in summer) and lower in the off season. The Toremar hydrofoil from Piombino to Cavo is 10€ per person each way year-round; the hydrofoil from Piombino to Portoferraio is 14€ per person each way year-round.

Tip: When driving into Piombino to catch a ferry to Elba, you can save time and hassle by buying your tickets at one of the roadside ticket offices on the outskirts of town. Otherwise, you can buy your tickets at the port, where you'll often find long queues even in low season. If bringing a car to Elba in high season, it's not a bad idea to book your ferry a few days in advance (at any travel agent in Italy, or online at either of the companies' websites), though the worst that might happen if you don't prebook is that you have to wait an hour or so for the next available ferry.

BY AIR   Elba's **airport** (℃ **0565/976011;** www.elbaisland-airport.it) at Campo nell'Elba, in the central part of the island, is served by flights from the Italian airports of Milan-Malpensa, Pisa, and Florence, as well as Bern and Zurich in Switzerland, and Munich and Friedrichshafen in Germany. With rare exceptions, Elba has regularly scheduled flights only between April and September. **Elbafly** (℃ **0565/977900;** www.elbafly.it) handles the routes between Elba and Milan (three flights per week), Pisa (nine per week), and Florence (four per week). **Intersky** (℃ **0565/977527** in Italy; 43/5574/4880046 in Germany; www.intersky.biz) serves Zurich, Munich, and Friedrichshafen. **Sky Work** flies between Elba and Bern (℃ **41/319610000** in Switzerland; www.skywork-airlines.ch).

GETTING AROUND

The best way to get around Elba is with your own car. If you haven't brought one on the ferry, you'll find dozens of rental agencies in Portoferraio. One I've used and liked is **Chiappi,** opposite the ferry dock at Calata Italia 1 (℃ **0565/914366;** www.rent chiappi.it). Chiappi is a full-service agency that also does scooter, camper, and boat rentals, as well as sailboat charters. If you've arrived at the airport in Campo nell'Elba, you can rent a car from **Elba by Car** (℃ **0565/977973;** www.elbabycar.it). In high season, expect to pay 50€ to 60€ per day for a compact car; prices go down by about 20% in the off-peak months. Renting a car on the mainland is usually cheaper, but then you have to pay for its ferry passage (around 40€ each way).

Elba also has a reliable bus network, run by **A.T.L.** (Azienda di Trasporti Livornesi; ℃ **0565/915392** or 199/108081; www.atl.livorno.it) that will get you to the principal destinations, but you'll need to allow for much longer travel times between places, and, of course, you won't have as much freedom to explore every little cove and mountain road. Ticket prices depend on the distance you're traveling but usually cost between 2€ and 4€. In summer, a system of smaller buses called **Elba Subito** (also run by A.T.L.; contact info above) links the town centers with many major beaches; this is an effort to reduce the amount of private automobile traffic clogging those

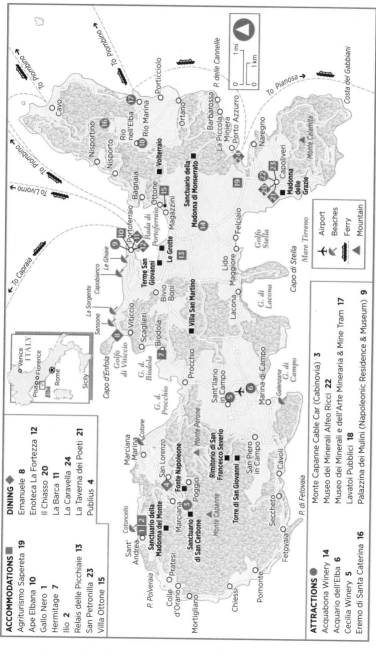

To Piombino
To Piombino
To Livorno
To Piombino
To Capraia

ITALY
Venice
Florence
Pisa
Elba
Rome
Sicily

To Pianosa

0   1 mi
0   1 km

Cavo
Porticciolo
Nisportino
Nisporto
Rio nell'Elba
Rio Marina
Ortano
P. delle Cannelle
Barbarossa
La Piccola Miniera
Porto Azzurro
Naregno
Costa del Gabbiani
Bagnaia
Ottone
Volterraio
Magazzini
Sanctuario della Madonna di Monserrato
Felciaio
Capoliveri
Madonna delle Grazie
Monte Calamita
Portoferraio
Rada di Portoferraio
Le Grotte
Terme San Giovanni
Le Ghiaie
Capobianco
La Sorgente
Sansone
La Ghiaie
Lido
Golfo Stella
Capo di Stella
Mare Tirreno
Capo d'Enfola
Golfo di Viticcio
Viticcio
Scaglieri
Biodola
Bivio Boni
Villa San Martino
Lacona
Maggiore
G. di Lacona
G. d. Biodola
G. d. Procchio
Procchio
Sant'Ilario in Campo
Marina di Campo
Galenzana
G. di Campo
Marciana Marina
Cotone
San Lorenzo
Fonte Napoleone
Monte Perone
Romitorio di San Francesco Severio
San Piero in Campo
Cavoli
Seccheto
P. di Fetovaia
Sant' Andrea
Cotoncello
Sanctuario della Madonna del Monte
Marciana
Sanctuario di San Cerbone
Poggio
Monte Capanne
Torre di San Giovanni
Colle d'Orano
Pratesi
Mortigliano
Chiessi
Pomonte
Fetovaia
P. Polveraia

Airport
Beaches
Ferry
Mountain

ACCOMMODATIONS ■

Agriturismo Sapereta **19**
Ape Elbana **10**
Gallo Nero **1**
Hermitage **7**
Ilio **2**
Relais delle Picchiaie **13**
San Petronilla **23**
Villa Ottone **15**

DINING ◆

Emanuele **8**
Enoteca La Fortezza **12**
Il Chiasso **20**
La Barca **11**
La Caravella **24**
La Taverna dei Poeti **21**
Publius **4**

ATTRACTIONS ●

Acquabona Winery **14**
Acquario dell'Elba **6**
Cecilia Winery **5**
Eremo di Santa Caterina **16**
Monte Capanne Cable Car (Cabinovia) **3**
Museo dei Minerali Alfeo Ricci **22**
Museo dei Minerali e dell'Arte Mineraria & Mine Tram **17**
Lavatoi Pubblici **18**
Palazzina dei Mulini (Napoleonic Residence & Museum) **9**

beach access roads and parking lots. Elba Subito buses are recognizable by their graphics of dancing red starfish hitchhiking in bathing suits.

VISITOR INFORMATION

In Portoferraio, the **APT Elba** (local tourist board) office is located directly opposite the ferry landing at Calata Italia 43 (© **0565/914671;** www.isoleditoscana.it or www.aptelba.it). From April to October, they're open Monday through Saturday from 9am to 7pm; the rest of the year, the hours are Monday through Friday 9am to 2pm. In summer, seasonal branches of APT Elba are also open in Capoliveri (Piazza Matteotti; © **0565/967029;** June 15–Sept 30: Mon–Sat 9am–noon and 7–10pm), Marina di Campo (Piazza dei Granatieri; © **0565/977969;** July 15–Sept 4: Mon–Sat 9am–7pm), and Porto Azzurro, Via Vittorio Veneto (© **0565/958253;** July 20–Sept 15 Mon–Sat 4–10pm). At any of these offices, you can pick up free island maps and reams of brochures on museums, cultural events, boat rentals—you name it. Don't hesitate to ask the staff's opinions on what to see and do; they can often provide valuable season-specific advice.

The **Parco Nazionale Arcipelago Toscano (Tuscan Archipelago National Park)** is also headquartered in Elba, in Portoferraio at Via Guerrzzi 1 (© **0565/919411;** www.islepark.it or www.parks.it/parco.nazionale.arcip.toscano), and there are visitor centers in Rio nell'Elba and Marciana where you can pick up brochures and maps and arrange excursions with licensed park guides. In Marciana, there is a "Casa del Parco" at the Fortezza Pisana (© **0565/901030**); in Rio nell'Elba, the Casa del Parco "Franco Franchini" is inside an ancient washhouse adjacent to the newer (1906) public washhouse, Località Lavatoi (© **0565/943399**).

The Top Attractions

Beautiful nature, a wealth of beaches, panoramic drives along the coast and through pretty inland country, and the general holiday atmosphere are what make Elba worth visiting. For history buffs, however, there are two (mostly underwhelming) Napoleonic residences you can visit as well as a handful of medieval fortresses and Roman ruins. Elba is also a geology geek's dream come true: The island has a long history of mining for metals and semiprecious gems and quarrying for stone, and every town has at least one *Museo Minerario* that shows off this mineral heritage.

Monte Capanne Cable Car ★★★ Hikers take a good half-day to reach the top of the highest mountain in the Tuscan archipelago, but from June to mid-October a *cabinovia* (cable car; though the "cars" are open-air contraptions that resemble Easter baskets) whisks us lazier types up to the top (starting from 375m/1,230 ft., near Marciana) in just 14 minutes. Views from the exposed, granite summit (1,019m/3,343 ft.) are simply spectacular on a clear day, taking in all the islands of the archipelago and Corsica, even the Apuan Alps. If you can get past the rickety look of it, the cable-car journey may just be the highlight of your stay on Elba.

Cable car: Località Pozzatello. © **0565/901020.** June–Aug daily 10am–12:15pm and 2:30–6:30pm; Sept 1–Oct 15 daily 10am–12:15pm and 2:30–6pm. 10€ one-way, 16€ round-trip. No credit cards.

Museo dei Minerali e dell'Arte Mineraria and Mine Tram ★★ ☺ If you can choose only one mineral museum to visit on Elba, this is your best bet. The museum, in the Palazzo del Burò, has the predictable collection of all the types of gems and metals from the island; but what makes this such an evocative attraction are the faithful, full-size **reconstructions ★★** of mine tunnels, miners' shelters, and iron workshops. The museum is part of the Parco Minerario dell'Isola d'Elba, which also operates **Tutti sul Trenino ★★**, a 90-minute mine visit by tram, over the hills, and into a real (no longer active) mine nearby, where you can take home souvenir chunks of pyrite and hematite (daily May–Sept, reservations required; 12€).

Via Magenta 26, Rio Marina. ☏ **0565/962088.** www.parcominelba.it. Museum: 2.50€; mine tram 12€. No credit cards. Apr–Oct daily 9:30am–12:30pm and 4:30–6:30pm (until 7:30pm in July and Aug).

Museo dei Minerali Elbani Alfeo Ricci ★

A worthwhile detour on a stroll through Capoliveri, the gems and stones collected in the mid-20th century by an eclectic Elban named Alfeo Ricci are some of the rarest and most valuable ever pulled out of Elba's mines, including enormous hunks of vivid blue-green chrysocolla and bright blue azurite.

Via Palestro, Capoliveri. ☏ **0565/935492.** 2.50€. No credit cards. Apr–May and Sept–Oct daily 9:30am–12:30pm, 4:30–7:30pm; July–Aug daily 9:30am–12:30pm and 7pm–midnight.

Palazzina dei Mulini & Museo Nazionale delle Residenze Napoleoniche ★

An 18th-century palazzo on the hill above Portoferraio's *centro storico* was Napoleon's official Elban residence during his 10-month exile (May 4, 1814–Feb 26, 1815), and the office from which he governed the 110,000 citizens of Elba as honorary "emperor." It now also functions as the National Museum of Napoleonic Residences, housing many paintings and personal effects of the famous Frenchman. Inside, you can visit the emperor's personal library, the apartment of Pauline Bonaparte (among other rooms maintained in period style), and a theatrical ballroom. The original flag— three golden bees on a red and white background—that Napoleon chose for Elba is also kept here. The better maintained of Napoleon's Elban villas, Palazzina dei Mulini also has pretty gardens and gorgeous views over the open sea from its cliffside belvedere.

Piazzale Napoleone, Portoferraio. ☏ **0565/915846.** Apr–Oct Mon and Wed–Sat 9am–7pm, Sun 9am–1pm; Nov–Mar Mon and Wed–Sat 9am–4pm, Sun 9am–1pm. 6€ (11€ cumulative ticket also valid at Villa San Martino).

Museo Napoleonico di Villa San Martino

Of the two former Napoleonic residences you can visit on Elba, this was the emperor's country retreat, set in the wooded hills on the outskirts of Portoferraio. Villa San Martino must have been much more pleasant 200 years ago, but poor maintenance, busloads of loud tour groups, and an uncontrolled colony of souvenir stands by the entrance blight what would otherwise be a lovely country villa scene. Still, despite the sad state of upkeep at the site, Villa San Martino does have some redeeming qualities that make it worth a visit for the Napoleon aficionado. In Napoleon's residence—a more modest pink stucco farmhouse to the rear of the grounds—the rooms have been set up more or less as they were in his time. The period furnishings are, for the most part, surprisingly simple. The highlight of the visit is the **Stanza Egizia ★** (Egyptian Room), done up with hieroglyphics and fresco murals of scenes from Napoleon's Egyptian campaigns.

Località San Martino (5km/3 miles southwest of Portoferraio). ☏ **0565/914688.** 6€ (11€ cumulative ticket also valid at Palazzina dei Mulini). No credit cards. Apr to mid-Sept Tues–Sat 9am–7pm, Sun 9am–1pm; mid-Sept to Mar Tues–Sun 9am–4pm.

Beaches

With more than 70 beaches and coves, Elba offers swimmers and sunbathers myriad ways to enjoy that crystalline Mediterranean water. Not all *spiagge* (beaches) are wide expanses of white sand, and those that are also tend to be the most crowded in July and August. However, if you're willing to accept a mixture of soft sand and polished pebbles or smooth sunning boulders, you'll have no trouble finding almost-deserted stretches of seashore, even in highest season. (And your feet will get a nice exfoliation treatment.) Newsstands and bookshops sell tourist maps of Elba that feature handy information about what type of sand or pebble you'll find at all the different beaches; otherwise, if all you want is an accessible bit of coastline, simply follow any road sign with a brown background, blue squiggly lines, and the word *spiaggia*—universal Italian highway shorthand for "you can swim here." A great way to discover your own favorite coastal spot is to rent a *gommone* and putter around the island, dropping anchor at whatever cove captures your fancy.

My list of beaches below is by no means exhaustive, but I've included Elba's most popular-for-a-reason beaches as well as some more secluded and harder to reach coves, in every part of the island.

CENTRAL ELBA: NORTHERN COAST

Le Ghiaie is Portoferraio's gravelly town beach and can be quite crowded, but it's handy if you've got a few daylight hours to kill before catching a ferry back at the port. A few kilometers west of Portoferraio (follow road signs toward Enfola) is the dramatic beach of **Capo Bianco ★**, so named because of the white rocks that frame it. Several kilometers farther west (still on the road to Enfola), you'll see signs for **La Sorgente ★**, which is a short stretch of soft, white gravelly beach (no facilities) and gorgeously clear water in shades from light green to cobalt blue. La Sorgente is connected by another 200m (656-ft.) footpath to the bigger and better "insider's" beach of **Sansone ★★**, which has the same clear water but an even more peaceful, uncontaminated atmosphere. **Capo d'Enfola** is connected to mainland Elba by a very narrow strip of land, along both sides of which are short gravelly beaches. Enfola is recommended not so much as a beach as for the interesting manmade sights here, including World War II–era bunkers that are easily visible from the hiking paths here.

To the south of Enfola, **Biodola ★★** is one of Elba's top beaches, with sugary white sand that extends for 600m (1,969 ft.). The coast here has a very gentle grade, so the water is calm and shallow at quite a distance from the shore—great for families, though it's always crowded in summer. Continuing south, the next major beach is **Procchio ★★**, a kilometer-long curve of golden sand, whose proximity to the town of Procchio and its services make it convenient but also highly frequented in summer. Both Biodola and Procchio are chock-full of boat and watersports equipment rentals, snack bars, and other beach services.

CENTRAL ELBA: SOUTHERN COAST

Just south of the town of Marina di Campo is the beach of **Galenzana,** whose coarse golden sand is almost always empty, because you have to walk there—you can't drive to it. The largest beach on Elba is the beach of **Marina di Campo ★**, a 1,500m-long (4,921-ft.) crescent of wide, soft white sand stretching north of the eponymous town. It's often packed, but it's your best bet for watersports and boat rentals on the southern coast of Elba. A favorite of the camping set is **Lacona,** another lengthy section of white sand and calm, shallow water. Toward Capoliveri, **Felciaio ★** is unremarkable for its sandy shores; the unique feature here is a shallow reef against the shore that acts as a sort of diving board just beneath the water.

WESTERN ELBA

Just outside the town of Sant'Andrea (park there and follow the pedestrian path east along the rocks) is a unique little cove called **Cotoncello ★**, where a tiny strip of fine sand is practically enclosed by smooth reefs, creating a sort of natural swimming pool.

The beach of **Fetovaia** ★, a narrow inlet on the southern coast between Pomonte and Marina di Campo, is very pretty but perhaps too crowded for its small size in the summer months. Nearby, **Cavoli** ★★ is another beach with lovely natural scenery—smooth rocks slope into the light blue water; you'll see it on many a postcard of Elba.

EASTERN ELBA

The lower half of Elba's "fishtail"—the coastline around Capoliveri—is sprinkled with beaches and coves, none of them particularly outstanding for swimming and sunbathing unless you find yourself in the area and dying for a dip. The north part of the fishtail offers some better options. Just across the gulf from Porto Azzurro, **Naregno** is a good-size golden sand beach with lots of facilities. Immediately north of Porto Azzurro is **Barbarossa,** a little sandy cove whose name and evocative appeal come from the belief that the legendary Greek pirate Barbarossa once landed here. At the far northeastern tip of the island, the coarse-sand town beach of **Cavo** is clean and quiet and within striking distance of beach bars, restaurants, and the hydrofoil to Piombino. On the northwest edge of the fishtail, heading back toward Portoferraio, two decent beaches are **Nisportino,** a calmer alternative to the adjacent Nisporto, and **Ottone,** below the Villa Ottone hotel. The latter has wonderful views across the bay.

Exploring the Island

PORTOFERRAIO & AROUND

The majority of new arrivals disembark at **Portoferraio,** the busy harbor on the north side of the island. If you've brought a car on the ferry, you might be tempted to leave the chaotic port scene behind and drive right out of Portoferraio; but despite a few modern eyesores, this is the liveliest place on Elba, a real town with history, good shopping, and all the services you could need—from Internet cafes to salons to car rental agencies. I recommend spending at least a few hours exploring on foot. Modern Portoferraio isn't much to look at; the historic buildings around the old, horseshoe-shaped *darsena* (boat basin) are infinitely more picturesque.

Ferries land at the docks along Calata Italia, in the modern part of town. Once off the boat, pop into **APT Elba** (the local tourist board), Calata Italia 26 (✆ **0565/914671;** www.aptelba.it), directly opposite the ferry landing. Armed with maps and brochures, walk north and east along the waterfront—just keep following the imposing 16th-century walls toward the *centro storico,* which is arranged around the U-shaped marina. At the base of the "U" is the Renaissance entrance to the city, an archway called the **Porta a Mare.** Above the harbor are the imposing bastions of the Medicean fortresses. All along the marina, as well as on the streets just inland, you'll find shopping and cheerful places to eat. **Il Libraio,** Calata Mazzini 9 (✆ **0565/917135**), is a wonderful bookstore that has tons of books about Elba and the other Tuscan archipelago islands (most in Italian, but there are a few in English, German, and French).

Two blocks inland from the Porta a Mare is Piazza della Repubblica, the lively main square of old Portoferraio, with its modest Romanesque duomo. Continuing uphill, you'll eventually reach the **Villa dei Mulini** (see "Attractions," p. 126), Napoleon's official Elban residence during his exile here, and now a museum with period furnishings and memorabilia. Below the villa is the smaller of Portoferraio's beaches (p. 127), **Spiaggia Le Viste.** The other, larger beach in town is **Le Ghiaie.** To get there, it's

If you need to park your car in Porto-ferraio, try street parking in town first; if that fails, there are a number of large lots a bit west of the ferry docks. When leaving Elba from Portoferraio, you can park your car (locked) in the staging area lanes in front of the ferry and take a half-hour or so to stroll around the waterfront and town; just be sure you're back at your vehicle 15 minutes prior to the ferry's departure. If you're unsure about the lawfulness of your harborside parking job, the dock staff can usually point you in the direction of a legal spot.

a straight shot from the ferry landing: Just take Viale Manzoni all the way (500m/1,640 ft.) to the other side of the isthmus.

Portoferraio is at the eastern tip of an anvil-shaped protuberance on the northern side of Elba. The western tip of the anvil, about 10km (6 miles) away, is **Capo d'Enfola.** Between them are a number of good beaches, like La Sorgente. Hikers will want to take an hour or so to explore the paths of the promontory here, where there are bunkers from World War II hidden within the vegetation.

South of Enfola, scooping around toward Marciana Marina in the west, are three wide bays: Viticcio, **Biodola,** and **Procchio.** The latter two are well-equipped tourist areas with two of the island's best and broadest sandy beaches—perfect for a day of sunning, swimming, and watersports.

EASTERN ELBA

The sector of the island that looks like a fishtail on the map was the lifeblood of Elba's economy as far back as Etruscan times: Until relentless mining sapped its resources, eastern Elba was extraordinarily rich in ferrous minerals. Elba was renowned in the Mediterranean world as a source of iron that could never be exhausted; in fact, the enormous quantity of iron (in the form of magnetite) here was even known to interfere with the navigational equipment of ships sailing offshore or planes flying overhead. Well, after being in business for 3 millennia, the last iron mines closed in the early 1980s, but much of the old iron territory is preserved as a *Parco Minerario.*

FROM PORTOFERRAIO TO RIO NELL'ELBA   Driving from Portoferraio, follow the road signs toward Porto Azzurro, but after a few kilometers, be sure to turn left (following signs toward Bagnaia and Rio nell'Elba). The road that continues east and inland toward Rio nell'Elba is SP32, aka Via del Volterraio. This is an exhilarating climb along a winding, panoramic road (that locals regularly drive at alarming speed, considering all the blind curves). As the road ascends, you'll see the evocative ruins of the Pisan fortress known as **Il Volterraio ★★** (always open; free) on a mountain spur to the north. Park at the roadside pullout to admire the views of the castle and down to Portoferraio bay. A path leads from here up to Il Volterraio; it's a short scamper of about 400m (1,312 ft.). Legend has it that the castle, whose rubble masonry dates mostly from the 13th century (though there are 11th-c. and Roman ruins here, too), was first built in Etruscan times for a queen named Ilva, who subsequently gave her name to the island. The stronghold is the only one in Elba's history to remain unconquered, even during the invasions of the terrible pirate Barbarossa in 1543.

EXPLORING EASTERN ELBA   **Rio nell'Elba,** on the eastern side of the Volt-erraio pass, is an inland town (not to be confused with Rio Marina) with an ancient mining history. Since mining operations ceased decades ago, it's now a quiet hamlet with steep and narrow streets, a few low-key restaurants, and a museum of mining and minerals. On the outskirts of Rio, don't miss a quick look inside the **Lavatoi Pubblici** ★ (right off the main road skirting the lower edge of town, with easy and free parking; no phone; always open; free). The pink stucco building, with a long granite basin filled with fresh running water, was Rio nell'Elba's public laundry from 1909. Adjacent to the washhouse (inside an even older washhouse structure) is a visitor center for the Tuscan Islands National Park with didactic displays on flora, fauna, and geology.

A lovely detour from Rio nell'Elba is a visit to the **Eremo di Santa Caterina** ★★ (Hermitage of St. Catherine, 3km/2 miles north of Rio nell'Elba; ✆ 393/7352616; www.eremosantacaterina.it): Just outside Rio nell'Elba to the north, there's a turnoff for Santa Caterina. Follow that road for about 1km (¾ mile) and park in the dirt lot marked Santa Caterina, on the right side of the road. Then, it's a 500m (1,640-ft.) walk along a cypress-lined lane to the sanctuary (of Romanesque construction, though later modified in the 17th c.), now a cultural center.

From Rio nell'Elba, SP33 continues north toward the sleepy seaside town of **Cavo.** The town beach (north of the marina) is pleasant and there's a nice coffee bar, **Mokambo** (Lungomare Kennedy 2/4; closed Sun), with an outdoor terrace overlooking the sand.

Hugging the coast south of Cavo (on SP26), you quickly reach the old seaside mining town of **Rio Marina.** Etruscans and Romans made this their harbor when they extracted iron from the hills to make weapons and armor, and you can still see the "industrial archaeology" of now-defunct mining operations around town. Rio Marina has a certain appeal from its working-class roots of fishing and mining. Salty old locals who've seen the vicissitudes of Elba's mineral economy gather at the wine bar **Blu Marly,** Via Appiani 20 (✆ 0565/962545), to drink and tell stories. Also in the center of town, the **Museo dei Minerali e dell'Arte Mineraria** (see "Attractions," p. 126) is the best of Elba's many mining-themed museums.

From Rio Marina, head back inland toward Rio nell'Elba, then south on SP26 to Porto Azzurro. The narrow bay, Golfo di Mola, marks the "notch" in the fish-tail shape of eastern Elba. The picturesque harbor of **Porto Azzurro** ★ ("Blue Port") is on an inlet on the north side of the bay. Graced with a busy and cheerful waterfront promenade, and a bite-size town with ochre-washed alleys, good restaurants, and shops, Porto Azzurro sees a lot of tourists in high season. Golfo di Mola was an obvious natural harbor on Mediterranean sea routes, used from ancient Roman times up to the 1800s. The Spanish fortified it with two castles: The imposing **Forte San Giacomo** (now a prison) presides above the town of Porto Azzurro, while the much smaller **Forte Focardo** is on a promontory that juts into the southern edge of the bay, past the beach of Naregno. One of the major religious monuments on Elba, ranking up there with the Eremo di Santa Caterina outside Rio Elba, is the **Santuario della Madonna di Monserrato** ★, a few kilometers inland (north) from Porto Azzurro.

Just outside Porto Azzurro (on the road that leads back toward Rio nell'Elba and Rio Marina) is the **Piccola Miniera** ★, Via Provinciale Est, Porto Azzurro (✆ 0565/95350; www.lapiccolaminiera.it; Mar–Oct 9am–1pm, 3–6pm; 9€, 7.50€ kids 5–12, free for kids under 5), a mining-heritage attraction where mine cars take you through various dioramas of mining engineering and daily life of miners in the iron caves. It's a little hokier than the Museo dei Minerali e dell'Arte Mineraria (see

"Attractions," p. 126) in Rio Marina, but still worthwhile, and the mine *trenino* should be a novelty for kids.

The hill town of **Capoliveri** ★★, south of Porto Azzurro, is many people's favorite place on Elba—even despite its inland location. Founded as a mining town, Capoliveri has managed to thrive even after the cessation of mineral extraction on Elba. It very much fits the mold of a typical Tuscan hill town, with charming side streets (called *chiassi* here) and piazzas, great vistas, and great places to eat and drink. Park your car in a lot just outside the *centro storico* and walk the rest of the way in. Up in the historic center, Piazza Matteotti is the heart of Capoliveri and hosts jazz concerts many nights in summer. Pedestrian-only Via Roma is the main drag and lined with irresistible shops and cafes. This street, and Capoliveri in general, is the place to be on Elba for the sunset *passeggiata* (nightly walk).

South of Capoliveri, **Monte Calamita** (413m/1,355 ft.) is the highest point in eastern Elba. It's worth driving up to see the open-air vestiges of the region's long history of mineral extraction. In fact, Monte Calamita means "Magnet Mountain," for the large quantities of iron in the rock here.

The southeastern extremity of this peninsula is named the **Costa dei Gabbiani** (Coast of Seagulls) after the large population of yellow-legged gulls that nest here every spring. Within the Costa dei Gabbiani area is a "vacation village" centered around a converted wine estate, the Tenuta delle Ripalte (www.costadeigabbiani.it), that offers attractive (though somewhat remote) accommodations in restored villas, cottages, and farm buildings, as well as a wealth of sports and leisure facilities.

CENTRAL ELBA

Elba is narrowest at its center, with only 6km (3¾ miles) separating Marina di Campo in the south and Procchio in the north. Landscapes are gentler here, and wide sandy beaches have given rise to some of the island's more modern tourist developments.

On the south side of the island, west of the fingerlike Stella peninsula, is the wide bay of **Lacona,** where the large sandy beach is well equipped for swimming and watersports. Lacona is also the *campeggio* (campground) capital of Elba, and making it especially popular with young and budget-conscious travelers.

The road west from Lacona, SP30 or Via del Monumento, gently winds through forests and rock outcrops until it reenters "civilization" at **Marina di Campo,** the busiest single resort area on Elba, chockablock with mid-range hotels, pizzerias, and pubs. The atmosphere is jovial and, in high summer, a bit juvenile. Marina di Campo's 2km-long (1¼-mile) sandy beach is a big attraction and has all the watersports and boat rentals you could possibly need.

Balance the beach-bumminess of Marina di Campo with visits to the nearby inland villages of **Sant'Ilario in Campo** (from Marina di Campo, about 5km/3 miles: Follow signs to La Pila, then turn left toward Sant'Ilario) and **San Piero in Campo** ★ (follow signs from Sant'Ilario, about 3km/2 miles). Both of these, but especially San Piero, are lovely little medieval *borghi* with narrow streets and beautiful views over the gulf of Marina di Campo. Also on the outskirts of Marina di Campo is Italy's second-largest aquarium (after that of Genoa), the **Acquario dell'Elba** ★★, Località La Foce (✆ **0565/977885;** www.acquarioelba.com; Mar–May and Sept–Oct 9am–7:30pm; June–Aug 9am–11:30pm; 7€, 3€ for kids 3–12). It has well over 50 tanks with various types of marine life, from large pelagic tunas and sea turtles to eels and tiny crustaceans, typical in the waters off Elba. The attached Museo Faunistico (included in aquarium admission) has dioramas of Elban birds and land animals.

This part of the island was exploited throughout antiquity for its granite, and you can take a nice hike (about 5km/3 miles round-trip) west from San Piero in Campo through the old **granite quarries** and see some enormous Roman-era granite columns (now lying on the ground).

Up on the northern coast, Procchio owes its very existence to its protected sandy bay—many hotels and tourist facilities have been built here to take advantage of the excellent beach, which, along with some good shops (most notably La Casa del Vino; see "Shopping," p. 140), makes Procchio worth a stop.

WESTERN ELBA

From Procchio, the SP25 runs west along the water toward Marciana Marina (7km/4⅓ miles). With its sporty curves through the pines and oleanders, it's an exceptionally fun drive. At first glance, the port of **Marciana Marina** doesn't impress: The inner part of the town consists mostly of ugly 1960s architecture, but continue to the waterfront and you'll find an animated *lungomare*—it's one of Elba's most popular yacht-mooring marinas—and historic buildings from Marciana Marina's past as an important fishing and export center. The heart of old Marciana Marina is **Rione Cotone ★**, at the far east (to the right, looking at the water) of the harbor, with salt-faded old pastel houses and a general look of a time-gone-by. At the opposite end of the harbor rises the so-called Torre Saracena, erected in the 12th century as a watchtower against pirate incursions. If you're in the mood for a swim, La Fenicia is a small but clean beach on the other side of the tower. On summer evenings, Marciana Marina's bars and restaurants are very happening spots, frequented by locals and vacationers of all ages.

After Marciana Marina, continue inland on SP25 toward Poggio. This is where Elba starts to feel a little bit Alpine: As you begin to climb toward Elba's highest point, Monte Capanne, the trees change, the air is cooler, even the architecture takes on a more rustic look. After a series of ascending hairpin turns (do not turn right on SP34 when you see signs for Marciana), you reach the hill town of **Poggio.** Arranged in a series of concentric circles around the 13th-century church of San Niccolò, medieval Poggio is a supremely quiet place and good for stretching your legs and breathing fresh air—a brief stop here is recommended as a remedy for carsickness from the tortuous roads that got you here. One of the island's finest restaurants is here, Publius (see "Where to Dine," p. 138), with breathtaking panoramas over dense woods and onward to the sea. On the road out of Poggio, toward Marciana (not Marciana Marina), there is a celebrated source of drinking water, the **Fonte Napoleone,** a spring that was known to the ancients and rechristened for—you guessed it—Bonaparte himself, who appreciated the purported benefits of its mineral profile.

Still going along SP25 in the direction of Marciana, you'll soon reach the lower station of the **Monte Capanne** *cabinovia* **★★★** (cableway to the top of 1,019m/3,343-ft. Monte Capanne; see "Attractions," p. 126). In summer, when the lift is running, take an hour's detour here to see the summit of the Tuscan archipelago's highest peak. The next town you'll encounter along the climbing and careening SP25 is **Marciana ★★**, one of the oldest towns on Elba. Marciana has well-groomed pedestrian streets, elegant *palazzi*, and a temperate microclimate (it's at 380m/1,247 ft. above sea level but only a few kilometers from the sea), which means you often need a sweater even in mid-August. The imposing 12th-century **Pisan fortress ★** is at the high, southern end of town and has an ample interior courtyard where outdoor classical concerts are frequently held in summer. Check in at the APT office in Portoferraio (see "Visitor Information," p. 126) for schedules.

After Marciana, the SP25 heads back downhill toward the water. The first sign-posted seaside town is **Sant'Andrea,** a steep, casual resort with a pretty bay (and small beach). Along the water, the granite **rock formations ★**—studded with ortho-clase (a composite of aluminum and potassium)—send the geologically inclined into a frenzy; the unique minerals give the water intense turquoise tones.

Continuing west past Sant'Andrea, SP25 begins to curve around toward the south—you're now at the far western end of Elba, or the "head" of the fish. On clear days, magnificent **roadside vistas** across the cobalt Mediterranean include the other Tuscan islands of Capraia, Pianosa, and Montecristo, Corsica; and, on a very clear day, you can look northwest and make out the snowy peaks of the Alps. Past the quiet seaside towns of Chiessi and Pomonte, the road curves back toward the east. Within a few kilometers, you'll reach the gorgeous and intimate but well-trafficked beach areas of **Fetovaia** and **Cavoli,** before entering Marina di Campo.

Outdoor Pursuits

Elba is a veritable playground for nature lovers and sports types. What's really great about the island is that even when you're out trekking and enjoying unspoiled scenery, you're never too far from civilization (a hot cappuccino, a steaming plate of seafood pasta, a cold beer—you get the idea). The island's many equipment rental agencies make it possible to strike out on a DIY adventure; but for a little more structure and a little less hassle, there is no shortage of outdoor-activity outfitters and "environmental guides" licensed by the national park service. When it comes to organized excursions into the natural side of Elba, a great one-stop shop—whether it's mountain biking, hiking, kayaking—is **Il Viottolo,** in Marina di Campo at Via Fucini 279 (✆ **0565/978005;** www.ilviottolo.com).

BOAT EXCURSIONS   Dozens of boat excursions—motorboats, fishing charters, sailboats—can be arranged on the spot from the Elban ports of Portoferraio, Marciana Marina, Marina di Campo, Porto Azzurro, and Rio Marina. Many offer day trips around the island, or to other Tuscan islands, while others only do weekend or week-long packages complete with skipper and cook. The **Dollaro II,** out of Porto Azzurro (✆ **0565/958346** or 328/6890227), does 3-hour cruises (15€) along Elba's southern coast (including stops for swimming in coves that are inaccessible by land). For day trips to the other Tuscan archipelago islands (departing from Portoferraio and Marciana Marina), contact **Aquavision** at ✆ **328/7095470** or 328/2187923. The round-trip fare to Giglio is 30€; to Capraia 25€; to Pianosa 24€.

To get a glimpse of Elba's underwater world without getting wet, the **Motonave Nautilus** (✆ **328/7095470** or 0187/817456) is a glass-bottom boat with daily departures from Portoferraio (Apr to mid-Oct at 10:30am), and from Marciana Marina (Apr–July and mid-Sept to mid-Oct at 3:30pm; July to mid-Sept at 2:30 and 5pm). Tours last 2 hours and cost 15€ per person.

Outdoorsy outfitter **Il Viottolo** (see above) runs guided tours to the island of Pianosa once a week (usually Thurs). Choose from either a day of snorkeling (55€) or sea kayaking (65€); both include visits of the island's historic settlement and defunct prison structures.

Of course, you can also **rent a motorboat** to explore the coastline yourself, though this is admittedly a bit more daunting on Elba—because of its size and ferry traffic—than on smaller Italian islands. You might not want to attempt the full island circumnavigation (147km/91 miles), but you can certainly have an adventure putter-ing along smaller sections of Elba's perimeter, finding hidden coves, swimming, and picnicking. Rental agencies are in every port town and on major beaches like Biodola and Lacona. Expect to pay 50€ to 60€ (fuel not included) for a half-day's rental of a small *gommone* (three- to six-person rubber dinghy with a 15–40 hp motor).

DIVING & SNORKELING The clear, unpolluted, mostly calm waters off Elba boast more than 40 dive sites, ranging in difficulty from easy to expert. In addition to fascinating undersea rock walls (Elba's mineral diversity continues below the water) and gorgeous beds of *gorgonie* (delicate red and yellow corals with intricate branch structure), the waters hold the sunken wrecks of a Luftwaffe warplane, a cargo ship, and even a runaway mine cart. The sea life in most every site is very rich, with species such as lobster, octopus, rockfish, crab, grouper, and conger eels. One of the most popular sites is off the coast of Pomonte, in western Elba, where the 1972 wreck of the cargo ship *Elviscott* lies almost perfectly preserved just 10m (33 ft.) below the surface. Divers can swim down through the ship's smokestack to the engine room.

Several island-based diving operators (all PADI- or CMAS-certified) rent out all the necessary equipment, take you out for day excursions to the dive sites, and provide lessons and certifications. **Diving in Elba,** with offices in Portoferraio, Procchio, and Biodola (✆ **347/3715788** Riccardo; **339/6518187** Fabio; **333/6758555** Valentina; www.divinginelba.com), is the best dive outfitter on the island—with a colorful cast of multilingual instructors—and specializes in the sites along the northern and western coast. **Sub Now,** in Marina di Campo, Località la Foce (✆ **0565/979051** or 393/7608586; www.subnow.it) offers guided dives and excursions along the south coast of Elba. In Sant'Andrea, west of Marciana Marina on the northern coast, try **Il Careno,** Piazza del Mare 12 (✆ **0565/908125;** www.ilcareno.it), which offers diving courses, guided dives, snorkeling, and equipment rental.

You can also rent **snorkeling** equipment at many of the bigger beaches like Biodola, Procchio, and Marina di Campo, and even at a few of the smaller ones.

HIKING Elba has enough rural landscapes and rugged terrain to keep nature walkers and hikers satisfied for weeks—there are many more possibilities than I can list here—but in addition to all the established hiking trails on the island, don't forget that most of the scenic pullouts along Elba's roads have scamper-worthy paths, too.

You can pick up a trail map at most bookshops and newsstands and go it alone, or you can join one of the myriad guided hikes offered by the following operators: **Il Viottolo,** Via Fucini 279, Marina di Campo (✆ **0565/978005;** www.ilviottolo. com), is the big name in Elban outdoorsy stuff, organizing every possible type of hike, from the archaeology- to the mineral-themed. Most last 4 hours and cost 30€ to 40€. Multiple-day itineraries include the Grande Traversata Elbana (Great Crossing of Elba, from 495€ including hotel stays); from east to west, it's 62km (39 miles) broken up into 4 days of hiking, with overnight accommodations at mid-range hotels along the way. **Pelagos,** Località Bocchetto 57, Porto Azzurro (✆ **347/6004835;** www. pelagos.it), specializes in environmental education and offers longer hikes in Elba, including its own GTE (Grande Traversata Elbana), as well as treks in the other Tuscan islands of Giglio and Capraia. Portoferraio-based **Genio del Bosco** (✆ **0565/ 930837;** www.geniodelbosco.it) is another nature-themed outfitter, with a broad range of guided excursions on foot, mountain bike, kayak, and horseback, though most of their clients are Italian- or German-speaking.

For any hiking on Elba, any time of year, be sure to bring plenty of water, food, and sun protection. Having said that, hiking here isn't terribly extreme. Trails are well marked; most go through semi-inhabited areas where you can ask directions or re-provision, and you're always bound to run into at least a few fellow trekkers.

HORSEBACK RIDING For outings in the lovely countryside near Portoferraio, beach rides, and mountain treks where your trusty steed does all the work, call Susanna Lemmi at **Centro Ippico Elbano,** Località Monte Orello (✆ **0565/933449** or 347/6395704); all experience/skill levels are welcome. Alternatively, in central Elba, **L.E. Farms** operates out of Campo nell'Elba (✆ **339/3147179** or 0565/ 979090; June–Sept only). **Centro Ippico Costa dei Gabbiani,** Località Ripalte, Capoliveri (✆ **0565/942408**), offers scenic rides along the dramatic coastline of Capoliveri's peninsula.

MOUNTAIN BIKING Trails abound on Elba—from the easy and flat to the steep and strenuous—but it's recommended to go with a guide who knows the island's roads and potential traffic hazards along the route. **Il Viottolo,** Via Fucini 279, Marina di Campo (✆ **0565/978005;** www.ilviottolo.com), offers day rides (4 hr., 30€–40€) all over the island, and **Emozioni Mediterranee** (✆ **328/6781755** or 0565/978004; www.emozionimediterranee.it) organizes weekend biking package trips on Elba, with ferry passage, lodging, and meals included, and a fun group atmosphere (from 169€ for 3 days). Both operators can accommodate beginners.

SEA KAYAKING It's paddling heaven along Elba's intricate coastline (particularly along the northern and western shores), with its crystalline waters, calm sea conditions, and embarrassment of coves in which to rest and avail of beach snack bars and other simple pleasures. **Sea Kayak Italy,** Via del Sette 12 (✆ **0565/996609** or 348/2290711; in the U.S. 650/728-8720; www.seakayakitaly.it), which is affiliated with the U.S. outfitter California Canoe & Kayak, offers half-day (50€), full-day (63€), and weeklong (400€, a full-island circumnavigation, camping in tents along the way) excursions for all skill and experience levels. For skilled kayakers only, they also offer an equipment rental service from their location in Marciana Marina (rates 25€ for 3 hr., 30€ for 8 hr., 35€ for 24 hr., or 150€ for 1 week). **Il Viottolo,** Via Fucini 279, Marina di Campo (✆ **0565/978005;** www.ilviottolo.com), also hosts daily sea-kayaking excursions (easy and medium level) to various stretches of the Elban coast; they visit a different destination every day of the week, but most trips last 4 hours, usually departing at 2:30pm or so, and cost around 30€. On Thursdays, Il Viottolo and its kayaks go to Pianosa to explore that island's hidden coves and crevices. The 7-hour trip costs 75€.

Where to Stay

With so many beaches and outdoor activities, Elba is a great place to vacation for a week or more. The major villa rental agency for the island is **Villa & Charme** (www. elbavilla.it), which has properties all over the island, from luxury villas to modest holiday apartments. For the budget-minded who don't mind roughing it a little bit, there are several well-equipped campgrounds on the southern side of the island, around Marina di Campo and Lacona. Try **Camping Ville degli Ulivi,** Via della Foce 89, Marina di Campo (✆ **0565/976098;** www.villedegliulivi.it), which has its own water park.

Agriturismo Sapereta ★ Only 1km (¾ mile) from the Lido di Capoliveri beach, this working wine estate, farm, and guesthouse is a good place to soak up some typical Tuscan gastronomic atmosphere while still being relatively close to the beach. The apartments, carved out of two restored farmhouses, are nothing fancy but have plenty of room (all have a patio) and the feel of an authentic Italian household. Produce from Sapereta's organic farm is available for purchase and use in guests' cooking facilities. The grounds feature common areas and leisure activities for adults and kids alike.

Località La Mola (2km from Porto Azzurro). ℂ **0565/95033.** www.sapereonline.it. 15 units. Apts (weekly basis): 380€–970€ (2-person); 410€–1,140€ (4-person); 480€–1,330€ (6-person). MC, V. **Amenities:** Restaurant; pool; tennis; wine cellar; BBQ; garden; playground. *In room:* A/C, fan, TV, kitchenette, private outdoor sitting/dining area.

Ape Elbana An award-winning hospitality experience it isn't, but what the "Elban Bee" does offer is a prime position in the *centro storico* of Portoferraio. Decor is almost aggressively ugly (for example, pale pink satin bedspreads way past their prime), a pity considering the cute vine-covered, yellow-stucco exterior. Saving graces are the on-site restaurant (good quality and value), and the central location in Elba's busy port town.

Salita Cosimo de' Medici 2, Portoferraio. ℂ **0565/914245.** www.ape-elbana.it. 24 units. Doubles 70€–150€. Rates include breakfast. MC, V. Free parking. **Amenities:** Restaurant. *In room:* A/C, TV.

Gallo Nero ★★ The "black rooster" strikes a nice balance in the western resort town of Sant'Andrea, offering a tranquil setting and proximity to the sea. Rooms, distributed between the main hotel building and a series of cottages, are spacious and cool with terra-cotta floors and wrought-iron bed frames. All but the lowest bracket of rooms have at least a partial sea view. The hotel's strongest feature is its lush and extensive garden, stretching all the way to the water with fragrant flowers and herbs and places to sit, read, and sunbathe along the way. A path through the garden permits guests pedestrian access to the beach of Sant'Andrea.

Via San Gaetano 20, Sant'Andrea, Western Elba. ℂ **0565/908017.** www.hotelgallonero.it. 29 units. Doubles 96€–230€. Rates include half-board. AE, DC, MC, V. Free parking. **Amenities:** Restaurant; bar; lounge; pool; tennis court; beach access; garden.

Hermitage ★ This is a full-service, five-star hotel on the crystal-clear bay of Biodola, which makes it an ideal choice for a beach- and watersports-focused vacation. While the external grounds are handsome and well-maintained (with several pools, walking paths, sitting pavilions), the rooms themselves aren't as luxurious as the price tag would suggest, though each has its own garden- or sea-facing private terrace. I suggest booking the Hermitage only in the off or shoulder seasons, when you can get a hefty discount off the rack rate.

Località La Biodola. ℂ **0565/9740.** www.hotelhermitage.it. 112 units. Doubles 244€–650€. Rates include half-board. AE, DC, MC, V. Parking (fee). **Amenities:** 3 restaurants; bar; private beach; fitness room; garden; 4 pools; spa; watersports equipment (fee); free Wi-Fi throughout.

Ilio ★★ In the steep seaside hamlet of Sant'Andrea, the Ilio is a great little boutique hotel spread among several low-rise buildings. Well planned gardens and terraces give the place a homey, organic feel. Generously sized rooms are well appointed but uncluttered, and all have free Wi-Fi; the otherwise unremarkable bathrooms get extra points for having Acqua dell'Elba (p. 140) fragrance diffusers. The on-site **restaurant**—an intimate space with blond wood and sleek surfaces that doubles as an art gallery—is a world away from the tired and over-formal hotel restaurants elsewhere on the island, turning out a surprisingly sophisticated, updated Mediterranean cuisine (a good thing since nightly room rates include half-board). Guests of the Ilio have a major asset in owner Maurizio and his staff: Opinionated, friendly, and expert about Elba, they're an amazing resource for planning your days.

Via Sant'Andrea 5, Sant'Andrea, Western Elba. ℂ **0565/908018.** www.hotelilio.com. 20 units. Doubles 110€–240€, including buffet breakfast and dinner. AE, MC, V. Free parking. Closed mid-Oct to mid-Apr.

Amenities: Restaurant; bar; cellar; garden; lounge; terrace. *In room:* A/C, TV, hair dryer, minibar, free Wi-Fi.

Relais delle Picchiaie ★★ A pink stucco villa set in the green hills south of Portoferraio, this is an all-around very comfortable place to be based on Elba. The management is well connected to Elba and its assets, frequently organizing activities like nature outings and wine-tastings. Rooms are bright but bland, with incongruous business-hotel carpet and upholstery that is a throwback to a circa-1983 Hilton; opt for the "classic" doubles, which have small balconies or terraces. The panoramic grounds, with view of Volterraio castle, offer a wealth of leisure facilities.

Località Le Picchiaie, 8km from Portoferraio (follow the signs toward Porto Azzurro). ☏ **0565/933110.** www.relaisdellepicchiaie.it. 49 units. Doubles 130€–390€. Rates include breakfast. AE, DC, MC, V. **Amenities:** Restaurant; bar; bikes; concierge; fitness room; gardens; lounge; 2 pools; room service; spa; tennis. *In room:* A/C, satellite TV, hair dryer; minibar, free Wi-Fi.

San Petronilla ★★ CAPOLIVERI The romantic, medieval hill town of Capoliveri is one of Elba's greatest treasures, with some of the island's nicest places to stroll, shop, eat, and drink in charming narrow streets. San Petronilla is only a 5-minute walk to the town's lively epicenter, Piazza Matteotti. While the Petronilla could get by on location alone, the gracious white villa would look perfectly at home in the Tuscan countryside, with its terra-cotta tiles, exposed beams, and authentic character.

Località San Petronilla, Capoliveri. ☏ **0565/968351.** www.albergo-petronilla.com. 8 units. Doubles from 100€. Cash only. **Amenities:** Restaurant; terrace. *In room:* TV, kitchenette (in apts), minibar (in doubles).

Villa Ottone ★★ ☺ Gorgeous gardens that meet the sea, with views across the bay to Portoferraio, are the main selling point of this old-world hotel. The property's showpiece is an aristocratic 18th-century villa, directly above the beach, where the waves lull you to sleep in high-ceilinged rooms with wrought-iron four poster beds and period stuccoes and frescoes. However, only a small fraction of the hotel's rooms (the most expensive ones, naturally) are in the villa; the rest are in the '70s main building and adjacent one-story "cottage." Though not as special as the villa, these accommodations are still quite nice, many with balconies or terraces immersed in the lush gardens, and the atmosphere is more casual. Villa Ottone has its own strip of sand-and-gravel beach, a boat dock, two swimming pools, and a nicely equipped spa. *One caveat:* Avoid the hotel restaurant, other than at the free breakfast.

Località Ottone (13km from Portoferraio, follow signs toward Porto Azzurro then Bagnaia). ☏ **0565/933042.** www.villaottone.com. 80 units. Doubles 230€–630€, including buffet breakfast. AE, DC, MC, V. Free parking. **Amenities:** 2 restaurants; bar; beach; concierge; fitness center; gardens; lounge; patio; 2 pools; room service; spa; tennis; kids' programs (summer only). *In room:* A/C, satellite TV, hair dryer, minibar, free Wi-Fi.

Where to Dine

Emanuele ★★★ ELBAN/SEAFOOD Behind a beach-bum bar facade hides what many cite as the best dining on Elba. Friendly, family-run Emanuele excels at marrying the catch of the day and pick of the crustaceans with fresh pastas and seasonal vegetables. Reserve ahead for a table in the pocket-size courtyard, shaded by pine trees and umbrellas just feet from the waves lapping at the pebble beach. The *garganelli branzino e verdure* (sea bass scented with rosemary and tossed with zucchini, carrots, oil, and peperoncino) is outstanding, as is the simple *tagliolini bottarga e carciofi* (thin pasta strands twirled with grated tuna roe and artichoke hearts). For a *secondo,* have grilled or oven-roasted sea bream, grouper, or perch pulled in by local fishermen that morning, or try the island specialty *totani alla diavola* (cuttlefish with oil and hot peppers). Save room for the *torta di mele* (warm caramelized apple torte).

Località Enfola, 6km west of Portoferraio. 🕾 **0565/939003.** Reservations recommended. Entrees 7€–18€; prix-fixe menu without wine 25€. MC, V. Daily noon–3:30pm and 7:30–11pm. Closed mid-Oct to Easter and on Wed until mid-June.

Enoteca La Fortezza ★★ WINE BAR   The "fortress" part of this wine bar's name isn't a gimmick—it's literally *inside* the old Medicean fortresses above town. The cavernous space is hewn out of 16th-century masonry, with brick vaults and rough stone walls left exposed to marvelous effect; the terrace outside has views over Portoferraio Bay. Wine lovers should make time for a few glasses here before or after the ferry and, if you're staying in Portoferraio, it's a fantastic place to while away an evening, sampling all the varietals of *vino elbano,* and Tuscan cheeses and charcuterie.

Via Scoscesa (inside the fortress walls), Portoferraio. 🕾 **335/8393722.** www.enotecadellafortezza. com. Small plates 5€–10€. No credit cards. Tues–Sun 11am–3pm and 6pm–midnight. Nov–Mar Thurs–Sat 6–11pm.

Il Chiasso ★★ ELBAN/SEAFOOD   Elegant and expensive, this is the place to go for special-occasion seafood at the apex of freshness. For whole-fish entrees, let the chef prepare you whatever's newly caught that day, but Il Chiasso's mouth-watering fish-based pastas can be a meal all by themselves. If it's available, don't miss the spaghetti *ai ricci di mare* (with sea urchin, an amazingly delicate flavor). The restaurant occupies two sides of a characteristic little side-street of charming central Capoliveri, adding to the special atmosphere.

Via Nazario Sauro 9, Capoliveri. 🕾 **0565/968709.** Entrees 15€–22€. AE, MC, V. Wed–Mon 7–10:30pm. Closed Oct–Easter.

La Barca ★★ ELBAN/SEAFOOD   "The Boat" is one of Portoferraio's best restaurants. It sees its fair share of tourism but remains a place locals return to go for well-prepared fish dishes and a friendly atmosphere. You can dine alfresco under an awning on the quiet street or inside surrounded by island art. The *gnocchi all'Elbana* is a good preparation of the potato dumpling pasta with a mix of tomato sauce and pesto, while the spaghetti *alla bottarga* is more traditional—thin spaghetti in butter with dried tuna eggs grated over it. For a *secondo,* try the catch of the day or the *stoccafisso con patate* (dried cod cooked with potatoes, onions, and parsley).

Via Guerrazzi 60/62, Portoferraio (in the Old City, a block up from the dock on the landward arm of the "U"). 🕾 **0565/918036.** Reservations recommended in season. Entrees 8€–16€. AE, MC, V. Thurs–Tues 12:30–2pm and 7:30–10pm (June to mid-Sept, dinner served daily). Closed mid-Jan to mid-Feb.

La Caravella ★ SEAFOOD   You can't miss it—La Caravella is the boat-shaped restaurant sitting on piers in the middle of Porto Azzurro's charming little marina. Expect a more touristy atmosphere and higher bill than at other restaurants in this seaside town, but you can't go wrong with spaghetti *allo scoglio* (a mix that usually includes prawns, clams, and mussels, tossed with tomatoes and parsley), or for a bit of a splurge, spaghetti *all'aragosta.* The best entrees are whole grilled fish and, if you're in a fried state of mind, the *fritto misto di mare,* with a medley of fish and crustaceans.

Via Vitaliani 3, Porto Azzurro. 🕾 **0565/95066.** www.ristorantelacaravella.eu. Reservations required in July–Aug. Entrees 14€–20€. AE, MC, V. Apr to mid-Oct 11:45am–2:30pm and 6:45pm–midnight. Closed Tues in Apr, May, and Oct.

Publius ★★★ ELBAN/SEAFOOD Romantic, panoramic Publius, set high on the hill in the quaint inland town of Poggio, is Elba's most special dining experience (if you can forgo the seaside setting of Emanuele). Everything here is pitch perfect, from the warm welcome, the rustically elegant atmosphere, the timing and cordiality of the waiters, and, of course, the cuisine. The meal starts with an amuse-bouche of polenta crostini, after which you can choose from an antipasti, primi, and *secondi*, all of which are beautifully balanced pairings of simple, fresh ingredients. While flavor combinations and presentations are more creative than standard trattoria fare, there's nothing fussy about the cooking at Publius. Most dishes are seafood-based, but carnivores can also find typical Elban *montagna* fare. A terrace offers spectacular coastal views—a wonderful treat, since Poggio is a quasi-Alpine setting. On the sophisticated list of wines from all over Italy, many are available by the glass.

Piazza del Castagneto 11, Poggio (on the road btw. Marciana Marina and Marciana). ✆ **0565/99208.** www.ristorantepublius.it. Reservations recommended. Entrees 10€–17€. AE, DC, MC, V. Tues–Sun noon–2pm, 7–10:30pm.

La Taverna dei Poeti ★★ TUSCAN/SEAFOOD The wood-and-glass doorway is covered with travel guide stickers from all over—a reassuring sign. And luckily, despite the popularity of the place, it hasn't become a tourist-trap. This *taverna* is all about quality, simple cuisine and friendly service. Great for a romantic dinner or a convivial group outing, the place feels like your Tuscan nonna's parlor. Affable proprietor Paolo will no doubt stop by your table and chat at some point during the meal. With tantalizing juxtapositions of local ingredients, the menu is one of those that has your mouth watering at first sight, and the dishes explode with succulence, pleasing textures, and fresh, deep flavors. It would be just as easy to make a meal of all the artisanal cheeses and meats on offer, but the restaurant is better known for its seafood dishes. The best are those that bridge the gap between surf and turf, like the amazing *scaloppine* of amberjack with pancetta, porcini mushrooms, and lime sauce.

Via Roma 14, Capoliveri. ✆ **0565/968306.** www.latavernadeipoeti.it. Reservations recommended. Entrees 10€–19€. AE, DC, MC, V. Thurs–Tues noon–3pm and 7pm–midnight. Closed Nov–Mar.

Shopping

Portoferraio has the island's best shops, and luckily for visitors, they're all concentrated along the street lining the old harbor (Calata Mazzini) and the parallel street just inland (Via Guerazzi). The main promenades of Capoliveri and Marciana Marina are also eminently suitable places for doing vacation-inspired retail damage—in Capoliveri, the boutiques stay open until midnight or later in high season.

Every Italian island has a signature scent, and the line-up of perfumes, soaps, home fragrances, and beyond at **Acqua dell'Elba** ★★★ is exquisite. Founded in Marciana Marina in the 1990s, Acqua dell'Elba captures the unique aromas of the woods, flowers, and sea here. The goods, recognizable by their Tiffany blue packaging, are also reasonably priced (about 30€ for a 1.7-oz. eau de parfum) for the quality and high-end look. Shop the product line at the Acqua dell'Elba boutiques in Portoferraio (Calata Mazzini 36; ✆ 0565/916155), Porto Azzurro (Piazza Matteotti 12/13; ✆ 0565/920167), Marciana Marina (Viale Aldo Moro 75; ✆ 0565/99513 and Lungomare Regina Margherita 33; ✆ 0565/904190), Capoliveri (Via Pietro Gori 17; ✆ 0565/935043), and Rio Marina (Via Principe Amedeo 12; ✆ 0565/962293). The head laboratory is also in Marciana Marina, at Viale Aldo Moro 17.

Italians love to outfit themselves in nautical gear, especially when on an island holiday, and the absolute must-have brand is **North Sails;** you can stock up on pseudo-technical sailing apparel at the North Sails boutique on Calata Mazzini 19, Portoferraio (✆ 0565/916624). The merchandise—logo T-shirts, caps, bags,—isn't cheap, but you will *soooo* look the part of the casual Mediterranean habitué.

Elban wines make a nice souvenir—or a nice picnic accompaniment while you're out exploring the island. It's hard to find a good selection of *vino elbano* at wine shops on the mainland, so stock up before you sail away. The D.O.C. labels to look for are Elba Bianco, Elba Rosso, Ansonica, Aleatico, and Moscato. There are *enoteche* (wine shops) in every town, but Elba's top wine merchant is **La Casa del Vino,** Via del Mare 1, Procchio (✆ 0565/907241).

Elba After Dark

Elba isn't renowned for its nightlife, but there are plenty of simple bars in all the towns where you're bound to find an amiable crowd quaffing wine and beer. **Capoliveri,** though it's up on a hill away from the water, is the most lively town come sundown, with several little alfresco bar-gelaterias that are buzzing for *aperitivo* (happy hour) and *dopocena* (after dinner) on its principal square, Piazza Matteotti. **Enoteca Fandango,** Via Cardenti 1, Capoliveri (✆ 0565/968329), is the place to go to sample Elban wines. Just south of Capoliveri, **Sugar Reef Musicology,** Località La Trappola (✆ 338/9179026; www.sugar-reef.com), has live music (jazz, rock, Latin, soul) or DJs every night in summer and a splendid terrace overlooking the sea. Doors open at 11pm.

Marciana Marina also has a pretty happening, if casual, nightlife scene. The young crowd starts with an *aperitivo* (try a vodka kiwi daiquiri) at **Yachting Bar,** Viale Regina Margherita 68 (✆ 0565-99351); over-30s may prefer the scene at **Slocum** (Viale Regina Margherita 72; ✆ 0565/99067), which also has live music many nights in high season. The sailing set has a rollicking good time at **Skipper Pub,** Via Vadi 13 (✆ 0565/904065). Wine enthusiasts should make for **Enoteca Coltelli,** Piazza Vittoria (✆ 0565/99166).

In Portoferraio, my favorite place for an after-dinner drink is **Enoteca La Fortezza** (see "Where to Dine," p. 138).

There are a few clubs (*discoteche*) on Elba, but the club scene is not electrifying. Still, you'll find a fun-loving crowd at **Decò,** Località La Trappola, south of Capoliveri (✆ 339/3499552; Tues–Sun 11pm–4am), which plays house, electronic, and '70s and '80s dance classics. Or check out **Club 64,** Strada Capannone Biodola (✆ 0565/969988 or 347/3231284; www.club64.net; Fri–Sun 11pm–4am May–Oct), a sumptuous villa set in the hills above Biodola on the northern coast of Elba. Think Lady Gaga blaring on fabulous outdoor dance floors and sunburned northern Europeans doing shots poured by sexy bartenders in barely there getups.

PIANOSA ★

Its name says it all. Pianosa, roughly translated, means "flat-o-rama." The island is known as the *zattera* ("raft") of the archipelago, as its flat top doesn't slope down to the water but drops off to the sea abruptly around its coast. This unyielding flatness means that when you're on Pianosa, you can't even see the water until you're right at the edge of the island. Pianosa has Roman ruins, and interesting birdlife (some introduced when this was a hunting reserve of the Grand Duke of Tuscany).

The biggest presence on Pianosa is its palpable history as a penal colony. Italy has had many prison islands over the years—all but one, on the Tuscan island of Gorgona, are now defunct—but for its final decades of existence, Pianosa was Italy's Alcatraz, the place where big-time, high-profile criminal masterminds were sent. During the 1970s—the so-called *anni di piombo,* or "leaden years"—when Italian political dissent turned into terrorism, commandos from violent groups like the Red Brigades did time on Pianosa, which by then had been upgraded from a small-time penal colony to a maximum-security facility. Following the horrific 1992 car-bomb assassinations of Sicilian anti-Mafia magistrates Giovanni Falcone and Paolo Borsellino in Palermo, Pianosa was the penitentiary where convicted *mafiosi* were incarcerated. Prior to Pianosa's transformation into the *supercarcere* it became, the island had been a quiet colony of mostly smalltime crooks who lived harmoniously alongside civilian residents and support staff. But during those *supercarcere* years, helicopters buzzed incessantly overhead, sirens wailed, and a long, terrible wall was erected to more meaningfully separate the prison areas from the other inhabited parts of the island.

From the mid-19th century until 1998, the penal colony kept tourism away and the island unspoiled for 150 years. Since the closure of the prison, Pianosa has been wholly part of the Parco Nazionale dell'Arcipelago Toscano, and visits are restricted to guided tours of no more than 100 persons per day, most of whom visit as a day trip from Elba. There are no overnight accommodations on Pianosa, and only one bar/restaurant (at Cala Giovanna), but it makes for a nice day trip from Elba (you can also get there from the mainland port of Piombino, though all ferries from Piombino to Pianosa stop at Elba along the way).

Essentials

In summer, there is at least one day-trip boat daily from the Elban ports of Portoferraio, Rio Marina, Marina del Campo, and Marciana Marina. Year-round, **Toremar,** Rio Marina, Banchina dei Voltoni (© **0565/962073**), operates a ferry on Tuesdays only between Piombino and Pianosa, stopping at Rio Marina, Elba, along the way. The trip from Rio Marina to Pianosa takes about 2 hr. each way and costs 11€. Private full-day boat excursions to Pianosa (from 40€), bundled with walking, mountain bike, snorkeling tours, and so on of the island are also offered by several Elban operators. Try **Il Viottolo,** Via Fucini 279, Marina di Campo (© **0565/978005;** www.ilviottolo.com), or **Emozioni Mediterranee** (© **328/6781755** or 0565/978004; www.emozioni mediterranee.it).

Exploring the Island

Like the prisoners who used to call the island home, you won't be set free to roam Pianosa on your own. The national park restricts the number of daily visitors to 100, all of whom must be accompanied by licensed park guides.

The first thing you'll see upon arrival is Pianosa's port, where you are greeted by a picturesque collection of 19th-century buildings in their weathered pastel mantles. In town, the main sights are the dominating **Forte Teglia** (erected by Napoleon), bleak **prison structures,** defunct for just over a decade, and tunnels of 4th-century-A.D. **Christian catacombs,** where 700 tombs have been excavated thus far. In the center of the island are the extensive ruins of a **Roman villa** attributed to Agrippa, who was exiled here in the 1st century A.D. On the western coast of Pianosa, Cala della Botte is home to a unique grotto called **Lavanderia Vecchia** (The Old Laundry), which has a freshwater spring that the ancient Romans seem to have exploited.

On the natural side of things, your tour guide is sure to catalog the various plants that grow on Pianosa, which is surprisingly fertile considering its severe-looking limestone underpinnings. Even Napoleon recognized this fecundity and planted 1,000 olive trees on Pianosa, 300 of which are still alive and firmly rooted in the calcareous soil. The limestone of Pianosa is also littered with fossils of animals that no longer live here (bears, horses, and deer), evidence that the island once belonged to the mainland.

All tours, after the requisite circuit of the island's historic and naturalistic points of interests, permit visitors to swim at the only **beach** where swimming is permitted, **Cala Giovanna,** near the port and the island's sole **bar/restaurant** (a very simple affair serving lunch only). Cala Giovanna is a narrow but sugar-white stretch of sand caressed by calm, turquoise waters, ideal for a dip before saying goodbye to the "raft."

CAPRAIA ★

30km/19 miles east of Corsica and 42km/26 miles north of Elba

Of all the Tuscan islands, Capraia is the least touched by humans, and it wears its scant tourist development as a badge of honor. Which is not to say the island is completely virgin: The Romans were here (and who knows what other ancient people may have settled here—many archaeological finds in the hills of Capraia remain a mystery), and both the Pisan and Genoese Republics left their marks over centuries of fighting each other for control of the archipelago. Even pirates (the Muslim Saracens) wanted a piece of Capraia, which became a theater of repeated incursions by the corsair Dragut Rais. Capraia's fortifications and *garitte* (watchtowers) date from this period—the 15th and 16th centuries—when the island was under near-constant threat of invasion. More recently, in 1873, Capraia became the site of a penal colony, which closed in 1986.

With the closure of the prison, sleepy Capraia began opening its eyes to tourism ever so cautiously. Luckily for conservationists, the entire island was designated parkland in 1996, with the creation of the Tuscan Islands National Park, and thus protected from abusive development. To this day, a trip to Capraia is all about quiet encounters with wild nature. Don't come here looking for nightlife or broad expanses of sand—the only beach on Capraia isn't even always there. But if hiking, boating, diving, and the simplest trappings of civilization are your perfect getaway, Capraia is sublime, and you'll definitely be part of an exclusive club once you've been here.

With so little human contamination, combined with favorable tides and winds, Capraia has some of the purest coastal waters in the entire Mediterranean. Pardon the hackneyed gemstone comparison, but the color of the water in Capraia's coves may be best described as brilliant green tourmaline. Capraia's unspoiled coast is a haven for sailors, and even VIPs of politics and show business are known to bring their yachts, which quietly bob at such coves as Cala del Ceppo. Nautical novices can rent small motorboats to explore the shoreline, or simply join one of the regularly scheduled full-island tours, stopping to swim in spectacular coves along the way. The undersea world off Capraia draws plenty of divers, too.

The west side of the island is all sheer cliffs and sharp rocks, while the east side, where the town is, presents a softer landscape of valleys and protected coves. Hikers will find utter solitude along old stone mule paths that wend their way up through the island's hilly interior (highest point: 445m/1,460 ft.) past groves of pines and cork oaks to a velvety green carpet of Mediterranean *macchia* with fragrant herbs and flowers like wild rosemary, myrtle, and helichrysum. Bird-watchers can spend hours spotting Audouin's and yellow-legged gulls, red kites, buzzards, herons, and peregrine falcons.

Even with all these attractions, Capraia remains undervisited: The summer population tops out at about 1,000, a large percentage of whom don't even spend the night. (With careful planning, you can visit Capraia as a day trip; the ferries are timed in such a way that you can have 5 or 6 hours to explore before catching the boat back to the mainland.) Rugged Capraia is still hitting the snooze button on tourism, and is perfectly happy about it.

Essentials

GETTING THERE   Toremar (℗ 0586/896113; www.toremar.it) operates ferries from the Porto Mediceo in Livorno to Capraia; in high season, there's a boat every day at 8:30pm; additional boats run on Thursdays (departing Livorno at 4pm) and Saturdays (departing Livorno at 3pm). The trip to Capraia takes about 2½ hours and tickets cost 15€ one-way. On Tuesdays and Fridays, the Toremar ferry also stops at Gorgona along the way. A faster option, **Consorzio Marittimo Turistico 5 Terre** (℗ 0187/732987 or 0586/905089) also offers a private boat shuttle service between Livorno and Capraia in July and August. Daily departures from Livorno leave at 8:30am and arrive in Capraia at 10:10am; from Capraia to Livorno, the boats are at 4pm Monday through Friday and 5:30pm Saturday and Sunday, arriving Livorno at 5:40 and 7:10pm, respectively. Tickets are 15€ each way. The private shuttle service is suspended in inclement weather, while Toremar's tough old boats can handle rough seas just fine. Cars are technically permitted on Toremar's ferries (the faster boat service doesn't transport vehicles), but with Capraia's only paved road being about 800m long/2,625 ft., it would be rather pointless to bring a car here.

GETTING AROUND   The inhabited parts of Capraia are easy to reach on foot from the ferry dock; the **old borgo** (walled town) is up on the promontory that forms the eastern boundary of the bay of the port. Additionally, there are 14 **hiking paths** and *mulattieri* (old mule trails) throughout the island. But the best way to appreciate Capraia's natural endowment is by boat. The classic, can't-miss excursion is the 2-hour *giro dell'isola* (around-the-island tour); see "Exploring," below. A bus runs the short length of asphalt between the ferry landing and the town, handy if you're hauling luggage; otherwise, this distance is very pleasant to cover on foot. Neither mopeds nor bikes can be rented on Capraia—this is strictly a walking or boating island.

VISITOR INFORMATION   **Pro Loco Capraia,** Via Assunzione, Capraia Porto (℗ 0586/905138; www.prolococapraia.it), is the volunteer-run tourist office at the port. Stop in here for island maps that detail hiking paths and the best coves to hit by boat.

Exploring the Island

Getting to know Capraia means intimate encounters with nature, both on turf and in the surf. For land exploration, there are dozens of hiking paths that zigzag over the hilly interior, but don't offer access to much of the wild coastline, which is why boats are the best means for appreciating Capraia. The one "must" attraction on Capraia is the 2-hour **island circumnavigation tour ★★** that takes in all the best coves along the island's 30km (19-mile) perimeter, and, in warm weather, there's a stop for swimming at Cala Rossa. *Tip:* Even if you are planning to rent your own boat to putter around Capraia, I recommend doing the tour first, as the guides will be able to point out a ton of fascinating details (in Italian and broken English, but you'll get the idea) that you would otherwise miss, from hidden grottoes to magnificently colored sea-bottoms in certain parts of the island.

Small motorboats are a breeze to rent at the port; as long as you hug the coast, it's a perfectly safe and fun way for even novice navigators to discover the island's countless coves and grottoes. For the more energetic explorer, those boat rental agencies also have a number of **sea kayaks** available. Motorless and maneuverable, kayaks allow you to get to know Capraia's perimeter in silence, and to get even closer to the jagged shore than motorboats can go. Rentals are offered for a half-day (9am–1pm or 1–6pm) or a full day (9am–6pm), with motorboats from 50€ and kayaks from 20€ per half-day.

For boat rentals and other activities on Capraia, contact **Agenzia Viaggi e Turismo Parco,** Via Assunzione 42 (© 0586/905071; www.isoladicapraia.it), which runs the *Rais Dragut* catamaran tours around the island, or **Agenzia della Rosa,** Via Assunzione (© 0586/905266).With your own boat, allow a good half-day to explore the coast, eat a picnic (you can pick up simple sandwiches, fruit, and beverages at groceries or snack bars in Capraia Isola town or down at the port), and swim in a cove or three. The following are some highlights of a do-it-yourself boat tour around Capraia:

Setting out from the port, head north; the second bay you'll reach, just before the northern tip of Capraia, is **Cala della Mortola ★**, which has the distinction of being the island's only beach. But even then, Spiaggia della Mortola is small and subject to tidal and wind conditions that can sweep it away at any time. The sand-and-pebble shore is created every summer when the southwesterly *libeccio* wind blows in from Corsica; but if the contrasting *grecale* wind, from the northeast, picks up, it can swallow up the beach at La Mortola at a moment's notice! Even if the beach has disappeared, the waters in this cove are still crystal clear and excellent for a swim. Rounding the northern tip of Capraia at Punta della Teglia (with its watchtower), and heading back south along the western coast, you'll quickly notice that this side of the island (called the *ponente,* or setting side, because it faces the sunset) is much more rugged and inhospitable. For 10km (6 miles), it's a visual treat of steep and jagged rocks, though the inlets here don't offer much protection from the wind and surf; the best swimming spots are back over on the eastern coast. Rounding the southern tip of Capraia, at Punta Zenobito, you immediately confront the most celebrated natural feature and swimming cove on the island, **Cala Rossa ★★★**. "Red Cove" takes its name from the fiery color of volcanic stone in the cliff that plunges to the sea here. Cala Rossa is part of an extinct, sunken crater, and a swim in the deep blue waters here, below that vermilion rock wall, is the highlight of most people's visits to Capraia. About 5km (3 miles) north from here is another popular cove, **Cala del Ceppo ★**, where the multihued seagrass growing on the sandy seafloor imparts a wonderful range of colors to the limpid water. A bit farther north, just before returning to town and the port, stop at **Cala dello Zurletto ★★**. In this protected cove, gorgeous grey-brown rocks have been sculpted by the wind and waves, making a dramatic backdrop for a swim.

As for exploring Capraia by land, the island offers dozens of different hikes (see "Outdoor Pursuits") that can take 30 minutes or 7 hours, depending on what you have the time or energy for. A natural place to start is in the immediate environs of **Capraia Isola** (aka *paese* or *borgo;* this is a confusing term, since it has the world "island" in it, but it refers to the old town of narrow streets on the hill just east of the port). There are a few more services here than down at the port, but it's still a fairly sleepy locale. The main sight in town is the **Forte San Giorgio ★**, an imposing castle built by the Genoese in the 15th century over an earlier Pisan citadel.

Outdoor Pursuits

DIVING   **Capraia Diving Service,** Via Assunzione 100 (© **0586/905137;** www. capraiadiving.it), will rent you equipment and take you out for guided dives to several excellent sites along the island's eastern coast, where practically guaranteed sea life sightings include grouper, eel, and octopus. At a depth of 45m (148 ft.), just outside the port bay, is a relic of a German reconnaissance plane that crashed in the waters off Capraia during World War II.

HIKING   The highlands of Capraia's interior are a walker's dream—especially for anyone seeking a contemplative outing, as you're often the only one on the trails. All hiking paths on Capraia have Roman numerals, and destinations are marked with wooden signs at most, but not all trail junctions. Before setting out, pick up a trail map from the Pro Loco tourist office at the port (see "Visitor Information," above). *Note:* Bring plenty of water and wear good walking shoes.

To hike on Capraia is also to bird-watch; whether you like it or not, you can't help but spy the local feathered friends. The avian mascot of Capraia is the *gabbiano reale* (yellow-footed gull, the 747 of seagulls). Also commonly sighted are Audouin's gulls, sea eagles, herons, buzzards, falcons, shearwaters, and black storks. Rounding out the island's fauna are mouflon (small wild horned sheep), lizards, geckos, and grass snakes (none dangerous or venomous).

HORSEBACK RIDING   For panoramic excursions in which another beast's legs do the climbing, **La Stalla** (a goat farm, where milk and cheese are made and sold; © **0586/905094**) has a small stable of sturdy, docile Haflinger horses available for half-day guided rides, from 20€ per person.

Where to Stay

Vacation rentals—apartments either down by the port or in the *paese* of Capraia Isola—are more common than traditional hotels (of which there are only two on Capraia). A minimum stay of a week is normally required. **Agenzia Parco** (© **0586/905071;** www.isoladicapraia.it) and **Agenzia della Rosa** (© **0586/905266;** www. capraiavacanze.it) are the two vacation rental booking companies on the island.

Camping Le Sughere ★   Very Mediterranean in style, with oleanders and prickly pears growing along the rustic stone paths, this campground set in the hills behind the town is an excellent choice for budget-conscious and back-to-nature types. The views from the property's gardens are spectacular. Bungalows are also available (they sleep four) with kitchenettes, TV, and hot water. If for some reason you've brought a car or camper, they offer reasonable parking (there is nowhere else to drive on Capraia).

Capraia Isola 57032 Livorno.© **0586/905066.** www.campeggiolesughere.it. 11€–13€ per person; tents 6.50€–11€. Bungalows (min. stay 1 week): 450€–850€ per week. May–Sept only. **Amenities:** Restaurant; pizzeria; general store; hot showers.

Casa Vacanza Solmar ★   In a typical island-style ivory stucco building off the port, Solmar offers 10 simple but attractively furnished apartments, with tasteful Indonesian/ maritime decor (dark blue or ivory muslin linens, bamboo room dividers, and silk wall hangings of sea life) and cool terra-cotta floors. Units sleep two to six people. Despite their location near the water, Solmar's apartments do not have sea views.

Via Assunzione. © **0586/905198** or 335/1778024. www.solmar.it. 10 units. Double occupancy 120€– €180 per night; 600€–1,300€ per week. MC, V. **Amenities:** Restaurant; bar; boat rentals. *In room:* A/C, TV, kitchenette.

A Night in Livorno

Considering the timing of Capraia-bound ferries (they all leave Livorno early in the morning), you'll probably need to spend the night in Livorno before heading out to the island. A comfortable choice is the four-star

Gran Duca, Piazza Giuseppe Micheli 16/18 (☎ 0586/891024; www.granduca.it); a stone's throw from the ferry terminal, it has well-appointed doubles starting at 120€.

Il Saracino   In the old *borgo* of Capraia Isola, this is a decent second choice if La Mandola (below) is full. The hotel, with maritime decorative scheme that comes off as pleasantly kitschy, has a panoramic terrace with seawater pool overlooking the port and its bay; the "residence" annex consists of apartments with cooking facilities, but these are fairly dismal inside despite their charming stone exteriors. Il Saracino also has a good **restaurant** on-site, and there's a shuttle van to and from the port for all guests.

Via Lamberto Cibo 40, ☎ **0586/905018.** www.capraiaisola.info. 35 units plus 6 apts. Doubles 120€–190€. Rates include buffet breakfast. MC, V. **Amenities:** Restaurant; bar; pool; terrace. *In room:* A/C, TV, hair dryer, minibar.

La Mandola ★   The only real hotel on Capraia is a series of low pink stucco buildings arranged like a miniature village on the edge of Capraia town (on the promontory east of the port). La Mandola bills itself as a "resort," when "nice hotel with some extra real estate" would be more accurate. The aesthetic in the guest rooms is more hip business hotel than rustic island retreat, but the units are crisp and comfortable and many have balconies or terraces. It doesn't offer scads of amenities or activities, but, at the center of the grounds is a saltwater swimming pool. The property's real asset is its setting among pinewoods overlooking the sea, and a generous use of unfinished stone helps the hotel blend in with the nature around it.

Via della Mandola 1. ☎ **0586/905300.** www.maxhotels.it. 50 units. Doubles from 140€. Rates include breakfast. AE, DC, MC, V. **Amenities:** Restaurant; bar; beach; pool; spa. *In room:* A/C, satellite TV, hair dryer, minibar.

Where to Dine

The sit-down meal options listed here are best at dinnertime. Since there's so much hiking and boating to be done during the day, an essential element of the Capraia experience is the **picnic lunch.** Stop for supplies at the *forno* (bakery, on the road between the port and town), whose *schiacciate* (similar to focaccia, and topped with cheese and other ingredients) are to die for. Capraia also has three *alimentari* (small grocery stores: Two are along the same road between port and town; one is at the port). Pick up several bottles of water before setting out on a day's expedition by land or sea.

Al Vecchio Scorfano ★★   SEAFOOD   Under the same management for three generations, the Scorfano ("Scorpion Fish") used to cater to the prison staff of Capraia; when the penal colony closed in 1986, they opened their doors to tourists and became the premier restaurant on the island. Matriarch Paola still manages the place, and her son Marco, an internationally trained chef, is in the kitchen. The restaurant has a fun portside setting (book ahead if you want a table directly on the seafront promenade), lively atmosphere, and a "marine" dining room of dark oiled wood and blue linens.

Via Assunzione 44, Capraia Porto. ☏ **0586/905132.** Reservations recommended in season. Entrees 10€–18€. MC, V. Fri–Wed noon–2:30pm and 7–11pm. Closed Nov–Mar.

La Garitta ★ TUSCAN/SEAFOOD   Up in the town, this is a rustic tavern-style restaurant, with dark wood tables, frequented by the sailing set. This is your best bet for simple yet well-prepared traditional food in cozy surroundings.

Via Genova 14, Capraia Isola. ☏ **0586/905230.** Entrees 8€–16€. MC, V. Daily noon–3pm, 7:30–11pm, later in summer.

Capraia After Dark

In general, people don't come to Capraia to party; they come to catch up on sleep and to de-stress from their hectic lives in the city. What action there is (and we're not talking glitzy discos) begins with sun-downers at the **little bars along the port,** where everyone who is staying overnight on Capraia is sure to make an appearance, and where yachters sometimes hang out before calling it a night onboard their vessels. For late-night eats and a festive vibe (in summer), **La Garitta** (see "Where to Dine," above) stays open later than other eating establishments in town.

GORGONA

The northernmost and smallest of the Tuscan islands, a speck less than a square mile (220 hectares/544 acres) almost due east of Livorno, has one of the most varied ecosystems in the archipelago and is designated in its entirety as parkland of the Parco Nazionale dell'Arcipelago Toscano. But unless you're doing hard time for the Italian State, Gorgona is difficult to visit. The island has been an "agrarian" penal colony since the late 1800s and as such, it's pretty much off-limits to the casual traveler (though a few permits are granted; see "Essentials" below). Even sea traffic must maintain a distance of at least 500m (1,640 ft.) from the shore. While the Tuscan islands of Capraia, Pianosa, and Montecristo were all formerly penal colonies, Gorgona is the last remaining active prison island in Italy.

The only landing site on Gorgona is an inlet on the northeast side of the island called **Cala dello Scalo** (Landing Cove), also the island's only (pebbly, but clean) beach. Remains of a 19th-century fishing village stand in the notch behind the beach, and some less attractive modern structures are also here. A handful of diehard civilian Gorgonese are constantly petitioning the government to have the penal colony closed. Indeed, it's a very costly prison to run (there are only 50 inmates and about 70 staff), not to mention the logistics difficulties presented by the remote nature of Gorgona.

Far from living a bleak, Alcatraz-like existence, the inmates of Gorgona are pretty much free to roam during the daytime, when they perform work projects all over the island like desalination, power plant maintenance, even fishing.

Essentials

It *is* possible to visit Gorgona even if you're not a criminal, but some planning is necessary. Technically, a permit from the Italian Department of Justice is required to go ashore at Gorgona. **Cooperativa del Parco Naturale dell'Isola di Gorgona,** Via Santa Barbara 13, Livorno (☏ **0586/899760** or 0586/884522), holds a standing number of permits to the island and is the only authorized concessionaire for public tours and transit to the island. Italian-language tours (though you might have a guide who also speaks some English or French) go once per week (usually on Tues) in summer, less frequently in spring and fall, and almost never in winter. Groups are limited to 35 people and strictly supervised; penitentiary police escort you for the entire, naturalist-led hiking tour of the island. The only way to reach Gorgona is with the **Toremar** ferry (© 0586/896113; www.toremar.it) from Livorno, which stops at Gorgona one or two days a week (usually Tues or Fri) on its way to Capraia. The Livorno-Gorgona journey takes 1½ hours each way. Add those travel times to some lengthy and challenging hikes of the island's interior, making a visit to Gorgona an all-day affair.

GIGLIO ★★

The second-largest of the Tuscan islands, Isola del Giglio, lies at the southern end of the archipelago and is a favorite summertime haunt of Romans who want to unplug and unwind surrounded by unspoiled nature—and just the right amount of rustic civilization. *Il Giglio,* as it's known to Italians, may mean "lily," but the island wasn't named for a flower. The etymology actually goes back to the Greek *Aegylon*—"Place of Goats"—for the animals that once thrived on the island's rocky contours. Giglio is composed almost entirely of granite, out of whose cracks and crevices pine groves and dense *macchia mediterranea* shrubs have grown, or been reforested, over time.

On a map, the 24 sq. km (9-sq.-mile) island is shaped like a dill pickle trying to hitch a ride. The "thumb" of the western coast sits just below the broad sandy bay of Campese, and several sandy coves are on the east coast, to the north and south of Porto. The rest of Giglio's bumpy shoreline is composed of rocky palisades and inlets, many of which are only accessible by boat. In summer, the beaches get crowded, making a boat tour around the island (on your own or with an organized excursion) a must to escape the hordes. Giglio is the next most visited island after Elba, though it's a distant second.

The island's three *centri abitati* (towns) are arranged in a mostly straight line from east to west. On the east coast, Giglio Porto is a delightful little harbor town, where pastel blocks of waterfront buildings are backed by steep hills covered with vineyards where grapes for the local *Ansonaco* wine are grown (see "It'll Put Hair on Your Chest," p. 155). Porto is where the ferries land and where most of the sea-oriented activities on Giglio are organized. In the middle of the island, Castello tells the medieval history of Giglio with its narrow streets and Pisan fortification walls. Castello is the administrative center of both Giglio and Giannutri, and a real Tuscan hill town, with all the architecture, breathtaking vistas, charm, and gastronomy that implies. The more modern tourist development of Campese, on the west coast, was built behind the eponymous bay that boasts the island's biggest and best beach, a wide crescent of beautiful, orange-tinged sand.

Everything else on the island is fairly wild and rugged. Twelve hiking paths "spiderweb" over the island, covering terrain both exposed and mountainous or flat and sheltered under the sea pines. Giglio is green and aromatic year-round, but in spring, visitors are treated to an explosion of wildflowers in the *macchia* scrub that blankets the island's slopes. Offshore, Giglio's emerald waters teem with marine life, and diving is a popular pursuit here. The particularly untamed southwestern coast of the island is protected territory of the Tuscan Islands National Park.

Though Giglio is not overtly glamorous and anyone will feel welcome here, it still attracts an understatedly chic crowd. International and Italian VIPs frequent the island, so keep your eyes peeled for tanned and toned stars of the soccer field and screen.

Porto Santo Stefano, on the Monte Argentario promontory, is the jumping-off point for Isola del Giglio: The island's proximity to this popular resort, combined with frequent ferries and Giglio's manageable size, make it feasible as a day trip, albeit a long one, from Rome, southern Tuscany, and even parts of Umbria. Giglio, in turn, is the main base for day trips to Giannutri (p. 157).

Essentials

GETTING THERE Isola del Giglio is connected to Porto Santo Stefano (on the Argentario peninsula, 2 hr. by car from Rome or Siena) by **MareGiglio,** in Giglio Porto at Via Umberto 1 (© **0564/812920;** www.maregiglio.it), and **Toremar** (in Porto Santo Stefano, © **0564/810803;** in Giglio Porto, © **0564/809349;** www. toremar.it). The trip takes about an hour and costs 10€ each way. In summer, there are up to 15 boats per day; off season, there are at least three daily sailings. Maregiglio also runs a few boats per week between Giglio and Giannutri (1 hr., 9.50€ each way). From mid-July through the end of August, a permit is required to bring a car to Giglio (inquire with your hotel or apartment agency when booking, or call the Comune of Isola del Giglio at © **0564/806064**). Normally, this just means paying a small extra fee to the ferry company.

GETTING AROUND Though Giglio's main towns are served by reliable buses, a **car** gives you more freedom to explore those paved and dirt roads not served by public transportation (see "Getting There," above). Upon arrival, you can rent a car from **Andrea Ansaldo,** Giglio Porto (© **340/8732865**). Andrea also rents scooters, or you can try **Giglio Multiservizi,** Via Umberto I, 26, Giglio Porto (©**0564/809056**). Buses, which link the three towns of Porto, Castello, and Campese, are run by **Autolinee Brizzi** (© **0564/807620;** www.autolineebrizzi.it). Buses run in the evening, although not as frequently. At night, **taxis** are often a necessity, since most of the evening action is in Castello, and not within walking distance of most hotels; expect to pay between 10€ and 15€ for trips between Porto and Castello or Campese and Castello. Some numbers to try are © 340/8732865; 338/9706950; 347/1941888; or 330/731424. Giglio is small, and the cabbies tend to be the same guys who rent cars and scooters.

Handy boat service to the beaches (10€ round-trip, or 5€ one-way) is offered all day from 8am to 7pm from the **Boatmen** (www.boatmen.it) kiosk next to the ferry landing in Porto. When, in high season, the beaches are overcrowded, the guys at Boatmen will also take you to secluded coves where you can throw a towel on the smooth granite and have a back-to-nature day of sun and surf. Private taxi-boat service can also be arranged from Boatmen at Giglio Porto to anywhere on the island; you can usually just find their orange kiosk at the harbor, but if you want to book their services in advance, give Mauro a call at © **349/3508493.** In summer, Boatmen offers a 2½-hour *giro isola* island circumnavigation tour (20€) around Giglio (departure from and return to Porto), with a stop for swimming. You can also rent your own small *gozzo* or *gommone* at Porto; expect to pay about 50€ for a half-day's rental, which is plenty of time to cruise around the island's perimeter, stopping at various coves for swimming and picnicking along the way. There are numerous agencies—just look for signs marked *noleggio barche*—but Alvino (© **347/0547755**) at Boatmen is a good place to start.

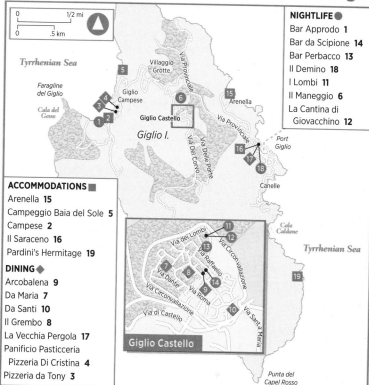

NIGHTLIFE●
Bar Approdo **1**
Bar da Scipione **14**
Bar Perbacco **13**
Il Demino **18**
I Lombi **11**
Il Maneggio **6**
La Cantina di
  Giovacchino **12**

ACCOMMODATIONS■
Arenella **15**
Campeggio Baia del Sole **5**
Campese **2**
Il Saraceno **16**
Pardini's Hermitage **19**

DINING◆
Arcobalena **9**
Da Maria **7**
Da Santi **10**
Il Grembo **8**
La Vecchia Pergola **17**
Panificio Pasticceria
  Pizzeria Di Cristina **4**
Pizzeria da Tony **3**

VISITOR INFORMATION The **Pro Loco Giglio** office is at Giglio Porto
(© **0564/809400;** www.isoladelgiglio.biz). Pick up the indispensable *Pro Loco Isola
del Giglio* map, which is marked with hiking paths, elevations, and the principal coves
and beaches for boating and swimming.

Exploring the Island

The island has three towns—Porto, Castello, and Campese—which is the order in
which you're likely to experience them. A bus, operated by Autolinee Brizzi (www.
autolineebrizzi.it) connects all three; the one-way ticket costs 1.80€, and each leg of
the trip takes 15 minutes (for example, Porto to Castello and Castello to Campese).

Ferries land at **Porto,** the busy harbor town with pastel-colored palazzi lining the
waterfront. Any and all waterborne activities can be organized from Porto, and it has
several lovely spots where you can eat and drink along the lively seafront promenade.
Nearby, the remains of a Roman villa are visible just beneath the water surface. **Castello** is the historic heart of Giglio; at an altitude of 405m (1,329 ft.) and 6km (4
miles) inland from Porto, it still preserves its citadel feel and has charming medieval
alleys, arches, and stairs around every turn. Castello is also the epicurean center of
the island, boasting the island's greatest concentration of high-quality restaurants,

wine bars, and nightlife. Island tourism is **Campese**'s raison d'être. This laid-back town on Giglio's western coast was developed in the 1970s around a picturesque crescent of golden sand that terminates in the north with the historic Torre del Campese. The watchtower was built to guard against the pirate invasions that plagued Giglio for centuries. The last pirates the island ever saw, Saracens from Tunisia, were repelled in 1799. The tower has been restored, but it's a private residence not open to visitors. Campese offers plenty of watersports and a few casual spots for eating and drinking, and—since it faces west—this is a prime place to be for a cocktail at sunset.

Of course, as an island with 28km (17 miles) of coastline and only two coastal towns, much of Giglio can only be seen from the sea. A **round-the-island tour** with Boatmen (see "Getting Around," p. 150) will point out all the most interesting geological features and, weather permitting, include several stops for swimming, well away from the typically crowded beaches of Arenella, Cannelle, Caldane, and Campese. If you decide to go for a **small boat rental** and circumnavigate Giglio yourself, a highlight is the western coast of the island, south of Campese. This part of the island is National Park, providing a stunning backdrop of forested cliffs for your swim or bob in secluded, crystalline waters. The sculpted granite platforms at **Punta del Capel Rosso,** at the southern tip of Giglio, are a favored spot for nude sunbathing and swimming.

Outdoor Pursuits

BEACHES Giglio has only four main beaches; consequently, in high season, don't expect to have much peace, quiet, or room on the sand for your arsenal of magazines and sun products. In July and August, it's far better to rent a boat and go exploring the lesser coves that dot the perimeter of Giglio, where you're likely to have a bit more privacy and beautiful cerulean waters for swimming. **Spiaggia di Campese ★★** is the largest beach, located in the eponymous tourist development on Giglio's western coast. This is the only real beach on the *ponente* (sunset) side of the island and has spectacular sunsets over its reddish-tinged sand. Campese has beach clubs as well as free public access stretches. **Cala delle Cannelle ★★** is the best beach on the eastern side of Giglio and is the second largest after Campese. Accessible via a 20-minute walk south from Giglio Porto, or by sea on one of the taxi boats bobbing in the harbor there, Cannelle is renowned for its clear, practically Caribbean-turquoise water. Portions of Cannelle have free beach access; the rest is taken over by beach clubs and their snack bars. A bit farther south from Cannelle (10 min. by foot; or take a water taxi from Cannelle or Porto), **Caldane ★** is a small cove of variegated greens and blues and usually less crowded than Campese or Cannelle. **Arenella ★** is a small beach with fine, reflective golden sand (made from granite particles) north of the port. Arenella is a bit of a trek on foot (and you have to walk on the side of a road that gets heavy car traffic in summer); instead, take a taxi or *barcaiolo* (water taxi) from Porto. Note that in peak season, tiny Arenella is taken over by the blue beach chairs and umbrellas of the *stabilimento* here, which tranquillity-seekers should avoid at all costs.

DIVING Blessed with the same pure and clean waters as nearby Giannutri and Elba, Giglio has about a dozen dive sites all around its perimeter. From rock walls crawling with lobsters and wriggling with eels to beds of vivid coral, sea sponges, all have great visibility. Other creatures you're likely to encounter while diving off Giglio are dentex (*dentice*), scorpionfish (*scorfano*), barracuda, and larger pelagic fish like tuna, which can reach 3m (10 ft.) in length even close to shore! In spring and summer, whether underwater or on a boat, it's not uncommon to spy passing dolphins and sperm whales. In Giglio Porto, **International Diving,** Via del Saraceno 60 (② **347/2461704;** www.internationaldiving.it), and **Max Shark,** Via San Lorenzo 13 (② **329/8022737;** www.maxshark.it), rent equipment and organize diving excursions; in Campese, try **Giglio Diving Club,** Via della Torre Campese (② **0564/804065**). Prices (which always include basic equipment) start at 30€ for a single dive, 75€ for a full-day excursion to Giannutri or to the interesting rock islets to the north known as the *Formiche di Grosseto.*

HIKING The Pro Loco office publishes a map of Giglio's 12 hiking paths (ask for the *cartina sentieri per trekking*), some of which are dirt trails, while others are paved-but-narrow roads, so be careful of vehicular traffic. The longest hike (6km/3.75 miles, up and over the central, panoramic ridge of the island) goes along the asphalt road from Castello, in the center of Giglio, to **Punta del Capel Rosso,** the southern extremity of the island. From Campese, a great picnic hike is the short 30-minute walk to the **Faraglione** (offshore rock stack), a few kilometers to the south. The other trails on Giglio are mostly easy- or medium-level hikes varying in length from 1.5km to 4.5km (1–2.75 miles). As always in the Italian islands, bring plenty of water and sun protection.

Where to Stay

Many real estate agencies book vacation rentals on Giglio. One of the most well-established agencies, with a strong local presence, is **Agenzia Baffigi** (② **0564/804140;** www.isolagiglio.com); as is standard on Italian islands, the minimum stay in summer is 1 week. The **Pro Loco office** (p. 151) can put you in touch with islanders who rent out individual apartments and rooms.

Arenella ★ 🏄 With an emphasis on serenity and well-being, Arenella is a cut above your typical midrange holiday isle hotel. Rooms are tranquil and subtly nautical, with sailcloth slipcovers, white walls, and hardwood floors. Most units have small balconies that look out over Arenella Bay, as does the panoramic terrace, where you can sip freshly made herbal infusions or a nice cold beer. Despite its clean and modern look, this is not a full-service resort, and, if you don't have a scooter, plan on taxis or half-hour hikes to town or the nearest beach.

Località Arenella 5 (3km/2 miles north of Giglio Porto). ② **0564/809340.** www.hotelarenella.com. 27 units. Doubles 90€–155€. Rates include buffet breakfast. AE, DC, MC, V. Minimum stay of 1 week from mid-July to Aug 31. Free parking. Closed Oct–Mar. **Amenities:** Restaurant; bar; terrace. *In room:* A/C, satellite TV, hair dryer, Wi-Fi (fee).

Campeggio Baia del Sole Facing the sunset, this campground north of the modern town of Campese has numerous shady terraces, set amid wild Mediterranean scrub and trees, where you can pitch a tent or park a camper. Cabin- or yurt-style bungalows (that is, walls, roof, and a door, but no bathroom or kitchen fixtures) are also available.

Località Sparavieri, just north of Giglio Campese. ② **0564/804036.** www.campingbaiadelsole.net. 6.80€–9.30€ per person; tent spaces 6.50€–19€. Bungalows (2–3 persons) 34€–62€. No credit cards. Open from Easter period through Sept. Free parking. **Amenities:** Bar; minimarket; hot showers; free Wi-Fi.

Campese ★ You'll find a warm holiday atmosphere at this honest, family-run two-star ("basic" in the Italian hospitality rating system) in seaside Campese. Its location, directly on the orange sand beach, makes it well suited for those who plan on a lot of sunbathing and water activities. Guests have free access to the hotel's own private stretch of beach, but you'll pay extra for sun chairs, umbrellas, and so forth. Half-board is mandatory, and the panoramic restaurant does a good job with standard pastas, pizzas, sandwiches, and salads.

Via della Torre 18, Giglio Campese. ✆ **0564/804003.** www.hotelcampese.com. 39 units. Doubles 150€–200€ (half-board). AE, MC, V. Free parking. **Amenities:** Restaurant; bar; games; library; free Internet station in lobby; TV lounge; pets allowed; seafront terrace. *In room:* A/C, TV, hair dryer, minibar.

Il Saraceno ★★ Boasting a wonderful seaside position just outside the busy town of Giglio Porto, and seeming to emerge from the rocks below, this is one of the most charming hotels on the island. This particular real estate was selected by the Romans, who built a villa here 2,000 years ago—remnants of its construction and decoration are visible around the hotel. The Saraceno is no design star, but the hodge-podge maritime decor nonetheless feels homey and comfortable. You'll pay a little extra for rooms with a sea view. The hotel's cordial staff is a major asset, providing invaluable assistance in helping you plan your time or arrange excursions.

Via del Saraceno 69, Giglio Porto. ✆ **0564/809006.** www.saracenohotel.it. 48 units. Doubles 75€–140€. Rates include buffet breakfast. MC, V. **Amenities:** Restaurant; bar; TV lounge; billiards; private sea access (no beach). *In room:* A/C, TV, hair dryer, minibar.

Pardini's Hermitage ★★ Pay attention to the second word in this place's name: If you like isolation and eccentricity, you'll be in heaven. If on the other hand you like to be in the thick of things, you'll hate Pardini's. A glance at the rather extraordinary lineup of "amenities" below—donkey rides? *Check*—gives you an idea of the kind of atmosphere you'll find at this beloved oddball inn, in the woods above the sea. The structure itself is a 1950s villa set high above a rocky, forested cove only accessible by sea or mule trail. (They'll send a motorboat to pick you up from the ferry terminal at Porto. Once you've landed, a donkey spirits you up a long stepped path to the villa, while your bags arrive via motorized pulley.) Guest rooms are wonderfully cozy though not very large, but Pardini's extensive grounds are especially well endowed when it comes to places to relax and enjoy solitude and nature. Or not—the place offers activities galore, and they even have their own farm, which produces olive oil, flour, vegetables, and goat's milk (in the form of cheese and yogurt), all of which are served in the estate's restaurant.

Cala degli Alberi, 5km (3 miles) south of Giglio Porto. ✆ **0564/809034.** www.hermit.it. 15 units. Doubles (with half-board) 240€–350€; full-board 270€–380€. **Amenities:** Restaurant; bar; lounge; fitness room; seawater Jacuzzi; library; arts and craft supplies; dance floor; donkey rides; fishing rods; games; sea access; yoga/meditation space. *In room:* A/C, TV, free Wi-Fi.

Where to Dine

The majority of the island's good restaurants are in Castello, though there are a number of locales in Porto with lovely waterfront atmosphere. Campese is more casual, with a few *pizzerie* and take-away joints.

Arcobalena ★★ GIGLIESE The Carfagna family has been running this adorable little spot, on an alley in Castello, for 2 decades. Their winning formula is simple—high-quality fresh ingredients, homemade everything, and great service. Arcobalena has plenty to offer in the way of fish, but it's also an excellent place to try local vegetables and other "turf" specialties of the island. In addition to the small indoor dining room, a handful of tables are set up in the characteristic little *piazzetta* outside.

Via Vittorio Emanuele 48, Castello. ☎ **0564/806106.** Reservations recommended in season. Entrees 12€–18€. MC, V. Daily noon–3pm, 7:30–11:30pm; closed Tues off season. Closed 2 weeks in Dec and Mar.

Da Maria ★★ SEAFOOD   This is one of the most elegant restaurants on the island (along with Da Santi, below), specializing in fresh seafood and homemade stuffed pastas like ravioli with shrimp. The *tagliatelle alla granseola* are perfection, letting the subtle flavor of the crab shine through without any unnecessary flourishes. The restaurant is also renowned for its *spigola al sale,* a *secondo* of sea bass baked in a salt crust. Save room for dessert: Maria's fruit-based *dolci* are the best on the island. Service is cordial and efficient.

Via Casamatta 12, Castello. ☎ **0564/806062.** www.ristorantedamaria.it. Reservations required in season. Entrees 12€–22€. Prix-fixe seafood menu 34€–45€. AE, DC, MC, V. Thurs–Tues noon–3pm and 7:30–11pm. Closed Jan and Feb.

Da Santi ★★ SEAFOOD   Its panoramic dining room, with a huge glassed-in veranda that seems suspended in mid-air, would be enough to sell you on this place. The cuisine also happens to be breathtaking, so come hungry. Start with an antipasto of octopus and shrimp in balsamic vinegar, then try a splurge-y *primo* of linguine *all'astice* (lobster) with vegetables. If you still have room for a *secondo,* it's tough to make a decision, but you'll sample the simple flavors and bounty of Giglio with a baked or grilled whole fish served with seasonal vegetables.

Via Marconi 20, Castello. ☎ **0564/806188.** Reservations required in season. Entrees 13€–20€. AE, DC, MC, V. Tues–Sun 12:30–3pm and 7:30–11pm. Closed Feb.

Il Grembo ★ GIGLIESE   The "Lap" has an obsession with detail and top-quality ingredients, as evident in antipasti like seafood salad—a tantalizing array of fresh shrimp, octopus, calamari, and parsley, glistening with lemon and the best olive oil you've ever tasted. Pastas (like *taglierini* with shrimp, carrot, and zucchini) and risottos are also phenomenal, and everything is beautifully presented. For optimal romance, opt for a table on the stepped side alley outside the restaurant.

Via Cecchi 30, Castello. ☎ **0564/806145.** Reservations required in season. Entrees 12€–18€. AE, DC, MC, V. Tues–Sun 12:30–3pm and 7:30–11pm. Closed Dec 10–Jan 30.

La Vecchia Pergola ★★ GIGLIESE   A pretty terrace on the water, *cucina casalinga* (simple, home-style cooking), and warm ambience make this the top choice for a meal at Porto. Local fresh seafood is offered, as are plates from mainland Maremma, Tuscany's cowboy country (so, they have great meat, too). Desserts are strictly homemade, and the wine list is comprehensive in every price range.

Via Thaon de Revel 31, Porto. ☎ **0654/809080.** Reservations required in season. Entrees 12€–18€. Fri–Wed noon–3pm and 7:30–11pm.

A Luxury Layover on the Argentario Peninsula

Ferries for the Tuscan islands of Il Giglio and Giannutri depart from the town of Porto Santo Stefano on the Argentario, a mountainous promontory that was once an island but became a peninsula (and thus was excluded from this book) several thousand years ago when silt deposits created three spits of land connecting it to mainland Italy. Island or not, the 60-sq.-km (37-sq.-mile) Argentario functions like one and is a favorite summer resort for stylish Romans and Tuscans. Its two towns, Porto Santo Stefano on the north side and Porto Ercole on the south side, are both picturesque villages with lively harbors and good seafood restaurants. When you're traveling through this peninsula on your way to Giglio or Giannutri, I recommend building in a few extra hours, whether for a meal or a driving tour along the *strada panoramica,* the dramatic coastal highway with glorious views of the southern part of the Tuscan archipelago.

If you really want to treat yourself well, book a night at the five-star **Hotel Il Pellicano ★★★,** a Relais & Chateaux property just outside Porto Ercole. Il Pellicano is truly one of the top 10 resorts in Italy, a place that makes even jaded globe-trotters smile with its luxurious amenities (including a restaurant with two Michelin stars and a state-of-the-art spa), gorgeous tableau (clusters of russet villas cascade down a private valley through panoramic terraces and a swimming pool to a glamorous bathing platform on the Med), inviting common areas, and above all, its genuinely warm, friendly staff, who make you feel like this slice of paradise is your home. For such a world-class hotel to feel so unpretentious yet deliver such impeccable hospitality is quite a rare feat in Europe. *Hotel Il Pellicano, Località Sbarcatello, 4km (2½ miles) west of Porto Ercole, Monte Argentario. ℂ 0564/858304. www. pellicanohotel.com. 50 units. Doubles 420€–865€. AE, DC, MC, V. Amenities: 2 restaurants; bar; fitness center; golf and horseback riding nearby; pool; room service; seaside swimming platform; spa; tennis; boat trips. In room: A/C, TV, DVD player, minibar, MP3 player, Wi-Fi (free).*

Panificio Pasticceria Pizzeria Di Cristina BAKERY/TAKE-AWAY The name says it all—bread, pastry, pizza—if you're looking to load up on delicious carbs, this busy little bakery in Campese is your spot. It's counter-service only, where pizza is sold by the slice, not the whole pie, and you can also get plain focaccia—perfect for eating on the beach while the sun goes down. The Gigliese baked good of note is *panficato* (literally "figged bread"), which is dough mixed with fresh figs.
Via Provinciale, Campese. ℂ **0564/804225.** Cash only. Daily 8am–midnight in summer.

Pizzeria da Tony ★ PIZZA Like an old friend, Tony's is cozy, buzzy, and friendly. On the beach in Campese, the pizzeria features Roman-style pies, cooked in a wood-burning oven. Try the seafood pizza (with calamari, mussels, and other marine critters), stick to classics like the *margherita* (tomato, mozzarella, and basil), or create your own—staff are happy to oblige. Pasta and panini available, too.
Via della Torre 13, Campese. ℂ **0564/806453.** Pizzas from 5€. MC, V. Mar–Nov 7:30am–midnight.

Giglio After Dark

The *locali* of Castello dominate the nightlife scene on Giglio, but to start out your evening, don't miss a sun-downer on the beach at Campese; it's the only west-facing waterside spot on the island. Watch the horizon turn pink and orange with a cocktail at **Bar Approdo,** Via di Mezzo Franco 2 (*©* **0564/804109**), directly on the sand at Campese. Up in Castello, elbow your way into **La Cantina di Giovacchino,** Piazza Lombi, Castello (*©* **0564/806001**), an atmospheric, multilevel (with panoramic terrace) wine and food bar, serving the robust Gigliese wine, *Ansonaco* (p. 155), as well as typical local salami and cheeses. **Bar Perbacco,** Piazza Gloriosa, Castello (*©* **335/377735**), is *the* place to be for *aperitivo,* while the younger, party-hardy crowd congregates at the steps outside **Bar Da Scipione.** Castello also has two *discoteche:* **Il Maneggio,** Località Il Pianello (*©* **377/1141435**), is a new open-air spot just outside the old town walls, and gay-friendly; in town, **I Lombi,** Via dei Lombi (*©* **347/5606601**), is an old-school Italian disco with cheesy summertime contests exalting the taut physiques of the Roman teens and 20-somethings who frequent the club.

Not to be left out, Porto has nighttime action, too, though more of the low-key variety. Try **Il Demino,** at Demo's Hotel, Via Thaon de Revel 31 (*©* **0564/809235**), on the beach facing the harbor.

GIANNUTRI ★

Half-moon-shaped Giannutri is the southernmost of the Tuscan islands and easily visited as a day trip from Porto Santo Stefano or Isola del Giglio, from which it is roughly equidistant (about 15km/9 miles). Its 260 hectares (642 acres) consist of an almost wholly unspoiled interior, and rocky cliffs with interesting coves and grottoes. The gorgeous sea and a coastline that drops off to reveal dramatic underwater scapes (including some cool shipwrecks) make Giannutri an especially popular destination for divers. In summer, the wide natural harbor formed by the island's curved shape is freckled with boats big and small, most visiting from other islands in the archipelago. Although Giannutri is 100% parkland of the Parco Nazionale Arcipelago Toscano, much of the island is privately owned and, in summer, it's taken over by an exclusive colony of wealthy wannabe Robinson Crusoes from the Italian mainland.

The island is a mass of jagged calcareous limestone, made less harsh by a thick blanket of *macchia mediterranea.* On walks through the interior, you'll inhale the aromas of wildflowers and herbs that grow rampant. On the northwest part of Giannutri, there are significant ruins of a Roman villa; dating from the 1st to 2nd centuries A.D., it most likely belonged to the prominent family of the Domitii Aheno-barbi, of which emperor Nero was a very notorious progeny.

There are no hotels or campsites on Giannutri, just a very small number of vacation-rental apartments and villas that need to be booked well in advance. Giannutri has two restaurants and a grocery store, but it's a good idea to bring your own essential provisions like water and sunscreen.

Essentials

Giannutri is connected by regular ferry to Porto Santo Stefano, in the Argentario peninsula. **MareGiglio,** based in Isola del Giglio, Via Umberto 1 (*©* **0564/812920;** www.maregiglio.it), runs the boats. Tickets are 9.50€ each way and the journey takes about an hour. In summer, there are daily departures from Porto Santo Stefano at 10 or 10:30am. (The return boats from Giannutri leave at 4:30pm.) In May, September, and October, there are four to six boats per week (always with weekend service), usually leaving Porto Santo Stefano at 10am. From November to March, service is greatly reduced, with only a few boats per week to Giannutri.

Though they aren't an official transportation link, there are private excursion boats at least once per day in summer from Giglio Porto on Isola del Giglio to Giannutri (a short trip of about 45 min.). In fact, Giannutri is more commonly visited as a day trip from Giglio than from Porto Santo Stefano. **Vegastar** (*©* **335/7589445;** www. veganavi.it) operates connections between Giannutri and Giglio as well as Porto Santo Stefano. Ferries (12€–14€ one-way) run daily from mid-June to mid-September and several times per week from the Easter period through mid-October. Service is suspended the rest of the year.

Note that from mid-May through the end of October on Giannutri, the National Park service imposes an island entrance fee of 3€ per person and a limit on the number of visitors allowed on Giannutri at any given time—a maximum of 300 persons per day. To visit certain protected land zones, even more restrictions apply: You must go with a guide in groups of no more than 25 persons. For more information on guided visits of Giannutri, contact licensed park guide **Marina Aldi** (*©* **0564/806096** or 328/0244996; aldimarina@virgilio.it).

Exploring the Island

Unless you're here for the diving, you'll only need to allow a few hours to "do" Giannutri—that is, hike the island end to end, go for a swim, and maybe have a bite or drink at one of the island's two restaurants.

Giannutri has two boat landing sites, **Cala dello Spalmatoio** in the northeast (along the inner curve of the half-moon) and **Cala Maestra,** where the ferries land; this is a naturally protected notch along the northwest, or outer curve of Giannutri. These harbors are also where the only swimming **beaches** are; they're pebbly, but the water is splendid. A short walk from Cala Maestra puts you at the ruins of the **Roman villa ★** (always open; free) that was built on the panoramic terrace, surrounded by Aleppo pines, 1,900 years ago by the descendants of Nero, the Domitius Ahenobarbus family. The most salient feature of the site are several marble columns with Corinthian capitals standing around an *impluvium* (basin for collecting rainwater); fragments of black-and-white mosaics represent marine deities and creatures, and the extensive masonry of the villa's substructure and canals for water distribution still remain.

Cala dello Spalmatoio is where most of the "action" is on Giannutri, although of course that's a relative term—but this is where you'll find a bar serving coffee, snacks, and alcohol; a restaurant/pizzeria; and a general store.

Many grottoes dot the island's rocky coastline, which is accessible only by sea, so inquire about informal boat tours at the port when you arrive. Unlike the other larger Tuscan islands, you can't easily rent boats on Giannutri for self-piloted exploration. The most famous area for grottoes is the aptly named **Cala dei Grottoni ★★** (Cove of the Big Grottoes) along the curtainlike rock wall of Giannutri's southernmost tip.

Outdoor Pursuits

DIVING   It may be tiny, but Giannutri has some of the best diving in the Med. Rich marine flora and fauna include vast "prairies" of *posidonia* (Mediterranean sea grass), coral, sponges, sea urchins, seahorses, starfish, amberjack, grouper, lobster, and, on rare occasions, turtles and dolphins. The island's 11km (7-mile) coastline is riddled with crevices and grottoes that make for spectacular underwater viewing. At **Punta Secca,** two cannons from an 18th-century galleon rest 50m (164 ft.) below on the seafloor. Near Cala Maestra, you can dive among the **wreck of the *Nasim II* ★★**, a 69m (228-ft.) freighter that hit the rocks and sank here in 1976. It was carrying 49 cars and 16 tow trucks, and much of the cargo—that which wasn't looted in the immediate aftermath of the accident—remains strewn on the seafloor between 33m and 60m (108 ft.–197 ft.). At **Cala Ischaiola,** you can dive down to the shipwreck of the ***Anna Bianca,*** a cargo vessel that went down in a matter of minutes in 1971. The **Archetti** (natural rock arches, 10m/33 ft. below the surface) are another popular spot with wonderful light effects, and eels and scorpionfish among the cracks.

A number of Argentario-based diving operators organize excursions to Giannutri. Try **Argentario Divers,** Piazza San Sebastiano 60, Porto Ercole (✆ **0564/832024;** www.argentariodivers.it), or **Abisso Blu,** Via Marconi 66, Porto Santo Stefano (✆ **333/ 3826314;** www.abissoblu.it).

HIKING   Giannutri's small size and relative flatness (the highest point is 88m/289 ft. above sea level) make it attractive for even reluctant walkers. Much of Giannutri, even the wildest terrain overgrown with *macchia,* is privately owned, but there are two perpendicular paths open to the public.

Where to Stay & Dine

Those with hopes of experiencing Giannutri's blessedly silent nights should plan well in advance; the number of beds here is extremely limited, and there are no hotels or campsites. Everything listed below shuts down from mid-October until Easter.

In Cala dello Spalmatoio, **La Torre** (✆ **0564/898892**) is a touristic complex comprising a restaurant/pizzeria, coffee bar, and gelateria; they also rent rooms on the island. The only other place to eat is over in Cala Maestra, at the restaurant **Taverna del Granduca** (✆ **0564/898890** or 0564/898421), a rustic joint with straightforward Tuscan seafood classics. Signor Morbidelli, owner of the taverna, is also an incomparable resource about all things Giannutri-related and can often help arrange overnight accommodations. **Le Dimore di Mimmina** (✆ **335/5878295** or 0575/ 410982; www.ledimoredimimmina.com) has two apartments in a private setting near the Roman villa, immersed in *macchia,* prickly pears, and agave plants. At both La Torre and Le Dimore di Mimmina, expect to pay about 150€ per room per night in high season, with minimum stay requirements.

MONTECRISTO

Legend has it that, before being taken by pirates in the 16th century, the monks who lived on Montecristo stashed away an unimaginable sum of gold somewhere on the island. The supposed existence of that lost treasure gave rise to Alexandre Dumas's *The Count of Montecristo* (his protagonist, Edmond Dantès, finds and uses the gold to exact his revenge on those who imprisoned him falsely). Thanks to that novel, Montecristo's name is internationally known, but forget any fantasies you might have of finding the monks' gold: The island is a biogenetic nature reserve (pretty much off-limits to humans) of the Tuscan Islands National Park. A view of its hauntingly jagged outline several kilometers away, from southern Elba or western Giglio, is as close as you're likely to get. Visits are strictly limited to 1,000 persons per year, who must demonstrate scientific or academic reasons for wanting to go ashore, and there is currently a 2-year waiting list to join one of the Forestry Service's guided tours.

To visit Montecristo, send a written request to the **Corpo Forestale dello Stato** at one of two addresses (this being Italian bureaucracy, it's better to cast your net wide): **Ufficio Territoriale Biodiversità di Follonica,** Via Bicocchi 2, 58022 Follonica, Italy (© **0566/40019,** fax 0566/44616; utb.follonica@corpoforestale.it), or **Ispettorato Generale del Corpo Forestale dello Stato Servizio V,** Via G. Carducci 5, 00187 Roma, Italy (© **06/4881804**). Then, wait about 2 years; if you ever make it to the island, leave an ex-voto for old St. Mamilianus as a thank-you.

TREMITI ISLANDS

The tiny Tremiti ★★ (pronounced *Treh*-mi-ti), with a whopping 310 hectares (766 acres) among them, are the only Italian islands in the Adriatic, a sea whose coast tends to be drearier than the Tyrrhenian. The Tremiti are a shining exception, however, presenting incredible natural beauty, significant history, and a laid-back vacation atmosphere. Although they're packed to the gills in August, the Tremiti still feel like a relaxing getaway from civilization. No one is here to parade his or her designer beachwear, and most of your time will be spent bobbing in rented *gommoni* (small boats), picnicking in rocky coves, and swimming in bright turquoise waters. After a requisite romp through the castle-monastery of Santa Maria a Mare, it's all about nature and the sea on the Tremiti.

The islands of the Tremiti—San Domino, San Nicola, and the uninhabited Caprara (aka Capraia)—are 20km (13 miles) north of the Gargano promontory, the "spur" of boot-shaped Italy. The Gargano itself is a National Park, and the Tremiti are a Natural Marine Reserve within that park. The transparent waters teem with marine life, making the archipelago very popular with divers of all skill levels, and the main tourist island of San Domino is so naturally gorgeous that it has rightly earned the marketing nickname of *Perla dell'Adriatico* ("Pearl of the Adriatic"). Pinewoods act as a canopy for a prolific *macchia mediterranea,* thick with fragrant junipers, capers, rosemary, and myrtle, while the squiggly coast is dotted with picturesque coves.

Its imposing abbey-fortress complex has made **San Nicola** the historic heart of the Tremiti, and it's still where most of the islands' year-round residents live. Off season, the population of the Tremiti goes down to about 400 souls, most of whom are descended from fishermen (or mobsters and ladies of ill-repute, depending on which version you believe) from Naples. To this day, the local dialect on the islands is much more Neapolitan than Pugliese, and the islands' restaurants turn out dishes that have more in common with the Campanian tradition than with the cuisine of Puglia.

Just 500m (1,640 ft.) across the water from San Nicola, verdant **San Domino** is the largest of the group and has most of the tourist infrastructure. This is where most ferries call and where all but one of the islands' overnight accommodations are located. San Domino's 7km (4⅓-mile) perimeter is a series of lovely inlets—though only a few sandy beaches—

A Homeric Connection

The *tremitesi* and many a Classical scholar believe that the Homeric warrior-hero Diomedes lived out his final days on the Tremiti islands, which were in antiquity once known as the Insulae Diomedeae. A more imaginative version of the legend is that the islands were created when the hero tossed a few pebbles into the Adriatic. An ancient Greek tomb is in fact preserved on the island of San Nicola and is venerated to this day as the *Tomba di Diomede*. It gets even more colorful: When Diomedes died, Aphrodite (Venus) turned his grief-stricken companions into birds that would guard his tomb. These birds, so the story goes, are the *diomedee*, or shearwaters *(calonectris diomedea)* that still breed and nest in the Tremiti. On evenings in the breeding season, you can hear their plaintive calls, which sound uncannily similar to the cry of a baby or the mew of a cat in heat.

that make for wonderful swimming. Although many of the coves can be reached on foot, the best way to discover San Domino's coastal treasures is by boat.

Caprara, just north of San Nicola, is generally considered the third and final Tremiti island (the others, Cretaccio and Pianosa, are usually dismissed as mere *scogli*, or rock outcrops). Though uninhabited, its unique rock formations make it a popular destination for boaters and swimmers. **Cretaccio** is a clay outcrop between the ports of San Domino and San Nicola, and far-flung **Pianosa** (another 20km/13 miles from the other islands) is a desolate platform where only the seagulls alight.

STRATEGIES FOR SEEING THE ISLANDS

The Tremiti are bite-size islands and very close together; whether you rent your own small motorboat, use a water taxi, or take one of the organized boat tours offered, you're bound to get a comprehensive look at each of the islands, even if you're only here for a couple of days.

The Tremiti islands' tourist season runs from May to October, though a handful of hotels and restaurants are open year-round. In the height of summer, the Tremiti aren't exactly a bargain; but if you come in the shoulder season (June and Sept, when it's still plenty warm), hotel prices drop (a 200€ room goes for 100€ or lower), and the islands exude even more relaxation and romance.

ESSENTIALS

Getting There

The closest Italian mainland (20km/13 miles away) is Puglia's Gargano promontory, where the towns of Vieste, Peschici, Manfredonia, and Rodi Garganico have ferry service in summer to the Tremiti. The ports of Pescara, Ortona, and Vasto, in Abruzzo, also offer sea connections to the Tremiti; but by far the most comprehensive (and only year-round) service to the islands is from **Termoli,** on the coast of Molise. Termoli is a 3-hour drive (or 5-hr. train ride, with connections) from Rome. Cars cannot

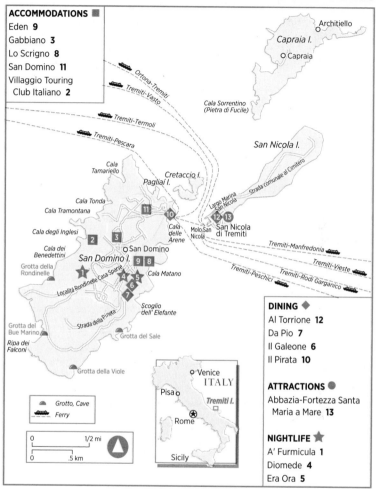

ACCOMMODATIONS
Eden **9**
Gabbiano **3**
Lo Scrigno **8**
San Domino **11**
Villaggio Touring
  Club Italiano **2**

Architiello
Capraia I.
Capraia

Ortona-Tremiti
Tremiti-Vasto

Cala Sorrentino
(Pietra di Fucile)

Tremiti-Termoli

San Nicola I.

Tremiti-Pescara

Cala
Tamariello
Pagliaí I.
Cretaccio I.

Cala Tonda
Cala Tramontana

Largo Marina
San Nicola
Strada comunale al Cimitero

Cala degli Inglesi

Cala
delle
Arene
Molo San
Nicola
San Nicola
di Tremiti

Cala dei
Benedettini
San Domino I.
San Domino

Tremiti-Manfredonia

Grotta della
Rondinelle
Cala Matano
Tremiti-Vieste

Località Rondinelle Casa Sparse

Tremiti-Peschici
Tremiti-Rodi Garganico

Scoglio
dell' Elefante

Grotta del
Bue Marino
Strada della Pineta
Grotta del Sale

Ripa dei
Falconi

Grotta della Viole

DINING ◆
Al Torrione **12**
Da Pio **7**
Il Galeone **6**
Il Pirata **10**

ATTRACTIONS ●
Abbazia-Fortezza Santa
  Maria a Mare **13**

Grotto, Cave
Ferry

Venice
ITALY
Pisa
Tremiti I.
Rome
Sicily

0   1/2 mi
0   .5 km

NIGHTLIFE ★
A' Furmicula **1**
Diomede **4**
Era Ora **5**

be taken to the Tremiti; leave your car at **Autoparcheggio del Porto** (✆ 0875/
703345), at the port in Termoli.

From Termoli, several different companies, with fast ferries or hydrofoils in summer in addition to traditional ferries, offer boat service to San Domino or San Nicola.
In high season, they make up to nine departures per day. The only year-round company between Termoli and the Tremiti, **Tirrenia** (✆ **0875/705343;** www.tirrenia.
it) has a fast ferry (45 min.) and slow ferry (1 hr., 40 min.) to San Domino. In summer
only, **Navigazione Libera del Golfo** (✆ **0875/704859;** www.nlg.it) has fast jets
and slower ferries (same travel times as Tirrenia) to San Domino and San Nicola;
Adriatic Shipping Lines (✆ **0875/705198**) has a hydrofoil (45 min.) and ferry
(1½ hr.) to San Nicola. Prices vary according to the season and speed of the boat, but

generally range from 13€ to 18€ per person, each way. Be aware that if you take a ferry that lands at San Nicola, you will most likely have to take a water taxi (from 5€, and sometimes a luggage fee is added) for the short distance across the water to San Domino, since that's where 99% of the accommodations are located.

You can also reach the Tremiti by **helicopter**—keep reading, it's affordable!—from Foggia (3 hr. by car or Eurostar train from Rome). The flights are operated by **Alidaunia** (☎ **0881/617961;** www.alidaunia.it) out of Foggia's Gino Lisa airport and land at the helipad on San Domino. Fares are 50€ each way in July and August (they knock 12% off this rate if you fly round-trip in these months), 25€ the rest of the year. Year-round, kids pay 50% and infants pay 10% of the normal fare. The Foggia airport tax of 10€, paid only on flights departing from Foggia, is extra. Arriving by helicopter is a very attractive option but must be booked well in advance for travel in summer; Alidaunia's AgustaWestland 139 is only a 15-seater. *Tip:* Be sure to pack light, as heavy bags will incur extra fees.

Getting Around

No automobiles are allowed on the Tremiti, but the islands are small enough to be explored on foot. Small buses connect the port of San Domino with the town in the central part of the island. However, most hotels and even campgrounds will send a minibus to pick up baggage-laden new arrivals at the port. To get between islands and putter around their coasts, your options are water taxis, organized boat tours that hit all the major coves and water-accessible attractions of the Tremiti, or small motorboat (*gommone*) rentals. About a dozen different outfits on San Domino and San Nicola offer these services. Water taxis cost between 5€ and 15€ per person, depending on the season and the distance traveled; small motorboat rentals cost between 70€ and 150€ for a full day, depending on the season. For water taxi service on San Domino, call **Sergio** (☎ **347/9387051**), **Da Tullio** (☎ **0882/463269** or 330/367320), or **Fabio** (☎ **349/3956021**). On San Nicola, water taxis are run by **Cooperativa A.Mar.Blu** (☎**0882/834487**). Da Tullio also rents *gommoni,* as does **Il Pirata** (☎**0882/463409**). Boat excursions—from the 1-hour *giro dell'isola* around San Domino to the 2-hour tour of San Domino, San Nicola, and Caprara—are easily arranged on the spot at the ports of either San Domino or San Nicola. Prices start at 7€ per person for the San Domino tour in a large boat.

Visitor Information

There are no local tourist board offices, but you can contact the Azienda di Promozione Turistica (APT), Via E. Perrone 17; 71000 Foggia (☎ **0881/723141;** www.pugliaturismo.com/aptfoggia) for brochures and maps. Several unofficial websites provide comprehensive information about the islands, but in Italian only. The best of these are www.leisoletremiti.it and www.tremiti.eu.

EXPLORING THE ISLANDS

The Tremiti consist of three main islands, two of which are inhabited: San Domino and San Nicola. The smaller boat trip destination of Caprara, where only wild rabbits live, is at the northeastern end of the group. Between the islands of San Domino and San Nicola, and acting as a natural bulwark for each of their ports, is the rock outcrop known as Il Cretaccio ("bad clay"). The islet is in fact made of clay and shaped like a heart-shaped locket that has been cleft down the middle. Another 20km/13 miles to the northeast, uninhabited Pianosa is the black sheep of the group, and not even included in some locals' list of the Tremiti. Except for Pianosa, the islands are very close together, making getting around by boat an easy and pleasurable way to see every nook and cranny.

To make things simple, think of each island in the Tremiti as having its own function: **San Domino** is where the hotels, hiking, and majority of beaches and swimming coves are; **San Nicola** is where you visit the fortress-sanctuary of Santa Maria a Mare and Diomedes' tomb; **Caprara** is where you take your boat (or a boat excursion takes you) to explore the natural arches and splendid inlets of its intricate coastline. Places to eat are on both San Domino and San Nicola.

San Domino

San Domino is the largest island (208 hectares/514 acres) and has the prettiest landscape. Its low limestone platform is covered with Aleppo pines and groves of ilex (holm oak), and its perimeter is a delightfully tortuous series of lovely coves where the limestone drops off ever so picturesquely to the sea. San Domino is much longer (2.8km/1¾ miles) than it is wide (1.7km/1 mile at its thickest point), with the port at the northeastern end and the town a 10-minute walk away, more or less in the center of the island. "Town" is a modern, laid-back affair consisting of hotels, vacation apartments, tourist residences, restaurants, and some shops and services, so don't worry about checking off any churches or other historic sights while you're here. Beyond the town, roads and trails lead to the wilder, southwest half of San Domino and to numerous inviting coves, otherwise accessible by sea. The pinewoods and dense shrubs of *macchia mediterranea* that cover the vast majority of San Domino offer the islands' only opportunity for hiking—although, given the gentle elevations (max 116m/381 ft. above sea level) and short distances, it's not so much rigorous hiking as a leisurely nature walk.

San Domino also has the Tremiti islands' only decent-size sandy beach, the 100m-long (328-ft.) **Cala delle Arene** ★, just south of the port. Cala delle Arene ("cove of the sands") is fully equipped with lounge chair and umbrella rental, but it's also overcrowded in summer. For swimming opportunities elsewhere on San Domino, it's all about the small *cale* (coves), natural inlets with interesting rock formations and calm, transparent water in shades running the gamut from light turquoise to almost purple. Many of these coves can be reached by pretty trails that descend down from the woods to water's edge (which may be a strip of pebbly sand or a smooth rock platform), but the easiest way to sample them all is by rental boat or a group boat excursion.

South of Cala delle Arene, **Cala Matano** ★★ is a gorgeous inlet with a small sandy beach backed by a sheer wall of white limestone and framed by pines that cling tenaciously to the rocks. This cove is accessible by land via a lovely trail that hairpins down from the woods above. Continuing south from Cala Matano, you'll see a rock outcrop known as **Scoglio dell'Elefante,** for its resemblance, if you let your eyes glaze over, to a pachyderm kneeling and drinking from the sea. Farther along is the **Grotta del Sale,** a sea cave where salt (*sale*) has piled up. Next up, don't miss the **Grotta delle Viole** ★, another small sea cave whose water takes on the most amazing violet tones, especially on summer mornings.

Rounding the southern tip of San Domino—the so-called Punta del Diavolo for the hellish sea conditions here in rough weather—and heading back up along the western coast, you'll soon arrive at the island's most celebrated cave, the enchanting

The Festival of Santissima Assunta

August can be downright mayhem in the Tremiti, but if you're here over Ferragosto (the national summer holiday, celebrated Aug 15), you're in for a treat, since August 14 to August 16 are also the *Festa Patronale della Santissima Assunta.* Over the 3-day event, an effigy of the Madonna is carried from the church on San Nicola, through the town streets, then over to San Domino and around the islands aboard a festively decorated fishing boat. On the evening of the 15th, a fireworks display goes off over the water and everyone feasts at a communal fish fry on San Nicola.

Grotta del Bue Marino ★★, named for the "sea-ox" or monk seals that used to make this their lair (the species is now almost extinct). At the end of the 75m-long (246-ft.), 6m-wide (20-ft.) grotto, there's a small sandy beach where you can picture pirates stashing treasure chests once upon a time, and throughout, the water takes on an electric-blue tone thanks to the peculiar light effects of the sun penetrating the water. You can swim in the cave as long as there aren't too many other boats around. The cliff outside the Grotta del Bue Marino is known as the **Ripa dei Falconi** and is famous as a nesting place for peregrine and Eleonora's falcons as well as *diomedee,* the shearwaters whose nocturnal calls sound like the wail of a child.

Farther up the western coast is another cave, **Grotta delle Rondinelle ★** (so named for the *rondine,* or robin, that nests here in spring), with a fat rock pilaster dividing its entrance into two archways. At sunset, the low rays of light create magical, polychrome effects on the water, walls, and ceiling of the cave. Next up are **Cala dei Benedettini** and **Cala degli Inglesi,** both coves with smooth rocks and protected waters that make them good swimming spots—and busy in high season. The pretty coves of **Cala della Tramontana** (part of which is Cala Tonda, almost wholly enclosed by the rocks as to form a sort of lake) and **Cala Tamariello** are also excellent for idling at anchor and swimming.

Punta del Diamante is the northernmost extremity of San Domino; a few hundred meters south, before reaching the port area, are striking rock formations known as the **Pagliai ★★** ("haystacks").They are a dramatic setting in which to swim or simply bob in your *gommone.* One of the *pagliai* is pierced by a narrow arch that you can swim or—very carefully—guide your boat through.

San Nicola

San Nicola is where the only major historical sights of the Tremiti are located. About a quarter of the size of San Domino, it is the municipal seat of the islands and where most of the full-time population lives. Its coastline consists mostly of limestone bluffs that plunge to the sea, with few suitable spots for swimming.

The principal draw on San Nicola is by far the abbey-fortress complex of **Santa Maria a Mare ★★**, Piazzetta Abbazia (© **0882/463063;** daily 10am–12:30pm and 5–10pm; 2€), which dominates the landscape of not only San Nicola but also the entire port area between San Nicola and San Domino. Its towers and fortification walls seem to rise right out of the chalky limestone cliffs, creating quite a formidable sight. The abbey was built in 1045, when the first Benedictine monks arrived on the island, but it was later enlarged, modified, and fortified over the centuries (the Benedictines were later replaced by Cistercian friars and then Lateran monks), though the overall architectural style remains fundamentally medieval. The monks of San Nicola enjoyed great power and prosperity, especially from the 15th to the 18th centuries, but the island's history as a religious stronghold was abruptly cut off in 1793 when King Ferdinand IV turned San Nicola into a penal colony.

Within the complex, most of which can be seen well enough by walking around in the open air, are a few structures worth peeking inside. The **church of Santa Maria a Mare,** accessed by a long limestone *scalinata* (gradual staircase), has a precious 11th- to 12th-century **mosaic floor ★** with animal motifs. Remarkably preserved at the altar is the original **wooden statue of Santa Maria a Mare** that the Benedictines brought to the island and used to consecrate the church. In the right-hand chapel **Il Cristo Grande ★** is a wooden Byzantine crucifix, standing 3.4m (11 ft.) tall.

Elsewhere around the abbey complex, check out the cloisters (with a nice cistern) and the various watchtowers—the highest is the **Torrione del Cavaliere ★**, rearing like a menacing animal above steep and impenetrable walls. The monks, forced to defend by themselves the considerable wealth that they had amassed on the island, frequently had to repel pirate invaders, pouring hot oil and shooting cannons from the towers onto their enemies. A moat known as the **Tagliata** runs along the east side of the abbey, effectively cutting it off from the rest of San Nicola.

Before leaving San Nicola, follow the signs to the **Tomba di Diomede,** where you'll find a small necropolis and Greek-era *tholos* (circular tomb with a domed roof) that the poetically inclined attribute to the Homeric hero, Diomedes, himself.

For those touring the perimeter of San Nicola by boat, the best place to drop anchor and go for a dip is at the **Spiaggia Marinella** (also accessible by a path from the town), halfway up the northern coast of the island.

Caprara

Uninhabited Caprara or Capraia (even locals switch back and forth between the two names) is a popular stop for boaters because of its fascinating rock formations and grottoes. The top attraction on Capraia is without a doubt the **Architiello di Capraia ★★**, a natural arch (5m-wide/16-ft. and 6m-tall/20-ft.) spanning the sea and acting as a gateway to a round inlet—a sort of sea lake enclosed by the low rock-wall coast. This is the "lover's lane" of the Tremiti, where couples who pass under the arch are guaranteed everlasting love. On the northern coast of Caprara, near the western tip, **Cala Pietra di Fucile** is another worthwhile stop. The name means "Cannonball

---

I Say Caprara, You Say Capraia . . .

Even locals can't agree on the spelling or pronunciation of the third, uninhabited island in the Tremiti. The difference is in the penultimate letter, which can be I or R, depending on whom you ask, or on what day you ask them. Either way, the name of the island is derived from *Capperaia,* due to the abundant growth of *capperi* (capers) on its rocky terrain.

To make things even more confusing, there are two other "Capr-" islands in Italy: Capraia in the Tuscan archipelago and, of course, the *famosissima* Capri in the Bay of Naples. Both of these islands' names, however, seem to be derived from *capra* (goat) for the fauna that clung to their rugged slopes in antiquity.

Cove," and the monks of San Nicola used to harvest the nearly perfectly round boulders from the beach here to use as ammunition against their seaborne enemies. If you're here off season, Cala Pietra di Fucile is a lovely spot for a swim, but in August, it's too crowded for comfort.

OUTDOOR PURSUITS

Apart from the easy hiking in the shade of San Domino's pinewoods (the longest trails take only 30 min. end-to-end and never climb more than about 50m/164 ft.), the main activity for sporty types is **diving.** The best outfitter in the islands is **Marlin Tremiti** on San Domino at the Hotel Eden (© **0882/463765** or **0882/463211;** www.marlintremiti.it).

The mostly shallow and remarkably transparent waters around the Tremiti present especially good opportunities for snorkelers and novice divers, though there are plenty of more challenging dives for experienced scuba enthusiasts. The entire area surrounding the Tremiti Islands has been protected since 1989, when the *Riserva Marina Naturale Isole Tremiti* was instituted here. The rich marine life includes octopus, lobster, congers and moray eels, grouper, dentex, bream, amberjack, even the occasional sea turtle, and the geologic formations below the water line are endlessly fascinating. Among the sunken relics off the Tremiti are remnants of a Roman ship (and its cargo) at **Punta di Ponente,** the southwestern tip of San Domino; the 19th-century steamer *Lombardo;* and at **Cala Zio Cesare,** a medieval ship that carried marble for the construction of the monastery on San Nicola. Deeper dives off San Domino take you to wreckage of planes and automobiles.

Off San Nicola, below the **Torrione dei Cavalieri,** is another Roman ship, at 50m (164 ft.) below the surface, with almost all of its cargo intact. Off Capraia, the **Secca della Vedova** and **Secca di Punta Secca** are medium-difficulty dives that show off the full range of typical Tremiti fauna and flora. **Gli Archi** is Capraia's most famous dive site, and its most difficult: At a depth of 60m (197 ft.), divers encounter a series of large natural rock arches opening onto diverse Mediterranean micro-habitats.

The religious-kitsch dive par excellence is found between Cretaccio and San Nicola, where a **statue of Padre Pio,** the immensely popular saint from the Pugliese town of Pietrelcina, is submerged at a depth of 15m (49 ft.). The 3m tall (10-ft.) statue was sunk here in 1998, 4 years before Padre Pio was canonized.

WHERE TO STAY

All but a small handful of the 800 beds available to tourists are on San Domino. In addition to the places listed below, it's also possible to rent apartments on San Domino (from 400€ per week for a two-person unit); a week stay is typically required in summer. **Lo Scrigno,** Via Vespucci 27, San Domino (© **0882/463429** or 348/4765201; www.loscrigno.info), above Cala Matano, has two- to three-person apartments with private verandas. The only accommodations on San Nicola are **homestays** (to be arranged on the spot, or contact Antonio Lembati at © **0882/463028**) or small **apartments** (max three persons, with kitchenettes), carved out of the old prison guards' barracks. Contact the Carducci family (© **0882/463025**) or the De Luca family (© **0882/463028**).

Eden ★ All rooms have sea views at this mid-range hotel overlooking Cala Matano, one of the prettiest coves on the eastern side of San Domino. The property itself isn't particularly wow-inducing, but the hotel gets extra points on the management side:

Staff is exceptionally helpful and friendly. Anyone interested in diving in the waters off the Tremiti would do well to book one of these rooms, since the archipelago's premier dive center, Marlin Tremiti, is headquartered here. The Eden is also one of few accommodations in the islands open year-round.

San Domino. © **0882/463211** or 0884/700911 (in winter). www.hoteledentremiti.it. 60 units. Doubles 100€–200€. Rates include breakfast. MC, V. **Amenities:** Restaurant; bar; conference room; diving center; free shuttle from port; terrace; TV room. *In room:* A/C, TV, hair dryer, minibar.

Gabbiano   It's probably the most attractive lodging in the Tremiti, but that doesn't mean chic: We are talking a 1980s south-Florida aesthetic. Still, the "Seagull" has bright and airy units, most with private terraces or balconies. The Gabbiano is renowned island-wide for its restaurant; however, hotel guests who choose the half- or full-board treatment do not eat in that restaurant but in a dreary, glorified mess hall with no view, and where the food is not up to the same standards. Were it not for this deceptive practice, I'd have given the Gabbiano a higher rating.

Piazza Belvedere, San Domino. © **0882/463410.** www.hotel-gabbiano.com. 40 units. Doubles 100€– 200€. Rates include breakfast. AE, DC, MC, V. Closed Oct–Apr. **Amenities:** Restaurant; bar; conference room; fitness room; free shuttle from port; terrace. *In room:* A/C, TV, hair dryer; minibar.

San Domino ★   Yet another mid-range option, the San Domino is located at the very entrance to the town, with an ample, well-tended garden where guests can relax on a sunny terrace or under the shade of the pines. Rooms and common areas have a somewhat institutional, generic Italian-beach-vacation feel, but everything is clean and functional and staff is pleasant. This is the only other hotel besides the Eden open year-round in the archipelago.

Via Matteotti. © **0882/463404.** www.hotelsandomino.com. 30 units. Doubles 98€–198€. AE, MC, V. **Amenities:** Restaurant; bar; excursions; free shuttle from port; garden; kayak and boat rentals; terrace. *In room:* A/C, TV, hair dryer.

Villaggio Touring Club Italiano ★★   T.C.I. is Italy's cooler version of AAA, and their compound under the Aleppo pines of San Domino is one of only four Touring Club *villaggi* in Italy. Each of the "bungalows"—round huts with simple but nicely finished interiors—has a private bathroom and a small outdoor terrace with lounge chairs and frequently a sea view. Other facilities, all of which blend beautifully into the wooded surroundings, include a restaurant (full-board is required, and meals are served family-style at long teak tables), amphitheater for evening entertainment (this is *the* place to be for the young crowd in summer), even an archery range. The low-impact, summer-camp vibe of the place is reinforced by "quiet hours" from 2:30 to 6pm and midnight to 8am. The village sits above Cala degli Inglesi on the island's western shore; this isn't a sandy beach, but there are several sunning platforms along the smooth rock.

San Domino. © **0882/463405** or 840/888802. www.villaggi.touringclub.it. Weekly rates (including full-board) from 315€ per person in May and Sept; from 500€ in June and the last week of Aug; from 700€ in July and mid-Aug; from 800€ in early Aug. Closed Oct to mid-May. AE, MC, V. **Amenities:** Restaurant; bar; TV lounge; archery; beach facilities; entertainment; kids' programs; hiking and boating excursions; playground; sea kayaks; tennis; terrace. *In room:* Fan.

WHERE TO DINE

Because most of the islands' 400 or so inhabitants are descended from 19th-century "colonists" from Naples, the local cuisine is quite similar to the Neapolitan culinary tradition—lots of fresh fish dishes, and heaping plates of pasta with crustaceans, shellfish, and *pomodorini* (cherry tomatoes). For pizza by the slice at the sandy beach of Cala delle Arene on San Domino, go to the nearby **Albergo Bar Pizzeria Rossana,** Via Federico II, 4 (© 0882/463298; www.isoletremitialbergorossana.it), which also has doubles from 60€ to 130€. The **kiosk** (no phone) by the dock at San Domino also does good panini and take-away fare for picnics aboard your rental *gommone.*

Al Torrione ★ TREMITESE   The energetic Nonna Sisina runs this takeout joint/ restaurant on San Nicola. Instead of trying to order a la carte from the menu, let Nonna and her staff bring you whatever they recommend: It will probably include big, shareable plates of seasonal vegetable-based pastas, mozzarella with different herb dressings, and homemade desserts. (Do let Nonna know if you're not famished or don't want to spend major euros, or else they'll keep bringing you course after course.) This is a place where you can escape the omnipresent seafood of the Tremiti, and fill up on hearty fare before or after a tour of Santa Maria a Mare.

Piazza del Castello, San Nicola. © **347/5501433.** Entrees from 10€. MC, V. Daily noon–3pm, 8–11pm Easter–October.

Da Pio ★★ SEAFOOD/TREMITESE   With its own fishing boat to haul in fresh seafood from around the archipelago every day, Pio is the best place for classic *cucina tremitese* on San Domino. The house specialty pasta is spaghetti *all'aragosta* (with lobster), but they also offer abundant grilled and baked fish dishes at attractive prices; try the *scorfano al forno con patate* (baked scorpionfish with potatoes). The restaurant is family run and the atmosphere is always lively and friendly. For a table on the external terrace, shaded by surrounding trees, be sure to book well in advance.

Via Aldo Moro 12, San Domino. © **0882/463269.** www.ristorantedapio.com. Reservations essential in season. Entrees 12€–18€. AE, MC, V. Daily 12:30–2:30pm and 7:30–10:30pm year-round.

Il Gabbiano ★ TREMITESE   The restaurant in the hotel of the same name (see "Where to Stay") is one of the island's most respected dining rooms, always serving top-notch seafood pastas and whole fish dishes in a panoramic, albeit retirement community-esque dining room. The garlicky sautée of shellfish is particularly mouthwatering; the wine list features excellent Pugliese varietals. When booking, be sure to request a table along the terrace, which has the best views over the water and Cala Matano, directly below.

Piazza Belvedere, San Domino. © **0882/463410.** www.hotel-gabbiano.com. Reservations essential in season. Entrees 14€–20€. AE, DC, MC, V. Daily 7:30–11pm May–Sept.

Il Galeone ★ PIZZA   In Italy, pizza is a money-saving option for a sit-down meal; it's also a chance to take a break from fish, which can become cloying after several days on an Italian island. "The Galleon" does excellent Neapolitan-style pies with fresh mozzarella and all the meat and vegetable toppings imaginable.

Via San Domino, San Domino. © **0882/463293.** Pizzas from 5€. MC, V. Daily noon–3pm and 7:30–11:30pm.

Il Pirata ★ SEAFOOD   On the waterfront at Cala delle Arene, the Pirate turns out Italian seafood standards to the summer crowd. Start with a cold salad of octopus and calamari, then warm up to a plate of shrimp risotto or the house specialty *tubetti della casa* (pasta tubes filled with fresh tomatoes and mussels). In August, management isn't particularly adept at serving the large number of tourists vying for a table (Il

Pirata is known as a social hot spot), resulting in long waits and sometimes rude exchanges; the restaurant is much more enjoyable outside peak season.

Cala delle Arene, San Domino. ℂ **0882/463409.** Reservations essential in season. Entrees 12€–18€. Daily noon–3pm and 7:30–11pm.

THE TREMITI ISLANDS AFTER DARK

There's no sophisticated nightlife on the Tremiti, but that also means you don't have to dress to the nines to fit in as you do at other, more chic Italian seaside locales. What action there is, however, is concentrated on San Domino; partying at the monastery of San Nicola is frowned upon. Start with an *aperitivo* at **Era Ora** (Piazza Sandro Pertini 6; ℂ **347/7314783**), then, after dinner, dancing queens can choose from one of the two open-air *discoteche* on San Domino, **A' Furmicula,** in the pinewoods outside town (℃ **0882/463312**), or **Diomede,** on the main square (Piazza Sandro Pertini 1; ℂ **0882/463403**).

SICILY

S icily is the *bisnonna* (great-grandmother) of all Italian islands, both in terms of size and richness of travel experiences, and a land unto itself, proudly different from the rest of Italy in its customs and traditions. It's also the largest island in the Mediterranean Sea; a place of beauty, mystery, and world-class monuments; and a striking mix of bloodlines and architecture from medieval Normandy, Aragonese Spain, Moorish North Africa, ancient Greece, Phoenicia, and Rome. In many ways, it fits your folkloric, mandolin-accompanied stereotype of "Sicily"—nearly all men seem to be named Salvatore, and plenty of elderly women walk around in black garb as if in mourning, even in the height of August heat, and the landscapes are sun-baked and picturesque, yet more colossal and forbidding than, say, Tuscany. However, there are surprises, too: The highways are beautiful and easy to navigate; blond-haired, blue-eyed native Sicilians are a common sight; and there is no tangible evidence of the Mafia anywhere.

In English, the word "Sicily" can carry some outdated connotations, so think of it as the Italians do: *la Sicilia,* that sunny, exotic appendage of the Italian Republic that may have its problems but gets under your skin from the first moment you arrive. Much of the island's raw, primitive nature has faded in modern times, as thousands of newfangled cars clog the narrow lanes of its biggest city, **Palermo.** Yet Palermo has enough artistic and historic sites to make your head spin. On the eastern edge of the island is **Mount Etna,** the highest active volcano in Europe. Many of Sicily's larger urban areas are relatively unattractive, but areas of ravishing beauty and eerie historical interest are found in the cities of **Syracuse, Taormina, Agrigento,** and **Selinunte.** Sicily's ancient ruins are rivaled only by those of Rome itself. Agrigento's **Valley of the Temples,** for example, is worth the trip alone.

Although the island's economy is moving closer to that of Europe and the rest of Italy, its culture is still very much its own. Its vague Arab flavor reminds us that Sicily broke away from the mainland of Africa, *not* Italy, millions of years ago. (On a map, the toe of the Italian "boot" actually seems poised to kick Sicily away; for now, it's separated from Italy by the 4km/2½-mile Straits of Messina, a dangerously unstable earthquake zone, making the eventual construction of a long-discussed bridge doubtful.) Yes, there are far too many cars in Palermo, and parts of the island are heavily polluted by industrialization, but Sicily is still a place where life is slower, tradition is respected, and the myths and legends of the past aren't yet forgotten.

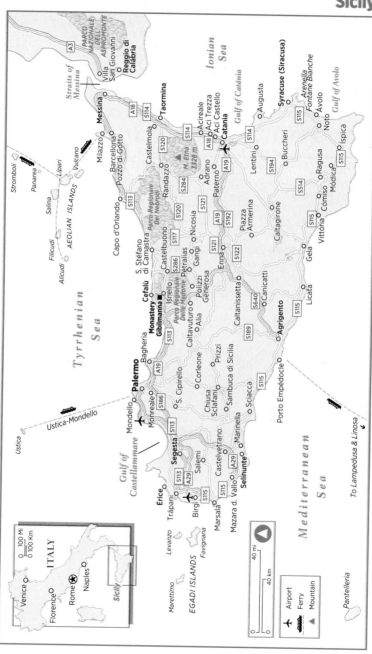

A Note on What's Included Here & What Isn't

In compiling this chapter, I sought to present the best cross-section of what Sicily has to offer, from stunning monuments, lovely towns, and authentic local culture, to cuisine, natural splendor, sun, and sand. In doing so, I had to omit certain parts of Sicily for the sake of space. As a result, you'll find that some places that look big on the map, or are important transportation hubs, such as Catania and Messina, are not included here. However, you can find detailed information about those cities and other Sicilian destinations that don't appear in *Italian Islands* in *Frommer's Complete Guide to Sicily* and at www.frommers.com.

Strategies

Unless you'll be visiting only one area, such as Palermo or Taormina, it would be criminal to spend less than a week in Sicily. Even better, 10 days will give you the time you need not only to sample the highlights around the island but also to travel between them. Sicily isn't Australia, but even with your own car, getting from region to region takes several hours.

If monuments and culture are your priorities, the shoulder months of April, May, September, and October are glorious. You're practically guaranteed gorgeous weather, cobalt skies, and fewer crowds. The seaside areas are full swing from June to August (*especially* Aug), which can be fun if beachgoing and partying are your things, but the heat of high summer makes some other quintessential Sicilian pursuits (such as traipsing about dusty archaeological sites) a lot less pleasant. Unlike other Italian islands, prices don't fluctuate very much from season to season in Sicily, though in popular resorts like Taormina, hotels tend to spike in August.

Essentials

GETTING THERE   Palermo and Catania airports are well connected with the Italian mainland and other European hubs. From May to October, low-cost airline Eurofly (www.euroflyusa.com) flies nonstop between New York's JFK and Palermo. You can also take the overnight train from Rome or Naples (which crosses into Sicily via ferry over the Straits of Messina), or the overnight ferry from Naples to Palermo, operated by Tirrenia (www.tirrenia.it) and SNAV (www.snav.it).

GETTING AROUND   It's best to explore Sicily by car. Once out of Palermo, it's a pleasurable and hassle-free affair, as the roads are well maintained and scenic, and traffic is minimal. Fuel is expensive in Sicily (as with all of Italy), and a few of the *autostradas* are toll roads. A detailed road map, such as Touring Club Italiano's Sicilia map, is essential, and available at airport bookshops and most newsstands. Sicily by Car (www.sbc.it) and Maggiore (www.maggiore.it), both with offices at Palermo and Catania airports and in the major cities, have the best rental rates.

Though a car gives you more freedom and flexibility, Sicily is also well served by trains and comfortable coach buses (usually preferable to trains), which are certainly an economical way to get around. Even for trips that traverse the entire island and take several hours, bus fares are seldom more than 10€, and most local routes cost less than 4€. For train timetables and ticket prices, visit www.trenitalia.com. The main bus companies in Sicily are **AST** (www.aziendasicilianatrasporti.it) and **Interbus** (www.interbus.it). Cuffaro (www.cuffaro.info) operates buses between Palermo and Agrigento's Valley of the Temples. Palermotourism.com also has a searchable interactive map for bus routes and which company serves them.

PALERMO ★★

Down through the ages, writers have tried to capture Palermo's singular allure. Vincenzo Consolo, in his *Strolling through Sicily,* was overcome with the city's rich red earth "with springs of water where the palm grove rises tall and slender." Though pockets of that oasis remain, the landscape Consolo wrote of is largely swept away today. In its place is one of the more difficult cities in southern Italy to explore. There's just too much traffic and pollution, and getting around in summer is an often dusty, humid affair, and even a risky one as you try to avoid cars, buses, and motor scooters. If you come to Palermo after having traveled elsewhere in slow-paced, user-friendly Sicily, the difficulties presented by this city come down like a ton of bricks. Yet there is magic in its madness, and those who brave it are rewarded with the discovery of artistic gems and memorable vignettes of street life. I can't guarantee you'll love every inch of this alluring yet hectic place, but what I can promise is that giving Palermo the significant effort it demands of tourists pays dividends in indelible travel experiences. And in the meantime, you'll get closer to the soul of Sicily.

The combination of distinctive sights in Sicily's capital—the result of more than a thousand years and countless Western and Eastern cultural influences—simply doesn't exist anywhere else. Not to be missed are the stunning Byzantine mosaics at the Norman Palace's Cappella Palatina (p. 177) or the cathedral of Monreale (p. 184), and the eye-popping rococo stuccoes at the *oratori* of San Domenico & San Lorenzo (see "The Oratories of Giacomo Serpotta: Palermo's Putti-palooza," on p. 179). Witness Palermo's striking Islamic-inflected architecture in the bulbous red domes of San Giovanni degli Eremiti and San Cataldo. In the crumbling, captivating Kalsa district, visit Palazzo Abatellis (p. 179), the masterpiece of Catalonian-Gothic architecture that houses Sicily's best art museum. Palermo's Museo Archeologico Regionale (p. 180) is the island's most comprehensive repository of ancient artifacts—a helpful complement to all the open-air ruins on Sicily.

Essentials

GETTING THERE   Most people arrive via Palermo's dramatically situated **Falcone-Borsellino airport** (aka Punta Raisi; ℂ **091/7020273;** www.gesap.it), on the sea among tall headlands 25km (16 miles) northwest of the city center. Palermo is well served by flights from all over Italy and many European cities, too. All the major rental car companies have operations here. If you won't be driving into Palermo with a rental car (and if you do, get clear directions and parking information from your hotel), an easy way to reach the center is with the shuttle bus run by **Prestia e Comandè** (ℂ **091/580457**). The buses depart every half-hour from 5am to 11pm; the trip takes 45 minutes and costs 5.80€ one-way. In central Palermo, the bus stops at the main train station, at Via Emerico Amari (port), and at Teatro Politeama. There's also a direct train called the **Trinacria Express** (ℂ **091/7044007;** www.trenitalia.com; 1 hr.; 5.50€) from Palermo airport to Palermo central station. Otherwise, taxis are plentiful; expect to pay about 45€ from the airport to town. If you're arriving in Palermo from another place in Sicily by rail, all trains come into Palermo Stazione Centrale, just south of the historic center. Buses from elsewhere in Sicily arrive at a depot adjacent to the train station.

GETTING AROUND   Walking is the best way to get around Palermo, since distances are never great within the historic center. To reach greater Palermo destinations (like the catacombs) or farther-flung locales (such as Mondello and Monreale), buses run by **AMAT** (✆ **091/350111**) cost 1.20€ per ride or 3.50€ for a full-day ticket. AMAT also runs a few **tourist bus lines** (.52€) that do loops of some of the main sights. Board them at Piazza Giulio Cesare, the tree-lined square directly outside the train station.

VISITOR INFORMATION   Official **tourist information offices** are located at Falcone-Borsellino (Punta Raisi) airport (✆ **091/591698;** Mon–Sat 8:30am–7:30pm, and in the city center at Piazza Castelnuovo 35; ✆ **091/6058351;** Mon–Fri 8:30am–2pm and 2:30–6:30pm; yes, they close for a collective half-hour lunch break). The website of Palermo's tourism board is www.palermotourism.com.

Exploring

Apart from the spectacle of amped-up humanity that Palermo is, it's also one of the great art cities of Europe, and ideally, you should give it at least 3 days. However, most people don't build that much Palermo time into their Sicily itineraries. Even if you only have a day to see Palermo, you can pick and choose from the sights listed below—they'll only whet your appetite for the next trip.

The gritty corner known as the **Quattro Canti,** where Via Maqueda meets Via Vittorio Emanuele, is the approximate geographic center from which the old town of Palermo radiates. This 5-sq.-km (2-sq.-mile) pocket of busy roads, quiet alleys, splendid monuments, and hidden treasures is where the lion's share of the city's tourist attractions is located. Everything listed here, except the Catacombe dei Cappuccini, is within walking distance of the Quattro Canti. Southeast of Quattro Canti is **Piazza Pretoria,** Palermo's most famous square. Its fountain, originally intended for a Tuscan villa, is bedecked with nude statues and mythological monsters—thus, it was called Fontana della Vergogna, or "Fountain of Shame," by outraged churchgoers.

If you don't want to bother with admission fees and museum crowds, the most atmospheric neighborhood for an unstructured walking tour is **La Kalsa ★★**. The key to understanding the contrasts of Palermo—if that's even possible—is this tangle of streets south of the main harbor, and northeast of the train station (Via Alloro is the main east-west street). The name is derived from the Arabic *khalisa,* or "pure," which the Kalsa is anything but. In the oldest and most intriguing part of the city, tarnished baroque gems like **Palazzo Gangi** (Piazza Croce dei Vespri), **Palazzo Ajutamicristo** (Via Garibaldi), and **Palazzo Mirto** (Via Merlo 2, off Piazza Marina; ✆ **091/6167541;** 3€; Mon–Sat 9am–7pm, Sun 9am–1pm) evoke Palermo's princely heyday, while entire blocks of the neighborhood are crumbled, never rebuilt after Allied air raids in 1943. Some of the bombed-out buildings are makeshift homes for families (and their livestock), who live together in a few rooms and sleep on simple pallets, while other scarred buildings have been repurposed as avant-garde art exhibition spaces. La Kalsa is quite an eye-opening place. Nearby, **Santa Maria dello Spasimo ★★** (Via dello Spasimo; ✆ **091/6161486**) is a swoon-inducing skeleton of a church, where mature trees grow out of broken Gothic vaults into the Palermitan sky. *Tip:* La Kalsa is safe during the day, but don't walk around here alone at night. If in doubt, just stick to Via Alloro or Piazza Marina.

Attractions

Palazzo dei Normanni ★★ CENTER This is Palermo's greatest attraction and Sicily's finest treasure-trove. Sumptuous and remarkably evocative of the golden age when Palermo was a splendid court city where West met East, the formidable Arab-Norman

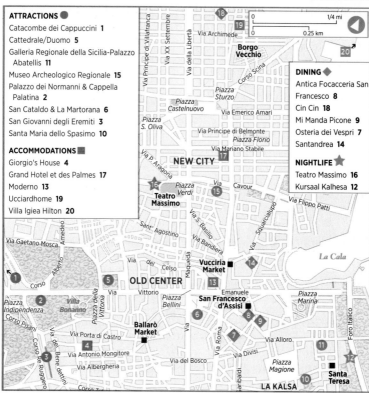

ATTRACTIONS ●

Catacombe dei Cappuccini **1**

Cattedrale/Duomo **5**

Galleria Regionale della Sicilia-Palazzo
Abatellis **11**

Museo Archeologico Regionale **15**

Palazzo dei Normanni & Cappella
Palatina **2**

San Cataldo & La Martorana **6**

San Giovanni degli Eremiti **3**

Santa Maria dello Spasimo **10**

ACCOMMODATIONS ■

Giorgio's House **4**

Grand Hotel et des Palmes **17**

Moderno **13**

Ucciardhome **19**

Villa Igiea Hilton **20**

DINING ◆

Antica Focacceria San
Francesco **8**

Cin Cin **18**

Mi Manda Picone **9**

Osteria dei Vespri **7**

Santandrea **14**

NIGHTLIFE ★

Teatro Massimo **16**

Kursaal Kalhesa **12**

9

SICILY | **Palermo**

palace consists of the Royal Apartments, where King Roger II slumbered and held court, and the **Cappella Palatina ★★★**, commissioned by Roger II from 1130 to 1140 and adorned with the most spectacular Byzantine mosaics outside Monreale, Ravenna, or Istanbul.

Piazza del Parlamento. ☎ **091/7054006.** Admission 6€. Mon–Sat 8am–noon and 2–5pm; Sun 8:30am–2:30pm. Bus: 104, 105, 108, 109, 110, 118, 304, or 309.

San Giovanni degli Eremiti ★★ CENTER   This is one of the most famous and certainly the most romantic of all the Arabo-Norman monuments still standing in Palermo and a short detour from the Palazzo dei Normanni. Since 1132, this church, with its series of five red, pencil-eraser domes, has remained one of the most characteristic landmarks on the Palermo skyline. With an atmosphere appropriate for the recluse it honors, St. John of the Hermits (now deconsecrated), this is one of the most idyllic spots in Palermo. A medieval veil hangs heavily in the gardens, with their citrus blossoms and flowers, as you wander around the cloister.

Via dei Benedettini 3. ☎ **091/6515019.** Admission 6€. Mon–Sat 9am–1pm and 3–7pm; Sun 9am–1pm. Bus: 109 or 318.

STREET eats

Are you steely of stomach? Is the phrase "barbecued goat intestines" more appetizing than revolting? If so, you'll definitely want to try out some of the street food *(cibo di strada)* in markets like Vucciria and Ballarò. Real Palermitans go crazy for this stuff, and you'll earn major street cred if you step up to the challenge.

Slaughterhouse leftovers play a starring role on the "menu" at these stands, so you might be better off not asking what's in there. No matter what stewed organ they're hawking—all organs and medleys thereof are fair game—Palermo's colorful *cibo di strada* vendors will unfailingly tell you it's the most *pregiato* (prized) piece of the animal. Sure, many of these non-descript meats will tempt you with their aromas, but it's only fair to disclose that *stigghiola* is essentially barbecued goat intestines, and that *pane con milza* sandwich consists of chopped spleen on a roll of bread. (You go in thinking, "Piece of cake, it's just a modified Sloppy Joe," but those

decommissioned red blood cells are an acquired taste.) Still, locals line up all day for the *pane con milza* (with optional cheese on top) at Antica Focacceria San Francesco, where the spleen bits are churned in a huge, ominous-looking cauldron.

On the less daring side, try *sfincione*, a typical Palermitan pizza with tomatoes, anchovies, onion and grated cheese, but you'll get bonus points for ordering *babaluci*, baby snails with olive oil, garlic, and fennel. Craving stadium food? Have *pane con salsiccia*, an herb-y Sicilian riff on bratwurst on a roll. If you are vegetarian, try a delicious *pane e panelle* sandwich. Panelle are discs of fried chickpeas and universally adored by *cibo di strada* newbies. Least bizarre of all, *arancini* are another typical Sicilian snack and easy to eat on the go. These deep-fried rice balls with mozzarella or meat inside will cost you about 1€ each. The best *arancini* in town are at Antico Caffè Spinnato (see "Escaping the Madness," p. 180.)

Cattedrale ★ CENTER   A few blocks east of the Norman Palace, the Arab-Norman duomo is a 12th-century structure much reworked and muddled in subsequent eras. As you enter, the first chapel on the right contains the tomb of Roger II, the first king of Sicily, who was crowned here in 1130 and died in 1154. Several of his descendants are also buried here. Accessed from the south transept, the Tesoro, or treasury, is a repository of rich vestments, silverware, chalices, holy vessels, altar cloths, and ivory engravings of the 17th century. The cathedral's grassy square is a welcome stop along one of the most maniacal roads in the city.

Piazza Cattedrale. 🕿 **091/334373.** Duomo: free admission; crypt and treasury: 1€ each. Mon–Sat 9:30am–1:30pm and 2:30–5:30pm. Bus: 101, 104, 105, 107, or 139.

Markets ★★★ CENTER   You can't do justice to Palermo without swinging through one of its street markets, if only for 15 minutes. Nowhere is Palermo's multi-cultural pedigree more evident than at the stalls of **Vucciria** ★★★ and **Ballarò** ★★. These markets go on for blocks and blocks, hawking everything from spices to seafood to sides of beef to toilet paper to handicrafts to electronics and meat snacks of questionable provenance. Ballarò, west of the train station, toward the Palazzo dei Normanni, is perhaps the more authentic of the two (where more real Palermitans shop), but the twinkling lights of Vucciria (from the French "boucherie," or butcher shop) and its covered souklike atmosphere is irresistibly charming. The vendors' colorful theatrics are very much for your benefit, so feel free to photograph away as they ham it up with swordfish heads and the like.

Ballarò: Piazza del Carmine to Piazza Ballarò. Vucciria: Via Argenteria (north of Via Vittorio Emanuele and east of Via Roma).

Galleria Regionale della Sicilia-Palazzo Abatellis ★★★ CENTER   There aren't very many "big names" here, but this is nevertheless one of most wonderful art museums in Italy and located in the heart of the captivating Kalsa district. The star work here is a 15th-century painting of the *Triumph of Death* (artist unknown), a gory, shrill, and immediately captivating scene of a skeleton on horseback, trampling hapless men and women—their fine clothing and jeweled necklaces notwithstanding. The rest of the collection concentrates on Sicilian art from the 13th to 18th centuries.

Via Alloro 4. ✆ **091/6230011.** 6€. Daily 9am–1pm; Tues–Fri 2:30–7pm.

San Cataldo & La Martorana ★★ CENTER   These side-by-side medieval churches, separated by a sultry little garden of tropical plants and trees, are more good examples of Palermo's striking Arab-Norman architecture. The bell-towered La Martorana, to the left as you climb the stairs from Piazza Bellini, has sumptuous mosaics, while San Cataldo is more interesting from the outside: It's the one with the red domes and the lacy Moorish crenellation around the tops of the walls. San Cataldo's opening hours are erratic; if it's closed when you arrive, ask the custodian

THE oratories OF GIACOMO SERPOTTA: PALERMO'S PUTTI-PALOOZA

You'll quickly notice that among Palermo's artistic attractions, there's a lot of talk about *oratorio* this or *oratorio* that. These private places for prayer at several churches around town are justly famous for their fantastic rococo decorations, alive with delightful and remarkably three-dimensional stuccoes, executed by native son Giacomo Serpotta in the early 18th century. In the case of the three listed below, the attached church is far less interesting than its *oratorio*. Admission to all three is free, but pay attention to the limited opening hours.

The **Oratorio di San Lorenzo** ★★★ (Via dell'Immacolatella; ✆ **091/332779;** Mon 3–6pm, Tues–Fri 9am–1pm, 3–5:30pm, Sat 9am–1pm) was his earliest such work—the walls are filled with playful white *putti* (cherubs) blowing

bubbles or kissing over the architectonic elements, which are also in white stucco. The effect is disarmingly dynamic, like the whole place is inhaling and exhaling around you. At the more polychrome **Oratorio del Rosario di San Domenico** ★★ (Via dei Bambinai; ✆ **091/332779;** same hours as Oratorio di San Lorenzo), another profusion of charming *putti* frames more introspective statues of the Christian virtues. The **Oratorio di Santa Cita** ★★★ (Via Valverde 3; ✆ **091/332779;** Mon–Sat 9am–1pm) is the other great Serpotta masterpiece, another all-white chapel where the cherubs steal the show—romping and climbing over the "architecture," coyly contorting their chubby bodies, they are joy personified, like a daycare full of the most adorable toddlers imaginable.

at La Martorana for the key. After visiting the churches, take a break at Pizzeria Bellini just below (Piazza Bellini 6; *②* **091/6165691**).

Piazza Bellini. *②* **091/6161692.** Free admission. La Martorana: Mon–Sat 9:30am–1pm, 3:30–6:30pm; Sun 8:30am–1pm. Bus: 101 or 102.

Museo Archeologico Regionale ★★★ CENTER It's one of Italy's best archaeological museums and a must if you're visiting any of the Greek sites on Sicily, especially Selinunte: The metopes from several of the temples there are on display here. The museum is a dusty, rambling, and not very well-marked place (a common feature of southern Mediterranean museums with world-class collections), which makes the adventure of "discovering" its treasures all the more fun and Indiana Jones–like. In addition to the native Sicilian artifacts, the Egyptian and Etruscan collections are also noteworthy. Some 11,000 works are on display.

Piazza Olivella 24. *②* **091/6116805.** Admission 6€. Daily 8:30am–2pm; Tues–Fri 2:30–6:30pm. Bus: 101, 102, 103, 104, or 107.

Catacombe dei Cappuccini ★★★ WEST OF CENTER Palermo's unforgettable "Library of Corpses" is the most bizarre final resting place in Italy, downright creepy to some, oddly clinical to others. Mummified, fully dressed cadavers hang from the walls, cantilevering eerily toward you as you walk the corridors of this ostensibly holy place. From the 16th to the 20th century, some 8,000 souls were "buried" here, most of them having elected while alive to be displayed thus—though the campy poses of some look more like a mortician's creative license.

Piazza Cappuccini 1. *②* **091/212117.** Admission 1.50€. Daily 9am–noon and 3–5pm. Bus: 327.

Escaping the Madness

Believe it or not, Palermo has plenty of genteel (and kid-friendly) places where one can go to escape the chaos of the *centro storico* and the tourist sights there. The modern part of town starts north of Via Mariano Stabile, where broad, tree-lined avenues like Via della Libertà make for pleasant strolling. The Arabs, a people who knew the joy of a green oasis, were the ones who introduced gardens into Palermo. The Normans extended the idea by creating parklands and summer palaces to escape the heat. Today, you can wander among the greenery and encounter incredible banyan trees and other exotic plantings. The most rewarding Palermitan parks are the **Orto Botanico ★★** (Via Abramo Lincoln 2B, just south of La Kalsa; *②* **091/6238241**) and the **Giardino Inglese ★** (off Via della Libertà in north-central Palermo).

To mix with Palermo's upper crust (and its wannabes), free from the menace of motorized traffic, strut your stuff down pedestrian-only **Via Principe di Belmonte,** the city's most fashionable retail strip and home to **Antico Caffè Spinnato ★★**, Via Principe di Belmonte 107/115 (*②* **091/329229**), the best coffee bar in town. Alternatively, get out of the city altogether with a day on the woodsy slopes of Monte Pellegrino or at the beach in Mondello (see "Side Trips," below).

Where to Stay

More than anywhere else in Sicily (even Italy), Palermo is one of those cities where you'll want a comfortable place to take midday breaks or to crash at the end of the day—so think twice about just booking the cheapest available.

Giorgio's House ★ CENTRO STORICO   Young and young-at-heart active types need look no further than this three-room B&B, a few blocks from the Palazzo dei Normanni, run by the infinitely energetic Giorgio Lo Cicero. Staying here is like finding that tour-guide-extraordinaire Sicilian cousin we all wish we had. Any activity you can think of, Giorgio will enthusiastically organize, though his passions are the outdoors and mountaineering. Decorated with a hodgepodge of grandmotherly furnishings, each of the rooms is spacious and impeccably clean. Note that Giorgio's House "moves" to Buenos Aires for the austral summer.

Via A. Mongitore. ☏ **091/525057.** 3 units. 30€ per person per night. 27€ per night for 3 nights or more. No credit cards. Closed Jan 16–Apr. **Amenities:** Activities galore; free Wi-Fi in lobby.

Grand Hotel et Des Palmes ★★ CENTRO STORICO   The top address for reliving bygone Palermitan glamour, this was once the city's prime setting for trysts and intrigue. A recent sprucing-up of the property has taken away some of the nostalgia—but made rooms much more modern and comfortable. Room rates are often slashed by 50% on their website, so budget travelers needn't shy away from this place. Even if you don't stay here, step in for a gander at the lobby or a drink at the bar. It's decadent and sultry, and as one Sicilian friend describes it, *palermitano da morire* ("ridiculously Palermitan").

Via Roma 398. ☏ **091/6028111.** www.hotel-despalmes.it. 180 units. Doubles 230€–265€. AE, DC, MC, V. **Amenities:** Restaurant; bar; concierge; fitness room; free parking; room service. *In room:* A/C, TV, hair dryer, minibar, Wi-Fi (17€ per day).

Moderno CENTRO STORICO   From fussy chandeliers to a preponderance of lugubrious gilt-framed oil paintings, this basic hotel right off the Quattro Canti doesn't live up to its name, but this is nevertheless a cool and comfortable choice for budget travelers. The Moderno has the most central Palermo location possible, but light sleepers beware: This corner sees whizzing traffic at all hours.

Via Roma 276. ☏ **091/588683.** www.hotelmodernopa.com. 38 units. Doubles 75€. AE, DC, MC, V. **Amenities:** Breakfast room; concierge; free parking; room service.

Ucciardhome ★★ NORTH OF CENTRO STORICO   At Palermo's "it" hotel for modernist aesthetes, dark wenge wood furniture contrasts with ivory fabrics for an ultra-relaxing, masculine feel. The comfortable rooms are filled with techno-gadgetry, and the sleek bathrooms are done up in metallic mosaics. The boutique Ucciardhome is in the less chaotic modern side of town, across from the Carcere Ucciardone, a prison and the hotel's namesake. For a contrasting dose of Palermo color, the lively street market of Via Ettore Ximenes is just around the corner.

Via Enrico Albanese 34-36. ☏ **091/348426.** www.hotelucciardhome.com. 14 units. Doubles 135€–190€. AE, DC, MC, V. **Amenities:** Babysitting; concierge; garden; gym; wine bar. *In room:* A/C, TV, CD player/ radio, hair dryer, minibar, free Wi-Fi.

Villa Igiea Hilton Palermo ★★★ WATERFRONT/OUT OF TOWN   Newly acquired by Hilton, this consummately Mediterranean property, a peach-toned castle surrounded by fragrant gardens and the sea, is the most luxurious stay in Palermo. Recently updated and spacious guest rooms have understated Art Nouveau decor and all mod-cons. Graceful columns of a Greek temple ruin stand alongside the hotel's kidney-shaped swimming pool, beyond which there's a sheer drop to the sea. The hotel can organize sailing tours of the coast for guests. The Villa Igiea is not in the center of town or near any transportation hubs, which guarantees the utmost tranquillity, but you'll need a car or taxi to go anywhere in the rest of Palermo.

Salita Belmonte 43, Acquasanta (4km/2½ miles NE of city center). ⓒ **091/6312111.** www.villaigiea. hilton.com. 124 units. Doubles from 295€. AE, DC, MC, V. **Amenities:** Restaurant; bar; babysitting; concierge; fitness room; pool; room service; tennis court. *In room:* A/C, TV, hair dryer, minibar, Wi-Fi (20€ per day).

Where to Dine

Antica Focacceria San Francesco ★ ☺ CENTER SNACKS/SICILIAN   All visitors need to make at least one stop at this local favorite, a tradition since 1834, in the Palazzo Reale/Monte di Pietà district. A casual place in a grand palazzo setting, this famous spot is great for your first primer in typical Palermitan food. From the self-serve area on the left as you walk in, you can assemble a sampler plate of swordfish roulades, various stuffed pizzas and baked pastas, and the delicious *panelle* (fried chickpea discs). More "advanced" palates can take their cafeteria trays to the counter where a taciturn staffer stirs a giant black cauldron full of stewed spleen for the *pane con milza* sandwiches. AFSF also has a proper sit-down restaurant with tables in the lovely piazza out front.

Via A. Paternostro 58. ⓒ **091/320264.** www.afsf.it. Sandwiches 3€–5€; entrees 8€–16€. AE, DC, MC, V. Daily 10am–midnight. Bus: 101, 103, 104, or 107.

Cin-Cin ★★ NORTH OF CENTER SICILIAN/CREOLE   One of the culinary treasures of Palermo, this is a favorite spot with locals. Pronounced "chin-chin," the restaurant's name is the Italian version of the toast "Cheers!" and suggests the camaraderie found here behind an unpretentious facade. It's reached by going down a flight of steps off Via Libertà, in the section between the Giardino Inglese and the Teatro Politeama. Sample the seafood pastas, into which all sorts of sea creatures (shrimp, clams, mussels, sea urchins) are tossed with a succulent sauce. Sicilians often treat beef and lamb as sideshows to their antipasti, pastas, and seafood dishes, but here the chef gives full attention to turning out perfectly cooked and aromatically seasoned meats. The owners, the Clemente family, once operated a restaurant in Baton Rouge, Louisiana, and Cin-Cin is the only restaurant in Sicily to offer such distinctly Louisiana dishes as oysters Rockefeller and chicken gumbo. Homemade Marsala and almond ice creams are a Cin-Cin specialty.

Via Manin 22, off Via Libertà. ⓒ **091/6124095.** Reservations recommended. Main courses 6€–15€. AE, DC, MC, V. Sept–June Mon–Fri noon–3pm and 8pm–midnight, Sat 8pm–midnight; July–Aug Mon–Fri noon–3:30pm. Bus: 101 or 107.

Mi Manda Picone ★ CENTER SICILIAN   I like to come here for three reasons: to sample the excellent and well-chosen Sicilian wines, to enjoy the tasty food at affordable prices, and to admire the facade of that Romanesque gem, Chiesa di San Francesco. The specialty here is wine, mostly from Sicily (450 kinds), accompanied by platters of hearty, robust food. Sit on the terrace in front of the church or retreat to the woodsy, medieval-style interior, which once functioned as a stable. Light snacks include stuffed and deep-fried vegetables; a marvelous flan of fava beans and Pecorino cheese; fresh salads; and antipasti platters. More substantial fare includes grilled tuna or swordfish steaks with capers and black pepper. The famous Antica Focacceria San Francesco is across the street.

Via Alessandro Paternostro 59 (Piazza San Francesco d'Assisi). ⓒ **091/6160660.** Main courses 9€–16€. AE, MC, V. Wine 4€–10€ per glass. Mon–Sat 7–11pm. Bus: 103, 108, or 164.

Osteria dei Vespri ★★ CENTER SICILIAN/ITALIAN This consistently delicious and atmospheric spot, on the ground floor of the elegant baroque Palazzo Gangi, is where Palermitans take out-of-towners for well crafted twists on local cuisine in an intimate, old-fashioned setting. The pasta dish that merits the most raves is ravioli with ricotta and fresh basil, homemade tomato sauce, eggplant, and crispy onion. An imaginative use of ingredients continues with such delights as swordfish Cordon Bleu, with almonds, oregano, and ginger, or the braised beef with Nero d'Avola red wine and wild fennel on a potato purée with glazed onions. The wine list, with literally hundreds of vintages, is the best in town.

Piazza Croce dei Vespri 6. ☏ **091-6171631.** Reservations recommended. Main courses 10€–18€. Fixed-price menu 45€. AE, DC, MC, V. Mon–Sat 1–3pm and 8:30pm–midnight. Closed 2 weeks in Aug. Bus: 103 or 105.

Santandrea ★★ 🍴 CENTER SEAFOOD/SICILIAN More chic than those restaurants listed above, this spot has alfresco and inside tables and daily specials on its menu. Thanks to its location in the heart of the Vucciria market, Santandrea features only the freshest vegetables and seafood. The waiter will recite the day's specials with obvious pleasure; go with the mixed antipasti, which always features fresh seafood. The pasta dishes are excellent, notably spaghetti prepared with sea urchins, a local delicacy, or spaghetti with fresh sardines. A friend describes Santandrea as "just the place you are always looking for—the right combination of great inventive dishes with amazing ingredients and a relaxed, hip setting."

Piazza Sant'Andrea 4. ☏ **091-334999.** Reservations required. Main courses 8€–18€. AE, MC, V. Mon–Sat 8–11:30pm. Closed Aug 13–17. Bus: 101, 103, 104, or 107.

Palermo After Dark

For such a large city, Palermo has a dearth of nightlife—not necessarily a bad thing since touring the city is a tiring enterprise that will have you tuckered out and ready for bed by about 10pm. In the hot summer months, the townspeople parade along the waterfront of Mondello Lido to cool off (p. 185). Although they are improving somewhat, many Palermo areas with bars and taverns (such as La Kalsa) are not safe for walking around at night. The safest (and most sanitary) places for drinking, making conversation, and meeting like-minded companions are the many bars in the deluxe and first-class hotels.

The liveliest squares at night—and the relatively safest because lots of people are here—are Piazza Castelnuovo and Piazza Verdi. Another "safe zone" is a pedestrian strip flanked by bars and cafes, many with sidewalk tables, along Via Principe di Belmonte, between Via Roma and Via Ruggero Settimo.

The principal venue for cultural presentations is the restored **Teatro Massimo** ★★, Via Maqueda (☏ **091/6053555**), which boasts the largest indoor stage in Europe after the Paris Opera House. Francis Ford Coppola shot the climactic opera scene here for *The Godfather: Part III*. The theater was built between 1875 and 1897 in a neoclassical style, and reopened after a restoration in 1997 to celebrate its 100th birthday. Ticket prices range from 15€ to 100€. The box office is open Tuesday through Sunday from 10am to 3pm; bus: 101, 102, 103, 104, 107, 122, or 225.

Side Trips

Palermo is graced with a number of satellite attractions (three of which start with *Mon-* for easy reference) that can be explored easily as side trips. Monreale, with its

While in Palermo, you might want to check out **Kursaal Kalhesa,** Foro Umberto I 21 (ⓒ **091-6167630;** Tues–Sun 11:30am–2pm and 4pm–1am). It's a bee-hive of activity and a great way to meet locals, most of whom are young and fluent in English. Situated in a restored palace near Piazza Marina, this is where Sicily meets New York's SoHo. An attractive crowd congregates at the bar, which is next to a bookstore-cum-lounge. You can read English-language newspapers, listen to live music, use the Internet cafe, or pick up tourist info at the travel agency.

For serious eating, head upstairs for Sicilian and Tunisian fare. The chef's delectable dishes are served in a cavernous room decorated with blue and white tiles; in warm weather, there's terrace dining. Main courses cost from 6.50€ to 12€.

9

SICILY | Monreale

bedazzled cathedral, is such an important sight that it is considered among greater Palermo's major attractions. In summer, the lively beach scene at Mondello Lido is only 15 minutes away. For a picnic spot with lofty views over the sea and skyline, take an excursion to the 600m (1,969-ft.) Monte Pellegrino, the forested headland towering over Palermo.

Even farther afield, there's the island of Ustica to the north, accessible by hydrofoil (75 min.) or ferry (2 hr., 30 min.) from Palermo's main port. See chapter 10 for full details about Ustica.

MONREALE ★★★

The most popular day trip is to the hill town of Monreale, 10km (6 miles) southwest of Palermo. The dazzling 12th-century **mosaics ★★★** in the Arab-Norman **Monreale Cathedral** (Piazza Guglielmo Il Buono, Monreale; ⓒ **091/6404403;** admission 6€; daily 9am–7pm) are perhaps the greatest artistic treasure in all of Sicily. Even if you have to miss all the other sights in the Palermo environs, try to schedule 2 or 3 hours to make the trek to Monreale. It dwarfs most other sights in Palermo and is, in fact, one of the major attractions of southern Italy.

The debate rages on as to who has the better mosaics—the other contender being the Cappella Palatina at the Norman Palace (p. 176) in Palermo—though it's undeniable that the vast scale of Monreale's mosaics creates the more astonishing impression. Overall, there are more than 2,000 mosaics here, covering 6,000 sq. m (64,583 sq. ft)—even more than in St. Mark's in Venice. The mosaic cycle is the second largest on earth, topped only by Istanbul's Hagia Sofia. The work of Byzantine artisans commissioned by Norman King Roger II, the mosaics culminate in a 13×9m (43×30-ft.) figure of *Christ Pantokrator* ("Ruler of All") in the apse. The rest of the mosaics—all of which are set on a glittering background of gold tesserae—depict scenes from the Old and New Testaments, though the overall geometry of the architecture has a Muslim feel. The cloister of the cathedral is gorgeous, with 228 columns enclosing a groomed courtyard and an ancient Arab fountain in the southwest corner.

Monreale is easy to reach from Palermo. Parking is tricky here, however, so unless you're driving to Monreale en route to somewhere else in Sicily, take the 30-minute ride on bus 389 from Palermo's Piazza Indipendenza. The bus departs every 20 minutes and costs 1€ each way. Bear in mind that the 389 is the most notorious bus line in Sicily for pickpockets, so keep a very close eye on your valuables.

MONDELLO ★

A crescent bay with shallow water and 2km (1¼ miles) of white sand, an Art-Nouveau bathhouse, and a carnival-esque atmosphere make Mondello Lido (12km/7½ miles west of Palermo) the quintessential "people's beach" of Palermo, especially for families. Windsurfing and snorkeling are popular here, and the grand **Stabilimento Balneare** (bathing club, now the excellent Charleston Le Terrazze restaurant), built on a pier in the middle of the bay in 1913, is a fabulous nugget of the old-fashioned European good life. Mondello is an easy 15-minute bus ride (no. 806 from Piazza Sturzo, near Teatro Politeama) or drive from Palermo.

Opening onto a half-moon-shaped bay between the soaring headlands of Monte Pellegrino and Capo Gallo, Mondello is the place for showing off your most daring swimwear and for living it up, including lots of late-night staggering along with the young Palermitani from bar to bar. Between the wars, Mondello was a snobbish retreat for the upper crust, evoking the most fashionable parts of the French Riviera. After World War II, it more democratically became a "beach for everyone."

MONTE PELLEGRINO ★

The parkland and nature preserve of the crown-shaped Monte Pellegrino, what Goethe called "the most beautiful headland on earth," looms over north Palermo. This green oasis and haven from the heat is where Palermitani retreat on a summer day (and on Sunday, when it's overcrowded and best avoided).

You can reach the mountain with bus 812 from Piazza Sturzo (Politeama) in Palermo (30 min.), or with your own car (15–20 min.), following signs to Monte Pellegrino or Santuario Santa Rosalia.

Along the way to the top, you'll be rewarded with some of Sicily's most **panoramic views ★★★**, taking in the old city of Palermo and a sweeping vista of the coastline. Families use the grounds and trails on Pellegrino as a picnic site, but the chief attraction of Monte Pellegrino is the **Santuario di Santa Rosalia** (ℂ 091/540326), a cave where the patron saint of Palermo lived. (Kitschy souvenir hawkers mar the scene somewhat.) Note the little pathway leading to the left of the chapel. If you take it, after about 30 minutes, you'll be at a cliff-top promontory with a view and a statue of the saint. The pathway to the right of the sanctuary leads to the top of Pellegrino, a leisurely hike of about 40 minutes.

CEFALÙ & THE TYRRHENIAN COAST FROM PALERMO TO MESSINA

The coastal road (A19, then A20) runs from Palermo eastward toward Messina. You can, of course, drive straight through the A19 and A20's 220km (137 miles) and not pull off to see a thing (nonstop, the trip is just over 2 hr.), but for anyone wishing to break up the trip, there are some treasures a short distance from this *autostrada*.

If you have time for only one stopover, make it **Cefalù,** the premier destination along the coast thanks to its white sandy beaches and charming village with a famous Romanesque cathedral. The coast also contains some of north Sicily's more impressive ruins, including those at **Himera** (near Termini Imerese) and at **Tyndaris,** west of the port town of Milazzo. Milazzo itself is industrial and unattractive, but it's the only place on Sicily where you can catch ferries and hydrofoils for the Aeolian Islands (p. 249). Inland, the forests and mountains of the **Parco Naturale Regionale delle Madonie** are a highly recommended detour for nature lovers, though you'll need to allow the best part of a day to explore them.

With mountains to one side and the glittering Tyrrhenian to the other (blighted here and there by modern intrusions), the views from the highway are also amazing, and if you like tunnels, you're in luck: The A20 has an insanely high number of long *gallerie* that cut through the massive coastal headlands. Claustrophobics beware.

CEFALÙ ★★

Picturesque Cefalù is where Giuseppe Tornatore shot most of 1988's *Cinema Paradiso* (rent it before you go), and despite a considerable influx of northern European sun seekers in summer, it's still a working fishing village where everyone seems to be named Salvatore. The seaside town is a great place to dip your toes in the Med as well as see one of the most imposing Norman churches in Sicily. Cefalù's 1131 Duomo (Piazza del Duomo; © **091/922021;** daily 8am–noon and 3:30–7pm; free admission) supposedly ordered built by the Norman King Roger II when he landed

CLIMBING THE crag

During the dog days of August, it's a long, hot, sweaty climb up to the top of Cefalù's Rocca, but once you're here, the view is panoramic, one of the grandest in Sicily. If you're stout-hearted, count on 20 minutes to approach the ruins of the so-called Temple of Diana and another 45 huffing and puffing minutes to scale the pinnacle. From Piazza Garibaldi, along Corso Ruggero, a sign— ACCESSO ALLA ROCCA—will launch you on your way. In summer, I recommend taking this jaunt either in the early morning or when evening breezes are blowing.

on a nearby beach after surviving a terrible storm at sea, has a fortresslike facade, emphasized by the two spired and mullioned towers that flank it. Immediately behind the cathedral is the Rocca, a towering, 278m (912-ft.) rock cliff that enhances the Duomo's formidable aspect. The Greeks thought the Rocca evoked a head, so they named the village *Kephalos,* which in time became Cefalù.

The swimming and sunbathing part of Cefalù is its western, modern end, along Lungomare G. Giardina, where gentle breakers lap at a narrow but well-used strip of white sand. Farther east, the beach is packed with European vacationers, while it's a bit broader and less crowded to the west. There isn't much to do, "sights"-wise, in Cefalù beyond the Duomo, Rocca, and beaches, but it's easy to park and get in and out of the town, making for a nice few hours' stopover. Many choose Cefalù as their base for touring this part of Sicily, so I've listed a few overnight options, too.

Cefalù is 1 hour (68km/42 miles) from Palermo. Take the E90 east to the A20 east, toward Messina. Exit at Cefalù and follow signs to the "centro." You can also take the train (1 hr.) or a bus (1½ hr.) from Palermo.

HITTING THE BEACH

Cefalù's crescent-shaped beach is one of the best along the northern coast. Regrettably, it's always packed in summer. In town, I prefer **Lido Poseidon,** where you can rent an umbrella and beach lounger from any number of clubs (May–Sept) for 10€. Other recommended beaches are found west of town at Spiaggia Settefrati and Spiaggia Mazzaforno.

SICILY'S MOST unusual HOTEL

Aesthetes might consider staying overnight in the Cefalù area if only to experience the most unusual hotel in Sicily, where guests sleep among modern art and political manifestoes. The **Atelier Sul Mare ★★★,** in the quiet seaside town of Castel di Tusa (20km/12 miles east of Cefalù), is sometimes defined as an "arts-oriented ashram" and occupies a boxy, concrete building that was erected in the 1960s as a conventional hotel with access to a nearby beach. Any vestiges of its original decor were ripped out long ago by the iconoclastic owner, Messina-born Antonio Presti. Today, the hotel combines aspects of Bauhaus architecture, pop art, psychedelics, hints of very permissive sexuality, and good doses of Italia Socialist politics. The black-and-white lobby's only adornments are hundreds of photocopies of articles about the place. About 25 of the guest rooms are comfortable, "conventional" units, each with original art and a sense of whimsy. The other 15 rooms were each decorated by an artist who lived on the premises for several months while completing the work. Examples include a sinuously curved all-black room by Chilean artist Raoul Ruiz, with a circular bed and a square-shaped skylight that blasts sunlight, representing a spiritual liberty from oppressive governments and cultures. A room decorated in honor of filmmaker and gay activist Pasolini was conceived as a grotto that might remind you of a miniature mosque. *Via Cesare Battisti, Castel di Tusa.* ✆ *0921/334295. www.atelier sulmare.com. 40 units. Doubles 110€–230€. MC, V.* **Amenities:** *Restaurant; bar. In room: A/C, no phone.*

WHERE TO STAY

Kalura ★ ☺ EAST OF TOWN   Set amid palm trees, Kalura is a friendly, inviting oasis with a North African feel. This snug retreat is 3km (2 miles) east along the coast, a 20-minute walk from the center of Cefalù (follow the street signs from town). Guest rooms are simple and well furnished; most open onto a sea view. A park is reserved for children at this very family-friendly place, and the private beach offers good swimming. The hotel is also the most sports-conscious in the area, and can arrange excursions to nearby attractions as well.

Via Cavallaro 13, Contrada Caldura. ☏ **0921/421354.** www.hotel-kalura.com. 73 units. Doubles from 190€. AE, DC, MC, V. **Amenities:** Restaurant; 2 bars; babysitting; mountain bikes; pool; rooms for those w/limited mobility; tennis; watersports equipment. *In room:* A/C, TV, hair dryer.

Riva del Sole ★ TOWN/SEAFRONT   The town's finest accommodation is in a three-story building rising along the seafront. Completely refurbished, it has its own discreet charm and harmonious styling in both its public and private rooms. Run by the Cimino family since it opened in 1966, it offers both attentive service and a welcoming atmosphere. Special features include a graceful garden, a solarium, a panoramic terrace, and an intimate bar. Bedrooms are midsize, tastefully furnished, and well-equipped, each with a private balcony or veranda opening onto the water.

Lungomare G. Giardina. ☏ **0921/421230.** www.rivadelsole.com. 28 units. Doubles 140€–150€. AE, MC, V. Free parking. Closed Oct to mid-Dec. **Amenities:** Bar; babysitting; all nonsmoking rooms; room service. *In room:* A/C, TV, minibar.

WHERE TO DINE

If you're heading out on an excursion, perhaps to Parco delle Madonie (p. 189), you can pick up the makings for a delightful picnic at **Gatta Gaetano Alimentari e Salumeria,** Corso Ruggero 152 (☏ **0921/423156**). This well-stocked deli offers the best of Sicilian cheeses and cured meats, to-die-for olives, and luscious fruits—everything except bread, which you'll find in many places all over town.

For the best cakes and cookies, stop by **Pasticceria Serio Pietro,** V. G. Giglio 29 (☏ **0921/422293**), which also sells more than a dozen flavors of the most delicious gelato in town. The drawback here? The staff never went to finishing school.

Al Porticciolo ★ SICILIAN   At the seafront of the old town, adjacent to the old port, this restaurant is set within a cavelike room that used to be a storage point for fish before the days of refrigeration. During the day, dine in air-conditioned comfort to avoid the heat, but at night, opt for an outdoor table. The pasta with sardines is well prepared here, but I'm also fond of the *tagliatelle* of octopus, the addictive grilled radicchio, and the country-style kettle of mussel soup—just right for a seafaring town. Their *cassata Siciliana* (layered sponge cake filled with ricotta, chocolate, and candied fruits) is among the best I've tasted.

Via Carlo Ortolani di Bordonaro 66. ☏ **0921/921981.** Main courses 8€–17€. AE, DC, MC, V. Thurs–Tues noon–3pm and 7pm–midnight. Closed Nov to mid-Dec.

Kentia ★★ ITALIAN   This restaurant manages to evoke a bit more glamour and style than some of its nearby competitors. It's a cool hideaway from the oppressive sun, thanks to tiled floors, high masonry vaulting, and an understated elegance. A dozen homemade pasta dishes are prepared daily. I generally stick to the *pesce del* *giorno* (catch of the day), which can be grilled to your specifications. The chefs also prepare a daily vegetarian fixed-price menu as well as one devoted entirely to fish. I've sampled both and recommend them heartily.

Via N. Botta 15. ⓒ **0921/423801.** Reservations recommended. Main courses 7€–15€; fixed-price vegetarian menu 18€; fixed-price fish menu 30€. AE, DC, MC, V. June–Sept daily noon–3pm and 7:30–11pm; Oct–May Wed–Mon noon–3pm and 7:30–11pm.

Osteria del Duomo ★★ OLD TOWN SICILIAN/INTERNATIONAL The hippest, most sophisticated restaurant in Cefalù is right in front of the town's famous cathedral, at the bottom of steps that have been trod upon by Norman knights and *La Dolce Vita* movie stars alike. Many tables sit in the open air on cobblestones, others under the vaulted ceiling of the air-conditioned interior. The chefs enthrall you with their smoked fish, their seafood salads are the town's best (and the ideal food on a hot summer day), and their truly excellent *carpaccio* of beef will appeal to serious carnivores. Count on freshly made salads and desserts as well.

Via Seminario 3. ⓒ **0921/421838.** Reservations recommended Sat–Sun. Main courses 8€–16€. AE, DC, MC, V. Tues–Sun noon–midnight. Closed mid-Nov to mid-Dec.

SIDE TRIPS

The excursions listed below are within an hour's drive of Cefalù but can just as easily be done while en route on the coastal road between Palermo and Messina.

Parco Naturale Regionale Delle Madonie ★★

Since 1989, some 39,679 hectares (98,049 acres) of the most beautiful land in Sicily has been set aside as a national park. The park contains more than half of the 2,600 plant species known in Sicily. Some of the most ancient rocks and mountains on the island are found here, along with some of the most spectacular peaks. Among them, **Pizzo Carbonara,** at 1,979m (6,493 ft.), is the highest mountain in Sicily outside of Mount Etna.

The park is far from a wilderness—it is inhabited and contains any number of charming villages. To reach it from Cefalù, follow the road directions south for 14km (8¾ miles) to the **Santuario di Gibilmanna.** From the belvedere at this town, in front of the little 17th-century church, you can take in a **panoramic view ★★** of the Madonie, including the peak of Pizzo Carbonara.

The Santuario di Gibilmanna is a shrine to the Virgin Mary. The Madonna is said to have shown signs of life in the 18th century when she was restoring sight to blind pilgrims and speech to a mute. Since the Vatican confirmed this claim, Gibilmanna has been one of the most important shrines in Sicily, drawing the devout.

After taking in the view, continue southeast, following the signs to **Castelbuono,** an idyllic town that grew around a *castello* (castle) constructed in the 1300s. You can stop over to visit its historic core, **Piazza Margherita.** The church, **Madrice Vecchia,** dates from the 14th century, and was built on the ruins of a pagan temple.

If you arrive during the lunch hour, your best bet for a bite to eat is **Romittaggio,** Località San Guglielmo Sud (ⓒ **0921/671323**), 5km (3 miles) south of Castelbuono. Specializing in simple mountain food, the restaurant is installed in a monastery from the Middle Ages. In summer, you can request a table in the arcades of the cloister. Meals range in price from 8€ to 16€. The restaurant is closed from June 15 to July 15 and on Wednesdays year-round.

The road continues south to **Petralia Soprana** ★★, at 1,147m (3,763 ft.) the loftiest town in Madonie and one of the best-preserved medieval villages of Sicily, with narrow streets and houses of local stone. A grand belvedere is found at Piazza del Popolo, with a **stunning vista** ★★ toward Enna in the east.

Himera

This was the site of a 7th-century-B.C. Greek settlement, 25km (16 miles) west along the coast from Cefalù (near the town of Termini Imerese, and 51km/32 miles east of Palermo). It's famous for the remains of the **Tempio della Vittoria** ★ (Temple of Victory), situated on a coastal plain at the mouth of the Imera River off Route SS113. Allow an hour or so to explore the site.

In 480 B.C., Himera was the site of one of the major battles of Sicily. The Greeks from Agrigento and Syracuse defeated a massive army led by the Carthaginian Hamilcar, who was killed in battle. The temple was constructed to honor this Greek victory; the labor was supplied by Carthaginians prisoners. But the triumph was short-lived. In 409 B.C., Hamilcar's nephew, Hannibal, attacked Himera in revenge for his uncle's death. He razed the city, killing most of its inhabitants.

Himera's temple contains little more than its foundation, with no standing columns. Yet the setting and the view make it worth a visit, especially if you have the imagination to bring it alive. If your imagination fails you, you can visit a modern antiquarium that shows diagrams of how the temple looked in its heyday. The remains of two other temples are also found in this archaeological park.

The site is open Monday to Saturday 9am until dusk, and Sunday 9am to 2pm; admission is 2€.

Tyndaris ★

At Capo Tindari, approximately 85km (53 miles) east from Cefalù, stand the **ruins of Tyndaris** (☎ **0941/369023;** daily 9am–1 hr. before sunset; 2.10€), on a lonely, rocky promontory overlooking Golfo di Patti. The view alone is reason enough to go; it stretches from Milazzo in the east to Capo Calavà in the west. On a clear day, there are stunning vistas of the Aeolian Islands, with Vulcano the nearest. Though Tyndaris goes back to the Greek era, most of what you see dates to the Roman Empire, including the basilica, beyond which is a **Roman villa** in rather good condition, with some original floor mosaics. Cut into a hill at the end of town is a 4th century B.C. **Greek theater.** The **insula romana,** an apartment building with ground-floor shops, contains the ruins of baths, patrician villas with fragments of mosaics, and what may have been taverns or drinking halls.

TAORMINA ★★★

Perched high on the edge of lush cliffs overlooking the Ionian Sea, the smoking top of Mount Etna looming in the background, Taormina is the most breathtaking town in Sicily, and one of the most dramatically situated hill towns in Italy, period. With such an enviable position, it was too good to remain a secret. Favored by holidaying Brits in the 19th century and popularized by the Hollywood set—Marlene Dietrich, Elizabeth Taylor, Cary Grant, and Clark Gable, to name a few—in the 1950s and '60s, Taormina is now the province of mainstream international tourists. Having said that, Taormina is a must on any first-time itinerary through Sicily. Its hotels are collectively the best in southern Italy, and conveniences (Internet that actually works!)

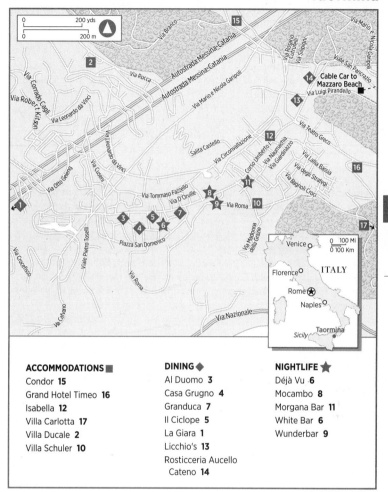

ACCOMMODATIONS ■
Condor **15**
Grand Hotel Timeo **16**
Isabella **12**
Villa Carlotta **17**
Villa Ducale **2**
Villa Schuler **10**

DINING ◆
Al Duomo **3**
Casa Grugno **4**
Granduca **7**
Il Ciclope **5**
La Giara **1**
Licchio's **13**
Rosticceria Aucello
  Cateno **14**

NIGHTLIFE ★
Déjà Vu **6**
Mocambo **8**
Morgana Bar **11**
White Bar **6**
Wunderbar **9**

and English-speakers abound, making for stress-free travel. Apart from its astonishing natural beauty, Taormina is undeniably jolly, with a European-summer-resort vibe that's hard not to like.

Like so many places in Sicily, Taormina has seen a long list of conquerors, like the Greeks and Romans, who built a spectacular theater here that is now the gorgeous venue for Taormina's summer music festival. In the Middle Ages, the Saracens, French, and Spanish left their marks in the town's storybook architecture. In the modern era, however, Taormina seems to have no other reason to exist than for the thousands upon thousands of visitors who flock here for dining, bar-hopping, shopping, breathing the tonic air that only seems to exist in hill towns by the sea, and enjoying the nearby beaches.

While there is almost no Sicilian soul left in Taormina, the town has retained its medieval look and charm. Corso Umberto I, the pedestrian main drag, is a clamorous, infectious parade of vacationers from early morning to well past midnight, and it can be great fun to get caught up in the revelry. If that's not your speed, there are also plenty of accommodations in the immediate vicinity that enjoy all the benefits of Taormina's physical position without the hordes of town.

Mt. Etna is equidistant from Taormina and Catania, but Taormina, with its fine hotels and restaurants and general ease of doing things, is often preferable as a base for day trips to see the volcano up close. Another worthwhile half-day excursion from here is the Alcantara Gorges. For either Etna or Alcantara, numerous agencies operate a variety of package tours, or you can do it yourself if you have a car.

With its mild climate, Taormina is a year-round resort, but at its busiest from May to October, when swimming is possible at the beaches below.

Essentials

Taormina lies near the northern tip of the eastern coast of Sicily. Catania (about 1 hr. by car) is the nearest airport, but you can also fly into Palermo (a straightforward 2½ hr. by car—all *autostrada*); consider a short stop in Cefalù to break up the drive. The Taormina-Giardini Naxos train station is well downhill from town, a 15-minute drive away (you'll need a taxi or hotel shuttle). If you bring a car (recommended), be aware that once in the labyrinth of steep, one-way, and pedestrianized streets in town, driving and parking is an adrenaline-pumping adventure that quickly turns into a headache. Get clear directions and parking information from your hotel before setting out. If your hotel doesn't have parking, try the **Lumbi** parking garage (© **0942/24345**) on the northern outskirts of Taormina, which runs a shuttle van for customers to town and back.

Exploring

With medieval stone gates at either end, pedestrian-only **Corso Umberto I** is the main artery of Taormina. Nearly all of what is considered central Taormina lies within a few blocks up- or downhill from the north-south arc drawn by Corso Umberto. **Porta Messina,** at the north end, is busier and more touristy, while **Porta Catania,** at the south end, is quieter, with some normal businesses and shops where you might even spy a few local Taorminese doing their daily business. Just outside Porta Messina is the long, triangular square that serves as the city's bus terminus, taxi stand, and hotel shuttle van stop for Taormina town. Regional buses arrive at a depot 400m (1,300 ft.) down the road (Via Pirandello); also down Via Pirandello, only 200m (650 ft.) from Porta Messina, is the upper station of the *funivia* (cableway) that connects Taormina with the beach at Mazzarò (see below).

Corso Umberto's 1km (¾ mile) would take less than 15 minutes to walk end-to-end if it weren't for the diversions along the way. But with so many shops, views, and

---

Travel Tip

Cafes and restaurants along Corso Umberto I itself tend to be surly tourist traps that, unfortunately, don't think twice about charging unwitting travelers close to 10€ for a simple takeaway sandwich. Stick to the side streets for your meals, snacks, and drinks, and you'll almost always find fairer prices and warmer service.

people to ogle, allow a good hour or more to amble along the length of it. Also, summer crowds slow the pace of the *passeggiata* here considerably. The **shopping ★★** here is the best in Sicily, ranging from high-fashion (no problem finding 500€ sandals) to high-kitsch (lava-themed liqueurs in Etna-shaped bottles, anyone?), and there are plenty of cafes and bars where you can grab a seat and watch the pageant go by.

About 50m (165 ft.) into town from Porta Messina is Piazza Vittorio Emanuele II. On the west side is the Moorish-Gothic **Palazzo Corvaja ★**, with its lancet windows and swallow-tailed crenellations. The building houses the city tourist office (✆ **0942/23243;** Mon–Sat 8:30am–2pm and 4–7pm). Immediately south of Palazzo Corvaja are the piazza and **Chiesa di Santa Caterina,** behind which are ruins of an ancient Roman *odeon* (small theater).

To the east of Piazza Vittorio Emanuele II, past the tree-shaded kiosks and down Via del Teatro Greco, is the marquee historical attraction of Taormina, the **Teatro Greco ★★★** (aka Teatro Antico or Teatro Greco-Romano; Via del Teatro Greco 40; ✆ **0942/23220;** 6€; daily 9am–7pm). As a purely archaeological site, it's not on par with Sicily's other star ruins—the theater is a summer concert and opera venue, so there are modern benches and stage equipment that detract from the atmosphere somewhat—but the position and the rapturous **views ★★★** from the top are what make this worth your time and euros. It's arguably the most spectacular playhouse of the ancient world and precipitously nestled on a promontory overlooking the sea and Mt. Etna. Built in the 3rd century B.C. by the Greeks and later modified by the Romans, the theater once accommodated 10,000 spectators and is today outfitted with bleachers for patrons of Taormina Arte summer festival (www.taormina-arte.com). In antiquity, performances took place on a stage in front of the *scaenae frons,* an evocative and now-skeletal wall of crumbling brick, marble columns, and niches. Modern productions use a wooden platform in the orchestra area and employ the romantic outline of the *scaenae frons* as a backdrop. (If you are lucky enough to catch a show here, the setting, onstage dramatics, and histrionic peanut gallery make for one very memorable evening. Hot-blooded Sicilians don't withhold audible commentary and wild gesturing when a performance stirs their passions.) The magnificent site also captured the attention of Woody Allen, who set the chorus scenes of *Mighty Aphrodite* here. Note that you can get a good overall idea of the theater from below without paying the admission fee, but to get to those awe-inspiring views over the bay and Etna (IMHO the best panorama in Sicily), you've got to cough up the 6 euros and climb to the top. Your digital camera will thank you.

A fun little detour into Mediterranean fabulousness after visiting the Teatro Greco is the **bar at the Grand Hotel Timeo ★** (Via Teatro Greco 59; ✆ **0942/625837**), on the south side of the road between the Teatro Greco and Corso Umberto I. The hotel itself is one of Taormina's way-overpriced grande dames, but the bar (also expensive, from 10€–15€ per drink) is open to the public and set on a lovely terrace overlooking the property's lush gardens. Going for a cocktail here is a classic Taorminese tradition and perfectly embodies the town's holiday spirit.

Just west (inland) from the Grand Hotel Timeo, turn left down the first side street, then left again on Via Bagnoli Croce to reach the **Giardino Pubblico ★★** (aka Parco Duchi di Cesarò; no phone; free admission; 8:30am–6pm). Taormina's quiet and shady municipal park is the perfect antidote to the crowds elsewhere in town. Bring a picnic and snag a spot on one of the benches, or just go for a walk. As with most everything in Taormina, the park has incredible views.

ABOVE & beyond TAORMINA TOWN

Most tourists venture *down* from Taormina town to the Ionian beaches below the resort, but for awe-inspiring views and a welcome break from the hordes of high season, I recommend going up the hill and inland to visit Monte Tauro and the village of **Castelmola ★**, each about 3km (2 miles) northwest of town. This short but rewarding foray (follow Via Leonardo da Vinci up to Castelmola, then look for signs for Monte Tauro, or take the Castelmola-Monte Tauro bus from Via Pirandello in Taormina town) affords some of the loftiest views in all of eastern Sicily. From **Monte Tauro**'s 390m (1,280-ft.) elevation, the contours of Mt. Etna are a formidable sight. There are also some hiking paths and ancient ruins scattered about here. At charming Castelmola, considered the "balcony of Taormina," the panoramas are equally sublime, and you'll find coffee and wine bars where you can have a seat and enjoy the atmosphere—for a lot less money than down in Taormina. For a full meal, head to **Parco Reale,** at the Hotel Villa Sonia, Via Porta Mola 9, *©* **0942/ 28082;** open daily for lunch and dinner.

Back up on Corso Umberto I, about halfway between Porta Messina and Porta Catania, is Taormina's largest and most beloved square, **Piazza IX Aprile ★★**, with the medieval **Torre dell'Orologio** (clocktower) and the churches of San Giuseppe and Sant'Agostino creating a postcard tableau beneath the steep exposed rock of Monte Tauro. The expansive piazza is paved with a checkerboard of pink and black stones and is open on one side to the east, providing a gorgeous view over the sparkling Ionian Sea; the full outline of Mt. Etna, smoking summit and all, is visible to the south. Resist the urge to rest your feet at one of the cafes here as they charge an arm and a leg for the privilege of using their sidewalk tables; instead, drink in that splendid view from a bench along the piazza's eastern side.

Another 250m (820 ft.) south along Corso Umberto, you'll reach the small **Piazza del Duomo,** home to a fortresslike 14th-century church with crenellations and exposed rubble masonry walls. A pretty baroque **fountain,** capped by an unusual female centaur, sits in the square out front.

Of course, many tourists in Taormina are here for the beaches. Although the "seaside resort" of Taormina is actually 200m (650 ft.) above the shore of the Ionian Sea, the handy *funivia* (cableway; *©* **0942/23605;** daily 9am–1am; 2€; no credit cards), a few minutes' walk from Porta Messina, makes it a snap to access the beaches below, whether for a swim or just a stroll. The upper station of the *funivia* is on Via Pirandello; right outside the lower station of the cableway is the beach development of Mazzarò, while a few minutes' walk south (to the right as you exit the station) leads to a larger bay and Isola Bella (see "Swimming in Taormina," for information on both beaches). To reach the larger resort of Giardini-Naxos to the south, take a bus (from the depot along Via Pirandello) or drive.

Swimming near Taormina

Don't let the town's vertical distance from the water discourage you: It's easy to reach the shore, whether by taking the *funivia* or buses from Via Pirandello. As with the best Italian coastlines, "beaches" tend to be narrow and crowded, with gravelly sand, but the surrounding scenery of forests and rocky cliffs and warm, cerulean water make up for it. Expect to pay 10€ to 14€ for use of a chair and umbrella at any of the beach clubs.

At the bottom of the cableway is **Mazzarò** ★, a small bay with several beach clubs and kayak rentals. The next bay south is larger, and punctuated in the middle by **Isola Bella** ★★, a gorgeous island and WWF nature reserve that Truman Capote was all set to buy for $10,000 back in the 1970s—until his check was returned marked "insufficient funds." Isola Bella is connected to the beach by a narrow spit of sand. Depending on water level, you can either walk or wade there. If you want to be where young Italians go to party, take a bus to **Giardini-Naxos,** a more modern resort development to the south, with thumping nightclubs on the beach.

North of Mazzarò are the long, wide beaches of **Spisone** and **Letojanni** ★, more developed but less crowded than Giardini-Naxos. In Letojanni, try **Paradise Beach Club,** Via Lungomare, Letojanni (✆ **0942/36944**), a 1920s villa and beach club where Greta Garbo once sunned and swam. A local bus leaves Taormina for Mazzarò, Spisone, and Letojanni, and another heads down the coast to Giardini.

Where to Stay

Hotels right in town tend to be pricey, but the good location can be worth it, as everyone gravitates to the top for dining and diversion. If you opt for an out-of-the-way address, be sure the hotel offers transportation to town—you won't want to deal with driving yourself or walking, and cabs are not only expensive but also few and far between in high season.

One of the celebrated names of Taormina hospitality, the historic San Domenico, is not listed here because I've consistently found it too stuffy and formal for the otherwise fun spirit of Taormina. The gardens there, however, are magnificent—if you want to check it out, stop in for an evening cocktail. The hotel is on Piazza San Domenico, 50m (165 ft.) south of Piazza del Duomo on the western end of town.

Condor TOWN   It's basic, but for expensive Taormina, this *pensione* a few minutes' walk north of Porta Messina does the trick for budget travelers. Rooms on upper floors have panoramic views and are far preferable to the darker units downstairs, which are functional enough but bring to mind an iffy motel on the outskirts of Reno. The young and relaxed clientele here always seems to be very friendly, with guests often socializing on the property's roof terrace.

Via Dietro Cappuccini 25. ✆ **0942/23124.** www.condorhotel.com. 12 units. Doubles from 85€. AE, DC, MC, V. *In room:* A/C, TV, hair dryer, free Wi-Fi.

Grand Hotel Timeo ★★ TOWN   If you must indulge in the pseudo-glamorous (and wildly overpriced) "grand hotel" experience in Taormina, skip the stuffy and overrated San Domenico and book a room instead at the buzzier and more central Timeo. Hidden in a tranquil private park just below the Greek Amphitheater, the old-world Timeo opened in 1873 and has hosted Audrey Hepburn, Marcello Mastroianni, and Sophia Loren. It's perched on a swoon-worthy panoramic terrace that's flooded with light and views upward to the Greek theater and down across town to the sea. With lush gardens and neoclassical architecture, the aura here is that of a sophisticated 19th-century villa that manages to be lighthearted and baronial at the same time. Elegant and spacious rooms have Baroque flourishes, and most have balconies or terraces. For the price tag and hotel classification, however, some of the furnishings feel too dated and services and amenities just not up to luxury snuff. Without a doubt, the Timeo coasts on its setting more than anything else. Guests have private beach access in Mazzarò; the staff will arrange tee times at nearby golf courses. Even if you don't stay here, visit the fabulous gardens and happening bar.

Via Teatro Greco 59. © **0942/625837.** www.grandhoteltimeo.com. 83 units. Doubles 380€–560€. AE, DC, MC, V. **Amenities:** Restaurant; bar; babysitting; concierge; private beach (1km/¾ mile away); pool; room service; wellness center. *In room:* A/C, TV, hair dryer, minibar.

Isabella ★ TOWN   All sunny yellows and creams, with a small-scale and chic feel, the Isabella is one of only two hotels located directly on pedestrian thoroughfare Corso Umberto I and welcomes visitors with a lobby that might remind you of the living room in a comfy country home. Guest rooms are not particularly large, though cozy and plush; some have views over the all-pedestrian hubbub of the town's main street. On the rooftop is the solarium-cum-breakfast terrace.

Corso Umberto I 58. © **0942/23153.** www.hotel-isabella.it. 32 units. Doubles 156€–280€. AE, DC, MC, V. **Amenities:** Restaurant; bar; babysitting; beach club w/watersports equipment/rentals; solarium; transfers; wellness center nearby. *In room:* A/C, TV, hair dryer, minibar.

Villa Carlotta ★★ 📷   Only Villa Ducale and Grand Hotel Timeo enjoy the same tranquil and romantic position as this house, situated in a mock castle at a busy corner in Taormina town. The entire property, owned by the same folks who run Villa Ducale, was updated in 2007 with strikingly sophisticated and varied interiors that never sacrifice style for comfort. Secluded back gardens (with swimming pool) add to the wonderful sense of privacy, given the hotel's central location. Staff is warm and professional; the only sour note is the price (Villa Ducale, up on the hill, is much more affordable), though Web deals are often available.

Via Pirandello 81. © **0942/626058.** www.hotelvillacarlottataormina.com. 23 units. Doubles 428€–613€. AE, DC, MC, V. **Amenities:** Restaurant; concierge; health club; library; nearby; pool; transfers and excursions. *In room:* A/C, TV, DVD player, hair dryer, minibar, free Wi-Fi.

Villa Ducale ★★★ 📷 HILLS ABOVE TOWN   Hands-down my favorite place to stay in Taormina is this romantic and sunny inn, serenely perched above town and decorated with folksy Sicilian flair. Bathrooms have Etro toiletries and shower jets or hydromassage tubs. Many units have terraces with jaw-dropping views of Mt. Etna. The charming, down-to-earth staff ensures a personalized stay, and a free shuttle bus makes reaching town a nonissue (the company of the convivial driver is a delight in itself). At 6pm every day, guests gather on the terrace for a complimentary sunset cocktail, accompanied by a spread of typical Sicilian appetizers. The Villa Ducale's sister hotel in town, the fancier and more expensive Villa Carlotta, is also lovely; both are extremely popular, so book well ahead.

Via Leonardo da Vinci 60. © **0942/28153.** www.villaducale.com. 17 units. Doubles 190€–280€. AE, DC, MC, V. **Amenities:** Beach access; transfers; Jacuzzi; room service; free shuttle to town; terrace. *In room:* A/C, TV, hair dryer, minibar, free Wi-Fi.

Villa Schuler ★★ TOWN   This lovely pastel palazzo hearkens back to a gentler era of Taormina tourism. Immersed in lush gardens below the madness of Corso Umberto, the family-run hotel is a haven of tranquillity with airy rooms (many with dramatic sea views) and huge bathrooms (many with Jacuzzi tubs). The most luxurious way to stay here is to book the garden villa suite with its own private access. It's spacious and beautifully furnished, with two bathrooms (one with a Jacuzzi). The villa comes with a kitchenette, patio, private garden, and veranda.

Via Roma, Piazzetta Bastione. © **0942/23481.** www.villaschuler.com. 27 units. Doubles 138€–196€. Villa suite 258€. AE, DC, MC, V. **Amenities:** Garden; piano and reading room. *In room:* A/C, TV, hair dryer, minibar, free Wi-Fi.

Where to Dine

Al Duomo ★ TOWN SICILIAN Known for its romantic terrace dining, this restaurant prepares its dishes using the freshest local produce and regional ingredients. It's an attractive place, with brickwork tiles and inlaid marble tables. Try the stewed lamb with potatoes and red Sicilian wine; fried calamari sautéed in extra-virgin olive oil; or rissolé of fresh anchovies.

Via degli Ebrei 11. ℂ **0942/625656.** Reservations recommended. Entrees 9€–18€. AE, DC, MC, V. Nov–Mar Mon–Sat noon–2:30pm and 7–11pm; Apr–Oct Thurs–Mon noon–2:30pm and 7–11pm.

Casa Grugno ★★ TOWN CREATIVE SICILIAN The hottest restaurant in town is helmed by an Austrian chef, Andreas Zangerl, who turns out a delectably haute version of Sicilian cuisine—traditional island recipes are prepared in artful, modern ways. The room is lively and intimate, with bright yellow walls and Saracen arches.

Via Santa Maria dei Greci. ℂ **0942/21208.** www.casagrugno.it. Reservations essential in season. Entrees 15€–25€. AE, DC, MC, V. Dinner Thurs–Tues.

Granduca ★ 🏛 SICILIAN This atmospheric spot, entered through an antiques store, serves excellent, carefully executed cuisine. In fair weather, request a table in the beautiful gardens. My favorite pasta here is spaghetti alla Norma (with tomato sauce, eggplant, and ricotta). If you want something truly Sicilian, ask for pasta with sardines. The best meat dish is the grilled roulades. At night pizzas are an economical option way to fill up, and baked to perfection in a wood-fired oven.

Corso Umberto I, 172. ℂ **0942/24983.** Reservations recommended. Entrees 8€–15€. Pizzas from 6€. AE, DC, MC, V. Daily 12:30–3pm and 7:30pm–midnight.

Il Ciclope 🍴 SICILIAN/ITALIAN This is one Taormina's better low-priced *trattorie*. Set back from the main street, it opens onto the pint-size Piazzetta Salvatore Leone. In summer, try to snag an outside table. The food is fairly simple, but the ingredients are fresh and the dishes well prepared. Try the fish soup, Sicilian squid, or grilled shrimp.

Corso Umberto I, 203. ℂ **0942/23263.** Entrees 7€–16€. AE, DC, MC, V. Thurs–Tues noon–3pm and 6:30–10:30pm. Closed Jan 10–Feb 15 and Wed Oct–May.

La Giara ★★ SICILIAN/ITALIAN Glossy, airy, and reminiscent of Rome during the heyday *la dolce vita*, this restaurant is almost excessively formal, and it has remained predictably stable since its founding in 1953. Views sweep from the veranda's outdoor tables over the bay of Taormina. The Art Deco ambience is also inviting, with marble floors and columns shaped from stone quarried in the fields outside Syracuse. The pastas are meals in themselves; I'm especially fond of the ricotta-stuffed cannelloni and the ravioli stuffed with pesto-flavored eggplant. The fresh fish of the day is grilled to perfection, and meats are cooked equally well.

Vico la Floresta 1. ℂ **0942/23360.** Reservations required. Entrees 18€–28€. AE, DC, MC, V. Apr–July and Sept–Oct Tues–Sun 8:15–11pm; Nov–Mar Fri–Sat 8:15–11pm; Aug daily 8:15–11pm.

Licchio's ★★ TOWN SICILIAN In terms of atmosphere, Licchio's is what you might call family-chic. Just off Porta Messina, you'll dine in a refined (though surgically bright) and bustling back garden on classic, seafood-focused Sicilian primi and *secondi* plus antipasti like tuna burgers and out-of-this-world carpaccio—try the *cernia* (grouper). Vegetarians and non-fish-eaters can also find plenty to order on the *terra* ("turf") side of the menu. This dinner-only restaurant draws a lot of real Sicilians, whether from Taormina proper or nearby towns, for a festive night out.

Via C. Patricio 10. ℂ **0942/625327.** Reservations essential in season. Entrees 7€–18€. AE, DC, MC, V. Fri–Wed 8–11pm.

Rosticceria Aucello Cateno ★ TOWN SNACKS/TO-GO With so many tourist-trap restaurants in Taormina, honest take-out joints are a godsend. My favorite is this jolly *tavola calda* (hot food deli) opposite the main taxi and hotel shuttle stop, where you can get freshly made lasagne, cannelloni, roast chicken, and *arancini* (fried rice balls) for a few euros each. Take your picnic to the beach, the Giardino Pubblico park, or your hotel room's terrace.

Via Cappuccini 8. ℂ **0942/623672.** To-go items from 1.50€ each. No credit cards. Daily 10am–8pm.

Side Trips

For information on visiting Mt. Etna from Taormina, see p. 199.

Less time-consuming than trekking up to Etna is the short trip out of town to the **Gole dell'Alcantara** ★ (ℂ **0942/985010**), which is a series of gorges with beautiful rapids and waterfalls. By car, head up SS. 185 some 17km (11 miles) from Taormina. Or take **Interbus** (ℂ **0942/625301**) for the 1-hour trip departing from Taormina three or four times per day. The round-trip fare is 4.50€. It's usually possible to walk up the river from May to September (when the water level is low), though you must inquire about current conditions before you do so. From the Gole dell'Alcantara parking lot, take an elevator partway into the scenic abyss and then continue on foot. You're likely to get wet, so bring your bathing suit. The waters are extremely cold, but they feel especially refreshing in July and August. If you don't have appropriate shoes, you can rent rubber boots at the entrance. From October to April, only the entrance is accessible, but the view is always panoramic. It costs 3€ to enter the gorge, which is open daily from 7am to 7:30pm. Allow at least an hour to "do" the gorge, plus travel time there and back.

Taormina After Dark

When night falls, many visitors are content to relax at cafe tables on outdoor terraces. The most popular form of evening entertainment is the *passeggiata*, or promenade, along Corso Umberto I. (Boutiques, very wisely, stay open until 1 or 2am in summer.) If you must indulge in the time-honored (and ghastly expensive) Taorminese tradition of going for a drink on the central square, Piazza IX Aprile, I prefer **Mocambo** (ℂ **0942/23350**) to **Wunderbar** (ℂ **0942/625302**). Both are historic, but Mocambo is friendlier and doesn't feel quite as touristy. Elsewhere in town, the happening nightspots go in and out of vogue, though the throwback piano bar, populated by leathery sugar daddies and German tourists wearing too much fragrance, is a common theme. Everywhere in Taormina is gay-friendly, and none of these spots really gets going until at least 11pm. Two words: disco nap!

A failsafe option for stylish surroundings and well-made drinks is **Morgana Bar** (Scesa Morgana 4; ℂ **0942/620056**). It has sumptuous interiors that scream "fashion" and a fabulous rear garden. A little less over-the-top, the current "it" place for trendy 20- and 30-somethings is **White Bar** ★ (Piazzetta Garibaldi 6/7; ℂ **0942/ 23767**), which has a sleek, modern look and patio tables on a charming little tree-filled square. Opposite White Bar is an also-popular bar called **Déjà Vu** (Piazzetta Garibaldi 2; ℂ **0942/628694**). It's sexy in a brothel-y kind of way (a dark labyrinth of rooms with dim red lighting, gilt-framed mirrors, and animal-print ottomans) and known as a "meet" market. Food is also served. The real discos are down in Giardini-Naxos, which has a younger vibe than Taormina proper.

MT. ETNA ★★★

Standing atop Europe's largest active volcano, as a fierce wind whips at your face and nearly knocks you over, it's hard to believe you're on a Mediterranean island. Yet this 3,324m (10,906-ft.) behemoth is inextricable from Sicily's identity, having wreaked destruction on nearby towns for millennia. The ancients explained its rumbling and molten output quite simply: It was where Hephaestus, god of fire, and his crack metalsmith, the Cyclops, forged thunderbolts for Zeus.

Mt. Etna isn't beautiful, per se, but a trip to the top of this awesome peak is an absolute must for nature lovers and a highlight for anyone traveling in Sicily. Etna is a classic day trip from Catania (Interbus runs coaches up the south side from Catania's central train station), but Taormina is a more congenial base for touring the volcano. Several bus companies in Taormina run a wide range of day tours to Etna, but be sure to get details about what's included before you book: The less expensive tours generally do not take you all the way to the top. If driving your own car, allow from 1 to 1½ hours from Catania or Taormina. Public buses take from 30 to 45 minutes longer, making Etna a full-day excursion pretty much any way you do it, and a tiring one. Although no significant hiking is necessary, conditions at the summit are often extreme, so bring a light jacket, sturdy shoes, sunblock, and water. Visibility is generally better before noon.

By car or bus, you can ascend Etna from its forested north side (follow signs to Linguaglossa) or its lava-covered south side (signs to Nicolosi then Rifugio La Sapienza); from either direction, brown signs marked "Etna" guide you to the staging areas where the summit tours begin. Both approaches have their merits, but coming from the south is a bit more fun since that's the side where the Funivia dell'Etna cableway is located. Park your car at Rifugio la Sapienza, the touristy outpost at 1,900m (6,234 ft.), then ride the *funivia* up to 2,500m (8,202 ft.). At the funivia office, you'll pay a steep 46€ for the various transport and guide fees that get you to the top.

First, the thrilling cableway climbs to the Torre del Filosofo station, where, in winter, you can hop off and ski down the snow-covered volcano. At Torre del Filosofo, you'll transfer to boxy white, high-clearance vans that look like something out of *The Empire Strikes Back.* These "Jeeps" (as locals call them) clamber up another 100m (328 ft.) to around 3,000m (9,843 ft.)—not quite the summit, but as close as tourists can safely go—where you're led around Etna's harsh upper reaches on foot by a grizzled old *guida alpina.* These mountains guides often don't speak any English but will manage to explain fumaroles and the like with emphatic gestures and a lit cigarette as prop. There's also a short walk at this point, over exposed and blustery volcanic dunes that really make you feel the force of nature, to some steaming craters. The extreme wind and sloping terrain makes it exhilarating and fun, but anyone with respiratory, heart, or balance problems should skip it. (Active types can make the ascent from 1,900m/6,234 ft. or 2,500m–3,000m/8,202 ft.–9.843 ft. on foot—and it'll knock a bunch of euros off that 46€ fee—but it's a shadeless and wind-beaten climb over a squirrelly footing of loose pumice and an astonishing number of dead ladybugs.)

Unlike Mt. Vesuvius, which destroyed ancient Pompeii back in A.D. 79, Etna is still quite active. Its summit crater emits a continuous plume of smoke that's visible throughout eastern Sicily when the sky is clear. Satellite images frequently show a bright orange, molten center in Etna's cone. Still, locals don't seem too worried about their formidable neighbor: As volcanoes go, Etna is a "friendly giant" that's only registered 77 fatalities in 190 eruptions since 1500 B.C. When she blows, the lava moves slowly, allowing plenty of time to get out of the way.

SIRACUSA ★★★

One of the centers of ancient Western civilization, southeastern Sicily is a sightseeing mecca filled with evocative ruins. The area's chief town is Siracusa (sometimes called Syracuse for English-speakers), one of the most important cities of the ancient world of Magna Graecia (Greater Greece), rivaling even Athens in its cultural and military muscle. In the 18th century, following the devastating earthquake of 1693, the entire town was rebuilt in the ebullient Baroque style that still characterizes Ortigia Island, Siracusa's irresistibly charming *centro storico.* When people talk about how much they love Siracusa, they're really talking about Ortigia and of course those glorious Greek ruins.

While Siracusa is plenty equipped for tourists, it's still a place (unlike Taormina or Cefalù) that even in high season doesn't feel overrun by foreigners. Locals very much do their thing: Families observe the afternoon *pausa,* when housewives cook up heavenly aromas in hidden kitchens; and come sundown, kids kick soccer balls against the Duomo—in short, living up to all your folksy Sicilian stereotypes. The cheer and authenticity of Siracusa, combined with its wonderful baroque architecture and impressive Greek ruins, make it hard not to fall in love with this seaside city.

The heart of "old" (though not ancient Greek) Siracusa is the island of Ortigia, an impossibly picturesque village whose main square, Piazza del Duomo, is the prettiest and most well-used public space in Sicily. Side streets, lined with balconied Baroque palazzi and opening onto sliverlike views of the sea, ooze Sicilian flair. While Ortigia spent much of the late 20th century crumbling, energetic restorations of those sultry palazzi have been underway for the past decade, and Ortigia is now brighter and cleaner than ever. (Although you can save money by staying at hotels in the modern town, I highly recommend staying somewhere on Ortigia, since this is where all the best dining, street life, and shopping are.)

The greatest single historical attraction of Siracusa is the **Parco Archeologico della Neapolis,** one of the most impressive archaeological gardens in Italy. The park is on the mainland of Siracusa, a half-hour walk or cab/bus ride north of Ortigia, and drips with the atmosphere of ancient times. It contains a massive Greek theater, a Roman amphitheater, and a quarry, once used as a prison, where lush vegetation has taken root. An adjacent museum contains artifacts from the entire region. Dedicated antiquities enthusiasts should also make it to the **Castello Eurialo,** a fun-to-explore Greek fortress, and where native son Archimedes first uttered "Eureka!"

Some of the most memorable cultural events in Sicily are staged in May and June, when ancient Greek plays are produced by Siracusa's **Istituto Nazionale del Dramma Antico** (Via Cavour 48; ⓒ **0931/487248;** ticket office open Mon–Fri 10am–1pm and 3–5pm; www.indafondazione.org). Performances, strictly from the ancient oeuvre of Euripides, Aeschylus, and their contemporaries, take place in the Teatro Greco (Greek Theater) in the Parco Archeologico della Neapolis (archaeological park). Tickets cost from 30€ to 62€.

Siracusa

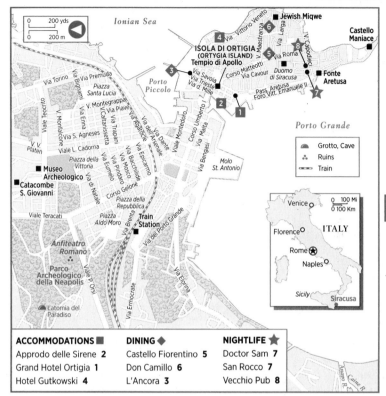

ACCOMMODATIONS ■	DINING ◆	NIGHTLIFE ★
Approdo delle Sirene **2**	Castello Fiorentino **5**	Doctor Sam **7**
Grand Hotel Ortigia **1**	Don Camillo **6**	San Rocco **7**
Hotel Gutkowski **4**	L'Ancora **3**	Vecchio Pub **8**

Taking in the rich sights and local flavor of Siracusa is a breeze and enormously satisfying—no wonder it's so many visitors' favorite destination in Sicily. Ortigia and the ancient ruins of Siracusa will be one of the highlights of your trip to this island, but the modern city that has sprouted around the two is unfortunately marred by ugly high-rises and temporary-looking supermarkets along speedways.

Though it's on the water, Siracusa proper doesn't have any sand, but some great beaches lie just a short distance away. Siracusa is also a convenient base for visiting the other celebrated Baroque hill towns of southeastern Sicily, including Noto. Allow 2 full days to see the principal sights of Siracusa alone, a few more if you're adding in side trips and beach days.

Essentials

GETTING THERE Siracusa is 1½ hours south of Taormina on the A18. It's 3 hours southeast of Palermo on the A19 and A18, and 3 hours east of Agrigento on the SS. 540, A19, and A18. Siracusa is also well connected with the rest of Sicily by bus and train, though buses are generally more efficient and frequent than trains.

GETTING AROUND   You won't need a car, just your own two feet and perhaps a few bus or cab rides to see the best of Siracusa proper. However, because Siracusa is a common base for exploring southeastern Sicily, many travelers arrive here by car and use it to get around the region. In that case, inquire about parking with your hotel or rental agency before arriving.

VISITOR INFORMATION   The **tourist office** is at Via San Sebastiano 43 (✆ **0931/481232**), open Monday to Friday 8:30am to 1:30pm and 3 to 6pm, Saturday 8:30am to 1:30pm. There's another office in the historic center at Via della Maestranza 33 (✆ **0931/65201**), open Monday to Friday 8:15am to 2pm and 2:30 to 5:30pm, Saturday 8:15am to 2pm.

Exploring

With splendors both ancient and Baroque, this cheerful coastal town is a one-two punch of architectural delights. Ortigia Island is Siracusa's *centro storico,* a mostly pedestrian zone where narrow alleys lined with romantic 18th-century palazzi spill onto such visual treats as Piazza del Duomo—in my opinion, the prettiest square in Sicily. The ancient ruins lay a good half-hour walk north of Ortigia, along grimy Corso Gelone. The walk is flat but not very attractive (although there are some decent mainstream shops along the way); in summer especially, it's best to take a bus or taxi to the Parco Archeologico. You'll find the bus stop and taxi rank on Ortigia at Piazza Pancali, the tree-lined square directly opposite the central bridge, Ponte Umbertino.

ORTIGIA ISLAND ★★★

Simply **wandering around Ortigia ★★★**, allowing yourself to get tangled up in the backstreets, is a great way to pass a few hours. You'll never get very lost—the island is only about 1 sq. km (¾ sq. mile)—and without even trying, you're likely to hit the major sights discussed below. Ortigia is roughly rectangular in shape, with three bridges on the western edge of the island leading over a narrow waterway to the "mainland." A 500m-long (1,640-ft.) spur of land, culminating in the Castello Maniace fortress and lighthouse (not all of which is accessible to the public), juts into the harbor on the southern side of Ortigia. Corso Matteotti is the main north-south drag that leads into the heart of Ortigia, ending at the round Piazza Archimede; this thoroughfare, planned in the Fascist era, is more modern than the rest of Ortigia (stick to the parallel side streets for more atmosphere), but it is nevertheless clean and attractive and has some nice boutiques and handy main-street services like ATMs and a pharmacy.

About halfway down the western edge of Ortigia and a few blocks back from the water is **Piazza del Duomo ★★★**, the first "big" thing you'll want to see when visiting Siracusa. The theatrical baroque perfection of Sicily's most beautiful piazza seems ripped from the illustrated pages of a Sicilian folklore tome. Dominating the square is the **Duomo ★★** (daily 8am–noon, 4–7pm) a sunny baroque cathedral built on top of the ancient Greek Temple of Athena. On the northwest side of the piazza is the delightful **Palazzo Beneventano del Bosco ★★**, a Baroque confection with convex, wrought-iron balconies. On the south side of the square is the sultry-looking church of **Santa Lucia alla Badia ★**. The many, interchangeable cafes on the square provide wonderful respite and people-watching—avoid mid-afternoon, when no one is here, but do make an effort to be here around sunset.

Also on Piazza del Duomo is an entrance to the **Hypogeum ★★** (no phone; admission 3€; Tues–Sun 9am–1pm, 4–8pm), a network of underground chambers and corridors dug as air raid shelters in World War II. The hypogeum visit exit is on Foro Vittorio Emanuele II, a tree-shaded seafront promenade that is pleasant to look at if not to smell—the birds love the green canopy here and they poop everywhere.

South of Piazza del Duomo and along the seafront is the lovely **Fonte Aretusa ★★**. This natural fountain near the harbor is one of Siracusa's most unique sights. Papyrus grows in the shallow pool, and the freshwater spring beneath once served as the city's main water supply. Fonte Aretusa is sunken about 6m below street level and encircled by an iron-and-stone parapet. At night, the cafes and sidewalks here are a breeding ground for the hot and bothered teens and 20-somethings of Siracusa.

A few blocks inland from Fonte Aretusa is the elegant **Galleria Regionale Palazzo Bellomo ★** (Via Capodieci 16; ✆ **0931/69511;** 8€;Tues–Sat 9am–7pm; Sun 9am–1pm), a recently overhauled 13th-century building that houses one of the great art collections of Sicily, dating from the high Middle Ages through the 20th century. The standout pieces here are Caravaggio's *Burial of St. Lucia* **★★** (1608) and Antonello da Messina's *Annunciation* **★** (1474). Caravaggio, bad boy of the baroque and a master of light, created a stunning canvas of grieving figures, illuminated from the right as if by a ray of sunlight.

Toward the opposite shore of Ortigia, in a ladder of streets between Via della Giudecca and Via Alagona, is where the old **Jewish Ghetto** of Siracusa was, and parts are still visible. The recently unearthed **Miqwe** (Via Alagona 52; ✆ **0931/22255;** 6€; daily 10am–7pm) consists of three freshwater pools, used for ritual bathing, and a private pool for the rabbi.

Back toward modern Siracusa and mainland Sicily, just off Piazza Pancali, are the ruins of the **Temple of Apollo ★**, the oldest Doric temple in Sicily, dating back to the 6th century B.C. The *Apollion* would have measured 58m by 24m when it was built. The massive ruins—of the temple platform, a fragmentary colonnade, and an inner wall, all in brown limestone—are not open to the public but visible and impressive enough from the street.

To see Ortigia from the sea, motor launches operated by a number of outfits along Ortigia waterfront will take you on a panoramic *gita in barca,* or **boat trip around Ortigia ★★**. Go at twilight, when the monuments of the old city are floodlit, but not when it's completely dark, as there are some sea caves along the route that you'll need a bit of daylight to see. Tours last about an hour and cost 10€.

THE ANCIENT RUINS ★★★

Walk north along Corso Gelone (or better yet, take bus no. 1, 3, or 12, or a cab from Ortigia's Piazza Pancali) to reach the sprawling collection of Greek and Roman ruins and abundant greenery known as the **Parco Archeologico della Neapolis ★★★** (Viale Paradiso; ✆ **0931/66206;** 8€; daily 9am–1 hr. before sunset). The main draw at Siracusa's wonderfully enjoyable archaeological park is the gigantic **Teatro Greco ★★★** (Greek Theater), whose 16,000-capacity *cavea* (seating area) was hewn right out of bedrock in the 3rd century B.C. This bowl of blazing white stone is a heat trap in summer, but there are some nymphaeums (alcoves with pools) at the top of the theater where you can splash yourself with water. The thickly vegetated area below the theater is the **Latomia del Paradiso ★★** ("Quarry of Paradise"), a lush and primeval garden where a

A GIGANTIC teardrop RUNS THROUGH IT

The tallest building in Siracusa is the bizarre **Santuario della Madonna delle Lacrime** (Our Lady of Tears Sanctuary, Via Santuario 33; ✆ **0931/21446;** free admission; daily 8am–noon and 4–7pm), a monstrous cone of contemporary architecture (built in 1993) halfway between Ortigia and the archaeological zone. Meant to evoke a sort of angular teardrop and rising 74m (243 ft.) with a diameter of 80m (262 ft.), it houses a statue of the Madonna that supposedly wept for 5 days in 1953. Alleged chemical tests showed that the liquid was similar to that of human tears. Pilgrims still flock here, and you'll see postcards of the weepy Virgin around Siracusa. Although criticized by architectural purists, the **interior** ★ is rather amazing. You might get dizzy looking up at the vertical windows stretching skyward to the apex of the roof. A charlatan TV evangelist and his rapt congregation would not look out of place here.

stegosaurus would not look out of place. Down here, follow the tour groups into the **Orecchio di Dionisio** ★ ("Ear of Dionysius"), a tall and vaguely ear-shaped cave where the Greek tyrant Dionysius supposedly kept and eavesdropped on prisoners. Near the park entrance is the 2nd century A.D. **Anfiteatro Romano** ★ (Roman Amphitheater), where gladiators fought and mock sea battles were staged.

A few hundred meters east of the ruins (back across Corso Gelone), the **Museo Archeologico Regionale Paolo Orsi** ★ (Viale Teocrito 66; ✆ 093/464022; 6€; Mon 3–5pm, Tues–Sat 9am–1pm, 3–5pm, Sun 9am–1pm) houses 18,000 artifacts that cover Sicilian prehistory to the Greek classical period, including some particularly gorgeous Greek archaic terra cottas. Observing the skilled execution and artistic sensitivity of the works here, it's easy to imagine the wealth and sophistication of ancient Siracusa.

Adjacent to the archaeological museum, don't miss the **Catacombe di San Giovanni** ★★ (Piazza San Giovanni, at end of Viale San Giovanni; no phone; 5€; Tues–Sun 9:30am–12:30pm and 2:30–4:30pm; closed Feb). Evoking the more famous Christian burial grounds along Rome's Appian Way, the Catacombs of St. John contain some 20,000 ancient tombs (long emptied by grave robbers), in honeycombed tunnels. In Roman times, Christians were not allowed to bury their dead within the city limits, so they went outside the boundaries of Syracuse to create burial chambers in what had been used by the Greeks as underground aqueducts. The early Christians recycled these into chapels. Some faded frescoes and symbols etched into stone slabs can still be seen. You enter the "world of the dead" from the **Chiesa di San Giovanni,** once the cathedral of Siracusa, now a ruin. St. Paul is said to have preached on this spot, so the early Christians venerated it as holy ground. *Warning:* Make sure that you exit the catacombs well before closing. Two readers who entered after 5pm were accidentally locked in.

Outskirts

About 6km (3¾ miles) west of Siracusa proper is the **Castello Eurialo** ★ (Piazza Eurialo 1, off Viale Epipoli in the Belvedere district; ✆ **0931/481111;** 4€, 10€ when combined with Parco Archeologico and Museo Archeologico; daily 9am–5:30pm). This 4th century B.C. fortress on the outskirts of Siracusa is the best preserved example of a Greek castle anywhere in the Mediterranean. It's also one of those great, undervisited Italian archaeological sites where you can romp all over everything, from the towers to the tunnels, without getting yelled at. Legend has it that Castello Eurialo is where Greek mathematician Archimedes famously cried "Eureka!" having discovered the law of water displacement while taking a bath. Without a car, the simplest way to reach the castle is with a taxi. Otherwise, you can take buses 11, 25, or 26 from the front of Siracusa's central train station.

Where to Stay

The countryside near Siracusa is an increasingly popular zone for villa rentals, which are a great way to enjoy this region, especially if you are traveling with kids or other couples. The feverish restoration work on historic buildings all over Ortigia has also resulted in a surfeit of short-term holiday lets and B&Bs with lots of character. A good agency for apartments in Ortigia is **Case Sicilia** (✆ **339/2983507;** www.casesicilia. com). For villas, **Think Sicily** (✆ **800/490-1107** in the U.S. and Canada or **44/ 020/7377-8518** in the U.K.; www.thinksicily.com) has a carefully edited list of well-equipped properties in the Siracusa region.

Approdo delle Sirene ★★ ORTIGIA   The modern and immaculate "Mermaid's Landing" was opened in 2004 by an energetic mother, Fiora, and son, Friedrich, from Rome. The semi-nautical decor features dark wood floors and striped linens in bold colors. Rooms with water view are considerably more spacious than standards, but all have contemporary bathrooms. The hosts can arrange all kinds of tours and excursions and also have bikes available for guests' use (no charge).

Riva Garibaldi 15. ✆ **0931/24857.** www.apprododellesirene.com. 8 units. Doubles 70€–125€. 2-night minimum stay June–Aug. AE, DC, MC, V. **Amenities:** Group dinners (on request); roof terrace. *In room:* A/C, TV, hair dryer, minibar, free Wi-Fi.

Grand Hotel Ortigia ★ ORTIGIA   This six-floor Art Nouveau palazzo facing the marina is the best choice on Ortigia for the services and amenities of a larger hotel. Don't expect luxury: It's a comfortable and classy place, but the grandeur faded a bit when the place got a (needed) update a few years back. While rooms have a sort of anonymous "nice hotel" flavor, the bathrooms have more character, with chrome fixtures and colored marble. Many units have a terrace overlooking the water.

Viale Mazzini 12 (at Via XX Settembre). ✆ **0931/464600.** www.grandhotelsr.it. 58 units. Doubles 130€–190€. AE, DC, MC, V. **Amenities:** Restaurant; bar. *In room:* A/C, TV, hair dryer, minibar, free Wi-Fi.

PADDLING AMONG THE papyrus

Just south of Ortigia is a nature reserve where dense papyrus grows along the banks of the *fiume Ciane* (Ciane river). Boat tours up this gentle waterway are a rustic and peaceful way to step back in time. You can also walk the path that follows the river course, past an ancient temple. Take Via Elorina (SS. 115) a few kilometers south to the bridge that crosses both the Anapo and Ciane rivers. Boats are usually stationed on the far (Ciane) side. Guided tours cost between 8€ and 15€ per person, depending on the number of passengers. For tickets and information on departure times, call ✆ **0931/69076.** To reach the departure site by bus, take line 21, 22, or 23 from Piazza della Posta and get off at Ponte delle Fiane.

Hotel Gutkowski ★ ORTIGIA   On the quieter "back side" of Ortigia, this robin's-egg blue palazzo is a haven of minimalist, spalike style. Some rooms (and especially bathrooms) are quite small, but all are equipped with minibar and TV. There's a roof terrace and informal wine bar on-site.

Lungomare Vittorini 26; ✆ **0931/465861.** www.guthotel.it. 25 units. Doubles 110€. AE, DC, MC, V. **Amenities:** Bar. *In room:* A/C, TV, minibar, free Wi-Fi.

Where to Dine

Castello Fiorentino ★ PIZZA   You can't get the full Italian dining picture without going to a great pizzeria—and this is one of the best in Sicily. Everyone, from teenagers to older couples, waits in the alley outside for a table (waits can be long, but that's part of the fun) and then sits down in an energetic, unpretentious room to stuff their faces with the local comfort food. The lengthy menu includes fritters, bruschetta, pizza, and pasta. Warm service makes you feel like a regular, and it's all yours for one very inexpensive tab.

Via Crocifisso 6. ✆ **0931/21097.** Pizzas from 6€. AE, DC, MC, V. Tues–Sun 7:30pm–midnight.

Don Camillo ★★ SEAFOOD   Its slightly formal dining room—high-vaulted stone ceilings, polished antiques along the walls—strikes an odd note in laid-back Ortigia, but this is the place to splurge on exquisite renditions of Sicilian specialties, including spaghetti with *ricci* (sea urchin—trust me, it's wonderful). It's a special night out, where the focus is on the food, not Sicilian theatrics and brio.

Via Maestranza 96. ✆ **0931/67133.** www.ristorantedoncamillosiracusa.it. Reservations recommended. Entrees 14€–24€. AE, DC, MC, V. Mon–Sat 12:30–3pm and 7:30–10:30pm.

L'Ancora ★★ ☺ SIRACUSAN/SEAFOOD   The full bounty of the sea plus lots of fresh local vegetables and herbs are employed at this bustling local favorite near the main post office on Ortigia. Decor isn't much to write home about, but there's an ample veranda, and the food is the absolute apex of freshness and Mediterranean tradition. It's best to book a table for weekend lunches, as the spot is a Siracusan go-to for family get-togethers, baptism parties, and the like.

Via G. Perno 7. ✆ **0931/462369.** www.ristoranteancora.com. Entrees 12€–18€. AE, DC, MC, V. Tues–Sun 12:30–3pm and 7:30–10:30pm.

Siracusa After Dark

For nightlife with a little more edge than people-watching on Piazza del Duomo, walk 1 minute south to **San Rocco,** Piazza San Rocco 3/5 (✆ **333/9854177**), a sleek indoor/outdoor enoteca and cocktail bar with a great *aperitivo* spread and a young crowd. Next door, the dive-y **Doctor Sam,** Piazza San Rocco 4 (✆ **0931-483598**), is perfectly friendly but big on tattoos, piercings, and reggae. Down the street, the English-style **Vecchio Pub,** Via delle Vergini 9 (✆ **0931/464692**), is where tourists and expats of all ages come to tie one on among their own species.

Side Trips

You could easily spend weeks making short forays into the countryside around Siracusa, discovering wonders both historic and natural, but if your time in Siracusa itself is limited, my number-one day-trip choice is the 18th-century *centro storico* of **Noto** (an easy half-day from Siracusa), whose line-up of ebullient palazzi represent the Sicilian Baroque at its sunniest. From May to September, a beach outing may be very compelling, and several seaside areas offer diverse settings at which to enjoy the coast of southeastern Sicily.

NOTO ★★★

The *centro storico* of this hill town is Sicily's crown jewel of baroque delights. An earthquake leveled most of Noto in 1693, clearing the way for the fanciful *barocco* style to establish a foothold in the early 18th century. In 2002, Noto was inscribed, along with seven other towns in the area, in the "Late Baroque Towns of the Val di Noto" UNESCO World Heritage Site for "outstanding testimony to the exuberant genius" of that period of art and architecture, which represented the "culmination and final flowering of Baroque art in Europe."

Whether with your own car or on a bus, it's about a 45-minute drive from Siracusa: If you're driving yourself, take the A18 *autostrada* south for 27km (17 miles), then exit and head north and up the hill, following blue signs toward Noto; once near town, be sure to follow the yellow signs toward Noto's "centro storico," not the brown signs to "Noto Antica," which is an archaeological site (it's the ruins of the old city destroyed by the earthquake) quite some distance from town. It's also easy to reach Noto by bus (55 min. each way; 6€ round-trip) from Siracusa. Two companies, AST and Interbus, serve the route, offering about a dozen buses per day from Ortigia or Siracusa train station. In Noto, both bus companies arrive at the Piazzale Marconi bus station, a 5-minute walk from the *centro storico*.

Noto's pedestrian-only main strip, Corso Vittorio Emanuele III, cuts east-west through a stage-set of honey-colored limestone confections, most of which are centered on Piazza Municipio. The most photographed spot in Noto, however, is hidden away on Via Corrado Nicolaci (a cross street of Corso Vittorio): About halfway up, on the left, is **Palazzo Villadorata** (or **Palazzo Nicolaci**) ★★★, with its diminutive but wonderful balcony supports carved with the heads of cheeky maidens, dwarves, lions, and horses—the individual figures' expressions are fabulous. For a fabulous (and expensive) overnight stay in the building that is the hallmark of *Noto barocca*, book a room at the new guesthouse inside the palazzo, **Seven Rooms Villadorata** (Via Nicolaci 18; ℂ **338/5095643;** www.7roomsvilladorata.it; inquire about rates).

Noto is even more bewitching when the sun goes down. If you're in Noto at mealtime, your best bet is **Al Buco** ★ (Via G. Zanardelli; ℂ **0931/838142;** entrees 8€–14€; MC, V), which serves mostly seafood and vegetables at lunch and dinner but is closed on Saturdays. Alternatively, for a snack, seek out one of Noto's celebrated pastry shops—**Mandorlo in Fiore** ★★ (Via Ducezio 2; ℂ **0931/836615**) is famous for its *cassata,* while **Pasticceria La Fontana Vecchia** (Corso Vittorio Emanuele 150; ℂ **0931/839412**) specializes in *pan di spagna* (sponge cake filled with sweet ricotta) and has great gelato, too.

BEACHES NEAR SIRACUSA ★

Some of the best unspoiled shoreline in all of Italy is on Sicily's southeastern coast. The color palette is lighter down here—the water is more pastel than cerulean, and the sand is white and sugary. From north to south, **Fontane Bianche** ★★ is the classic beach detour for those who stay in Siracusa, 15 minutes away. It's an almost-square bay with laid-back beach clubs and luxurious deep sand. **Lido di Noto,** 15 minutes from the baroque hill town, is a lively beach with great waterfront restaurants. Half the beach is private beach clubs (where you pay around 10€ for day use of a lounge chair, umbrella, and shower facilities), and half is free public access. Between Noto and Pachino is the **Vendicari Nature Reserve,** where beaches are small and hard to find but the scenery is beautiful. Thousands of migratory birds nest here every year. A few miles south of the *autostrada* on SP19, park at the Agriturismo Calamosche to reach **Calamosche ★★,** favored by local teens and 20-somethings. It's a 15-minute walk down a nature path to reach the intimate cove, framed by rock cliffs and sea caves. The water is a calm, perfectly dappled teal. **Isola delle Correnti ★★,** at the southeastern tip of the island, is one of the best beaches on Sicily. It's a bit more windswept and wavy than the other spots, which can be nice when you tire of perfectly still turquoise water and searing sunshine. On a clear day, you can even see Malta, which is just 100km (60 miles) to the south.

RAGUSA ★

Ragusa is really two towns in one: an upper town, the newer **Ragusa Superiore,** mapped out after a devastating earthquake in 1693, and the medieval and baroque **Ragusa Ibla,** constructed on an isolated spur. Ibla, in glaring contrast to the modern city, is one of the best-preserved old towns in Sicily, and well worth a day of your valuable time. The two parts of town are linked by a steep winding road or else by steps. Even if Ragusa Ibla weren't fascinating, the site would make an interesting trip because of the craggy valley that separates the two towns.

From the twin towns, panoramas of the countryside unfold. These are the landscapes most often evoked in Sicilian literature and cinema, an oft-filmed terrain that has positioned Ragusa and its outlying districts in the forefront of Italian filmmaking.

If all this weren't enough, you can take a 25km (16-mile) drive to **Marina di Ragusa,** a thriving beach resort. Many visitors prefer to anchor here, visiting Ragusa Ibla for the day. Unlike the historic core of Ragusa Ibla, Marina di Ragusa is relatively modern, with its long, narrow, and unusually sandy beach strip. A boardwalk is lined with shops, bars, and restaurants. A party atmosphere prevails here in summer, when, by 10pm, the action is just getting started.

Essentials

GETTING THERE   Ragusa is a 1½-hour (82km/51-mile) drive from Siracusa, the nearest major city. Take the SP14 west, toward Canicattini Bagni and Palazzolo Acreide, then follow blue highway signs to Ragusa. Ragusa is also served by train and bus from Siracusa. **AST** (© 0932/681818) runs seven buses per day on the 2-hour run; the fare is 5.80€ one-way. Trains also take 2 hours and cost 7.05€. The stations in Ragusa are at Piazza del Popolo and the adjoining Piazza Gramsci.

VISITOR INFORMATION   The **tourist office,** at Via Capitano Bocchieri 33 (© 0932/221511), is open Monday, Wednesday, and Friday 9am to 1:30pm and Tuesday and Thursday 9am to 1:30pm and 4 to 6pm.

GETTING AROUND   If you don't want to make the steep climb linking Ibla with Superiore, you can take city bus no. 3—and it's one hairy ride!—departing from in front of the cathedral or from Piazza del Popolo; the fare is .80€ one-way. The bus will let you off in Ibla at Piazza Pola or Giardini Iblei, most central for exploring the medieval and baroque town.

Exploring the Two Towns

If your time is limited, you can skip the upper town (Superiore) and spend all your hours in Ragusa Ibla, as the older town holds far more intrigue. Those with more time can hike through the upper town, looking for the attractions that follow.

RAGUSA SUPERIORE

The long main street, **Corso Italia,** cuts through the upper town and makes for Ragusa's best promenade. The main attraction here is **Cattedrale di San Giovanni,** Via Roma 134 (© 0932/621658), dating from the 18th century and dedicated to St. John the Baptist.

RAGUSA IBLA ★★

I prefer to reach the old town by taking a long stairway, **Santa Maria delle Scale ★**, heading down from Ragusa Superiore to the historic core of Ibla. Take this walk for the **panoramic vistas ★★** alone, some of the finest in southeastern Sicily. The town is in deep decay, but it's a nostalgic remnant of bygone Sicily. Wander its narrow streets and check out its crumbling baroque palaces.

Head east until you come to the 18th century **Duomo di San Giorgio ★**, Piazza del Duomo (© 0932/220085), which is open daily from 9am to noon and 4 to 7pm. Characterized by an impressive neoclassical dome and tiered wedding-cake facade, this is one of the best examples of the Sicilian baroque.

If you continue walking all the way east through Ragusa Ibla, you'll reach the beautiful public gardens, **Giardino Obleo ★**, which are studded with religious buildings. At the edge of the gardens, enjoy the **panoramic view ★** sweeping across the Valley of Irminio. The gardens are the perfect place for a picnic and can be visited daily from 8am to 8pm; there's no entry fee.

Where to Stay

Hotel Terraqua ★ MARINA DI RAGUSA   This is the most appealing hotel in the seaside resort of Marina di Ragusa, half an hour south of Ragusa. Configured as a cement-and-glass cube dotted with balconies, it was built in the 1980s, and identifies itself mainly as a beachfront hotel with clean rooms and frequent breezes. Don't expect any personalized service from the staff—they're familiar with hordes of vacationers coming and going. But as a base for exploration of the neighborhood, including Ragusa Ibla, the hotel is a worthwhile choice. The hotel is not directly on the sands of the beach—it's inside its own walled garden, a 5-minute walk from the water. It also has the best and biggest pool in town.

Via delle Sirene 35, Marina di Ragusa. © **0932/615600.** www.hotelterraqua.com. 77 units. Doubles 120€–160€. AE, DC, MC, V. **Amenities:** Restaurant; bar; babysitting; pool; tennis court. *In room:* A/C, TV, hair dryer, minibar.

Where to Dine

Il Duomo ★★★ IBLA   SICILIAN   With its newly awarded 2 Michelin stars, this restaurant in the old town is one of the finest in Sicily—its devotees say *the* best. It lies on an impossibly narrow street, uphill and about a block behind the Duomo. Come here for the intensely patriotic cuisine of Ciccio Sultano, a native *Ragusano* who commits himself passionately to the old-time traditions. Several varieties of bread are baked each day, using old-fashioned, increasingly hard-to-find strains of wheat. At least 20 types of olive oil are on display, and if you ask for help, a staff member will advise you on which variety is best with which particular bread or platter. Menus are based on the changing seasons, and many dishes make ample use of such local products as cherry tomatoes, pistachios, bitter almonds, wild fennel, and mint. Believe it or not, one of the most praised specialties is roasted baby pig with a chocolate sauce which has been caramelized with Marsala wine. I found one of the most succulent pastas to be studded with freshly caught tuna and zucchini and served with a savory herb-laden pesto sauce.

Via Capitano Bocchieri 31. ℂ **0932/651265.** Reservations recommended. Main courses 9€–19€; fixed-price menus 110€–120€. AE, DC, MC, V. Aug Sun noon–2:30pm; July–Sept Mon 7–11pm, Tues–Sat noon–2:30pm and 7–11pm.

PIAZZA ARMERINA

Graced with impressive but decaying *palazzi,* the town of Piazza Armerina (103km/64 miles NW of Ragusa, 134km/83 miles NW of Siracusa) itself is worth a short visit if you've got some extra time, but the marquee attraction isn't in town: What everyone comes here for are the Roman mosaics at the Villa del Casale, 5km (3 miles) to the southwest.

The extraordinary mosaics at the 4th century A.D. villa, the former country retreat of a wealthy Roman citizen, are some of the most important Roman pictorial art in the world. And we're not talking precious, restrained imagery of emperors and the like: This is like an uncut, down-and-dirty Roman reality show about gladiators and wild animal fights, hunting parties, alcohol and sex, skimpy gym clothes, and more. Few archaeological sites brush the dust off our notions of "antiquity" quite like these mosaics. Villa Romana del Casale is without exaggeration the richest collection of Roman mosaics anywhere and is one of the top 10 Roman sites in Italy.

Seeing the Sights

Piazza Armerina is set on a plateau some 700m (2,297 ft.) above sea level. The city was founded during the Norman era, and today is filled with mansions showing both baroque and Renaissance architectural influences. Its historic **medieval quarter** ★ is graced with many beautiful churches, the most impressive of which is the **Duomo** (Via Cavour; ℂ **0935/680214;** daily 8:30am–noon and 3:30–7pm), crowning the highest point in town at 720m (2,364 ft.).

Villa Romana del Casale ★★★   Located 6km (3½ miles) from Piazza Armerina, this is one of the most wonderful archaeological sites in the world: You're not here to see evocative columns and arches, but mosaics, mosaics, and more mosaics. Some 9,065 sq. km (3,500 sq. miles) in total, the mosaics are all polychrome marble and all on display *in situ* on the floors of 40 rooms that made up the private countryside mansion and hunting lodge of a rich and powerful Roman patrician who lived, or at least vacationed, in Sicily in the late 3rd or early 4th century A.D. The original roof of the villa is long gone, so the site is now covered by a labyrinthine greenhouselike structure, and visitors must view the mosaics from narrow catwalks suspended above the floors.

Among the thoroughly engrossing scenes, animal, hunting, sporting, and mythological themes predominate. Unsurprisingly for a men's weekend getaway pad, gore and blood abound in the artwork, though there are also some tender vignettes captured in the mosaics and even a dash of PG-13 erotica. Do yourself a favor and acquire a site map before setting out—there are many, many rooms in all different directions here, and you wouldn't want to miss any of these treasures. The catwalks tend to be crowded with tour groups (which of course linger in the best viewing spots for the best mosaics) and it can get pretty warm and stuffy inside the enclosure, but try not to let these factors addle you into rushing through the site.

The villa's central architectural feature was a garden courtyard, or peristyle, from which all the other rooms branch out. After parking along the road and walking south toward the actual villa grounds, you will most likely enter from the northwest corner of the structure and tour the mosaics in a sort of clockwise fashion. Among the first discernible rooms you'll encounter are the **Terme,** or steam baths (rooms 1–7), which supplied water and also heated the villa with steam circulating through cavities (now exposed) in the floors and walls. In the **Sala delle Unzioni** (Anointment Room, room 4), a slave is oiling up his master for a shoulder massage.

The corridors of the peristyle (room 13) contain the splendid **Peristyle mosaic ★★**, which can be viewed on all sides of the portico. It's a romp of birds, plants, wild animals, and more domesticated creatures such as horses. Adjoining it to the baths is the **Palestra ★★** (exercise area, room 15). In these highly detailed mosaics, a chariot race at Rome's Circus Maximus is depicted.

Along the north side of the peristyle are a few rectangular rooms with fragmentary mosaics of mostly geometrical motifs. The **Sala delle Quattro Stagioni** (room 23) contains mosaic medallions representing allegories of the four seasons. Next to it, the **Sala degli Eroti Pescatori ★** (Room of the Fishing Cupids, room 24) is a busy scene of little winged men harpooning, netting, even underwater-wrestling various species that are destined to become ancient Roman seafood.

Just past those rooms is one of the highlights of the villa, the **Sala della Piccola Caccia ★★★**, room 25. *Piccola Caccia* means "small hunt," referring to the type of game being captured—fowl, deer, rabbits, and the like. Spend some time studying all the action in the various registers of this mosaic and all the individual creatures and facial expressions.

The long hall to the east of here (it's where all the crowds tend to gather) is the villa's most spectacular feature, the **Corridoio della Grande Caccia ★★★**, or Corridor of the Great Hunt (room 28), measuring 65m (197 ft.) in length. The mosaics here, depicting big game—exotic African beasts here, not the common European fauna you see in the Small Hunt mosaics of room 25—are among the most splendid from the ancient world. From panthers to camels to ostriches, the animals are all captured alive and shown in various stages of transport across land and sea to the port of Rome, where they will be part of the games in the Colosseum.

A cluster of three rooms east of the north (right-hand side) end of the Grande Caccia corridor includes the **Vestibolo di Ulisse e Polifemo ★** (Vestibule of Ulysses and Polyphemus, room 47), where the Homeric hero proffers a *krater* of wine to the Cyclops (here with three eyes instead of one, and a disemboweled ram draped casually over his lap) in hopes of getting him drunk. Adjacent is the **Cubicolo con Scena Erotica ★** (Bedroom with Erotic Scene, room 46)—despite the titillating name, it's a very tame affair. Most of the mosaic is geometric patterns, but at the center is a seductress, with vampy side gaze and a nicely contoured rear end for all to see, embracing a young man.

Off the southwest side of the Grande Caccia corridor is one of the most amusing rooms of all, the **Sala delle Dieci Ragazze in Bikini ★★**, Room of the 10 Girls in Bikinis, room 30. Wearing skimpy strapless bikinis that would be appropriate for a

CALTAGIRONE: A ceramics SIDE TRIP

A lovely drive 30km (19 miles) southeast of Piazza Amerina takes you to **Caltagirone,** an enchanting little town that earthenware potteries built. Glazed pottery is offered at shops throughout the town, whose most celebrated attraction is **Scala di Santa Maria del Monte** ★★, a stunning set of ceramic steps leading from old town to new town. There are 142 lava stair treads graced with majolica tiles—no two alike—that evoke everything from Moorish designs to baroque patterns.

As you go along, you'll encounter **Branciforti** ★, Scala di Santa Maria del Monte 3 (✆ **0933/24427**), which sells stunning ceramics in deep shades of blue with swirling arabesques. To learn more about ceramics, head for the little **Museo della Ceramica,** on Via Roma

(✆ **0933-58418**), open daily from 9am to 6:30pm and charging an admission of 3€. Later you can relax in the shade of the **Giardino Pubblico,** a public garden nearby.

The **tourist office** is in Palazzo Libertini, Piazza Umberto (✆ **0933/53809**). Parking is available in a public lot near Chiesa San Francesco di Paola, approached before you reach Piazza Umberto. If you'd like to spend the night, the **Grand Hotel Villa San Mauro,** Via Portosalvo 10 (✆ **0933/26500**), has 91 first-class rooms from about 100€ per night. The best place to eat is **La Scala,** Scala Santa Maria del Monte 8 (✆ **0933/57781**), where meals cost around 35€. It's near the base of the famous stairs, and even has a mountain stream running through it.

beach in the 21st century, the girls are engaged in various exercises—curling dumbbells, tossing a ball, and running.

South of the central block of the villa and peristyle is the trefoil-shaped **Triclinium** ★★★, room 33, a large dining room known for a magnificent rendition of the Labors of Hercules. In the central apse, the mosaics depict the **Gigantomachy** ★★★ (Battle of the Giants), five mammoth creatures in their death throes after being pierced by Hercules's arrows, poisoned with the blood of the Lernaean hydra.

As you pore over the mosaics at Villa del Casale, it's easy to forget that the villa itself, architecturally, must have been splendid—an enormous space, it was replete with fancy water features, marble-clad walls, and opulent vaulted ceilings. There are other, more intact Roman villas in Italy where you can get a more complete picture of the architecture, but nowhere else are there mosaics like these.

Note: The site is normally open daily from 10am to 4pm but is currently closed for renovation and is expected to reopen in Spring 2011. Check www.villaromanadel casale.it for updates. Admission is 3€ but will likely go up to 6€ when the current restoration project is completed.

Where to Stay & Dine

The fare at the archaeological site cafeteria is pretty dismal—the hot buffet especially—but they have basic sandwiches that'll do in a pinch.

Al Fogher ★ 🏠 SICILIAN   This rustic restaurant, 3km (1¾ miles) north of Piazza Armerina, serves dishes based on local recipes. The *carpaccio* of swordfish or tuna will get you started. The chef's creativity is further expressed in such dishes as risotto with pumpkin, ricotta and gooseliver seasoned with fresh rosemary, and pork in a pepper sauce with pistachio crust. The real specialty of the house is duck breast with a champagne vinegar sauce, dried tomatoes, and a green apple mousse. The wine cellar holds 400 different local and international choices.

Contrada Bellia, Strada Statale 117. (✆) **0935/684123.** Reservations recommended. Main courses 10€–35€. AE, DC, MC, V. Tues–Sat 12:30–2:30pm and 8–11pm; Sun 12:30–2:30pm. Closed July 20–Aug 5.

Park Hotel Paradiso   This modern hostelry has the best location for those who want to be near the Villa Romana del Casale. Located right outside of town and surrounded by a forest, this is a well-kept building with comfortably furnished guest rooms. The hotel has good on-site dining and drinking facilities, so you don't have to wander around Piazza Armerina at night.

Contrada da Ramaldo, 1km (½ mile) beyond Chiesa di Sant'Andrea. (✆) **0935/680841.** www.parkhotel paradiso.it. 95 units. Doubles 95€–110€. Rates include breakfast. AE, DC, MC, V. Free parking. **Amenities:** Restaurant; 2 bars; fitness center; pool; nonsmoking rooms; rooms for those w/limited mobility. *In room:* A/C, TV, hair dryer, Jacuzzi in superior rooms, minibar.

AGRIGENTO & SELINUNTE

Two of the great cities of Magna Graecia—or what's left of them—can be explored along Sicily's southwestern coast. Both Agrigento and Selinunte knew greater glory than they experience today, but the remains of what they used to be are still rich in spite of the looters and conquerors who have passed through. Of the two, Agrigento is the far greater attraction. Its remarkable series of Doric temples from the 5th century B.C. are unrivaled outside of Greece. All of the modern encroachments have seriously dimmed the glory of Agrigento, but much is left to fill us with wonder.

Selinunte, in contrast, was never built over as Agrigento was, and holds extensive remains of the acropolis, though none quite equal the charm of Agrigento's Valley of the Temples. As you stand in the midst of a carpet of mandrake, acanthus, capers, and celery growing wild at Selinunte, you'll have to work hard to imagine what the city must have looked like at the apex of its power.

Agrigento

The ruins of ancient Akragas—commonly known as the **Valley of the Temples**—are justifiably Sicily's most celebrated (and photogenic) archaeological site. The 2,500-year-old temples, their simple Doric columns striking a timeless figure against the cobalt sky, have come to be a calling card for Sicilian tourism itself.

The modern town of Agrigento is well equipped with lodging and dining options. If you elect to spend the night here, do it for the sake of seeing the incomparable beauty of the temples illuminated after dark. (The site closes at dusk, but you'll still be able to see those gorgeous silhouettes from afar.)

With your own car, Agrigento is 2 hours south of Palermo on the SS. 121 and SS. 189 and 2½ hours west of Siracusa (via Catania, Enna, and Caltanissetta; or via Gela) on the A18, A19, and SS. 640. By rail or bus, the best and most frequent connections are from Palermo (1½ hr., and 7.60€ by train). **Cuffaro** ((✆) **0922/403150**) runs four buses per day from Palermo, 2 hours and 9€ each way.

Exploring

THE VALLEY OF THE TEMPLES ★★★

You've seen them on countless postcards as you've traveled around Sicily, and now here they are before you: the evocative skeletons of seven temples that together comprise the most important Greek ruins outside Greece itself. The weathered podiums, colonnades, and architraves of these magnificent buildings are the poignant legacy of the once-powerful city of Akragas, founded in the 6th century B.C. as a beachhead. Sadly, the temples were systematically quarried for their stone throughout the Middle Ages, and many went on to live new lives in the mundane structures of coastal towns nearby, such as Porto Empedocle.

While the temples deservedly get top billing here, there are other elements of ancient city life, such as houses, streets, and tombs, whose outlines can be discerned. The name "valley of the temples" is a misnomer, as everything is set on a ridge with olive and almond trees and views of the sea. As you wander the site, imagine the glorious beacon that the temples, embellished with gold sculptural details, must have been for those approaching by sea.

Ticket booths (© **0922/26191** or 0922/497226) are found at the west and east entrances of the archaeological park; admission is 6€, and the site is open daily from 8:30am to 7pm. Board a bus at the gate or drive your own car to explore the site. Allow several hours to tour the ruins. If you have only have limited time, start from the east, as that's where the oldest and most impressive temples are found. Otherwise, start from the western end and check out the humbler ruins there before working your way east to the site's more stellar attractions.

In the western zone, the four extant columns of the **Temple of Castor and Pollux ★** still carry a corner of the entablature and pediment, making them among the most evocative and photographed ruins in Agrigento. Just east of here, the **Temple of Zeus ★** would have been the largest ever built, with 20m-high (66-ft.) Doric columns, but it was never completed (war with Carthage and an earthquake sealed its unfinished fate). This is where you'll find one of the famous 8m-tall (26 ft.) *telamones* (atlases) meant to support the structure.

Across Via dei Templi is the eastern zone of the archaeological park. The **Temple of Hercules ★★** once ranked in size with the Temple of Zeus, but today only 8 fluted columns still stand along the temple's flank. Incredibly, scorch marks from fires set by Carthaginians over 2,000 years ago are still visible. The most impressive temple at the site, and on par, preservation-wise, with the Temple of Hephaestus in Athens, is the **Temple of Concordia ★★★**. Unlike the other temples here, it was spared destruction by later occupants of Agrigento because its *cella*, or cult chamber, was reconsecrated as a Christian basilica in the 4th century A.D. It's not clear to which deity the temple was dedicated in antiquity: It was only named the Temple of Concordia in 1748, when its 34 columns were picked up and restored to the state you see today. The last of the major temples in this zone is the **Temple of Juno ★★**, with a romantically skeletal look despite its 30 re-erected columns and sections of entablature. It was likely used for wedding ceremonies and sacrificial offerings (though the red stains on the stone are the scars of fires during various wars).

Between the ruins and Agrigento town, the **Museo Archeologico** (Via dei Templi; © **0922/40111**; admission 6€; Mon 9am–1:30pm, Tues–Sat 9am–7:30pm) has detailed explanations in both Italian and English of the many artifacts unearthed in this area. However, after a long and dusty outing at the ruins, this isn't a necessary stop unless your thirst for all things Akragas is stronger than your thirst for a cold beer, water, anything, back at your hotel or at a bar somewhere in town.

Where to Stay & Dine

Agrigento's hotels leave plenty to be desired—they know they have a captive, non-returning audience each and every night—but if you do decide to sleep here, a pleasant anomaly is **Fattoria Mosè** ★ (Via M. Pascal 4; ℂ **0922/606115;** www. fattoriamose.com; doubles from 75€; no credit cards), a comfortable and welcoming agriturismo in the countryside 4km (2½ miles) from the temples. The working organic farm offers seven simple but cozy rooms and produces olive oil, almonds and pistachios, jams, and even loofah sponges. In Agrigento itself, between the temples and the medieval town, **Colleverde Park** (Via Panoramic dei Templi; ℂ **0922/29555;** www.colleverdehotel.it; doubles 140€–180€; AE, DC, MC, V) is one of the better values in this overpriced town.

Restaurant at the Villa Athena Hotel ★ SICILIAN   Expect surly service at best, but there's no denying the magic of seeing the temples lit up at night from the torch-lit terrace of this hotel. The food can also be more than decent, with creative antipasti and primi that employ local vegetables and seafood.

Via Passeggiata Archeologica 33. ℂ **0922/596288.** Reservations required. Entrees 14€–22€. AE, DC, MC, V. Lunch and dinner daily.

Trattoria dei Templi ★ SICILIAN   This earnest and well-run restaurant is so proud of its location, it's taken Sicily's classic *penne alla Norma* (with eggplant, tomato, and mozzarella) and given it a new name and pasta type, *cavatelli alla Valle dei Templi.* It's a reliable spot for attentive service and a menu of hearty pastas and fresh local seafood, plated with great flourish.

Via Panoramica dei Templi 15. ℂ **0922/403110.** Reservations recommended. Entrees 8€–22€. Lunch and dinner daily.

Wine Touring Between the Ruins

A visit to the Planeta winery is a fun inland detour on the way from Agrigento to Selinunte. Planeta makes some of the best Sicilian wines, including exquisite Chardonnay and Syrah, and their "Cantina dell'Ulmo" estate in Sambuca di Sicilia has a 16th-century farmhouse set up for tastings and tours (by appointment).

To get there, exit the SS. 115 a few kilometers east of Menfi and follow the SS. 624 and SS. 188 to Sambuca di Sicilia. In Sambuca, follow signs for "Azienda Agricola Planeta-Terre Sicane" (ℂ **091/327965;** www.planeta.it; Tues–Sat 9am– 3pm). Book visits at least 3 days in advance; e-mail visits@planeta.it or fax 091/ 6124335.

SELINUNTE

Guy de Maupassant called the splendid jumble of ruins at Selinunte "an immense heap of fallen columns, now aligned and placed side by side on the ground like dead soldiers, now having fallen in a chaotic manner." Regardless of what shape they're in, the only reason to visit Selinunte is for its ruins, not for the unappealing modern towns that have grown around it.

Travel Tip

In warm weather, for an unforgettable only-in-Sicily moment, stop at the crystal-watered beach in Marinella around sunset, swim about 50m (164 ft.) offshore, and look to the west— you'll see the Temple of Hera outlined on top of the hill.

One of the superb colonies of ancient Greece, Selinunte traces its history to the 7th century B.C., when immigrants from Siracusa set out to build a new colony. They succeeded, erecting a city of power and prestige adorned with temples. Much of Selinunte's history involves seemingly endless conflicts with Segesta (p. 223). Siding with Selinunte's rival, Hannibal virtually leveled the city in 409 B.C. The city never recovered its former glory and ultimately fell into decay.

Selinunte is on the southern coast of Sicily and is best explored by **car,** as public transportation is awkward and slow. From Agrigento, take Route 115 northwest into Castelvetrano; then follow the secondary road marked SELINUNTE, which leads south to the sea. Allow at least 2 hours from either Palermo or Agrigento. All buses and trains to Selinunte connect in Castelvetrano, 20 minutes away. Most visitors come here on a day trip while based elsewhere, but there is a handful of accommodations in the seafront village of Marinella, 2km (1¼ miles) east of Selinunte.

Exploring the Archaeological Garden ★★

Selinunte's temples lie in scattered ruins, the honey-colored stone littering the ground as if an earthquake had struck (as one did in ancient times). Some sections and fragments of temples still stand, with great columns pointing to the sky. From 9am to 1 hour before sunset daily, you can walk through the monument zone. Some of it has been partially excavated and reconstructed. Admission is 6€.

The temples, in varying states of preservation, are designated by letters (confusingly, you'll encounter them in reverse alphabetical order); most date from the 6th and 5th centuries B.C. Near the entrance, the Doric **Temple E** contains fragments of an inner temple. Standing on its ruins before the sun goes down, you can look across the water that washes up on the shores of Africa, from which the Carthaginian fleet emerged to destroy the city. **Temple G,** in scattered ruins north of Temple E, was one of the largest erected in Sicily and was also built in the Doric style. The ruins of the less impressive **Temple F** lie between Temples E and G.

After viewing Temples E, F, and G, all near the parking lot at the entrance, you can get in your car and drive along the Strada dei Templi west to the Acropoli (or walk there in about 20 min.). The site of the western temples was the **Acropoli,** which was built from the 6th century to the 5th century B.C.

The most impressive site here is **Temple C.** In 1925, 14 of the 17 columns of Temple C were re-erected. This is the earliest surviving temple at the site, built in the 6th century B.C. and probably dedicated to Hercules or Apollo. The pediment, ornamented with a clay Gorgon's head, lies broken on the ground. Temple C towers over the other ruins and gives you an impression of what all the temples might have looked like. Also here is **Temple A,** which, like the others, lies in scattered ruins.

An Amazing Meal on the Beach

The best restaurant in the vicinity of Selinunte is on the water at Porto Palo di Menfi, a few kilometers east of Marinella and Selinunte. **Ristorante da Vittorio ★★★** (Via Friuli Venezia Giulia 9, Porto Palo di Menfi. ✆ **092/578381;** www.davittorioristorante.com; entrees 10€–25€; lunch daily year-round; dinner daily June–Sept; by reservation only Oct–May; AE, DC, MC, V) draws gourmands from all over for its superb seafood-only menu and open-air, family-friendly beachfront locale. The 40€ prix-fixe menu (excluding wine) is the best way to sample Vittorio's food. Vittorio and his family also offer overnight accommodations in 12 simple but comfy rooms (75€).

WESTERN SICILY

Exploring the less-traveled end of the island practically ensures the kind of authentic cultural interaction and discovery that's harder to find in the more well-known destinations of eastern Sicily. Western Sicily is rich in Greek ruins, including the glorious temple at Segesta, and also lays claim to what some consider Sicily's most breathtaking hill town, Erice. On the western coast, Trapani is a busy port and the gateway to the Egadi Islands (p. 279), while nearby Marsala is the home of the eponymous dessert wine. On the northern coast, the sparkling beach of San Vito lo Capo provides a relaxing break from the cultural touring.

TRAPANI

Some liken the port city of Trapani (*Trah*-pah-nee) to a watered-down version of Palermo—in a good way: There's local flavor but less traffic and sketchiness. Allow a few hours to walk the *centro storico,* which occupies the western (seaward) end of Trapani's sickle-shaped bay. The major city along the western coast of Sicily, Trapani lies below the headland of Mount Erice, with the Egadi Islands a short hop by ferry or hydrofoil ride from here. Trapani's economy is based largely on fishing and winemaking along with salt mining, with tourism growing annually. If you have only a day for the west, your time is better spent in Erice to the north. But if you have an extra day, consider devoting it to historic Trapani, once a Phoenician outpost. Trapani's most dubious reputation is as a major Sicilian center of the Mafia.

Architecturally, the worst blows to Trapani were the Allied bombardments in 1940 and 1943. The entire historic district was razed. Regrettably, the new Trapani bounced back with the building of several ugly modern blocks—think Soviet Union in the heyday of the Cold War. As a result of all this destruction, Trapani has fewer historic sites to visit than most Sicilian cities of its size—but there are some nuggets.

You can fly into Trapani's Florio Airport from Rome and the offshore island of Pantelleria. Trapani is well linked by public transportation to Palermo, 2 hours by bus or train to the east. You can also make the drive from Palermo along the A29 *autostrada.* Marsala is 45 minutes to the south, while Erice lies 30 minutes away, up the hill to the east of the city. Trapani is a major embarkation point for ferries and hydrofoils (*aliscafi*). Most departures are for the Egadi Islands (Favignana, Levanzo, and Marettimo). Service is also available to Ustica, Pantelleria, and even Tunisia. Ferries depart from the docks near Piazza Garibaldi. **Francesca Badalucco,** Via Ammiraglio Staiti 91 (*©* **0923/542470**), across the street from Trapani's harbor, is the best agency for ferry information and tickets.

Exploring Trapani

Most visitors head first for the ***centro storico*** ★, the medieval core lying on the headland jutting into the sea. The most ancient part of this "Casbah" was constructed in a typical North African style around a tightly knit maze of narrow streets. The most intriguing street is 18th century **Via Garibaldi** (aka Rua Nova, or "New Road"), which is flanked with churches and palaces. The best shops in the old town line **Via Torrearsa,** which leads down to a bustling *pescheria* **(fish market)** where tuna—caught in waters offshore—is king. The spacious central square, **Piazza Vittorio Emanuele** is a relaxing palm-treed oasis.

The main street of Trapani is **Corso Vittorio Emanuele,** sometimes called Rua Grande by the Trapanese. Many elegant baroque buildings are found along this street, which makes for a grand promenade. At the eastern end of the street rises the **Palazzo Senatorio,** the 17th-century town hall, done up in pinkish marble.

Across from the port is the **Chiesa del Purgatorio** (in theory, open daily from 8:30am–12:30pm and 4–8pm). The entire atmosphere of this church remains medieval, with suffocating incense and otherworldly music. It houses the single greatest treasure in Trapani: the *Misteri* **★★,** 20 life-size wooden figures from the 18th century depicting Christ's Passion.

Where to Stay

Crystal Hotel ★ This is the most architecturally dramatic and urban-style hotel in Trapani. Constructed in the early 1990s, it's characterized by an all-glass facade that curves above a piazza in front of the rail station. (Few trains come into Trapani daily, so the neighborhood is very quiet.) Guest rooms are comfortable and efficiently organized. Each unit comes with an immaculate bathroom with a shower. Overall, this is a worthy choice and a modern refuge in the midst of an otherwise antique city.

Piazza Umberto I. ℭ **0923/20000.** www.crystalhoteltrapani.it. 70 units. Double 150€–200€. Rates include breakfast. AE, DC, MC, V. Free parking. **Amenities:** Restaurant; bar; babysitting; room service; nonsmoking rooms. *In room:* A/C, TV, minibar, Wi-Fi (11€ per day).

Hotel Vittoria Set on the waterfront road, a short distance from the center of town, this hotel is less preferable to the Crystal but still acceptable in every way. This is a well-built, solid structure lacking any particular architectural charm or style. Nevertheless, it is exceedingly comfortable, and the staff is helpful. Guest rooms are furnished in a minimalist way, though the beds are inviting, and each unit comes with a small bathroom, most with showers rather than tubs.

Via Francesco Crispi 4. ℭ **0923/873044.** www.hotelvittoriatrapani.it. 65 units. Doubles from 100€. Rates include breakfast. AE, DC, MC, V. Free parking. **Amenities:** Bar; breakfast lounge. *In room:* A/C, TV, hair dryer, minibar, free Wi-Fi.

Where to Dine

Ai Lumi Tavernetta ★ SICILIAN   Many locals cite this artfully rustic tavern, established in 1993 on the ground floor of a palazzo, as one of Trapani's best restaurants. During the 17th century, it functioned as a stable, but today the venue is filled with wines from virtually everywhere, dark furniture, and a clientele that includes actors, politicians, and journalists. And, thanks to thick masonry walls and air-conditioning, it's a cool retreat from the blazing heat outside. Flavorful dishes include roast lamb in a citrus sauce, local rabbit that's larded and then roasted, and seafood pasta with shrimp and calamari that tasted so fresh, they could have just leapt from the boat.

Corso Vittorio Emanuele 75. ✆ **0923/872418.** Reservations recommended Fri-Sat nights. Main courses 7€–18€. AE, DC, MC, V. Sept-July Mon-Sat 7:30–11pm; Aug daily 7:30–11pm.

Taverna Paradiso ★ SICILIAN   This tavern, established in 1996 in an old warehouse on the seafront, is the town's most prestigious restaurant. The medieval-looking stone rooms are decorated with rustic artifacts that show off the antique masonry. The food is excellent, and prices not nearly as high as you might expect from a place of this quality. House specialties include a maritime version of the North African couscous; spaghetti with tangy sea urchins; and a marvelous pasta dish with lobster, shrimp, and fresh artichokes. In winter, well-flavored meat and poultry dishes are featured when fish catches are slim due to rough waters.

Lungomare Dante Alighieri 22. ✆ **0923/22303.** Reservations recommended. Main courses 9€–15€. AE, DC, MC, V. Mon-Sat 1–3:30pm and 8–11:30pm.

MARSALA

At the westernmost tip of mainland Sicily, Marsala is the home of the world-famous Marsala wine, a rival of port and Madeira. The name Marsala dates from the port's occupation by the Saracens, who called it *Marsa el Allah,* or "Port of God," and to this day, Marsala evokes a North African town with its tangle of narrow streets and alleys. But it was the Carthaginians who founded the town on Cape Lilibeo (also called Cape Boeo) in 396 B.C. Marsala then fell to the Romans after a siege that lasted a decade (250–241 B.C.). The year 47 B.C. saw the arrival of Julius Caesar, who pitched camp here en route to North Africa.

In 1943, Marsala sustained heavy damage from Allied bombers before their land invasion of Sicily. Today, Marsala is a thriving little town, and its namesake wine is still the major fuel for the local economy. Although Erice (p. 221) is a more popular attraction, Marsala merits a half-day or so if you can spare it. You can also reach the Egadi Islands from here; several boats per day sail from Marsala port to Favignana.

Whether by train, bus, or car, it takes about 45 minutes to reach Marsala from Trapani. By **car,** head south from Trapani along Route 115. Marsala and Trapani are equidistant from Trapani's Birgi airport.

Exploring the Town

The heart of this wine-producing town is **Piazza della Repubblica,** site of the Chiesa Madre (see below) and the Palazzo Senatorio, dating from the 18th century and nicknamed "Loggia."

Branching off from this square is the main street, **Via 11 Maggio.** In the heyday of the Roman Empire, this street was called *Decumanus Maximus.* From Piazza della Repubblica, **Via Garibaldi** heads south to **Porta Garibaldi,** a magnificent gateway crowned by an eagle. Garibaldi is honored because it was at Marsala that he and 1,000 volunteers, dressed in red shirts, landed from Genoa. Their aim was to overthrow the Bourbon rulers, thus liberating the "Kingdom of the Two Sicilies."

If you'd like to watch Marsala grapes crushed and turned into the town's "sweet nectar," head for the **Cantine Florio,** Lungomare Via Florio (✆ **0923/781111**), which offers free guided tours of the winery. The 30-minute tours are offered Monday and Thursday at 11am and 3:30pm, Friday at 11am. Devotees of Marsala also flock to **Cantina Sperimentale Istituto Regionale della Vite e del Vino,** Via Trapani 218 (✆ **0923-737511**), open Thursday through Monday from 7:30am to 2pm and Tuesday and Wednesday from 7:30am to 2pm and 3 to 7pm. You are allowed to sample a number of experimental wines here.

Marsala's **Museo Archeologico di Baglio Anselmi,** at Lungomare Boeo (✆ **0923/952535**), is open Monday, Tuesday, and Thursday from 9am to 1:30pm and Wednesday and Friday through Sunday from 9am to 1:30pm and 4 to 7pm. Admission is 3€. Its chief attraction is the remains of a well-preserved **Punic ship ★** discovered in 1971 in the waters north of Marsala. It measures 35m (115-ft.) long and was artfully reconstructed in 1980. The ship may have been originally constructed for the Battle of the Egadi Islands in 241 B.C.; it's amazing to think that a vessel dating back to the First Punic War is still around in any form. Once manned by 68 oarsmen, this is the only known such war vessel ever uncovered.

Open for a free look 24 hours a day is the **Insula di Capo Boeo,** at the end of Viale Vittorio Emanuele. Here are the ruins of a trio of Roman *insulae* (apartment complexes), including that of a spacious villa dating from the 3rd century B.C. Around the *impluvium* (basin built into the floor) you can see mosaics depicting a fight between wild beasts. Also here are the ruins of *terme* (baths) and salons containing mosaics. The head of Medusa is visible, so be careful not to look her in the eye.

Where to Stay

Villa Favorita ★ 🏨 NORTH OF TOWN   This elegant and offbeat choice was established in the early 19th century, when it became a rendezvous for Sicilian intellectuals and aristocrats. Today the elegant retreat is part of the cultural heritage of Marsala and has been given a new lease on life as a four-star hotel. Much of the original architecture of the main building has been preserved, with its wide oak floors and arched loggias opening onto a courtyard. Choose between a traditional room in the main building or a more private whitewashed bungalow in the garden. The restaurant serves first-rate Sicilian and Italian dishes.

Via Favorita 23, N of Marsala. ✆ **0923/989100.** www.villafavorita.com. 42 units. Double 80€–102€. Rates include breakfast. AE, DC, MC, V. Free parking. **Amenities:** Restaurant; bar; bowling green; playground; pool; rooms for those w/limited mobility; tennis court. *In room:* A/C, TV, minibar, free Wi-Fi.

Where to Dine

Tenuta Volpara ★ 🍴 EAST OF TOWN   SICILIAN   Follow a labyrinth of winding country roads, then pass between a stately pair of masonry columns to reach Marsala's quintessential country inn—a jumble of light, noise, and energy in an otherwise isolated rural setting, 5.6km (3½ miles) south of the city. Vast and echoing, it was rebuilt in 1993 on the site of a ruined tavern that had been here for centuries. Many of your fellow diners might be here as part of a wedding reception or baptism, which adds to this place's sense of fun. You'll dine on such items as steak braised in a Barolo wine sauce, homemade sausages roasted with an herb-flavored liqueur, fettuccine with fresh mushrooms, and the dessert specialty, *zabina,* a pastry laced with ricotta cheese.

Situated in an annex somewhat removed from the bustle of the restaurant are 18 motel-style guest rooms, each with a shower-only bathroom, air-conditioning, minibar, TV, and phone. With breakfast included, a double costs 80€.

Contrada Volpara. ℂ **0923/984588.** Reservations recommended Fri–Sat nights. Main courses 7€–12€. AE, DC, MC, V. Daily 1:30–3pm and 8:30pm–midnight. Closed Mon Oct–Mar.

ERICE ★★★

In a Sicilian hill town beauty pageant, the tiara could either go to Taormina or Erice (*Eh*-ree-cheh). Originally an ancient Elymian settlement, Erice is 751m (2,465 ft.) above sea level, but only about 3km (2 miles) inland—so we are talking some dramatic heights—with a wonderfully preserved medieval *centro.* It's one of the highlights of western Sicily to stroll the cobblestoned lanes here, catching glimpses of stunning views in every direction—that is, when Erice isn't engulfed in a misty cloud created by its own microclimate. Erice is a lovely place to spend an afternoon wandering the medieval streets, with their baroque balconies and flowering vines. While Erice may be prettier than Taormina, it's a very quiet place with little to do but stroll—a few hours here is plenty.

Buses to Erice depart from Trapani's Piazza Montalto; the trip lasts 50 minutes and costs 2€ one-way. If you're driving, park your car near the Chiesa Madrice and Porta Trapani, on the southwest edge of the old town, then head into the medieval core on foot.

Exploring

Erice's chief attraction is the **medieval town ★★★** and its **rapturous views ★★★**, although there are some individual points of interest worth seeking out as you make your way along its cobblestone streets.

After leaving Porta di Trapani, your first discovery will be immediately to the northeast. **Chiesa Matrice di Erice,** Via Vito Carvini (ℂ **0923/869123;** Mon–Fri 9:30am–12:30pm and 3:30–5:30pm, Sat–Sun 9:30am–1pm and 3:30–6pm), is the main church of Erice, constructed in 1314 using stones from the ancient Temple of Venus that once stood here. If you climb the church's campanile, or bell tower, you'll be rewarded with a stunning view across the Gulf of Trapani to the Egadi Islands.

If you walk north from the church, you can follow **Mura Elimo-Puniche ★**, the defensive walls constructed by the Elymian culture (8th–6th c. B.C.) around the northeastern flank of Erice. The best-preserved part of the walls lies along Via dell'Addolorata, stretching from Porta Carmine to Porta Spada, which is at the far northern end of the massive fortifications.

At Porta Spada, the end of your "wall walk," you'll find yourself at **Chiesa di Santa Orsola,** a 1413 church with its original Gothic rib-vaulting still on view in the nave. Directly to the east of this church is the **Quartiere Spagnola.** Launched in the 17th century but never finished, this "Spanish Quarter" building is no grand sight, but a **panoramic vista** ★ unfolds from here over the Bay of Cofano.

The **Villa Balio** gardens, on the southwest side of town, are worth a look. Situated on the summit of a hill, the gardens open onto one of the most **spectacular views** ★★ in western Sicily, embracing the peaks of Monte Cofano with distant views of the Egadi Islands. On a clear day you can see all the way to Cap Bon in Tunisia, a distance of 170km (106 miles). The gardens are always open; entrance is free.

Saving the best for last, follow the path beyond the gardens to the **Castello di Venere,** or Castle of Venus, built atop Mount San Giuliano on the same spot where in ancient times a temple to the goddess stood. Dating from the 12th century, the present *castello* was constructed as a defensive fortification by the Normans. Massive and majestic, it became the seat of Norman authority in the west. It's still encircled by mammoth medieval towers. The castle provides an even more **memorable view** ★★★ than from the Villa Balio gardens; you can see the plains of Trapani and the Egadi Islands to the southwest. In fair weather, you can even spot the island of Ustica (p. 244). After all the looting, burning, and destruction this castle has witnessed over the centuries, little is left of the ruins. But the view makes it worthwhile. The castle is open daily from 9am to 8pm, with no admission fee.

The **FuniErice cableway,** Piazza Umberto I, 3 (✆ **0923/869720;** www.funiviaerice.com; Mon 1:10pm–1am, Tues–Fri 7:45am–1am; Sat–Sun 8:45am–2am; 3€), connects Erice with Trapani's Casa Santa neighborhood; the 11-minute ride is great way to experience the town's thrilling altitude, especially at sunset.

Where to Stay & Dine

If you're staying overnight, a good bet, and quite a decent value, is **Torri Pepoli** ★★ (Viale Conte Pepoli, Giardini del Balio; ✆ **0923/860117;** www.torripepoli.it; 7 units; doubles 100€–150€; AE, DC, MC, V). As stunning to look at as it is to look out from, this 13th-century Arab-style castle has been refitted as a four-star hotel, with large and colorful rooms, modern bathrooms, and neo-Gothic furnishings.

Restaurants in town tend to be rather touristy, but there are a number of renowned pastry shops, including **Pasticceria Michele Il Tulipano,** Via Vittorio Emanuele 10 (✆ **0923/869672;** daily 7:30am–9pm), where you can pick up a heavenly *cassatella* (fritter filled with sweet ricotta). My favorite sit-down meals in town are at **Monte San Giuliano** ★ (Vicolo San Rocco 7; ✆ **0923/869595;** reservations recommended; main courses 8€–15€; AE, DC, MC, V; Tues–Sun 12:15–2:45pm and 7:30–10pm; closed Jan 7–21). To reach this rustic garden hideaway, negotiate your way through a maze of alleys that begin a few steps downhill from Erice's Piazza Umberto I, then pass through an iron gate and stone walls to the restaurant's terraces and dining rooms. The seafood is excellent, and my favorite pasta is homemade *busiate* made with *pesto alla Trapanese,* which in this case means garlic, basil, fresh tomatoes, and—surprise, surprise—almonds.

SAN VITO LO CAPO ★

At first glance, a panorama of this beach town looks like a postcard from Rio de Janeiro—a broad expanse of white sand lines a curving bay, with a massive mountain promontory at one end. But this Sicilian resort is a much smaller, quieter affair. The mellow *centro* consists of boxy, whitewashed houses with Saracen arch doorways that bear the influence of Arabic culture. That influence carries over to the cuisine as well—couscous is bigger than pasta here, and there's even an international festival held here every September (www.couscousfest.it).

San Vito's gorgeous **beach ★★**—a kilometer-long stretch of clean, fine sand—makes it a popular summer destination for Italian families and couples. Swimming in the turquoise waters here, with the imposing contours of Monte Monaco to the east, is an unforgettable experience. Organized boat tours of the nearby Zingaro and Scopello nature reserves are a great way to access hidden coves and see unspoiled Sicilian flora and marine fauna.

Spending the Night

Consider staying in San Vito so you can sample the signature couscous dishes at a local restaurant. At the **Ghibli Hotel ★** (Via Regina Margherita, 80; 𝄐 **0923/ 974155;** www.ghiblihotel.it; doubles from 90€; AE, DC, MC, V), rooms are tastefully decorated in a North African style. Use of a beach club, just minutes down the road, is included in the room rate. The hotel's alfresco restaurant, **Profumi di Cous Cous,** is a perfect foray into *cucina sanvitese* under a canopy of citrus trees.

SEGESTA ★★★

Segesta's one and only raison d'être on the tourist route is its **archaeological park** (Contrada Segesta; 𝄐 **0924/952356;** 6€; daily 9am–5pm), which contains a single, amazing **Greek temple ★★★**. First of all, the setting is unreal: a fairy tale landscape of rolling hills, splendidly enveloped by a green valley and framed by the peaks of Monte Barbaro and Monte Bernardo. The 5th century B.C. temple at the center of this scene, at 300m (900 ft.), is just as impressive: It's perhaps the best-preserved ancient Greek temple anywhere, with 36 Doric columns supporting unadorned entablatures and pediments (scholars say the temple lacks decoration—and a roof—because construction was interrupted, and never resumed, when a war broke out with nearby Selinunte). A short bus ride (1€) farther up Monte Barbaro, to 431m (1,414 ft.), is Segesta's **ancient theater ★★**, hewn straight into the side of the mountain in the 3rd century B.C. In ancient days, the theater could hold as many as 4,000 spectators, and the site is still used summer theatrical productions.

Several trains and buses per day make the half-hour run from Trapani (p. 217). The train station, Segesta Tempio, is only a 1km (½-mile) walk from the Doric temple. Buses to Segesta leave from Piazza Montalto in Trapani. By **car,** take the *autostrada* (A29) running between Palermo and Trapani. The exit for Segesta is clearly marked.

OTHER SICILIAN ISLANDS

with Darwin Porter and Danforth Prince

10

This chapter covers the "stragglers" off Sicily: Pantelleria, Lampedusa, Linosa, and Ustica. These four islands are the loners among the Italian islands, not members of any cohesive archipelago. Flung far out at sea, they are remote worlds unto themselves. Both in terms of landscape and atmosphere, they have little in common with each other beyond the geographic distinction of being very isolated outcrops of land in the southern Mediterranean. Each is seductive in its own way, with diversely compelling assets for the traveler looking for something a bit more "out there."

Pantelleria (110km/68 miles southwest of Mazara del Vallo, Sicily) is the darling among these four. Dubbed the "Black Pearl of the Mediterranean," it's an exotic island with a strong Arabic feel and a forbidding terrain of rough black lava. Despite the fact that Pantelleria has no sandy beaches, the island has nevertheless risen in popularity as a summer retreat among chic and moneyed Europeans who cherish its very otherness—and its exclusivity. Flights to Pantelleria aren't cheap, and decent accommodations—most common is the Arab-style *dammuso* stone house, converted into boutique guesthouses and villas all over the island—are expensive. Yet there is striking beauty in the black lava, especially where it meets the cobalt sea, and unexpected charms like a neon-blue volcanic lake where you can take a mud bath. Food and wine lovers will find a surprisingly sophisticated gourmet scene. Pantelleria town is the contrast to all of this—the impoverished burg where local kids walk down sidewalks barefoot while tourists toast the sunset at harborside bars. Put all of this together, and few islands can deliver such a profound sense of escape.

Lampedusa and Linosa are grouped together as the *isole Pelagie* (Pelagic, or "High-Sea" islands), although they're quite different from each other and 40km/25 miles, 1½ hours by ferry apart. Suspended about halfway between Pantelleria and the island nation of Malta, the Pelagie are the southernmost islands in Italy. Lampedusa, in fact, is closer to Africa than to Italy. Lampedusa is not the most initially welcoming place: It's dry and flat, with a mostly raggedy port town. But tourists don't come for the

charms of the village. They come for Lampedusa's coastline, where shelves of soft tufa dramatically meet the sea, making for paradisiacal swimming beaches and coves. Nowhere is this more spectacularly demonstrated than at Isola dei Conigli beach. Lampedusa used to be a very offbeat choice for a holiday, but as more money has been invested in tourism here in the past several years, and there are now smart accommodations and hip bars. Lampedusa, in high summer anyway, has become a bit more mainstream.

Mainstream isn't the word you'd use to describe Linosa. Tidy, tiny, lush Linosa is a fertile volcanic island with immaculately maintained streets (all six of them), good hiking, a few beaches, and that's about it. Linosa has proudly stayed off the radar of mass tourism, and because of its size and remoteness, probably always will. Come here for a few days of summer-camp-like relaxation, free of stress and technology.

Ustica, a 2½-hour ferry ride north of Palermo, is small and volcanic (read: no beaches), but it has a pleasant, village-y atmosphere, and for scuba enthusiasts, there is no better diving in the Italian Islands. Famous dive sites include the Scoglio del Medico, an offshore basalt outcrop with an undersea maze of grottoes, tunnels, and canyons, and the Underwater Archaeological Museum, where ancient Roman artifacts lie undisturbed on the seafloor. Non-divers can take a boat tour around Ustica to discover the island's many fascinating sea caves. If you've got an extra day in Palermo, a side trip to Ustica will definitely be memorable.

PANTELLERIA ★★★

Stark and windswept Pantelleria may be the chicest island getaway in all of Europe. All over this 86-sq.-km (33-sq.-mile) island, striking black rock sets off the green vegetation and glorious blue of the Mediterranean. Pantelleria is an exotic place caught between two continents and two cultures, and behind a down-and-out port town lies a countryside with some of the most exclusive accommodations in the world. Although *ciao*s are exchanged on the street (and it's mostly Italians who vacation here), Pantelleria's whole look and feel are a world away from the entrenched civilization of mainland Italy or even Sicily, from which it is removed by 110km (68 miles) of open sea. Architecturally and gastronomically, Pantelleria has more in common with North Africa, just 70km (43 miles) to the east.

Pantelleria's rich ancient history includes the usual suspects of Mediterranean squatters—Phoenician settlers named it Cossyra and were later subjugated by Rome, then Byzantium, and then Arabs, who called the island *Bent El Rion* ("daughter of the winds"), from which "Pantelleria" derived. The Arabs were here from 700 to 1123, and they left a significant legacy on the island, first and foremost in the *dammusi* (a form of stone house that exists nowhere else in the world) that riddle the island. Nearly all of these ancient structures have been converted into vacation rentals or miniresorts, and staying in one is integral to the Pantelleria experience.

These days, the most well-known squatters on Pantelleria are the glitterati of European fashion and media. An elite set of designers, actors, photographers, and editors come here to escape the flash and chaos of their real worlds. Giorgio Armani was the first Big Name to buy property here, and he stills summers in an elaborate compound of *dammusi* called Casa Armani, and he still goes for *aperitivo* at Bar Aurora in working class Pantelleria town. But don't come to Pantelleria expecting any overt glamour or you'll be sorely disappointed: Pantelleria is the anti-Sardinia, Capri, and Panarea in its lack of nightlife, glitzy boutiques, and showy scene. You will meet real locals here, and they are friendly and warm. But they aren't walking around in Tod's resort wear and chic linen caftans. The real Pantelleria is endearingly indifferent to what an exclusive place it has become.

Before you go booking the next flight to this still-insider place, some disclosure is in order on the physical nature of Pantelleria: It isn't for everyone. The summer sun is unequivocally oppressive, and even on otherwise mild spring and fall days, the *scirocco* wind, carrying dust from the Sahara, can send you running for cover. Near constant wind keeps the skies clear, so clouds are unheard of, but then so are sandy beaches on this lavic outcrop—a key detail to keep in mind when thinking about what your days will look like here. Pantelleria's lava shores are inhospitable for the normal "island" pursuits of baking in the sun, and even going for a swim is a bit of a process here, almost always involving a drive along a steep and winding road, then a 10-minute scamper down a bumpy trail to water's edge, then donning aqua socks to protect your feet from the jagged bottom once you actually wade in. The antagonism of nature on Pantelleria, more than its remoteness, has kept mass tourism at bay.

However, the rewards for your suffering of heat, wind, rough rocks, and carsickness are indelible experiences. The sea off Pantelleria is uncontaminated in extremis: Near the shore, the water seems like a liquid form of internally flawless emerald, while a bit farther out, the color changes to deep cobalt, as the sea bottom drops off sharply.

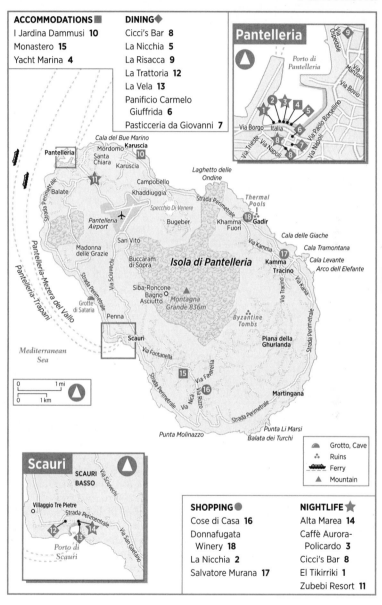

ACCOMMODATIONS ■
I Jardina Dammusi **10**
Monastero **15**
Yacht Marina **4**

DINING ◆
Cicci's Bar **8**
La Nicchia **5**
La Risacca **9**
La Trattoria **12**
La Vela **13**
Panificio Carmelo Giuffrida **6**
Pasticceria da Giovanni **7**

SHOPPING ●
Cose di Casa **16**
Donnafugata Winery **18**
La Nicchia **2**
Salvatore Murana **17**

NIGHTLIFE ★
Alta Marea **14**
Caffè Aurora-Policardo **3**
Cicci's Bar **8**
El Tikirriki **1**
Zubebi Resort **11**

Grotto, Cave
Ruins
Ferry
Mountain

10

OTHER SICILIAN ISLANDS | Pantelleria

Stunning nature, from the elephant's trunk rock formation called Arco dell'Elefante to the warm sulfuric lake of the Specchio di Venere, makes a lasting impression. And the sense of isolation is profound. Pantelleria is about as close as you can get to the end of the Earth while still being technically in Europe.

227

Strategies

Pantelleria in August is stratospheric—in terms of both temperature and expense. Yes, you want it to be warm when you're here, but considering the sparse and low vegetation and the black rock underfoot, "sweltering summer" takes on a whole new meaning on this island. Being this close to Africa, Pantelleria has very long shoulder seasons (Apr to mid-June and mid-Sept to Nov) of warm weather in which the pursuits of swimming and sunning are perfectly feasible. Prices in August are also nearly double the normal rate for lodging, car rentals, and boat tours. *Dammusi* that rent for thousands of euros per week in August become much more affordable in the spring and fall seasons, too. Pantelleria may have a reputation for exclusiveness, but a vacation here doesn't have to set you back thousands if you're smart about trip timing and can forgo the ultra-luxury accommodations.

Essentials

GETTING THERE Pantelleria is most commonly and conveniently reached by air, though flights here are fairly expensive. The island's airport is served by many Italian airports, but the most frequent connections are from the Sicilian airports of Palermo and Trapani, on **Meridiana** (✆ 0871/2229319 outside Italy or ✆ 892928 within Italy; www.meridiana.it), which is the only airline offering year-round service to Pantelleria. Fares for the 45-minute flight are normally 125€ round-trip regardless of season. From late May to late September, there are nonstop charter flights to Pantelleria (operated by Alitalia and AirOne, but book through **Agenzia La Cossira;** ✆ 0923/911078 or 0923/913629; www.lacossira.it) from Rome, Milan, Venice, Bologna, and Verona (from 300€ round-trip).

You can also get to Pantelleria by sea from the western Sicilian port of Trapani. **Siremar** (in Trapani, Molo Sanità; ✆ 0923/24968; www.siremar.it) runs ferries (4 hr., 45 min.; 34€ one-way) from Trapani to the island year-round. In Pantelleria, Siremar has an office at Via Borgo Italia 22 (✆ 0923/911120). **Traghetti delle Isole** (in Trapani at Via Ammiraglio Staiti 13; ✆ 0923/21754 or 0923/22467; in Pantelleria at Agenzia Marittima Adriano Minardi, ✆ 333/2875261; www.traghetti delleisole.it) also operates a daily ferry to and from Trapani; the journey takes from 6 to 7 hours.

GETTING AROUND Your own transport is essential on Pantelleria. Due to the steep and rough roads, not to mention constant sun and wind exposure and lack of nighttime road illumination, a rental car is a better idea than a scooter. Book one—the official car of Pantelleria seems to be a boxy, early-'90s Fiat Panda, preferably in pistachio green—at **Policardo,** Via Messina 31, Pantelleria Town (✆ 0923/912844). In August, rates are 55€ to 70€ per day, but only 35€ to 44€ the rest of the year, with more favorable rates for full-week rentals. Policardo also rents quads and scooters. **Taxis** can be called at ✆ 0923/912716, ✆ 338/6116825, or ✆ 380/4687576. The island also has a limited and unreliable bus service, with all lines departing from Piazza Cavour in Pantelleria town. In theory, the buses serve much of the island, but I wouldn't want to depend on a Pantelleria public bus for my ride home in the afternoon heat of summer.

VISITOR INFORMATION The **Pro Loco** is at Piazza Cavour in Pantelleria town (✆ 0923/911838; Apr–Oct daily 9am–1pm and 5–8pm).

FAST FACTS The **carabinieri** (police) are at Via Trieste 13 (✆ 0923/911109). There's an **Internet point** at Via Dante 7 (✆ 0923/911367; daily 9am–2pm and

4:30–9:30pm); if you have your own laptop, there's free Wi-Fi at **Cicci's Bar** (see "Where to Dine," p. 232). The Banca Nuova on Via Catania (© **0923/912732**) has an **ATM,** and there are several other banks with ATMs in town. For medical care, the **hospital** is at Piazzale Almanza 21 (© **0923/911110**), though this is a very backwater facility only recommended for minor injuries; serious cases are transported by helicopter to Trapani. The main pharmacy, **Farmacia Greco,** is on Piazza Cavour 28 (© **0923/911310**). The **post office** is at Via Verdi 2 (© **0923/695232;** Mon–Fri 8am–1:30pm, Sat 8am–12:30pm).

Exploring the Island

Pantelleria town is a working port that isn't love at first sight for those who vacation here, thinking Pantelleria is a chic insiders' getaway. There are delivery trucks belching fumes as they idle on the harborside streets, poor local children shuffling along in rubber sport sandals, and block after block of apartment buildings in that unattractive, utilitarian postwar style so common in southern Italy. What Pantelleria town lacks in glamour, it makes up for in authenticity—which makes it the polar opposite of more obviously posh Italian islands like Capri and Panarea—and if you're the type of traveler who's always in search of real local culture, you'll love Pantelleria town. Even the elite habitués of the island who own lavish *dammuso* compounds in the countryside never miss morning coffee and evening drinks at one of the unassuming bars of Pantelleria town. The town, which is built along the crescent-shaped harbor and continues inland for a few hundred meters, has all the services you need—supermarkets and delis, marine hardware stores, laundries, even a 99-cent store—and exactly one historical monument, the ancient **Castello Barbacane** (not open to the public), which dominates the harbor with its imposing, windowless walls in black lava.

Outside town, the best introduction to Pantelleria's striking landscape is a drive along the coastal road (the *strada provinciale* or *strada litoranea*) that hugs the shore all the way around the island, passing through a few of the larger villages. It's a journey of about 60km (37 miles) that takes roughly 2½ hours, if you only make a few quick stops along the way. Stopping for a swim anywhere along the route will add at least an hour, and probably more. Along the way you'll get to know the many facets of Pantelleria—the fancy *dammusi* and sparking sea are clearly visible through the low vegetation, yet so are ratty yards and power lines.

The Coastal Road & Swimming Coves

Pantelleria's best swimming spots are concentrated on the northeast coast, from Pantelleria town to the Arco dell'Elefante. Though the coves here are, as elsewhere on the island, either rocky or pebbly (aqua socks are a must!), they're relatively easy to access from the paved *strada litoranea* (coastal road). Heading out clockwise (east) from Pantelleria town, one of the first enticing inlets is **Cala del Bue Marino** ★, where centuries of wind and water have sculpted sinuous reliefs into the lava rock walls. Next up, **Karuscia** is a wide and shallow bay accessed by a gently sloping but bumpy deposit of lava rocks. A bit farther east is Punta Spadillo; park where you see signs pointing to **Laghetto delle Ondine** ★. At the end of a 10-minute trail is this seaside "infinity pool" formed when sea water in high tide washes over the rock wall into a smooth basin. Continuing south on the coastal road, follow the signs to **Gadir,** where there are ancient **thermal pools** ★, reinforced in concrete, at water's edge. Beyond Gadir is the bathing mecca that consists of three promontories, two gorgeous bays (**Cala Tramontana** ★★ and **Cala Levante** ★★), and one awesome natural rock formation—the **Arco dell'Elefante ★★★**. The "Arch of the Elephant" is the visual calling card of Pantelleria and every bit as impressive in real life as in the postcards and Web images. Here, at the southern tip of Cala Levante, the sloping lava, with a natural arch forming a "trunk" where it meets the water, looks exactly—I mean, *exactly*—like an elephant kneeling in the Med for a drink of water. From the big flat ears to the oblong eye sockets, this rock is pachyderm all the way. (Drive through Tracino, then park at the end of the road marked Cala Levante; this is the north side of the bay and 300m/984 ft., by sea or rocky shore, from the "elephant." A swim under the arch is a must, while some more adventurous local kids are known to cliff-dive from the top of the elephant's nose.)

Given the time involved in getting to most of these swimming spots, packing a picnic is a good idea. Near water's edge, you can usually find some flat rocks suitable for lounging on. If you're bringing food, a fun local custom is pouring a bit of olive oil into small bowl-shaped divots in the rock, which is already perfumed with sea salt, and dipping fresh bread in.

The Interior

You might catch a glimpse of the incongruously bright turquoise water of the **Specchio di Venere ★★★** upon final approach at Pantelleria airport. Nestled in a verdant valley in northeast Pantelleria, "Venus's Mirror" is an extinct crater that is now a circular lake, bordered by sulfur-rich mud that is said to have healing properties for dermatological or rheumatic disorders. (Note that the sulfur of Pantelleria, like sulfur anywhere else, smells like rotten eggs—don't say I didn't warn you.) To partake of the rite as the Pantescans do, first swim in the water so that all your skin is wet, then harvest some mud from the shallow lake bottom; cake yourself in the mud, let it dry until brittle and plastery, then go for a cleansing swim in a different part of the lake, which is kept warm year-round by sulfuric hot springs. The greyish-white mud you see on shore continues all the way under the water, accounting for the extraordinary swimming-pool color of the Specchio di Venere.

All throughout Pantelleria are villages with fewer inhabitants and services but more interesting architecture than what's in Pantelleria town. Many of these villages still bear the names the Arab settlers gave them—Bugeber, Khamma, Bukkaram, Rekhale, Gadir. The best-equipped village is the seaside **Scauri ★**, on the west coast. Several good restaurants (including the island's only waterfront dining, at La Vela—see "Where to Dine," p. 232) and a busy fishing port (though no good swimming) make Scauri a lively spot and worthwhile detour on any island tour.

Several paved roads, from all directions, get close to the green parkland of Pantelleria's highest peak (836m/2,743 ft.), **Montagna Grande ★★★**. The easiest access is from the end of the road that continues south of Sibà. From there, it's a short hike to the summit area, where the glorious **views ★★★** sweep for miles and miles in every direction. Outside of the hot summer months, it's fun to spend some time up here on the hiking paths that traverse the peak.

The Pantelleria hinterland's rite of passage is going for a sweat in the **Bagno Asciutto ★★** (also known and signposted as **Grotta di Benikulà**), a natural "dry bath" on the western slope of Montagna Grande. Follow signs from Sibà; the paved road eventually peters out so you'll have to make the final stretch, a rocky 10-minute trail, on foot. Here, steam vents in the rock grotto create a perfect sauna—good for eliminating the toxins of too much local wine consumed the night before, perhaps. Bring a towel, as recommended practice is to lie face down on the cave floor.

DAMMUSO OR die

A rented *dammuso* is our top accommodations choice on Pantelleria; a minimum stay of 1 week is required in summer, but you can often swing a shorter stay of 3 to 5 days outside of July and August. Elite travelers go to great lengths (and great expense) to stay at the uber-chic **Monastero** resort (℡ **349/5595580;** www.monastero pantelleria.com; rates available on request), owned by the fashion photographer Fabrizio Ferri, or at one of the spectacular *dammuso* compounds that belong to other luminaries of European style. More modest budgets can get the same general idea by renting one of the myriad *dammusi,* through such agencies as the highly recommended **Il Dammuso** (www.ildammuso.com), which has the most comprehensive catalog of these vacation units in all price ranges, ranging from barebones, Flintstones-like units that cost 500€ per week to lavishly remodeled villas with stunning kitchens and magazine-worthy design throughout (upwards of 2,000€ per week). Be aware, however, that even some of the more sumptuous properties are a good distance from the sea.

On the southern side of Pantelleria, or *dietro isola* ("behind the island"), there's a fertile plain called the **Piana della Ghirlanda.** With green farm plots that present a striking contrast to the barren, lavic look of the rest of Pantelleria, this is the "garden district" of the island. Surrounding volcanic slopes protect the valley from the winds, creating favorable conditions for growing the main crop, *il cappero* (the caper), as well as every other fresh vegetable and herb that shows up on island menus. Also here is Pantelleria's only real archaeological site, a cluster of **Byzantine tombs** (always open and free) hewn into the volcanic rock. You may also see some **dwarf olive trees;** the Panteschi place heavy rocks on them as they grow, so their resulting low profile is less battered by the winds and ensures their survival.

Dietro Isola in general is the wild side of Pantelleria, where tenacious Aleppo and maritime pines cling to the cliffs. In one spot, called **Salto della Vecchia** ("Old Lady's Leap"), the cliffs drop off about 300m (984 ft.) to the sea. Near here, the best place to swim is Balata dei Turchi, a sheltered cove backed by those same towering rock walls. The access by land is admittedly difficult and time consuming, so I recommended visiting the Balata dei Turchi by sea (see "Island Tour by Boat," below).

Wine Country

As you drive around the countryside of Pantelleria, you'll see signs with grape clusters, indicating that an *azienda agricola* or *vitivinicola,* or winery where the famous *passito* wine is produced, is nearby. Wine producers are scattered here and there all over the island, as any south-facing, terraced volcanic earth on Pantelleria is good for growing the *zibibbo* white grape from which sweet *passito* is made. One of our favorite Sicilian winemakers, **Donnafugata** (Contrada Khamma; ℡ **0923/915649;** www. donnafugata.it), has an estate in eastern Pantelleria, not far from the Arco dell'Elefante, and welcomes visitors in summer. Tours (June 23–Sept 30, Tues–Sun at 10:30am, 5, and 7pm) of the vineyards and cellar last about 1½ hours and include tastings of two or three wines. The tours are free but must be booked in advance.

Island Tour by Boat

Pantelleria's jagged coastline is much easier to explore by sea than by land, and taking a day to rent a boat, or better yet, hire a local boatman to take you on a small group tour, is a must while here. The 52km (32-mile) perimeter of the island makes the Pantelleria *giro dell'isola* tour a full-day affair, departing at 10am and returning at 5pm. Rates are usually around 30€ (50€ in Aug), which includes a *spaghettata* (lunch of pasta and other *cucina pantesca* specialties), served picnic-style on the boat. You'll stop for a swim at the iconic Arco dell'Elefante and on the south side of the island, under 300m-tall (984-ft.) rock walls in the sheltered waters of Balata dei Turchi.

Tours can be arranged informally and on-the-spot at Pantelleria harbor. Just arrive around 9:30am and see which captain or craft you like best. They basically all charge the same rates. **Futura** (② **0923/912324**), skippered by a fisherman named Franco, is one of the more fun-oriented boats and serves fresh fish for lunch. If you opt to go it alone and rent your own boat, try **La Tortuga** (on Pantelleria harbor; ② **333/6750836**), from 40€ for a half-day rental. Because of the size of Pantelleria (bigger than most boat-rental islands of Italy) and the potentially strong currents and winds, it's best to limit your cove-hopping to the eastern side of the island.

Where to Stay

I Jardina Dammusi ★★★ The best of both Pantelleria-accommodations worlds (independent *dammuso* vs. resort) meet at this collection of seven luxury *dammusi,* 3km (2 miles) east of Pantelleria town. Staggered on terraces overlooking the sea (200m/656 ft. away), the units are spaced out to ensure privacy, and each has its own pool and ample outdoor space. (De rigueur for any *dammuso,* each unit has a *ducchena* bench on the terrace, with hammock, shaded by *cannizzato* cane roofs, and a circular-stone-walled *giardino arabo* with fruit trees.) Interiors are rustic but elegant; in the open kitchens, the stone walls and countertops are washed with textured ochre for a bit of that subtly Arabic look so characteristic of Pantelleria. Guests can avail of I Jardina's service center for everything from excursion booking to grocery delivery.

Località Karuscia, Strada Provinciale km 2.4. ② **0923/913627.** www.ijardinapantelleria.it. 7 units. Weekly rentals from 700€, double occupancy.

Yacht Marina ★ If you don't stay in a countryside *dammuso,* the best traditional, affordable choice in Pantelleria town is this hotel right on the harbor. The anonymous business-hotel interiors may be out of keeping with the surroundings of this working port town, but you'll have plenty of space, marble-clad bathrooms, and all modern comforts. The location couldn't be more convenient, putting you within a stone's throw of the waterfront bars and island boat tours.

Via Borgo Italia. ② **0923/913649.** www.marinahotelpantelleria.com. 37 units. Doubles 100€–200€. AE, DC, MC, V. **Amenities:** Bar; lounge. *In room:* A/C, TV, hair dryer, Internet, minibar.

Where to Dine

Mainstays of typical Pantelleria cooking are fish couscous (usually only offered once a week at any given restaurant, so if you want to order it, call around to see where it's going to be available during your stay) and a condiment known as *ammogghiu* or *pesto pantesco* (made with tomatoes, capers, black olives, pine nuts, fresh local herbs, garlic, and peperoncino), used on fresh fish and pasta or spread on bread. The local cheese is *tumma,* made from cow's milk.

For a quick lunch in Pantelleria town, stop in at locals' haunt **Cicci's Bar,** Via Cagliari 7 (✆ **339/5885821;** Mon–Sat 5:30am–midnight), or pick up pizza by the slice at **Panificio Carmelo Giuffrida** (Via Borgo Italia 21; ✆ **0923/911311**) and have it wrapped up for your picnic by the sea somewhere. **Pasticceria da Giovanni,** on Piazza Cavour (✆ **349/4759904**), is the place for typical Pantescan pastries.

La Nicchia ★★★ SCAURI PANTESCAN   Without a doubt the most serious restaurant on Pantelleria, "the niche" is a gourmet place in Scauri (on the west coast), serving up tantalizing Pantescan classics and creative twists in a romantic courtyard with a gnarled old orange tree. Everything here is exquisite, and made from only the finest and freshest, rigorously local ingredients. For an *antipasto,* try the *caponata* with toasted almonds; for your *secondo,* order the *gamberoni* (prawns)—whether seasoned with *gelatina d'uva* (a delicate jelly made from *zibibbo* grapes) or potato puree with capers and black olive cream sauce; they are to die for. The wine list has more than 70 labels, almost all from Pantelleria and Sicily. La Nicchia sells its own gourmet products at a shop in Pantelleria town (see "Shopping," below).

Contrada Scauri Basso. ✆ **0923/916342.** Reservations required. Entrees from 15€. AE, DC, MC, V. Thurs-Mon 7:30-10:30pm. Closed Jan 15-Feb 15.

La Risacca ★ PANTELLERIA TOWN SEAFOOD/SICILIAN   This is your best bet for an atmospheric meal in the port town. Fare is straightforward Mediter-ranean—pastas and fresh fish—with Sicilian inflections (eggplants appear in many dishes) and island standbys like *pesto pantesco.* Seating is on a large patio facing the port, so book a table early enough to watch the sunset.

Via Milano 65. ✆ **0923/912975.** Entrees from 10€. AE, DC, MC, V. Tues-Sun 12:30-3pm and 7:30-10:30pm. Closed Oct.

La Trattoria ★ SCAURI PANTESCAN   Fresh, authentic island flavors, a menu to suit all tastes and levels of gluttony, cordial service, and at the end of the meal, a bill that doesn't flabbergast you. What's not to like? You could easily fill up on the tempting *antipasti,* but save room for the ravioli filled with ricotta and mint. Ask to book the private room (for two to four diners), which has heaps more atmosphere than the bland and overly lit main dining room.

Contrada Scauri. ✆ **0923/916101.** Reservations recommended. Entrees from 10€. AE, DC, MC, V. Din-ner nightly 8pm-midnight, Fri-Sun 12:30-2:30pm.

La Vela ★ SCAURI PANTESCAN   The only waterside dining on the entire island, above the bobbing boats in the fishing harbor of Scauri, makes "the sail" a Pantelleria standout. It's a rustic joint with wooden tables and paper tablecloths, but the breeze, shade, and simple, good food—grilled fish and a particularly flavorful *insalata pantesca* (salad with potatoes, tomatoes, olives, capers, and onions)—make this my favorite sit-down lunch spot while out and about on the island.

Contrada Scauri. ✆ **0923/916566.** Reservations recommended. Entrees from 10€. No credit cards. Wed-Mon 12:30-3pm and 7:30-10pm. Closed Jan-Feb.

Pantelleria After Dark

For an island that gets such chic visitors, there isn't all that much in the way of nightlife. Later in the evening, the posh crowds are having fabulous private parties at their swank *dammusi,* but earlier on, almost everyone makes their way down to one of the bars of Pantelleria town for a drink at sunset. The marina-facing **Caffè Aurora-Policardo ★**

(Via Borgo Italia 36; ✆ **0923/911098;** daily 5:30am–2am) is renowned for its *granite* (and for being Armani's favorite place for *aperitivo*). Also facing the water, **El Tikirriki** ★ (Via Borgo Italia 2/3; no phone) is another beloved spot for *prosecco* and happy-hour snacks. Just off the main piazza, **Cicci's Bar** (Via Cagliari 7; ✆ **339/5885821**) is where local *panteschi* go for drinks and snacks, but there's no view of the sunset from here.

Out on the island, **Alta Marea** ★★ in Scauri (Calata del Porto; ✆ **0923/916151**) is the closest thing on Pantelleria to an "it" scene. It's open from 7pm to 7am and serves as an *aperitivo* bar, restaurant, and *discoteca*. For something a little fancier, the bar at **Zubebi Resort** (near the Specchio di Venere lake, Contrada Zubebi; ✆ **0923/913653**) draws a chic crowd most evenings in summer.

Shopping

Elegant specialty-foods shop **La Nicchia** ★, in Pantelleria town at Via Borgo Italia 31 (✆ **0923/912968**), sells capers, caper pâtés, caper sauces, caper pesto, dried herbs, citrus jams, and a wide range of wines and spirits, all of which make great souvenirs. (La Nicchia products are also sold at some Dean & Deluca and Williams-Sonoma stores in the U.S., but they're much less expensive here at the source and relatively easy to pack.) If you fall in love with *passito* while here, go to **Salvatore Murana** ★ (Contrada Khamma 276, ✆ **0923/915231**), the most serious wine shop on Pantelleria. The *dammuso*-owning set get their cool outdoor pillows and light fixtures at **Cose di Casa** (Contrada Rekhale; ✆ **0923/916651**).

LAMPEDUSA ★

Lampedusa itself isn't beautiful. It is a dry platform of barren rock in the middle of the Mediterranean nowhere (roughly equidistant from southern Sicily, Tunisia, and Malta, it's about 200km/124 miles on average from the nearest major landmass). Vegetation is practically nonexistent save for a few sparse palms and agave plants and a rather burnt-looking coverage of *macchia mediterranea*. The island's one town, at the port, is downtrodden, and Lampedusa is best known to Italian news followers as the place where illegal immigrants from Africa wash ashore in hopes of asylum in the European Union. So why on earth would you want to vacation here? The short answer is for the sea.

The coast of Lampedusa looks as though it has been carved with a capricious cake knife. Tall walls of striated yellow tufa are pierced by caverns and caressed by the brightest turquoise water in Italy. The blond tufa stone continues underwater, in many places in low shelves that create wide and shallow swimming zones that look like something out of French Polynesia. The most famous of these magazine-cover natural swimming pools is Spiaggia dei Conigli—without exaggeration one of Europe's top beaches. It's this unlikely tropical-paradise effect that makes Lampedusa such a magnet for sun-seeking summer vacationers. The island has become especially popular with northern Italians, who delight in how inexpensive Lampedusa is compared with other more established Mediterranean beach locales.

At 20 sq. km (7¾ sq. miles), Lampedusa is the largest of the Pelagie Islands, which consist of Linosa (39km/24 miles to the north) and the islet of Lampione (18km/11 miles to the west and, in practice, only visited by divers). Lampedusa also has the most tourist infrastructure and the Pelagie's only airport. While tourism accounts for a major source of income (and nearly all of it rung up in Aug), Lampedusa is a working island

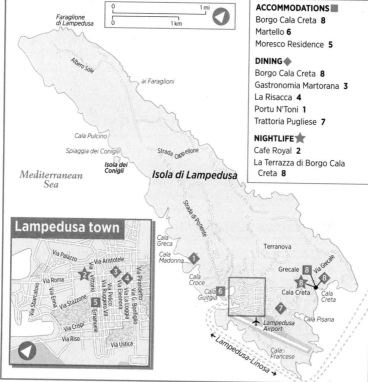

ACCOMMODATIONS ■
Borgo Cala Creta **8**
Martello **6**
Moresco Residence **5**

DINING ◆
Borgo Cala Creta **8**
Gastronomia Martorana **3**
La Risacca **4**
Portu N'Toni **1**
Trattoria Pugliese **7**

NIGHTLIFE ★
Cafe Royal **2**
La Terrazza di Borgo Cala Creta **8**

10

OTHER SICILIAN ISLANDS

Lampedusa

year-round. Fishing is a big business here, and Lampedusan boats haul in impressive catches of shrimp, squid, lobster, and grouper every morning, whether it's July or January.

At first glance, Lampedusa port (the island's only real inhabited area) is a "nothing town" that could be anywhere in southern Italy, with anonymous post-war apartment blocks and narrow streets choked with *motorino* fumes, but there's quite a bit of life and character here. The pedestrian main drag of the town is called Via Roma and lined with lively cafes and boutiques, and peopled around the clock by locals and visitors out for a social stroll. Beyond Lampedusa town, the rest of the island is mostly uninhabited. But you'll venture out to the west, to the celebrated beaches of the southern shore, and if you join a boat tour, you'll see the dramatic cliffs of the northern coast, inaccessible by land.

Lampedusa is the southernmost place in Italy, and accordingly, it's much closer to Africa in feel, from the weather to the landscape. Virtually no one else besides Italians comes here on vacation, so you'll need to come armed with a phrasebook to navigate the island's menus and services. But if you're adventurous enough to give it a try, Lampedusa will reward you with an exceptionally warm welcome.

In spite of some undeniable blight, there's always that amazing water, and even when the *scirocco* blow in dust from the Sahara, there's something about Lampedusa that gets under your skin.

Strategies

August is frankly horrendous on Lampedusa, unless your main goal is partying in the bars of Via Roma or on the Spring-Break-y beach of Cala Guitgia. Otherwise, try any other month between April and October. May is wonderful, and when the island's few flowers are in bloom, coloring the otherwise dusty terrain.

Essentials

GETTING THERE Unless you're already going to be in southern Sicily, where ferries depart for the Pelagie islands, it's most convenient to fly here. Lampedusa has an airport, which is served by **AirOne** (✆ **199/207080** or 06/65681448; www.flyair one.it) and **Meridiana** (✆ **892928** or 095/530017; www.meridiana.it) year-round from Palermo and Trapani. During the peak tourist season of June to October, non-stop flights from Milan, Rome, and Bologna are also available. Flying to Lampedusa is generally quite expensive; expect to pay around 200€ round-trip from Sicily, more for the seasonal service from other cities.

If coming by sea, all boats depart from Porto Empedocle, on the southern coast of Sicily (not far from the Valley of the Temples at Agrigento), stopping first at Linosa before continuing on to Lampedusa. **Ustica Lines** (✆ **0923/873813;** www.ustica lines.it) operates the faster hydrofoils (3 hr.; 34€ to Linosa; 4 hr., 15 min.; 54€ to Lampedusa). In Porto Empedocle, buy tickets at Agenzia Pietro Barbaro, Via IV Novembre 3 (✆ **0922/636110**); in Linosa at Mare Viaggi, Via Re Umberto 70 (✆ **333/5703885**); and in Lampedusa at Agenzia Marittima Strazzera, Via Stazzone 2 (✆ **348/3538218**). **Siremar** (✆ **0922/970003;** www.siremar.it) runs one ferry per day from Porto Empedocle (6 hr.; 34€ to Linosa; another 2 hr. and an additional 5.60€ to Lampedusa). If you would like to book a reserved seat (*poltrona*) or a sleeping compartment (*cabina*, minimum two persons) on Siremar's ferries, you'll pay about 35€ or 50€ more, respectively, for each ticket. In Porto Empedocle, buy tickets at Tricoli e Nuara, Via Molo 13 (✆ **0922/636683**); in Linosa at Gaetano Cavallaro, Via Principe Umberto (✆ **0922/972062**); and in Lampedusa at Sebastiano Strazzera, Lungomare L. Rizzo (✆ **0922/970003**).

GETTING AROUND Bus service is extremely limited, and the best beaches are well removed from town, so you'll definitely want your own wheels. I recommend renting a scooter, quad, or Méhari (a sort of convertible Jeep, made by Citroën) as opposed to a car, which interferes with the splendid views as you drive around. **Licciardi** (Via Siracusa 18; ✆ **0922/970678**) has competitive rates for all of the above (a Méhari goes for 210€ per week off season to 280€ in Aug, while a small scooter rental runs from 140€ off season to 210€ in Aug). Note that even with your own transport, it's still a decent walk to most of the best swimming spots. Spiaggia dei Conigli, for instance, is a good 20-minute hike from the nearest dirt road. The north and west coasts of the island are pretty much only accessible by sea, and it's easy to join a *giro dell'isola* tour that stops at the most picturesque coves, or you can go it alone by renting a *gozzo* or *gommone* from any number of agencies at the port; try **Licciardi** (information above) or **Dag** (Via Nino Bixio 1; ✆ **0922/970755;** www. autonoleggiodag.it), which also rents cars and scooters.

VISITOR INFORMATION The **tourist office** is at Via Vittorio Emanuele 87 (✆ **0922/971171**).

FAST FACTS If you need the police, call the **carabinieri** at ✆ 0922/970001. For medical problems, the **Guardia Medica** is at Via Grecale 2, ✆ 0922/970604. The main **pharmacy** is at Via Vittorio Emanuele 35, ✆ 0922/970195. The Banca Popolare S. Angelo at Via Roma 50 (✆ 0922/970102) has an **ATM.** The **post office** is at Via Piave 1 (✆ 0922/970081).

Exploring the Island

Lampedusa town is, well, ugly on the whole, but past that overall impression is the character and soul that comes with being a real working port. Of course, chances are you haven't flown or sailed all the way to Lampedusa to pound the pavement of a traffic-clogged seaport, but the *passeggiata* along the main street, Via Roma, is a ritual not to be missed. Anyone and everyone on Lampedusa comes here in the evening for a stroll, shopping, and drinks (Cafe Royal, at number 83, is the classic spot). Whatever you need, you'll find it on Via Roma, whether a new beach bag, designer sunglasses, a *cannolo,* or a rental car agency. Take a wander down the side streets and you'll discover bakeries where the emanating aromas of pastries are irresistible and time-warp general stores where you can get kitschy Sicilian beach gear—you know you want some.

The port of Lampedusa is divided by jetties into three discrete marinas. Ferries from Linosa and Porto Empedocle arrive at the far south and east edge of the harbor, while the majority of tourist boats, rentals, and fishing boats are in the central *Porto Nuovo.* The western sector of Lampedusa harbor is **Cala Guitgia,** which has a pretty crescent of white sand backed by a modern tourist development known as Contrada Guitgia. (This beach is certainly convenient to town, but absolutely to be avoided in summer unless you don't mind sharing your square foot of sand with hyper teenagers in over-thought "beach" outfits and blaring European radio hits. If, however, you are 18 and looking to score, it's Cala Guitgia or bust.)

Beaches

Elsewhere on the island, "things to do" are limited to basically one activity: getting to know the stunning coves and beaches of Lampedusa. The most noteworthy swimming spots—all accessible by land though it may involve a significant hike—are concentrated on the southern and eastern coasts, while the wilder west and north sides of the island are only accessible by sea.

If your time on the island is limited, make a beeline for **Spiaggia dei Conigli ★★★**. A stunning cove on the southwestern coast, this is Lampedusa's marquee attraction and truly one of the best beaches in Europe. It's not easy to get to—the only access is via a rugged and steep trail, so allow at least half a day for this excursion—but the natural splendor of "Rabbit Beach" more than compensates for your exertion. Even veterans of the Caribbean and Polynesia can't believe their eyes as they descend the rocky trail toward the beach: What comes into view is a gorgeous crescent of sugary white sand set against perfectly clear waters no deeper than your torso for more than 100m (328 ft.) from shore, and in every possible shade of turquoise. A dramatic amphitheater of tufa rock above the beach, where *macchia mediterranea,* agave plants, and prickly pear thrive in the yellow stone, completes the fabulous quasi-lunar tableau. And as long as the tide isn't high, you can wade through the water to the adjacent island, Isola dei Conigli.

CARETTA CARETTA, LAMPEDUSA'S
CUTEST beachgoers

The name of Lampedusa's most famous beach, Spiaggia dei Conigli, may mean Rabbit Beach, but it's another adorable animal, the endangered *caretta caretta* or Loggerhead sea turtle, that is a regular visitor here. In late spring, these turtles lay their eggs on the eastern end of the beach, at which time that stretch of sand is cordoned off and guarded by volunteers for the environmental group Legambiente. In late summer—usually between the last week of August and first week of September—the eggs hatch, and hundreds of tiny hatchling turtles make their way into the water. Only a small percentage will survive predatory birds and fish. Females that

do survive will return to this same beach to lay their eggs one day.

In Contrada Grecale, north of Lampedusa town, the **Centro Recupero Tartarughe Marine** (Sea Turtle Rescue Center; ✆ **338/2198533;** opening hours vary but public visits are normally possible in summer) takes care of injured and sick turtles. When they are sufficiently convalesced, the turtles are released back into the sea; sometimes there are so many individuals being released at one time that the center's staff asks the public to assist in the event—a once in a lifetime opportunity, the annual release usually takes place sometime in mid-summer.

Tourist and fishing boats aren't allowed in this bay, which is part of the Area Marina Protetta Isole Pelagie (Pelagie Islands Protected Marine Area), making it perfect for aimless floating (the snorkeling is great, too) and families with young children. One boat is permitted to approach the beach, however: At 12:30pm every day in summer, *la barca dei panini* brings sandwiches and cold drinks to the beachgoers. The beach is divided into two areas: On the right (west), you can pay 7€ for an *ombrellone* (umbrella); otherwise, the area on the left (east) is free access (and where the *caretta caretta* sea turtles lay their eggs every spring see above). Thinking about the southern Mediterranean heat and how long it takes to get out of the sun once you're down here, that 7€ *ombrellone* isn't such a bad deal . . . . Rental kayaks and pedal boats are available for puttering around Isola dei Conigli (allow at least an hour). But that's it as far as services go: Definitely bring plenty of water and snacks, as *la barca dei panini* only calls at these shores once a day.

To reach Spiaggia dei Conigli, take the Strada di Ponente east from town, and after about 5km (3 miles), turn left where you see signs for the beach; you'll soon reach a dirt parking lot, which is as far as vehicles can go. As you descend the trail, which takes about 15 minutes going down and a half-hour coming back up, the spectacular bay and Isola dei Conigli come into view. The villa above the beach was built by the popular Italian singer-songwriter Domenico Modugno, who died here in 1994.

Note: The magnificent effect of this spot is greatly diminished when the hordes descend in August; try it any other month between May and October.

Once you've "done" Spiaggia dei Conigli, check out some of the island's other outstanding swimming and sunning places. One of the best, though it's even more arduous to reach than Conigli, is **Cala Pulcino** ★★ (Flea Cove); west of the promontory that delineates Spiaggia dei Conigli, it's a narrow, fjordlike inlet with a small but pristine beach of white sand. *Stupenda.* (I recommend getting here by sea, but if you insist on hoofing it, follow the signs that lead off the path down to Spiaggia dei Conigli; in all, it's about a half-hour walk down, 45 min. back, from the main road.)

On the east side of Lampedusa, **Cala Creta ★** doesn't have a beach but there are smooth shelves of tufa sloping to the sea, which is diamond-clear and a gorgeous emerald shade in this part of the island. Caverns in the rock provide shade. There's a certain casual elegance here, thanks to the higher-end hotels and resorts in the zone, and there are plenty of seaside pizzerias and *trattorie,* but it can get very crowded in summer. Aviation enthusiasts might want to check out the sand-and-pebble, palm-backed beach at **Cala Francese ★★**, just 400m (1,312 ft.) south of the runway at Lampedusa airport. "French Cove" is one of few bathing locales that remain quiet even in peak season. (Quiet, that is, except for the occasional roar of jet engines overhead.) Variegated textures in the rocky seabed make for great snorkeling, and the shallow and calm waters are perfect for kids. The snack kiosk here makes killer *panini.*

Immediately west of the port "suburb" of Contrada Guitgia are three deep notches in the coastline of Lampedusa, each with sheltered strips of sand and calm, pristine waters. From east to west, they are **Cala Croce ★** (gorgeous sand and sea and good services), **Cala Madonna ★** (for snorkeling), and **Cala Greca** (a small white sand beach with crystalline water)—the big advantage here is that they can be reached on foot from town (allow 15 min. to reach Cala Croce and 30 min. to reach Cala Greca; it's located just past Camping La Roccia campground).

Boat Tours

I highly recommend taking a **round-island boat tour of Lampedusa ★★**, mostly because almost half of the coast (the west and north sides plus certain coves on the south side) isn't accessible by land. The north coast, with its tall cliffs and grottoes, is breathtaking. Dozens of outfits at the port, each with their own character of a captain, offer these *giro isola* excursions, which normally depart from the Porto Nuovo at 10am and return by 5pm. Rates range from 15€ per person in low season to 30€ in August—very economical considering the fact that most of the tours include an abundant on-board lunch with seafood and other local specialties. All in all, it's quite festive. Several stops for swimming are guaranteed, but note that no tourist boats are allowed in Lampedusa's most famous swimming bay, between Isola dei Conigli and Spiaggia dei Conigli; that one can be reached by land only.

Excursions are generally by motorboat, but **Lampedusa Summer (☎ 338/ 3260571;** www.lampedusasummer.com) organizes sailboat trips (same schedules and rates).

Diving

The undersea world around Lampedusa holds wonders of geology, flora, and fauna. Much of the surrounding water is protected as a nature reserve, which, combined with the natural clarity of the Caribbean-colored water, makes for some of the Med's most amazing dives. Just about every species of Mediterranean fish can be found here, but some of the most frequently sighted are grouper and lobster. Twelve nautical miles east of the Lampedusa is the celebrated **Secca di Levante,** a platform (only 10m/33 ft. deep, surrounded by 50–60m/164–197-ft. sea bottoms) where dolphins, caretta caretta turtles, and enormous versions of local fish swim in totally peaceful waters. Any serious diver on Lampedusa will definitely want to sign up for

DEALING WITH THE scirocco

When the *scirocco* wind blows in from Africa, it renders most of the beaches on the southern coast of Lampedusa unusable. The water loses its clarity and becomes rough, and flotsam from the open sea washes ashore. So what's a vacationer to do? A good option is to **rent a boat** and head for the north coast. The northern waters are completely unaffected by the *scirocco*, so you can putter around the coves and grottoes (there are no beaches, but the swimming is excellent) on perfectly calm seas. If your heart is set on sand, try locals' spot **Cala Pisana,** an inlet on the east coast, just south of Cala Creta. Totally protected from the *scirocco*, it has a small white sand beach here and wonderful turquoise water for swimming. (Tourists don't typically choose Cala Pisana because it's right next to the island's desalination plant, and there are two discharge pipes here that flush water into the bay, but it's only clean salt water left over from the desalination process.)

an excursion to the islet of **Lampione,** 20km (12 miles) to the west. Sandbar sharks, huge grouper, lobsters, and vibrant corals thrive in these waters, which are protected under the Riserva Marina Isole Pelagie. The best dive operator on Lampedusa is **Moby Diving Center** (Via delle Grotte, Lampedusa town; ✆ **333/9564543;** www. mobydiving.it), which offers single dives (50€ with equipment) and multiple dive packages (130€ for three; 370€ for 10; including equipment). Non-divers accompanying divers can always be accommodated.

Where to Stay

Lampedusa is an old-fashioned vacation island in the sense that most accommodations are set up for weeklong stays. This is changing somewhat—some hotels and resorts will now accept shorter stays in off-peak months; but in August, unless you book a full week or more, expect to be turned away. **Lampedusa Summer** (www. lampedusasummer.com) is one of several vacation rental agencies on the island, offering a wide range of properties (independent villas and *dammusi,* apartments in town), from 30€ to 40€ per person, per night.

Borgo Cala Creta ★★ Accommodations in this "village" overlooking beautiful Cala Creta are in stone *dammusi* (traditional African-style stone houses) with simple, cool interiors (think blue tiles and whitewashed archways) and terraces shaded by cane roofs. The low profile of the structures here—all faced with irregular fieldstones of Lampedusa's native tufa—and the verdant and aromatic *macchia mediterranea* all over the grounds give the property an authentic, natural feel. The restaurant is quite good (see "Where to Dine," below), drawing non-guests for dinner, and the bar, "La Terrazza," is one of Lampedusa's top spots for a romantic cocktail.

Contrada Cala Creta, 3km/2 miles east of Lampedusa town. ✆ **0922/970883.** www.calacreta.com. 23 units. Doubles 420€–826€ per week, with daily breakfast and 3 dinners. AE, DC, MC, V. **Amenities:** Restaurant; bar; airport transfers; excursions; shuttle service. *In room:* Ceiling fan, minibar, radio.

Martello ★ Cheerful and centrally located, the Martello is a good choice for those who want to be near the action of town. Rooms are very generously sized but decor has that generic, Italian-Mid-Range-Hotel look. "Comfort" rooms have balconies, while "superiors" have sea-view balconies. Half-board is required, and the restaurant is delicious and lively, with big picture windows facing the port. In August especially, the place has a real holiday feel, with the staff organizing occasional karaoke nights that go on into the wee hours.

Piazza Medusa 1, Lampedusa town. ☎ **0922/970025.** www.hotelmartello.it. 27 units. Doubles 130€– 240€ per night with half-board. AE, DC, MC, V. **Amenities:** Restaurant; bar. *In room:* A/C, TV, hair dryer.

Moresco Residence ★
Strategically positioned near the heart of town and main artery Via Roma, but just enough removed from the noise and chaos, Moresco is its own little, wonderfully tranquil world. The spotless complex looks like a De Chirico painting with its pink stucco architecture and minimalist pool and deck, and consists of lovely two- to four-person apartments decorated with subtly Oriental touches. Moresco is a nice oasis to return to after exploring Lampedusa during the day, but it's not equipped with enough amenities to make it a resort where you'd want to hang out; there are no public areas beside the pool, and breakfast is served in your room.

Via Vittorio Emanuele 56, Lampedusa town. ☎ **0922/971799.** www.morescolampedusa.com. 14 units. 2-person units 550€–920€ per week; 4-person units 770€–1,260€ per week. Weeklong stay (Sat–Sat or Sun–Sun) required. AE, DC, MC, V. **Amenities:** Car, scooter, and boat rental; excursions; pool; room service; transfers. *In room:* A/C, TV, kitchenette, terrace.

Where to Dine

Given the lack of civilization out on the island, it's a good idea to stock up on picnic fixings in town before heading out for a day at the beach. The *panini* and ready-made Sicilian specialties at **Gastronomia Martorana ★★**, Via Roma 92, are to die for. For a casual meal on the beach, try the restaurant/bar at **Portu N'Toni** (no phone; open all day in summer), between Cala Madonna and Cala Croce on the southern coast.

Borgo Cala Creta ★★ SICILIAN/LAMPEDUSAN
On the terrace of the Borgo Cala Creta village of *dammusi* (see "Where to Stay," above), this exceedingly friendly and delicious restaurant offers a prix-fixe menu that changes every day of the week but always includes an assortment of typical Sicilian *antipasti*, a *primo* (usually a seafood pasta), a fish *secondo*, a *dolce* of fruit or pastry, and wine. Monday is fish couscous night, while Wednesday features an ample spread of authentic Tunisian cuisine (lamb couscous, tagines with chicken and spinach).

Contrada Cala Creta. ☎ **0922/970883.** Reservations required. Prix-fixe 30€ (kids' portion 15€); special raw fish and crustaceans menu 60€. AE, DC, MC, V. Open for lunch and dinner.

La Risacca ★★ LAMPEDUSAN
In a rustic-chic dining room (or on an ample patio) in the heart of Lampedusa town (just off the eastern end of Via Roma), La Risacca serves up a tantalizing menu of traditional Lampedusan seafood specialties. From *primi* like linguine with calamari and bottarga or gnocchi with prawns to comprehensive offerings of fresh grilled whole fish, everything is mouthwatering. Service is friendly, and prices moderate.

Via Enrico La Loggia 15. ☎ **0922/975798.** Reservations recommended. Entrees from 11€. MC, V. Open for lunch and dinner.

Trattoria Pugliese ★ PUGLIESE/SICILIAN
This is a favorite local joint, right next to the airport, though the atmosphere isn't much to write home about. The menu features dishes from the Puglia region (as its name would suggest); among the *primi*,

try the *orecchiette alle verdure* (ear-shaped pasta with vegetables). It's also one of few Lampedusa restaurants where there are other options besides seafood! Portions are huge, service is warm, and the prices very budget friendly.

Via Cala Pisana 3. © **0922/970531.** Entrees from 8€. No credit cards. Daily 8:30pm–midnight, June–Sept only.

Lampedusa After Dark

Come nightfall, any one of the handsome bars on Via Roma is bound to be happening, so just walk up and down and see which you like best. But the classic place to drop in for a drink, beginning with the *aperitivo* hour and continuing until about 2am in high season, is **Cafe Royal ★** (Via Roma 83; © **0922/970354**); by day, it's Lampedusa's favorite coffee bar. The young and beautiful congregate at **13.5 ★** (Via Roma 47; © **339/1953007**), a serious wine bar (with hard-to-find Sicilian labels) and gelato and pastry shop that's open 24/7 in summer, playing the latest trendy music for a party-loving crowd. For romantic drinks in a quieter setting, head for the bar at **La Terrazza di Borgo Cala Creta** (part of the resort of the same name; Contrada Cala Creta; © **0922/970394**).

LINOSA

The smaller sister in the Pelagie islands group is nothing like its more famous, more trodden sibling, Lampedusa. In contrast to Lampedusa's flat and barren appearance, Linosa is a hilly, green, and clean island practically untouched by tourism or the trappings of "progress" in the modern age.

Not only is nature on Linosa different from that of Lampedusa, so is its spirit. Linosa's proud residents (about 400 year-round) keep their pastel town tidy and wear their helmets when driving their scooters. It's a bit like a tiny Sicilian island version of Switzerland. The colorful, immaculately maintained cottages of Linosa's single town are a photographer's dream.

Whereas Lampedusa makes its non-tourist dollars from fishing, Linosa makes its off-season money from agriculture: Capers, lentils, figs, and grapes for wine are all grown in the fertile valley between the island's three extinct craters. The top of a 1,000m-tall (3,281-ft.) undersea volcanic mountain, Linosa was an important agricultural outpost of the southern Mediterranean throughout antiquity and the Middle Ages. Up until a few years ago, when a disease wiped out the prickly pear plants they fed upon, Linosa was renowned for its beef cattle.

Rich marine life and the striking undersea "architecture" of Linosa's basalt foundation makes this island popular with divers, but there are also some gorgeous seascapes above the waterline to attract swimmers and hikers. The water here, thanks to the basalt rock underneath, takes on the most unreal emerald tones. With an area of 5 sq. km (2 sq. miles) and perimeter of 11km (7 miles), Linosa is easy to explore on foot, but round-island boat tours can also be arranged.

Strategies

Certainly, Linosa is so small and tranquil as to drive restless types stir-crazy. There are almost no shops or services (forget trying to find an ATM, though cash is the only tender accepted island-wide); cellphone, TV, and radio reception is scratchy at best. But if you're looking for something remote, and you have some time to fill on either side of a trip to southern Sicily or Lampedusa, I definitely recommend a stop at Linosa, but limit your stay to a day or two.

Contrary to the wisdom that normally prevails about visiting Italian islands in August (that is, to be avoided like the plague), Linosa is one exception where August is actually one of the best months. Even during this, Linosa's peak season, there are no more than a few hundred tourists on the island at once, which combined with the island's time-warp feel creates a real sense of summer-camp camaraderie.

Essentials

GETTING THERE   Linosa has no airport, so the only way to get here is by boat, either from Porto Empedocle in southern Sicily, or from Lampedusa. **Ustica Lines** (✆ **0923/873813;** www.usticalines.it) operates the faster hydrofoils (3 hr.; 34€ from Porto Empedocle; 75 min.; 20€ to Lampedusa). In Porto Empedocle, buy tickets at Agenzia Pietro Barbaro, Via IV Novembre 3 (✆ 0922/636110); in Linosa at Mare Viaggi, Via Re Umberto 70 (✆ 333/5703885); and in Lampedusa, at Agenzia Marittima Strazzera, Via Stazzone 2 (✆ 348/3538218). **Siremar** (✆ **0922/972062;** www. siremar.it) runs one ferry per day from Porto Empedocle (6 hr.; 34€ to Linosa; 2 hr.; 5.60€ to Lampedusa). If you would like to book a reserved seat (*poltrona*) or a sleeping compartment (*cabina,* minimum two persons) on Siremar's ferries, you'll pay from 20€ to 40€ more, respectively, for each ticket. In Porto Empedocle, buy tickets at Tricoli e Nuara, Via Molo 13 (✆ 0922/636683); in Linosa at Gaetano Cavallaro, Via Re Umberto (✆ 0922/972062); and in Lampedusa at Sebastiano Strazzera, Lungomare L. Rizzo (✆ 0922/970003).

GETTING AROUND   Linosa's 5-sq.-km (2-sq. -mile) territory is easily covered on foot; roads and hiking paths connect the town with all the points of naturalistic interest. If you'd like to go with a guide, **Errera** (Via Scalo Vecchio 1; ✆ **0922/972041**) offers sea tours and minibus tours of the interior.

FAST FACTS   The **carabinieri** are at Via Re Umberto (✆ 0922/972083). The **Guardia Medica** are at Via V. Alfieri (✆ 0922/972115). Also on Via Alfieri are the **pharmacy** (✆ 0922/972203), and the **post office** (✆ 0922/972084). There are no banks, and credit cards aren't accepted anywhere on the island.

Exploring the Island

Linosa town is where all the island's (few) services are, including a few restaurants, B&Bs, and bars. Past this small grid of vividly colored houses, the landscape becomes more agricultural, with small holdings where capers and grapevines are cultivated, and eventually leads to the fertile heart of Linosa, the so-called **Fossa del Cappellano.** Wandering through that valley, you'll still see the stone troughs where the famous cows of Linosa, now long gone, once fed. For a comprehensive panorama of Linosa (and on a clear day, Lampedusa), hike to the top of **Monte Vulcano.** At an elevation of 186m (610 ft.) and only 1km (¾ mile) east of town, it's an easy undertaking.

The Linosan beach par excellence is **Cala Pozzolana di Ponente ★★**, on the west coast. It's an extraordinary feat of geology, where sculpted slopes of jagged basalt are "intruded upon" by a giant monolith of yellow tufa—all above a crescent of black sand. Like Spiaggia dei Conigli on Lampedusa, this is another spot where *caretta caretta* sea turtles make their nests in late spring. (Thanks to the warmer temperatures of the volcanic sand, more turtles tend to survive on Linosa than on Lampedusa.) Other popular spots for swimming and generally marveling at the nature on Linosa are **I Fili** ★ (accessible only by sea), a labyrinth of multicolored reefs backed by dramatic upheavals of striated brown rock, and **I Faraglioni** ★, where imposing outcrops of basalt offshore shelter the island coastline to create a sort of natural swimming pool, with water less than 1m (3 ft.) deep in many places.

To reach dive sites like **La Sicchitella** (especially rich in sea sponges, fat grouper, and dense schools of dentex), arrange an excursion with Marenostrum (✆ 0922/972042) or Linosa Diving Center (✆ 0922/972061).

Where to Stay & Dine

There are no real hotels on Linosa, just a few vacation apartments and bed-and-breakfast accommodations. **Errera** (see restaurant listing, below) rents apartments from 80€ per night, while **Residence La Posta** (✆ 0922/972507; www.linosaresidencelaposta.it) is a B&B with doubles from 100€ to 160€ per night. Units have A/C, TV, and minibar, and breakfast is served on a garden terrace.

With a popular restaurant and separate bar in front of the port, **Errera** ★ (Via Scalo Vecchio 1; ✆ 0922/972041; entrees from 10€) has practically cornered the market on Linosan dining. Quality remains high, and the family-run kitchen turns out excellent *zuppa di lenticchie* (lentil soup, an island specialty) and Sicilian standards like *spaghetti ai ricci* (with a delicate sea urchin sauce) and simply grilled fish. In addition to Errera, a few other casual snack/pizzerias round out the scene.

The Linosan spot to hang out at is **Dammuso Wine Bar** ★, Via Re Umberto 10 (✆ 0922/972195), open daily from 10am to 2am in summer, although Bar Errera (address above) gets its share of the happy-hour crowd, who sit under an awning to watch the sunset.

USTICA ★

The black-lava top of a submerged volcano, Ustica is the oldest of the Sicilian outer islands. It is tiny (9 sq. km/3½ sq. miles, pop. 1,370) and rather foreboding looking, thanks to its dark volcanic composition. The Romans, in fact, named it *ustum* ("burnt"), perhaps because it looked to them like a large piece of spent charcoal. But where there's volcanic soil, there's fertility, and parts of Ustica are actually quite lush and green. A visit here is a trip to unknown, offbeat Sicily. Even many Palermitans have never made the 75km (47 miles) ferry ride north to Ustica.

The Phoenicians were the first recorded civilization to settle Ustica, and in time they were followed by the Greeks, who named the island *Osteodes* ("ossuary"), in memory of the skeletons of 6,000 Carthaginian mutineers who were brought here and abandoned without food or water. Attempts to colonize Ustica in the Middle Ages failed because of raids by Barbary pirates. As late as the 1950s, Ustica was a penal colony, a sort of Alcatraz of Sicily. Antonio Gramsci, the theorist of the Italian Communist Party, was once imprisoned here. And, in one of the most secret meetings of World War II, British and Italian officers met here in September 1943 to discuss a switch in sides from Mussolini to the Allies.

Because its jagged coastline is riddled with creeks, bays, and caves, Ustica is best explored by a rented boat circling the island. In 1987, Sicily designated part of the island a national marine park, and today its clear waters and beautiful sea, filled with aquatic flora and fauna, attract snorkelers and scuba divers from around the world.

Divers are also drawn to its ancient wrecks and the now-submerged city of Osteodes, an underwater archaeological park 1.6km (1 mile) west of the island.

Essentials

GETTING THERE   Palermo is the most common gateway to Ustica. Hydrofoils and ferries operate daily from Palermo's Stazione Marittima. The ferry is the cheapest and slowest transport, costing 17€ each way and taking 2½ hours. The hydrofoil, at a cost of 23€, does it in half the time. For tickets for either transport, go to **Siremar,** at Via Francesco Crispi 118 in Palermo (© 091/336632), and on Piazza Bartolo in Ustica (© 091/8449002). Hydrofoil service runs from April to December; ferries run year-round, but not on Sundays in winter. From June to September, **Ustica Lines** (in Ustica at Via Cap. Vincenzo 15; © 091/8449002, or in Naples at Varco Angioino; © 081/5517164; www.usticalines.it) also runs a hydrofoil from Naples to Ustica (it continues to the Egadi islands and then Trapani but does not serve Palermo); the 4-hour journey costs 72€ each way.

GETTING AROUND   Arrival from Palermo is at Ustica village, the only port and home to 90% of the islanders. Once you arrive, you can always do as the locals do and rely on your trusty feet. The heart of the village is reached by climbing a flight of steps from the harbor. Otherwise, take one of the orange minibuses that circumnavigate the island, hugging the coastline. These leave from the center of Ustica village daily on the hour. Figure on 2½ hours for the entire bus ride (1€) around the island.

Ustica is one of those Italian islands where you'll definitely want your own *imbarcazione* (watercraft) to get around. There are no beaches here, just coves created by the jagged volcanic rock, and most of them are difficult if not impossible to reach by land. Summer boat excursions are run by local fishermen who not only know the most scenic beauty spots, but also will allow you time out for swimming during an island trip. **Hotel Ariston,** Via della Vittoria 5 (© 091/8449042), organizes sightseeing boat trips (2½ hr., 15€). Scuba divers can go to **Ailara Rosalia,** Banchina Barresi (© 091/8449605), which rents boats for 60€ a day, diving gear not included.

VISITOR INFORMATION   There is no official tourist office on Ustica, but you can visit the headquarters of the **Parco Marino Regionale,** on the main square of town (© 091/8449456). The staff here can provide information about the marine park. Hours are daily from 8am to 8pm.

FAST FACTS   For a medical emergency, call the **Guardia Medica** (© 091/8449248). The police or **Carabinieri** can be reached at © 091/8449049. The **Banca Monte dei Paschi di Siena,** which has the island's only ATM, is at Piazza Longo 9 (© 091/8449070). The pharmacy, **Farmacia Zattoni,** is on Piazza Umberto I, 30 (© 091/8449382).

Near the Port

It's fun just to stroll around the village, taking in views of the bay, Baia Santa Maria. The little town is made more festive by a series of murals that decorate the facades of the buildings. The main piazza is actually an agglomeration of three squares: Piazza Umberto I, Piazza Longo, and Piazza Bartolo. A fun photo-op in town is beneath the street sign for *Via Confusione.*

Directly south of the village stands **Torre Santa Maria,** housing the **Museo Archeologico** (no phone). It's open daily from 9am to noon and 5 to 7pm; admission is 3€. Its most fascinating exhibits are artifacts recovered from the ancient city of

Osteodes, now submerged beneath the sea. Many of the finds, such as crusty anchors, were recovered from ships wrecked off the coast.

To the east of the tower are the ruins of a Bronze Age settlement, **Villaggio Preistorico,** at Faraglioni. Excavations began in 1989 on what was a large prehistoric village dating from the 14th century to the 13th century B.C. The foundations of some 300 stone-built houses were discovered, and the defensive walls of the settlement are among the strongest fortifications of any period known in Italy. Admission is free; the site is always open.

If you walk north of Ustica village, you'll come to the remains of the **Rocca della Falconiera** fort, at 157m (515 ft.). Figure on a 20-minute walk. The defensive tower was constructed by the Bourbons to protect the island from raids by pirates. This site was first settled back in the 3rd century B.C. by the Romans. If you look toward the sea, you'll see the lighthouse, **Punta dell'Uomo Morto (Dead Man's Point)** on a cliff, where a cave contains vestiges of centuries-old tombs. From the fort you can take in a view of **Guardia dei Turchi,** at 244m (801 ft.). This is the highest point on the island. That object you see in the distance, evoking a mammoth golf ball, is in fact a meteorological radar system installed by the Italian government.

Exploring the Island

Since it is the lavic tippy-top of an extinct volcano, Ustica doesn't have sandy beaches. But as you traverse the island, you'll find jumping-off points for swimming. The biggest attraction is the grotto-lined coastline, and because distances are short, hiking is a viable option. Wildflowers cover the island except in late July and August, when the blistering sun burns them away. You'll also see produce grown by the islanders, such as lentils, figs, capers, grapes, prickly pears, wheat, and almonds. Of all the caves or grottoes on the island, the most celebrated and fascinating is the **Grotta Azzurra ★★**, the first cave south of Ustica village as you head down the coast by boat. Like the more fabled cave in Capri, the grotto hosts an incredible iridescent glow from light reflections from the sea. Almost as stunning is the sea cave directly to the south, **Grotta Pastizza ★**. This is a stalactite cave behind a great pyramidal rock. Down the coast is **Grotta della Barche** ("of the boats"); Ustica fishermen anchor in this safe haven during storms.

Parco Marino Regionale

The Marine National Park was created in 1987, the first marine reserve ever established in Italy. Since Ustica lies in the center of an inward current surging through the Straits of Gibraltar directly from the Atlantic Ocean, its waters are always clean and free of pollution.

Underwater photographers flock to the park to film the stunning **aquatic flora and fauna.** A splendid seaweed, *Poseidonia oceanica,* is called "the lungs of the sea" because it oxygenates the water. You may also see an array of magnificent red gorgonians, stunning black coral, plentiful turtles (now that they are protected), swordfish, lobster, and *cernia* (grouper). Some divers claim to have had close encounters with grouper as big as a Fiat 500.

Active Pursuits

J. Y. Cousteau claimed that the waters off the coast of Ustica were among the most beautiful he'd ever seen, ideal for both diving and underwater photography—and we agree. Renowned dive sites include **Grotta dei Gamberi ★★**, off the southern tip of the island beyond Grotta del Tuono. Near Punta Gavazzi is the famous **Underwater Archaeological Museum ★★**. Many anchors and even Roman amphorae can still be seen in these waters. The best dive spot on the north coast is **Secca di Colombara ★★**, to the west of Grotta dell'Oro. Here you can see a vast array of gorgonians and Ustica's most beautiful sponges. **Scoglio del Medico ★★**, or "doctor's rock," is an outcropping of basalt, riddled with grottoes, gorges, tunnels, and canyons.

Hiking Around Ustica

You can circumnavigate the island in 3 to 4 hours, depending on your pace. The best hike is along the coastal path heading north of town, where you'll see the Municipio, or island headquarters. Head left here, taking the trail along the north coast that leads past an old cemetery. This hike hugs the steep cliffs on the northern side of the island, part of the marine reserve, and the views are stunning. Eventually you'll come to **Punta di Megna,** on the western coast, on the exact opposite side of the island from Ustica village. The offshore rock so appreciated by scuba divers, **Scoglio del Medico,** can be seen from here. The road continues along the southwestern coast as far as the battered ruins of the old tower, **Punta Spalmatore,** where you can go swimming. (There is no beach here, however.) Below this point, at **Punta Cavazzi,** along the southern rim of the island, is **Piscina Naturale ★★**, a sheltered seawater pool and the best place on Ustica for swimming. If there are a lot of tourists on the island at the time of your visit, this "hole" is likely to be crowded with bathers in the briefest of swimwear. At this point, the route no longer follows the coast and cuts inland all the way northeast to Ustica village once again.

Where to Stay

Hotel Clelia ★   This is the most typical of Ustica's little island inns, situated off Piazza Umberto I, the main square of Ustica village. It was the first little boardinghouse on the island to receive visitors, who began arriving in 1950 during the lean postwar years. It is also one of the island's best bargains. For most of its life, it was a *pensione,* or boardinghouse. But after so many improvements, it has been upgraded to three-star status. Nonetheless, its prices have remained reasonable in spite of the installation of soundproof windows and modern furnishings. Guest rooms are small but comfortable, each with a little shower-only bathroom. Hotel extras include a lovely patio, a shuttle bus that makes trips around the island, and scooter and boat rentals. This is one of the few places that remain open year-round.

Via Sindaco I, 29. ✆ **091/8449039.** www.hotelclelia.it. 26 units. Doubles 50€–120€. MC, V. **Amenities:** Restaurant; bar; excursions; free Internet station in lobby; port shuttle; scooter and boat rentals. *In room:* A/C, TV, hair dryer, minibar.

Where to Dine

Da Mario USTICAN   In the very center of Ustica village on its heartbeat square, this spot offers good regional fare at reasonable prices. You can sit at a table on the square, watching island life parade before you. Mario can be found in the kitchen, preparing such dishes as homemade pasta with freshly caught swordfish, grilled fish done to perfection, and roasted squid and spaghetti with fresh crabmeat. And, of course, everything tastes better when washed down with the local Albanella wine.

Piazza Umberto I, 21. ✆ **091/8449905.** Reservations recommended in summer. Entrees 8€–12€. AE, MC, V. Daily 12:30–3pm and 8–10:30pm. Closed Jan and Mon from Nov–Mar.

Schiticchio SEAFOOD This modest establishment, near town hall in the center of Ustica village, offers a rustic decor, a staff that seems to try hard to please, and good homemade food prepared with the freshest ingredients on the island. Ask about the fresh fish of the day, which is often grilled to perfection. The pizza oven turns out succulent pies, and we delighted in a homemade pasta with a tangy pesto sauce.

Via Tre Mulini. © **091/8449662.** Reservations recommended. Entrees 8€–12€. AE, DC, MC, V. Daily 12:30–3pm and 7:30pm–midnight, later in summer.

AEOLIAN ISLANDS

by Agnes Crawford

Off the northeast of Sicily, the extraordinary and evocative Aeolian Islands provide a dramatic setting for an island holiday. The archipelago is made up of seven islands: Lipari, Vulcano, Salina, Panarea, Stromboli, Filicudi, and distant Alicudi—the visible part of a volcanic system on the cusp of the Eurasian and African plates. The tectonic activity far below has left a major geological legacy, and volcanic activity reigns supreme. Whether in the form of the extinct verdant twin peaks of Salina, the disconcerting rumbling mass of still-active Stromboli, or the bubbling sulfurous mud at Vulcano, each island has its own geographical and geological quirks and its own very distinct character and atmosphere.

The rugged terrain of the volcanoes means that the Aeolians are not the spot for the traditional beach holiday; there are few sandy beaches for idle lounging, and wherever you go you tend to be walking uphill. However, for those who like to explore, there are countless coves, inlets, and peaks to investigate both from land and sea, all set off against the blue sky by glorious and rampant vegetation. Lipari, the main island, offers the widest range of accommodations and most of the nightlife, and as such, is especially favored by young travelers and backpackers. Stromboli and Vulcano are the main draws for geology buffs, but also the focus of the mass tourism of the archipelago, and hordes of German and Italian groups descend in high season. Salina offers relaxation, glorious settings, and spectacular hikes, but little in the way of nightlife. Beautiful Panarea is adored by the very chic in-crowd, while those seeking isolation and communion with nature make for Filicudi and Alicudi.

High season, as with all Italian islands, is July and August—and especially the last 2 weeks of August. The Aeolians are at their best in late May and June, or in September and October, when the weather is milder (but still plenty warm for swimming and sunning) and prices aren't as painful. If you must go in July or August, expect blazing heat and crowds, but also an irresistible island-vacation atmosphere in full swing.

STRATEGIES FOR VISITING THE ISLANDS

Splendid in their isolation, the Aeolians are not the easiest place to get to, which is an integral part of their charm. Once you're there, however, it's fairly straightforward to hop between one island and the next. Hydrofoil and ferry connections are regular (especially from Apr–Oct), and the ports are small and quickly navigated. However, it is important to bear in mind that the Greeks did not name the islands after Aeolus, god of wind, for nothing. Winter storms can, on occasion, also see the islands cut off from "mainland" Sicily for days, and even in spring and summer the seas can be unpredictable. It is wise to leave a reasonable margin of freedom around travel plans as hydrofoils in particular can be subject to delays and cancellations; and, when a sailing is cancelled, ferry workers greet the plaintive squeals of city folk with a disdainful shrug.

Milazzo, on the northeast coast of Sicily, is the main port for ferries to the Aeolians, though seasonal service is available from Naples as well.

From Milazzo: You can choose between ferries and hydrofoils run by **Siremar** (© 91/7493111; www.siremar.it) and hydrofoils run by **Ustica Lines** (© 090/9287821; www.usticalines.it). As per usual, ferries take a little longer, and cost a little less than hydrofoils. Because schedules change without notice, it's best to call or check online for current crossings and prices. It is a good idea to buy tickets in advance, especially in high season (July and Aug) and at weekends throughout the summer.

From Naples: SNAV (© 081/4285555; www.snav.it) runs a hydrofoil from Naples's **Mergellina** port from late May/early June to early September, with service to Vulcano, Lipari, Salina, Panarea, and Stromboli. Note that tickets from the mainland are much costlier than those from Sicily.

Eat Aeolian

Sicilians take their food *very* seriously indeed, and however they make it in their town is the best way. As a result, pretty much anywhere you go on these islands you'll automatically find yourself eating Aeolian. If an Aeolian talks about "foreign" food, chances are he's got Calabria, or even Palermo, in mind rather than Beijing. A couple of the key local flavors are *finocchio selvatico* (wild fennel) and *capperi* (capers), including the larger and even more delicious *cucunci*. And of course fish . . . lots of fish. Some to keep an eye out for are *gamberi di nassa* (deliciously sweet prawns), *mupa* (a deepwater fish), *scorfano* (scorpion fish—hideous to look at, delicious to eat), and *cernia* (grouper).

Sweet Malvasia is *the* Aeolian wine, and although some dry wine is also made on the islands, you're best off opting for something from the Sicilian mainland with your entree, and having a drop of *dolce* Malvasia with your dessert. And since nobody does dessert like the Sicilians, you'll be spoiled for choice: *cassata* (sponge cake with ricotta and candied fruit), cannoli, and *granite* just for starters. The *granite* in these parts, a sort of mix between a sorbet and ice cream, is traditionally made from local almonds, coffee, or any fruit you can think of. Served with a brioche, it makes a fabulous breakfast; on its own, it is a cool, refreshing treat.

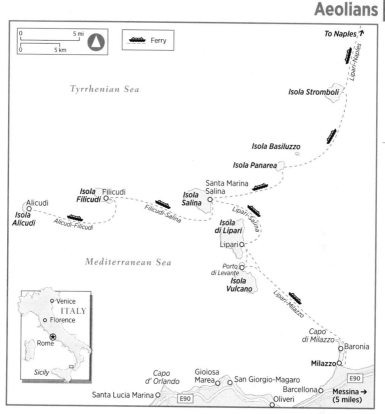

Inter-Island: All inter-island journeys, whether by ferry or hydrofoil, are handled by **Siremar** and **Ustica Lines** (contact info above). Schedules vary from season to season and are known to change with little notice. For the most up-to-date planning info, especially for your inter-island journeys, consult each company's website.

If you prefer to explore the islands from one base rather than island-hop, Lipari is a good choice. While not the most attractive of the islands, it has a wide range of accommodations at all price ranges and abundant services. However, Salina's position at the heart of the archipelago makes it a charming and practical choice.

Note: Arriving with a car is a bad idea; several of the islands prohibit cars, and many are small enough to negotiate on foot. Notable exceptions are Lipari and Salina, where the best way to get around is to rent a small car or a scooter.

Most of the islands wind down in late October, and you'll be hard pressed to find anywhere to stay beyond Lipari. In high season (July and Aug), prices rise alarmingly; in the most popular places (Lipari, Vulcano, Stromboli), you can barely hear yourself think, and the smaller islands, especially Panarea, can be overrun with day-trippers. However, go midweek in June or especially September (after 3 months of sunshine, the sea will be at its warmest) and you'll be in paradise.

VULCANO ★

Known to the Greeks as Hierà (Holy Island), Vulcano crops up often in the rich mythological tales associated with the Aeolian islands. Aristotle spoke of an eruption on Vulcano so violent it covered nearby Lipari with ash. Ulysses stopped by Vulcano—said to be the entrance to Hades—while on his *Odyssey,* and Strabo described it as "the island of fire, with three breaths emerging from three craters." The island was named by the Romans in honor of Vulcan, the god of fire (Hephaestus for the Greeks), and from the Middle Ages its name became the generic term for this type of phenomenon, giving us the word "volcano." In fact, the island is the result of the fusion of several volcanoes, the largest of which is the **Vulcano della Fossa.** Technically still active, it last erupted in 1890. A climb to the top offers a dramatic view down into the crater. The others are **Vulcanello** to the north of the island (123m/403 ft.); the inactive **Monte Aria** (500m/1,640 ft.), which forms a vast plain of lava, tufa, and all sorts of other things that send geologists into raptures; and the 481m (1,578-ft.) **Monte Saraceno.**

The southernmost of the Aeolians, and the closest to the Sicilian mainland, Vulcano is also the most visited of these islands, particularly in high season. A rag-tag approach to building since the mass tourism boom came to the island in the early '80s gives the island's town a slightly down-at-heel vibe. However, the island does have some of the best beaches in these islands, with black rather than golden sands.

Essentials

GETTING THERE Vulcano is the first port of call for ferries and hydrofoils arriving from the Sicilian mainland. Boats dock at the **Porto del Levante,** on the northern side of the island, on the eastern side of the isthmus that joins to **Vulcanello.** The routes continue on to Lipari, Salina, and then either Panarea and Stromboli or to Alicudi and Filicudi.

GETTING AROUND Most of the tourist activity is centered on the northern side of the island, around the neck of the isthmus between Porto Ponente and Porto Levante, an area best explored **on foot.** While the island's total area is 21 sq. km (8 sq. miles), the distance between the two ports is barely 500m (⅓ mile). However, **Scaffidi** (℘ 090/9853073) runs **bus service** from the port to Piano, an inland village 7km (4⅓ miles) southwest of Porto Levante, and to Gelso, at the southern tip. You can rent a **bike** or **scooter** at **Da Paolo,** Via Porto Levante (℘ 090/9852112), May through November daily from 8am to 8:30pm. Mountain bikes cost from 5€ to 10€ per day; scooters start from 20€. If you would like to explore the island by boat, rent a dinghy from **Centro Nautico Baia di Levante** (℘ 393/9151901; www.baialevante.it), on the beach by the hydrofoil jetty. The Centro Nautico also organizes **boat trips** to other islands.

FAST FACTS The **Banco di Sicilia,** Via Marina Garibaldi 152 (℘ 090/9811140), has an ATM and keeps regular banking hours Monday through Friday. Money can also be exchanged at the **Thermessa Agency,** Via Porto Levante (℘ 090/9852230), daily from 6:30am to 8:30pm. You can purchase hydrofoil tickets here as well, or try **Siremar,** Via Roma 74 (℘ 090/986016), for both hydrofoil and ferry tickets. For **medical services** from June to September, a doctor is on call at ℘ 090/9852220. The island **pharmacy,** Bonarrigo, Via Favaloro 1 (℘ 090/9852244), is open daily from 9am to 1pm and 7 to 9pm. The **Carabinieri** (army police corps) can be called at ℘ 090/9852110. The **post office** is on Via Piano, off Porto di Levante (℘ 090/9853143).

Exploring the Island

AROUND PORTO LEVANTE

The area around the **Porto del Levante,** the island's main port, is the focus of the tourist activity on the island, but cannot be described as picturesque. From the dock follow your nose to the fabled **Laghetti dei Fanghi ★** (Little Lakes of Mud), said to offer all sorts of health benefits. Whether or not skin complaints and rheumatism are cured by luxuriating in the bubbling mud, it is undoubtedly radioactive, and bathers are advised to spend no more than 15 minutes at a time. It is also incredibly smelly and will discolor clothing and jewelry, not to mention add an unfortunate green tinge to artificially colored blonde hair. Despite all that, a trip to the *laghetti* is a sensory-transporting experience, and an essential ritual on Vulcano. The lakes are open daily from 6:30am to 8pm from Easter to October, and admission is 1€.

An attractive 20-minute walk from the port across the isthmus from the Porto di Levante, by the **Porto di Ponente,** is an excellent black sand beach (which gets extremely hot in the middle of the day), the **Spiagge Nere ★**, with a number of *stabilimenti* (beach clubs) that rent sun loungers and umbrellas, and the pizzeria/bar **A Zammara,** a popular hangout. The beach's proximity to the hotels of the ports of Levante and Ponente means it's crammed with bathers in high season.

North of Porto Levante, and linked to the main body of the island by a thread, **Vulcanello ★★** rose out of the sea following a particularly violent eruption in 183 B.C. It last erupted in 1888 and the curiously shaped lava flows it left are known locally as the **Valle dei Mostri ★★** (Valley of Monsters).

THE GRAN CRATERE

Aside from the mud, chances are the **Gran Cratere ★★** (Big Crater) of the island's largest volcano, the **Vulcano della Fossa,** is what you are here to see. It is 418m (1,371-ft.) high at the summit and can be reached by foot from the Porto di Levante. The climb takes a little over an hour at a brisk pace. It is strongly advised to attempt it only in the early morning or in the evening, and to allow 3 hours for the trip there and back. The sandy soil makes the going tough in some parts, so wear decent footwear (closed shoes rather than sandals). Also bear in mind it can get very dusty; people with respiratory problems are advised not to attempt the climb, and contact lenses are a very bad idea. Sunscreen is a must, and make sure you take plenty of water, although there is a small cafe halfway up. To get there, follow the signs that say *"al cratere."* Five or 10 minutes after leaving the port area to the south, a gravel track slopes up to the left and leads to the crater. The lowest point of the crater's edge is at 290m (952 ft.). When you reach the edge, the smoking fumaroles and the lunar landscape lend an evocative sense of otherness. Lean over the edge and look into the main crater and ponder the ancient legends that associated the gaping maw with the entrance to Hades. Walking around the crater gives splendid views across the archipelago to the north, but as you scamper about, don't get too close to the fissures hissing with escaping gas—the temperatures at these fumaroles are stratospheric.

If you would prefer to visit the crater with a guide, seek out one of the various organizations that take tours to the top, including **Nesos,** based on Lipari, at Corso Vittorio Emanuele 24 (© **347/576860;** www.nesos.org), and **Gruppo Trekking Vulcano** (© **333/7656762** or 090/9852378; fpalmer60@virgilio.it).

SOUTH TO GELSO

Islanders who live inland are likely to reside in the remote village of Piano, 7km (4⅓ miles) from the port. Piano lies between two peaks, **Mount Saraceno,** 48m (157 ft.), and **La Sommata,** 387m (1,270 ft.). There's not much for tourists here, but if you continue on the bus to the southernmost village of **Gelso,** you can view the inland scenery of Vulcano along the way. At Gelso, the end of the line, you'll find some summer-only places to eat and good sea bathing. *Gelso* is Italian for "mulberry," one of the crops cultivated in the area along with capers. Far less crowded than the beaches near Porto Levante, the **Spiaggia del Gelso ★** is a mix of black sand and pebbles along the southern coast of the island; by land it is reached either by car or scooter, or for a few euros the fishermen and boatmen at the Spiagge Nere will give you a ride. Immediately east of Gelso the **Spiaggia Punta dell'Asino ★** is a cove reached by a steep path from the village of Gelso, not to be undertaken by the faint-hearted; although once you're down on the beach, sun loungers and umbrellas can be rented from a kiosk on the sand in summer (which also sells snacks and drinks), and dusty feet can be refreshed in crystalline waters. From the beach the energetic can follow a path to **Capo Grillo;** its sweeping **panorama of the Aeolians ★★** is one of the best views on the island.

Where to Stay

Hotel Aura ★   A short stroll from the Porto Levante, the Aura offers simple Aeolian charm: whitewashed walls and blue windows, and a pool and Jacuzzi with a view up toward the looming volcano. Rooms are simple but spotless, and many have a private (if not secluded) terrace with a table and chairs. The hotel also offers half-board in conjunction with a nearby *trattoria*.

Via Eucaliptus 49. ✆ **090/9853454.** www.auravulcano.com. 25 units. Double 85€–190€. Rates include breakfast. MC, V. Closed mid-Oct to Apr. **Amenities:** Jacuzzi; pool. *In room:* A/C, TV, minibar.

Hotel Eros ★   Modern Mediterranean in style and a stone's throw from the port, all rooms at the Eros have their own terrace, equipped with deck chairs to enjoy your sun-downer. Rooms and bathrooms are spotless, if slightly anonymous. Relax by the pool or venture out to nearby beaches, as the hotel's "private beach" is hardly a full-service affair, and on a stretch of water that is far from the most inviting on the island. Breakfast is taken on the covered terrace where the evening meal is also served, by the garden leading to moored yachts.

Via di Porto Levante 64 ✆ **090/9853265.** www.eroshotel.it. 28 units. Double room 200€–270€. Rates include breakfast. AE, DC, MC, V. Closed mid-Oct to mid-May. **Amenities:** Restaurant; bar; boat, bike, and car rental; pool; rooms for those w/limited mobility. *In room:* A/C, TV, minibar, free Wi-Fi.

Therasia Resort Hotel ★★   On the promontory of Vulcanello, and away from the sulfurous stench of the Porto Levante, the low white forms of the Therasia Resort provide spectacular views of Lipari. The restaurant is good—though not as good as it should be for a five-star hotel—but the views from the infinity pool more than make up for any shortcomings. Transfers are offered to a nearby black-sand beach with sun loungers; otherwise, a ladder leads down black rocks into the sea for the more adventurous. On the way down, sun loungers, and the ever-necessary umbrellas, are dotted on ledges cut into the rocks and providing vantage points for the spectacular views. All rooms have terraces, and superior units offer sea views.

Loc. Vulcanello. ✆ **090/9852555.** Fax 090/9852154. www.therasiaresort.it. 94 units. Double 230€–380€; superior 350€–540€; suite with Jacuzzi on terrace 600€–800€. Rates include breakfast. AE, DC, MC, V. Closed Nov to late Apr. **Amenities:** Restaurant; bar; boat, bike, and car rental; free Internet station in lobby; Jacuzzi; 2 pools; smoke-free rooms; spa. *In room:* A/C, TV, minibar.

Where to Dine

Da Gaetano ★★ 🏚️ SEAFOOD/AEOLIAN   A little pricier than the average Vulcano restaurant, but worth it for the freshest of fresh fish, Da Gaetano is at Gelso on the south coast of the island. Specialties include *fettuccine alle eoliane* with no fewer than 27 herbs, and *carpacci* of whatever sea creature was hauled in that morning. A terrace offers views over the sea toward the Sicilian mainland.

Strada Provinciale, loc. Gelso. 🕐 **347/7216532.** Reservations recommended. Main courses 14€–20€. MC, V. Daily noon–3pm and 7–10pm.

Vincenzino ★ SEAFOOD/AEOLIAN   This is the best of the *trattorie* near the touristy ferry port. Known for its hefty portions and affordable prices, Vincenzino has an appealingly rustic setting. You might begin your meal with spaghetti with crayfish, capers, and tomato sauce. The risotto *alla pescatora* (with crayfish, mussels, and other sea creatures) is also recommended. Another good choice is the house spaghetti with ricotta, eggplant, tomatoes, and herbs. From October to March, the menu is limited to a simple array of platters from the bar.

Via Porto di Levante. 🕐 **090/9852016.** Reservations recommended. Main courses 10€–18€. AE, DC, MC, V. Daily noon–3pm and 7–10pm.

Vulcano After Dark

Cantine Stevenson, Via Porto di Levante (🕐 **090/9853247;** Apr–Sept daily noon–3am), are the wine cellars that bear the name of James Stevenson, a Welshman who bought most of Vulcano in 1870 for the export of pumice and sulfur. He also sought to reform the island's agricultural output, and planted the first vineyards. His attempts were thwarted by the eruptions between 1888 and 1891, and after his death in 1903 his properties on the island were sold. In his former wine cellars, live music is featured nightly—whether folk, Sicilian, pop, rock, jazz, or blues—and more than 600 types of wine are sold. The cantina has a rather curious colonial-style decor, somewhat surreal with the volcano looming above. Near the Laghetti dei Fanghi mud baths, **Il Castello** (www.castellobar.interfree.it; no phone) is partly a popular open-air disco and partly an indoor club; don't even dream of showing up before 11pm though. A similar sort of thing is to be found at **Manà Manà:** An open-air nightclub inside the Centro Termale, it occasionally has live music.

If commercial house music and self-consciously designer-clad Italian teenagers are not your thing, the bars around the Porto Levante—mostly of the neon-signed snack-bar variety—are good for a casual drink. A good choice is **Ritrovo Remigio** (🕐 **090/9852085;** from early morning to 2am) with tables overlooking the port. Remigio also does excellent *gelato* (with a brioche, Sicilian style, it also makes a great breakfast) and pastries (do not miss the **cannoli**).

LIPARI ★

The largest and most populated island in the Aeolians, and the effective "hub" of the archipelago, Lipari was supposedly named for the 12th-century B.C. ruler Liparos. The son of Auson, king of an Italic tribe, he invaded from the Italian peninsula in the 12th century B.C. Because of its mineral wealth and its strategically useful position in the Mediterranean, the island continued to be invaded throughout the centuries by Greeks, Arabs, and Spaniards, among others. Its historical importance has made

Lipari the administrative center for all of the islands with the exception of Salina, which is autonomous. Lipari town is the only reasonably sized town of the archipelago. While not the most picturesque Italian burg you'll ever clap eyes on, it nevertheless has a small-city feel, and, beyond the gaudy souvenir shops, its historical center has a certain charm.

Outside of Lipari town, the rest of the island offers rough-around-the-edges natural beauty, and the relics of the pumice industry (halted in 2008) dot the northern coast around **Acquacalda.** On the east coast, 4km (2½ miles) north of Lipari town center, **Canneto** is an agreeable seaside stretch with a few cafes and a campsite. Inland and to the southwest is the small town of **Quattropani.**

Back in Lipari town, **Marina Lunga** (Long Marina) is where ferries and hydrofoils dock. On the southern side of the *castello* promontory is the smaller, and much more picturesque, **Marina Corta** (Short Marina). The cliff-top **citadel** is surrounded by Spanish-built, 16th-century fortifications. Inside the walls are the *duomo* and the **archaeological museum** (the major historical site on the island; p. 257). The major artery of Lipari town, **Corso Vittorio Emanuele** (aka **"Il Corso"**) leads up from Marina Lunga. The site of most of the businesses catering to visitors (including the tourist office, bars, and banks), it's paved with the islands' volcanic basalt, and its slightly down-at-heel 19th-century merchants' houses have crumbling pastel stucco and wrought-iron balconies.

Essentials

GETTING THERE   As the main island of the archipelago, Lipari is the hub of ferry and hydrofoil services between the islands, making it a good spot from which to explore the other Aeolians; it offers the largest number of sailings all year round. The main port is the **Marina Lunga.** Hydrofoils from Milazzo and Naples dock at the jetty, and ferries call at another port, 100m (328 ft.) to the south, known as **Sottomonastero** ("Under the Monastery").

GETTING AROUND   The bus system is somewhat limited, and many hotels, *pensioni,* and the campsite will pick you up from the port. By the hydrofoil ticket office on the jetty is the ticket office for **Urso Guglielmo.** A round-trip ticket to Canneto is 2.10€; it costs 2.60€ for other destinations around Lipari, or you can buy a card with 6, 10, or 20 single journeys at a discount. The ticket hut will give you a timetable, as will the main office at Via Cappuccini 9 (© **090/9811262**). Several **scooter rental** outfits are at the hydrofoil jetty and at the ferry jetty, such as **Da Luigi,** directly opposite the hydrofoil jetty (© **090/9880540**). Prices vary depending on the season and availability, but 20€ should get you a day's rental of a 50cc bike. You will need to present a driver's license and leave a passport as security. Another excellent way to explore the island is by boat, which allows access to coves and bays inaccessible by land, and gives splendid views of the spectacular coastline. Most of the scooter rental outfits also rent **small motorboats.**

VISITOR INFORMATION   The spartan **tourist information office** at Via Vittorio Emanuele 202 (© **090/9880095**) serves the entire archipelago. Perplexingly for a holiday island, it is closed on Saturdays, Sundays, and public holidays (Mon–Fri 9am–1pm and 4:30–7pm). In July and August it is—in theory at least—also open on Saturday, 9am to 1pm.

FAST FACTS   **Ferry** and **hydrofoil** tickets are available at the **Siremar** office, Via Mariano Amendola, Marina Lunga (© **090/9811312;** Mon–Fri 9am–1pm and

4:30–7:30pm). Hydrofoil tickets can also be bought on the pier at the **Terminal Aliscafi,** Marina Sottomonastero (© **090-9812200;** daily, hours vary according to timetable but the office will be open for at least 30 min. before a scheduled sailing). Next to the tourist office at Corso Vittorio Emanuele 202 is a **supermarket,** open 8am to 9pm Monday to Friday, and 8am to 9.30pm on Saturdays. Two **pharmacies** are in Lipari town at Via Roma (© **090/986713**), and at Canneto on Via Marina Garibaldi 72 (© **090/9811428**). For a **hospital** emergency, call © **090/983040;** for **first aid,** © **090/9811010.** For the local **Carabinieri** (police corps), call © **090/9811333.** The **post office** is at Corso Vittorio Emanuele 207 (© **090/ 9810051;** Mon–Fri 8am–1:30pm and Sat 8am–12:30pm). For **Internet access,** go to either Corso Vittorio Emmanuele 63 or 179 (7 days a week, 9am–1:30pm and 4:30–9pm in winter; 9am–1pm and 5:30pm–midnight in summer). The major bank is **Banca Monte dei Paschi di Siena,** Via Vittorio Emanuele 209 (© **090/9880432**), which has an ATM.

Exploring the Island

As the "hub" of the Aeolians, Lipari has a number of companies (all in Lipari town) offering **boat trips** to the other islands, both for daytime swimming and exploring, and evening viewing of the lava flows on Stromboli. Among these is **Da Massimo,** Via Maurolico 2 (© **090/9813086;** www.damassimo.it), which also rents boats. **Nesos** (www.nesos.org) offers regular **guided group walks** of the west coast of Lipari on Tuesday mornings, and to the crater on Vulcano on Fridays. Other excursions can be organized on request. The Nesos office at Corso Vittorio Emanuele 24 is rarely open, but a mobile-phone number is © **347/5768609.**

LIPARI TOWN ★

CITADEL/UPPER TOWN   Between the Marina Sottomonastero and the Marina Corta juts the hulk of the **castle rock.** It is accessible from the ferry terminal by the Salita Melagunis staircase that leads up to the elegantly leafy Piazza Mazzini, home of the celebrated restaurant Filippino (p. 260). From Piazza Mazzini are good views along the coast and the fortifications of the castle rock. Dating from the mid-16th-century Spanish occupation of the island, the walls are entered by the ramp up from Piazza Mazzini. At the top of the ramp is the ticket office for the **Archaeological Museum ★★** (Mon–Sat 9am–1pm and 3–7pm; ticket office closes at 6pm; Sun and public holidays the museum is open 9am–1pm only; admission 6€).

The collection traces the island's inhabitants from the 5th millennium B.C. through Greek and Roman occupation and depicts the significance of the Aeolians, especially Lipari, throughout the course of ancient Mediterranean history.

At the southern end of the castle rock and included with admission to the Archaeological Museum is the **Parco Archeologico** (open-air archaeological park), which houses many of the Greek sarcophagi found in the Contrada Diana (5th–3rd century B.C.; see "Lower Town," below). A reconstruction of the Greek theater holds concerts and classical plays in the summer months (for information, contact the tourist office; p. 256) with the Mediterranean as the backdrop.

Next to the museum building is the Norman/Baroque **Cathedral of St. Bartholomew ★** (daily 9am–1pm), the patron saint of the island. In front of the cathedral, the **Via del Concordato**'s wide steps cut through the hefty fortifications down to Via Garibaldi.

LOWER TOWN After Corso Vittorio Emanuele, the second major artery of the lower town is **Via Garibaldi,** which curves around the bottom of the castle rock between Piazza Mazzini and Marina Corta. At the small harbor of **Marina Corta,** cafes line the piazza and fishing boats bob—altogether a very pleasant spot to regain your strength, perhaps with a *granita* (Italian ice), while admiring the prickly pears clinging to the vast mass of the castle rock. A number of roads link Via Garibaldi with the **Corso,** including Via Maurolico where the Approdo bar (see "Lipari After Dark," p. 260) is a popular hangout. Opposite is the delicious and elegant Kasbah Café (see "Where to Dine," p. 260), a popular choice for visitors and Liparoti alike.

AROUND THE ISLAND

The major destination on Lipari is 4km (2½ miles) north of Lipari town: The small town of **Canneto** is where the best beaches are found. Canneto can be reached by bus or a 30-minute walk, following the seafront past the sailboat marina and through the road tunnel. Just north of Canneto is **Spiaggia Bianca ★**, named for the soft white sand, a by-product of the old pumice mines. To reach the beach from Canneto town, take the waterfront road, climbing the stairs along Via Marina Garibaldi, and then veer right down a narrow cobbled path for 300m (980 ft.). Alternatively, regular boat shuttles from Canneto will take you and bring you back for a few euros. Other than its beaches, Canneto has a small seafront with a couple of agreeable cafes serving decent *arancini* (fried rice balls, a Sicilian fast-food specialty) and *granite*.

Buses run north of Canneto, passing the **Cave di Pomice** (pumice quarry) at Campobianco, between Spiaggia Bianca and Porticello. From Cave di Pomice, you can see **Mount Pilato,** at 476m (1,562 ft.). This is the ancient crater of a volcano that last erupted in A.D. 700. On the north coast is the tiny, blink-and-you-miss-it town of **Acquacalda,** literally "Hot Water" for the sporadic periods of volcanic activity that warm the sea. It's little more than a single street with a couple of snack bars, the eerie skeletons of the now defunct pumice mining equipment jutting out into gloriously colored seas. Leaving Acquacalda, the road follows the coast with views toward Salina, and Panarea and Stromboli in the distance. The road then leads to the small town of **Quattropani,** to the west of 602m (1,975-ft.) Mount Chirica. The town consists of a grocery store, a restaurant, two churches, and a cemetery. The older of the churches is the destination of an annual pilgrimage on September 8 dedicated to the **Madonna della Catena** (the Virgin of the Chains); a particularly Sicilian veneration of the Virgin, it refers to the 14th-century miracle at Palermo where three condemned men were freed from their chains by an apparition of the Virgin. The road continues round to the town of **Pianoconte,** where there is a good-value and pleasant restaurant, **Le Macine** (✆ 090/9822387; www.lemacine.org; lunch and dinner all year except Jan).

At Pianoconte a turnoff from the main road is signposted for the **Terme di San Calogero.** As the road winds down for a couple of miles, the islands of Alicudi and Filicudi are visible in the distance on a clear day. Though the original *terme* (baths) are in ruins, they form one of the oldest thermal complexes in the Mediterranean. Believed to have been used since the 17th century B.C., the baths are also the only known surviving example of Mycenean architecture beyond Greece. Despite these splendid claims, the site is abandoned, although an elderly man selling capers and Malvasia wine out of his trunk will let you in to see the 15th-century B.C. domed steam room *(tholos)* for a small donation.

A path runs 4km north along the **wild western coast** ★★ of Lipari from the terme up to **Caolino,** toward Quattropani. Walking shoes are advised, and it takes a reasonably experienced hiker about 2 hours. Back on the principal road, you come to the panoramic point of **Quattrocchi,** which offers views across the island, including the **Formiche** ("The Ants"), the rocks off the southern coast of Lipari. Three hundred meters (984 ft.) toward Lipari town is a turnoff down to the coast, leading to the nicest beach on the island, **Spiaggia di Valle Muria** ★★. The beach is a crescent of wide golden sand on the southernmost tip of Lipari and is often deserted because of its out-of-the-way position.

Where to Stay

At the port, arrivals are greeted by swarms of people with **rooms to rent,** which can offer a cheaper alternative to a hotel. Recommended among these is **Le Terrazze** (www.eoliecasevacanze.com), at the end of Marina Lunga, toward the small yacht port. Rooms are clean, equipped with air-conditioning, and cost from 20€ per person off season to 50€ per person in August, without breakfast.

Casajanca ★   On the seafront at Canneto, this two-story "White House" (Casajanca is *casa bianca* in Aeolian dialect) has wrought-iron balconies that drip with bougainvillea. Its small internal courtyard has a tiled Jacuzzi with naturally hot water, ideal for soothing the feet after a hard day of volcano spotting. Overlooking the courtyard is a small communal balcony with a few tables and chairs. Opening directly onto the *lungomare* (seaside promenade), the breakfast room is where you can watch the world go by.

Marina Garibaldi 115, Canneto. ☏ **090/9880222.** www.casajanca.it. 10 units. Double 80€–200€; triple 95€–240€. Rates include breakfast. AE, DC, MC, V. Year-round. **Amenities:** Bar; room service. *In room:* A/C, TV, minibar.

Hotel Poseidon ★   Near the hydrofoil jetty, the Hotel Poseidon is on a side road off Corso Vittorio Emanuele. Twelve of the rooms are carved out of a 19th-century merchant house; a couple of rooms are large with frescoed walls, while six other rooms are in a new wing built in the 1990s. An internal courtyard is dominated by a vast palm tree, and communal terraces are good for enjoying the evening air.

Vico Ausonia 7, Lipari. ☏ **090/9812876.** www.hotelposeidonlipari.com. 18 units. Double 75€–150€; triple 90€–180€. Rates include breakfast. AE, DC, MC, V. Closed Nov 15–Feb 28. **Amenities:** Bar; babysitting; room service; smoke-free rooms. *In room:* A/C, TV, hair dryer, minibar.

Hotel Tritone ★★ ☺   Opened in 2004 by the Bernardi family, who also run the celebrated restaurants Filippino and E' Pulera (see "Where to Dine," below), the newly built hotel is a 10-minute walk from the Lipari town center. Rooms, each with a patio and balcony looking over the volcanically heated pool, are comfortably furnished with all mod cons and nice bathrooms. Service is prompt and polite, and the family's strong culinary tradition makes itself felt in wonderful breakfasts. The hotel **restaurant** is also excellent, with the emphasis on local produce and fish. When weather permits, meals are served on the terrace.

Via Mendolita, Lipari. ☏ **090/9811595.** www.bernardigroup.it. 39 units. Double 120€–240€. Rates include breakfast. AE, DC, MC, V. Year-round. **Amenities:** Restaurant; bar; babysitting; pool; pool bar (July-Aug); parking; rooms for those w/limited mobility; smoke-free rooms; transfers to and from the port. *In room:* A/C, TV, hair dryer, minibar.

Villa Meligunis ★   The Villa Meligunis is in the old fisherman's quarter behind the port of Marina Corta, which is also very close to the ferry port. The 32 rooms have terra cotta–tiled floors and heavy cream-colored bed linens; the superior rooms have private terraces, and the nearby Residence Agave, run by the same management, houses six self-catering apartments. The hotel's finest feature is its panoramic roof garden. It also offers a restaurant, pool, bar, and splendid views.

Via Marte 7, Lipari. ☏ **090/9812426.** www.villameligunis.it. 32 units. Double 150€–290€; suite 225€–365€. Rates include breakfast. AE, DC, MC, V. Free parking. **Amenities:** Restaurant; 2 bars; babysitting; pool; room service; smoke-free rooms. *In room:* A/C, TV, minibar, hair dryer, free Wi-Fi.

Where to Dine

Filippino ★★★ SICILIAN   The most famous restaurant on the island, Filippino celebrated its centenary in 2010. Very much a family affair, the dining room is run by Filippino's grandson, Antonio Bernardi. The atmosphere is traditionally elegant, with a large covered terrace full of wrought-iron lamps and crisp white linen. The accent is on local produce, fresh fish, and traditional dishes produced with flair. Sicily's Arab influence comes through in couscous with prawns, eggplant, and zucchini, and many of the seafood offerings, like the mupa, are specific to the deep waters around the volcanic islands. Finish with that great Sicilian classic, *cassata,* and a drop of Malvasia. The heavily Sicilian wine list is well priced, and it's possible to escape with a bill of 35€ a head if you're careful; otherwise, with fresh lobster and top end wines, the sky's the limit.

Piazza Mazzini, Lipari. ☏ **090/9811002.** Reservations required July–Aug. Main courses from 12€. AE, DC, MC, V. Daily noon–2:30pm and 7:30–10:30pm. Closed Nov 10–Dec 26.

Kasbah Café ★ MEDITERRANEAN   Run by Alessandro del Bono on Via Maurolico, just off the Corso, the Kasbah Café is a welcome addition to Lipari's dining scene. Freshly elegant with crisp linens and sparkling glasses, the cafe offers fresh food at reasonable prices. Fresh spaghetti with pot-caught prawns are excellent, and fish is served either grilled or *alla eoliana* (with tomatoes, olives, and capers).

Via Maurolico 25, Lipari. ☏ **090/9811075.** Reservations recommended. Pizza 7€–8€; main courses from 12€. AE, MC, V. 8pm–midnight. Closed Nov–Mar.

La Nassa ★ SICILIAN   At this enchanting restaurant, the delectable cuisine of Donna Teresa matches the friendly enthusiasm of her son Bartolo. The food is the most genuine on the island, prepared with respect for both old traditions and modern tastes. After the *sette perle* ("seven pearl") appetizer, a combination of fresh fish, sweet shrimp, and spices, you can try your choice of fish, cooked to your specifications. For dessert, try cookies with Malvasia wine.

Via G. Franza 41, Lipari. ☏ **090/9811319.** Reservations recommended. Main courses 10€–18€. AE, MC, V. Apr–June Fri–Wed 8:30am–3pm and 6pm–midnight; July–Oct daily 8:30am–3pm and 6pm–midnight. Closed Nov–Easter.

Osteria Mediterranea ★★ 🍴 SICILIAN   On the main drag Il Corso (otherwise dominated by tourist menus), the Osteria offers elegant rusticity and great value. Sample dishes include potato *gnocchetti* with prawns, and *carpaccio* of tuna. Try the Sicilian house wine from the well-priced selection of bottles from the region. The good-value *prix fixe* is 16€ for two courses and pudding.

Corso Vittorio Emanuele 148. ☏ **090/9880026.** Reservations recommended. Entrees 8€–12€. MC, V. Daily 8pm–midnight. Closed Nov–Mar.

Lipari After Dark

On balmy summer nights, the bars on Marina Corta overflow with the carefully dressed showing off their tans. The **Café du Port,** Piazza Sant'Onofrio (☏ **090/9811801**), occasionally has live music, as does the **Chitarra Bar,** Salita San Giuseppe (*℃ 090/9811554*). Opposite the Kasbah Café (see above), **L'Approdo ★** (*℃ 090/9817061*) spills out onto Via Maurolico, with frequent live music and good cocktails. Otherwise, just join in the *passeggiata* flowing along the Corso and Via Garibaldi.

SALINA ★★★

The richly verdant twin mounts of Salina are at the center of the Aeolian Islands making it a good, and infinitely classier, alternative to Lipari if you prefer to do your island hopping from a fixed base. If your idea of island life is dancing 'til dawn to pounding bass, Salina is definitely *not* for you; this is about as far as you can get from Ibiza. If, however, smart hotels, a couple of tiny towns, good food, and soaking in gorgeous scenery are your style, this is the Aeolian island for your relaxing and romantic break. Explore the inland mountains by renting a small car, or a boat and putter around the island's bulk seeking out crystalline coves—or just admire the view and sigh.

At Salina's heart are two extinct volcanoes—the island was known in antiquity as *Didyme* (meaning "Twin"), when the mountains were interpreted as the breasts of a goddess. These twin mountains are now a protected nature reserve. The taller peak, **Monte Fossa delle Felci** (Mountain of the Valley of Ferns), is to the east of the island. At 962m (3,156 ft.), it is the highest point in the Aeolian Islands; the slightly smaller **Monte Porri** (Mountain of Leeks) is to the west.

The island's modern name is more pragmatic, and was given by the Romans in reference to the abundant quantities of salt extracted from the brackish lake at **Lingua,** on the southeast of the island. For the Romans, this salt export was fundamental, but nowadays the major exports are Malvasia wine and capers. The popularity of Malvasia saw a massive boom in merchant activity on Salina in the 19th century, but the boom came to a dramatic end with the outbreak of phylloxera, a disease that destroyed the Malvasia vines. The resulting famine saw a mass emigration from which the island never recovered; the population today is 2,400 in contrast to a late-1800s population of 9,000. The **Museum of Emigration** at Malfa commemorates this extraordinary turn in the island's fortunes.

Essentials

GETTING THERE   Of Salina's two ports, the main one is **Santa Marina Salina,** which has a marina for yachts. Santa Marina is convenient if you are staying in either Santa Marina or Malfa. Most of the sailings listed below also stop at the tiny port of **Rinella,** on the south of the island, ideal if you are staying there, or at Leni; for Rinella, expect a very slight modification to journey times and cost.

GETTING AROUND   There is a **taxi stand** on the jetty at Santa Marina, and the **ferry companies'** offices are just beyond, on either side of the church. The **bus stop** at Santa Marina is outside the Siremar office and the Mercanti di Mare hotel, and services run regularly between Santa Marina, Malfa and Leni. However, to explore the 27-sq.-km (10-sq.-mile) island more thoroughly, and less frustratingly, rent a car or a scooter. At Santa Marina Salina, **cars and scooters** can be rented at **Antonio Bongiorno,** Via Risorgimento 240 (*℃ 090/9843409;* www.noleggiobongiorno.it/index.html); follow the road up from the port to the left. Prices range from 26€ to 30€ a day for a 50cc scooter, and 60€ to 100€ for a car, depending on vehicle size and season. If you need a transfer from the port, **Tourist Service,** Via Roma 112, Malfa

(© **090/9844034;** www.touristservicesas.it), will pick you up; and they also rent cars and scooters for getting around the island during your stay. At Santa Marina, **Nautica Levante** (© **090-9843083;** www.nauticalevante.it) **rents boats** and organizes guided **boat tours** of the island. They all rent **holiday apartments.**

VISITOR INFORMATION The tourist office is on Piazza Santa Marina (© **090/ 9843175).**

FAST FACTS **Ferry** and **hydrofoil** tickets are available at the Siremar office on the piazza at the port at Santa Marina (© **090/9843004)** and at Rinella (© **090/ 9809170).** The major **pharmacies** are in Santa Maria Salina on Via Risorgimento (© **090/9643098),** in Leni at Via Libertà 7 (© **090/9809053),** and in Malfa on Via Umberto (© **090/9844188).** For **first aid,** call © **090/9844005.** The **Carabinieri** (police station) is in Santa Marina on Via Lungomare (© **090/9843019).** The **post office** in Santa Marina is on Via Risorgimento (© **090/9843402);** others are in Malfa (on Via Roma) and in Leni (on Via Libertà). For **Internet access,** Salina Computer in Santa Marina is at Via Risorgimento 110 (© **090/9843444;** www. salinacomputer.it) and is open from 11am until late. At Santa Marina, **Banca Antonveneta** is on the main piazza by the port, next to the Hotel Mercanti di Mare; it has an **ATM,** as does the **Banco di Sicilia,** Via Risorgimento 158/160. In **Malfa,** the **Banca Nuova** is at Via Provinciale 2/4.

Exploring the Island

SANTA MARINA SALINA ★★

The island's main town, Santa Marina Salina, has the island's main port and, of course, the marina. Overlooking the port is the restaurant Porto Bello (see "Where to Dine," p. 264), and Layla, one of the island's most popular bars (see "Salina After Dark," p. 265). Just beyond is the Piazza Santa Marina, in front of the church. Just up behind the main piazza and the Lungomare is the town's main drag: The car-free **Via Risorgimento** is lined with elegant 19th-century merchant houses, relics of the island's moment of glory. Many of these have recently, and lovingly, been restored, as has the charming Cinque Balconi Hotel (see "Where to Stay," p. 263). The street has an agreeable mixture of boutiques, including super-cool **amanei** at number 71 (www. amanei.com), and traditional grocery stores.

Following the eastern coastline south from Santa Marina, the road ends just beyond **Lingua ★,** a small town on the salt lake that was a fundamental part of the island's development. Overlooking the lake is the small **Ethnographic Museum** (© **090/9643396)** that traces the island's history. At Lingua, the main piazza is home to **da Alfredo**'s world-famous *granite* (see "Where to Dine," p. 264); the town also has a small shoreline, a few restaurants, pretty fishing boats, and a stony beach. Swamped in July and August, the tiny town is pleasantly sleepy in the shoulder season. For excursions to the verdant center of the island, best undertaken in spring and autumn, take the road to **Valdichiesa,** just north of Leni, where you can take one of the routes to the top of the **Monte Fossa dei Felci,** passing through paths rich in the ferns that give the mountain its name. The crater of the extinct volcano is 100m (328 ft.) deep, with a diameter of over 600m (1,969 ft.). From the rim of the crater, spectacular views take in the entire archipelago in a setting rich in centuries-old chestnuts, oaks, and pines. Occasionally the *Falco della Regina* (a type of Mediterranean falcon) is visible circling above.

MALFA

One of the three administrative districts on the island, the small town of **Malfa** is slightly inland from the center of the northern coast. Its name is theorized either to come from the Arab *marfa,* meaning port, or from the Marine Republic of Amalfi, from which settlers came to Salina in the 12th century. Malfa town is built around Via Roma and has at its center the **Church of the Immacolata** on the small principal piazza, which is the site of the celebrations of the feast of St. Joseph on March 19. From Malfa, a small stony **beach** is accessible by foot, and **boat rental** is available at the tiny fishing port.

To the west of town, the road leads up to **Semaforo,** which offers dramatic views down onto the remains of the long-sunken crater of an extinct volcano. The road continues down to **Pollara,** where the annual *Sagra del Cappero,* Festival of the Caper, is held the first weekend of June (in the piazza in front of the church of Sant'Onofrio). The spectacular **beach ★** beneath Pollara, with its towering wall of striated rock, was one of the sites in the 1994 movie *Il Postino.* Sadly no longer accessible because of the risk of landslide of the spectacular overhanging ledge, it is best seen from the water. Just beyond the spur after the beach at Pollara, and only accessible by boat, is a pretty **rock arch** carved by millennia of pounding waves.

Close to the inland town of **Leni** (the third administrative district of the island), little **Rinella,** in the center of the southern coast, is a port of call for some hydrofoils. The pizzeria **Da Marco** is a popular destination for a cheap supper.

Where to Stay

Capo Faro Resort ★★★   Opened in 2004 by an aristocratic Palermitan wine-producing family, the Tasca d'Almerita, the resort takes its name from the nearby *faro* (lighthouse). Its 18 chic rooms occupy seven white stucco cottages dotted among 7 hectares (17 acres) of carefully tended olive trees, bougainvillea, fruit trees, and, above all, the Tasca Malviasia vines. With the Monte Fossa delle Felci towering behind, views stretch across to Stromboli and Panarea. Spectacular and abundant breakfasts are taken by the pool, and a no-under-14s rule means you will be able to absorb the splendid views in peace. Throw in a seriously smart **restaurant,** massages, boat trips, and wine tastings, and you'll never want to leave.

Tenuta Capofaro, via Faro 3, Salina. Ⓒ **090/9844330** or 090/9844331. www.capofaro.it. 18 units. Standard double 220€–320€; superior double 290€–390€; deluxe double 350€–250€. Rates include breakfast. MC, V. Closed Oct to early Apr. **Amenities:** Restaurant; bar; pool. *In room:* A/C, TV, hair dryer, minibar, free Wi-Fi.

Hotel Signum ★★★ 📷   One of the star hotels in the Aeolian islands, the Hotel Signum is down an alley off Malfa's main drag. It was opened in the 1980s by Malfa native Clara Rametta, who restored a jumble of long abandoned small village houses connected by open staircases. The crisp, cool rooms are all different in size and aspect, but all have elegantly rustic furniture. Some have sea views; others are set under the shade of lemon trees and open onto the garden. The infinity pool is undoubtedly one of the hotel's highlights and offers views across to the belching silhouette of Stromboli, as does the beautiful terrace where the abundant breakfasts are served under the vine-covered pergola. A spa at Hotel Signum exploits the naturally warm waters of the island. Massages and various other treatments are offered, and they're only too happy to bring you an aperitif to enjoy in the Jacuzzi as you ponder the great verdant mass of the volcano rising above after a hard day by the pool. Staff are courteous and knowledgeable, and anything Clara Rametta doesn't know about Salina isn't worth knowing.

Via Scalo 15 Malfa, Salina.© **090/9844222** or 090/9844375. www.hotelsignum.it. 30 units. Standard double 130€–280€; superior double 170€–320€; deluxe double 210€–360€. Rates include breakfast. MC, V. Closed early Nov to mid-Mar. **Amenities:** Restaurant; bar; boat trips. *In room:* A/C, TV, minibar, free Wi-Fi.

I Cinque Balconi ★★ 🛏   In two beautifully restored 19th-century merchant houses on Via Risorgimento, Santa Marina's car-free main drag, the Cinque Balconi opened in 2008. It takes its name from five balconies that afford sea views. The rooms vary in size and decor, but all show attention to detail and local traditions. Original tiles in parts of the houses were copied by local workmen for the decoration of the bathrooms. The bar/breakfast room is in the old merchant's shop, and across the communal courtyard with its fig and orange trees is the old oil mill, now a suite.

Via Risorgimento 36, Santa Marina Salina.©/fax **090/9843508.** www.icinquebalconi.it. 9 units. Standard double 130€–200€; superior double 120€–180€; junior suite 170€–250€. Rates include breakfast. MC, V. Closed Nov–Mar. **Amenities:** Bar. *In room:* A/C, TV, hair dryer, minibar, free Wi-Fi.

La Locanda del Postino ★ 🛏   In the bowl of the crater on the northwest coast of the island, down from the tiny village of Pollara, the Locanda takes its name from the celebrated movie that was partly filmed here in the early 1990s. The 10 large rooms are sparsely but pleasantly furnished. Each has a private terrace looking across to the famed beach at Pollara. Meals can be served on your terrace; otherwise, guests eat on a communal terrace under the traditional Aeolian cane-thatched roof. The proprietors are bristling with enthusiasm and full of useful information.

Via Picone 10, Pollara, Salina.©/fax **090/9843958.** www.lalocandadelpostino.it. 10 units. Double 120€–200€. Rates include breakfast, half-board 25€ per person. MC, V. Closed Nov–Apr. **Amenities:** Restaurant; bar; boat trips. *In room:* A/C, TV on request, hair dryer.

La Salina Hotel Borgo di Mare ★★   On the southeastern point of the island, by the salt lake at Lingua, La Salina is a carefully renovated *borgo di mare* (seaside hamlet) that once housed a salt works. Owned by the Cataffo family, who run the Porto Bello restaurant at Santa Marina (below), the complex is nestled among vines, oleander, and bougainvillea. Rooms all have a balcony or terrace, many with sea views, and are decorated with elegant simplicity. Breakfast, lunchtime snacks, and evening drinks are served on the hotel terrace. The hotel also offers direct access to a small stony beach. A swimming pool is planned for 2011.

Lingua, Salina.©/fax **090/9843441.** www.lasalinahotel.com. 24 units. Standard double 130€–200€; superior double 180€–230€; junior suite 250€–350€. Rates include breakfast. MC, V. Year-round. **Amenities:** Bar; parking. *In room:* A/C, TV, hair dryer, minibar, free Wi-Fi.

Where to Dine

Alfredo in Cucina ★★ 🍴   Part of the ever-growing Alfredo empire (of *granita* fame) at Lingua, this bustling informal bistro offers local classics with a modern twist. Pasta with swordfish, citrus fruit, and almonds, and tuna with wild fennel and potatoes were on the menu when I dropped in. In August the terraces are given over to an extension of the seafront bar where *pan cunzato* (dried bread, lightly soaked in vinegar and topped with dressed tomatoes) takes on myriad forms and provides the hungry hordes with a cheap and delicious lunch.

Via Marina Garibaldi, Lingua. © **090/9843307.** www.alfredoincucina.com. Entrees 10€–18€. MC, V. Daily noon–3pm and 7:30–11pm. Closed Nov–Mar.

Capo Faro ★★ CREATIVE ITALIAN   A gourmet extravaganza awaits you on the covered terrace by the pool at Capo Faro. The restaurant is under the control of Luca Fantini, second in command under Heinz Beck at Rome's La Pergola, repeatedly voted the best restaurant in Italy. Elegant distillations of Aeolian classics include *ricciola* (amberjack fish) with classic Sicilian caponata, *paccheri* (giant pasta tubes) with both raw and cooked fish, and an almond *granita* to make your heart sing. As to be expected from a resort owned by the Tasca family, the wine list is ample, and above all Sicilian.

Tenuta Capofaro, via Faro 3. © **090/9844330/1.** Fax 090/9844339. www.capofaro.it. Entrees 18€–28€. MC, V. Reservations advised. Daily noon–3pm and 7:30–11pm. Closed Nov to early Apr.

Hotel Signum ★★ AEOLIAN   The family-run restaurant at Hotel Signum is one of the finest on the island. In good weather, dinner is served on the beautiful terrace; otherwise, it's in the elegantly cozy dining room with its mismatched old school desks, antique dressers, and exposed beams. Dishes never stray far from Aeolian traditions and focus on the glorious local fish and produce—I particularly enjoyed linguine with red prawns and mint. The wine list is ample and Sicilian, and the charming sommelier is only too happy to help you choose.

Via Scalo, 15 Malfa, Salina. © **090/9844222** or 090/9844375. Fax 090/9844102. www.hotelsignum.it. Reservations advised. Entrees 14€–18€. MC, V. Daily 7–11pm. Closed mid-Nov to mid-Mar.

'nni Lausta ★★ AEOLIAN   "The Lobster" in local dialect, this small restaurant on the *corso* at Santa Marina has an ever-changing, and reassuringly short menu that focuses on seasonal produce, fresh fish, and traditional Aeolian flavors. A small covered terrace is upstairs.

Via Risorgimento, Santa Marina Salina. ©/fax **090/9843486.** www.isolasalina.com. Reservations advised. Entrees 10€–18€. MC, V. Daily 8–11pm. Closed Nov–Mar.

Porto Bello ★★ SEAFOOD   The *porto* of Santa Marina is indeed *bello,* and, overlooking it since 1977, Porto Bello has since become an institution. Founded by the Cataffo family—who take their food very seriously indeed—it offers a romantic terrace that is frequented in high season by yachting types whose boats bob about by the pier below. As to be expected, fish is the order of the day, the freshness advertised by a number of raw dishes such as the *cassata del tonno,* a layering of tuna, mint, and tomatoes, finished with slices of orange. If you fancy a break from fish, try the house pasta, spaghetti *al fuoco* (on fire), a fusion of tomato, basil, garlic, chili, and ricotta.

Lungomare Giuffrè, Santa Marina Salina. © **090/9843125.** portobellosalina@tin.it. Reservations advised. Entrees 10€–18€. AE, MC, V. Mar–Nov daily noon–3pm and 7:30–11pm.

Salina After Dark

Salina has none of the bustling nocturnal activity of Lipari, but there are a couple of Santa Marina bars that sometimes have live music. At the marina, next to the Porto Bello restaurant, is the island's coolest bar, **Layla.** On the piazza overlooking the Lingua, **Alfredo's** bar (© **090/9843075**) is home of *granite* famed across the globe and also a popular haunt for sun-downer drinks. The bar is the heart of the family business that spawned Alfredo in Cucina (above).

PANAREA ★★

The smallest of the Aeolians, Panarea is an island paradise of whitewashed walls dripping with Mediterranean flora, and a coastline dotted with preposterously gorgeous cerulean coves. The fauna, however, may be an acquired taste: It's a popular haunt for the *figli di papà* (rich kids) and Peter Pans from Italy's bigger cities who overrun it in July and August, flush with Daddy's money. Petite Panarea is chic, and it definitely isn't cheap. Book your stay in advance, especially in high season. Prices in late May, June, or September are much more bearable, and you'll have the island almost to yourself. No cars are on the island's narrow whitewashed-walled streets, just golf carts, smoking scooters, and the ubiquitous three-wheeled *ape* mini-trucks.

Resist the temptation to visit Panarea as a day trip from another island; when the boats offload day-trippers in high season, the island is swamped and loses its sleepy Mediterranean charm. If you're going to "do" Panarea, you should stay at least 1 night. During the day, avoid the throng and hire a boat to putter around the gorgeous coves: Cooling off in the crystalline waters, having a floating picnic as you bob around, is the way to enjoy Panarea. As the sun goes down, and the last boats have whisked away the day-visit hordes, the island takes on its chic evening mantle.

Essentials

GETTING THERE   Panarea is between Salina and Stromboli, and is served by the summer **SNAV** (© 081/4285555; www.snav.it) hydrofoil service from Naples, and by the ferries and hydrofoils from Milazzo, usually with a connection at Lipari.

GETTING AROUND   Hydrofoils arrive at the single pier at the village of San Pietro, on the east coast. Most everything on Panarea is walkable, but the best coves are accessible only by sea: Rent a motorboat (**Da Diego,** just a few meters west of the ferry dock; © 338/5774880) or avail of the informal **group shuttle services** from the port to popular swimming areas like Cala Junco and the offshore rock islets of Basiluzzo and Lisca Bianca (about 5€ round-trip): Just hang around the waterfront and follow the swarthy men yelling out "Lisca," "Junco," and so on (see "Exploring the Island," below).

FAST FACTS   Hydrofoil and ferry tickets can be bought at the small ticket office opposite the jetty (hours vary to coincide with departures). The island is serviced by **Siremar** (© 090/983007) and **SNAV** (© 090/983009). For the **Carabinieri** (police), call **090/983181.** It's best to stock up on anything you might need before arriving. There is an **ATM** on the island (although not a bank), at the southern end of the seafront at San Pietro next to the small **supermarket.** Boutiques in the winding streets of San Pietro tend to sell expensive and studiedly carefree boho-chic, although there are a couple of **grocery stores** where you'll be able to find last-minute sun-cream or batteries, and a couple of places selling sandwiches and snacks. The only **pharmacy** on the island is Farmacia Sparacino, Via Comunale Iditella, 12 (© 090/983148), just up beyond the port.

Exploring the Island

San Pietro is the only substantially developed area of tiny Panarea, and even then, it's still very much a village where almost nothing is more than a 5-minute walk from the port. It's not flat, however, and those with luggage will want to snag a **golf-cart taxi:** Many hotels offer this service free of charge; otherwise, the "taxi" stand is by the pier in San Pietro. From San Pietro, you can **walk** to a few beaches and lookout points and the scant remains of a Bronze Age village on the south side of the island. Otherwise, the best way to get around is to **rent a *gozzo* ★★★** (small wooden boat with a sunshade and 25-hp motor). A number of operators at the port rent out these easy-to-drive, no-experience-necessary motorboats, which are the ideal way to explore the inlets on the wilder, uninhabited stretches of coastline that are inaccessible by land. The curve that makes the northwest corner of the island marks the now-sunken crater of the extinct volcano, visible from above when the water is calm. Any time you see a cove with inviting waters—which is just about everywhere around Panarea's perimeter—just drop anchor and dive off your *gozzo*. A full day's rental in high season will cost from 50€ and can double in the height of August, excluding fuel costs, which are higher here than on the mainland. Before you set out on a day's exploration, stock up on water and snacks at one of the minimarkets in town.

SAN PIETRO

The largest of the three hamlets on the east coast of the island, and the site of the single-jetty port, San Pietro is home to the majority of the island's hotels, bars, restaurants, and shops. A couple of agreeable bars look over modest fishing boats toward the moored yachts of oligarchs, and the occasionally smoking hulk of Stromboli beyond. When the sun sets, San Pietro becomes a ridiculously entertaining catwalk for the Italian fashionista-turistas who think nothing of changing outfits three times (three different studiedly carefree bathing suit/pareo combinations, mind you) between 5pm and midnight as they migrate from *aperitivo* to dinner to clubbing at the Hotel Raya. Even if nightlife isn't your thing (but it should be, at least temporarily, while you're on Panarea), **happy hour at the portside bars ★★** is de rigueur. All the day-trippers have left, and Panarea becomes an intimate, fabulous party.

OUT ON THE ISLAND

Heading north from the port, a flight of steps leads up past the whitewashed houses of **Ditella.** Terraces drip with hibiscus, bougainvillea, and jasmine. Passing the sleepy Carabinieri station, the road narrows to become a steeper footpath. Reaching the road there is a view to the right from **Calcara** looking over the fumaroles that give the sea occasional hot zones, and sometimes release steam. The fumaroles are accessible from the road by a very steep footpath. More serious walkers can bear left from the road above Calcara to follow a fairly rugged and steep footpath that climbs up to the **Timpone del Corvo,** giving glorious views across the island and east to Stromboli. The screelike nature of the path means it is best attempted in decent footwear. Go in the morning, and bring water. Following the path, one reaches the splendid **Cala Junco ★★** for a cooling swim. The full circuit back to San Pietro takes a good 4 hours.

Much less demanding than the above-described hike is the route to **Cala Junco** (pronounced "*yoon*-ko") heading south from San Pietro. Leaving town, the road has views down to the sea on your left and red rocks on your right dripping with prickly pears. Passing into the cluster of low white houses at **Drauto,** you come to the simple **Sirena** bar/restaurant, which has an agreeable terrace on which to seek refreshment. The Sirena also rents rooms (www.hotelsirena-panarea.com). The road then leads to **Zimmari ★**, the only sandy beach on Panarea: Though it suffered a great deal from the storms of the winter of 2008 to 2009 and is somewhat reduced in size, it is packed in busy periods. The pleasant bar/restaurant **Da Nunzio** (see "Where to Dine," p. 270) overlooks the beach. Picking your way over the large volcanic stones that make up the second part of the beach leads to a steep stepped path that gives views across the bay toward the Basiluzzo and Lisca Bianca outcrops. Best avoided by vertigo-sufferers, the path curves past a large red rock with views down to **Punta Milazzese** ★. Excavations carried out here in 1948 uncovered the remains of 23 Bronze Age huts, their circular forms clearly visible from the path. Continue down the path from the Bronze Age village to the "beach" of Cala Junco, where there is no sand but large, smooth boulders that make surprisingly comfortable (really!) lounge chairs. The cerulean bay of **Cala Junco** ★★ is a favored place of the boating set, who anchor their yachts and cigarette boats here—the cove offers shelter from the ever-present winds of Aeolus—for lazy afternoons of sunning, swimming, and champagne-sipping. You and your *gozzo* are welcome, too, or just hop on one of the shuttle service boats from San Pietro.

THE ISLETS OFF PANAREA

Across the water from San Pietro are the striking *isolotti* (mini-islands) of Dattilo (directly east), Lisca Bianca (also to the east, past Dattilo), and Basiluzzo (a long, wedge-shaped wall of rock and two adjacent rock stacks, to the northeast—Stromboli is directly behind it). Tourist boat excursions to these islets depart all day long from San Pietro harbor, although in high season, **Lisca Bianca** is horrendously crowded—you'll be fighting for a spot on the pebbles. There is, however, a tradition with the Arco degli Innamorati (Lovers' Arch) that honeymooners won't be able to resist: A

Diving in the Aeolians

The Aeolians are a good spot for divers of all levels of experience between late May and September. The visible islands above sea level are, so to speak, the tip of the iceberg. That means that close to the shore the rock face plunges into vast depths, and this deep cool water is home to all sorts of interesting marine life, including grouper and lobster. Furthermore, the intense human activity in these areas over recent millennia has made it a treasure-trove for archaeological finds, some of which still languish on the seabed. (There are fragments of Roman ships under the water here, but they're strictly off-limits to divers.) Just off **Filicudi** there is even an **underwater annex of the archaeological museum** (suitable for fairly experienced divers with a guide). At **Panarea**, explore the area around the **Basiluzzo**, the rocks known as the **Formiche** (Ants), and the bubbling **fumaroles**. Off **Stromboli**, venture out to **Strombolicchio**, and off **Salina**, explore the collapsed crater at **Pollara**. The following diving centers cover all of the islands except Filicudi and Alicudi, both of which can be visited as diving excursions from the larger islands.

Amphibia (✆ 335/1245332 or 335/6138529; www.amphibia.it) has two fully accredited diving centers in the archipelago. The older of the two opened in 1997 on **Panarea**, just by the jetty at San Pietro. The other is on **Salina**, by the jetty at Santa Marina, and opened in 2004. Also on **Panarea**, the **Hotel Lisca Bianca** (✆ 090/983004; www.liscabianca.it), just by the jetty at San Pietro, has a diving center. On **Stromboli, Diving Club La Sirenetta** (✆ 090/986025; www.lasirenetta diving.it) is at the Sirenetta Park Hotel. On **Lipari, Diving Center La Gorgonia** (✆ 090/9812616; www.lagorgonia diving.it) is at the Marina Corta, on Salita S. Giuseppe. On **Vulcano, Diving Center Saracen** (✆ 090/9852189 or 347/7283341; www.divingcenter saracen.it) is close to the Spiagge Nere, by the Bar Saracen.

swim underneath the arch, local legend has it, means that the couple will be together forever. A better option is **Basiluzzo** ★★, where you can swim in the gorgeous emerald water beneath a sheer wall of striated limestone. Some vestiges of Roman ruins are visible here, and Roman artifacts nestled on the seabed below.

Where to Stay

Da Francesco ★★ 🍴 Directly overlooking the port, this *trattoria* also has 12 spotless, recently redecorated, air-conditioned rooms that offer a more wallet-friendly alternative to the big hotels. Most rooms have a small outside area, and room 11 has a sea-view terrace. Breakfast is served on the terrace of the *trattoria,* which offers good home-cooked food (see "Where to Dine," below).

Lungomare San Pietro. ⓒ **090/983023.** www.dafrancescopanarea.com. 12 units. 30€–80€ per person per night. Rates include breakfast. MC, V. **Amenities:** Restaurant; bar. *In room:* A/C.

Hotel Raya ★★ 📷 In the 1960s, the first hotel on the island was opened by Myriam Beltrami, who sought to create a refuge among the unspoiled nature of the island. Today's hotel still uses all-natural materials, from the paint to the biodegradable shampoo and organic produce. Soon after it opened, the hotel became a mecca for the key players of the swinging decade, and the hotel has since been synonymous with all that is uber-chic. In high season, the rooftop bar with views over the sea toward Stromboli is *the* place to be seen. Despite being so thoroughly in with the in-crowd, it remains elegantly understated; rooms are amidst the bougainvillea, prickly pears, and hibiscus, and each has sea views—but there isn't a TV or Wi-Fi network in sight. Despite the good restaurant, and the sea-view pool with volcanically heated water, the Raya has never sought a revision of the two stars (low on the totem pole of the Italian hospitality rating system—most high-end hotels have five) assigned to it in the 1960s, and proudly wears them as a badge of inverted snobbery. Though room rates are high, you're paying for the Raya's gorgeous setting and cult status.

Via S. Pietro. ⓒ **090/983013.** www.hotelraya.it. 30 units. 180€–540€ double; 420€–750€ suites. Rates include breakfast. No children 11 or under. MC, V. Closed Nov–Mar. **Amenities:** Restaurant; bar; pool. *In room:* A/C, hair dryer.

Hotel Tesoriero ★★ A stone's throw from the single jetty at San Pietro, the Hotel Tesoriero is a pretty jumble of white painted cubes set in a garden of colorful bougainvillea. Run by the Tesoriero family since the mid-1980s, it was retiled and refurbished in 2006. There is a communal sea-view terrace and ground-floor outdoor area, and four rooms have terraces. Rooms are simple but spotless and comfortable, and breakfast is of the continental variety. Upon request, half-board is available with Da Paolino (see "Where to Dine," below).

Via S. Pietro. ⓒ **090/983098** or 090/983144. www.hoteltesoriero.it. 13 units. 90€–240€ double. Rates include breakfast. No children 11 or under. AE, DC, MC, V. Closed mid-Sept to mid-Mar. **Amenities:** Bar. *In room:* A/C, TV, hair dryer.

Lisca Bianca ★★ Despite being part of the Best Western franchise, the Lisca Bianca remains very much a family affair. Directly opposite the jetty at San Pietro, all rooms have a terrace or small patio. Three price levels—standard, superior, and executive—reflect room size and whether views are of the sea or the garden. Breakfast is served on the cool tiled terrace with views toward Stromboli, beyond the hulk of Basiluzzo rock. Come sundown, the terrace with its blue-cushioned iron chairs and tiled tables becomes one of the island's *aperitivo* hot spots. The hotel also has an annex at the next village over, **Ditella,** with sea views and a double and triple room, two bathrooms, sitting room, and small kitchen that can be booked as a family unit. The hotel's diving center and boat rental will set you up for exploring the seas.

Via Lani, 1, 98050 Panarea, Italia. ⓒ **090/983004** or 090/983005. Fax 090/983291. www.liscabianca. it. 35 units. 180€–540€ double; 420€–750€ suites. Rates include breakfast. AE, DC, MC, V. Closed Nov-Mar. **Amenities:** Restaurant; bar; babysitting; boat rental; room service. *In room:* A/C, TV, hair dryer, minibar, Wi-Fi (fee).

Where to Dine

Da Adelina ★★★ 🍴 CREATIVE AEOLIAN   Right on the sea-front, chef Giovanni Sorano, a native of Messina and previously of Filomena in Washington, D.C., conjures up sophisticated reworkings of traditional Aeolian dishes using local ingredients in the cozy dining room overlooking the port. The wild fennel so characteristic of these islands crops up again and again, as do home-salted anchovies. The menu changes regularly to accommodate seasonal produce, much of which comes from the restaurant's own garden. I enjoyed gnocchi made with squid ink and served with artichoke hearts and mussels, and crispy *lasagnette* (mini-lasagne) with seafood.

Via Comunale del Porto 28. ⓒ **090/983277.** Reservations recommended. Entrees 14€–20€. AE, MC, V. Daily 8–11pm. Closed mid-Oct to late May.

Da Francesco ★★ 🍴 SICILIAN   The *trattoria,* which spawned the small hotel of the same name (see above), provides good-value local staples on a terrace overlooking the *porticciolo* (small port). Many of the vegetables come from the adjacent garden, and specialties include spaghetti *alla disgraziata* ("disgraceful woman") with capers and tomatoes, and fresh fish cooked simply. Da Francesco's empire continued to expand in 2009 with the opening of a "fast food" joint, ideal for a picnic lunch of *polpette alle melanzane* (meatballs with eggplant) as you bob about on your *gozzo.*

Lungomare San Pietro. ⓒ **090/983023.** www.dafrancescopanarea.com. Entrees 8€–16€. MC, V. Daily 12:30–3pm and 8–11pm. Closed late Oct to May.

Da Paolino ★★ 🍴 AEOLIAN   A 10-minute walk from San Pietro toward Calcara, Da Paolino is a charming *trattoria* offering good value and honest-to-goodness homecooking on a beautiful terrace with views toward Stromboli. Specialties include spaghetti *millebaci* ("a thousand kisses"), a sort of Aeolian pesto with wild fennel and capers. Fish is fresh and cooked simply, and you can enjoy the view while the eponymous Paolino and his family feed you.

Via Iditella 75. ⓒ **090/983008** or 339/1325473. Reservations advised. Entrees 10€–16€. MC, V. Daily 12:30–3pm and 7.30–11pm. Closed mid-Oct to late May.

Hycesia ★★ 📷 AEOLIAN   In the tangle of streets above the port, the Hycesia has been providing beautifully cooked fresh fish to the beautiful people on its elegantly rustic and splendidly charming covered terrace since 1979. First opened by Maria Maisano, it is now run by her sons Marcello and Gaetano, and Gaetano's wife Andrea. The emphasis is on the innovative use of high-quality, fresh ingredients, and the menu varies constantly. Specialties include the simple marine flavors of spaghetti *ai ricci di mare* (with sea urchins), and the wildly delicious *scorfano* (scorpion fish) with wild fennel. The proprietors will be happy to guide you through their excellent selection of Sicilian wine.

Via San Pietro. ⓒ **090/98304** or 090/983226. www.hycesia.it. Reservations advised. Entrees from 15€. AE, MC, V. Daily 8–11pm. Closed late Oct to Apr.

Looking the Part

Seriously expensive faux hippie-chic is the Panarea look; wander around the handful of boutiques just off the port and it can be yours. As the sun goes down, women show off their tans (and taut bellies) in barely there floating silk numbers (of the sort sourced in Indonesia by the Raya's founder Myriam Beltrami, high priestess of "the look"; the Raya has its own boutique). "Casually" thrown over the tenth bikini of the day, the sarong is accessorized with big sunglasses, surprisingly expensive beads, and flip-flops hand-woven from a rare grass grown by a nearly extinct tribe in the Amazon basin, and yours for only 100€.

Panarea After Dark

As the sun begins to set, it is time for an *aperitivo*. The most fashionable spot is the rooftop terrace at the **Hotel Raya.** To start the evening off, try the loosely Moroccan-themed **Bar Banacalii,** on the wooden veranda overlooking the port, at the **Hotel Lisca Bianca:** The best tables are upstairs on the elegant terrace. The rich, under-25 set flocks with religious devotion to a "sushi bar" above the port called **The Bridge** for *aperitivo*. A little farther afield, **Da Nunzio** at Zimmari is a good spot for a sun-downer overlooking the beach. Equally pleasant, but with much less flash, there are a few more "normal" Italian bars (where you can get an iced coffee or a beer, simple cocktails or a smoothie) on the port opposite the jetty. Panarea's only nightclub is at the **Hotel Raya,** where the key word is *posh.*

STROMBOLI ★★

The most isolated of the archipelago, Stromboli (the accent is on the first syllable) is at the northeast extremity of the Aeolians, and is Europe's most active volcano. Its name derives from the Greek *strongyle,* meaning circular, and seen from afar it is a child's drawing of what a volcano should look like. Its single cone rises 926m (3,038 ft.) out of the sea, belching clouds of white smoke you can set your watch by. A recurring feature in classical literature, Stromboli is sometimes identified with the treacherous "wandering rocks" described to Ulysses, by the sorceress Circe.

Today, volcano buffs swarm to the island to witness the spectacular eruptions, best seen at night when the cascades of molten lava illuminate the hillside. For active types, the evening trek to the *Sciara del Fuoco* will be the highlight of traveling to the Aeolians. The island is particularly favored by German visitors, and is very much in keeping with the Romantic Teutonic tradition of dramatic landscapes. The island is an active volcano, bubbling and belching away under your feet. The black soil is rich in minerals and produces bigger, brighter, bolder vegetation. This rampant fecundity, combined with the intermittent rumbling of the beast beneath, and a distinct sense of isolation, can be extremely disquieting. It has been known for visitors to arrive in the morning only to set sail the same evening in search of somewhere a little less unnervingly wild. Car-free, the island has one "main" road running from the port along the shore to Ficogrande, and another from the port at Stromboli up to the upper part of the town at San Vincenzo. Hotels have electric buggies to pick you up; otherwise, local traffic is limited to scooters and *api,* the little scooter-powered vans.

Essentials

GETTING THERE   The most northeasterly of the archipelago, Stromboli is the first stop for the summer SNAV service from Naples, and is served by the ferries and hydrofoils from Milazzo, often with a connection at Lipari.

GETTING AROUND   The island covers an area of 13 sq. km (5 sq. miles). Stromboli town is a sprawling series of hamlets running along the shoreline and up to the main piazza at San Vincenzo. From the port at Scari up to San Vincenzo is a 10-minute uphill walk, while along the shore to the area of Piscità, the farthest extremity is about 2.4km (1½ miles). Several agencies at the port hawk deals ranging from cruises to boat trips; a reliable one near the jetty at Stromboli, and identifiable by the girl-riding-shark logo, is **Sabbia Nera,** Via Marina (✆ **090/986390;** www.sabbianera stromboli.com). Open from Easter to September, daily from 9am to 1pm and 3 to 7pm, they rent boats and scooters, organize boat trips by day and night around Stromboli and to surrounding islands, organize excursions to the top of the volcano with accredited guides, and do pretty much everything else you could require on the island. Boat rentals for tours around Stromboli begin at 150€ a day (fuel extra). You can also rent a scooter here from 20€ a day (plus fuel).

FAST FACTS   The hydrofoil and ferry companies **Siremar** (✆ 090/986016) and **SNAV** (✆ 090/986003; www.snav.it) both have offices along the harbor road at the port and are easy to spot. Boats arrive from Milazzo April to September only. From June to September, SNAV runs a hydrofoil direct between Stromboli and Naples. The **Carabinieri** (police) are reachable at 090/986021. The local **pharmacy,** Via Roma 2 (✆ 090/986713), is open daily from 8:30am to 1pm and 4:30 to 8pm (longer hours in Aug). The **post office,** Via Roma (✆ 090/986261), is open Monday to Friday 8am to 1:30pm and Saturday 8am to 12:30pm.

Exploring the Island

There are two main settlements on opposite sides of the island, **Ginostra** and **Stromboli,** both served by hydrofoils and ferries. **Ginostra** ★ is only accessible by boat and boasts what Ginostrians like to refer to as the smallest port in the world, the **Scalo di Pertuso.** Naturally hewn from the rock, it is far too small for ferries and hydrofoils to dock alongside, so passengers are transported to the tiny port by way of a pilot ship, *Il Rollo.* On land, a flight of stairs leads up to the village, the only one in the Aeolians without central electricity. The village is a picturesque, and very rustic, cluster of summer homes with two restaurants and two shops. It's favored by aging hippies, and suffice it to say that if you require all mod cons this is not the right place for you. If, however, you want some real no-frills rusticity, you will be in your element.

East of Ginostra, and only accessible by boat, on the extreme southern point of the island, the dramatic grey granite rocks of **Punta Lena** ★ provide a rugged and relatively under-populated spot for bathing in the crystalline waters. The western shore of the island is dominated by the **Sciara del Fuoco** ★★★, where the volcano's spectacular show is played out, while tourist activity is concentrated in the town of **Stromboli** on the northeastern coast. Served by the single jetty port at **Scari,** Stromboli town is actually an agglomeration of three settlements, **Ficogrande, San Vincenzo,** and **Piscità,** rather than a town with a center. **Ficogrande** runs north along the coast from the port along the small coast road at sea level. Rounding the bend, an extinct sunken volcano called **Strombolicchio** comes into view just out to sea.

The most popular beaches on the island are the black sandy coves at **Piscità,** although be warned: They are very busy in the summer. Always less crowded is the **Forgia Vecchia** beach, a 10-minute walk from the pier at **Scari,** heading south along the coast. This black-pebble beach has a spectacular natural setting, with views up to the looming volcano above, and the water is crystal clear (although usually teeming with yachts in high summer). Continuing north along **Ficogrande,** after passing La Sirenetta Hotel on your left, the *lungomare* leads up a narrow street with houses and gardens on either side. The area of **Piscità ★** with its charming houses glimpsed behind high walls is home to Domenico Dolce and Stefano Gabbana's summer retreat. The walled street offers occasional access down on the right to the popular dark sandy beaches, the great hulk of the volcano rising up on your left. Occasional green signs marked "waiting area" (as in, assemble here and wait for the all-clear in case of a big eruption!) are a reminder of the rumbling beneath your feet. At the fork in the road, bear left and continue past the church of St. Bartholomew to the upper town at **San Vincenzo,** or keep right on the path up to the **Semaforo.** The road to Semaforo gives way to the *Mulattiera* (literally "The Mule Track"). The fairly steep path takes about an hour, and pauses for breath are rewarded with splendid **views ★★** down over the houses of Piscità and the slopes of the island. Before dusk, swarms make their way up to witness the fiery lava flows at **Sciara del Fuoco ★★★**, which reach maximum spectacle at night. Remember to take a flashlight to find your way back down again.

To reach the **summit of the volcano,** you need to go with an accredited guide in groups of no more than 20; various companies offer guided walks, including **Magmatrek,** Via Vittorio Emanuele (② **090/9865768;** www.magmatrek.com), and **Stromboli Adventures,** corner of Piazza San Vincenzo and Via Vittorio Emanuele (www.stromboliadventures.it; ② **090/986264**). Book in advance in high season to be sure of a spot. The group tours cost 25€ and take 5 to 6 hours—including between 30 minutes and an hour at the summit—and start from either Stromboli or Ginostra. Reasonable physical condition is required, children 9 and under are not allowed, and contact lens wearers should bear in mind that lenses are incompatible with volcanic dust. It is also worth bearing in mind that it can get a bit chilly, even in the dead of August.

Diving expeditions are offered by the diving center at La Sirenetta Park Hotel (below); favorite sites include the caves of the Secca del Scirocco, suitable for expert divers. The steepness with which the volcano plunges into the sea (the seabed is 2,000m/6,562 ft. deep under Sciara del Fuoco) favors a number of deep-sea fish, including barracuda, *cernia* (grouper), and the occasional lobster.

Where to Stay

There are many holiday rentals on the island; for example, **Stromboli Paradise** (② **340/159-5757;** www.stromboliparadise.com) rents houses at Ficogrande and Piscità.

La Locanda del Barbablu ★   In the upper part of Stromboli town, close to the church of San Vincenzo, the deep-pink and orange stucco exterior of this charming 19th-century inn suggests the idiosyncratic yet simple rustic charm of the interior. Rooms are small but comfortably furnished with charming rustic antiques. A wide terrace opens onto dramatic views of the volcano and the sea. All rooms have well-maintained bathrooms with shower/tub combinations. The restaurant is good and only offers an evening tasting menu (50€, drinks excluded; booking required); it changes daily but is usually based on fresh fish. Early-nighters might bear in mind that sounds of revelry may make their way up to the rooms from the bar.

Via Vittorio Emanuele 17–19, Stromboli, 98050. ⓒ **090/986118.** Fax 090/986323. www.barbablu.it. 5 units. Double 140€–240€, minimum 2 nights. AE, DC, MC, V. Closed mid-Oct to mid-Apr. **Amenities:** Restaurant; bar. *In room:* Hair dryer.

La Sirenetta Park Hotel ★★   On the coast at Ficogrande, a short electric-cart ride from the port, the Sirenetta was the first hotel on the island. It was opened in the 1950s by Domenico Russo, the island's schoolteacher, who had rented out adjoining houses in the upper town at San Vincenzo to Ingrid Bergman and Roberto Rossellini for the filming of *Stromboli*. When the crowds began to descend following the movie's success, he built a collection of rooms around a small courtyard at Ficograndi, and gradually the hotel expanded to its current 50 rooms. Now run by Domenico's son, Vito Russo, the "Little Mermaid" has whitewashed buildings that drip with colorful bougainvillea and palm trees; most units have sea-view terraces. When making reservations, specify the (pricier) renovated rooms: The older ones look a bit tired. An abundant breakfast is served on the covered terrace at the front of the hotel, looking across to Strombolicchio. Half-board is offered.

Via Marina 33, 98050 Ficogrande (Stromboli). ⓒ **090/986025.** Fax 090/986124. www.lasirenetta.it. 60 units. Double 130€–310€ (depending on category and season); double with half-board 170€–380€. Rates include breakfast. AE, DC, MC, V. Closed Nov 1 to mid-Apr. **Amenities:** 2 bars; fitness center; free Internet station in lobby; saltwater pool; room service; rooms for those w/limited mobility; smoke-free rooms; tennis court; watersports. *In room:* A/C, TV, hair dryer, minibar.

Where to Dine

Da Zurro ★ 🍴 SEAFOOD   Close to the port, near the Ossidiana Hotel, this restaurant's brusque lighting and slightly battered exterior air belies a wealth of deliciousness inside. Zurro himself is a fisherman turned cook, and boy does he know his fish. Here you'll find an excellent *spaghetti alla strombolana* (capers, tomatoes, anchovies, garlic, toasted breadcrumbs), as well as the creative use of whatever the ships brought in that morning.

Via Picone 18, Stromboli. ⓒ **090/986283.** Reservations recommended. Main courses 15€. MC, V. Daily 7–11pm. Closed Nov–Easter.

Punta Lena ★★ 🍴 AEOLIAN   On the coastal road leading toward Ficogrande from the port, Punta Lena is arguably the best restaurant on the island. The charming blue-and-white dining room leads out onto a terrace over the sea that is the setting for Chef Stefano's locally inspired creations. Order whatever was landed that morning, and you won't go wrong.

Via Marina 8 (Località Ficogrande). ⓒ **090/986204.** Reservations recommended. Main courses 15€. AE, DC, MC, V. Daily 12:15–2:30pm and 7:30–10:30pm. Closed Nov–Mar.

Stromboli After Dark

As the sun starts to go down, and the glow of the volcano lights up the evening sky, thoughts turn to the *aperitivo*. A popular spot is **Ritrovo Ingrid,** Piazza San Vincenzo (ⓒ **090/986385**), which offers great views from its terrace and is named after you-know-who. Open evenings only, until 3am, it is closed one week on a Sunday, the next on a Monday. If Ingrid's having her day off, try **Il Malandrino,** Via Marina (ⓒ **090/986376**), also open 6 days a week—it alternates days off with Ritrovo Ingrid. Live music is often found at **La Tartana,** Via Marina 33, Ficogrande (ⓒ **090/986025**);

open from June to September daily from 9pm to 2am, it is on the beach opposite La Sirenetta hotel.

FILICUDI ★

Known by the Greeks as Phoenicusa, meaning rich in ferns, uncompromisingly rustic Filicudi has a permanent population of just 200 souls, divided between nine *contrade* (districts) that occupy the southeastern area of the island. The larger of these are Filicudi Porto and Pecorini a Mare. The population of the island rises during the summer to a couple of thousand, and on the south of the island, to the east of Pecorini a Mare, the locality Stimpagnato is entirely made up of holiday homes. Unless you are feeling intrepid, the uninhabited remainder of the island is best explored by boat. The coastal landscape is characterized by rugged terraces rampant with gorse, stony beaches, and steep cliffs that plunge down into caves, of which the most celebrated is the **Grotto del Bue Marino,** near Punta Perciato. *Sciare,* paths carved into the rock by the distant eruptions of the island's volcanoes, run down to the sea. Filicudi is dominated by the extinct volcano of the *Fossa Felci* (774m/2,540 ft.), the largest—but by no means the only—volcano on the island; the other seven are long extinct and largely eroded.

Such is Filicudi's isolation (7 nautical miles west of Salina) that in the early 1970s, 15 members of the Greco Mafia clan from Corleone on the Sicilian "mainland" were interned on the island, far from their criminal empire, much to the chagrin of the *Filicudiani.* No longer an internment camp, the island is favored by graying members of the literati. The ever-so-slightly eccentric are joined by members of émigré island families who all come for the peace and quiet. And quiet it is . . . electricity first came to the island in 1986, and if you are looking for Wi-Fi, all mod cons, and nightlife, Filicudi is not your choice. But if rustic isolation is your thing, bring lots of books, and you'll be in your element.

Essentials

GETTING THERE   Ferries and hydrofoils from Milazzo dock at the single jetty port at Filicudi Porto. Filicudi is on the Milazzo, Vulcano, Lipari, Salina, Filicudi, Alicudi route. For Panarea and Stromboli, and the SNAV hydrofoil to and from Naples, it will be necessary to change and spend the night on Salina.

GETTING AROUND   The island is best explored on foot or by boat; the single tarmac road that snakes between the nine contrade gives a false impression of longer distances when, in fact, you can easily **walk** between them on the much more direct *mulattiere* (paths originally intended for mules) that cut through the terraces of the island. From the port to Pecorini, it will take about 20 minutes. If you would like to **rent a scooter or a boat,** try **I Delfini** diving club by the port (✆ **090/9889077;** www.idelfinifilicudi.it).

FAST FACTS   For **ferry** and **hydrofoil** tickets and information, the Siremar window at the port is only open just before sailings (✆ **090/9889975**). In a medical emergency, call the **guardia medica** (✆ **090/9889691**). For the **Carabinieri** (police), call ✆ **090/9889942.** At the time of writing, there was no **pharmacy** on the island, a subject of distinct local protest, and no **ATM.** The island's **post office** is on Via Pecorini (✆ **090/9889053**). Credit cards are accepted at some hotels and restaurants, but for everything else come prepared with cash. The fishermen who give boat trips will not smile upon your Amex, and if you are renting a room privately, cash is the norm.

Exploring the Island

The inhabited part of the island is in the southeastern corner, on either side of the isthmus that leads to the point of **Capo Graziano.** This was the site of excavations of two early Bronze Age settlements, and the area gives its name to the "Capo Graziano culture," a period of settlement in the archipelago in the early 2nd millennium B.C.

An **underwater archaeological museum** ★★ lies off the coast of Capo Graziano. Accessible to experienced scuba divers accompanied by a local guide, it serves as a reminder of the innumerable shipwrecks off these coasts. Relics date from Greek ships of the 5th century B.C. to a 17th-century Spanish galleon. For information on visiting the site and other dives off Filicudi, contact I Delfini (above).

The **Spiaggia del Porto** and **Spiaggia di Pecorini** on either side of Capo Graziano are good pebbly beaches (no sandy beaches are on the island), and countless coves and inlets are ready to explore on boat trips around the island. Keep an eye out to the north of the island for a vast pointed basalt rock known as **Il Giafante,** Sicilian dialect for "elephant," the animal it (very approximately) resembles. On the west coast of the island, **Punta Perciato,** a natural arch carved out of the volcanic rock by infinite waves, sticks out into the sea. Nearby is the **Grotta del Bue Marino** ★★. The most celebrated of the myriad caves around the island's coastline, "the Cave of the Sea-Ox" is named for the oxenlike "lowing" made by the echo of the waves. Rent a boat at the port, or catch a ride with a fisherman to get close, then swim into the cave to appreciate the beautiful light effects that turn the water an extraordinary shade of deep turquoise. The **Festa del Mare** is a moveable feast, celebrated here each August, when a candlelit procession of decorated boats makes its way toward the cave where a statue of Eolus is deposited on the seabed.

The sunset from **Stimpagnato** ★, on the south of the island, to the east of Pecorini a Mare, is spectacular. The sun sinks into the sea by the rock known as La Canna, with Alicudi in the background.

Where to Stay

La Canna Up on a hill high above the port, this traditional whitewashed Aeolian hotel is open year-round, and offers splendid views. On arrival you will be met at the pier and driven to the hotel. For the rest of your stay, a steep flight of steps leads down to the beach; if just thinking about it sounds like too much effort, you can concede to enjoy the fabulous views from the pool.

Via Rosa, 43, 98050, Filicudi. 🕐 **090/9889956.** Fax 090/9889966. www.lacannahotel.it. 14 units. Double 45€–80€ per person per night. In high season, prices include obligatory half-board and a minimum 1 week stay, 85€–105€ per person per night. Rates include breakfast. **Amenities:** Restaurant; bar; boat trips; pool; scooter rental. In room: A/C, TV.

La Sirena ★ Earning a star for its splendid location directly on the beach at Pecorini a Mare, La Sirena offers simple but comfortable rooms, each with a sea-view balcony. "The Mermaid" is run with enthusiasm and charm by Antonio and his wife Alina. In July and August half-board is obligatory, no great sacrifice considering the restaurant is among the best on the island (see "Where to Dine," below). Antonio and Alina also rent rooms and small houses around the island.

Via Pecorini Mare. 🕐 **090/9889997.** pensionelasirena.it. 35€–40€ per person Sept to late June and July–Aug 80€–90€ per person, including dinner. Rates include breakfast. AE, MC, V. **Amenities:** Restaurant; bar. In room: A/C and/or fan.

Where to Dine

La Sirena ★ CREATIVE SICILIAN   La Sirena's terrace by the beach at Pecorini is full of enthusiastic and successful reworkings of Sicilian classics: Spaghetti is served with squid ink or almond pesto, and fish dishes include a juicy sausage of fresh tuna served with caramelized onion jam, and marinated swordfish. Service is friendly and unhurried, and the quality of the food top-notch.

Via Pecorini Mare. *©* **090/9889997.** pensionelasirena.it. Reservations recommended in season. Main courses 15€. AE, MC, V. Daily noon–3pm and 7:30–11pm.

Villa La Rosa ★ SEAFOOD/SICILIAN   Villa la Rosa's ample terrace combined with chef Adelaide Rando's enthusiasm for Filicudian cooking makes this a delightful supper choice. The inevitably fish-based menu varies according to the catch of the day. When I sampled, the risotto of black rice with fresh prawns and caper flowers was excellent, as was the swordfish served with couscous and fresh chili, a reminder of Sicily's proximity to North Africa.

Via Rosa 24. *©* **090/9889965.** www.villalarosa.it. Reservations recommended in season. Main courses 18€. MC, V. Daily noon–3pm and 7:30–11pm. Closed late Sept to May.

ALICUDI

An uncompromisingly rugged cone—so textbook "volcano"-looking and surrounded by water so gorgeously blue as to seem almost fake—at the western-most reaches of the archipelago, Alicudi makes sleepy Filicudi look like New York City. Thirty-four nautical miles separate the island from Lipari, but the feel is light years away. A hundred or so inhabitants live year-round on the 5-sq.-km (2-sq.-mile) island, served by just one hotel/restaurant, and one road, which runs the short distance between the helipad (for emergencies) and the pier. Not a single motorized vehicle or bicycle is on Alicudi. If you do not lug your bags up the steep steps cut into the lavic rock yourself, chances are one of the island's mules will do the job for you.

The island was formed about 150,000 years ago by the long extinct, and almost perfectly round, *Montagnola* volcano. Inhabited since the 17th century B.C., the modern name comes from the Greek *Ericusa,* meaning "rich in heather"—which still proliferates on the slopes of the island. Alicudi's fertile soil is today chiefly exploited for the cultivation of olives and vines, and is reflected in the colorful bougainvillea and prickly pears that soften the island's inhospitable slopes. Alicudi reaches a height of 675m (2,215 ft.), about a quarter of the volcano's total height, which plunges to a depth of 1,500m (4,921 ft.) below sea level. The steepness with which the shore drops away makes the deep waters close to the island ideal for pulling in sea creatures usually found in open water; *ricciola* (the greater amberjack), *cernia* (grouper), and even lobster are harvested in these waters. Divers can enjoy the fauna, or even a spot of underwater fishing near the rock of Jalera.

Essentials

GETTING THERE   If you're planning a day trip to Alicudi, you can organize a private boat trip from the island where you are staying. Alternatively, start early and, in high season, you can generally fit in a visit with the scheduled sailings. The usual Aeolian caveat applies, however: The best laid plans are at the mercy of the wind and the waves. Alicudi is on the Milazzo, Vulcano, Lipari, Salina, Filicudi route (**Siremar;** www.siremar.it; *©* **090/9889795**).

GETTING AROUND   Ferries and hydrofoils arrive at the pier in sleepy Alicudi Porto. From there the only hotel is a short **walk** down the only stretch of tarmac (which leads to the island's **emergency helipad**). To rent a boat, or take a trip, simply negotiate with the fishermen at the port.

FAST FACTS   The island's only two small grocery stores, the Bar Airone, and the post office are in tiny Alicudi Porto. In a medical emergency, call ✆ **090/9889913.** The **post office** at the port (✆ **090/9889911**) is open Monday through Saturday 8:30am to 1pm. There is no **bank** or **ATM** on the island.

Exploring the Island

Beyond Alicudi Porto, the island's **beaches** (more stony inlets than real beaches) are largely concentrated on the eastern coast of the island, near the port area but only accessible by sea. You can either **hire your own boat** or catch a ride with the fishermen at the port for a few euros. A full trip around the island is strongly advised; the full glory of the steep and inhospitable western coast can only be appreciated from the sea. The best beach is at **Bazzina,** which—compared to the rest of the island—has relatively shallow waters close to the shore and is excellent for snorkeling (rental equipment is not always available on Alicudi; it's best to rent your mask, snorkel, and fins from another island). A stiff climb not for the faint-hearted to the highest area of the island, **Filo dell'Arpa** ("Harp String," 675m/2,215 ft.), reveals a marked difference in vegetation from the lower 300m (984 ft.), as the olives and prickly pears give way to ferns and chestnut trees.

Where to Stay & Dine

Casa Mulino   Just up from the port and the beach, this traditional whitewashed Aeolian house is surrounded by Mediterranean vegetation and has been converted into one-, two-, and three-bedroom self-catering mini-apartments (complete with kitchen). *Spartan* is once again the watchword here. Ask for a room with sea-view terrace protected from the midday sun by traditional Aeolian cane roofs.

Via Regina Elena. ✆ **090/9889681.** www.alicudicasamulino.it. Double 70€–100€; 4-person apt 100€–200€ per day; 6-person apt 140€–250€.

Hotel Ericusa   This is the only hotel on the island (and the only restaurant and bar), located on the beach close to Alicudi port. Rooms are spartan and basic. Prices are either half- or full-board, and meals are served on the covered terrace looking out toward the distant Sicilian mainland. Ericusa's dining room is also the only restaurant on the island; the local dishes vary from day to day and are limited to what the fishermen have landed.

Via Regina Elena. ✆ **090/9889902.** www.alicudihotel.it. 21 units. Double with half-board 75€–95€ per person; full-board 95€–115€ per person. MC, V. **Amenities:** Restaurant; bar.

EGADI ISLANDS

Within tantalizing reach of the western coast of Sicily, the Egadi Islands are a laid-back archipelago with striking natural beauty and plenty of manmade charms. Sailing toward the sun-beaten, windswept Egadi from nearby Trapani or Marsala, the islands—Favignana, Levanzo, and Marettimo—can appear somewhat harsh, but as you pull closer to shore, you'll find crystalline water in the most gorgeous shades of emerald and turquoise, real towns with real character, and surprisingly dramatic landscapes.

Unlike the Aeolian islands, that other Sicilian archipelago with which they're often compared, the Egadi are new to the tourist scene and still have the feel of authentic, working islands that just also happen to welcome visitors warmly. Life goes on in the picturesque fishing villages of Favignana, Levanzo, and Marettimo (each island has one, eponymous town) as it has for generations, with residents following daily rhythms and making a living off the sea. While the Egadi are within day-trip distance of both Trapani and Marsala, a few days' stay is recommended, as each island has its own unique offerings, whether manmade or natural.

STRATEGIES FOR SEEING THE ISLANDS

Unlike the Aeolian Islands, the Egadi are relatively close to, and easy to reach from, the Sicilian "mainland." They're also a lot cheaper than the Aeolians (except in Aug, when hotel prices here are just as criminally expensive). With the most developed tourist infrastructure and best swimming in the Egadi, Favignana is the most common base for a trip to these islands, but you can also stay on small, quiet Levanzo for more solitude. Magnificent Marettimo, by comparison, is positively remote, though there are a few overnight accommodations and tourist services here, too.

Boat service between the Egadi is regular and reliable, so it's perfectly convenient to base yourself on Favignana, as many vacationers do, and make daytime forays to Levanzo and Marettimo. Favignana and Levanzo are only 10 minutes apart by hydrofoil (30 min. by ferry), while the trip from Levanzo to Marettimo is a bit longer (35 min. by hydrofoil, 1 hr. by ferry). If, however, you're looking for a destination where you can unplug completely, surrounded by stupendous nature and an authentic community, book a stay on Marettimo and forget the other two islands.

With frequent connections from "mainland" Sicily (Trapani and Marsala), it's also realistic, if you're staying anywhere in western Sicily, to make a day trip of one or two of the Egadi. No airports or heliports are in the Egadi; most visitors to these islands fly to Palermo or Trapani.

FAVIGNANA ★★

Butterfly-shaped Favignana is the hub and beating heart of the Egadi. It's the largest of the group and has the most services and consequently receives the most visitor traffic. Whereas the other Egadi are more specialized in their attractions, Favignana's appeal is broad: There are easily accessible azure coves, a pretty town with a lively scene, plenty of places to stay and eat, strong cultural traditions, and the archipelago's most frequent connections to mainland Sicily. Favignana is your best bet for a well-rounded Egadi vacation, and it also makes a handy base for day forays to Levanzo and Marettimo.

Favignana's 33km (21-mile) perimeter is an unfinished jigsaw puzzle of alluring coves with sparkling, multitoned water. It's also the flattest of the Egadi, and nearly all its coastline is accessible by land. Bus service is scant here, so you'll want to rent a bike or scooter to sample the various grottoes and inlets. Cala Rossa, with turquoise water set against the dramatic mini-Manhattan of an old tufa quarry, is Favignana's iconic place for a swim. Inland, the island's topography has a less overt "wow factor" than Levanzo's or Marettimo's, but the low *macchia* scrub that covers much of Favignana is an explosion of heady herbal aromas and, in spring, a riot of wildflowers in bloom. Figs, capers, and pomegranates flourish alongside palms and agave plants—just as you would expect on an island between Sicily and North Africa.

Tourism now makes up a good chunk of Favignana's economy, but it wasn't always this way. The Favignanese for centuries made their living off tuna fishing and tufa quarrying (a porous blond stone called *pietra di Favignana,* used throughout Sicily). Favignana was first settled by the Phoenicians (then called Aegusa, "butterfly," for its shape) and considered a strategic island by the Arabs and Normans. The late 19th century was Favignana's fishing heyday, when the powerful Marsala wine baron family, the Florio, built a tuna processing plant and residence here, since closed and requalified for other uses. In the modern era, traditional tuna fishing off Favignana has been greatly reduced by large-scale commercial fishing operations elsewhere in the Mediterranean and Atlantic, and the quarries of Favignana's native stone are

---

La Mattanza: A Grisly & Mesmerizing Ancient Ritual

Animal lovers may wish to avoid the Egadis in late May or early June, when the *la mattanza,* or tuna slaughter, takes place. Bluefin tuna, prized throughout the world for their flavorful red flesh, swim all over the Atlantic and Mediterranean but return every spring to western Sicily to spawn. The *mattanza,* which was an Arab invention, is still carried out in the waters off Favignana, usually in May or June. Led by the *rais* (the Arabic word for "head," in this context, the high priest of tuna-corralling), the team of skilled *tonnaroti*

(tuna fishermen) stops to pray at a floating cross bearing images of various saints, palm fronds, and flowers before heading out to the *tonnara* (trap) to butcher the powerful fish with bare hands and harpoons. The season comes to a close by June 13, the feast day of Sant'Antonio. *Note:* Collapse of bluefin tuna stocks in the Mediterranean may eventually spell an end to *la mattanza;* efforts are now underway to list the bluefin as an endangered species.

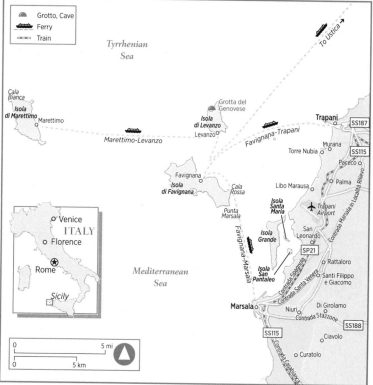

defunct. Their evocative skeletons remain all over the island, however, and some have even been converted into snazzy "quarry hotels."

Favignana may have gotten a recent dose of chic with those quarry hotels and a few stylish new "residence" accommodations, but this everyman's resort seems to be teetering on the brink of midrange overdevelopment. Yet if the general atmosphere on Favignana lacks sophistication, the food has it in spades. Even simple restaurants turn out amazing dishes, firmly rooted in the bounty of the waters offshore. The classic souvenir of Favignana is a specialty tuna item, whether *bresaola di tonno* (essentially prosciutto in fish form), *ventresca* (the mother lode of tuna cuts, from the belly), or, for the more adventurous, a delicacy known as *lattume* (pickled tuna gonads).

Tip: Avoid Favignana in August, when the heat, tourist masses, and high prices diminish the island's magic. *Do,* however come in late May or June, when the weather is divine, the flowers are blooming, and you're likely to catch some of the fervor that accompanies the *mattanza* season.

Essentials

GETTING THERE Siremar, Molo Sanità, Trapani (✆ **0923/24968;** www. siremar.it), has at least a dozen daily boats (ferries and hydrofoils) between Trapani and Favignana. Boats from the Sicilian mainland call first at Favignana (55 min. by ferry/8.20€, 15–20 min. by hydrofoil/10€) before proceeding to Levanzo and Marettimo. Siremar also has a ticket office on Favignana at Molo San Leonardo (© 0923/921368). **Ustica Lines,** Via Ammiraglio Staiti, Trapani Porto (© 0923/873813; www.usticalines.it), is the other carrier offering sea connections from Sicily to Favignana, running hydrofoils only from both Trapani and Marsala. From Trapani, trip frequency, crossing times, and ticket prices are the same as Siremar's hydrofoils, listed above. From Marsala (Piazza Piemonte Lombardo; © 348/3579863), the hydrofoil to Favignana takes 30 minutes and costs 10€. Ustica Lines has an office on Favignana at Molo San Leonardo (© 0923/921277).

GETTING AROUND   Favignana is mostly flat and fairly small, but just big enough that you can't get everywhere you want to go **on foot.** It's the perfect island for **biking**—that is, leisurely pedaling on easy roads. Two wheels make all of Favignana's coastline (and all those enticing coves and beaches) much more accessible. Brits and Northern Europeans usually opt for bikes (available for rent all over Favignana town), while Italians choose—what else?—the *motorino.* Scooters will, of course, get you from point A to point B faster, but the daily rental rate is also significantly higher. In the blistering heat of August, however, that *motorino* becomes a godsend. In Favignana town, **Noleggio Grimaldi,** Piazza Europa 34 (© 0923/921635 or 339/1609239), or **Noleggio Da Pietro,** Via Garibaldi 10 (© 347/3716841), both rent bikes and scooters. Depending on the season, bikes are 5€ to 8€ per day, while scooters run from 15€ to 40€ per day for 50cc models and 25€ to 50€ for 100cc/125cc bikes. Small **motorboats** are readily available for rent at the port, or join one of the organized **island-circumnavigation excursions** offered by those boat rental agencies. These usually last several hours and may include lunch on-board, with tastings of Favignana tuna.

VISITOR INFORMATION   The **Pro Loco** tourist office, Piazza Madrice (© 0923/921647), acts as an information center for Levanzo and Marettimo as well. The Pro Loco can arrange guided tours of the recently restored Florio tuna plant (see below).

FAST FACTS   The **Banca Nuova,** Piazza Europa 2 (© 0923/921251), keeps regular banking hours and has an ATM. The **post office,** which also has an ATM, is at Via G. Marconi 2 (© 0923/921209) and opens Monday through Friday 8am to 1:30pm and Saturday 8am to 12:30pm. For medical assistance, the **Guardia Medica** is at Via delle Fosse (© 0923/921283). A **pharmacy** is at Piazza Madrice 70 (© 0923/921265). For the **police,** call © 0923/921202.

Exploring the Island

Favignana—the port town where all boat traffic arrives—is the island's only town. You'll see the elegant pink **Palazzo Florio** ★ when you sail into harbor. It was built by the wealthy Florio family in 1876 as a tuna-season residence. The palazzo and gardens are now headquarters of the Egadi Islands *Area Marina Protetta* (protected marine area), but you can have a peek at the ground floor and courtyard. Patriarch and island benefactor Ignazio Florio (of whom there is a statue in town) was and is beloved by the Favignanesi, while his son Vincenzo, who cared more about automobile racing than tuna fishing and ruined the business, is not quite as well regarded. The other Florio relic on Favignana is the **Ex Tonnara Florio** ★, or tuna processing plant and cannery, at water's edge on the west side of the marina. After a long period of decay and abandonment, the plant was restored and reopened to the public as a cultural center. The imposing building, with its noble arches and vaults, is an excellent example of 19th-century industrial archaeology.

Making your way from the port area into the heart of Favignana town, you'll quickly arrive at the main square, **Piazza Madrice ★**. This handsome plaza, paved with patinated *pietra di Favignana,* is lined with lively cafes and a pretty church, the 18th-century **Chiesa Matrice.** In the evening, everyone on Favignana comes to Piazza Madrice and nearby Piazza Europa for an *aperitivo,* dinner, or gelato.

West of Favignana town is the island's highest point, **Monte Santa Caterina** (314m/1,030 ft.), which has an old fortress at its peak. The fort, which was originally a 9th-century pirate watchtower, was enlarged by the Normans in the 12th century and later the Bourbons in the late 1700s. Now a military zone, it is off-limits to the public.

Outdoor Pursuits

"Out on the island" there is gloriously little to do but putter around and discover places to swim. If you only have limited time on Favignana, make a beeline to the northeast tip of the island and **Cala Rossa ★★★**. This is the classic postcard shot and symbol of Favignana, a spectacular semicircular bay with smooth rock platforms and crystalline turquoise waters. The drama of the spot is completed by the orthogonal stone pilasters of the old tufa quarries standing as surreal backdrops on shore. The waters here weren't always crystalline, however: "Red Cove" takes its name from the blood that was spilled here during battle in the First Punic War (3rd c. b.c.). Just east of the promontory is **Cala Bue Marino,** another enchanting rocky cove. **Cala Azzurra ★★**, on the southeastern point of Favignana, is famed for its bluest-blue waters (hence the name) and another favorite swimming spot, but it's prone to algae, which mars some of the experience. Heading back west along the southern coast, the next major sight is the **Grotta Perciata** (Pierced Cave). A bit farther west of here—yet only a 15-minute walk from town—is **Lido Burrone ★★**; the largest and prettiest sandy beach on the island, it is fully equipped with beach clubs renting chairs and umbrellas, kayaks, and snorkeling equipment. (Alternatively, **Praia** is a small beach adjacent to town, on the north coast.)

The western wing of Favignana is more windswept and desolate than the eastern half, meaning you'll almost always have a few sheltered coves to yourself, including **Cala Faraglioni** (swim into the caves to the north of the bay) and **Cala del Pozzo,** a wild spot where the strong wind is said to *favorisce l'abbronzatura* (favor suntan). **Cala Rotonda ★** is by far the most popular inlet on the western coast—at this near-perfect circle of rocks, the caves are accessible only to swimmers.

The Tufa Quarries

Beyond the roadside walls of eastern Favignana, the ground often plummets down to gaping cavities that were once tufa quarries, odd and wonderful landscapes of sheer walls that bear the score marks of rock-extraction. Many have now been converted into gardens, vineyards, or hotels. In other places, the scars of quarrying are at street or sea level: Once-massive outcrops of tufa are now reduced to evocative adventure-movie sets of trapezoidal cave entrances and lush vegetation. Along the water near Cala Rossa, a sort of Manhattan of tufa-pilaster creates an amazing "skyscraper" effect.

Where to Stay

Note that the highest prices listed below are only valid for August; rates drop by about 50% during the rest of the summer, late spring, and early fall—all gorgeous times for a stay on Favignana. For a vacation rental, try **Casa Vacanze Francesca** in Favignana town (© **349/6713297;** www.egadicasavacanze.com). **Villaggio Miramare** (Strada Provinciale Punta Sottile 10; © **0923/921330;** www.villaggiomiramare.it) has attractive apartments in a seaside "holiday village" on the southern side of the island.

Albergo Egadi ★★ FAVIGNANA TOWN   Airy and fresh are the watchwords at this elegant home-away-from-home in the center of Favignana town. The owners are an italo-*francese* couple, and the Gallic influence is evident in the French-country decor and color scheme. Request a room on the top floor, where there's a terrace with a sea view. The hotel also rents out "Nene House," a four-person villa in a refined-rustic, panoramic setting on the mountainside above town.

Via Cristoforo Colombo 17. © **0923/921232.** www.albergoegadi.it. 12 units. Doubles 100€–200€, including breakfast. AE, DC, MC, V. Year-round. **Amenities:** Restaurant; bar. *In room:* A/C, TV, hair dryer, minibar.

Cave Bianche ★★★ EASTERN FAVIGNANA   Aesthetes and design buffs will get a kick out of this quarry hotel, a sexy boutique affair set in the flat bottom of an old tufa *cava*, about 5km (3 miles) east of Favignana town. Think modernist L.A. or Miami surrounded by the high walls of the island's native blond stone, scored from the last blocks that were extracted. You descend from street level to the floor of the quarry, which is the hotel "quad," with gardens, a swimming pool, and a restaurant set against a reflecting pool. Guest units are in a terraced structure in the quarry cavity, and the spare but comfortable interiors are boldly modern—clean, long lines, pop furniture, and saturated colors. The hotel is also earnestly green, from its construction that blends in with the defunct quarry to low-energy lamps, water recycling, and solar panels.

Strada Comunale Fanfalo. © **0923/925451.** www.cavebianchehotel.it. 32 units. Doubles 126€–282€, including breakfast. AE, DC, MC, V. Closed Nov–Mar. **Amenities:** Restaurant; bar; vehicle and boat rentals; diving, fishing, and boat excursions; Jacuzzi; pool. *In room:* A/C, TV, hair dryer, minibar, Wi-Fi.

Hotel delle Cave ★ EASTERN FAVIGNANA   A sort of cousin to the Cave Bianche, this is another, newer and smaller quarry hotel. The peculiar modern architecture is a bit austere and reminiscent of some of Sicily's Arab monuments. Fresh-feeling rooms are simple and modern, and a few design flourishes set them apart from your average Italian three-star. As at Cave Bianche, you have no indication a hotel is here until you descend from the parking lot and discover the manicured civilization within: A communal lawn has sun beds and two small hydromassage pools, but no real place to swim. Fortunately, it's a short walk or ride from here to Cala Rossa, one of Favignana's best coves.

Vicolo dell Madonna, Contrada Torretta. © **0923/925423.** www.hoteldellecave.com. 14 units. Doubles 105€–230€, including breakfast. Closed Oct–Mar. **Amenities:** Restaurant; bar; vehicle and watercraft rentals; excursions; Internet; Jacuzzi; parking; transfers. *In room:* A/C, TV, hair dryer, minibar.

Il Borgo del Principino ★★ WEST OF TOWN   One of the chicest choices on Favignana opened in 2009, on the western slope of Monte Santa Caterina—a 10-minute walk from town, still convenient but quiet. The Borgo, a restored minivillage of historic buildings arranged around a garden courtyard, consists of two- to four-person apartments, with comfortable, modern furnishings and small outdoor living areas. Interiors are perhaps a bit too metro-sleek—minimalist espresso wood, brushed steel—for the otherwise rustic surroundings, but the bathrooms are a gorgeous mixture of native stone and contemporary fixtures. In the communal courtyard, a lawn is planted with olive and palm trees, agave plants, and fragrant local shrubs, all of which manage to look native and spontaneous without being unkempt. Owners Leo and Puccio are Sicilian hospitality incarnate and full of great advice.

Contrada Boschetto. ✆ **0923/921046,** 331/4662820, or 348/7704924. www.borgoprincipino.com. 9 units. Doubles 60€–160€; quadruples 90€–260€ (minimum stay of 3 nights in high season). MC, V. Closed Nov–Apr. Free parking. *In room:* A/C, TV, hair dryer, kitchenette.

Il Portico ★ FAVIGNANA TOWN   Located in the center of town, this is a great choice for those who want to be in the middle of the action and don't mind a little extra noise. Il Portico is a cheerful, clean, welcoming place with helpful staff (they'll tell you which beach to hit when the *scirocco* wind is blowing). Modern rooms have some nice extra touches like Frette towels and small balconies. The roof terrace is a well-used social hangout with sun loungers, hot tub, and outdoor shower. Bustling piazzas and restaurants are all within a stone's throw.

Via Meucci 3. ✆ **0923/921701.** www.hotelilportico.it. Double 80€–200€. AE, DC, MC, V. Closed Nov–Easter. **Amenities:** Bar; vehicle and watercraft rentals; diving and fishing excursions; Wi-Fi. *In room:* A/C, TV, hair dryer, minibar.

Where to Dine

The most celebrated restaurant in Favignana town, seafood-specialist **El Pescador** (Piazza Europa 38; ✆ **0923/921035**) is a bit of a tourist trap—good food, but prices are way too high. The best gelato and *granite* are at **L'Arte del Gelato,** Via Roma 16. For delicious local fare in a no-nonsense atmosphere, I love the self-service restaurant **Il Quadrifoglio** (Via Roma).

Aegusa ★★ FAVIGNANESE   Attached to the hotel of the same name, Ristorante Aegusa serves up spot-on renditions of traditional Favignanese and Sicilian cuisine in a romantically lit garden courtyard. The *caponata* is perfection, and the well-rounded list of *primi* and *secondi* employ only fresh local seafood (from grouper to lobster to sea urchin); *bottarga,* dried tuna roe, is even used as a condiment on spaghetti. Service is warm and friendly, and prices are reasonable.

Via Garibaldi 11. ✆ **0923/922430.** www.aegusahotel.it. Reservations recommended. Entrees 11€–18€. AE, DC, MC, V. Open for lunch and dinner.

Egadi ★★ FAVIGNANESE   Certainly not a place for a rustic, down-home island meal, Egadi is widely regarded as the best restaurant on Favignana. Though it's now under new management, it was opened in the 1990s by the Guccione sisters, who are legends of Egadi gastronomy. In an elegant dining room with crisp and professional waitstaff, you'll feast on sophisticated seafood (principally tuna and swordfish) and vegetable dishes, and forget for a few hours that you're on Favignana. The wine list is as fancy as the food.

Via Cristoforo Colombo 17. ✆ **0923/921232.** Reservations required. Entrees 14€–22€. AE, DC, MC, V. Tues–Sun 7:30–10:30pm.

La Sirenetta ★ PIZZA   This busy pizzeria/snack bar, with outdoor tables on a little piazza, is a great choice for the budget-minded or those who can't bear the thought of one more tuna-based meal. Stop by and reserve a table during your pre-dinner walk through town, or risk a long (though lively) wait.

Piazza Europa 27. ✆ **0923/922399.** Reservations recommended. Pizzas from 3.50€. No credit cards. Dinner only.

LEVANZO ★

Although it may lack the other islands' more obvious natural attractions and tourist infrastructure, tiny Levanzo is well worth a visit, and its proximity and frequent connections to Favignana make a day trip ideal.

At only 6 sq. km (2⅓ sq. miles), Levanzo (*Leh*-van-zo) is the smallest of the Egadis, with a jagged coastline of some rather forbidding cliffs. The adorable village of Cala Dogana ("Customs Cove") is at the southern end of the island and measures less than 500m (1,640 ft.) end to end. Yet there are good dining options and homey accommodations, a few bars and bakeries, and no shortage of *escursioni* offered by colorful boats moored in the harbor.

There are no cars on Levanzo, besides a few Jeeps that take tourists to the Grotta del Genovese (p. 287), and the resulting peace and quiet is extraordinary.

Essentials

GETTING THERE   Levanzo is most commonly visited as a side trip from Favignana (6km/3¾ miles to the south), but you can also get here directly from western Sicily. Day-trippers can avail of Siremar's and Ustica Lines' scheduled boat service (6.20€ for the 15-min. hydrofoil ride from Favignana); otherwise, it's easy to arrange private boat transfers between Favignana and Levanzo. **Siremar** (Molo Sanità, Trapani; ☎ **0923/24968;** www.siremar.it) has at least a dozen daily boats (ferries and hydrofoils) between Trapani and Levanzo (90 min. by ferry/8.20€, 25 min. by hydrofoil/10€). Siremar has a ticket office on Levanzo at Via Calvario 29 (☎ **0923/924128**). **Ustica Lines** (Via Ammiraglio Staiti, Trapani Porto; ☎ **0923/873813;** www.ustica lines.it) is the other carrier offering sea connections from Sicily to the Egadi, running hydrofoils only from both Trapani and Marsala. From Trapani, trip frequency, crossing times, and ticket prices are the same as Siremar's hydrofoils, listed above. From Marsala (Piazza Piemonte Lombardo; ☎ **348/3579863**), the hydrofoil to Levanzo takes 55 minutes (changing boats at Favignana). Ustica Lines has an office on Levanzo (Molo Aliscafi; ☎ **348/8042681**).

GETTING AROUND   Boats arrive at Cala Dogana, an inlet on the south side of the island. This is also where Levanzo's only village is, with its few *pensioni,* restaurants, and basic shops. Round-island tours, offered by **Levanzo in Barca** (☎ **339/7367785** or 0923/924028; www.levanzoinbarca.it), cover the island's coastline in under 2 hours, but Levanzo is the one Italian island where, if pressed for time, you can forgo the boat tour. In fact, I prefer exploring Levanzo via its well-kept, scenic hiking paths. Mountain bikes, available for rent at the port, can also be taken on the trails. With a total surface area of just 6km (3¾ miles) and a maximum altitude of 278m (912 ft.), distances and heights are never great, and the swimming spots can all be reached by land. Levanzo in Barca also provides "taxi" service to the swimming coves and beaches, picking you up at an agreed-upon time for transport back to town, as well as nighttime connections to Favignana when the hydrofoil isn't running.

FAST FACTS   There are **no banks** on Levanzo, so hit the ATM on Favignana or in Trapani before making a trip here. A few restaurants accept credit/debit cards, but you'll need cash for excursions, coffee, and snacks. The **post office** is at Via Salita Scuole 5 (☎ **0923/924051**). The nearest **pharmacies** are on Favignana, but for medical assistance on Levanzo, contact the **Guardia Medica** at ☎ **0923/924092.** An **Internet point** is at Panetteria Olimpia, Via Pietre Varate 5 (☎ **0923/924024**).

Exploring the Island

The main sight on Levanzo is the **Grotta del Genovese ★★** (*✆* **339/7418800** or *✆* 0923/924032; www.grottadelgenovese.it; 10am–1pm and 3–6pm; cave admission only 5€; cave plus round-trip transportation by boat or off-road vehicle 13€; booking essential), famous for its Paleolithic (c. 10,000 B.C.) graffiti and Neolithic (c. 6,000 B.C.) wall paintings. Together, these make up the most important prehistoric figurative art in Italy. The site is a low-arched cavern in the karstic limestone about 30m above sea level. The cave had been used as an agricultural shelter until 1949, when a Florentine painter named Francesca Minellono discovered the 33 engravings and 100 painted figures. Tours are conducted by the fanny-packed custodian, Sig. Natale Castiglione.

HIKING Of all three Egadi, Levanzo has the best walks. The rocky, often harsh perimeter of Levanzo belies a surprisingly flat interior, with fertile agricultural plains. Don't let the island's highest peak, Pizzo del Monaco (278m/912 ft.), fool you; most of the topography and trails on Levanzo have only gentle *saliscendi* (rises and falls). The longest hike (about 7km/4.3 miles round-trip) runs due north of Cala Dogana (the island's only village) to the lighthouse at **Capo Grosso.** There is no water access here, as the lighthouse stands high above the sea on the vertical cliffs that mark the northernmost point of the island. Another of the island's lengthier walks goes to the **Grotta del Genovese** on the east coast. Hikes from Cala Dogana to the main swimming areas of the southern half of the island—Il Faraglione, Cala Minnola, and Cala Calcara—take from 15 to 30 minutes each way.

MOUNTAIN BIKING The wide, well-maintained trails of Levanzo are perfect for even novice mountain-bikers; rent some wheels at La Plaza Residence (see "Where to Stay," below).

SWIMMING The best spots for a dip in Levanzo's crystalline sea can all be reached by land (with moderate hikes), by boat tour, or by *servizio spiagge* (beach service) boats from the port. On the northwest coast, **Cala Tramontana ★** is a wide bay, backed by imposing limestone forms, with a pebble beach and gorgeous transparent water. It's also the farthest good swimming area from the port, so unless you have time to hike there and back (about 6km/3.75 miles round-trip), consider taking a beach-service boat (see "Getting Around," above). **Cala Calcara,** on the east coast, is a low amphitheater of Dolomitic limestone and a favorite shelter for boats cruising the Egadi. A few hundred meters to the south is the attractive picnic spot of **Cala Minnola ★**; the "beach" consists of smooth natural rock platforms that slope conveniently into the water, and immediately behind it is a pretty pinewood ideal for a picnic. A 15-minute walk west of the port leads to the **Faraglione;** its pebble beach with calm, clear waters is a favorite spot for families with children.

Note: Whatever you do, don't swim at the port. Its waters may look clear and enticing, but a sewage problem in town means waste is washed directly into the harbor.

Where to Stay

Albergo Paradiso ★ Above and behind the eponymous (and recommended) *ristorante,* the 15 rooms of this inn have simple maritime decor and a great sense of tranquillity. Large picture windows afford sea views and refreshing breezes. Guests have the option of full-board, with all meals served in the panoramic, refined restaurant.

Via Lungomare 8.© **0923/924080.** 15 units. Doubles from 60€. AE, DC, MC, V. Closed Dec 15–Mar 5. **Amenities:** Restaurant; bar. *In room:* A/C, TV.

La Plaza Residence   On a pretty stepped alley in Levanzo town, these are spacious and contemporary self-catering apartments with comfortable living areas and small bathrooms with shower. A few units have partial sea views.

Via Salita Poste.© **0923/1941526** or 335/6718308. www.levanzoresidence.com. 7 units. 80€–180€ per night or 420€–1,120€ per week. AE, DC, MC, V. **Amenities:** Bike rentals; excursions. *In room:* A/C, TV, kitchenette.

Lisola ★   Carved out of the workers' quarters of the old Florio winery, on the hill above the port, this residence consists of handsomely furnished apartments with historic flair, just the right amount of Sicilian kitsch, and modern comforts. Each unit has its own veranda amid the cactus and bougainvillea. The property, which has a desert-oasis feel, has lots of communal outdoor space (garden, hammocks, barbecue, eating area, sun terrace, swimming pool). Lisola is a good 10-minute hike from town, but they have a Jeep to transport you there and back, with your luggage.

Contrada Case. © **320/1809090.** www.lisola.eu. 7 units. Double-occupancy apts 550€–750€ per week. AE, MC, V. **Amenities:** Swimming pool. *In room:* A/C, TV, kitchenette, outdoor living area.

Where to Dine

Pick up groceries and snacks at the **alimentari** (deli/food shop) on Via Lungomare, or get *kabbuci cunzati* (panini stuffed with tomatoes, mozzarella, oregano, and other fillings) at **Panetteria Olimpia,** Via Pietre Varate 5 (© **0923/924024**).

Ristorante Paradiso ★★   Paradiso has no written menu, just to-die-for seafood, from mouthwatering classics like *calamari fritti* (fried calamari) to local specialties like pasta made with fresh island herbs and tuna, scorpionfish, or whatever's been caught that day by *levanzari* fishermen. Save room for dessert: The *cassatelle* (ricotta and chocolate-filled "ravioli," fried and dusted with powdered sugar) are incredible. Tables are on a panoramic deck overlooking the water near the port.

Via Lungomare 8.© **0923/924080.** Reservations recommended in summer. Entrees from 9€. AE, DC, MC, V. Open for lunch and dinner.

MARETTIMO ★★★

Mountainous Marettimo is the most far-flung and difficult to reach of the Egadi, but don't let this put you off. Its very isolation, combined with stunning unspoiled nature, makes Marettimo the real jewel of the archipelago. Time truly has stood still on this authentic island, where fishermen still make a living off the sea, and where there's still only one hotel. "Activities" on Marettimo are few but include the simple pleasures of boating around the island's perimeter, which is riddled with extraordinary grottoes and swimming coves, hiking over the rugged interior, or hanging out in the island's one village, which is a picturesque collection of whitewashed, blue-shuttered houses and narrow streets. In fact, some visitors never even make it past the village, where it's quite possible to pass hours in a bar or *trattoria* getting to know Marettimo through conversation with locals.

In summer, Marettimo is popular as a day trip from Favignana, and in August it's really too crowded here to find that quietness so unique to Marettimo. Visit in the off-peak months of June and September and stay overnight, several days if possible.

Respect Thy Elders

Although tourists have become more commonplace on Marettimo in recent years, and the majority of locals will welcome you heartily, there is still a certain hostility among elderly *marettimare* (women) toward mainlanders and city-folk. I've heard stories about female tourists in beach attire or jeans being spat at or receiving harsh Sicilian oaths for their "vulgarity." Since outsiders were unknown on this island for decades, discreet behavior and dress are the best policies when off the beach.

Essentials

GETTING THERE Siremar (Molo Sanità, Trapani; ℂ 0923/24968; www.siremar.it) has several scheduled ferries and hydrofoils per day between Trapani and Marettimo (2½ hr. by ferry/13€; 1 hr. by hydrofoil/18€). Siremar has a ticket office on Marettimo at Piazza Umberto 2 (℃ 0923/923144). **Ustica Lines** (Via Ammiraglio Staiti, Trapani Porto; ℃ 0923/873813; www.usticalines.it) runs hydrofoils only from Trapani and Marsala. From Trapani, trip frequency, crossing times, and ticket prices are the same as Siremar's hydrofoils, listed above. From Marsala (Piazza Piemonte Lombardo; ℃ 348/3579863), the hydrofoil to Marettimo takes 1 hour, 10 minutes and costs 18€. Ustica Lines has an office on Marettimo at Corso Umberto I, 15; ℃ 0923/923361). Day-trippers from Favignana or Levanzo can take the hydrofoil to Marettimo (12€) for the 30- to 45-minute crossing.

Note: Build flexibility into your travel schedule since rough seas (most common Nov–Apr) interrupt hydrofoil and ferry service, cutting the island off for sometimes days at a time. Hydrofoils may be canceled if the sea is even slightly *mosso* (rough).

GETTING AROUND Hydrofoils and ferries arrive at the Scalo Nuovo (New Port) on the south side of the island's one village. Outside of the small pedestrian-friendly grid of Marettimo town (1 sq. km/⅔ sq. mile), there is exactly one paved road, which becomes a dirt road a few hundred meters outside the port area. There are no other inhabited areas, just stunning scenery, much of which is traversed by moderate-to-strenuous hiking paths, though a much better way to get around Marettimo is to join an island-circumnavigation tour offered by one of the boatmen at the port.

VISITOR INFORMATION The **Associazione Culturale Marettimo,** Via Campi 3 (℃ 0923/923000), sells maps and can arrange guided tours of the island by land or sea. It also houses the small Museo del Mare (see "Exploring," below).

FAST FACTS **Banca Nuova,** Corso Umberto 2 (℃ 0923/923004), has an ATM and keeps regular hours Monday through Friday, though it's a good idea to bring some cash to the island; a few places accept credit/debit cards. For **medical services,** call the Guardia Medica at ℃ 0923/923117. The **pharmacy** is at Via Gaetano Maiorana 22 (℃ 0923/923024). The **police** can be reached at ℃ 0923/923122. The **post office** is at Via San Simone 30 (℃ 0923/923086; Mon–Sat 9:30am–12:30pm). **Wi-Fi** is available at Baia del Sole wine bar, Piazza Umberto 5 (℃ 0923/923014).

Exploring the Island

Marettimo is shaped like a parallelogram, or, for the more poetically inclined, a flying carpet. The village of Marettimo is about halfway down the eastern coast on the only place flat enough for a settlement. A sharp ridge of Dolomitic limestone, covered in the green of pines and Mediterranean scrub, forms a spine that bisects the island from north to south. From the vantage point of the sea, the western coast of Marettimo is the most spectacular, with tall cliffs plunging to the sea and fascinating caves and karstic features that have been formed over the millennia.

In Marettimo town, everyone stops for breakfast at **Caffè Tramontana,** Via Campi, on the old port on the north side of town (🕿 **389/9612272**); at sunset, an *aperitivo* is de rigueur at **Bar Baia del Sole,** Piazza Umberto 5 (🕿 **0923/923014**), with tables on the central piazzetta. While wandering around town, pay a visit to the charming **Museo del Mare ★** (Via Campi 3; 🕿 **0923/923000**). The collection is a single room with poignant photographs of *marettimari* fishermen through the years, dating back to the early 1900s. Many of these fathers and sons emigrated to California and Alaska, where the fishing business was more profitable, in the early 20th century.

BOAT TOURS   Seeing Marettimo's full complement of coves and grottoes from the sea is a must. While it's theoretically possible to rent your own small motorboat at Marettimo's port, your best bet for getting to know the 19km (12-mile) perimeter of the island is to have a local boatman take you on a *giro dell'isola* (island-circumnavigation) tour, which departs from either Scalo Nuovo, the "new port" where the hydrofoils dock, on the south side of town, or Scalo Vecchio, the "old port" where the island's fishermen are based, on the north side of town. You'll go counterclockwise around the whole island into the most beautiful and interesting inlets and sea caves. As long as the weather is warm, at least two stops for swimming are included. *Note:* Much of the island's coast is Nature Reserve, but locals have permits that allow their boats to get closer to certain areas than your rented motorboat could.

Excursions can be arranged ad-hoc at the harbor, whether with young men in designer T-shirts or salty old fishermen who'll shove aside their nets to make room for passengers. Many of these skippers have great stories to tell, and a few speak excellent English: **Pietro Guerra** (Scalo Nuovo; 🕿 **0923/923046;** www.marettimotour. it), who captains the *Nardina G. Alaska,* spent many years in Alaska as a salmon fisherman before transporting his beloved *Nardina G.* back (via container ship and the Panama Canal) for service as a tourist excursion boat. **Medi@tour** (🕿 **0923/923196** or 339/7729404; www.marettimoweb.it) has four boats that accommodate 7 to 16 passengers. Expect to pay 15€ per person for the round-island itinerary (3 hr. total, with stops for swimming) to 20€ per person for a more extended, 5-hour tour with longer breaks in the swimming coves.

Heading north from town, first up is the celebrated **Grotta del Cammello ★★★**. The roof has fallen in a cavern of limestone, creating gorgeous light effects and water colors that range from emerald to deep cobalt. On the northern side of Punta Troia is **Grotta del Tuono ★★**, Cave of Thunder, for the sound that the pounding waves make when the mistral wind blows. A bit farther along is the **Grotta della Pipa,** named for a pipe-shaped rock here; then, around the promontory of Punta Mugnone, the south-facing inlet, **Cala Bianca ★★★**, is one of the most spectacular places for a swim on Marettimo. The white sea bottom creates a natural swimming pool, edged by high walls of karstic limestone. Next is the **Barranche ★★★**, those massive monoliths of limestone that create the amazing impression of a majestic Wild West by the sea. In this cathedral-like zone is the **Grotta Perciata ★★** ("pierced" by clefts in the rock), followed by the **Grotta del Presepe ★**, or Creche Cave, where the limestone formations resemble a nativity scene, and the **Grotta della Bombarda ★** (the waves

> ## Canine Companions
>
> Marettimo's hikes offer glorious solitude, but there is one caveat: You won't be completely alone on your outing because one of the island's stray dogs (a sort of Spaniel left over from the days when hunting was permitted on the island) is bound to accompany you at least part of the way; they'll even show you where the freshwater springs are. Though these dogs don't belong to anyone in particular, they're healthy, clean, collared, and respected members of the community.

make a "bombarding" sound) with its interesting undersea rock formations visible from the boat. The remainder of the island tour takes in **Punta Libeccio,** with its lighthouse, and the southern half of the western coast, dotted with **idyllic swimming spots** (including several minicaves only accessible to swimmers) and around the southern tip of Marettimo. Along this last stretch is usually a stop at **Praia Nacchi ★,** a pebbly but beautiful beach with crystalline turquoise water gently lapping the shore.

HIKING Avid hikers will find Marettimo's rugged profile quite seductive. No matter where you go, the views are to die for, and the aromas and sounds of this island are testament to its uncontaminated nature. Many of the island's 12 sq. km (4¾ sq. miles) are impassable, steep, forested terrain, but there are several trails worth tackling, from moderate to challenging. Although poorly maintained in the past, Marettimo is well on its way to having a very respectable network of hiking trails.

DONKEY RIDES Any of Marettimo's hiking trails can also be negotiated on the back of one of the island's trusty donkeys. The best way to arrange a donkey ride is through the staff at your accommodations, or, if you're not staying overnight, inquire in town about *escursioni a dorso d'asino.*

DIVING If the Baroque artist Caravaggio painted underwater scenes, they might have resembled the high-keyed marine scapes in the depths off Marettimo. The formidable slopes and splendid grottoes around the island's coast only continue and intensify underwater, creating magnificent habitats for vibrant marine life. **Voglia di Mare** (Via Mazzini 50; ✆ **339/4213845;** www.vogliadimare.com) offers day dives from 70€, with full equipment rental included, as well as weeklong packages. Another recommended outfit is **Stella Marina Diving Club** (✆ **0923/923144** or 0923/923276), run by island native and former Alaska fisherman Pietro Torrente.

FISHING The **Società Cooperativa San Giuseppe** (✆ **0923/541155**) organizes fishing trips—in the traditional *marettimaro* style: You get up very, very early—from 20€ per person.

Where to Stay

Until quite recently, the only place to stay on Marettimo was in the houses of fishermen, whose families still welcome tourists off the hydrofoil at Scalo Nuovo. You can also contact such agencies as **Medi@tour** (✆ **0923/923196** or 339/7729404; www.marettimoweb.it) to arrange a homestay. By far the most sought-after digs on Marettimo are the **Hiera Apartments ★★★** (✆ **0941/361681;** www.dicasainsicilia.it; two-person apartment 480€–1,350€ per week, four-person apartment 570€–1,500€ per week). The two units are straight from a boho-chic fashion shoot. Book well in advance.

Il Gabbiano Blu   The Blue Seagull consists of a free-standing *villetta* (two units with kitchen and veranda) just outside the village and four one-bedroom units with cooking facilities in town. These accommodations are simple and a bit cramped but certainly economical.

Via del Timo 22. ✆ **0923/532769.** www.ilgabbianoblu.com. 6 units. Double-occupancy apts 40€–75€ per night. No credit cards. Closed Nov–Apr. *In room:* Ceiling fan, TV, kitchenette.

Marettimo Residence ★★   The island's only accommodations with comprehensive amenities and services, the Residence is a complex of eco-friendly self-catering apartments in a garden setting near the water south of town. The bright and spacious one-, two-, or three-bedroom units, whitewashed and blue-shuttered in keeping with the Marettimo style, all come with a private terrace or veranda and kitchenette. A communal barbecue and gazebo area make DIY seafood dinners a real possibility. The property is 200m (656 ft.) south of the port, but the affable proprietor, Fausto, will meet you at the dock to transfer your luggage by golf cart.

Via Telegrafo 3. ✆ **0923/923202.** www.marettimoresidence.com. 42 units. Double-occupancy units 75€–190€ per night, 360€–1,200€ per week. AE, DC, MC, V. Year-round. **Amenities:** Children's play area; Internet; pool. *In room:* Ceiling fan, TV, hair dryer, kitchen.

Where to Dine

On Marettimo, it's all about seafood—and lots of it. For **picnics,** you can buy prepared food at La Scaletta (see below) and take-away pizza at **La Lampara** (Via Chiusa 35; ✆ 347/0873742), or just stop in at one of the *alimentari* (deli/groceries) for simple *panini*, fruit, and bottled water. **La Cambusa** at Via Garibaldi 5/b (✆ 0923/923441) is a good one-stop shop for those and Sicilian specialty items. Visit **Pescheria La Torre** (Via Municipio 2; ✆ 0923/923200) for fresh fish to cook in your apartment. The best coffee is at **Caffè Tramontana** (Via Campi, on the old port on the north side of town; ✆ 389/9612272). **Bar Baia del Sole** (Piazza Umberto 5, ✆ 0923/923014) is the spot for pre-dinner drinks. **La Scaletta** has the best gelato and *granite*.

Il Pirata ★★ SEAFOOD   Recognizable by the Jolly Rogers and American flags flying out front, The Pirate is all about seafood. The brusque owner is, like several other men his age on the island, a veteran of the Alaska salmon-fishing business. The house specialties are *zuppa di aragosta* (couscous with lobster broth), couscous with seafood, and spaghetti with fish-and-vegetable sauces, but also try the wonderful raw fish appetizers and the San Francisco–style clam chowder (many emigrants from the Egadi ended up in the Bay Area). In addition to the rustic dining room, about a dozen tables are under a gazebo on the adjacent beach. A meal here is hearty, lively, and memorable.

Via Scalo Vecchio 27. ✆ **0923/923027.** Reservations recommended. Entrees 10€–16€. AE, MC, V. Open for lunch and dinner.

La Scaletta ★★ SEAFOOD   The multitasking Scaletta, in addition to being a gelateria, coffee bar, and snack bar, also serves sit-down meals—great, gastronomically sophisticated ones at that. Owner Giovanni personally presides over the dining room, which is above the bar and has a view over the waterfront north of the port. To eat here is to feast on a set menu that changes every day. Giovanni and his staff will bring you plate after plate of refined vegetables and seafood, always seasoned with the freshest local herbs, until you're stuffed to the gills.

Via Telegrafo ¾. ✆ **0923/923233** or 0923/923181. Reservations required. Prix-fixe dinner 40€ excluding wine. No credit cards. Mar–Sept daily 7–10:30pm.

Shopping

Locally produced honeys (from island thyme, rosemary, and heather) can be purchased at **Dolce e Salato** (Via Municipio 10; ✆ **328/2370676**); **Marettimo Gioiello** (Corso Umberto I, 28; ✆ **0923/923222**) sells gold and coral jewelry.

SARDINIA & SARDINIAN ISLANDS

13

Ask any Italian, "Why go to Sardinia?" The answer, over and over? "Il mare. E' stupendo." There's no denying that Sardinia as a whole has the best beaches, not only among the Italian islands but also among all the coastlines of mainland Italy. And while elsewhere in Italy, spiaggia doesn't always mean you're going to have sand, spiaggia in Sardinia invariably means a cushiony beach of golden, pink, or white sand. Sardinia's 1,870km (1,162 miles) of coastline is riddled with sugary beaches—whether they're uninterrupted for several kilometers, or mid-size half-moons, or tiny coves—where transparent seas gently lap and marine breezes blow. Some complain about the constant wind on Sardinia, but that perpetual erosion is why there is so much fine sand along the island's shores. There are so many beaches that almost never are they crowded (other than weekends in Aug). Whether you want a swinging social scene, sports, or solitude, there's a beach for you in Sardinia.

Of course, there's much more to Sardinia than its coastline, but tourists rarely go inland. Sardinia is one of the 20 *regioni* of Italy, but it feels like another country, so different are its traditions and cultural history from that of the mainland. At 24,090 sq. km (9,301 sq. miles), Sardinia is only a fraction smaller than Sicily (25,060 sq. km/9,675 sq. miles), making it the second-largest island in the Mediterranean. With its massive expanses of severe-looking terrain, Sardinia feels even larger than it is—*aspro* is the word Italians often use, which is equal parts "rugged" and "harsh." Sergio Leone shot some of his spaghetti westerns in Sardinia because of the island's resemblance in many areas to the American frontier. Yet for its size and ancient history, Sardinia isn't, like Sicily or the rest of Italy, a gauntlet of must-see art and architecture, nor is it strong on storybook town squares with picturesque churches where, you know, there just happens to be a Caravaggio hanging above the altar, or cafes where you'll want to sit for hours, sipping coffee and wine and watching the pageant of Italian daily life go by. Certainly, Sardinia has strong traditions and customs, but they're harder to access here than in the rest of Italy. Indeed, the fact that *la Sardegna* represents an escape from the culture-gawker tourism of so many parts of Italy is a great part of the appeal for those who vacation here. You don't have to worry about all the churches and museums you

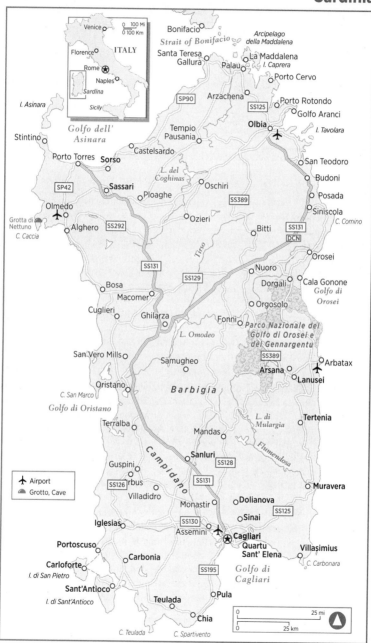

LAND OF THE nuraghi

While Sardinia may not boast the archaeological riches of mainland Italy and Sicily, the island is totally unique in the world for its Bronze Age *nuraghi* (singular: *nuraghe*). These beehive-shaped towers and intricate ancillary structures of local fieldstone are scattered all over the island (several thousand survive in ruins, though there were once more than 30,000). If you only have time for one, the most celebrated *nuraghe* in Sardinia is Su Nuraxi (see "Side Trips" under "Cagliari," below), an easy half-day trip north from Cagliari. Elsewhere, *nuraghi* tend to be less impressive, overgrown, and in decay, often surrounded by sheep and their droppings in the middle of someone's pasture.

might be missing, because there really aren't many. The mysterious *nuraghi*—Bronze Age stone structures in the shape of beehives, located all over the island—represent the main archaeological attraction on Sardinia.

The interior of Sardinia contains some stunning, humbling landscapes, and its brawny mountain ranges are well suited to the independent eco-tourist (that is, don't expect much in the way of infrastructure and organized trips, though hiking and horseback riding opportunities abound), but Sardinia's ace in the hole—here we go again—is its coastline. Vacationers who love Sardinia treasure it because of its quasi-tropical sea and abundant beaches—literally, as Italians say, *una piu' bella dell'altra* (one more beautiful than the next)—and because it's an utterly relaxing and sort of mysterious place that is right in their Mediterranean backyard, only an hour's flight from any major airport on the Italian mainland.

Serious gourmands and lovers of casual, unforgettable dining experiences will have no problem packing on a few extra kilos while in Sardinia. Food is generally high quality no matter where you go, and the island's regional cheeses, breads, and pastries are famous nationwide. Sardinian menus can at first be difficult to navigate, but they're not that far from "continental" Italian cuisine; they just have slightly odd names for everything. For example, a common dish is *malloreddus*. Sounds exotic, but it's just shell pasta flavored with a hint of saffron, usually tossed with something simple and hearty like tomato and meat sauce. And this being an island caressed by the seafood-rich Mediterranean on all sides, fish of all kinds is almost always available at any restaurant. But go inland, and the classic dish is *porceddu*, roast pig.

Even with all of Sardinia's enticing attributes—Caribbean waters and Italian food—what's not to love? The casual foreign traveler who otherwise loves all things Italian, and who is already traveling a considerable distance to be in this part of the world, will have a harder time "getting" Sardinia. The island is a bit of an aloof soul that can feel a bit disconnected, like a piece of the sensuous package you've come to expect from Italy is missing. But for water- and sun-themed relaxation seekers, Sardinia is paradise.

STRATEGIES

Unless you're going on an organized tour, a car is essential on Sardinia. Buses and trains exist, but they don't run all that frequently and certainly aren't a comprehensive network for areas of principal interest to the tourist. So much of the

Sardinian experience is following your whims—for example, down coastal roads to small signposted beaches where you might be the only people there—that you need the flexibility of your own wheels. (While, with some planning, Sicily can be done with public transportation, Sardinia can't.) Highways and secondary roads are well maintained and generally traffic free, and parking isn't a hassle. An exception to both those statements is the Costa Smeralda in July and August.

Like Sicily, Sardinia is big, and simply covering the distances here is time consuming. Unless you have 2 weeks to spend here, you have to pick one half of the island, and most travelers find the north of Sardinia more satisfying than the south. In a week, it's feasible to sample a bit of each region, getting a taste for the geographic variety of the island, which is quite rewarding from a scenic point of view. But you'll be spending several hours a day in the car, and your trip is likely to feel superficial and incomplete from a cultural perspective—Sardinia doesn't reveal itself to visitors quite as readily as Sicily does, for instance. If a long weekend, say 3 or 4 days, is all you can spare, a short trip to Sardinia can be quite satisfying as long as you limit yourself to one general area of the island, such as the Costa Smeralda and the Maddalena archipelago in the northeast or Villasimius in the southeast, or Alghero and its environs, in the northwest.

Cagliari airport has the most flight connections to Italy and Europe, so you might find it convenient to spend 1 night in the capital coming or going—fine, as there is enough of interest in Cagliari to make it worth a half-day of sightseeing, but don't stay more than 1 night if you only have a week or so on the island. Alghero is by far the prettiest city in Sardinia, so consider flying into Alghero's Fertilia airport and basing yourself in the north. You'll have both beaches and wine country within easy day-trip distance.

GETTING THERE   You can either fly or take a ferry to Sardinia. Flying is faster and usually just as economical as the ferry, as ferry connections exist mainly for Italians who want their own cars with them once they arrive in Sardinia. Flight time from Italy is about 45 minutes, while ferries can take from 5 to 15 hours.

By Air   In the south, **Cagliari-Elmas** airport (© 070/211211; www.sogaer.it), 3km (2 miles) from the capital, is the island's busiest airport and served from most major Italian and European cities. Just outside Alghero, in the northwest, **Alghero Fertilia** airport (© 079/935282; www.aeroportodialghero.it) is linked with dozens of Italian and European cities, mostly by low-cost carrier RyanAir (www.ryanair.com). **Olbia,** in the northeast near the Costa Smeralda, has a small airport (Aeroporto Costa Smeralda; © 0789/563444; www.olbiairport.it) with flights to many places in Italy, as well as the U.K. and Germany. Most of Olbia's air traffic is during the

SA LINGUA sarda

It only takes a few minutes of studying a Sardinian map or menu to figure out that this is an island with a strong dialect that is quite different from Italian. Place names are tongue twisters: Each seems to have about 11 syllables, and they're filled with *X*s and *U*s—even

Italians have a hard time spitting out Sardinian words and end up laughing at themselves. The dialect is colorful and jolly; in the Italian dubbed version of *The Simpsons,* the Scots-speaking janitor Groundskeeper Willie has a Sard accent.

SARDINIA'S LITTLE GREEN train

The **Trenino Verde** ★★ (www.trenino verde.com) is a narrow-gauge railway, complete with old-fashioned rail cars, that has four different routes that cover scenic and wild areas of the interior as the tracks snake their way past lakes and up wooded mountain slopes. It's an intimate journey that has a time-warp feel; the lines pass through small villages whose depots haven't changed in a century. The longest and most popular segment is the 159km (99-mile) trip between Mandas (about 60km/37 miles north of Cagliari) and Arbatax (a port city, about halfway up the east coast), which takes passengers through the lovely landscapes of the Gennargentu foothills. The trips take 5 hours each way and are timed in such a way that you can make a day of it: Trains depart from Mandas at 8:35am, arrive in Arbatax at 1:30pm, depart Arbatax at 2:35pm, arriving back at Mandas at 7:30pm. (From Arbatax, the morning trains leave at 7:50, arrive in Mandas at 12:45pm, depart Mandas at 3:25pm, arriving back at Arbatax at 8:20pm.) One-way fare is 9€. The other lines are Mandas-Isili-Sorgono (95km/59 miles in the central part of the island); Macomer-Bosa (a short 46km/29 miles that ends up on the western coast); and Nulvi-Tempio-Palau, which starts near the city of Sassari (take a regular train from there or Alghero to reach the Trenino Verde station at Nulvi or Tempio Pausania). The highlight of this last route is the final panorama, entering Palau, of the Maddalena archipelago off the northern coast.

summer. Airfares to Sardinia vary widely but are often less than 50€ one-way, although "budget" airlines like RyanAir charge exorbitant fees for checked luggage.

By Sea Several Sardinian cities are connected by efficient, clean ferries to ports up and down the western coast of Italy, and even Sicily. Crossing times average about 5 to 6 hours for fast ferries, or from 9 to 15 hours for traditional slow ferries. Fast ferries are not available for every combination of departure/arrival port nor are they always running throughout the year, but they usually run several times per day in summer between the Italian mainland ports of Civitavecchia (near Rome), Piombino, and Livorno (both in Tuscany), and the northern Sardinian seaports of Olbia and Golfo Aranci.

Olbia, on the northeast coast of Sardinia, has the fastest and most frequent connections to Italy; from Genoa (10 hr.), Piombino (4½ hr.) and Livorno (6½ hr.), and Civitavecchia (5–7 hr.). Most Olbia-bound boats are operated by **Moby Lines** (ⓒ 49/61114020 call center in Germany; www.mobylines.com) and Tirrenia. **Golfo Aranci,** immediately east of the Costa Smeralda, can be reached by **Corsica Ferries** (ⓒ 199/400500; www.corsica-ferries.it) from Civitavecchia (5½ hr.) and Livorno (6½ hr.) and by **DiMaio Lines** (ⓒ 848/151818 or 081/8822220; www.traghettiweb.it/traghetti/dimaio.htm) from Naples (13½ hr.). **Arbatax,** about halfway down the east coast of Sardinia, is connected by Tirrenia ferries to Civitavecchia (11 hr.) and Genova (19½ hr.). Porto Torres, near the northwest tip of Sardinia, has ferries to Genova (10 hr.) and Civitavecchia (7½ hr.), operated by **Grandi Navi Veloci** (ⓒ 010/2094591; www.gnv.it), Grimaldi Lines (ⓒ 081/496444; www.grimaldi-lines.com), and Moby. In southern Sardinia, **Cagliari** is served by **Tirrenia** ferries (ⓒ 892123 in Italy or 02/26302803 from abroad; www.tirrenia.it) from Civitavecchia (15 hr.) and Naples (16½ hr.), and the Sicilian ports of Palermo (14½ hr.) and Trapani (10 hr.).

Ferry prices range widely depending on the departure and arrival ports, the day of the week, and, above all, the time of year: Fares are highest in August. In general, expect to pay anywhere from 25€ (super-promotional fare, midweek) to 100€ (fewer restrictions, weekend rate) per person. A reserved seat (*poltrona,* recommended in summer) is an additional 7€ or so. Cabins can be booked for an extra 62€ to 110€ per person, based on quadruple occupancy. Bringing a car on board can cost anywhere from 5€ to 40€, depending on the season and specials.

You can book ferries through the U.K.-based **Direct Ferries** (www.directferries. co.uk/sardinia), which has a handy summary of all passenger/vehicle boat connections to Sardinia on its home page.

GETTING AROUND   With so many nooks and crannies you'll want the flexibility to explore, Sardinia is definitely a place where you'll want your own car. All the major rental companies are represented at Sardinian airports and often at the major ferry terminals (the seaports of Olbia, Golfo Aranci, Arbatax, and Cagliari). One I've used, which has more competitive fares than most, is Auto Europa (www.autoeuropa.it). Buses and trains do exist in Sardinia, but service is extremely limited and connections time consuming when it comes to reaching anywhere beyond the hub cities of Cagliari, Alghero, Sassari, Olbia, and Nuoro. For more information on trains, look at the English version of www.trenitalia.com.

VISITOR INFORMATION   The multi-lingual main portal for tourism in the Regione Sardegna, www.sardegnaturismo.it, has a wealth of information for trip planning, history and culture, and brochures for various special interests.

CAGLIARI ★

The capital of Sardinia lies on the southern tier of the island, surrounded by sea and hills. Known to the Phoenicians and Romans, today it appears modern except for an evocative medieval quarter, Castello, which occupies a long, narrow hill running north to south. In spite of ugly contemporary buildings on the outskirts, Castello is much as D. H. Lawrence saw it in 1921, built up on fortification walls of sunbleached stone, overgrown with weeds and vines. Its narrow, often dilapidated streets are filled with *palazzi* from the 1300s and 1400s and several churches, including the city's atmospheric Duomo.

For visitor information, the **tourist office** at Piazza Matteotti (near the waterfront, across from the main bus station and taxi rank; ☏ **070/669255**) has English-speaking staff and is open Monday to Saturday from 9am to 1pm and 5 to 8pm; winter hours are more limited. The official tourist board website is www.visit-cagliari.it.

Exploring

If, like most people who visit the capital, you only have a few hours to explore, make a beeline for the Castello district of the *centro storico.* Castello means castle, and this was the citadel of old Cagliari (whose Sard name *Casteddu* also means castle)—fortified by the Pisans in 1217—and the city's richest trove of architectural and historic sights. Situated high above the rest of town, Castello is a district of panoramic piazzas, quaint alleys, and aging palazzi. To reach this area, simply walk straight inland from the port up the gentle slope of shopping street Largo Carlo Felice. Near the top of Largo Carlo Felice, bear right on Via Marino, then take a slight left onto Via Giovanni Spano, where you'll see signs for the elevator (free, always open) that whisks you up through the fortification walls to the heights of Castello and to the top of the bastions of this quarter. This is the southern end of Castello, where the **Porta dei Leoni** (Lion's Gate) dovetails with the splendid Bastione Saint Remy and Terrazza Umberto I above. (There are also free elevators from "lower" Cagliari to the northern end of Castello, at Porta S'Avanzada and the Torre di San Pancrazio. If you can't find the elevator entrances, just ask a local, *"Ascensore?"*) Castello is just as much fun to explore, and perhaps even more so, in the evening as during the day.

The Porta dei Leoni elevator will deposit you before the **Bastione Saint Remy ★★** (sometimes referred to as Terrazza Umberto I), the piazza-like southeast corner of the citadel walls that affords 270-degree views over Cagliari and its harbor. This is the beating heart of Castello and a favorite meeting place, day or night, for Cagliaritani. At the north end of the square is the very hip **Caffè degli Spiriti ★★** (𝄐 070/655884), with an alfresco terrace and tables under a tented and glassed-in dining area. Grab a seat and an iced coffee here while you drink in the view from this lofty position. They also serve light meals and all kinds of cocktails.

Heading west from Bastione Saint Remy, up Via dell'Università, you soon reach the Pisan-era **Torre dell'Elefante ★**, which impresses with its original wooden portcullis still in situ. The tower is named for the sculpture of a marble elephant sitting on a ledge on one of the tower walls. (Like the Torre San Pancrazio a few blocks north, the Torre dell'Elefante only has one solid facade—that which faces "intruders" on the Castello district; the inside of the tower, with its wooden stairs and landings, is left exposed to the elements.) At the northern, higher end of Castello is the tallest monument and architectural symbol of the city, the Pisan **Torre di San Pancrazio ★** (Piazza Indipendenza; 𝄐 **070/6776400;** 2€; Apr–Oct Tues–Sun 9am–1pm and 3:30–7:30pm; Nov–Mar Tues–Sun 9am–4:30pm). Dating from 1305, this Pisan defense tower is a sort of twin to the Torre dell'Elefante at the southeast edge of Castello. Climb the steps for a wonderful view of the city and its bay—the same view watchmen saw while looking for enemies approaching from the sea.

Adjacent to the Torre San Pancrazio is the **Cittadella dei Musei ★** (Piazza Arsenale; 𝄐 **070/662496;** Tues–Sun 9am–8pm), a recently restructured conglomerate of museums and **panoramic grounds ★** in the former Piedmontese arsenal. Within the *cittadella,* the **Museo Archeologico Nazionale di Cagliari ★** (4€) houses artifacts from all over the island, dating from prehistory to the Middle Ages; especially worth a look, and unique to Sardinia, are the small but sophisticated **bronzes ★★** from the Nuragic culture. Across the courtyard, the **Pinacoteca Nazionale** (National Gallery; 2€) contains the island's most important paintings, textiles, armor, ceramics, and jewelry.

Right in the middle of Castello, the **cathedral ★** (*cattedrale,* or *duomo*; Piazza Palazzo, off Via Martini; 𝄐 **070/663837;** free; Mon–Fri 8am–12:30pm and 4:30–8pm; Sat–Sun 8am–1pm and 4–8pm) was constructed in the 13th century in the Pisan style. The church isn't monumental per se, but its combination of Romanesque and Gothic architecture and major artworks make it a memorable detour. Chief among these are splendid **pulpits ★** by Maestro Guglielmo (these were once owned by Il Duomo at Pisa). The carved panels magnificently illustrate the life of Christ. A door leads down to the **Santuario ★**, with its impressive 18th-century baroque tomb of Martin II of Aragon. There are tombs here of the princes of the House of Savoy, plus nearly 300 Christian martyr graves.

After visiting Castello, take a wander around **Stampace,** the district below and west of Castello. Known as the "quarter of the seven churches," Stampace is even older than Castello. With charming pastel buildings and authentic workshops where craftsmen can be seen and heard tinkering with metal and wood, Stampace has preserved its medieval roots. The most colorful square here is the small Piazza Sant'Efisio, home to the **church of Sant'Efisio** (Tues–Sun 9am–1pm and 3:30–7:30pm), dedicated to the patron saint of Sardinia. The **crypt** where Efisio was imprisoned before his execution lies 9m (30 ft.) underground here in Stampace, and can be accessed via steep stairs leading down from the church.

The main archaeological site in Cagliari, and one of the most striking Roman ruins in all of Sardinia, is the 3rd-century **Roman amphitheater ★** (Via dell'Anfiteatro; 📞 070/652956; Tues–Sun 9:30am–1:30pm and Sun also 3:30–5:30pm), set in a primeval valley 300m (984 ft.) northwest of the Cittadella dei Musei end of the Castello district. It was originally elliptical—like a scaled-down version of the Colosseum in Rome—but the southern half is all but gone, leaving just the horseshoe-shaped curve of the northern end, where the original stone seats have largely been built over in the modern era to accommodate concertgoers for the venue's summer season of cultural events. Its capacity in Roman times, when it was used for gladiatorial and animal fights, was 20,000 spectators.

A Day at the Beach

Cagliari in high summer is sweltering. Do as the locals do and trade the tight spaces of the city for the broad expanse of golden sand and turquoise water at **Il Poetto beach.** Poetto is 9km (5½ miles) east of central Cagliari, just north of the Sella del Diavolo headland. To get there, take the bus marked Poetto from Piazza Matteotti, near the waterfront in central Cagliari. The trip takes about 20 minutes and there are several stops where you can get off to access the beach. Along the 6km (3¾-mile) stretch of Il Poetto, markets and kiosks sell beach gear, drinks, and snacks, and there are several restaurants and watersports outfitters, too. Much of the beach is free public access, though you can also find *stabilimenti* (clubs, generally open Apr–Sept), such as **L'Aquila** (Viale Poetto 10; 📞 070/371698), that have lounge chairs, changing rooms, kids' play areas, volleyball, and watersports equipment.

Where to Stay

Due Colonne ★ MARINA   You won't find a more strategic location in Cagliari—the Due Colonne occupies the prime real estate where Via Roma intersects Largo Carlo Felice, in the heart of Cagliari's Marina district, putting guests within steps of the city's most vibrant shopping and dining and the portside promenade. Rooms are classic and comfortable, with big bathrooms; many units have a view over the busy harbor, though these are also a bit noisier.

Via Sardegna 4. 📞 **070/658710.** www.hotel2colonne.it. 23 units. Doubles 110€–130€. AE, DC, MC, V. **Amenities:** Breakfast room; Internet (30 min. free; 2€ per 12 hr. after that). *In room:* A/C, TV, hair dryer, minibar.

La Peonia ★★ NORTH OF CENTER   This is an exceptional B&B in a neo-Gothic palazzo outside central Cagliari. Anton and Vanna, the fantastic hosts who own and manage La Peonia, have a loving touch with their property. With antique beds and floor tiles and red floor-to-ceiling drapes, the rooms have a regal feel, but the bathrooms are especially luxurious, with what many describe as the best shower in Sardinia. The location may be a bit out of the way, but it's only a 15-minute cab (or 20-min. bus) ride into the port area and old Cagliari.

Via Riva Villasanta 77. 📞 **070/513164.** www.lapeonia.com. 3 units. Doubles 72€–88€. MC, V. **Amenities:** Breakfast room; garden; lounge. *In room:* A/C, TV, hair dryer, minibar, free Wi-Fi.

Regina Margherita ★ CENTER   Long the leader of Cagliari hotels before it was knocked off its throne by the T Hotel, this favorite is still the choice for traditionalists. In the center of the city, it's a hotel from the '80s that opens onto water views. A post-millennium overhaul added modern tech to both the public and the private rooms, which are midsize, comfortable, and inviting without being particularly distinguished. The location is halfway between the Terrazza Umberto (Bastione Saint Remy) and the port.

Viale Regina Margherita 44. ✆ **070/670342.** www.hotelreginamargherita.com. 99 units. Doubles 180€–200€. AE, DC, MC, V. **Amenities:** Restaurant; bar; babysitting; room service. *In room:* A/C, TV, hair dryer, minibar, free Wi-Fi.

T Hotel ★ NORTH OF CENTER   A cylindrical skyscraper with a showy contemporary lobby, the T makes quite a statement and is without a doubt the "cool" address in this town. The T has a slick ground floor cafe (tables are set on catwalks surrounded by shallow pools) that draws the dashing and trendy of the city for business lunches and after-work drinks. The lower level houses a futuristic-looking spa. Once off the elevator on the guest unit floors, however, the T disappoints somewhat: Standard rooms, while done up in bold colors and equipped with the latest in "design" fixtures, are on the small side. The king-size mattresses are ridiculously comfortable, however. The staff is eager to please, and there's definitely an appealing energy to the place that's hard to find elsewhere in Cagliari. Note that the hotel is in an anonymous modern neighborhood, about a 10-minute cab or bus ride to the historic district.

Via dei Giudicati 66. ✆ **070/47400.** www.thotel.it. 207 units. Doubles from 180€. AE, DC, MC, V. **Amenities:** 2 restaurants; bar; concierge; pool; room service; spa. *In room:* A/C, TV, hair dryer, minibar, free Wi-Fi.

Where to Dine

Dal Corsaro ★ CENTER   SARDINIAN   One of Cagliari's preeminent dining addresses, this restaurant is classically elegant, catering to both locals out for a special occasion or tourists out for a bit of a splurge. The Deidda family has been in charge since 1967, and they are ambassadors of Sardinian regional cuisine, using only the freshest ingredients. They excel in their fresh fish dishes, including filet of red tuna with an onion fondant, black olives, and tomatoes, and in their filet of white fish with mussels and caramelized eggplant. Especially delicious is their homemade spaghetti with calamari and fresh lemon.

Viale Regina Margherita 28. ✆ **070/664318.** Reservations required. Entrees 15€–30€. AE, DC, MC, V. Mon–Sat 12:30–3:30pm and 8–11pm. Closed first 2 weeks of Jan.

Opera Prima ★★ CENTER   Even better (and less expensive) than Dal Corsaro is this friendly spot along the water just east of the main port area. Opera Prima is the rare dining establishment that does fish and meat equally well, so feel free to toggle back and forth between the *mare* and *terra* selections on the menu. Everything, from the antipasti to the dessert, is mouth-wateringly memorable.

Via Campidano 9. ✆ **070/684619.** Reservations required. Entrees 10€–18€. AE, DC, MC, V. Tues–Sun 12:30–3:30pm and 8–11:30pm.

Pizzeria Il Fantasma ★ CENTER   PIZZA   For cheap and tasty pizzas and a loud and lively atmosphere, Cagliaritani rely on "the Ghost." Much more than the standard array of pizza toppings can be had here (for example, horse meat), and the chef is happy to oblige custom orders and multi-topping combos on a single pie. When there isn't a crowd outside (which is rare), you might well think you have the wrong address—there's no sign, giving it the look of a private office or residence—but trust me, number 77 is where you want to be when you get the urge for pizza.

Via San Domenico 77. © **070/9536618.** Pizzas from 6€. MC, V. Tues–Sun 7:30pm–midnight.

Trattoria L'Infinito ★★ NORTH OF CENTER It may have a slightly inconvenient and unattractive location, near the Santa Gilla marsh between the airport and old Cagliari, but the classics of Mediterranean cuisine—especially seafood in its myriad incarnations—are done so well and for such reasonable prices here that you won't mind the cab ride there and back. *Infinito* certainly describes the house antipasti sampler, which is an abundant service of four heaping plates of fish and vegetable starters (swordfish with eggplant and peppers; tuna with onion; grilled scallops; sautés of crayfish, shellfish, shrimp . . . just to name a few of the possibilities). Many diners are sated after the antipasti alone, but if you can, save room for the glorious pastas, like lobster tagliolini. Portions are always heaping, and the waiters efficient and jovial. But best of all is how honest the prices are: For about 25€ a head, you'll eat like a king.

Via Santa Gilla 39. © **070/283261.** Reservations required. Entrees 10€–16€. AE, DC, MC, V. Daily 12:30–3:30pm and 7:30–11pm.

Cagliari After Dark

The best place to soak up what nightlife there is in the Sardinian capital is atop the ramparts of the Castello district. Ground zero of the action is Bastione Saint Remy and the **Caffè degli Spiriti** ★★ (see "Exploring," above), whose open-air bar is abuzz with scenesters well into the wee hours. Not far away, the cavelike bar **Librarium Nostrum** ★ (Via Santa Croce 33; © 070/650943) is a hip hideaway with expertly mixed cocktails. From the outside tables, set against the retaining wall of Castello, there's a nice view over the Stampace quarter. After a day at the beach of Poetto, **Twist Bar** (Lungomare Poetto, 5th stop; © 348/2749236) is a relaxed place to hang with locals.

SIDE TRIPS

In addition to the ideas below, you can also theoretically use Cagliari as a base for daylong forays to the beaches of Chia (p. 305) or Villasimius (p. 311). Each is only about a 90-minute drive from the capital; however, most beach-minded vacationers prefer to base themselves in those resort areas, which are well equipped with accommodations and dining.

North to Su Nuraxi Nuraghe & the Giara di Gesturi

The largest, oldest, and most celebrated of Sardinia's unique *nuraghi* (and Sardinia's only UNESCO World Heritage site) is **Su Nuraxi** ★★ (© 070/9368128; daily 9am–sunset; 4.20€ includes obligatory guided tour, offered every half-hour) and its attached *nuraghic* village, near the town of Barumini. Su Nuraxi, which just means "the *nuraghe*," is an easy half-day trip from Cagliari (90-min. drive each way) or detour off the main north-south highway, the SS. 131/E25, if you're driving between Cagliari and Oristano or northern Sardinia. About 40km (25 miles) north of Cagliari, exit the highway and follow SS. 197 to Barumini for 20km (12 miles), then follow brown signs to "Su Nuraxi" or "Nuraghe." The site is located on the SP44, just west of Barumini, before the town of Tuili. You can park outside the site and get an overview of the exterior anytime; but to step beyond the chain and see the inside of the *nuraghe,* you must pay and join one of the free guided tours, offered every half-hour. Within the 1500 B.C. *nuraghe,* which is dominated by a conical central tower, or *mastio,* 19m (62 ft.) high, there are all sorts of mystical-feeling corridors and stairs, and guides will point out ingenious engineering touches. The complex is a dream for photographers, both for the evocative masonry and for the commanding views over the surrounding countryside.

Immediately north of Su Nuraxi is the basalt plateau called the **Giara di Gesturi** ★★. This is an absolutely idyllic area for hiking, with cork oak woods alternating with savannah and little mirrorlike ponds. The Giara di Gesturi is home to a species of miniature horse, *is quaddeddus,* which is only about 1m (3 ft.) tall and unique to this habitat. The easiest way to reach the area is from Gesturi, north of Barumini.

West to the Ruins at Nora

Sardinia's most important Roman ruins are at the **archaeological area of Nora** ★★ (© 070/921470; daily 9am–8pm, in winter until 5:30pm; 5.50€), scattered along the water at Capo di Pula promontory, an easy 36km (22-mile) drive from Cagliari. Follow highway signs to Pula; after about 25km (16 miles) on the SS. 195, follow brown signs to Nora, *città romana* or *zona archeologica.*

The site of Nora has Phoenician and Carthaginian origins, but most of that archaic city disappeared underneath the Romans' ambitious building program, which reached its zenith in the 1st and 2nd centuries A.D. The standout monument of Nora is the **Roman theater,** which has much of its *cavea* (seating area) and stage substructures intact. Nora also had several bath complexes, the best preserved of which are the **Piccole Terme** (small baths). Around the site, you can also make out a **water tank** *(serbatoio),* a **marketplace and warehouse** *(macello),* and a house, the **Casa dell'Atrio Tetrastilo,** from the 3rd century A.D.

Nora is part of a larger town, **Pula** ★, which is a fun detour in its own right. The main piazza is always lively and there are good restaurants and shopping.

Southwestern Sardinia & the Sulcitan Islands ★★

Unless you're heading for one of the cushy "resort-villages" in Santa Margherita di Pula, southwestern Sardinia feels remote and offbeat. Brawny foothills, shady pinewoods, and windswept dunes predominate on this largely uncontaminated stretch of coast; hotels and resorts are oases unto themselves, and there isn't much in the way of village life. If you're looking for a social atmosphere and "action," this probably isn't where you want to be. On the flipside, the atmosphere in the southwest is utterly romantic and relaxing, and the top attractions here—the beaches—are plenty compelling for anyone in search of a place to chill and unwind. The best stretches are along the Costa del Sud, around Chia and Teulada, and on the Sulcitan islands of Sant'Antioco and San Pietro. Completing the beach vibe, there are even pink flamingoes living in a marsh behind the beaches of Chia. This part of the island gets a lot of wind, making it a destination for windsurfers and kitesurfers, but nearly all of the beaches have calm, kid-friendly waters.

All the places listed here are less than a 2-hour drive from Cagliari's Elmas airport, and most are only about an hour away. One of the main roads in southwestern

Sardinia, the coastal SP71 highway between Chia and Teulada, ranks as one of the most spectacular drives in Italy. Many hotels here provide bicycles for their guests, which are a viable option for getting from beach to beach and for experiencing the panoramic SP71. Sant'Antioco is connected by causeway to the mainland; to reach San Pietro island and its charming village of Carloforte, you can take a ferry from Calasetta on Sant'Antioco or from Portoscuso on the mainland.

Chia & the Costa del Sud ★★

Virgin dunes and stunning white-sand beaches lapped by waters in amazingly variegated shades of turquoise make the seaside around Chia and Capo Teulada the most popular zone in southwest Sardinia. Santa Margherita, which you'll drive through on the way down here from Cagliari, is almost entirely private beach, either belonging to all-inclusive resorts (like the way overrated and overpriced Forte Village—don't even consider it) or vacation homes. The beaches of Santa Margherita di Pula are nowhere near as pretty as those near Chia and Teulada, so don't let those snobby gated properties make you feel like you're missing out!

Beyond the vacation homes, hotels, and beaches, Chia itself isn't a real town. The **Mongittu** coffee bar and market (at the turnoff for "Chia" on the SP71) are pretty much the extent of services here, and there are no real cultural attractions. Don't expect much more in Domus de Maria, the slightly larger *comune* of which Chia is part. Luckily, the hotels and beach clubs in the area have all the services you need. Teulada is more of a village, albeit a quiet one, and is known for its handicrafts.

It may be difficult to tear yourself away from the beaches, but this area also boasts an inland natural treasure in the **Is Cannoneris forest ★★** (Località Sedda Is Tovus; ✆ 070/9270285), an easy half-hour detour from Chia. At 4,768 hectares (11,782 acres), it's one of the largest holm oak forests in Europe and is home to many

> ### Ch-Ch-Ch-Chia
>
> The Costa del Sud town of Chia is pronounced *kee*-a, like the Korean car maker, not *chee*-a, like the '70s planter "pets."

examples of endemic fauna, like the Sardinian deer. An extensive network of well-maintained paths makes this a hiker's dream and a great option when you've had too much sun. (To reach Is Cannoneris, drive to the town of Domus de Maria, then follow signs to Sedda Is Tovus and Is Cannoneris.)

BEACHES

The prime beach zone begins just before (east of) the Torre di Chia, an old Spanish watchtower. (From the SP71 highway, follow signs to Torre di Chia.) The beach directly below the tower is called **Su Portu,** a perfectly rounded sickle of the kind of brilliant and fine white sand that is the hallmark of this part of Sardinia. Along the access road to Su Portu, another road branches off to the left and to the longer beach of **Sa Colonia ★**. Sa Colonia is backed by the Stagno di Chia (Chia Pond), which is full of **pink flamingoes,** herons, and cormorants.

Back on SP71, continue west for another 1.7km (1 mile) to reach the turnoff for Su Giudeu. In fact, this road leads to several beaches (and several hotels), including Campana, Su Giudeu, and Cala Cipolla. Each of these is signposted, but drive slowly so as not to miss them; Cala Cipolla is the farthest away, though it's only 2km (1¼ miles) in from the main highway. **Campana ★** is the first one you'll come to, and it's essentially an extension of the larger beach to the west, **Su Giudeu ★★**; together, they form a wide expanse of gently sloping golden sand and placid water that is generally regarded as the best beach in Cagliari province. Su Giudeu has all the facilities you need. At the far western end of Su Giudeu, follow a short stretch of dirt road to **Cala Cipolla ★★**, a delightful cove set within a narrow bay, framed by granitic promontories and dense *macchia mediterranea*.

After Cala Cipolla and Capo Spartivento promontory, Chia ends and the coast becomes rather squiggly and mostly rocky, with no beach access for several kilometers. Return to the SP71, following signs for Teulada, and go west about 5km (3 miles); turn left where you see signs for Tuerredda, the most celebrated sunning and swimming locale of the Costa del Sud. **Tuerredda ★★★** is a south-facing cove, within a larger and protected bay of powdery sand and quasi-Polynesian sea. In the middle of the bay, accessible by a short swim through crystalline blue-green waters, is the Isolotto di Tuerredda, an islet where you can dry off on the smooth, sun-warmed rocks or sand. Tuerredda has a snack bar, a restaurant, and boat rentals. Spread your towel on the sand or rent a beach chair from one of the vendors.

The next bathing spot west of Tuerredda is **Cala Piscinnì** (7.5km/4¾ miles west of Tuerredda), with small and rocky coves alongside the sandy beach. Several kilometers north along this coastline, which is the eastern boundary of the Golfo di Teulada, **Campionna** and **Porto Teulada** are both decent sandy beaches that don't get many crowds. Rounding the western side of the Golfo di Teulada, the beach of **Porto Tramatzu ★** is well equipped with services and has a narrow strip of sand and wonderfully transparent waters. It sits opposite Isola Rossa, which can be reached with organized tours.

A bit farther afield, on the west side of Capo Teulada, is **Porto Pino** beach (from Teulada, follow signs to Sant'Anna Arresi, then signs to Porto Pino). The popular Porto Pino has exceptionally high dunes, woods with rare Aleppo pines, and lots of services. It gets pretty windy over here—surfers love it.

WHERE TO STAY & DINE

Even the simplest hotels in this area are rather pricey in high season. For something more affordable, try the **Locanda Sa Colonia** (© **070/9230001;** www.sacolonia chia.it; doubles 140€–190€), on the beach in Chia. A campground, **Campeggio Torre Chia** (Viale del Porto 21; © **070/9230054;** www.campeggiotorrechia.it) also rents bungalows that sleep two to four and have kitchenettes for 85€ to 125€ per night. Chances are you'll take most of your meals at your hotel, but there are a few restaurants to choose from in the area.

Agriturismo Sa Mitza e S'Orcu ★ 🏠 INLAND Near the entrance to Is Cannoneris forest, this farm, restaurant, and guesthouse is a lovely mountain retreat only 15 minutes from the beaches of Chia. Each of the units is rustic and cozy and has a balcony with sweeping views of the valley and sea below. Meals, made strictly with handmade or local ingredients, are served in the vaulted farmhouse dining room. Even if you don't sleep here, try out their restaurant.

Strada Montana per Is Cannoneris, outside Domus de Maria. © **070/9236207.** www.samitzaesorcu.it. 6 units. Doubles from 80 €. MC, V. **Amenities:** Restaurant; garden. *In room:* Terrace/balcony.

Aquadulci ★★ CHIA Discreet luxury is the hallmark of this hotel near the beach of Su Giudeu. The Aquadulci features minimalist, eco-friendly style in its airy, contemporary guest rooms and common areas. Within steps of your room is the hotel's

LUXURY lighthouse

In 2009, Alessio Raggio, the owner of the hip and wildly successful Cagliari bar Caffè degli Spiriti, opened the five-star guesthouse **Faro di Caposparti-vento** ★★★ (Viale Spartivento, Chia; ✆ **333/3129638;** www.faro capospartivento.com) inside the old lighthouse on the point between Chia and Capo Teulada. Consisting of six gorgeous suites worthy of an *Architectural Digest* spread (where it was once featured), the residence can be booked as a whole or on a single-unit basis. Rates range from 300€ to 800€ per night. The facility comes with full-time chefs and housekeeping staff and can be rented out for special events.

subtropical garden, where hammocks are suspended between palms, and its swimming pool. The whole place has the feel of a spa, and in fact there is an onsite *centro benessere* with the full gamut of massages and body treatments. The famous beaches of Chia are less than a 10-minute walk away, on a boardwalk over the dunes. Guests are mostly Italian, especially young families and honeymooners. *Tip:* Classic rooms are really too small; opt for a superior or junior suite if budget allows.

Località Capo Spartivento, Chia. ✆ **070/9230555.** www.aquadulci.com. 41 units. Doubles 180€–450€. AE, DC, MC, V. **Amenities:** Restaurant; bar; babysitting; beach facilities; bike rentals; concierge; garden; pool; room service; spa. *In room:* A/C, TV, hair dryer, minibar, free Wi-Fi.

Ristorante Crar'e Luna ★ CHIA   SARDINIAN/SEAFOOD   In a converted agricultural warehouse where vineyards meet the dunes of Chia, this is a lovely country-style eatery where you can expect warm, familiar service and memorable meals. You feel like you're in the middle of nowhere, so protected is it from noise and traffic, but it's right off the main road. Most noteworthy among the culinary offerings are excellent fish and a huge antipasto spread. Kids can romp on the spacious lawn surrounding the place.

Viale Chia. ✆ **070/9230056.** Reservations recommended. Entrees 10€–18€. AE, DC, MC, V. Daily 7:30–11pm; Tues–Sun noon–3pm.

Ristorante Mirage ★ CHIA   SARDINIAN/SEAFOOD   Seafood reigns at what many regard as the best freestanding restaurant in Chia. It's not cheap, but the cuisine is to die for and a dinner here the perfect way to cap off a day of rest and relaxation on the beach. The word is out—it's a must to book your table in advance. The place is open year-round, which is a good sign: Long after the tourists have gone home, a dedicated customer base of locals keeps the Mirage in business.

Viale Chia 10. ✆ **070/9230249.** www.miragechia.it. Reservations recommended. Entrees 12€–20€. AE, DC, MC, V. Wed–Mon noon–3pm, 7:30–11:30pm.

THE SULCITAN ISLANDS ★

Just when you thought Sardinia couldn't feel any stranger or more detached from the rest of the world, along come the Sulcitan islands. Lying just off the southwestern tip of the mainland, the islands of Sant'Antioco and San Pietro are well worth a visit, whether as a day trip from Chia (an hour's drive) or overnight, both for their beaches and interesting historical sights. Sant'Antioco has significant archaeological attractions in its Phoenician *tophet, Punic* necropolis, and the ancient basilica and catacombs of Sant'Antioco. Since Roman times, Sant'Antioco (88 sq. km/34 sq. miles) has been connected by artificial isthmus and causeway to the mainland, so it feels less like an island than San Pietro (51 sq. km/20 sq. miles), which can only be reached by ferry (30 min. from Calasetta on Sant'Antioco or Portoscuso on the mainland) and has a more dramatic coastline of deep-set coves and rocky promontories. On San Pietro, the only town is delightful Carloforte. Originally settled by a party of Genoese in the 18th century (they were exiles of the pirate-battered coast of Tunisia), the port retains its Ligurian traditions, both in the language spoken by locals and the architecture. With orderly and clean blocks of pastel houses and a picturesque waterfront, it's like a smaller, more exotic version of Portofino, and it's getting trendier by the minute. Rich Milanese are especially fond of Carloforte and have built some gorgeous vacation homes along the water on the outskirts of town. San Pietro is also famous for its oft-photographed 16m-high (52-ft.) off-shore rock stacks, *Le Colonne* ("the columns").

Relaxation and warm, authentic hospitality prevail along these coasts. Each island's villages come alive for the evening *passeggiata,* but the rest of the time, the Sulcitan islands are calm and quiet but for the sound of the wind and the sea.

Sant'Antioco ★

Sure, there are beaches here, but the most compelling reason to make the trip across the 3km (2-mile) causeway to Sant'Antioco is for its history and archaeological attractions. It's an island with ancient roots and much of its interesting heritage is on display for visitors. The Phoenicians founded a city on Sant'Antioco in the 8th century B.C., calling it Sulky (hence the "Sulcitan" islands). Then came the Carthaginians in the 6th century, and they stayed for 400 years until the Romans took over. Both the Phoenicians and Carthaginians left meaningful traces of their cultures, mostly in their funerary arts and customs.

In the Roman era, the island got another name, Plumbaria, for its valuable lead deposits. Along the way, the Romans martyred a Christian evangelist named Antiochus here in the 2nd century. After the Romans, the island became a Byzantine stronghold that eventually succumbed to repeated Saracen raids. A few devotees of St. Antiochus remained and renamed the island Sant'Antioco. His 5th-century basilica and catacombs are both very evocative of the island's millennial history.

Life is slow and simple on Sant'Antioco today. The island has several good sandy beaches and a typical village atmosphere in the main town, also called Sant'Antioco, though none of the magic of its sister island, San Pietro. Ferries for Carloforte on San Pietro depart a few kilometers away, at modern resort development of Calasetta.

The **tourist office** is in Sant'Antioco town at Piazza della Repubblica 31a (© **070/182031;** Mon–Fri 9am–noon and 5:30–9pm).

Exploring

The archaeology of Sant'Antioco begins with your very crossing onto the island. The causeway was first built in the Punic era and later reinforced by the Romans, whose characteristic masonry arches can be seen in the structure. In town, you can visit the **Archaeological Area of Sulci ★** (© **0781/800596;** admission is 1.50€ to each site; daily 9am–8pm in summer, with more restricted but still daily hours in winter), which consists of several scattered excavations relating to ancient Sulky, including the Phoenician **tophet** (crematorium and cemetery for infants), remains of the **Phoeni-cian-Punic city and necropolis,** the **Museo Archeologico Comunale,** and, not of the Sulky period, the **Forte Su Pisu,** a roofless 19th-century fortress built by the house of Savoy.

The most venerated attraction on the island is the **sanctuary of Sant'Antioco** ★ (℃ **0781/83044;** daily 9am–12:30pm and 3–7pm), comprising the 5th-century Byzantine basilica (modified in the 11th and 18th c.) dedicated to the saint and the catacombs underneath, used by the Christians for their tombs from the 2nd to the 7th centuries A.D.

After touring the dusty ruins and dank churches, rinse off and refresh with a dip at one of Sant'Antioco's low-key beaches. The best are **Coaquaddus** ★ and **Maladroxia** ★ on the southeastern side of the island, **Cala Lunga** on the west side, and **Spiaggia Grande** and **Le Saline** on the northeast side, near Calasetta. As always in Sardinia, the prevailing wind can be a factor in which beach you choose—luckily Sant'Antioco has beaches facing all directions, so you can always find a protected spot no matter which way the wind is blowing.

San Pietro ★★

Of the two Sulcitan islands, San Pietro is the prettier sibling. Not only is San Pietro endowed with more natural splendor than scrubby Sant'Antioco, but the atmosphere and architecture are more attractive, too. Mostly thanks to the charming Ligurian-style port town here, Carloforte, there's a subtly chic feel to San Pietro. In summertime, gleaming yachts pull into harbor, and it reminds you a bit of St. Tropez—or what St. Tropez might have been like 100 years ago. Most restaurants on San Pietro feature *cucina tabarkina*—dishes developed by the Genovese colonists of Tabarka, Tunisia, who migrated to San Pietro in the 18th century. Mainstays include *cascà*, a sort of couscous, and lots of local seafood.

To reach San Pietro, take the **Saremar** (℃ **0781/88430;** www.saremar.it) or **Delcomar** (℃ **0781/857123;** www.delcomar.it) ferry from Calasetta, on Sant'Antioco. Boats leave every half-hour for the 30- to 40-minute crossing; one-way fares are 5.30€ per passenger and 8.40€ per vehicle. You can also reach San Pietro from Porto Vesme (the name of Portoscuso's port) on the mainland (5.90€ per passenger, 9.80€ per vehicle; 45 min. crossing time) with the same companies. Take a car, because you'll need one to get to the best beaches.

Exploring

Carloforte ★★ is the only town on San Pietro, and you'll want to spend at least a few hours wandering the cobblestoned streets of this elegant port. Go for a walk along the palm-lined **waterfront** and ogle the boats, then stop in for a meal at one of the harbor-facing restaurants; there are several to choose from along Corso Cavour. Besides the seafront promenade, the main pedestrian drag in town is **Corso Tagliafico,** leading up from the ferry dock and Piazza Pegli. Lined with smart cafes and shops, Corso Tagliafico and its terminus, **Piazza della Repubblica,** act as a sort of open-air living room for Carloforte residents and visitors. The **Pro Loco** visitors' office, which can furnish maps of the island and point out various attractions, is at Corso Tagliafico 1 (℃ **070/854009**).

As for the rest of the island, it doesn't take more than about 15 minutes to drive to any given spot, and the main reason you'll want to get out on the island is for San Pietro's wonderful and secluded beaches.

If you only have time for one beach on San Pietro, head to **Bobba** ★★, near the southern tip of the island. It's small but sandy, framed by dark rocks, and has the distinction of being the only beach with a view of the **Colonne** rock stacks in the waters just offshore. Nearby, a trail leads along the top of the cliffs (the walk is short, flat, and not scary) to Punta delle Colonne, directly overlooking the rock columns. Another popular beach is **La Caletta ★**, also known as Lo Spalmatore, on the western side of the island. La Caletta is set in the middle of a wide, calm bay with beautiful turquoise water, given interesting color and light effects by the smooth rocks on the seafloor. For something totally different, **Cala Fico ★** on the northwest coast is a fjordlike cove with a pebbly beach.

Touring the perimeter of San Pietro is also possible by boat, and the only way to see the most striking cliffs and geological formations of the island, concentrated mostly along the impenetrable northwest coast, is from the water. You'll find plenty of outfitters for *gommone* rentals and organized tours at Carloforte marina.

Where to Stay & Dine

On both islands, quick casual eating and drinking can be found at bars along the main promenades—Corso Cavour and Corso Tagliafico on San Pietro and Corso Vittorio Emanuele on Sant'Antioco. In addition to the listings below, the **restaurant at the Moderno hotel** in Sant'Antioco (Via Nazionale 82; ✆ **0781/83105**) is a good, if expensive, bet for seafood in a pretty garden setting.

SAN PIETRO

Al Tonno di Corsa ★★ SEAFOOD Tuna—the historic lifeblood of San Pietro— is the main event at this handsome, old-school *ristorante* with cozy indoor dining as well as outside tables with an oblique view of the port. Let the waitstaff guide you through the myriad tuna offerings (like *capunnadda*, a variation on the classic *caponata* antipasto, with tuna instead of eggplant); but if you're not in a fishy mood, they also serve excellent renditions of traditional non-seafood dishes like *bobba*, a puree of fava beans and vegetables. Most pastas and *secondi* feature fresh fish and vegetables.

Via Marconi 47, Carloforte, Isola San Pietro. ✆ **0781/855106.** Reservations recommended. Entrees 14€–24€. AE, DC, MC, V. Daily 12:30–2:30pm and 8–10:30pm; closed for part of winter, exact dates vary.

Hieracon ★★ This pale mint Art Nouveau palazzo directly on the waterfront of Carloforte has an air of aristocratic history about it, and in fact it was a noble family residence and consulate before being converted to a hotel in the 1980s—luckily, without sacrificing the period flair of the place. In the guest rooms, marble floors, tall ceilings, and antiques are lightened by warm textiles, and though a few modern comforts have been installed, the overall feel is sober and classic. Opt for a deluxe sea-view room, as they don't cost much more than classics and superiors. The top floor "classic" rooms are the least desirable of the bunch.

Lungomare Corso Cavour 62, Carloforte, Isola San Pietro. ✆ **0781/854028.** www.hotelhieracon.com. 24 units. Doubles 95€–160€. AE, DC, MC, V. **Amenities:** Restaurant; bar; concierge. *In room:* A/C, TV, hair dryer, minibar, free Wi-Fi.

SANT'ANTIOCO

Del Corso ITALIAN Sant'Antioco doesn't have any real standout accommodations, but the Del Corso is a no-frills Italian three-star with a prime location and good-value rooms. The attached **Café del Corso** is the best coffee and pastry bar on the island and a social hot spot around the clock.

Corso Vittorio Emanuele 32, Sant'Antioco. ✆ **0781/800265.** www.hoteldelcorso.it. 11 units. Doubles 69€–100€. MC, V. **Amenities:** Breakfast room; excursions. *In room:* A/C, TV.

Pasqualino ★ SEAFOOD Your best bet for fish and classic island cuisine on Sant'Antioco is probably the most popular restaurant in Calasetta, so book a table in advance. What Pasqualino lacks in superficial style it makes up for in reliable, spot-on cooking. The house couscous, flavored with seafood and local herbs, is wonderful.

Via Roma 99. © **0781/88473.** Reservations recommended. Entrees 10€–18€. AE, DC, MC, V. May–Sept daily 12:30–2:30pm and 7:30–10:30pm; closed Tues the rest of the year; closed Feb.

Southeastern Sardinia: Villasimius & the Costa Rei ★★

When waxing rhapsodic about Sardinia's Caribbean-like seas, island aficionados are usually talking about the southeast part of the island. This beach paradise—namely around Villasimius and the Costa Rei—is mighty tempting for the weekend sun seeker or anyone looking for complete relaxation. Only an hour's drive from Cagliari, this stretch of the island has a gorgeous landscape that is somewhere between the South Pacific and the Costa Smeralda, full of turquoise coves fringed by fine sandy beaches and backed by lush vegetation and granite outcrops. Pirate ships wouldn't look out of place along this coast, but all you'll find are well-worn fishing boats bobbing around, often in front of casual beach-hut restaurants where you can eat simple, good food while rubbing sand between your toes and listening to a soundtrack of gently lapping waves. This Mediterranean idyll can be yours for prices considerably lower than what you'll pay on the Costa Smeralda or even in the southwest, around Chia. If there's a downside to all this, it's that the southeast has been developed recently and quite rapidly (a situation common to Sardinia's prettiest coastlines) as a sort of more democratic, family-oriented cousin of the Costa Smeralda. The coast around Villasimius and Punta Rei, a bit north, is chockablock with modern holiday homes and vacation villages. Having only been built up in the past few decades, the actual towns here have little personality and not much in the way of cultural activities. However, they're sunny, clean, and have plenty of services to make for a stress-free, if slightly soulless, vacation. And oh, those beaches!

EXPLORING

No need to worry about hitting the sights or wasting any of your precious daylight hours dutifully traipsing through interesting towns. There aren't any. Instead, it's all about the amazing, endless beaches down in the southeastern corner of Sardinia. The multifaceted coast around Villasimius has one long stretch of sugary sand beach after another. Farther north, the pearly white beach at Costa Rei goes on for miles, lapped by the most stunning emerald waters, but it's also much more crowded up here: The Costa Rei is new-vacation-construction central. But the good news is you don't have to pick just one spot: The distances in this beach paradise are so short (only 25km/16 miles from Villasimius to the far northern end of Costa Rei), you can easily sample everything even during a short trip.

The best beach in the seaside development of Villasimius is **Porto Giunco ★**, sometimes called the "beach of two seas" because the Mediterranean on the eastern side and the Notteri pond on the western side, are separated by a tongue of sand just a few dozen meters wide. Porto Giunco's very white, fine sand and striking looks have made it a popular location for Italian TV spots promoting the glamorous beach life. Services abound here, and there are many hotels and restaurants nearby. A bit north of here, **Spiaggia Simius ★** is the well-equipped town beach of Villasimius, with a wide band of superfine sand—great for long beach walks.

Leaving some of that development behind, head north to **Punta Molentis ★★** and the eponymous beach there, a little peninsular promontory with sea on both sides (sand to the west, rocks to the east) and a charming little thatched-roof *ristoro* (casual restaurant) called I Due Mari (by reservation only, see "Where to Stay & Dine," below), accessible by a boardwalk over the rocks. Punta Molentis is hardly ever crowded, nor is the excellent beach at **Cala Sinzias ★★★**, about 15km (9⅓ miles) north of here. Cala Sinzias is one of those vacation-in-paradise poster-child beaches—a smooth expanse of pale golden-pink sand lapped by gin clear turquoise water. Rent beach chairs from the Hotel Garden Beach Cala Sinzias (see "Where to Stay & Dine," below).

This paradisiacal setting is the beginning of the Costa Rei, which refers to the long parenthesis of sandy shore between Cala Sinzias and Capo Ferrato. However, farther north, the Costa Rei gets a lot more crowded and its beaches much more prone to strong winds, especially the *maestrale* from the north that can blow sand all over you and make it difficult to enjoy the gorgeous setting unless you're a windsurfer. The flourlike sand of **Costa Rei ★★** beach goes on for 8km (5 miles), backed by thousands of cookie-cutter vacation homes, most of which have been erected in the past 20 years. A boardwalk runs up and down, and there are services and water equipment rentals galore, making the Costa Rei perfect for long walks and a social, sporty vibe.

WHERE TO STAY & DINE

Vacation houses abound in coastal southeastern Sardinia; an agency with comprehensive listings for modern, well-appointed villas is **Rent Sardinia** (✆ **848580081** toll-free in Italy or 070/684545; www.rent-sardinia.com). A property that sleeps six can range from about 800€ per week in low season to upwards of 3,000€ per week in high season, depending on the location, distance from the water, and amenities.

Hotel Garden Beach Cala Sinzias ★★ CALA SINZIAS   The setting alone, between the eucalyptus woods and gorgeous sands of Cala Sinzias beach, is enough of a selling point, but the Garden Beach is also a very well run, attractive hotel with comprehensive services and amenities. Guest rooms are in low-slung Spanish style buildings and decorated with charming Sardinian flair. Handsome pavilions around the property house bars and restaurants, though nothing makes as big an impression as the swimming pool, as big as a small sea. A robust lineup of kids' club activities (soccer camps, dance) will keep the little ones busy.

Strada Panoramica Villasimius-Costa Rei, Cala Sinzias. ✆ **070/995037.** www.hotelgardenbeach.it. 106 units. Doubles 85€–220€. AE, DC, MC, V. **Amenities:** 3 restaurants; bar; babysitting; beach facilities; beach volleyball; boutique; fitness room; kids' programs; playground; pool; tennis; watersports equipment.

Hotel Mariposas ★ VILLASIMIUS   A contiguous jumble of pink and yellow stucco under red tile roofs, the Mariposas does its best to look like it's always been part of this beautiful Mediterranean landscape. All rooms, done up in homey Mediterranean beach house style, have a terrace overlooking the grassy garden and pool, and about 1km (¾ mile) away, the sea. It's an easy 10-minute walk to the beach or 15 minutes to Villasimius town. Best of all, the exceptionally welcoming staff will do anything to make your holiday more relaxing.

Viale Matteotti, Villasimius. ✆ **070/790084.** www.hotelmariposas.it. 23 units. Doubles 86€–216€. AE, DC, MC, V. **Amenities:** Babysitting; bicycle and scooter rentals; diving center; garden; pool; free Wi-Fi. *In room:* A/C, TV, minibar.

I Due Mari ★ PUNTA MOLENTIS   On the far outer curve of Punta Molentis beach, this open-air cafe is open by reservation only for lunch and dinner. The set menu includes an appetizer, loads of grilled fish, dessert, wine, water, espresso, and a *digestivo*. It's not a gourmet experience but the intimate setting in this quiet cove, weathered fishing boats bobbing within spitting distance, is sublime.

Punta Molentis, 3km (2 miles) east of Villasimius. ⓒ **393/4077632** or 346/5221679. Reservations essential. Prix-fixe lunch 20€; dinner 40€. No credit cards. June–Sept at 1pm for lunch; 9pm for dinner.

Il Miraggio ★★★ ☺ 📷 VILLASIMIUS   SEAFOOD/SARDINIAN   Torchlight flickering around you, your toes in the sand, feast on amazing seafood pastas and grilled fish at this wonderful beach restaurant near Villasimius. During the day, it's a kiosk that sells *panini* to beachgoers and serves quick lunches, but at dinner, the food gets a bit more serious and all tables are moved out on the sand and under the stars. When booking your table, specify *prima fila* (front row) so that you can gaze out past the dwarf palms and flaming tiki torches to the sea—and perhaps also keep an eye on your kids, who are welcome at this informal place and often play in the sand between courses. As low-key and family-friendly as it is, Il Miraggio is also a bit trendy; I've even spotted a few Italian celebrities here.

Località Campus, Villasimius. ⓒ **070/798021.** Reservations essential. Entrees 8€–16€. AE, DC, MC, V. Apr–Oct daily 11:30am–3:30pm (snack bar/lunch) and 8–11pm.

NORTHEASTERN SARDINIA: COSTA SMERALDA & MADDALENA ARCHIPELAGO ★★★

When I first lived in Italy in my 20s, my beach reading of choice was *Chi,* Italy's version of *US Weekly.* Invariably, the hot-actress-and-star-soccer-player fling du jour was always photographed somewhere off the northern coast of Sardinia—the dateline would be Porto Cervo, or Palau, or La Maddalena—canoodling for the paparazzi on the back of someone's yacht, romping in the turquoise waters of some sugary beach that looked like the Caribbean, or partying at Flavio Briatore's infamous disco, Billionaire. To me, that part of Italy, Sardinia's Costa Smeralda ("Emerald Coast"), represented the ultimate in Italian fabulosity. Everyone was so tanned and radiant. I had to see it for myself.

When I got there, it wasn't quite what I expected, in ways both good and bad. Overall, I love it, and I love to hate it. But for better or worse, the Costa Smeralda is foremost in my mind when I think of a trip to Sardinia. Most Sards would cringe at that, because admittedly there's little authentic Sardinian culture up in these parts, but the Costa Smeralda is such a stunning and rarefied pocket of the world (that just happens to be in Sardinia) that it's a must-see on this island.

The landscape on this coast also happens to be drop-dead gorgeous—striking pink granite outcrops recalling the red rocks of the American Southwest, mixed with vibrant oleanders, gnarled juniper trees, and umbrella pines bent by the wind. It's the desert meets the Med, and it's rapture for the eyes. The coast is riddled with mostly small, though pretty, sandy beaches with calm bays for swimming, and although you can certainly drive from beach to beach, regulars putter around these glittering waters in boats.

As impressive as the natural setting and the cleanliness of it all is, the developed areas feel utterly fake, un-Italian, and despite an obvious veneer of wealth, not very glamorous at all—this for me was a *grande delusione* (big disappointment). How could Heidi Klum and Naomi Campbell, not to mention all those Adonises of the Italian soccer field, spend their summers *here?* Of course, the fake feel should come as no surprise, because the Costa Smeralda was built up only a few decades ago, and marketed from the get-go as a hideaway for the international jet set. The Aga Khan purchased this 35-mile stretch of then-virgin coastline, as well as 12,950 hectares (32,000 acres) of land along it, in the 1960s. The area was dubbed *Costa Smeralda* ("Emerald Coast"), and ersatz villages sprouted up around the natural harbors and gated villa compounds went up on the promontories. Sure enough, the package attracted the rich and famous, and became the luxury playground it is today.

The main developments along the Costa Smeralda are Porto Cervo and Porto Rotondo, each with a requisite jumble of new pastel buildings that is really just a cleverly disguised outdoor mall with a *Vogue*-perfect lineup of designer boutiques arranged around a simulated piazza. You can get expensive drinks and machine-made gelato at sterile cafes, and gleaming sailboats bob in the modern harbors. Between the two of them, Porto Cervo and Porto Rotondo have about 2 grams of soul. Yet in July and August, the entire coast is chockablock with sun seekers and revelers, oligarchs and skippers, and the Costa Smeralda is, out of all Italian island and seaside locales, *the* place to be. No contest.

The scenic and friendly Maddalena archipelago, an easy hop from anywhere along the Costa Smeralda, is perhaps the most compelling attraction in northeastern Sardinia. The vibe is low-key and the nature is lovely—lots of exposed peach-toned rock, maritime pines, and quiet sandy coves, and almost all of it is protected as parkland of the Parco Nazionale dell'Arcipelago della Maddalena. La Maddalena and its secondary islands offer a kinder, gentler way to experience the glorious sea and scenery of northeastern Sardinia.

GETTING THERE   The northeast is well served both by air (Olbia airport) and sea (ports of Olbia and Golfo Aranci). The **Maddalena archipelago** is exclusively reached by sea. Regularly scheduled ferries leave from Palau every 15 minutes and arrive at La Maddalena 20 minutes later. Ferries are operated by **Saremar** (✆ **0789/709270;** www.saremar.it) and **Enermar** (✆ **0789/708484**); the trip costs 2.50€ per person each way; a car costs an extra 6€ each way. From Palau, from La Maddalena island itself, or from most any cove with a dock along the Costa Smeralda, you can arrange group or private boat trips to the other islands in the group; see "Boating," below.

Costa Smeralda ★★

Loosely speaking, the Costa Smeralda is the coastal zone between Porto Rotondo and Baja Sardinia. Purists, however, point out that the real borders of the original Costa Smeralda development are much more restricted: It basically includes Porto Cervo and environs, from the beach of Liscia Ruja in the south to Liscia di Vacca and the Hotel Pitrizza in the northwest. Along the roads of the Costa Smeralda, giant granite boulders engraved with *Pirates of the Caribbean*–style lettering announce the various swanky subdivisions, like Cala di Volpe and Romazzino. Because the scenery and vibe are similar all along this stretch of coastline, I am going to upset the purists and lump some technically non-Costa Smeralda locales (such as Baja Sardinia and Porto Rotondo) into this section.

Costa Smerelda & La Maddalena

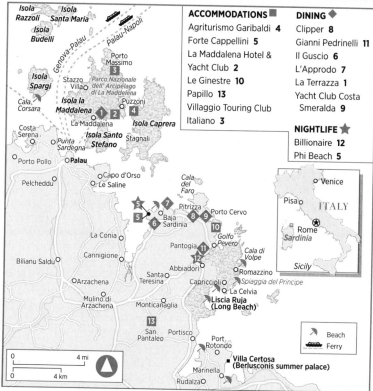

13

SARDINIA & SARDINIAN ISLANDS

Northeastern Sardinia

Exploring the Region

The principal activities on the Costa Smeralda and its environs are beachgoing, boating, shopping, posing, and partying. Beaches are abundant and almost all of them are free to the public. All but the smallest beaches offer something in the way of refreshments and activities; I recommend visiting some of the well-known beaches like Liscia Ruja (Long Beach) along with less-trafficked coves. The waters here are universally gorgeous, shallow, and calm, and afford gorgeous views of the surrounding granitic promontories. Whether you go by sea or land, the distances are never great (for example, Porto Cervo to Palau is just 30km/19 miles, and that's one of the longer trips in this area), but be aware that in July and August, car traffic can be a nightmare, as there's usually only one road to get from point A to point B. Parking, too, in the centers of Porto Cervo, Porto Rotondo, and Baja Sardinia is a challenge in summer unless you have hotel parking. After dark, it's practically gridlock as revelers make their way to the various "it" bars and clubs.

Aside from the stupendous natural scenery, this part of Sardinia doesn't offer much in the way of "sights"—at least not in the traditional, Italian-tourism sense of the word, though there is plenty to ogle here—but there are a few places you should definitely check out to get the full sense of the Costa Smeralda. Ground zero is **Porto Cervo,** which essentially has two nuclei: On the south side, the **Piazzetta** mall is the hub of all high-fashion, high-end retail action (get your 400€ Versace bikini here); there are also a number of hotels and restaurants in this very congested area. (Many of these shops close for the winter; in high season, hours are from 9am–1pm and 5–9pm daily; in shoulder months like May and Sept, you can find them open Mon–Sat 9am–1pm.) A new museum here, the **Monte di Mola Museo** (Via del Porto Vecchio 1; ✆ **0789/92225;** www.mdmmuseum.com; mid-June to mid-Sept Tues–Sun 6pm–midnight), hosts contemporary art exhibitions. The north end of Porto Cervo, accessible via a panoramic road or by free boat shuttle from the old marina below the Piazzetta, is dominated by the modern **marina ★**, complete with a fancy yacht club and the latest in seaborne behemoths moored in the harbor. Be sure to have a good look around.

Beaches

AROUND PORTO ROTONDO

In the zone around Porto Rotondo, the best beach is **Spiaggia Ira ★★** (follow signs toward Porto Rotondo, then Rudargia). Fringed by sugary white sand, the bay here is a swimming pool of electric turquoise water, and facilities include a snack bar and boat rentals. Farther south, **Spiaggia di Marinella ★** (off the SS. 125, follow the SP16 to Porto Rotondo, then to Marinella) is a larger beach with good facilities and watersports opportunities.

AROUND PORTO CERVO

The better beaches of Porto Cervo lie south of the town center, around the Cala di Volpe area northward to Romazzino. **Liscia Ruja ★★** (just south of Cala di Volpe, off the SP94), also referred to as Long Beach by Costa Smeralda regulars, is the see-and-be-seen beach for the fashion set. It's also Porto Cervo's biggest and best equipped beach, so if you only have time for one Costa Smeralda sun and sand day, you can't go wrong with Liscia Ruja. Continuing through Cala di Volpe and back south along the east side of the bay, **La Celvia ★★** is an intimate sandy beach enveloped by *macchia mediterranea* and the most amazing private villas in the area. Keep your eyes peeled—this is where a lot of Italian showbiz personalities hang out. Another great spot, though it involves a bit of a walk, is the **Spiaggia del Principe ★★** (from Cala di Volpe, follow signs to Romazzino, then turn right on Via degli Asfodeli; park at the end of this road, then follow a 600m/1,969-ft. pedestrian path to the beach). This is a perfect crescent of bleach-white sand, neon blue water, and a little granite reef in the middle of the beach. Farther north is the beach of **Romazzino ★** (from Cala di Volpe, follow signs to Romazzino), equipped with plenty of options for eating, drinking, and playing on the water.

In Baja Sardinia, the resort town west of Porto Cervo, **Cala Battistoni** is the beach directly below the developed center. It's lively and clean, with lots of facilities, boat trips, and the convenience of being steps away from shops and restaurants. Parking can be a bit difficult, however. Also in the Baja Sardinia area, though a bit removed from the town center, is a highly recommended outdoor bar/club called **Phi Beach ★★** (see "Northeastern Sardinia After Dark," below). The actual beach here is scant, but the setting is divine, and it's a fun place where vacationers of all stripes gather on big sun beds and sip communal mojitos while a DJ spins summer anthems. Phi Beach has a full bar and restaurant, serving stylish delicacies like seafood *carpaccio*. To get there, follow signs from Baja Sardinia west to Forte Cappellini.

Active Pursuits

BOATING

Part and parcel of the Costa Smeralda experience is *la barca.* Motorboating or sailing around the jigsaw-puzzle-piece coves is practically a religion here, so the nautically inclined will be in hog heaven. You don't have to be a yacht owner to get out on the water—myriad charters operate out of Porto Cervo and Porto Rotondo and the secondary marinas nearby, whether you want a big or small boat, sails or motor, a day trip or a weeklong tour with a skipper. In Portisco (between Porto Rotondo and Porto Cervo), **Boomerang Charter** (© **0789/24293;** www.boomerangcharter.com) has good rates for weeklong tours on a variety of sailboats. Prices start at around 1,500€ per week for self-piloted vessels that can sleep six people. If your party is only one or two, and you don't mind a little less privacy, they also organize group cruises for 8 to 10 people. In Porto Cervo, **Sea World Services** (Piazzetta Clipper, Porto Cervo; © **0789/91693;** www.swsportocervo.com) is a higher-end agency that arranges all kinds of boat charters (though no rentals), from 600€ per day, crew included, for an eight-person boat.

Group boat tours to the Maddalena archipelago are much more affordable than private charters from the Costa Smeralda and are an easy day trip from just about anywhere in northeastern Sardinia. See "Doing the Maddalena Islands by Organized Boat Tour," p. 321.

Still want to be your own captain? No problem: The mainstays of Italian island do-it-yourself boat tourism, *gommoni* (rubber Zodiac motorboats), can be rented easily at any port and many beaches along the Costa Smeralda. Larger engine sizes require a nautical license, but the smaller ones don't require any boating experience at all. Rates are higher here than elsewhere in Italy, however, from 100€ for a half-day.

Where to Stay

There are a number of wildly expensive five-star resorts along the Costa Smeralda, like the **Cala di Volpe,** the **Romazzino,** and the **Pitrizza** (all near but not directly in Porto Cervo), that bill themselves as exclusive luxury retreats where all the VIPs go. However, none of them offers a setting or services quite splendid enough to justify their rates, which can be upwards of 1,000€ per night; it's hard to recommend them on cache alone. Almost all the fancy hotels in the area, including those listed above, are Starwood properties, so if you have a bunch of extra rewards points, it might be an option to consider.

Sardinian Villas (www.sardinianvillas.com) has a number of lovely properties (many very exclusive and expensive) on the Costa Smeralda and also handles bookings for the **Le Case della Marina ★**, attractive and modern apartments with sweeping views, shared pool and ample outdoor living space, conveniently situated on the hill directly behind the harbor.

Forte Cappellini ★ BAJA SARDINIA This "vacation village" is a complex of bungalows dispersed among the *macchia mediterranea,* a few minutes' walk from a series of small, sandy coves just west of Baja Sardinia. The units are all very fresh feeling with brightly tiled bathrooms, white walls and terra-cotta floors; understated Sardinian textiles add a homey touch. However, the rates are a bit stiff given the short list of in-room amenities. A swimming pool, surrounded by lawn, sits at the center of the property. The popular open-air bar Phi Beach is on the water adjoining Forte Cappellini's grounds.

Via Tre Monti, Baja Sardinia. ☏ **0789/99490.** www.hotelfortecappellini.it. 57 units. Doubles 200€–250€. AE, DC, MC, V. **Amenities:** Restaurant; bar; pool. *In room:* Hair dryer, minibar.

Le Ginestre ★★ PORTO CERVO OUTSKIRTS   Fabulously positioned amid dense Mediterranean greenery about 1km (¾ mile) south of Porto Cervo center, this resort offers generously sized rooms and plenty of amenities. It's the kind of place where you'll want to unpack your entire suitcase and hole up for a week. All rooms in the low-slung peach stucco villa feature clean, contemporary furnishings and fixtures, and have ample terraces. The hotel's private beach lies 250m (820 ft.) away. A swimming pool and tennis court (no fee) are also directly on the hotel grounds. Le Ginestre's staff helpful and unobtrusive staff can arrange all kinds of activities.

Località Pevero, near Porto Cervo. ☏ **0789/92030.** www.leginestrehotel.com. 80 units. Doubles 180€–300€. **Amenities:** Restaurant; bar; beach; fitness room; pool; room service; spa; tennis. *In room:* A/C, satellite TV, hair dryer, minibar, free Wi-Fi.

Papillo ★★ 🍴 PORTO CERVO OUTSKIRTS   Formerly known as the Borgo Antico, this yellow stucco retreat in the inland village of San Pantaleo (between Porto Rotondo and Porto Cervo) is an oasis of friendliness and relaxation. Almost all units have a balcony overlooking the inner courtyard and swimming pool. The Papillo is an immaculate and convenient base for touring the Costa Smeralda. One drawback is that it's not directly on the water, but in summer, the hotel runs a free shuttle to Rena Bianca, one of the prettiest and largest beaches in the area.

Via la Petra Sarda, San Pantaleo. ☏ **0789/65400.** www.papillohotelsandresortsborgoantico.hotelsin sardinia.it. 27 units. Doubles 110€–220€. AE, DC, MC, V. Closed mid-Oct to Mar. **Amenities:** Restaurant; bar; excursions and transfers booking; pool. *In room:* A/C, satellite TV, hair dryer, minibar, free Wi-Fi.

Where to Dine

Clipper ★★ ITALIAN/SEAFOOD   Set within one of the hairpin turns on the road leading down to Porto Cervo marina, Clipper does a brisk business with resort habitués and serves very good Mediterranean cuisine at slightly more honest prices than other places in town. The seafood on offer is displayed on ice, so you can pick exactly which fish or lobster you want and how you want it cooked. The house specialty pasta, the *spaghetto Clipper,* is a tasty blend of shrimp, cherry tomatoes, avocado, and curry. An extensive wine list includes dozens of Sardinian wines at good prices. As the name would suggest, decor here is maritime themed, but the result—lots of varnished mahogany, artsy and oversize photos of sailboats, and nautical striped upholstery—is handsome, not tacky. Request a table outside or at one of the large picture windows inside.

Via della Marina, Porto Cervo. ☏ **0789/91644.** Reservations essential in July and Aug. Entrees from 12€. AE, DC, MC, V. May-Oct daily 7:30pm-1:30am.

Gianni Pedrinelli ★★★ SARDINIAN   For a gourmet splurge, look no further than this institution of Costa Smeralda gastronomy. This is quite an elegant spot, despite the rustic framework of the old farmhouse it occupies in the hills above Porto Cervo, but thankfully it's mostly free of the flash and pretense that pervades other famous restaurants in the region. The scene and cuisine are country-chic, and the food tends more to turf than surf, although fish is present in starters like seafood *carpaccio* and grilled octopus. The artisanal antipasti table is enough to warrant a meal here, but among the *primi,* try the ravioli in fresh ragu; for a *secondo,* choose from chicken, pork, or beef dishes in rich and delectable reductions. Consider dining here at the end of your trip, because you might not want to put on a bathing suit after you've had an indulgent meal at Gianni Pedrinelli.

Località Piccolo Pevero, on the road btw. Porto Cervo and Abbiadori. © **0789/92436.** www.gianni pedrinelli.it. Reservations essential. Entrees from 14€. AE, DC, MC. V. Daily 7:45-10:45pm and for lunch by reservation only. Closed Nov-Feb.

Il Guscio ★ ITALIAN/PIZZA

Lively even in the off season, this is a great choice for an inexpensive, reliable meal of standard pastas and pizzas. Despite the location several blocks inland, Il Guscio is hugely popular with young movers and shakers. Expect fast (though not hurried) service and enormous portions, which you'll eat under TV monitors playing music videos and fashion shows.

Viale dei Cedri, Baja Sardinia. © **0789/99325.** Pizzas from 6€, entrees from 8€. MC, V. Daily for lunch and dinner. Closed Oct-Mar.

L'Approdo SARDINIAN/SEAFOOD

Among the waterfront options in Baja Sardinia, this is your best bet. "The Landing" doesn't break down any culinary boundaries, but it is a very pleasant place with indoor-outdoor dining and an enticing menu of typical local dishes and fresh seafood. The atmosphere is what Italians call *signorile* ("grown-up"), catering to a mostly older clientele with damask tablecloths and exceedingly polite waiters in white shirts and black ties. You can't go wrong with their seafood pastas, like *linguine alle vongole* (with clams, tossed in a light sauce of white wine, garlic, and parsley).

Via Baja Sardinia, Baja Sardinia. © **0789/99060.** Entrees from 12€. AE, DC, MC, V. Daily 12:15-3:45pm, 7:45pm-midnight.

Yacht Club Costa Smeralda CONTINENTAL

One of the top things to do in Porto Cervo is to simply lurk around the marina, ogling the mega-yachts and the uniformed crews that are perpetually hosing and buffing them. Stop in for lunch at the restaurant at the spiffy Yacht Club, and you will really infiltrate the Costa Smeralda scene (or pretend to, anyway). Here, you'll actually spy yacht owners and their VIP guests. The cast of characters is as stereotypical as you would expect: lots of Middle-Eastern and Russian tycoons of a certain age and their supermodel consorts in absurd but glamorous "beach" get-ups, noshing on overpriced salads and club sandwiches. There's also a bar (9am–2pm and 6pm till late) on the pool deck in the center of the complex.

Via della Marina, Porto Cervo. © **0789/902208.** www.yccs.it. Reservations recommended in July and Aug. Entrees from 15€. AE, DC, MC, V. Apr-June and Sept 12:30-2:30pm and 7:30-10pm; July-Aug 12:30-3:30pm and 7:30-11pm.

Northeastern Sardinia After Dark

The Costa Smeralda has no shortage of trendy places to party among the beautiful people. However, if you're traveling outside of high season, you can skip this section. The places listed here are only open in summer. If you do plan to hit the bars and clubs, prepare for lots of traffic, even after midnight.

Any discussion of Costa Smeralda nightlife has to include Flavio Briatore's infamous nightclub, **Billionaire** (Località Sottovento; © **0789/94192;** www.billionaire life.com). From all the paparazzi photos that are taken here and end up in European tabloids, you would expect something a bit more glamorous than the reality. The most hyped *discoteca* in Sardinia lies at the end of a cracked driveway, past some ratty buildings, off the road between Porto Cervo and Abbiadori. Once you're inside, however, it's pretty impressive: Billionaire is a terraced villa, with a view of the bay below, aglow with hundreds of candles and an army of preposterously beautiful, tanned, and toned partiers. Decor is all Moroccan lamps and gossamer swaths of cloth meant to evoke the caravans of the spice route (you know, the glitzier caravans, where spice traders plied concubines with Dom Perignon), gold appliqués on the walls, glass beads dangling from windows and doorways, and palm fronds everywhere. Soccer stars, TV starlets, and titans of industry populate the VIP section, which is decorated with gilded statues of the Buddha (because ritzy discos are a required stop on the eightfold path to nirvana). Resident DJs spin house music. The name "Billionaire" says it all: This club is ridiculously expensive and selective. Unless you're an exceptionally attractive young female, you must be (or act) rich and famous in order to get in; if you do, expect to pay a 30€ cover, which includes the first drink. (So generous, that Flavio!) Billionaire is only open in July and August, from midnight until dawn.

If you'd like to have some actual fun (as opposed to just ogling glamazons), head instead to the outdoor water's edge bar and *aperitivo* hot spot of **Phi Beach** ★★ (✆ **0789/955012;** www.phibeach.com; late May to mid-Sept only 10am–late), attached to the Forte Cappellini bungalow village west of Baja Sardinia. The crowd here is much more diverse and laid back—it's not strictly a skin show; families with kids are just as welcome as sporty singles. Though Phi Beach doesn't have much sand (it's mostly granitic boulders around here), the multi-level decks are equipped with dozens of white-cushioned platform sun beds and shell-shaped wicker furniture that fully look the part of a trendy Miami-inspired beach bar. Phi is open all day as a beach club and restaurant, but the best time to come is for happy hour (6pm onward), when the action heats up and the sunset over the water is truly spectacular.

La Maddalena Archipelago ★★★

A stone's throw from the Costa Smeralda, the Maddalena archipelago consists of one main inhabited island, **La Maddalena,** which has a cute port town and is connected to the rural island of **Caprera** by a short causeway, and about 60 other islands and islets, the most visited of which are **Spargi, Budelli,** and **Razzoli.** Boat excursions to the Maddalena archipelago can be arranged at any of the small ports and through most hotels, or you can take the 20-minute car ferry (recommended, so you'll have wheels once you get there) from Palau to La Maddalena, and from there you drive all over La Maddalena (lots of beaches and pretty scenery) and then over to Caprera. The other islands in the Maddalena group are nearby but only accessible by private boat.

EXPLORING

If you're taking the ferry from Palau, your first introduction will be the island of La Maddalena itself, with its characteristic port village. In refreshing contrast to the contrived towns of the Costa Smeralda, La Maddalena has the authentic feel of a real maritime community. Park your car in one of the lots adjacent to the ferry dock, and head east into town on foot for a short walking tour. There aren't any big sights, but you'll see local life played out around the newsstands, coffee bars, and find some interesting shops to browse, including the excellent deli, **Specialità Alimentari Sarde** ★★ (Piazza Garibaldi 10; ✆ **0789/731008**), which has the best selection of typical Sardinian specialty foods, from cured meats to cheeses to breads and condiments to wine and liqueurs. The friendly staff will help you buy provisions for a picnic or a unique souvenir to take back home.

DOING THE MADDALENA ISLANDS BY
organized BOAT TOUR

Daylong group boat tours are the cheapest and easiest way to get an overview of the entire archipelago. In high season, these can be arranged through any hotel and at any of the marinas along the coast of northeastern Sardinia, from Olbia to Palau. Palau is where the lion's share of these tours are based, and there you'll find dozens of outfits all offering the same basic itinerary, which starts at 10am, ends at 5pm, and includes at least two long stops for swimming (you'll have 2 hr. at Cala Corsara on Spargi, the loveliest beach in the archipelago), lunch on board, and coastal tours of Budelli, La Maddalena, and Caprera. Prices range from 35€ to 45€, lunch included.

In summer, these excursions can be organized ad hoc on the day of travel, but from October to May, there are far fewer options for boating the Costa Smeralda or reaching the lesser islands of the Maddalena archipelago: Be sure to inquire with your hotel before arrival about tour availability if this is something that's important to you.

DRIVING AROUND LA MADDALENA & CAPRERA

Out on the island, which you'll need your car to explore, there are dozens of little coves, both sandy and rocky, where you can swim or just relax on the shore. It's all very rustic out here; plan to park along the roadside, squat behind a bush when nature calls, and bring any food and drink with you from town. Before heading back to the ferry, drive over to the island of **Caprera ★**, which is connected to La Maddalena Island by causeway. The main attraction here is the **Casa-Museo di Giuseppe Garibaldi** (✆ 0789/727162; Tues–Sun 9am–1pm; 4€). Here, in the house where the legendary 19th-century general lived his final years, you can see all kinds of historical artifacts and personal effects; also on the grounds (and visible without paying the entrance fee) is the tomb of Garibaldi, who died at home on Caprera in 1882, and the graves of six of his children. The rest of Caprera is gloriously wild, with wonderful stands of pine trees and plenty of places to have a picnic in the shade. If you're here around lunchtime, go to the rustic **Agriturismo Garibaldi** (near the Casa-Museo; ✆ 0789/727449), where you can sit down at red-check-cloth-covered picnic tables for a filling meal of Sardinian charcuterie, pasta, roast pig, boar, or lamb, country vegetables, wine, dessert, and coffee for 25€.

Where to Stay & Dine

If you plan on staying for a week or more and don't mind more spartan accommodations, the **Villaggio Touring Club Italiano** on La Maddalena (Località Punta Cannone; ✆ 840/888802; www.villaggi.touringclub.it/la-maddalena) has a lovely location, with huts and bungalows immersed in a lush hillside above a picturesque cove. Lots of sports and activities are offered, and rates, which start at about 400€ per person, per week, include all meals at the on-site restaurant.

In addition to the restaurant recommended below, consider picking up picnic fare at **Specialità Alimentari Sarde ★★** (Piazza Garibaldi 10; ✆ 0789/731008) or going for the 25€ prix-fixe lunch at **Agriturismo Garibaldi,** on Caprera (details above). For a fancy meal, look no further than La Grotta (Via Principe di Napoli 3;

© **0789/737228;** www.lagrotta.it), the preferred dining locale for Russian yacht owners calling at La Maddalena.

La Maddalena Hotel & Yacht Club ★★   The bones of this brand-new "design hotel," built within the island's former navy yard and arsenal, were originally constructed to host the 2009 G8 summit. When the summit venue was moved to L'Aquila, the central Italian city that was devastated by the earthquake of April 2009, the building project morphed into a luxury resort (opened in the summer of 2010). With striking contemporary architecture and interiors—lots of glass and long horizontals in the public areas, and Asian influences in the supremely tranquil guest rooms—La Maddalena Hotel & Yacht Club aims to be the next big thing in northeastern Sardinian upscale hospitality, and for now, its rates are nowhere near the stratospheric prices of ritzy Cala di Volpe, et al, in Porto Cervo. The complex includes a panoramic swimming pool and a spa (both at water's edge), and a touristic port, the Porto Arsenale, where you can rent small craft or arrange sailboat trips.

Piazza Faravelli, Località Moneta. © **0789/794273.** www.lamaddalenahyc.com. 110 units. Doubles from 190€. AE, DC, MC. V. Closed Oct–Apr. **Amenities:** Restaurant; bar; babysitting; garden; kids' play area; pool; spa; tennis; watersports. *In room:* A/C, TV, minibar, free Wi-Fi.

Ristorante La Terrazza ★ SARDINIAN   With its namesake terrace (a second-floor veranda) overlooking the *centro storico,* La Terrazza is the top spot in town for solid cucina sarda in a charming setting. The traditional menu includes a wide range of antipasti, fresh pasta *primi,* and meat and fish *secondi* (order your seafood either grilled or fried). In addition to the dozen or so tables on the terrace, there's an airy internal dining room done up in warm colors and nonna-chic decor.

Via Villa Glori 6. © **0789/735305.** Entrees 9.50€–18€. AE, DC, MC, V. Daily 12:30–3pm, 7:45–11:30pm.

Alghero ★★

If you've been traveling up and down Sardinia, enjoying the beaches and relaxation but secretly pining for something more reminiscent of the Italy you know and love back across the Med, Alghero will have you exclaiming "finally!" Here, at last, is a historical center with picturesque architecture and an air of nobility that feels very much lived in. However stereotypically Italian the atmosphere, Alghero is more Catalan than anything else. When the people of Alghero rebelled against their Aragonese/Catalan rulers in the 15th century, the population was summarily replaced by Catalans, who remained ever since. Only a century ago did Alghero's Catalan purity begin to be diluted by intermarriage with Sards and adoption of the Italian language.

Whatever its roots, Alghero has enough character and diverse offerings to make it a year-round destination—while the nearby swimming is good, there's more to this town than beaches. Surrounded by imposing seawalls—the *bastioni,* which make for romantic strolling—the cobblestoned *centro storico* is chock-full of great cafes, restaurants, and shops. If jewelry, especially coral, is your thing, your wallet could take a serious hit here. Nearby to the north and south are some spectacular beaches, world-class wineries, and evocative ruins. The most popular excursion from Alghero, however, is to the Grotta di Nettuno sea cave; whether by boat trip or by the 656-step staircase that provides access by land, this enormous cavern of multi-hued stalactites and stalagmites is one of the highlights of Sardinia.

What's perhaps most appealing about Alghero is that there's a real energy and authentic, lived-in quality to the city that's missing from other popular tourist areas in Sardinia. In recent years, low-cost flights into Alghero's Fertilia airport have

Alghero

Map labels:
Torre del Porticciolo
Punta Cristallo
I Piani
Sella e Mosca Winery
Alghero Fertilia
Anghelo Ruiu Necropolis
Sa Segada
SP55bis
SS291
Monte Doglia
Isola Piana
Monte Timidone
Mugoni
SP42
SP44
Porto Conte
Maristella
Nuraghe Palmavera
Tramariglio
Localitá Capo Caccia
Regione Maristella
Spiaggia di Bombarde
SS127
Fertilia
Viale Primo Maggio
Spiaggia Maria Pia
Pischina Salida
Isola di Foradada
Grotta di Nettuno
Capo Caccia
Lazzaretto
Lido San Giovanni
Mediterranean Sea
Grotto, Cave
Beach
Ferry
Mountain
Alghero
SS105
6
7

Porto di Alghero

Via Garibaldi
Via Catalogna
Bastioni Pigafetta
Via Manno
Cattedrale di Santa Maria
Via Vittorio Emanuele
Via La marmora
Via Roma
Via Principe Umberto
Via Doria
Via Mazzini
Via Gilbert Ferret
Via 20 Settembre
Bastioni Marco Polo
Viale Giovanni XXII
Bastioni Cristoforo Colombo
Via Fratelli Kennedy
Viale Sassari

Alghero

ACCOMMODATIONS ■
Carlos V **7**
San Francesco **3**
Villa Las Tronas **6**

DINING ◆
Al Tuguri **4**
Andreini **3**
La Lepanto **5**
Mirador **2**

NIGHTLIFE ★
Bar Mirador **2**
Buena Vista Sunset Club **2**
Cafe Latino **1**

brought a flood of British and Northern European vacationers to this area, but so far Alghero has weathered the crowds gracefully and untainted by mass tourism.

EXPLORING

The nondescript if cheerful modern outskirts of Alghero belie the charm and beauty of the old city that lies on the tip of the promontory. You can't drive into the *centro storico,* so park at the free marina lot, from which it's a 5-minute walk to the heart of town. Tourist information can be found at the exceedingly helpful **AAST** (Piazza Porta a Terra 9; ☏ **079/979054;** Mon–Sat 8am–8pm, until 2pm Nov–Mar), conveniently located just outside the city walls, at the point where most visitors enter old Alghero.

Within the walls, wander the old streets (whose signs are bilingual—in Italian and Catalan), still lined with patrician palaces from the Spanish period, shop at hip and elegant boutiques, and stop in at the Gothic-Catalan **cathedral of Santa Maria** (daily 9am–6pm; free admission), but above all in Alghero, don't miss a **walk along the bastions** ★★ that run between the western edge of the old town and the sea below. The views from here are panoramic any time of day, but it's especially captivating at night when the promenade and walls are floodlit. You can also "do the walls" from a seated position—at one of the stylish cafes along the bastions.

ATTRACTIONS

While Alghero's old city is a major attraction in itself, the most compelling individual sites are actually a bit out of town. Just a short drive to the north are several places of significant historical, cultural, and naturalistic interest, including a *nuraghe,* a Neolithic necropolis, and an international-level winery. The cliffs of Capo Caccia, also to the north, conceal the splendid cave of Grotta di Nettuno. And then there are the beaches, covered separately in the next section.

Anghelo Ruiu Necropolis ★★   With 38 tombs in the form of miniature houses called *domus de janas* (fairy dwellings) built inside caves and outfitted with sophisticated stone carvings, this site is totally worthy of Indiana Jones. Artifacts from the site are at the archaeological museum in Cagliari, but there are fine replicas at the Sella e Mosca winery (see below).

SP42 (road to Porto Torres), 10km (6 miles) north of Alghero. ℂ **079/980040.** 3€. Apr–Oct daily 9am–7pm; Nov–Mar daily 9:30am–4pm.

Grotta di Nettuno ★★   One of the greatest natural attractions of Sardinia is Neptune's Cave, set inside the base of the cliffs of Capo Caccia. It is, however, a bit expensive and can be chaotic in summer, and if you've seen stalactites and stalagmites elsewhere, you might want to think twice before you commit. You can arrive by boat, with one of the regularly organized excursions from Alghero's marina, or by land, down the legendary *Escala del Cabirol* ★★: This hand-cut "stairway of goats" has 656 stone steps leading down the cliff face. Either way you get there, this spectacular cavern has a 120m-wide (394-ft.) saltwater lake, a forest of stalactite columns, and concretions in the form of "organ pipes." Guided tours of the cave are included in the admission fee and last about 30 minutes. For those who wish to brave the stone stairs, a public bus marked Nettuno runs here from Alghero, costing 4€ round-trip. Allow 20 minutes to descend the stairs, and longer for the trip back. For the boat trip crowd, excursions depart from Bastione della Maddalena in Alghero several times daily, though not in rough weather. The boat tour of the caves takes 2½ hours total, costing 10€ to 14€ per person, depending on the company.

Capo Caccia, 27km (17 miles) northwest of Alghero (the top of the staircase to the grotto is clearly signposted). ℂ **079/946540.** 12€. Apr–Sept daily 9am–7pm; Oct–Mar daily 9am–4pm.

Nuraghe Palmavera ★   If you missed Su Nuraxi (p. 303), this is the best place on the island to see a prehistoric stone-built *nuraghe,* some 50 individual dwellings crowded close together. A central tower surrounds these huts, forming a limestone complex from 1500 B.C. Built with huge blocks of stone, the truncated cone tower is in the shape of a beehive and opens onto a panorama of the countryside. The remains of a 14th century B.C. "palace" can also be seen.

SS. 127bis, km 45; from Alghero follow signs to Porto Conte. ℂ **079/980040.** 3€. Apr–Oct daily 9am–7pm; Nov–Mar daily 9:30am–4pm.

Sella e Mosca Winery ★★   This is one of the oldest and biggest wine estates in Sardinia, with beautifully maintained grounds, multi-lingual tours of the cellar, a wine shop and tasting room, and a surprisingly good museum. The museum, included in the cellar tour, is noteworthy not for its exhibits about winemaking but for its reproductions of fascinating artifacts found at nearby Anghelu Ruju, a pre-Nuragic necropolis, as well as the personal effects and military regalia of Messrs Sella and Mosca, who were active in the Italian unification of the late 19th century.

Don't let the moderate prices in the wine shop mislead you: Sella e Mosca is a serious winemaker; the Cannonau D.O.C. is well balanced, spicy, and herbal—even fuller-bodied are the cab-Cannonau blend, *Tanca Farrà,* and the 100% cabernet *Marchese di Villamarina.* My favorite wine here, however, isn't a Big Red, but the wonderfully versatile and hot-weather-friendly *Terre Bianche.* It's made from the white *torbato* grape, which as it turns out is an amazing winemaking grape but incredibly temperamental. The only place it has been successfully grown in Italy is Sardinia. If you have a car and will be on the island for a while, pick up a case of Terre Bianche— it's only about 3€ per bottle here at the winery!

Località I Piani, on the SP42, 11km (7 miles) north of Alghero. ⓒ **079/997700.** Free tours Mon–Sat at 5:30pm June–Sept, call for times in other months; shop open June–Sept daily 8:30am–8pm; Oct–May Mon–Sat 8:30am–1pm and 3–6:30pm.

BEACHES

The best beaches near Alghero all lie to the north of the city. For a quick dip near the center, the city beach of San Giovanni will do in a pinch, but far better is the beach of **Maria Pia** ★★ (4km/2½ miles north of Alghero). Here, a strip of truly flourlike sand is caressed by gentle turquoise waves, a pinewood behind the beach provides some respite from the sun, and the trees emanate a fragrance that, blended with the marine air, should be bottled and sold as *Acqua di Sardegna!*

Alghero's most beloved beach, Le Bombarde, lies at the top of the bay that extends north of the city, 7km (4⅓ miles) away. **Le Bombarde** ★★ has lots of amenities, soft sand, and clean turquoise water. It's also the main beach hangout for the young and socially inclined locals and vacationers. Just west of here, past some dense vegetation (take the inland road; don't try to bushwhack your way through) is **Lazzaretto** ★, a sort of a smaller cousin of Le Bombarde, with the same fine sand, crystal clear water, and ample services.

Side Trips
THE PANORAMIC ROAD TO BOSA

The **Alghero-Bosa *strada litoranea* (corniche road)** ★★, a 45km (28-mile) stretch of cliff-hugging, curving highway, ranks right up there with the most breathtaking drives in Italy. From either city, follow signs to *strada litoranea;* the highway numbers are SP105 and SP49. There's another road between Bosa and Alghero, slightly inland and parallel to the *litoranea* (following the SP12), so I recommend taking that inland route south from Alghero and then returning from Bosa to Alghero on the *litoranea.* Forty-five kilometers (28 miles) of perpetual drop-offs to the sea are beautiful, but stressful to have to negotiate twice. Coming north, you have the "comfort" of being in the land-side lane, and of having the view of Alghero below as you descend the hill. There are no services along the *litoranea Alghero-Bosa,* though there are a few pebbly swimming spots you can hike down to along the way (these are not well marked if at all, so just look for clusters of parked cars and then locate a path to the water). Bosa itself is a pleasant, tourist-friendly seaside town with an attractive old quarter and a 12th-century castle.

NORTH TO STINTINO & ASINARA ISLAND

At the northeast tip of Sardinia, just an hour's drive (56km/35 miles) from Alghero, is the village of Stintino—it's pleasant enough, with a nice little marina and sleepy streets with basic shops and services. The reason you make the trek to Stintino is for the beach of **La Pelosa** ★★★ (4km/2½ miles north of town), which looks like it might have been concocted by Mother Nature after she took some hallucinogenic substances. A broad expanse of soft, crystalline white sand gently gives way to a veritable wading pool of perfectly clear water that goes on and on and on for hundreds of meters without getting deeper than about knee height. The color effects in the water are absolutely breathtaking, floating between palest grey-aqua to brilliant tourmaline. Depending on how the clouds and sun are behaving, the colors can look even more electric. Because such a large area is shallow, La Pelosa isn't the ideal beach for avid swimmers, and it gets inevitably crowded in July and August, but it is without exaggeration among the top beaches in Europe.

From the beach of La Pelosa, you can see the island and national park of **Asinara** ★ (℗ 079/503388; www.parcoasinara.org), about 10km (6 miles) to the northeast. Once a penal colony and closed to the public for a century, Asinara has recently reopened to the public, who come primarily to catch a glimpse of the **albino donkeys** that roam the island's scrubby contours. Just decades ago, there were only 60 of these donkeys left on the island, but heartening news has come with the latest census: There are now 120 albino donkeys on Asinara, equally divided among males and females. To reach Asinara, take an authorized boat from Stintino or Porto Torres; these usually leave around 10am, so plan to be at the marinas around 9:30am. There are no car ferries to Asinara, but once there you can take a tram around the island (www.treninoasinara.it; 40€ including boat transfer from Stintino; on Asinara there are stops to visit the old prison, view wildlife, and swim), rent bikes, or set out on any number of hiking trails.

Where to Stay

Most hotels are located on the outskirts of old Alghero, in high-rises on the beach in the modern town. Consider renting a vacation apartment in old Alghero—Casa Maiorca Apartments (Via Maiorca 24; ℗ **349/8060989**) consists of two totally renovated units with modern fixtures and historic charm, from 80€ to 160€ per night (sleeps four to six).

Carlos V ★   A nice *via di mezzo* (compromise) between the spartan San Francesco and the pricey Las Tronas, which it's located opposite, this large sea resort hotel on the waterfront is surrounded by well-landscaped gardens and terrace. It's been around since 1971 but was completely renovated in 2006. Rated five stars by the government, its front rooms open onto the Bay of Alghero. If possible, try for a room with a view and avoid the units in the rear. Bedrooms are midsize to spacious and tastefully and comfortably furnished with modern pieces.

Lungomare Valencia 24. ℗ **079/9720600**. www.hotelcarlosv.it. 179 units. Doubles 80€–200€. AE, DC, MC, V. **Amenities:** Restaurant; bar; babysitting; pool; room service; tennis. *In room:* A/C, TV, hair dryer, minibar, free Wi-Fi.

San Francesco   It gets points for being the only hotel in old Alghero and a former convent, but the accommodations are definitely ascetic. If you can live without a TV and phone, the San Francesco is a fine base that exudes peace. The cloister is a well-used common area where you can read and mingle with other guests, and the ghosts of the nuns don't mind if you open a bottle of wine.

Via Machin 2. © **079/980330**. www.sanfrancescohotel.com. 20 units. Doubles 80€–100€. AE, DC, MC, V. **Amenities:** Room service. *In room:* A/C, hair dryer.

Villa Las Tronas ★★★   The top choice for luxury in the Alghero area, this is the most romantic and elegant hotel in northeastern Sardinia, a place where Italian royalty used to spend their summer vacations. Built in the 1800s, the villa remained in private hands until 1940. It is erected on a private promontory virtually surrounded by the sea, but only a short walk from Alghero. Piers and terraces attract sun worshipers. Much of the aristocratic atmosphere remains, including marble floors, tall ceilings, crystal chandeliers, and antiques. Bedrooms are elegantly styled with traditional pieces, and the hotel has the best facilities in Alghero.

Lungomare Valencia 1. © **079/981818**. www.hotelvillalastronas.com. 25 units. Doubles 170€–400€. AE, DC, MC, V. **Amenities:** Restaurant; bar; babysitting; fitness center; pool; room service; spa. *In room:* A/C, TV, hair dryer, minibar, free Wi-Fi.

Where to Dine

Note that everything listed here except Al Tuguri is closed on Monday.

Al Tuguri ★ ALGHERESE/SEAFOOD   This three-level restaurant in the old town, the domain of chef/owner Benito Carbonella, offers the most authentic recipes in town. It's housed in a building whose history dates from the 15th century. The ground floor is like a drawing room with sofas and a fireplace. Climb the bare sandstone steps to the dining floors above, especially the most exclusive upper floor. Grilled fish from the Alghero coast appears nightly; the pasta delight is *taglierini* with artichokes or mussels and peas. The sautéed calamari stuffed with fresh vegetables is sublime, as are the linguine with ricotta, fresh tomatoes, and arugula. Desserts are homemade daily.

Via Maiorca 113. © **079/976772**. Reservations recommended. Entrees 12€–28€. MC, V. Mon-Sat 12:30–3pm and 7–10:30pm. Closed Christmas–Feb.

Andreini ★★ CREATIVE SARDINIAN   A modish eye has gone into everything at this chic restaurant—the garden, the exposed stone in the dining room, the menu font—that just walking by, you want to love it. Luckily, the food holds its own with the overt style of the place. The kitchen, helmed by Cristiano Andreini, turns out clever combinations of seafood and vegetables with haute presentations, but if you're not a fish person, steer clear—nearly everything served here has some sort of sea creature, whose names you might not always recognize. In addition to a la carte offerings, the chef has two set menus (60€ and 70€ per person, excluding wine), but the entire table must participate.

Via Ardoino 45. © **079/982098**. Reservations recommended. Entrees 14€–22€. AE, DC, MC, V. Tues-Sun 7:30–11pm.

La Lepanto ★★ SEAFOOD   This is Alghero's go-to address for a special night of feasting on fish. The setting is contemporary-elegant, complete with artful lobster tanks and panoramic windows overlooking the water. While there are great meals to be had here, service seems to have gone a bit downhill recently. Still, most people love it, and if you love classic Mediterranean seafood in all its various species and unfooled-around-with preparations, you'll love it, too.

Via Carlo Alberto 135. ✆ **079/979116.** Reservations required. Entrees 14€–22€. AE, DC, MC, V. Tues–Sun noon–2:30pm and 7:30–11pm.

Mirador ★ ALGHERESE/SEAFOOD   With terrace seating on the bastions of old Alghero, Mirador has a lengthy menu of Algherese standards (paella, pastas with crustaceans and local herbs and spices) and Italian seafood classics. Among a handful of non-fish dishes, the *tagliata di manzo* (sliced rib-eye steak) with balsamic vinegar, arugula, and parmigiano, is outstanding. The setting is lovely, and the restaurant itself is quite handsome. Prices are surprisingly moderate, and the attached bar is one of the nicest spots in town for a drink, before or after dinner.

Bastioni Marco Polo 63. ✆ **079/9734018.** Reservations recommended. Entrees Tues–Sun 11:30am–1:30pm and 7–11pm.

Alghero After Dark

The cafes along the seawalls draw a lively crowd in summer. The hippest is **Cafe Latino** ★ (Bastioni Magellano; ✆ **079/976541**), where you can sip coffee or cocktails on outdoor tables facing the marina. Another good bet is the **Bar Mirador** ★, attached to the restaurant of the same name (see above). For the young crowd, if you can get past the overwrought name, the party is at **Buena Vista Sunset Club** (Via Cavour 15), where they mix a mean mojito complete with barman acrobatics worthy of Tom Cruise in *Cocktail.*

FAST FACTS: ITALIAN ISLANDS

American Express There are no AmEx offices in the Italian islands. In mainland Italy, offices are found in Rome at Piazza di Spagna 38 (✆ **06/67641**), in Florence on Via Dante Alighieri 22 (✆ **055/50981**), in Venice at San Marco 1471 (✆ **041/5200844**), and in Milan at Via Larga 4 (✆ **02/721041**).

ATMs The easiest and best way to get cash away from home—the **Cirrus** (✆ **800/424-7787;** www.mastercard.com) and **PLUS** (✆ **800/843-7587;** www.visa.com) networks span the globe. Be sure you know your personal identification number (PIN) and your daily withdrawal limit before you depart. **Note:** Banks that are members of the **Global ATM Alliance** charge no transaction fees for cash withdrawals at other Alliance member ATMs; these include Bank of America, Scotiabank (Canada, Caribbean, and Mexico), and Barclays (U.K. and parts of Africa).

Business Hours Regular business hours are generally Monday through Friday from 9am (sometimes 9:30am) to 1pm and 3:30 (sometimes 4pm) to 7 or 7:30pm. In July and August, **offices** might not open in the afternoon until 4:30 or 5pm. **Banks** are open Monday through Friday from 8:30am to 1 or 1:30pm and 2 or 2:30 to 4pm, and are closed all day Saturday, Sunday, and national holidays. The *riposo* (mid-afternoon closing) is often observed in the islands, though less so in more tourist-oriented locales like Capri. Most shops are closed on Sunday, except for certain ones that remain open on Sunday during the high season.

Car Rentals The three major rental companies in Italy are **Avis** (✆ **800/331-1084;** www.avis.com), **Budget** (✆ **800/472-3325;** www.budget.com), and **Hertz** (✆ **800/654-3001;** www.hertz.com). U.S.-based companies specializing in European car rentals are **Auto Europe** (✆ **888/223-5555;** www.autoeurope.com), **Europe by Car** (✆ **800/223-1516,** or 212/581-3040 in New York; www.europebycar.com), and **Kemwel Drive Europe** (✆ **877/820-0668;** www.kemwel.com).

Currency At the time of this writing, the **euro,** the official currency of Italy and 11 other participating countries, was worth approximately US$1.30 (per 1€). Inversely stated, US$1 was worth approximately .77€.

Driving Rules Italy, like the rest of continental Europe, drives on the right. On multilane highways, drive on the right; only use the left lane to pass, then get back in the right lane or incur the wrath of big black BMW SUVs. Driving into cities and towns with restricted historic centers can be tricky, but police are usually lenient with tourists who, for instance, find themselves driving the wrong way down a one-way street. Use your seat belts. Careless or reckless drivers face fines; serious violators could land themselves in prison.

Drugstores   At every drugstore *(farmacia)* there's a list of those that are open at night and on Sunday.

Electricity   The electricity in Italy varies considerably, usually alternating current (AC), varying from 42 to 50 cycles. The voltage can be anywhere from 115 to 220. It's recommended that any visitor carrying electrical appliances obtain a transformer. Most laptops and cellphone chargers are dual voltage, operating at either 100 volts or 200 volts. That means that only an adapter is required. Check the exact local current at the hotel where you're staying. Plugs have prongs that are round, not flat, so an adapter plug is also needed (available for a few euros at any Italian hardware store).

Embassies & Consulates   In case of an emergency, embassies have a 24-hour referral service.

The **U.S. Embassy** is in Rome at Via Vittorio Veneto 121 (📞 **06-46-741;** fax 06-46-74-2244). **U.S. consulates** are in Florence, at Lungarno Amerigo Vespucci 38 (📞 **055-266-951;** fax 055-215-550), and in Milan, at Via Principe Amedeo 2–10 (📞 **02-29-03-51;** fax 02-2903-5273). There's also a consulate in Naples on Piazza della Repubblica 1 (📞 **081-583-8111;** fax 081-761-1804). The consulate in Genoa is at Via Dante 2 (📞 **010-58-44-92;** fax 010-55-33-033). There is also a consulate in Palermo (Sicily) at Via Vaccarini 1 (📞 **091-305-857;** fax 091-625-6026). For consulate hours, see individual city listings.

The **Canadian Consulate** and passport service is in Rome at Via Zara 30 (📞 **06-854441**). The **Canadian Embassy** in Rome is at Via Salaria 243 (📞 **06-85444-2911;** fax 06-445-982912). The **Canadian Consulate** in Naples is at Via Carducci 29 (📞 **081-401338;** fax 081-410210).

The **British Embassy** is in Rome at Via XX Settembre 80 (📞 **06-422-00001;** fax 06-42202334). The **British Consulate** in Florence is at Lungarno Corsini 2 (📞 **055-284-133;** fax 055-219-112). The **Consulate General** in Naples is at Via Dei Mille 40 (📞 **081-4238-911;** fax 081-422-434). In Milan, contact the office at Via San Paolo 7 (📞 **02-723-001;** fax 02-869-2405).

The **Australian Embassy** is in Rome at Via Antonio Bosio 5 (📞 **06-852-721;** fax 06-852-723-00). The Australian Consulate in Milan is at Via Borgogna 2 (📞 **02-77-70-41**).

The **New Zealand Embassy** is in Rome at Via Zara 28 (📞 **06-441-7171;** fax 06-440-2984). The **Irish Embassy** in Rome is at Piazza di Campitelli 3 (📞 **06-697-9121;** fax 06-679-2354).

Emergencies   Dial 📞 **113** for ambulance, police, or fire. In case of a car breakdown, dial 📞 **803-116** at the nearest telephone box; the nearest Automobile Club of Italy (ACI) will be notified to come to your aid.

Etiquette & Customs   Some churches may require that you wear **appropriate attire:** Men need to wear long pants, and women must have their knees and shoulders covered in order to enter. On some islands, like Marettimo, where tourism is not as established, it's important to dress and behave respectfully.

Hospitals   For emergencies requiring an ambulance, call 📞 **118.**

Insurance   See Planning.

Language   Italian, of course, is the language of the land, but English is generally understood at most hotels and restaurants and businesses that cater to visitors. Even if few staff members at a restaurant, for example, speak English, one person almost always does and can be summoned. As you travel in remote towns and villages, a Berlitz Italian phrase book is a handy accompaniment.

Legal Aid   The consulate of your country is the place to turn for legal aid, although offices can't interfere in the Italian legal process. They can, however, inform you of your rights and provide a list of attorneys. You'll have to pay for the attorney out of your pocket—there's no free legal assistance. If you're arrested for a drug offense, about all the consulate will do is notify a lawyer and perhaps inform your family.

Liquor Laws   Wine with meals has been a normal part of family life for hundreds of years in Italy. Children are exposed to wine at an early age, and consumption of alcohol isn't anything out of the ordinary. There's no legal drinking age for buying or ordering alcohol. Alcohol is sold day and night throughout the year because there's almost no restriction on the sale of wine or liquor in Italy.

Lost & Found   Alert your credit card companies the minute you discover your wallet has been lost or stolen and file a report at the nearest police precinct. Your credit card company or insurer may require a police report number or record of the loss. Most credit card companies have toll-free numbers to call if your card is lost or stolen, and they may wire you a cash advance immediately or deliver an emergency credit card in a day or two. If you have lost your card, use the following numbers: **Visa:** ✆ 800/819-014; **Master-Card:** ✆ 800/870-866; **Amex:** ✆ 06-7228-0848.

If you need emergency cash over the weekend when all banks and American Express offices are closed, you can have money wired to you via **Western Union** (✆ **800/325-6000;** www.westernunion.com).

Mail   Mail delivery in Italy is notoriously bad. Postcards and letters weighing up to 20 grams sent to the United States and Canada cost .85€; to the United Kingdom and Ireland, .65€; and to Australia and New Zealand, 1.05€. You can buy stamps at all post offices and at *tabacchi* (tobacco) stores.

Measurements   See www.onlineconversion.com for details on converting metric measurements to nonmetric equivalents.

Newspapers & Magazines   In major cities and popular international tourist destinations, it's possible to find the *International Herald Tribune* or *USA Today,* as well as other English-language newspapers and magazines, including *Time* and *Newsweek,* at hotels and news kiosks.

Police   Dial ✆ **113** for police emergency assistance in Italy.

Restrooms   All airports, ferry terminals, and rail stations have restrooms, often with attendants who expect to be tipped. Bars, nightclubs, restaurants, cafes, gas stations, and all hotels have facilities that anyone can use for free. Public toilets are found near many of the major sights. Usually they're designated as WC (water closet) or *DONNE* (women) and *UOMINI* (men). The most confusing designation is *SIGNORI* (gentlemen) and *SIGNORE* (ladies), so watch that final *i* and *e!* The nicer public toilets, in some train stations, charge a small fee or employ an attendant who expects a tip. It's a good idea to carry some tissues in your pocket or purse.

Taxes   As a member of the European Union, Italy imposes a value-added tax (called IVA in Italy) on most goods and services. The tax that most affects visitors is the hotel tax, which ranges from 10% to 19%.

Non-E.U. (European Union) citizens are entitled to a refund of the IVA if they spend more than 155€ at any one store, before tax. To claim your refund, request an invoice from the cashier at the store and take it to the Customs office *(dogana)* at the airport to have it stamped before you leave. ***Note:*** If you're going to another E.U. country before flying home, have it stamped at the airport Customs office of the last E.U. country you'll be in. Once back home, mail the stamped invoice (keep a photocopy for your records) back to the original vendor within 90 days of the purchase. The vendor will, sooner or later, send you a refund of the tax that you paid at the time of your original purchase. Reputable stores view this as a matter of ordinary paperwork and are businesslike about it. Requesting that the refund be credited back to your credit card is usually a faster procedure.

Many shops are now part of the "Tax Free for Tourists" network (look for the sticker in the window). Stores participating in this network issue a check along with your invoice at the time of purchase. After you have the invoice stamped at Customs, you can redeem the check for cash directly at the Tax Free booth in the airport (in Rome, it's past Customs; in Milan's airports, the booth is inside the duty-free shop) or mail it back in the envelope provided within 60 days.

Time Zone   In terms of standard time zones, Italy is 6 hours ahead of Eastern Standard Time (EST) in the United States. Daylight saving time goes into effect in Italy each year from the end of March to the end of October.

Tipping   In **hotels,** the service charge of 15% to 19% is already added to a bill. In addition, it's customary to tip the chambermaid .50€ per day, the doorman (for calling a cab) .50€, and the bellhop or porter 1.50€ to 2€ for carrying your bags to your room. A concierge expects about 15% of his or her bill, as well as tips for extra services performed, which could include help with long-distance calls. In expensive hotels, these euro amounts are often doubled.

In **restaurants and cafes,** 15% is usually added to your bill to cover most charges. If you're not sure whether this has been done, ask, *"È incluso il servizio?"* (ay een-*cloo*-soh eel sair-*vee*-tsoh?). An additional tip isn't expected, but it's nice to leave the equivalent of an extra couple of dollars if you've been pleased with the service. Checkroom attendants expect 1€, and washroom attendants should get .50€.

Taxi drivers expect at least 10% of the fare.

Water   Most Italians have mineral water with their meals and buy plastic bottles of *acqua minerale* for days at the beach; however, tap water *(acqua dal rubinetto)* is safe almost everywhere, as are public drinking fountains. Unsafe sources will be marked ACQUA NON POTABILE. If tap water comes out cloudy, it's only the calcium or other minerals inherent in a water supply that often comes untreated from fresh springs.

Index

See also Accommodations and Restaurant indexes, below.

General Index

A

Abisso Blu (Giannutri), 159
Access America, 39
Accommodations, 48–49. *See also* Accommodations Index
  Agrigento, 214–215
  Alghero, 326–327
  Alicudi, 278
  best, 4
  Caltagirone, 212
  Capraia, 146–147
  Capri, 80–82
  Cefalù, 188
  Costa Smeralda, 317–318
  Elba, 136–138
  Erice, 222
  Favignana, 284–285
  Filicudi, 276
  Giannutri, 159
  Giglio, 153–154
  Ischia, 94–95
  Lampedusa, 240–241
  Levanzo, 287–288
  Linosa, 244
  Lipari, 259–260
  Marettimo, 291–292
  Marsala, 220
  Noto, 207
  Palermo, 180–182
  Panarea, 269–270
  Pantelleria, 232
  Ponza, 110–111
  Procida, 99–100
  Ragusa, 209
  Salina, 263–264
  San Vito lo Capo, 223
  Sardinia
    Cagliari, 301
    Chia, 306–307
    La Maddalena, 321
    southeastern, 312
  Siracusa, 205–206
  Stromboli, 273
  Taormina, 195–196
  Trapani, 218
  Tremiti Islands, 168–169
  Ustica, 247
  Ventotene, 118–119
  Vulcano, 254
Acquacalda, 256, 258
Acqua dell'Elba, 140
Acqua Dolce (Ventotene), 117
Acquario dell'Elba, 132
Acropoli (Selinunte), 216
Adriatic Shipping Lines, 163–164
Aeolian Islands, 249–278
  brief description of, 55
  strategies for seeing, 250–251

traveling to, 35
website, 29
A' Furmicula (San Domino), 171
Agenzia Baffigi (Giglio), 153
Agenzia della Rosa (Capraia), 145, 146
Agenzia La Cossira (Pantelleria), 228
Agenzia Parco (Capraia), 146
Agenzia Viaggi e Turismo Parco (Capraia), 145
Agrigento, 213–215
Agriturismo Garibaldi (Caprera), 321
Ailara Rosalia (Ustica), 245
Air Canada, 34
Air France, 34
AirOne, 236
Air travel, 33–35
Alfredo's (Salina), 265
Alghero, 322–328
Alicost, 86
Alicudi, 277–278
Alidaunia, 164
Alilauro, 71, 86, 115
Alitalia, 34, 35
Al Piccolo Bar (Capri), 78
Alta Marea (Pantelleria), 234
AMAT (Palermo), 176
Amedeo Canfora (Capri), 84
American Airlines, 34
American Express, 329
Amphibia (Aeolian Islands), 268
Anacapri (Capri), 79–80
  accommodations, 81
  restaurants, 83
Andrea Ansaldo (Giglio), 150
Anfiteatro Romano (Siracusa), 204
Anghelo Ruiu Necropolis (near Alghero), 324
Anginola (Capri), 76
Ansonaco, 155
Antico Caffè Spinnato (Palermo), 180
Antonio Bongiorno (Salina), 261
Apartment rentals, 48
  Costa Smeralda, 317
  Tremiti Islands, 168
APT Elba, 126, 129
Aquavision (Elba), 134
Archaeological Area of Sulci (Sant'Antioco), 308
Archaeological Museum. *See* Museo Archeologico
Archetti (Giannutri), 159
Architiello di Capraia (Caprara), 167
Arco dell'Elefante (Pantelleria), 230
Arco Naturale (Capri), 76
Arenella (Giglio), 152
Argentario Divers (Giannutri), 159
Art and architecture, 16–18
  best, 6
Asinara, 326
The Association of British Insurers, 39

AST, 208
AST (Sicily), 174
A.T.L. (Elba), 124
ATMs (automated-teller machines), 329
Australia
  customs regulations, 31
  embassy and consulates, 330
  health-related travel advice, 41
  passports, 30
  visitor information in, 29
Autolinee Brizzi (Giglio), 150
Autolinee Ponza, 105
Autoparcheggio del Porto (Termoli), 163
Azienda Autonoma di Cura Soggiorno e Turismo dell'Isola di Capri, 73

B

Bagno Asciutto (Pantelleria), 230
Bagno Vecchio (Ponza), 110
Ballarò (Palermo), 178
Banca Monte dei Paschi di Siena (Lipari), 257
Bar Approdo (Giglio), 156
Bar Baia del Sole (Marettimo), 290
Bar Banacalii (Panarea), 271
Barbarossa (Elba), 129
Bar Da Scipione (Giglio), 157
Bar Franco (Ischia), 97
Bar Mariposa (Ventotene), 116
Bar Mirador (Alghero), 328
Bar Perbacco (Giglio), 157
Barranche (Marettimo), 290
Bar Tripoli (Ponza), 112
Basiluzzo (Panarea), 269
Bastione Saint Remy (Cagliari), 300
Bay of Naples Islands, 29, 35, 55, 68–100
Bazzina (Alicudi), 278
Beaches and coves. *See also specific beaches and coves*
  Alghero, 325
  Alicudi, 278
  best, 1–2
  Cagliari, 301
  Capri, 77–78
  Cefalù, 187
  Elba, 127–129
  Favignana, 283
  Giannutri, 158
  Giglio, 152
  Ischia, 87, 89–91
  La Maddalena Archipelago, 320, 322, 325, 326
  Lampedusa, 237–239
  Linosa, 243
  Panarea, 267
  Pantelleria, 229–230
  Pianosa, 143
  Salina, 263
  Sant'Antioco, 309
  San Vito lo Capo, 223
  Sardinia and Sardinian Islands, 305–306, 310–313, 315, 316

Restaurants

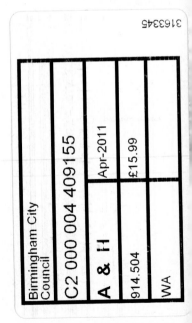